CREATING
AMERICA

CREATING AMERICA

AMERICA

Reading and Writing Arguments

FOURTH EDITION

JOYCE MOSER *and*
ANN WATTERS

Stanford University

Upper Saddle River, New Jersey 07458

Library of Congress Cataloging-in-Publication Data

Creating America : reading and writing arguments / [edited by] Joyce Moser and Ann Watters.— 4th ed.
    p. cm.
    Includes bibliographical references and indexes.
    ISBN 0-13-144386-0
    1. Readers—United States.   2. United States—Civilization—Problems, exercises, etc.   3. English language—Rhetoric—Problems, exercises, etc.   4. Persuasion (Rhetoric)—Problems, exercises, etc.   5. College readers.   I. Moser, Joyce.   II. Watters, Ann.

    PE1127 .H5C74 2004
    808'.0427—dc22

                                                            2004009466

Editorial Director: Leah Jewell
Senior Acquistitions Editor: Brad Potthoff
Assistant Editor:
Editorial Assistant: Steve Kyritz
Executive Marketing Manager: Brandy Dawson
Marketing Assistant: Allison Peck
Production Liaison: Fran Russello
Manufacturing Buyer: Mary Ann Gloriande
Cover Design: Robert Farrar-Wagner
Cover Image: Colonial Flag by Warren Kimble/Kimble House, Inc.
Permissions Specialist: Michael Farmer

Photo Resercher: Beaura Kathy Ringrose
Director, Image Resource Center: Melinda Reo
Manager, Rights and Permissions: Zina Arabia
Manager, Visual Research: Beth Brenzel
Manager, Cover Visual Research and Permissions: Karen Sanatar
Image Permission Coordinator: Joanne Dippel
Project Management: Karen Berry/ Pine Tree Composition, Inc.
Composition: Pine Tree Composition, Inc.
Printer/Binder: Courier Companies, Inc.
Cover Printer: Coral Graphics

Credits and acknowledgments borrowed from other sources and reproduced, with permission, in this textbook appear on page 605.

Pearson Education LTD., London
Pearson Education Singapore, Pte. Ltd
Pearson Education, Canada, Ltd
Pearson Education–Japan
Pearson Education Australia PTY, Limited
Pearson Education North Asia Ltd
Pearson Educación de Mexico, S.A. de C.V.
Pearson Education Malaysia, Pte. Ltd
Pearson Education, Upper Saddle River, New Jersey

PEARSON
Prentice
Hall

10 9 8 7 6 5 4 3 2 1
ISBN 0-13-144386-0

For Janice Hayes, a quintessential American

For Tom, Mike, and Andy Watters;
Tom Moser, Tom Jr., and Cathy;
Frederika, Rick, and Lucy;
Polly and Toby

Contents

✿✿✿

PART II
Argument in the American Tradition

Chapter 5: Identities   115

American Identities through History   116

BENJAMIN FRANKLIN   "Join, or Die" (1754)   119

> Franklin's eighteenth-century woodcut, reportedly the first American cartoon.

ALEXIS DE TOCQUEVILLE   "Origin of the Anglo-Americans" (1839)   121

> An introductory chapter to the renowned work *Democracy in America.*

HOWARD CHANDLER CHRISTY   "Victory Liberty Loan" (1919)   126

> An early-twentieth-century poster designed to garner financial support for World War I.

LUTHER STANDING BEAR   "What the Indian Means to America" (1933)   129

> An American Indian's view of the conflict of Anglo and Indian cultures.

RALPH ELLISON   Prologue to *Invisible Man* (1947)   134

> A fictional representation of an African American's experience in the dominant culture.

JOHN F. KENNEDY   "Inaugural Address" (1961)   138

> A speech that powerfully invoked a national call to service.

Chapter 6: American Dreams   171

Chapter 8: Work and Play 315

Work and Play through History 317

Alternative/Rhetorical Table of Contents

※※

Fiction and Poetry

Speeches

Preface

We developed the fourth edition of *Creating America* to provide a book that focuses on argumentation and persuasion in the context of American history and tradition: a book that brings together materials about issues that have always concerned Americans and that Americans continue to revisit and reinterpret. This edition maintains the focus of the previous three editions on argumentation in context. For those of you who are unfamiliar with the structure of the book, we will review it and follow with the most significant additions and changes. Part I, Contexts for Reading and Writing Arguments, is composed of four separate chapters. Chapter One, "Arguments in American Cultures," is an overview of the historical scope, design, and intent of the book. Chapter Two, "The Art and Craft of Persuasion," is a three-part assessment and analysis of distinct persuasive components. The first part of the chapter, "Persuasion and Audience," provides the rhetorical underpinning for argumentation, with explanations and examples of the relationship between rhetor and audience, the purpose and effect of Aristotelian appeals, and common uses and abuses of logic. The second section in this chapter, "Persuasion in Diverse Genres," discusses specific genres included in the text—essays, legal cases, fiction, poetry, film, advertisements, speeches, and so on—and illustrates the persuasive elements they share as well as those advantages that are unique to each of them. The final part of the chapter, "Elements of Persuasion," concentrates on those components that all writers use to some degree, such as assertions, examples, assumptions, definitions, and refutations, and that constitute the practical continuum of those underlying rhetorical assumptions discussed in the first part of the chapter. Chapter Two also contains student essays as illustrations: an analysis of visual persuasion in a famous Vietnam War photograph, an analysis of refutation in the Supreme Court case *Brown v. Board of Education,* and an analysis of an advertisement.

Chapters Three and Four are devoted to different but related aspects of essay writing. Chapter Three, "Writing Essays," moves students through the whole writing process, from strategies for prewriting to developing a thesis, organizing an essay, and shaping an argument. In order to concretize these suggestions, we have also included, under the sections which discuss expository, analytical, and argumentative writing, examples of each kind of essay, followed by discussion of their rhetorical and developmental strategies. The expository essay, from the 1920s, is a paean to New York energy by a Korean immigrant—"A Korean Discovers New York." The analytical essay is a student's deconstruction of a well-known Vietnam antiwar poster which plays off the very famous James Montgomery Flagg World War I poster of Uncle Sam. And in the argumentative essay, a philosopher makes the case for "Affirmative Action in Context."

Chapter Four, "Research," is about integrating research into writing. Building on Chapter Three, it guides the student through all the steps of the research process: approaching a topic and gathering information (including online information); strategies for Internet research, search engines, ways of evaluating Web-based information, and sample Web sites; detailed discussions and samples of library sources; and sections on drafting, revision, and documentation.

The revisions of Part I include the following:

- an alternative rhetorical table of contents for instructors who want to assign particular modes of discourse or expression, or varied strategies of development;

- new photographs and images to illustrate Aristotelian appeals;

- an expanded section on visual rhetoric, including revised sections on paintings and posters;

- enlarged sections on photography and advertisements;

- a new student essay analyzing a contemporary fashion ad;

- a new section on film techniques and vocabulary to enable students to analyze the persuasive nature of our most pervasive visual idiom;

- new Web sites devoted to visual persuasion;

- a revised section on plagiarism; and

- an expanded section on Internet and Web sources, including examples of Web-site sources that offer guidelines for MLA and APA style, and Web sites helpful to student writers.

Teachers integrating the rhetorical material with readings, as well as teachers wishing to use the readings alone and to teach with a different model of argument, such as the Toulmin model, will find a rich range of materials in Part II, "Argument in the American Tradition."

Part II offers textual and visual arguments for analysis and discussion. Chapter 5, "Identities," includes a range of materials from early discussions of what is uniquely American to contemporary struggles of building community yet maintaining cultural identity. Chapter 6, "American Dreams," includes selections on both political and material dreams and success. Chapter 7, "Images of Gender and Family," offers different perspectives on what makes a family and what constitutes the particular roles and rights of men, women, and children. Chapter 8, "Work and Play," looks at the business of America—business; and at the business of play, or contemporary American sports. Chapter 9, "Justice and Civil Liberties," brings together core readings and images of American freedoms and the struggles that precede and accompany them. Chapter 10, "War and the Enemy," offers visual and textual arguments about how we idealize our friends and demonize our enemies. Chapter 11, "Frontiers," analyzes both the idea and the reality of the frontier and the West.

Each chapter includes an introduction to the core theme or issue. Selections follow, with headnotes for context and background information; journal prompts to guide reflective writing; and questions for discussion and writing, with a focus on analysis and argumentation. In each chapter we include a recommended film that should be available as a video or DVD rental in most colleges or communities. Most chapters also include at least one student essay, generally written in response to a chapter writing suggestion; inclusion of these essays is based on the premise that student writing is an appropriate focus for analysis and discussion.

Part II, Argument in the American Tradition, includes the following revisions and additions:

- Chapter 5, "Identities," incorporates new selections on American patriotic images, diversity, and hegemony, as well as a new film selection, to give a broader perspective about American identity in the world and to provide a context for discussion.

- Chapter 6, "American Dreams," has updated articles and illustrations on the American search for happiness, a contemporary look back at Dr. Martin Luther King, Jr.'s, "I Have a Dream" speech, the American search for community, and a new film selection.

- Chapter 7, "Images of Gender and Family," incorporates recent articles that provide a historical context on women and gender from both dominant and nondominant cultures and a recent student essay on marginalized groups.

- Chapter 8, "Work and Play," includes new illustrations and new articles on office work, minimum wage work, the work of a high school basketball coach, and the future of Title IX.

- Chapter 9, "Justice and Civil Liberties," includes a new film selection and articles on technological conflicts with constitutional rights, especially with regard to the Internet.

- Chapter 10, "War and the Enemy," returns to its focus on war and conflict, and responds to the events of 9/11 and the war on terrorism; it also has a new film selection.

- Chapter 11, "Frontiers," includes a new painting, an excerpt from Lewis and Clark, nature writing by Edward Abbey, and an article on the development of gambling casinos on American Indian lands.

Creating America, fourth edition, is designed for use in a first-year course in composition, particularly one emphasizing argumentative writing. The underlying pedagogy is based on an Aristotelian model, but it is informed by the theories of Kenneth Burke, Carl Rogers, and feminist critics. Our premise is that people use, to quote Aristotle, "all of the available means of persuasion" to argue a point; therefore, we do not treat argument and persuasion separately. Rather, we focus on the appeals to ethos, pathos, and logos, introducing induction and deduction under logos as the basic principles by which to evaluate and through which to develop arguments. The selections represent a range of arguments, from rather combative debate to more dialogic, narrative explorations of difficult questions and complex issues.

Acknowledgments

We gratefully acknowledge our colleagues at Stanford University: Dr. Elena Danielson, Director of the Hoover Institution Archives; Cissy Hill and Carole Leadenham; and Maggie Kimball, Head Archivist, Stanford University Libraries.

We also offer our profound thanks to our colleagues, mentors, family, and friends who have supported or contributed to this project and enabled us to get through it: Tom Moser, Sr., Fredrika Moser, and Tom Moser, Jr.; Tom, Andy, and Mike Watters; Susan Wyle, Barbara Gelpi, Albert Gelpi, Andrea Lunsford, Carol Schloss, Rob Polhemus, Judith Cain, Sue Koppett, Linda Jo Bartholemew, George Dekker, Wendy Goldberg, Linda Paulson, Joan L'Heureux, John L'Heureux, Marvina White, Arnold Rampersand, Willard Wyman, and Diana Maltz; the Vice Provost for Undergraduate Education at Stanford, John Bravman, and Associate Provost Ellen Woods; the staff of Freshman and Sophomore Programs: Sharon Palmer, Gari Gene Reynaud, Dena Slothower, Mona Kitasoe, Jasmine Lu, Carlos Seligo, and Sam Newman; and Susan Cohn, Rosa Lee, Drs. Elizabeth Lee and Laurie Spencer, Jennifer Raiser, Carolyne Cohn, and Beth Springer.

Our editors at Prentice Hall, Karen Schultz and Corey Good, offered us encouragement, counsel, and patience, and we owe them a special debt. We also thank Leah Jewell and Steve Kyritz at Prentice Hall and Karen Berry of Pine Tree Composition. Writers both need reviewers and dread what they have to say. Our reviewers—Moumin M. Quazi, University of the Incarnate Word; G. Matthew Jenkins, Old Dominion University; Patricia G. Ocañas, Our Lady of the Lake University; Lacy Landrum, Oklahoma State University; Kelly Richardson, Winthrop University; Virginia Chappell, Marquette University; Carmella Braniger, Oklahoma State University; and Diane Williams, College of Lake County—were simply superb, and their tremendous help is largely responsible for whatever improvements there are in this edition.

Above all, we thank our students, who continue to challenge and inspire us, and our families, who sustain us.

Joyce Moser, Stanford University
Ann Watters, Stanford University

1

✿✿✿

Arguments in
American Cultures

W hen the founding fathers were about to publish the Declaration of Independence and set themselves on a course that would put them in direct conflict with the British government, Benjamin Franklin is reported to have said, "Gentlemen, we must all hang together, or assuredly we shall all hang separately."

In a sense, this book takes Franklin's observation and applies it more generally to thinking and writing about the nation that Franklin and his corevolutionists were in the process of establishing. The pieces of American life—people who come from many countries, cultures, and religions; states that differ from one another in topography, industry, and demographics; huge variations in urban and suburban lifestyles, in income and interests—are so heterogeneous that they could have hardly been expected to coexist as they have for more than two hundred years, but they have done so. *Creating America* offers a way of examining and writing about what it is that has caused those pieces to hang together.

Reading American Cultures

The selections assembled in this book are not limited to any one time period; there are eighteenth-century cartoons, nineteenth- and twentieth-century advertisements, and contemporary films; great political speeches from the 1770s to the present; essays on relations between the genders and generations; paintings from the nineteenth century; propaganda posters from the two world wars; Henry David Thoreau on civil disobedience, Frederick Douglass on the horrors of slavery, Pulitzer Prize–winning photographers on the horrors of war, and Studs Terkel on the pleasure and pain of a good day's work.

Our central premise is that certain ideas run back to the earliest days of America as a political and social entity and continue to do so

1

today, and that those threads can be read across centuries and across genres. Every generation of Americans reinterprets and reargues these ideas in the light of its own experience. This book provides a wide array of materials that vary in kind and across time—fiction, essays, cartoons, posters, journals, paintings, poetry, legal proceedings, advertisements, movies—and that thus form a core sample of American culture.

The ability to analyze these materials can work both ways. An eighteenth-century etching about what constitutes appropriate behavior for a young woman instructs us about earlier norms and helps us to understand more recent conflicts about feminism, freedom, and self-expression. And a contemporary advertisement that sells sex in order to sell clothing also helps us understand the limits within which earlier generations of women defined themselves.

In the same way, Jon Gertner's article about the futile pursuit of happiness is highly informative regarding the American association of happiness and money; but so is advertising music on MTV. Reading Susan B. Anthony on the First Amendment and freedom of speech may offer insight into the argument about whether the Internet should be censored; and reading Martin Luther King, Jr., on nonviolent resistance may help readers understand why his intellectual ancestor, Thoreau, refused to pay taxes and insisted, with some relish, on going to jail to protest a war he could not support. And a contemporary article on why the Internet will continue to spread information for free extends and transforms questions about freedom of speech into the twenty-first century.

Persuasion

As you study the selections in this book, you will find that most of the authors are engaged in arguments of one kind or another about a particular political stance, a contemporary ethical problem, or the status quo. Frequently the fight is not so much about an individual opponent as about an idea or a belief. However varied the subject matter or the historical events surrounding it, this kind of argument is characteristically a manifestation of disagreement in a democracy. It is argument that encourages rather than stifles disagreement and allows the expression of different, even completely opposing, points of view, and it protects the right of individual Americans to say and express ideas that other Americans find highly offensive. It is argument designed not to bludgeon opposition into submission but rather to persuade.

The target of such persuasive argument is often the American public at large or a particular group of citizens within a larger political unit. Americans take for granted their right to argue publicly and privately and to criticize their government, their elected officials, their school boards, their neighbors. There is a long if not always polite tradition of Americans' criticizing their elected leaders in often virulent terms, and those comments make for sometimes vicious political commentary, but ultimately they constitute one of the great experiments of a democracy. This chapter provides suggestions for analyzing and using persuasion as a basis for your own experiments in reading and writing critically about American materials.

Persuasion is a process in which a *rhetor*—a speaker, a writer, or an artist—tries to elicit a desired response from an *audience* by identifying commonalities in the interests of both parties. It is a process that deals not in certainties but in probabilities—in arguing from evidence or reasons and assumptions to a conclusion. This textbook is designed to enable you to develop your ability to understand and analyze the strategies of persuasion in what you read and to develop your own ability to write persuasively. Studying persuasive texts can help you to become a more critical reader and listener and to communicate more clearly and effectively. By focusing on diverse kinds of arguments in American culture, by looking at context and purpose, by looking beneath the surface at strategies and appeals, you will see persuasion all around you in daily life—not only in books you read, but also in advertising, flyers, posters, news magazines, newspapers, and so forth. A persuasive text is one that asserts a point of view and seeks a desired response; it attempts to induce the readers to agree with whatever is being expounded on. A description of orderly governance in an American Indian tribe, for example, implicitly argues for respect for that culture. Sometimes the desired response is self-sacrifice; a poster advertising war bonds appeals to the interests of the audience—whether self-interest or desire to belong—to garner financial support for the war effort. Ultimately, persuasion can change beliefs, behavior, or even government policy; in *Brown v. Board of Education*, a legal argument citing inequities in segregated education changed the law of the land and the future of millions of Americans.

Persuasion and American Cultures

American cultures have common threads that are woven in tremendous diversity. Persuasive appeals in public discourse must take this fact into account in order to succeed, tapping into the assumptions and common values and beliefs while acknowledging divergent views. More so than the speakers and writers in more homogeneous cultures, Americans wishing to persuade their fellow Americans must understand something about their audience(s): who they are, what they believe and assume, how they communicate, and what they value. Some assumptions and values remain constant over time, but each age brings with it a different view anchored in that particular time and culture. The right to vote has always been an important American construct; however, what it meant for the founding fathers, who restricted voting to property-owning white males, what it meant to slaves and the abolitionist movement before and during the Civil War (see Frederick Douglass's Fourth of July speech in Chapter 9), and what it meant to supporters of women's suffrage after the Civil War (see Susan B. Anthony's speech, also in Chapter 9) are all significantly different from one another. Examining persuasive texts from different time periods in American history and from different cultural perspectives may help us to understand better our own age and culture while considering them in a larger historical context.

As the preceding discussion suggests, the themes in this text represent some of the core debates in American history. Who are Americans? What are their dreams? What makes an American family? What are Americans' values about work and success? What are their concepts of justice and liberty? Why do they construct an "other" or enemy, and how do they take action against the other? What is their image of the frontier, and how, having reached the geographic limits of the continent, do they search for new frontiers? Each type of question or problem lends itself to a particular aspect of argumentation.

In the second chapter, we begin to explore those aspects, including the relationship between the rhetor and the audience—a fluid and often an exasperating connection that changes with time, history, and experience. The connection is especially complicated if, as is often the case with selections in this book, a document written for one audience in one generation has proved to be so important that it continues to be read by future generations who were not part of the original equation. What you need to recognize is that you, as a contemporary reader, have a relationship with the text that is as valid and as important as that of any member of the original audience. And the way you read that text will depend, in part, on the experience, beliefs, and assumptions you bring to it.

It will also depend on other issues raised in Chapter 2: the differences between past and present audiences; the appeals that others make to you and that you can use to persuade others; the logical errors that can throw an argument off or intentionally mislead you as the reader, and the ways you can recognize them in your work or anyone else's; and persuasion in action—for example, the way all or some of these techniques work even in a supposedly objective piece of writing such as a news story.

Besides persuasive techniques, there are all the ways in which we shape them. Essays are probably the form you're most familiar with as a writer, but even essays come in different permutations—expository, argumentative, reflective, or, in much of the best work, some combination of them. Legal cases, of which there are several in this book, would seem to lend themselves entirely to logical arguments, but in fact no legal argument that isn't also persuasive is going to convince a jury or a reader. And a great legal narrative has a lot in common with a good story.

Fiction and poetry are often posited as forms that rely on emotion or aesthetics, but in fact a really persuasive poem or story has a logic and an inevitability that many essays don't have; fiction and poetry can deal indirectly with such abstract issues as justice or love or political freedom, and can end by making them more concrete and specific than a direct statement written in expository form (see the story "In the Land of the Free" in Chapter 6).

Finally, this next chapter deals with the enormous persuasive power of visual texts and the many forms they can take—illustrations, comics, posters, advertisements, photographs, music videos, movies. Keep in mind that an advertisement has a writer, designers, a producer, and other people who make creative decisions about how to present the product and what audience to gear the ad toward. Similarly, a movie involves hundreds of people, from the director and the writers to the cinematographers and film editors; every line of dialogue and every camera angle is the result of someone's choices. Because you see only the final product, you may believe that there was something inevitable about it, but in fact, once you realize how much choice is involved, you also become more aware of alternatives. The film or the advertisement or the poster could have been done differently, and its success in reaching you, the audience, will depend partly on your awareness that art is no more haphazard than a closely reasoned legal argument.

Whatever the form, aesthetic achievement always depends on a set of assumptions, conscious or unconscious; there are always particular appeals to you, and there is an underlying structure that may be either completely convincing or so full of logical errors that all persuasive content is lost. As you look at the next chapter, remember that reading, writing, and viewing are all interactive; in exploring the text, you are also developing your own argumentative and persuasive capabilities.

2

The Art and Craft of Persuasion

There are three interrelated parts to this chapter. The first part, Persuasion and Audience, focuses on how closely the rhetor's, or speaker's, effectiveness is tied to his or her ability to identify the audience correctly and how to appeal to it appropriately. A rhetor who fails to do so will not connect, and therefore will not persuade. Many factors, cultural, personal, and intellectual, go into being a successful rhetor. This section identifies and explains the most significant ones, including the eternally useful Aristotelian appeals, as well as the logical errors that can derail your argument and make it very difficult for you to get your point across.

The second part of the chapter, Persuasion in Diverse Genres, is a practical overview of how many venues there are in which to use persuasive strategies: not only texts, such as essays and legal cases, but also visual representations, such as advertisements, films, cartoons, and photographs. To show you how to analyze an image, we have included a student essay on the famous Vietnam War photograph "Saigon Execution" in which a man is killed at the instant the picture is being taken (you will find that photograph in Chapter 10). This essay is an example of one way in which a visual representation can be analyzed for its rhetorical appeals in much the same way as a written text.

Finally, the section entitled Elements of Persuasion breaks out the constituent parts on which both textual and visual persuasion rely: assumptions, assertions, examples, and refutations. Another student essay, this time on the most famous Supreme Court case of the last hundred years, *Brown v. Board of Education,* shows how rhetorical strategies—appeals to ethos and logos—can combine with a persuasive element, refutation, to overthrow a legal precedent, and, by the way, to change American history.

Persuasion and Audience

Rhetor and Audience

Understanding the arts of persuasion entails understanding how others persuade you and how you can persuade others through your own arguments. Although some scholars have stated that argument relies on logic and that persuasion relies on emotion, Aristotelian rhetoric makes no such clear-cut distinction. Aristotle's *Rhetoric* suggests that reason, beliefs and values, and emotion—*logos, ethos,* and *pathos*—work together to engage the whole person and guide him or her toward appropriate judgment of the issue at hand. A traditional view suggests that argument entails an adversarial relationship between two sides— generally writer or speaker and audience. In debate, for example, each of the two opposing sides offers arguments that the other side then refutes; in propaganda, the audience is inundated with generally one-sided, unsupported assertions. Such persuasion is rhetoric "to gain advantage, of one sort or another," as critic Kenneth Burke notes, and to some degree, it reflects Aristotle's primary definition of rhetoric as "understanding all of the available means of persuasion."

More recently some scholars have argued for different approaches to argumentation. Drawing on the work of psychologists such as Carl Rogers, they outline a model that suggests that both rhetor, or communicator, and audience are participants in the argument and should work together, much like a client and therapist, to pursue knowledge and truth. Some feminist critics suggest that our traditional views of argumentation are male-centered, adversarial, and combative; these critics emphasize a more collaborative approach to argumentation, with negotiation rather than debate as the dominant mode. In such an approach, both sides identify their common interests and attempt to close the distance between their respective positions.

Another view suggests rereading Aristotle to understand the connection between rhetor and audience. (The term *rhetor* will in this textbook refer to an individual attempting to persuade orally or in written text or image.) In this view, the rhetor and audience work together to pursue and develop a solution to a problem, a difference of opinion, or an issue. Audience and rhetor are dynamically involved in argument, and no argument can begin from scratch; the rhetor relies on and presumes a certain background on the part of the audience, including certain assumptions, beliefs, values, and reservoir of knowledge.

Audiences and Cultures

Scholars of rhetoric assert that persuasion in homogeneous cultures tends to leave many reasons and assumptions unexpressed; a shared heritage tends to include a fair number of shared assumptions

and values. In a heterogeneous society such as the United States, arguments rely on some common ground, but they tend to be more forcefully and clearly articulated, with premises and steps in the logic more
often stated than assumed. The argumentative style and organization
tend to be more indirect in countries where a direct approach could be
considered offensive and where the rhetor might instead broach a subject, move away from it, then return to supporting points later. The
point, again, is to analyze audiences carefully, to visualize them and
consider their beliefs, values, attitudes, and style of interaction, rather
than concentrating only on one's own point of view. Understanding
audience assumptions and expectations is crucial in developing persuasive argumentative strategies.

Audiences from Other Times

Analyzing arguments written for readers from other time periods
brings with it its own complexity. Although the basic strategies of argument remain much the same through time, the role of public debate
and the particular concerns and issues vary with each age and culture.
The early America of European colonial culture was largely agricultural, with people living on farms and in towns isolated from each
other; it took days for information to reach New York City from
Philadelphia. Today Americans and the rest of the world are con
nected by global media. Colonial culture was more homogeneous, but
space and time separated its communications; American society today
is more diverse, but most Americans are exposed to the same news
and popular culture. Superficially, then, we have more in common,
but the increased variety in cultures means that we come to the discussion with different cultural perspectives. People who seek to persuade
others in American cultures and media cannot count on the kinds of
shared assumptions held by the audiences of Benjamin Franklin or
Thomas Jefferson. Understanding persuasive texts from other times,
then, will require not only analyzing the texts themselves but also considering the assumptions, values, beliefs, and needs of the audiences
for whom they were intended.

Audience and Appeals: Ethos, Pathos, and Logos

In order to induce others to identify with them or their point of
view, rhetors use a number of strategies. Aristotle outlined three
modes of persuasion that relate to the connection between writer and
audience: appeals to ethos, pathos, and logos.

Appeals to Ethos   Appeals to ethos are appeals to the underlying
values and beliefs of the audience. There are two benefits to this kind
of appeal. First, it helps rhetors to establish their own credibility and

authority—or, as Aristotle puts it, "the personal character" of the speaker. A politician who presents himself or herself as the product of an economically poor environment is appealing to the American belief in success as a product of hard work. Academic writers who present themselves as well informed and capable of using the language and convention of their disciplines, as well as relying on credible scholarly resources, are appealing to a belief—which some observers might call typically American—in expertise, research, and inquiry.

The appeal to ethos has a second function as well, one that is subtle, but important. Rhetors draw on the values and beliefs they share with the audience, not only to establish their own authority but also to suggest the underlying premises that will support whatever arguments and conclusions they are trying to make. And two different rhetors can appeal to the same underlying value or belief for entirely different purposes. For example, when Franklin Delano Roosevelt vilified the Japanese during World War II, he was appealing to the deep-seated American belief in fair play, which had been violated by the Japanese sneak attack on Pearl Harbor. When Martin Luther King, Jr., appealed to that ingrained sense of fairness, he was arguing, not for the purposes of identifying an enemy, but for the civil rights of all Americans.

Let's look at an example of persuasion that uses appeals to ethos as unspoken premises to support a conclusion. Consider, for example, the statement as illustrated in the accompanying photo.

This stenciled statement-plus-images can be found painted near drains in many cities and towns. Such appeals target local concerns; in some areas, *bay* would be replaced with *river* or *ocean,* and sometimes the images would be different—birds rather than a dolphin, for example. The argument includes an assertion (do not dump waste here), a reason (because it will drain to the bay), and implied consequences (and damage the waterways and wildlife).

Although the argument seems to rest primarily on reason, appeals to values and beliefs pervade this argument. The rhetor assumes that the audience values the environment, represented in the water symbol and the small animal outline, and that viewers will accept some responsibility for protecting natural resources.

Consider alternative messages for this argument: for example, instead of "drains to bay," the rhetor could have stated, "$500 fine." Why might the rhetor appeal to ethos rather than threaten violators with a fine? What are the advantages, as well as the disadvantages, of appealing to values and beliefs in this rhetorical situation?

Appeals to Pathos An effective rhetorician, according to Aristotle, seeks to understand the emotions and then to put the audience in the right frame of mind to hear an argument. Appeals to pathos, like appeals to ethos, relate to identification. If one can empathize, then one can identify with another, put oneself in the other's position, and understand the other's feelings and point of view. Critics have argued that emotional appeals are less appropriate than logos or ethos appeals, perhaps over concern about manipulating audience emotions or relying on emotional appeals to cover up a lack of logic and evidence. Yet persuasion engages the whole individual, and pathos appeals can create a more balanced argument or a more ethical decision. Cost-benefit analyses may argue against any intervention in postcommunist Eastern Europe, but showing the human costs and suffering, in text or images, may provide a kind of evidence that eludes the rigorous economical and political analyses. By the same token, logically staking out the political benefits of uninterrupted oil shipments to the United States may not present the whole picture unless one includes the human costs, on both sides, of a war in Iraq and other countries in the region.

In the "no dumping" argument cited earlier, the rhetor didn't select images of snakes and rats, for example, but rather chose a more appealing animal that evokes a desire to protect, such as a dolphin. Further, most of these arguments are painted in blue and white, which mirror colors found in nature and suggest pristine surroundings, rather than mudslides or other unappealing natural phenomena. Are there any disadvantages to using emotional appeals in this rhetorical situation? Do these appeals go far enough in persuading the reader? How might physical location, culture and local customs, economic status, or other elements of the rhetorical situation affect the selection of appeals? How do such appeals operate in the accompanying example?

The rhetor cannot generally invoke emotions directly by asking the readers to feel a certain way or to empathize with someone. He or she must use language, examples, and details that clearly convey situations with which the audience can identify. Appeals to pathos are frequently made through specific detail or connotative language— language that evokes feelings or emotional responses. In the Prologue to *Invisible Man*, for example, Ralph Ellison invites the reader to identify with a man who is invisible in his society; Ellison persuades readers to see another point of view by invoking their empathy for the narrator's situation.

Appeals to Logos   Appeals to logos refer to the logic and shape of the argument. Nearly every argument at least pretends to possess some logic in the form of reasons why the audience should change their views. Consider the sign in the photo posted in the parking lot of a large, Swedish home design store.

The rhetor offers a reason to support the assertion; the sign makes a request and then offers a reason why the viewer should grant the request. Appeals to logos may overlap with other appeals; the reason given also appeals to self-interest, and in that sense it also appeals to emotion. In the next photo, the appeal to self-interest approaches an appeal to self-preservation.

Analyze the caution sign on page 14. What is the image's main assertion? What support is offered? What assumptions are left unstated? Why do you think that the author chose these strategies for this rhetorical situation?

Aristotle cites two basic methods of developing logos appeals: induction, arguing from evidence; and deduction, arguing from general principles.

In *induction*, the rhetor generalizes from a number of observations, specific cases, or examples and then draws inferences or conclusions based on data. Induction deals not with certainties but with probabilities; the rhetor cannot test every single case or provide an infinite number of examples, so he or she uses examples and evidence to draw conclusions about another case or a larger population.

When the rhetor reasons from examples to a conclusion, he or she asks the audience to make an inductive leap—a leap of faith from the known and verifiable specific cases presented in the argument, across an unknown and unknowable stretch, to a probable conclusion. The relevance, breadth, and number of examples reduce the leap that audiences must make and therefore strengthen the credibility of the argument. Because rhetors have a limited amount of time and space to devote to their examples, they must select those that are most persuasive and most suited to the audience and purpose. When Martin

Luther King, Jr., describes driving all night because he can't find a motel that will accept his business, or having to explain to his child why she can't play in a playground that is for whites only, or seeing that his people's wives, mothers, and sisters are denied the respected title of "Mrs." and that grown men are called "boy," his vivid, specific examples make a strong case for the conclusion that Americans of African descent endure relentless and pervasive racism. In academic writing as well, each author must include relevant, sufficient, and representative examples to build a persuasive case for the conclusion. Scientists carefully record data about sampling, methods, and observations to substantiate credibly the conclusions they draw from their data.

Inductive arguments can go astray in one of two ways: either the evidence is inadequate for the conclusion drawn, or the reasoning from evidence to conclusion is faulty. Readers of academic prose as well as other kinds of arguments must be critical of the kinds of examples offered and be mindful of biased or inadequate sampling. They should also examine critically the "leap" they are asked to make from evidence to conclusion.

Say, for example, a friend of yours works in a hospital transcribing medical notes written by physicians. On his first day of work, this friend sees six patient charts, and all six contain doctors' notes in handwriting that is almost illegible. He might conclude that doctors have terrible handwriting. If he tells you, "All doctors have terrible handwriting," he would be guilty of overgeneralizing. In fact, he hasn't seen all doctors' handwriting. If he said, "All of the doctors whose handwriting I have seen write illegibly," then he would be making a statement that is accurate (assuming that others share his standards) but that is limited to the sample he describes. Induction, like other forms of argumentation, is open to question; if it weren't, there would be no reason for debate. But reasonable people will be likely to accept the conclusions that one draws if they are based on sufficient evidence and if the conclusions logically follow from the evidence. What we most want induction to do is to enable us to generalize from a sample to larger populations and other cases; we want to be able to say, with some degree of certainty, that the conclusion is true on the basis of our evidence.

Deduction, the other primary method of organizing arguments, takes a general principle (also called a premise or an assumption) and draws a conclusion or makes an assertion that is based on it. The *syllogism* is a classic outline of deduction used to test the logic of the argument. It entails a statement of a general premise, a specific case, and a conclusion derived from the general premise and specific case. For example, consider the following statements:

> All physicians have terrible handwriting.
> Dr. Weller is a physician.
> Therefore, Dr. Weller has terrible handwriting.

Clearly the generalization forming the conclusion of the argument is highly questionable. Sketching out an argument in this form frequently enables readers to examine both the premises being made and the conclusions being drawn. Generally, though, arguments don't occur in this explicit form. More often, writers persuade through collapsed arguments, with generalizations and assumptions left out or buried within the argument.

Such a compact deductive argument, known as an *enthymeme,* unites the author's statement and conclusion with a part of the argument that is understood or assumed by the audience. The syllogism generally spells out the general principle, the specific case, and the conclusion. The enthymeme leaves out one of the premises, often the generalization or underlying assumption. Drawing from the example, the argument would appear something like this:

> Dr. Weller, being a physician, has terrible handwriting.

or

> Of course Dr. Weller has terrible handwriting—she's a physician.

Both statements have buried within them the outlined argument in the syllogism, but rather than sketching out all the steps, the rhetor relies

on assumptions shared with the audience. The rhetor's task is to analyze the audience and to know how much background information to
supply, what definitions to include or exclude, what the audience already accepts or believes, and what points must be argued and supported with evidence. In the compact argument of the enthymeme, the
rhetor assumes that the audience will supply certain links in the chain
of argument.

A number of selections in this book provide examples of deductive arguments. The Declaration of Independence (Chapter 9) argues
extensively from principle, explicitly stating premises and assumptions, testing those premises against a specific case (the British government of the colonies), and then drawing the conclusion that the break
with Britain is justified. If one accepts the premises—that governments
derive their authority from the consent of the governed; that there are
inalienable rights to life, liberty, and the pursuit of happiness; and that
there is legal contract between governor and governed that obliges
each side to fulfill its obligations—then one must accept the validity of
the conclusion: that governments that do not protect these rights and
refuse to keep their part of the bargain no longer deserve their authority, and it is not only right but necessary that the governed should establish themselves as an independent country.

Errors in Logic

Arguments can go wrong in a number of ways. Critical readers
and careful writers need to question the arguments they read and to
take care with the evidence, assumptions, and reasons they offer and
the conclusions they draw. In a deductive argument, a critical reader
can argue with the reasons and assumptions, sometimes called
premises, on which the conclusion is based, or question the reasoning
process from premises to conclusions. In inductive reasoning, one can
question the evidence offered or the conclusion drawn about that evidence. Both methods can lead to a number of errors in logical argumentation, or fallacies. Following are some of the most common
fallacies.

1. *Hasty generalization.* Leaping in logic from a very few cases to
a broad conclusion can be considered hasty generalization. If, for example, we find that two senators have financial assets worth millions
of dollars and we conclude that all public officials are wealthy, we
have made a leap that is unsupported by the evidence. We have
moved too hastily from examples to a conclusion.

2. *Inadequate or biased sampling.* This fallacy is related to hasty
generalization. If a writer's conclusions are based on too few samples
or a skewed or biased collection of samples, the conclusions are not

necessarily generalizable to the larger issue or population. If we sampled only the senators included in a list of the fifty wealthiest Americans to draw conclusions about all senators, we would be using a biased sample. We need to cast our net wider and draw from a more representative sampling. Drawing at random a sample of ten or twenty from the list of one hundred senators and examining their financial statements would give us more representative and complete data and enable us to make generalizations about the larger population of senators.

3. *Straw man.* A straw man in argumentation is a false target: the writer sets up a misstatement of the opponent's view and then attacks that misstatement instead of the real argument. An argument attacking someone who does not support specific pro-choice legislation might suggest that the opponent wants "all women barefoot and pregnant" instead of discussing the specific legislation in question.

4. *Ad hominem.* In the ad hominem argument, literally meaning "against the man," the writer attacks an individual holding the position rather than the position. If a writer says, "Governor Jones is in favor of nationalized health insurance, so it must be a bad idea," that writer is attacking the governor but not addressing the merits of the governor's specific arguments.

5. *False analogy.* Argument by analogy is one of the weakest strategies and is highly vulnerable to attack. A false analogy entails erroneously suggesting that two people, situations, or issues are analogous or comparable in certain ways. In recent years, any number of potential military conflicts have been argued against because they might represent "another Vietnam," whether or not there are, in fact, any similarities between the two situations. In order for an analogy to work, it must match up in all significant areas with whatever it is being compared to; otherwise, it produces a kind of false coherence that is at best lazy thinking and at worst downright misleading.

6. *Post hoc, ergo propter hoc.* Literally, this expression translates into "after this, therefore because of this." The mistake in logic lies in suggesting that because A happened before B, A caused B. The watchword in statistics and many social sciences, however, is that correlation does not equal causation. Because the divorce rate increased after the advent of widespread television viewing, there is no reason to conclude that television viewing causes divorce. Even though there are times when we are instinctively sure that the causation exists—for example, nine months after the great New York City electrical blackout of 1965, the number of children born rose dramatically—there has to be some more definite causation than the fact that one phenomenon happened after another.

7. *False dilemma.* A false dilemma is an either-or situation in which the writer implies that we have only two choices: "Either we get

rid of television once and for all, or we resign ourselves to being a nation with the leading divorce rate in the civilized world." This kind of reasoning suggests that you either haven't considered all the factors or that you are deliberately leaving some of them out to make the options appear much more limited than they really are.

8. *Slippery slope.* In this lapse in logic, the writer argues that one first step will inevitably lead to further disastrous consequences. For example, someone opposed to genetic engineering might argue, "Once we allow scientists to map human chromosomes, we will see people wanting designer children with blond hair and blue eyes." In law, the slippery slope is an argument often used against either the loosening or the tightening of legal restrictions on personal behavior; it comes up frequently with freedom of speech issues, both political and commercial. If X, who is a telemarketer, cannot call strangers at random during the dinner hour, then maybe the next step will be to prohibit advertisers from sending free mailings, and then maybe the next step will be to forbid door-to-door selling, and so on.

9. *Begging the question.* Begging the question is essentially assuming something as a given that has not been proved. A related strategy, circular reasoning, restates the proposition as a conclusion: "Students who have bad grades and don't study should not be allowed to watch television because viewing might be detrimental to their schoolwork."

10. *Non sequitur.* Literally, this term means, "It does not follow." Advertisements are full of fallacious reasoning but make something of a specialty of non sequiturs: "Crock Cola tastes great: America's fastest-growing cola company!" Taste and corporate growth are juxtaposed as if one leads to the other; regrettably for consumers, such is not necessarily the case. Sometimes the term *non sequitur* is used more generally to indicate any lapse in logic.

Understanding Persuasion in Practice

In addition to evaluating the appeals to ethos, pathos, and logos in an argument, taking arguments apart on a structural, sentence-by-sentence level to see how they work can be instructive. Understanding both general principles of persuasion and specific, sentence-level strategies enables us to evaluate the arguments that confront us daily, in college studies and in our communities.

Examples of persuasion surround us in academic texts, mass media, personal conversations—even as we walk down the street. Let's examine a specific piece of persuasion encountered on a college campus recently. A flyer posted on the wall of a campus building has the following message spray-painted on it, in red letters on a white background, as if through a stencil:

Oil in Kuwait
Oil in Panama
No Oil in Bosnia
Get it?

Unpacking the argument takes a bit of thought and involves reader response and input to make the argument work. First, we observe that this is not an impromptu message, because it was created through a stencil, which presumes multiple applications of the message in various locations. The somewhat diffuse red spray paint draws attention to the message and suggests blood; the rhetor, through the parallel structure of the phrases, argues that the situations are analogous: that the United States intervened militarily in other countries when doing so was in its own best interests; and that it has not intervened in Bosnia because there is no economic motive to do so. In a rather taunting manner, the rhetorical question of the last line invites audience engagement in the discussion.

As it happens, some audience members—people of the academic community who passed by the notice—did engage in the argument. Written in ballpoint pen ink between lines two and three are "No oil in Vietnam" and "No oil in Grenada," a reference to other U.S. military involvement without apparent economic benefit. More recent viewers might assert that there is "No Oil in Afghanistan"—or might refute the rebuttal by writing in "Oil in Iraq!"

Except for the rhetorical question, each of the other elements in the argument is a phrase, which the audience has to fill in to complete a statement. Those statements might look something like this:

The United States intervenes militarily in other countries only to protect its interests, such as access to suppliers of oil.
Bosnia is not a supplier of oil.
Therefore, the United States will not intervene militarily to protect its interests in Bosnia.

For the conclusion to be true, the premises leading to the conclusion must be true. If they are not, the argument breaks down. When critiquing an argument, the audience can question the premises or the reasoning process that leads to the conclusion or claim. The scrawled messages in ballpoint pen refute the argument by attacking the premise that the United States intervenes militarily only when oil is at stake.

Examining the style of the message, we see that the rhetor made use of an excellent stylistic tactic, parallelism. The grammatical structures of the first three lines are equivalent: noun, preposition, noun, with a negative added to the last line. Parallel structures can help to clarify and emphasize connections and equivalence between ideas, as the rhetor was trying to suggest.

Let's examine another use of helpful grammatical structure, a balanced sentence:

When guns are outlawed, only outlaws will have guns.

What is your immediate reaction to this slogan? Imagine that you saw it on a bumper sticker of a car. Does it seem sensible or logical? Now read it aloud, and take it apart.

When guns are outlawed.
Only outlaws will have guns.

First, examine the rhythm. Which words are stressed? How do the stresses contribute to the rhythm? What words are then distressed and de-emphasized? How does the sense of balance, of equivalence, contribute to the sense of logic or make it seem that the slogan "makes sense"?

Now look critically at the diction, or word choice. First look at the ambiguous term, *guns.* Does it refer to handguns? Shotguns? Rifles? Semiautomatics? Uzis? What does *outlawed* mean? Does it mean people must register for a gun? That they must wait ten days before purchasing one so that the seller can check for a criminal record? Does it mean children can't buy guns? Then examine that unstressed word, *only.* Is it true that only outlaws or criminals will have guns? What about police officers? Forest rangers? Brinks guards? The assumptions and assertions of the slogan do not bear up under close examination. In a fleeting statement as on a bumper sticker or in a cartoon, such arguments can sometimes make an impression or erode the position of the opposition just a bit.

Consider another recent political slogan:

No Blood for Oil.

Trace the steps of the argument, the assumptions, the premises and conclusions. What does "blood" mean in this context? What does "oil" mean? Does "no blood" mean no defense of vital interests? No defense of allies? Does fighting for oil mean fighting for a luxury? For a necessity? For the ability to defend one's country? Or does it mean special interests with connections to powerful politicians?

Though you need to avoid falling into fallacious arguments, or those in which the logic breaks down, as in the example of the bumper sticker, you can use structures such as parallelism and balance to show viable relationships between things and ideas. You can choose whether to use *denotative* language, which is explicit language that attempts to convey objectivity, or *connotative* language, which is emotion-laden language that attempts to evoke an image or idea. By the same token, you can understand when you are being hornswoggled or fooled by eloquent language disguising a weak argument.

Let's look at the way that another rhetorical strategy, antithesis, which is a balanced structure with opposing elements, can reinforce the effects of language:

> We observe today
> not a victory of party
> but a celebration of freedom.

These opening lines to John F. Kennedy's "Inaugural Address" stress the orderly changing of administrations, emphasizing not the rancorous 1960 presidential race against and defeat of Richard Nixon, not the onset of Democratic rule, but the sense that the inauguration itself is a link in history, part of the ritual of democratic government. A few lines later, Kennedy makes use of highly connotative language to evoke a sense of tradition, grandeur, and solemnity:

> For I have sworn before you and Almighty God the same, solemn oath our forebears prescribed nearly a century and three quarters ago.

Why would a modern president—one who used the relatively new medium of television to his advantage, one who represented youth and change, one who frightened some citizens simply by virtue of being Catholic—speak in archaic, formal diction? How do you think that you would have reacted to such a speech? What tone, approach, and mood does this rhetor evoke? And how do these strategies support his goals?

Sometimes simple repetition of a key phrase can drive a point home forcefully and eloquently. You may have been told in the past to avoid being repetitious; now is a good time to examine the difference between needless, annoying repetition that occurs when you have not taken care with your essay or paragraph organization, and repetition that reinforces points and ideas, suggests connections between ideas, clarifies meaning, and delivers pleasing balance and rhythm to the audience. As we saw with the bumper sticker, rhythm and balance are no substitute for logic and evidence; nevertheless, well-crafted prose is itself more persuasive than plodding, hard-to-follow prose. And unless you are deliberately trying to obfuscate or muddy up the issues, clarity is a virtue too. Let's look at an eloquent example of *anaphora,* or a repeated sentence opener, from Martin Luther King, Jr.'s, "I Have a Dream" speech.

> So let freedom ring from the prodigious hilltops of New Hampshire.
> Let freedom ring from the mighty mountains of New York.
> Let freedom ring from the heightening Alleghenies of Pennsylvania!
> Let freedom ring from the snowcapped Rockies of Colorado!
> Let freedom ring from the curvaceous peaks of California!
> But not only that;
> Let freedom ring from Stone Mountain of Georgia!

Let freedom ring from Lookout Mountain of Tennessee!
Let freedom ring from every hill and molehill of Mississippi.
From every mountainside, let freedom ring!

This section follows King's recitation of the lyrics to "America" and picks up the thread of the last line of that song in the repeated "let freedom ring," and the image of "from every mountainside" in the last line of the song. Examine the progression of King's lines. What geographical regions are included? Then examine the break, midway, and the change in direction. In what ways does this repetition, attached to the diverse regions, reinforce a theme?

You can read the full text of this speech in Chapter 6. As you review this and other selections, remember to analyze not only themes and overall structure but also patterns of sentences, words, and images; all contribute to and underscore the persuasive message of the rhetor.

Persuasion works on many levels: to engage the audience, to get them to identify with the point of view of the rhetor, and, if possible, to move them in belief or in action to the position suggested by the rhetor. Because argument relies on moving beyond the supporting materials to draw conclusions, whether that support is based on examples or derived from a general proposition, the strength and effectiveness of appeals to ethos, pathos, and logos are crucial in persuading audiences. Such appeals operate at the level of the main points, the supporting points, and down to individual words and sentences.

Persuasion in Diverse Genres

There are any number of genres in which a writer or an artist can be persuasive; some of them are clearly argumentative, like a pro-and-con debate or a legal case; some of them less obviously so, like fiction, poetry, or film. But all of them can be successful at conveying a point of view or swaying an audience. In this book we include a variety of genres with strong persuasive elements. The brief explanations that follow are designed to help you read these materials, regardless of medium, for ideas, themes, and argumentative and persuasive content, as well as for the pleasure of encountering American writers and artists on their home ground.

Essays

Essays may be reflective, analytical, expository, or argumentative. The essay was invented by the Renaissance writer Michel de Montaigne, who used it as a way to reflect on and explore ideas and especially to learn about himself. Informal, ironic, funny, full of anecdotes and charm, Montaigne's essays started as quotations on which he made comments and ended as an exploration of his psychological makeup and view of the world. He tested out his thoughts, pains, prejudices, and pleasures against the measure of his own intelligence. Great essays demand a high level of honesty from the writer, but they also provide a kind of immediacy and intimacy, a one-on-one exchange between reader and writer that is very satisfying. The essay persuades through a form of verbal seduction—by enabling the reader to look with the writer's eyes and the writer's own viewpoint. Reflective essays also present the personality of the writer distinctively; when you get to know a great essayist, invariably you will recognize his or her voice, and hopefully as time goes on, you will also begin to write in a voice that is distinctly and uniquely yours.

In most expository essays, particularly those written in academic venues, the writer gives information in order to explain a point of view on a topic. This kind of essay presents you, as the writer, with an opportunity to work out your ideas in a broad context—on the environment, for example, or privacy, or relations between men and women. Your research, reflections, and analyses all contribute to the assertions you make and how you make them, but the goal of an expository essay is to express or explain your ideas clearly and to persuade the reader to accept the merit of your thesis or main point, rather than to change the reader's opinion or behavior.

An argumentative essay argues a point of view or presupposes an opposing point of view, and is geared directly to anticipating and refuting it. Like the expository essay, it clearly puts ideas in the public arena, but with the goal of stimulating debate, eliciting criticism, convincing readers to change the way they think or what they do, or persuading them to take action in a particular direction. The best argumentative essays, however, are not divorced from the writer; they engage readers most thoroughly when the author is passionate about the subject matter.

Occasionally an author is able to write an essay that is simultaneously analytical and expository or argumentative, for example, the excerpt from Thoreau's *Civil Disobedience* in Chapter 9. Thoreau tells us about himself—his potential beliefs, his conviction that they demand action if they are to be valid as principles, and why he believes that civil disobedience to unjust laws is the most accurate and honest expression of his individuality and personality available to him. He is so eloquent on the importance of the lone conscience in a democracy, the trouble with Congress, and the moral obligation to stand up and be counted at any cost, that his personal creed also becomes a persuasive argument for nonviolent resistance as a general political tool. Few essayists can manage to combine all forms of the essay in one, but

Thoreau will give you some idea of how many forms of self-expression and powerful persuasion a good essay can entertain simultaneously.

Fiction and Poetry

We don't often think of fiction or poetry as persuasive writing because the arguments they make are more subtly stated, enveloped in character and language and plot. They are *about* someone or something. In fact, a great story or poem can move people profoundly and change their ideas, or enlighten them, in ways that more direct forms of address cannot. For example, Ralph Ellison's *Invisible Man* is a novel about an African American man who finds himself both literally and figuratively invisible in white America. Nowhere in the text does Ellison deliver a lecture on prejudice, or the corrupting influence of racism, or the tragic denial of ordinary freedoms. (See Chapter 5 for the Prologue of this novel.) But his characters, the voice of the narrator, and the story are so lucid and so affecting that the theme argues more profoundly than any explicit statement could. Similarly, "The Land of the Free" (see Chapter 6), Sui Sin Far's tragic story of a Chinese immigrant family, never explicitly criticizes the cultural insensitivity of the social workers who take a Chinese woman's child or the greed of the lawyer who is supposed to help get him back. But both issues become profoundly clear through the narrative of the story and the dialogue of the characters.

Poetry is characterized by a kind of compression that makes its point through concentrated images and language. Langston Hughes, a major figure in the Harlem Renaissance and one of America's foremost poets, writes "Let America Be America Again" (see Chapter 6) through the separate voices of Americans denied their full participation in their national experience. It is the music of those individual voices, first telling their different stories and then eventually joining together in a chorus, which communicates their longing and their determination, far more effectively than any polemic could. In her poem "Dear John Wayne," Louise Erdrich makes a forceful argument against the treatment that Native Americans have received in the media, in popular culture, and in the way that other Americans perceive them (see Chapter 11). Rather than assemble statistics about life on the reservation, she sets out an illustration whose point is vividly clear: the experience of Indian teenagers at a drive-in movie, watching John Wayne, the all-American hero, shoot apparently endless numbers of their ancestors in a movie battle. The oversimplification of the movie's portrait of good guys and bad guys, combined with the ordinariness of watching a movie at a drive-in, urges us to rethink our perspective and reevaluate our ideas—the goal of every well-written argument.

Legal Cases

Legal cases are a good way to clarify the elements of persuasive argument because that's exactly what they are about: two opponents in a court of law, arguing against each other in order to persuade a judge or jury to decide in their favor, knowing that only one side can win, and using every psychological and intellectual strategy they can think of to get the decision to go their way.

Trials are adversarial by definition; there have to be two sides and a neutral third party—a judge or a jury guided by a judge. Once the verdict has been reached, on the basis of the evidence—once the third party has been persuaded by one side or the other—the trial is over. If the losing side is dissatisfied with the verdict, it can write an appeal, a piece of purely persuasive writing that goes to a panel of judges who then decide whether they want to overrule the trial court decision or to have the case tried again (see Chapter 8, *Rusk v. State of Maryland*).

The U.S. Supreme Court is the court of last resort for appeals, but certain threshold conditions must be met for an appeal to be submitted to it; for example, the Court can decide to rule on a case involving the interpretation or application of the Constitution of the United States to a particular situation. Two of the cases in this book are Supreme Court cases. As you read the decisions that the Court made in *Plessy v. Ferguson* and *Brown v. Board of Education*, keep the following four points in mind (see Chapter 9).

First, the Court often relies on the accumulated body of law already decided in related cases—called *precedent*—to explain why it is not overturning the verdict in the case before it. Occasionally—and *Brown* is the most famous example in American law—the Court rejects all precedent and makes a new law or takes the law, and the country, in a new direction.

Second, every year the Court receives many requests to hear cases on appeal but accepts only a fraction—usually those involving issues of substantial national importance. When it refuses a case, whatever the previous state or federal court decided remains unchanged.

Third, once the Supreme Court makes a decision, it is the law, until or unless Congress passes a different one. There is no higher court of appeal. It is a remarkable feature of our political life that Americans accept the Court's authority, though many of them may disagree with individual decisions.

Finally, Supreme Court decisions are rarely unanimous. With nine justices, the vote on a given case can be anything from 9-to-0 to 5-to-4.

When you turn to *Plessy*, you will first read the majority decision, which prevailed. Then you will see Justice John Harlan's minority dissent—an opinion written by a justice who disagrees with the majority or is not persuaded by its reasoning and wants to set the reasons down clearly. *Brown*, in contrast, was decided unanimously.

Sometimes a dissenting opinion in one case forms the basis for a majority decision in another case years later. That outcome is what happened between the *Plessy* decision and the *Brown* case almost fifty years afterward; Justice Harlan's argument against racial segregation was rejected in his lifetime, but in 1954 the Supreme Court found his language persuasive and used it in reversing the *Plessy* decision.

Visual Rhetoric

This text includes a range of images, both historical and contemporary. We are persuaded daily by images—advertisements, editorial cartoons, Web sites, television programs, music videos, movie trailers, and the like. Advertisements convince us to buy certain food, drink, or clothing, or to cultivate a certain appearance; they suggest to us how we could look thinner, richer, better dressed; they suggest lifestyles, encourage guilt, foster patriotism, sell almost anything.

Films and television programs are both so ingrained in our lives that they are seen as enactments of our values and experiences, our fears, and sometimes our prejudices. They attract us by creating heroes, by reinforcing or undercutting accepted ideas, by showing us friends who are more like the ideal family, or families so dysfunctional that they make us feel better; they invoke our fantasies and our need to escape. Of course, the films and television of all countries fulfill similar national and local needs, but because American film and television are so dominant and popular in other parts of the world, they are, along with popular music, the cultural currency by which countries measure us and by which we measure ourselves.

Posters and editorial cartoons communicate social expectations or political ideas to vast audiences. American political cartoons are traditionally commentaries on contemporary situations—war, the economy, the behavior of famous figures. Visual images can persuade where words might fail.

Perhaps in response to rising expectations for the use of visuals in academic, business, and professional settings, scholars now attend to many different varieties of visual persuasion. Discussions of visual rhetoric may include elements with a much longer history in our culture, like photographs, paintings, cartoons, advertisements, and posters. But they also include Web sites and business documents that persuade visually through conventional images and also through the appearance, format, and placement of text. Graphics, visual display of data, and other elements of a document are more and more commonly used to increase the clarity and the persuasiveness of textual documents as well.

You've grown up watching videos and DVDs, film, and television, and reading magazines, and consciously or unconsciously passing judgment on visual materials. For example, you've seen automobile advertisements all your life; you don't have to have lived in the 1950s to get the point of an advertisement for a 1958 car complete with enormous fins and a huge front grill. And when you see an eighteenth-century etching showing a woman confined within the outlines of a compass, you will probably have little difficulty in figuring out that it illustrates the limits of what women were allowed to do. Although pictures from different times are directed to different audiences and your own reaction to those from the past may be different from those of the original viewers, keep in mind that the skill involved in "reading" images is one you practice every time you look at the advertisements in a magazine, on a television show, or in a movie.

What follows is a brief overview of the varieties of visual images in this book, as well as some strategies for analyzing and enjoying them.

Paintings, Photographs, and Cartoons   As with other expressive media, perhaps it is less common to think of paintings as persuasive, even when they capture specific events or appear to be recording a simple moment in time. Painters who went west with exploration or geological parties painted canvases of Western landscapes that seemed to East Coast audiences almost unbelievable in their grandeur. They loved the paintings but trusted the photographs more (see the following page). Alfred Bierstadt, one of the greatest of the Western landscape painters, often used tiny human figures to give his viewers a key to the enormous scope of the wonders of Yosemite or a redwood forest, whether or not there were actually figures in the landscape when he made his sketches. This technique doesn't make his work any less valid; on the contrary, like all artists, painters select and reorganize as one way of communicating their ideas. The interpolation of tiny Native American figures did more than articulate the scale of the trees. Because the viewer of the painting would typically be white, those Native American figures help to explain what the wilderness used to be like and how it was changing. Bierstadt also included details when he focused on living creatures, as he did in his panoramic picture, *The Last of the Buffalo* (see Chapter 11). The title of the painting, the image of the animals about to be killed in a traditional Native American hunt, with the bodies of dead buffalo on the ground, give us a sense of desolation at the loss of a way of life that is none the less powerful because Bierstadt drew the buffalo in his studio and modeled it on a buffalo skull he had in front of him.

Photographs seem to possess a peculiarly strong validity for Americans. When artists in the nineteenth century, like Bierstadt, painted the natural glories of the West, people back in the East often had trouble believing that such spectacular scenery and color weren't the product of someone's overactive imagination rather than the rendering of actual places. But no such disbelief greeted later photographs of the same spots. The fact that a photograph looked more "real" gave it a kind of currency that a great painting might not have for the same audience.

The historical reliability of photographs was given a huge impetus during the Civil War, when photographers set up their studios at battlefields and soldiers had their pictures taken to send back to their families. If, as was often the case, the soldier was killed, his photograph became a kind of memorial for his family as well. Photographers also took pictures of the battlefields, including photos of corpses, of dead horses, and of maimed men. The most famous photographic exhibit of the Civil War, held in New York, explicitly showed the death and devastation of the war. It brought civilians the kind of intimacy with a national tragedy that would hardly be duplicated until a century later, in November 1963, when television's role in news enabled people all over the country to participate as a single community by watching the coverage of President Kennedy's funeral.

Today it would be inconceivable for any popular print medium like newspapers and magazines to omit photographs from their news coverage. Whether still photos by watching a newspaper or "live-action video" on a television news program, photographs bring the story to life and capture the event in ways that complement the textual material and sometimes supplant it entirely. Two photographs from the Vietnam War (see Chapter 10), both winners of Pulitzer Prizes, caught the horror of war so profoundly—one is a picture of an execution and one is of naked and burned children—that they became timeless evocations of the tragedy inevitable in all war, not in just one particular war.

No matter how much photographs function for us as objective records—and that is one reason Americans trust them—they are also artful. The photographer "edits" by choosing precisely how much he or she wants to show: even Civil War photographers were not above posing surviving soldiers to reenact battle scenes in order to make better pictures. Photographs are taken from a certain perspective, from a specific point of view; they record, but they also select. They capture the event, but at the same time they leave out part of the picture, often the larger context. Photos taken to report the news can move viewers to change their point of view and, in some cases, to change policy. The war photographs in Chapter 10 are examples of photography's immense persuasive power.

Editorial cartoons make no pretense of objectivity. Often visual images with brief text, they must capture attention and make a point in only a second or two. Benjamin Franklin's woodcut in Chapter 5 and most of the editorial cartoons in contemporary newspapers tap into cultural references common to rhetor and audience as a kind of shorthand for longer arguments. In a sense, they are visual enthymemes, because the audience supplies the missing links in the argument in order to get the point.

Posters   Posters developed out of nineteenth-century technology and the need to communicate with a larger audience. They advertised performances and goods, appealed for labor and military recruits, and in time of war and national distress sought to maintain morale and to denounce the enemy. Posters were a dominant communication device from the late nineteenth century until the rise of the newsreel, radio, and later television. They were still useful, as a quickly and cheaply produced mass medium, but their impact declined as the other media appeared. For posters to persuade, they had to be able to attract attention and to inform. Since the audience generally would have been passersby on their way somewhere else, or people standing in line at the post office or other public building, the posters, rather like political cartoons and advertisements, had to catch the viewer's attention and make a point quickly, in a matter of seconds. Effective posters generally convey a strong impression and a single strong element, through the size of the type, the placement of a figure on the background, or the strategic use of color. A bold color accent on a muted background can immediately draw the eye to the core issue or theme. Other elements can be more subtle; in the Hoover Archives collection, for example, there is a German poster stressing soldiers' efforts to save women and children of the fatherland that includes a small cross hanging around a woman's neck, tapping into the "Christian" identity of the woman and, presumably, of her soldier-savior. In World War I, when recruiting posters were designed by famous illustrators like Howard Chandler Christy and James Montgomery Flagg, the results could be astonishing. Christy, who specialized in drawing pretty, fashionable girls, who became known as Christy girls, put one of them in a male sailor's outfit and headed the poster with the words "I wish I was a man—so I could join the Navy." He took the most famous slogan, "I Want You," which was associated with a serious Uncle Sam pointing his finger, and transformed it into a young woman wearing an officer's uniform; her collar is unbuttoned, her blond hair is in disarray, and the words "I Want You," with an obviously different connotation, are written in a loose lipstick-colored script at the top of the poster, thereby offering a very different kind of encouragement to young men thinking of enlisting. At a time when women who went bathing wore

concealing two-piece outfits and bathing caps that resembled pincush-
ions, the need for young men to join the armed services gave artists
the opportunity to experiment with presentations of gender and sexuality that would have been shocking to an audience before the war.

In evaluating posters as persuasive discourse, we look to some of
the same criteria we use in judging other works of art. Although we
can't always know the artist's personal beliefs or the extent to which
the poster represents mass opinion, we can examine the rhetorical
strategies employed by the artist and the themes implicit in the poster.
We can assume that the posters were meant to inform or persuade and
that the appeals employed by the artist were designed to evoke audience response. We can then make inferences about the intended audience, remembering that we are generalizing from the data that the
posters provide. We can look to color, placement of objects in the
poster, designs, motifs, and themes to analyze their effectiveness.

Advertisements   Like posters, advertisements reveal much about
the cultures in which they appear and can serve as an index of social
values, preoccupations, worries, and fantasies. Often shortchanging
logic in favor of associations and emotional appeals, ads can appear in
print or on video or DVD, radio, or film; they can be made up of text
or image or both; and their arguments can be expected and explicit, or
unexpected and implicit. Ads featuring famous people, particularly
athletes and actors, can present pictures of physical perfection, wealth,
or unattainable glamour that play on the viewers' insecurities, while
suggesting that those insecurities can be reduced just by buying whatever is being advertised. Or ads can go in the opposite direction and
portray just one object on a page, like a woman's very dressy, extremely high-heeled shoe, and that isolated image is enough to convey
a sense of glamour and an evening out. In men's and women's fashion
magazines, the emphasis on selling products is so strong that articles
may occupy only a quarter of the pages, with the rest devoted entirely
to ads for clothing, makeup, food, drink, cars, and personal products.

Purveyors of products also go to great effort to have them featured
in films; the positive reinforcement for the car that the hero drives, or
the soda that the heroine drinks, can act almost subliminally to reinforce a positive association with the product in the viewer's mind. In
the same way, ads have moved to a more explicit form in DVDs. And
an enormous battle has been waged as schools and school boards have
debated whether to accept offers of free television equipment in exchange for including a certain amount of advertising in the television
"curriculum." The trade-off between the financial benefits of supplies,
books, and facilities that a school gains, as opposed to the dangers of
turning an educational institution into the equivalent of a daily advertisement for fast food, highlights the difficulties that schools face in
balancing commercial and noncommercial priorities. Even the histori-

cally advertising-free medium of public television, which simply used to list the names of its major benefactors, has found that in return for corporate contributions, it must offer longer and longer "thanks" to its sponsors, and the thanks looks more and more like full-fledged advertisements.

As in writing about art, posters, and texts, writing about advertisements entails evaluating purpose, appeals, and aesthetics. The purpose is generally evident: the purchase of a product. Much fruitful analysis of advertising focuses on the assumptions; the flaws in logic; and the ethos, pathos, and logos appeals in the ads. Many of the points made earlier about these appeals pertain to advertising. Logical fallacies are rampant. Emotional appeals are often evident but are also often hidden beneath ostensibly logical claims. For example, an advertisement for soup might claim that soups will warm up a child before the child runs outside on a cold day; such an ad relies on emotional appeals (warmth, nurturing, home and health) more than physiological fact. Cigarette ads in the 1920s and 1930s used beautiful showgirls puffing away to encourage the emotionally pleasing association between cigarettes and glamour.

Critically assessing the layout, color, and image of advertisements can yield rich information about its persuasive tactics. Often products are strategically placed on the page or near certain parts of the anatomy of a model; other times, a product (lipstick, beverage) is deliberately presented in a sexually suggestive position. Sometimes the advertiser wants part of the ad to recede into the background. For example, look at some magazine advertisements for cigarettes, and then try to find the surgeon general's warning.

If you want to get an idea of what kinds of advertising appeals are effective on you, pick up one of the magazines you like, flip the pages, and notice which ad you stop at and which part of the page you see first; then assess what key feature of the product is made prominent and which is pushed to the side. See if you can figure out what persuaded you to stop and look: not just the product or person, but what the page evokes from you—laughter, admiration, envy, curiosity, comfort, good memories. You will learn about what appeals to you as a viewer and to what degree the ad's target audience shares your interests.

The language of advertising is highly connotative, associative, and image-laden; writers have to convey maximum impact in the fewest words possible. Student writers could indeed learn a lot about conciseness by examining well-written advertisements. The structure of textual arguments in advertising, though, is something to avoid in academic arguments; it is commonly designed to shortchange logic and to get consumers to draw a particular inference (they should buy a certain product) from the limited "data" presented.

There is no getting away from advertising in mainstream American culture. There are different ways of approaching the issue—from economic, sociological, psychological, political, and aesthetic perspectives, to name a few. You may wish to investigate some of these perspectives as you develop longer, documented essays for college courses. Professor Jean Kilbourne, for example, examines damaging attitudes toward and treatment of women in advertisements in the lecture/film *Still Killing Us Softly* that may be available through your college library. And the Web sites for various dolls, like the traditional, if varied, Barbie dolls and the contemporary and much more sexually dressed Bratz dolls, illustrate the complex relationship between young girls' self-image and the power of advertising to affect and profit from it.

We close this section with an essay on a Dolce & Gabbana clothing advertisement that makes an extreme fashion statement; student Jordan Blackthorne analyzes its somewhat unusual visual rhetoric and its appeals. For copyright reasons, we are unable to show this ad (which depicts an androgynous figure in tight clothes in a room with both very old and new furniture), but students can find it in *Vanity Fair* or on the Dolce & Gabbana Web site.

Modern Advertising and the Curious Allure of Clothing We Would Never Wear

JORDAN BLACKTHORNE

In the pages of *Vanity Fair*, sandwiched between a slightly grainy, faux family portrait and an intense-looking beauty in black-and-white, is a quite incongruous two-page fashion advertisement. The color photograph depicts an expressionless model posed in a bizarre outfit and room. The design is so eccentric that at first it was difficult to see the appeal, or understand how the ad would possibly motivate a person to buy anything at all, which is presumably its purpose. But perhaps the intended attraction lies in the strangeness itself. There is something inarguably attention-grabbing about an image that has no apparent basis in my reality; never in my life have I encountered clothing, a room, or an overall scene like this one. The allure, however, is lost on me, because although the advertisement certainly stands out, it takes fashion to such an extreme that it fails to evoke any feelings other than mild curiosity, confusion, and disbelief at the absurdity of modern advertising.

This advertisement tries to be and do a number of things that other fashion ads avoid. Instead of trying to display the most beautiful people and attractive clothes, the makers of this ad chose to show a rather androgynous young model dressed in an outrageous outfit. The model, probably a woman, has been stripped of everything that typically defines feminine beauty: her hair is hidden under a tight cap, huge dark sunglasses conceal her eyes, she wears no obvious make-up or jewelry, and her clothing fits in a way that hides most signs of sexuality and even gender. Her outfit is a strangely cut black top, large and loose around her arms and chest, and tighter—though not at all revealing—around her midsection, with lavender tights and oversized, shin-high, white and gray boots that look like ski boots. This is clearly not an attempt to relate to the "average consumer," because it still takes fashion to an extreme that is as impossible as other ads' perfection.

Overall, her appearance almost invites a challenge. Her face a blank, emotionless mask, she sits straight-backed on an ornate antique table. One ski-booted foot is propped commandingly on an overturned, very modern metal coffee table, and although her legs are angled sideways, her body is turned so that her torso is open to the viewer. This position is definitely provocative, fully prepared for a confrontation. Every bit of her, from the firm set of her mouth to her squared shoulders to the way her foot is propped defiantly on an expensive piece of furniture, exudes self-possession. In this picture, this space, she is in control.

Our model has staked a claim on two pieces of furniture in the room, and they illustrate a play on opposites that absolutely permeates this advertisement. The overturned metal table is at sharp contrast with the antique wooden table on which she is seated. At the opposite edge of the page, an antique chair matches the table, and the walls are classically paneled like an old drawing room. Yet the floor is highly modern like the metal table: the surface is clear glass, under which lie rows of fluorescent lights. This clash of old and contemporary styles is also apparent in the model's outfit. The loose top half of her shirt resembles a kimono, while the tighter, almost restrictive fit of the bottom half suggests a corset, both of which are very classic, recognizable looks. Her leather ski boots, on the other hand, are extremely modern, with large buckles and heavy soles. The contrast, combined with the model's dominance over the room, suggests that this line of clothing is good enough for anything.

A funny but important part of the common consumer mentality is that, under the right brand name, the stranger something seems, the more expensive, cutting-edge and therefore desirable it becomes. The ad displays things that seem pricey and unfamiliar, and we are expected to want them. But while the strange photograph attracts us initially and our brains may race to make sense of the image, the visual focus of the ad is ultimately on the words "Dolce & Gabbana." The company is not selling the clothing it depicts; it is selling its label. In an appeal to pathos, it is selling a statement and a lifestyle that fascinates people because strangeness and distance are intriguing when portrayed as fashion. No one would dress in these clothes in public, and the makers of the advertisement are certainly aware of this, but the ad surreptitiously puts an idea into viewers' heads that they could be more fashionable and intriguing than they are, and that Dolce & Gabbana can help them do it. Although this ad fails to persuade *me,* many other people may be attracted by such a striking photograph, and all of the less tangible benefits it offers.

Films

We have included a film selection in each chapter. Film critic Robin Wood says that movies express not only the dreams of the people who make them but also the dreams of the audience watching them. No other art form is more wholly or characteristically American. Hollywood became known long ago as the "Dream Factory," and there is no aspect of American life that is not refracted sooner or later through the lens of a camera. Sometimes the result is realistic; sometimes it is more an expression of wish fulfillment or escapism. Sometimes it is insulting; minorities watched movies for generations, looking for images of themselves and seeing nothing or seeing themselves portrayed in stereotypical or debased characterizations. But it would be impossible to imagine modern American culture without movies. And every theme in this book has provided and continues to provide material for the vast film audience. Movies are so embedded in our lives that many of the most profound notions that Americans have about themselves are as much a result of what they see on the screen as of what they read or learn from experience.

Since you have been watching films all your life, the ones in this book will have certain pictorial values, lights and shadows, cuts from one scene to another, close-ups and long shots, that will be familiar to you. But in order to help you look at these films critically and aesthetically, what follows is a basic vocabulary of film definitions from the *Film Studies Dictionary.*

Aspect ratio—the ratio between the width of a film image and its height. Thomas Edison's ration of 1.33:1 has been considered so generally pleasing that the Academy of Motion Picture Arts and Sciences has kept it as the standard, but wide-screen movies have different ratios.

Assembly edit—the first stage in film editing; the unwanted material is eliminated and the rest is organized roughly into the approximate final length and shape of the film.

Auteur—a director whose themes and style are so distinctive that they characterize his or her whole body of work, such as Alfred Hitchcock.

Back light—a light, usually a bright spotlight, positioned behind and usually above an actor or object; it can provide a dramatic effect by making the object or actor stand out from the background.

Black-and-white film—film that shows colors as a range of grays; *Citizen Kane* by Orson Welles (see Chapter 6) makes especially brilliant use of it.

Breakdown—the way a scene is cut up into shots.

Bridge—a shot that links two sequences separated by time or space.

Camera angle—the degree to which an angle of a shot varies from the mythical standard shot, which is at the shoulder height of an average human being and straight ahead.

Continuity—the quality of a film that is designed to make it look as seamless and natural as possible.

Coverage—collecting different shots of a scene so that the editor will have a lot to choose from.

Crosscutting—in editing, the alternation of shots from at least two different scenes to suggest that the scenes are happening simultaneously but in different spaces.

Cut—the most common way of connecting images—splicing the end of one shot to the beginning of the next.

Cutaway—a shot that briefly interrupts the main narrative to show something else, like what another character is thinking or seeing.

Deep focus—a way of shooting that keeps a number of planes of action in one shot in sharp focus, allowing a number of significant actions to take place in different planes; *Citizen Kane* is one of the greatest examples of the use of deep focus.

Dissolve—a device by which one shot appears to fade out as another one fades in and replaces it; dissolves commonly suggest a change of setting or a lapse of time.

Establishing shot—a shot at the beginning of a scene that situates when and sometimes where the action is going to take place.

Extreme long shot—a panoramic shot from a great distance, sometimes used to emphasize human vulnerability.

Fade-in, fade-out—the gradual disclosure or obscuring of an image as the screen becomes gradually eliminated or darkened.

Flashback—the representation of some action or scene which occurred before the present time in the narrative. The flashback could be accompanied by the voice of a character or a narrator, it can reveal personal history, or it can give various versions of the chronology of the story.

Focus—the point behind the lens at which rays of light reflected from a subject converge to form an image.

Frame—the basic unit of film: a single still rectangular image.

Freeze frame—a frame of film that is repeated numerous times, making it appear as if the movement in the shot has stopped.

Genre film—a category of film with certain elements in common. Genre films are defined in different ways, i.e., horror films are identified by their effects and westerns by their settings.

High key lighting—lighting design that emphasizes brightness with little use of shadow or strong contrasts.

Interior monologue—what a character is thinking, usually revealed to the audience through voice over shots of the character.

Jump cut—a break in the continuity of a shot done by removing a section of a shot and then splicing together what's left.

Long shot—a shot in which the camera is a great distance from the object being photographed, or a shot in which the subject is seen in its entirety in small scale.

Low angle—a shot in which the camera is situated below eye level or below the object being photographed.

Low-key lighting—appearing dimly lit, though the overall appearance of darkness and shadow may be contrasted with brighter areas.

Midshot—the camera is relatively near the subject or the scale of the object shown is of moderate size; a human figure is usually shown from the knees up or the waist up and fills most of the screen.

Montage—a concentrated sequence using such techniques as jump cuts and dissolves to create a kaleidoscopic effect or to summarize a particular experience.

Narrative space—not only actual locations but also places implied or suggested, like all the colleges that expel Kane in *Citizen Kane.*

Narrator—the character or implied character who delivers the narration at various points in the film.

Overhead shot—a shot taken from directly above the action.

Perspective—the illusions of depth and distance on a flat surface; different camera lenses produce different kinds of perspective.

Point of view—the eyes through which we view the unfolding of the plot.

Shallow focus—when only the narrow area within the image is in sharp focus and the background (and sometimes the foreground) is out of focus.

Split screen—two or more images being shown on-screen at the same time; this can, for example, show more than one perspective, such as two things happening simultaneously.

Storyboard—a series of shots, photographs, drawings, or computer-generated drawings for a film; Hitchcock used storyboards to prepare scenes in advance.

Subjective camera—the use of the camera to give the impression that the images on-screen represent the field of vision or imagination of a character.

Tracking shot—in practice, any shot in which the camera moves on wheels.

Voyeurism—the act of watching people without their knowledge or permission; Hitchcock recognized the voyeuristic element in the way an audience watches film characters and paid special attention to it in *Rear Window*, a film in which a photographer discovers a murder by watching his neighbors through a camera lens.

We can look for common themes shared by the posters, political cartoons, films, fiction, essays, and arguments to find the common denominators in the way different media treat particular themes. You can pursue research by looking up particular themes or issues (women in the workforce, access to the Internet, support on the home front, civil rights, vilification of the enemy, American attitudes toward wealth) that interest you and then analyzing treatment of them in the different media. Maybe your library has access to back issues of *Life* magazine, for example. One student researched issues of *Time* magazine from the 1940s, found an article entitled "How to Tell Your Friends from the Japs," and was able to trace racial stereotypes from posters and cartoons as well as the popular general interest magazines of the times. Other sources for this kind of research include Sam Keen's book *Faces of the Enemy* and the film of the same name, a thoughtful look at the ways in which we create an enemy through various media, including posters and cartoons. Bryan F. LeBeau's book *Currier and Ives: America Imagined* gives a century's worth of illustrations on American life that shaped how ordinary Americans saw their history and their hopes. Another excellent source for propaganda and war-era posters is *Persuasive Images,* by Peter Paret et al.

Numerous Web sites are devoted to visual persuasion. You may find some useful examples on some of the following Web sites:

http://cartooning.about.com/arts/cartooning/mbody.htm (cartooning)

http://www.nara.gov/exhall/powers/powers.html (powers of persuasion)

http://www.nara.gov/ (national archives and record administration)

Analyzing an Image

The essay that follows, written by student Ray Tsao, is an example of how a photograph, one of the most famous photographs from the Vietnam War, can be analyzed for its use of visual rhetoric, particularly the Aristotelian appeals to ethos and pathos. This is a visceral image, and still a shocking one; Tsao's essay captures the complicated political and emotional charge that this photograph carried in a highly partisan time, as well as those elements that make it a timeless picture of war. (The photo may be found in Chapter 10).

❊❊ *Persuasiveness in "Saigon Execution"*

RAY TSAO

The Vietnam War divided the United States as never before; civilian sentiment diverged sharply from government action. Undoubtedly, Edward T. Adams presented a stark contrast to wartime propaganda in his photograph, "Saigon Execution." Whereas the U.S. government had focused on appealing to logic, in arguing that the fall of a democratic Vietnam would result in the proliferation of communism, Adams's photograph relies more on appeals to ethos and pathos, offering a powerful antiwar message precisely because of its ability to refute logical arguments.

Taken in the broadest sense, Adams's photograph was the almost reasonable portrayal of the execution of a Vietcong suspect. The context of war overrode what was essentially the murder of the human being. The execution was a path in which the audience followed quite readily; in order for the war to be won, enemies had to be killed. Therefore, the Vietcong suspect's death was but one of thousands in Vietnam; clearly, more would follow as the war was waged. However, Adams was able to present the suspect's death in another light.

The details in the photograph gave a dose of realism to the audience back home. Indeed, the gritty details of war apparent in "Saigon Execution," the broken windows, half-destroyed buildings, ravaged streets and patrolling soldiers, were substantially different from the picturesque "clean" war depicted in government propaganda. This was no conflict staged in an unnamed jungle or battleground; it was set amidst the friendly confines of "home." Furthermore, the audience could empathize with the Vietnamese, imagining their houses in the middle of a battlefield. More compelling, however, were the two individuals in the photograph, Police Chief Colonel Nguyen Loan and the Vietcong suspect.

The suspect easily attracts the attention and sympathy of the audience. He looks like little more than a teenager, his arms clasped behind his back and hunched over, his expression nothing but fear and horror. In addition, his casual plaid shirt is markedly different from Loan's combat fatigues. This is neither a heavily armed commando nor a vicious criminal, but a frightened boy. The idea that people similar to the suspect were being executed was one both alien and disturbing to the audience back home, not only for the loss of life but also the loss of innocence.

By the same token, Loan came across as a forbidding figure—as the symbol of South Vietnamese and U.S. power, but hardly justice. With both his face and body averted, it is difficult to relate to him. Much like the grim reaper, the police chief is a faceless agent of death. Obviously, Loan's emotions remain unclear to the audience, and whether he felt sympathy or took pleasure in executing the suspect became irrelevant. However, with his right hand gripping the gun, there was no question which man has the power.

"Saigon Execution" succeeded in disputing propaganda on the home front and giving the audience a taste of the realism that came with the Vietnam conflict. More than ever, it became unclear which side was "right." Was it necessary to occupy someone's homeland and impose a government which the civilians disavowed? The photograph—which won a Pulitzer Prize—did little to help the U.S. government's position. Adams's photograph achieved what antiwar activists had hoped: by confusing the line between "friend" and "enemy," it forced American viewers to reevaluate the necessity of the Vietnam conflict.

The purpose of this short essay is to demonstrate that a photograph can make an argument, and a persuasive one at that. Because it was not staged—the photographer was shooting a roll of film when the execution took place—the killing was on the evening news all over America, and it shocked the viewers. Ray Tsao's point is that this picture appeals to ethos and pathos, and thereby undercuts the official government argument for the war, which was based on logic. But what you should keep in mind when you look at the photo and read the essay is the way Tsao goes about proving his point—by looking closely at all the details of the photograph, including the street and buildings in the background, the shirt of the Vietcong, the look on his face, and the body language and posture of the colonel. It is those details that give him the basis for analyzing the underlying appeals in the picture, and that kind of close reading is crucial to analyzing the persuasiveness of any image, in or out of this book—an advertisement in a magazine, a painting, a cartoon.

Tsao's reading of the photo is not exhaustive. Is the look on the Vietcong's face one of terror, or is it the physiological result of being shot? Is the colonel's face averted, or is he just aiming his gun? What difference does it make that the photo is shot from up close and not a hundred feet away?

Tsao's methodology is invaluable for helping you to analyze visuals yourself. The next time you see an advertisement that gets to you, that you think is either wonderful or terrible, take the time to stop and look at it, really look at it. Look closely, and ask yourself why you think it worked, or why it didn't. What clues do you find? How did you come to the conclusion you did? See how many details you can list: where figures and objects are, where shadows and light are, what the perspective is, what the language says, where the words are placed on the page. This close reading will also begin to formulate ideas about who the audience is, why you react the way you do, and what underlying assumptions, values, and beliefs you bring with you that affect the way you see the world you live in.

Elements of Persuasion

As you examine the visual and textual arguments in this book, you may find it helpful to be able to recognize the rhetorical building blocks on which they rely: assumptions, assertions, examples, and refutations. You will never read an essay or a novel or a poem, or see an advertisement or a film, that does not make use of some or all of these elements. You use them yourself in ordinary conversation every time you talk to a friend. The difference is that in conversation, they are generally spur-of-the-moment, extemporaneous. In your own writing, you have the choice and control over which elements you use, how you use them, and in what combinations. They are the DNA of persuasion, both essential and capable of infinite versatility.

Once you have thought about material presented earlier in this chapter—who is your audience, how do you want to appeal to it and why, what genre you want to use—you can use the elements that follow to structure and guide your writing. It is not a question of choosing one over the other; if you make any assertions or if there are assumptions you start out with, you will always need examples to back them up. If you are arguing against someone else's ideas, then you need ammunition—assertions, examples—to show that your idea is better. As you become more conscious of these elements, which you use intuitively in your everyday life, you will also find it more natural and effective to use them in your writing.

Assumptions and Assertions

In everyday life we make countless assumptions: that the water will flow out of the tap when we turn it on, that the bus will come more or less on time to take us to school or work. That sometimes the water main breaks or the bus is quite late does not change the fact that we take these things for granted. When we arrive at school, we assume that a paper we turn in will be read and evaluated; we assume that the data we obtain from reliable sources—books, reputable journals, people we trust—are reported accurately. Sometimes we explicitly state the assumptions on which we are operating; for example, we might say, "With inflation holding steady for the rest of the quarter, we predict stable interest rates."

Assumptions are the unseen glue in an argument, providing the connection between the evidence or proof and the conclusions drawn from that proof. They are underlying principles on which we base our claims and part of the shared values or wisdom of a community, whether a society, culture, workplace, or academic discipline. We might conclude, for example, that a family might be dysfunctional on the basis of our own criteria for functional families. Or we might assume that nuclear families have always been the norm, until we reflect on other community structures such as clans, tribes, and the like, or research alternative families in American history.

There is nothing inherently bad about assumptions; life would be extremely difficult if we had to start from scratch every day. But critical readers and careful writers do need to recognize assumptions in arguments, particularly those that are unstated. Careful readers question assumptions in the arguments they read, interrogating the text (or image) and writing notes in the margins or a notebook: "Who says? Why do you say that? Do you have any proof? Why did you draw that conclusion?" They will check for missing links between evidence and claim, or for a jump from reason to conclusion that does not seem warranted by the reason itself. In addition to asking questions, one can diagram a selection by blocking out on paper the conclusion and the specific reasons that support it, and then examining them for underlying assumptions.

Assertions are the conclusions one draws on the basis of some combination of reasons and assumptions. The main assertion in an essay is often referred to as a *thesis statement*. Reasons are the support that the writer offers—the evidence on which she or he has based those assertions. Assumptions are the often unstated beliefs, values, and principles we hold that interplay with other assumptions and reasons. Some writers refer to assumptions and reasons as premises; the term *premise* is prominent in discussions of formal logic and the syllogism, or deductive argument in outline form. For the sake of clarity, we will use *assertions* consistently throughout this text but will note synonyms that other writers sometimes use.

Assertions vary in tone and in language because of differences in the assumptions that underlie them and because of differences in temperament, background, and purpose. Some assertions are factual; some are statements of values; some are drawn from research; and some are meant as calls to action, to suggest changes in policy or procedure.

The whole middle section of the Declaration of Independence is a list of assertions about all the terrible things that King George III did to the colonies which finally forced the colonists to declare their independence. Chapter 9, Justice and Civil Liberties, includes the first draft of the Declaration along with the final version, so that you can see how different in tone and effect the two versions are.

In the same chapter, Susan B. Anthony's speech after she got arrested for trying to vote in 1872 makes assertions that were unacceptable to most Americans at the time—that the Constitution meant to include women in the phrase "We the People," that the Declaration meant to include women in the phrase "All men are created equal," and that being denied the right to vote was a violation of the Fourteenth and Fifteenth Amendments. By using the language of our most revered documents in her assertions, Anthony was laying claim to a political legitimacy that could not be expressed in any other terms.

Examples

Technically, an example is a single part chosen to show the nature or character of a whole, or a sample of a larger unit, or a typical sample of something; George Washington is an example of an American president, and Chris Rock is an example of a comedian.

Practically, though, examples fulfill two crucial functions in writing. First, they enable an audience to identify emotionally and/or intellectually with the writer or the writer's subject. This identification is especially important if the writer wants to move the audience to action, or knows that the audience is hostile or indifferent or just unfamiliar with the material. For instance, in the speech "I Have a Dream," Martin Luther King, Jr., included examples of how prejudice affected the lives of African Americans doing ordinary things—like trying to book a hotel room or to get a seat on a bus—to explain the effects of racial segregation to an audience, many of whose members had no personal experience of segregation. These common and easily understandable examples help persuade through *identification*—identification between King and his audience, between the people he is talking about and the people he is talking to.

The second role that example fills is to support persuasion through *evidence;* examples can act as proof for general statements or assertions. Just as abstractions without examples are emotionally uninvolving, assertions without examples are unconvincing. Examples are as essential to a persuasive argument as results are to an experiment.

The following two paragraphs show the difference between a paragraph without clear examples and the same paragraph rewritten by the author to include examples. The argument concerns whether dropping the atomic bomb on Japan hastened the end of World War II. The writer, Paul Fussell, is criticizing John Kenneth Galbraith, the economist, who thought that the atomic bomb made no difference.

Without Examples

On the other hand, John Kenneth Galbraith is persuaded that the Japanese would have surrendered by November without an invasion. He thinks the atomic bombs were not decisive in bringing about the surrender and he implies that their use was unjustified. What did he do in the war? He was in the Office of Price Administration in Washington, and then he was director of the United States Strategic Bombing Survey. He was thirty-seven in 1945, and I don't demand that he experience having his ass shot off. I just note that he didn't. In saying this I'm aware of its offensive implications ad hominem. But here I think that approach justified. What's at stake in an infantry assault is so entirely unthinkable to those without any experience of one, even if they possess very wide-ranging imaginations and sympathies, that experience is crucial in this case.

With Examples

On the other hand, John Kenneth Galbraith is persuaded that the Japanese would have surrendered surely by November without an invasion. He thinks the A-bombs were unnecessary and unjustified because the war was ending anyway. The A-bombs meant, he says, "a difference, at most, of two or three weeks." But at the time, with no indication that surrender was on the way, the kamikazes were sinking American vessels, the *Indianapolis* was sunk (880 men killed), and Allied casualties were running to over 7,000 per week. "Two or three weeks," says Galbraith. Two weeks more means 14,000 more killed and wounded, three weeks more, 21,000. Those weeks mean the world if you're one of those thousands or related to one of them. During the time between the dropping of the Nagasaki bomb on August 9 and the actual surrender on the 15th, the war pursued its accustomed course: on the 12th of August eight captured American fliers were executed (heads chopped off); the fifty-first United States submarine, *Bonefish,* was sunk (all aboard drowned); the destroyer *Callaghan* went down, the seventieth to be sunk, and the Destroyer Escort *Underhill* was lost. That's a bit of what happened in six days of the two or three weeks posited by Galbraith. What did he do in the war? He worked in the Office of Price Administration in Washington. I don't demand that he experience having his ass shot off. I merely note that he didn't.

The first paragraph gives no evidence to support or refute Galbraith's contention that the use of the bombs was unnecessary. The second, with its example upon example of the numbers and types of casualties that occurred in the last days of the war, certainly puts the writer in a stronger position to persuade the reader that Galbraith was wrong.

Refutation

Refutation is proof that an argument or statement is wrong. It comes into existence only when there is an opponent or another side. Refutation means that someone else has gone first; it is the answer to an assumption, or a point of view, or a statement with which one disagrees.

In one sense, then, refutation is not a completely independent rhetorical strategy; it needs to bounce off and argue against something else. The emphasis in refutation is less on stating one's own principles than on taking the material presented by an opponent and dismantling it.

In another sense, refutation is based on instinct, on the impulse to react negatively when we hear an idea that infuriates us or strikes us as stupid or unethical or unjust. But refutation is more disciplined than that. An artful, well-prepared writer or speaker uses refutation to overturn an opponent's argument or to take his or her ideas and reverse them to advantage.

It is possible to refute an argument logically without necessarily having a deep intellectual belief in the view expressed by the refutation. For example, an excellent logician could refute the argument of someone he or she agrees with by pointing up inconsistencies; a member of a debating team could be randomly assigned either side of an argument and would be expected to find ways to damage the other side's approach. And criminal attorneys are routinely expected to fulfill their duty of defending people whom they dislike, distrust, or even believe to be guilty, mostly by refuting the prosecution's evidence and raising doubt in the mind of a jury or judge.

The higher forms of refutation, however, are neither mechanical nor uncommitted. They come from one's involvement with an issue or a principle, and they do more than decimate the opposing viewpoint; they can change the way people think and can move them to action.

In extraordinary cases—like those expressed in Chapter 9 by Henry David Thoreau, Frederick Douglass, and Martin Luther King, Jr.—refutation can acquire a significant symbolic authority, which resonates over time to larger and more distant audiences. It can even move and inspire otherwise ordinary people to risk their own security and freedom in the name of an idea. Thoreau, for example, argued so powerfully for the effectiveness of nonviolent resistance over the use of force that both Mahatma Gandhi and Martin Luther King, Jr. were able to apply his approach to two of the most powerful civil rights movements of the twentieth century.

In the following essay, student writer William West analyzes Chief Justice Earl Warren's successful use of refutation in *Brown v. Board of Education* to overthrow a legal precedent that had stood for fifty years. You will notice that refutation is not the only element from this chapter that Warren employs; he also relies heavily on Aristotelian appeals, and he gives many examples. But refutation of an older legal decision is his main purpose, and all the other tools at his disposal are chosen and organized with that purpose in mind.

✳✳ *Refutation in* Brown v. Board of Education

WILLIAM WEST

A court of law does not have open to it the same avenues for supporting its opinions that an ordinary rhetor has. Legal argumentation and writing are governed by conventions, one of the most important of which is precedent. Because the Supreme Court case of *Brown* v. *Board of Education* overturned *Plessy* v. *Ferguson*, which had stood for over half a century, the court had to be careful to fully justify its rejection of precedent. In his opinion for the court, Chief Justice Earl Warren carefully creates an argument which uses logical appeals to justify overturning *Plessy*, and appeals to ethos to give the ruling more validity.

The contested issue in the case is whether so-called "separate but equal" educational facilities are truly equal and afford black students the equal protection under the law required by the Fourteenth Amendment.

The first part of the Court's opinion outlines the general facts of the case and the arguments presented by both sides. This approach both appeals to the belief in impartial and balanced justice and forms the groundwork for later argument. Only after he has laid this groundwork does Justice Warren begin to criticize the *Plessy* ruling.

In calling *Plessy* into question, Justice Warren repudiates the idea that it should stand simply because it is based on tradition. He begins with a logical reminder of how much times have changed since *Plessy* was decided. That leads to his point that the test *Plessy* used, that of counting only tangible factors in judging whether separate public facilities can also be equal facilities, is also out of date. He argues that "We cannot turn the clock back . . . to 1896 when *Plessy* v. *Ferguson* was written. We must consider public education in light of . . . its present place in American life and throughout the nation."

Having introduced the idea that times have changed, and thereby implied that precedents can be changed too, Warren proposes that the test for separate but equal schools deserves a more modern test than the one in *Plessy*. In this way, he compensates for getting rid of the old logical appeal to precedent by substituting a newer logical appeal to the realities of the modern world.

However, Justice Warren then goes on to make an additional appeal, this time to widely held American values. He writes that education is "required in the performance of our most basic public responsibilities" and is "the very foundation of good citizenship." Phrases such as these evoke commonly held beliefs about the importance of education and participation in democracy. No one can easily argue, at least in the abstract, against the ideal of preparing young girls and boys to be good citizens. Warren implicitly asks whites who support these notions in the abstract to extend them to the particular case of segregated black students.

Finally, after having laid the necessary groundwork, Warren makes his assertion: certain intangible differences between segregated schools "deprive the children of the minority group of equal educational opportunities." This is the conclusion of the logical inquiry that he proposed earlier. He then supports this conclusion by presenting other court rulings, which, although they did not overturn *Plessy* outright, nonetheless identified inequality in specific cases. In addition he supplies psychological evidence, "amply supported by modern authority," that segregation gives black students a feeling of inferiority. The cases presented as evidence serve as concrete examples of how facilities can be truly unequal and serve as new precedents.

Throughout this opinion Warren uses appeals to ethos and logos together to justify the controversial act of overturning a long-standing precedent. On the one hand, he appeals to logic. On the other hand, he invokes the American belief in good citizenship and democratic participation. This ethical appeal provides the implied support for Warren's conclusion that separate cannot be equal, and that *Plessy* is unconstitutional. The significance of combining the appeals to logos and ethos in a legal context is clearly what underlies the structure of Warren's argument.

The chapter on Justice and Civil Liberties from which this student essay is drawn contains some of the most effective examples of persuasive argument that this country has produced, including the Declaration of Independence and Martin Luther King, Jr.'s, "Letter from Birmingham Jail." West's topic is particularly interesting, not only because of the importance of the Supreme Court's decision in *Brown v. Board of Education* but also because it unpacks the most significant rhetorical element in that decision. We can see its constituent parts— the appeals, the examples, the assertions. But the focus is on the ultimate goal of justifying the refutation of an older Court decision and replacing it with a new decision that reads the Constitution in a completely different way. By analyzing the rhetorical parts that together combine to form a good refutation, West gives us an insight into how any refutation can be constructed.

We hope that these suggestions for analyzing persuasive strategies, audiences, cultures, and genres will help you to learn to read diverse arguments critically and to become more aware of your own abilities as readers, viewers, and writers. Chapter 3 offers suggestions for developing your essays, from prewriting to thesis to organizing your ideas, and Chapter 4 is a guide to incorporating research materials into your writing.

In order to integrate critical reading and persuasive writing, the chapters in Part II, "Argument in the American Tradition," combine critical readings with suggestions for analytical and persuasive writing. Each chapter develops a core thematic issue and links that issue to important aspects of argumentation through an introduction, diverse persuasive materials, an end-of-chapter discussion, and assignments that develop your ability to construct your own effective arguments. We hope that the arguments you find included in this book, as well as the suggestions for good writing, will stimulate your imagination, your critical thinking, and your understanding of persuasion in what you read and what you write. Argument about American culture rages on, and we hope that you will jump in and become part of our ongoing discussion and debate—part of the American tradition.

3

⁂

Writing Essays

Essay Development

In writing an essay, you start with an idea, an assignment, or something you've wondered about. A possibility occurs to you, maybe from reading or from a discussion you had in class or with a friend. You read, review, perhaps take notes—and in the process integrate what you are learning with what you already know. Writing is a process, not a single discrete event, and as you put word to paper you simultaneously uncover some thoughts and clarify others. Essays and other forms of prose force you to develop, organize, and transmit clearly ideas, evidence, and interpretations so that other people can understand them. Composing even one paragraph that says exactly what you mean in the clearest way that you can is immensely satisfying, and trying to find the best words in the best order is what keeps a lot of writers going. Writing is also a way to record information and demonstrate knowledge, and it remains the primary means of disseminating knowledge and information in the academic world. Despite the pervasiveness of visual and audio media, writing remains the crucial means of communication in the rest of society as well.

There are several different kinds of persuasive writing, including reports, exposition, and argumentation. The writing situation—the audience, purpose, and subject—dictates the form. This book focuses on argumentation, but we believe that persuasion in communication is not a separate genre but a continuum with varying degrees of argumentative edge. All good argumentation is also persuasive, or it has failed as argument.

Along the continuum of persuasion in written discourse, *reports* tend to be the least overtly persuasive. A report writer presents information accurately in a relatively unbiased manner; indeed, the writer's thoroughness and accuracy may in themselves be persuasive of a certain conclusion, but the report does not necessarily suggest that

49

conclusion. A lab report is an example of the kind of report writing commonly used in college; a good lab report includes all the relevant information, but it is not a record of your opinions about biology. In business, people other than the report writer often make decisions based on what the report says, although some reports also include recommendations, explanations of complex issues, pros and cons, and summaries of different parties' positions. A really well-written report by a reliable writer can carry a lot of weight in the decision-making process.

An *expository essay* asserts a point of view and is persuasive insofar as the writer wants to convince readers of the merits of his or her case. The expository or analytical essays that most college students write often work in conjunction with other texts and materials; that is, the writer is responding to a text, an idea, a concept, or a situation. Such essays often entail developing a point of view or an assertion about a subject and then supporting that point of view with evidence from personal observation, other texts, or a prominent theory or expert in the field. Essays analyzing a literary work, a historical event, a political idea, or an economic theory are good examples of the kinds of expository writing you can expect to encounter in your courses.

An *argumentative essay* clearly attempts to persuade its readers to identify with the writer, to change their minds, to change their behavior, and to adopt or abandon a policy or course of action. The argument rests on assumptions, assertions, and evidence. As opposed to a report, it is expected to take one side over another.

All three kinds of essays can integrate research. We suggest that you consider research a process you undertake whenever the response to a question or the testing of a hypothesis requires that you look beyond your own knowledge and experience for supporting evidence. Instead, outside experts and evidence present a far more convincing case. In the sections that follow, we first discuss developing essays that may not require outside research, and then we outline suggestions for integrating research.

Techniques for Developing Essays

All forms of writing involve a process of prewriting, writing, and revising. During this process, it may be helpful to use some of the following prompts and questions to help you think about, focus, structure, and develop your paper.

Strategies for Prewriting
1. *Free write.* Start with a focused free write, that is, writing without attention to grammar, style, or spelling. Keep pen to page, or fingers to keyboard, and write for five or ten minutes to get started, even

if half of what you write is "I don't know what to say, I haven't got any ideas, I hate this." Do you have some general topic area to think about? Jot down everything you can think of about your area, however general to start with. Then review your notes, and try again with a more focused view of some aspect of the topic that came up in the free write; see whether there are any phrases or even words that you could play with. If you don't have an assignment or a specific topic in mind, free writing can help you figure out what you might find interesting to write about.

2. *Brainstorm.* Write down ideas, images, possible directions—anything that comes to mind about your potential topic—in a list down the page, rather than in the continuous flow of the free write. Review your list and try again, focusing on something interesting that came up in the brainstorming. If you exchange brainstorming lists with someone else in your class, you can probably help each other out by noticing good points in each other's lists.

3. *Do invisible writing.* If you have access to a computer, this exercise may be useful. Turn off the monitor or screen brightness, and write continuously without viewing what you are writing. This technique is useful for people who tend to get writer's block or to censor their writing and ideas even before they can get the words out.

4. *Review what you have written.* Do you see possibilities to focus on? Do you see connections or angles you didn't think of before? If so, select one of the preceding exercises—free writing, brainstorming, or invisible writing—that seemed the most productive for you, and do another session of writing on the focused area you discovered in the exercises. Review the topic, and see whether it looks promising for further development. Devise a tentative core point or hypothesis; it may change later, but at least it will give you something to work with. Remember that since your writing, like your ideas, is constantly evolving, there is no one method that will work for you every time, and you should feel free to use any of them.

5. *Consider your own biases.* After you have developed a tentative focus, the next couple of exercises may be useful. First, write out all of your biases or preconceived notions about the topic. This step is particularly important if you are developing an argumentative researched essay. It is crucial that you conduct your research in an open-minded manner, one that enables you to seek out material and data on both sides of the question. An argument implies an opposition, so take care to look at both sides in your research as well as in your structuring of your argument.

6. *Construct a dialogue between the two sides.* Personify each side of the argument, and have the two sides debate the issue. That is, assign a position or a personality to each side, and let them argue for a while, with you writing the script.

7. *Refine your topic and your focus.* In a sentence, try to write what the focus and approach of your paper will be. If you can't write it now, at least narrow it to something that seems manageable for the length and depth of the paper assigned.

8. *Try the journalistic method.* After generating some material about your topic, it might be useful to adopt a systematic approach based on the journalistic method, which asks and responds to the following questions: what, who, when, where, why, and how.

- *What* is happening, or what has happened, in terms of your topic?

- *Who* (or perhaps *what*) was or is involved in your topic? Who or what does something, or to whom or to what does something happen?

- *When* did it happen?

- *Where* did it happen? What is the background of the situation?

- *Why* did it happen? Why did the agent (*who*) cause it to happen? What are the implications of this purpose?

- *How* was the action or event brought about? What were the means, methods, resources involved?

While working with whichever prewriting and planning methods you find most helpful, you will find that one or more areas of focus emerge. As you review your prewriting and planning material, you are in a good position to develop a tentative thesis statement. You will likely go back and forth between prewriting and drafting, adjusting the thesis and content as you go, but explicit attention to your thesis now will pay off when you strive to organize and develop your essay later.

Developing a Core Assertion: The Thesis Statement

Critical readers learn to detect and analyze the main idea in a text. Persuasive writers develop a thesis statement to focus and guide the development of their essays. By *thesis statement,* we mean the core assertion, the main point being argued for and supported. In an expository or informative essay, the thesis statement indicates your limited topic and your approach to that topic; it still asserts a point of view or perspective, but it tends not to have an argumentative edge to it. A thesis statement in a persuasive piece of discourse seeks to argue for a certain position or point of view, not merely informing but pushing for some change in viewpoint or attitude on the part of the audience. An expository thesis statement does not necessarily provoke a response or an argument; a persuasive thesis statement generally does.

Whereas readers of informative or explanatory information will want to see the evidence or support that led to the thesis statement, the persuasive essay will also need to respond to counterarguments; its thesis will generally be a stronger assertion of a position than the expository thesis statement. Clearly there is overlap between expository and argumentative thesis statements, but the edge of an opinion, statement of belief, or more forceful assertion generally signals to the reader that an argument follows. For example, an essay might include one of the following core assertions:

- "Martin Luther King, Jr.'s, 'I Have a Dream' speech was the turning point of the March on Washington."

- "Martin Luther King, Jr.'s, 'I Have a Dream' speech confronted white America with its own sorry record on civil rights for black Americans."

- "If America is to support the ideals for which Martin Luther King, Jr., fought, it must do more than pay lip service to civil rights rulings—it must enforce them."

The first statement could serve as the thesis for an expository essay; it selects and limits a topic, and conveys an approach and an attitude toward that topic. The writer may try to convince the reader as to the merits of his or her case but does not invite counterarguments or try to change attitudes. The second statement also focuses the topic and indicates an approach; in addition, it addresses beliefs and values, and it engages the reader through value-laden terms (*confronted, sorry*), though it could soften them (i.e., *poor record*) and still argue a point. This sentence invites debate, if not dialogue. The third sentence doesn't argue a point of view or value judgment, as does the second sentence, but it proposes a course of action: enforcing civil rights legislation. Buried within the third statement is the assumption or principle that all Americans should support the values for which King fought.

Many expository thesis statements look something like the first sentence; some arguments about values, beliefs, and principles look like the second; proposals or attempts to move the reader to a specific course of action often look like the third. There are many different variations and types of sentences, and we will examine them throughout this book. Essentially, though, a thesis is an assertion that focuses the topic; it indicates an approach to be followed in the essay or other discourse, and in the case of persuasive and argumentative works, it argues for a position, a belief or value, or a course of action. It also serves as a signpost to your reader about what direction the rest of the essay will be headed in, and makes the rest of your essay much easier to follow.

A thesis is not a statement of acknowledged fact; if it were, there would be little point in discussion. It is not an effusion of emotion or a matter of taste; those too defy reasoned debate. It is an element that reflects and guides the essay. An essay exists to amplify or prove the thesis; the thesis is an encapsulation of the essay. The two must echo and reinforce each other if the essay is to be coherent, to be linked throughout.

Not all pieces of writing explicitly state a thesis. Some use implication, meaning that the audience has to infer, or figure out, from the essay what the point or assertion is. Generally, argumentative essays clearly state a position, but pieces that are less explicitly persuasive often do not. The etching *Keep Within Compass* in Chapter 7 states its point, though the values and beliefs supporting that point are implied through other text and the artwork.

As you practice writing, you will generally need to develop a clear statement of purposes, focus, approach, or proposal. Not every piece of writing you will ever do will need an explicit thesis statement, but generally college writing (and much out-of-college writing) will require you to state your position or point clearly and then to support it with appropriate evidence. When do you devise a thesis statement? That depends. If you have an idea of what you want to assert, even if it is not fully formed or is tentative, write it down, perhaps trying several variations. Often free writing a bit after you have jotted down several possibilities will help you to discern what it is you are trying to say. If you are exploring a topic—for example, an analysis of an argumentative piece or a research issue—read, discuss, and take notes until you feel ready to develop a working thesis statement. There is no way that you can do your best work without digesting the information on which you base your essay, and that consideration means you have to really take the time to read the material. Otherwise, your readers will know right away that you are either skimming along on the surface of the research or, worse yet, making statements you and the reader both know are unsupported. Some students find that a simple outline for a thesis statement can help them focus it. Although writing down a topic or a phrase is a good start, it is more difficult to get off the fence and state an assertion or proposal. Two outlines that students have found useful are the following:

1. I shall argue that _____.

This format reminds you that you need to assert something, not just throw out a topic, even a narrowed topic, although that is a useful stage in the process before you develop a thesis.

2. Although _____, I believe I shall argue that _____ because _____.

This outline can guide you by making sure that you are looking at potential objections to your argument, that you assert something, and that you have lined up some evidence to support your view.

These are working outlines and need not appear in your essay. In fact, the second outline could produce an exceedingly cumbersome thesis, or at least an inelegant one. But you will be able to decide how explicit to make your thesis statement as you revise, and you will be able to refine the language in revision as well. The Hofstadter selection in Chapter 11 is a superb example of an explicitly stated thesis.

As noted earlier, writing is generally not a linear process that takes you from point A to point B in orderly succession; rather, it is a recursive process—writers return to earlier parts of the process as needed—perhaps reviewing and refining the focus or brainstorming examples to support a key point. But after some productive effort at prewriting and crafting a thesis statement, you will be in a good position to consider how you want to structure your material. Some writers have found the following techniques helpful.

Organizing and Drafting the Essay

Break your topic into parts.   After generating yet more information, through prewriting and as appropriate through research and note taking, think about how you might break down or analyze the parts of your topic. Draft out the major divisions or aspects of your topic on paper or on screen. Don't worry about the form of the outline; just get the major divisions on paper so that you can see where your project is going and so that you have a sense of the magnitude and direction of the topic at this state.

In order to help you keep track of your material, you can also make up headings that won't appear in the final version of your paper. If you're writing about Thomas Jefferson, you can have one heading that says "Early Life," another that says "Declaration of Independence," another that says "Louisiana Purchase," etc. If you cluster all the bits of information about one of those topics under a heading, you will at least know where to find them later. And the headings will help keep you from writing a stream of consciousness paper in which you repeat sentences because you have information about the topic scattered all over the place and don't remember how much of it you have already used.

Go back to the question of focus.   Does your tentative thesis statement still capture the gist of your ideas? If not, review your notes, your preliminary thoughts and ideas, and the materials you have developed. Try to understand where they are taking you. What connections can you make? What inferences can you make from your findings? Draft several thesis statements; one or two probably will come close to representing the direction in which your research is taking you.

Consider coherence. Having listed the major divisions of your subject area, consider whether all of the parts you have set forth still belong in your paper. Are all parts closely related to the key question of your preliminary focus? If not, will you adapt your thesis or throw out the irrelevant material?

Review your main topic divisions. Does an order suggest itself? Does there seem to be a best way to present your points to the reader?

Pay attention to contradictions and opposing views. At what point do they suggest themselves? If you are writing a persuasive essay, opposing views may come up at any time in the process; if they don't come to mind, you'll need to seek them out. Ask yourself questions. Why isn't what I propose already in place? Why wouldn't people want what I am advocating? If I were trying to persuade readers to the opposite view, what points would I make? If you don't consider and deal with opposing views, the reader will certainly be thinking of them, and you will undercut your credibility if you don't concede to or refute opposing arguments.

Refocus your thesis statement. Try to write a more focused thesis statement to state the argument or point that you want to make (review the notes on thesis statements in the introduction).

Write out a plan. If at this point you see the overall pattern of your paper emerging, take the time now to write a prospectus—a plan that summarizes the purpose, organization, and main points of your paper. If you are not yet ready to do so, answer some of the following questions:

- Why is the subject important to you or to potential readers? Why have you chosen to write about it, and what do you plan to transmit to others?

- How much additional reading will you need to do, and where will you go to find the information you need?

- How much background information do your readers need in order to understand the significance of your topic or the issues involved?

- What points will you be making about your topic, and what kinds of evidence will you include?

Consider methods and sources of research. For researched essays, review the rest of the chapter for advice about taking notes, integrating sources, and documenting sources.

Revising the Draft

After you get the basic structure of the rough draft down, review the logic of your assertions. Determine whether they still support the thesis and whether the thesis still allows you to engage the parts of your topic that you want to cover. Thesis and support must remain connected and mutually reinforcing. Review your draft and determine if you need more evidence or if you should cut out parts that don't seem relevant. Ask yourself, do I absolutely need this paragraph? Have I said something very similar to this elsewhere in the paper? You know if you're padding, so be honest with yourself. That's not always easy, so peer feedback at this stage can be useful. Exchange drafts with a classmate and try to give each other "big picture" feedback on the thesis, basic structure, and supporting evidence. Then revise your essay as needed to attend to criticism from your peers. Remember, though, that as the author, you have the final decision over changes you make. Accept feedback, but use your own judgment in deciding how much and what kind of advice to take.

You should certainly spell-check your paper if you are using a computer to write it, but such tools do not find all the errors and lapses in good style that your draft may have. Peer feedback is also helpful for detecting errors that you may not find, since at this point in the draft your eyes may see what they expect to see (or want to see) rather than what is on the page. A peer who is less invested in your writing than you are will be able to see it more objectively than you can. You and a peer should both go over your paper in fine detail, attending to issues of style, appropriateness of language, level of diction, proper syntax, and correct documentation style.

Organizing Tools

Writers use different approaches for organizing their essays. The following are some of the most common. There is no hard-and-fast rule here about which approach to take; the point is that some organizing principle will work for you, and any one you use is better than none. The alternative is writing an essay at two o'clock in the morning, and finally getting sleepy enough to convince yourself that those loosely related ideas you've been looking at on your computer screen really form a unified presentation. That approach is about as effective as it sounds. Here are a couple of techniques to help you lay more effective groundwork for your writing.

Outlines

An outline indicates the framework of your essay. It summarizes the core assertion and key supporting points. When you make an outline, you can put in the points you're sure of, and doing that may help you to see what's missing. Constructing an outline can help you sort out the relationships between various ideas as well as determine whether your thesis is narrow enough and where you need to provide additional specific support (i.e., more examples). An outline can also help you to reorder and reorganize points, keeping related ideas together and enabling you to check the overall order and flow of ideas.

Some students prefer a very rough kind of outline of the major sections that indicates the purpose of each section. It is possible to limit yourself very successfully to a working thesis statement and several topic sentences—essentially listing what could be the main sentence in each paragraph. That kind of outline gives you a road map to follow as you build the essay.

A more formal outline indicates the subordinate elements under each major heading; a detailed outline might include Roman numerals for section headings, numbers for subsections, and letters of the alphabet for individual ideas. If you can organize this kind of outline, you will have a lot of the work for your essay in front of you before you even start writing out the text in paragraphs.

A topic sentence outline, in which you actually write out your points in complete sentences instead of listing topics or ideas in fragments, has a real advantage. It forces you to make your assertion or to state your assumption, and that step means you have to set forth your claims and examine them and the evidence you have to support them. This is a highly objective way of seeing what you really have, because it is the closest you can come to reading your work as though it had been written by someone else.

Index Cards and Notebooks

Index cards are an informal approach that many writers use. If you feel that you can't put down every idea because you don't really know yet what you think or because you really don't like outlines and don't do them thoroughly, try writing on a bunch of index cards. Put one idea on each card in big letters. Number the cards. In that way you can always add supporting evidence or secondary ideas without losing track of your materials. For your own sake, however, keep a rubber band around the cards or stash them in one place; there are few occurrences more discouraging to the use of this or any other system than losing all the work that went into it.

The alternative—and the more writing you do the better this is—is to have one notebook dedicated to your writing. Carry it with you, and put everything, including library information, brainstorming ideas, and possible thesis sentences, in it. Scribble sentence fragments, try out opening paragraphs. A notebook is private and inexpensive, and all the information is together in one place. Professional writers almost always have a notebook with them so that they can put down ideas whenever they occur. That habit—writing down ideas as you have them, rather than hoping you'll remember them until you have time later—can help preserve your thoughts when they are freshest and most likely to suggest other connections.

Laptops and Computers

Computers are clearly helpful for storing large quantities of information in multiple formats. Many students have access to computers either at home or at school, and they use them for writing drafts. They are a good repository for your preliminary work, as well as for any potential reference you come across, and also for any idea that you got from free writing, brainstorming, or any of the other exercises earlier in this chapter. If you are fortunate enough to have a laptop, take it to the library with you and put everything on it, just as if you were using index cards. You can use the computer to see what kind of outline, if any, would work for you. You can try a rough or detailed outline, or make files for each of them.

Sample Essays

Generating and organizing material for your essay depends to some degree on the type of essay you are writing. Earlier we discussed reports, expository essays, and argumentative essays. Often essays will be both argumentative and expository (see Susan B. Anthony and Mary Pipher selections), but there is usually a dominant mode. Expository essays can be reflective; they can tell about a place or an incident. The dreaded "What I Did on My Summer Vacation" topic from elementary school calls for an expository response—you're not mounting an argument over whether you did or didn't go to Disneyland with your grandparents. "Nurses in Vietnam," Jacqueline Navarro Rhoads's narrative about her experiences during the Vietnam War, is also expository. It's a story about what happened to her and to people she knew, and how she felt. Analytical essays are a type of expository essay that involve taking something apart—a poem, a picture, a set of assertions, a group of assumptions, even an argument—and explaining how it works, what it aims to do, and how well it succeeds. Argumentative essays are aimed at proving a point or points, and sometimes at doing so by dismantling someone else's argument or by taking on someone else's ideas. In the next section, we provide samples of each of these modes, so that you can see them side by side and get a better sense of their strategies.

Expository Essays   The following example of an expository essay is by Korean American Younghill Kang, who emigrated to the United States in 1921 and whose writing is an attempt to mediate between Asian and American experience from an immigrant's perspective. This essay describes his arrival in New York.

✼✼✼ A Korean Discovers New York

YOUNGHILL KANG

From an old walled Koran city some thousand years old—Seoul—famous for poets and scholars, to New York. I did not come directly. But almost. A large steamer from the Orient landed me in Vancouver, Canada, and I travelled over three thousand miles across the American continent, a journey more than half as far as from Yokohama to Vancouver. At Halifax, straightway I took another liner. And this time for New York. It was in New York I felt I was destined really "to come off from the boat." The beginning of my new existence must be founded here. In Korea *to come out from the boat* is an idiom meaning to be born, as the word "pai" for "womb" is the same as "pai" for "boat"; and there is the story of a Korean humorist who had no money, but who needed to get across a river. On landing him on the other side, the ferryman asked for his money. But the Korean humorist said to the ferryman who too had just stepped out, "You wouldn't charge your brother, would you? We both came from the same boat." And so he travelled free. My only plea for a planet-ride among the white-skinned majority of this New World is the same facetious argument. I brought little money, and no prestige, as I entered a practical country with small respect for the dark side of the moon. I got in just in time before the law against Oriental immigration was passed.

But New York, that magic city on rock yet ungrounded, nervous, flowing, million-hued as a dream, became, throughout the years I am recording, the vast mechanical incubator of me.

It was always of New York I dreamed—not Paris nor London nor Berlin nor Munich nor Vienna nor age-buried Rome. I was eighteen, green with youth, and there was some of the mystery of nature in my simple immediate response to what was for me just a name . . . like the dogged moth that directs its flight by some unfathomable law. But I said to myself, "I want neither dreams nor poetry, least of all tradition, never the full moon." Korea even in her shattered state had these. And beyond them stood waiting—death. I craved swiftness, unimpeded action, fluidity, and amorphous New. Out of action rises the dream, rises the poetry. Dream without motion is the only wasteland that can sustain nothing. So I came adoring the crescent, not the full harvest moon, with winter over the horizon and its waning to a husk.

"New York at last!" I heard from the passengers around me. And the information was not needed. In unearthly white and mauve, shadow of white, the city rose, like a dream dreamed overnight, new, remorselessly new, impossibly new . . . and yet there in all the arrogant pride of rejoiced materialism. These young, slim, stately things a thousand houses high (or so it seemed to me, coming from an architecture that had never defied the earth), a tower of Babel each one, not one tower of Babel but many, a city of Babel towers, casually, easily strewn end up against the skies—they stood at the brink, close-crowded, the brink of America, these Giantesses, these Fates, which were not built for a king nor a ghost nor any man's religion, but were materialized by those hard, cold, magic words—opportunity, enterprise, prosperity, success—just business words out of world-wide commerce from a land rich in natural resource. Buildings that sprang white from the rock. No earth clung to their skirts. They leaped like Athene from the mind synthetically; they spurned the earth. And there was no monument to the machine-age like America.

I could not have come farther from home than this New York. Our dwellings, low, weathered, mossed, abhorring the lifeless line—the definite, the finite, the aloof—loving rondures and an upward stroke, the tilt of a roof like a boat always aware of the elements in which it is swinging—most fittingly my home was set a hemisphere apart, so far over the globe that to have gone on would have meant to go nearer not farther. How far my little grass-roofed, hill-wrapped village from this gigantic rebellion which was New York! And New York's rebellion called to me excitedly, this savagery which piled great concrete block on concrete block, topping at the last moment as in an afterthought, with crowns as delicate as pinnacled ice; this lavishness which, without a prayer, pillaged coal mines and waterfalls for light, festooning the great nature-severed city with diamonds of frozen electrical phenomena—it fascinated me, the Asian man, and in it I saw not Milton's Satan, but the one of Blake.

It is clear as one reads this essay that for Kang, who came from an ancient culture, the newness and enormous energy of New York were immensely attractive to him before he ever came to America. Let's look at a couple of his assertions:

> It was in New York I felt I was destined really "to come off from the boat." The beginning of my new existence must be founded here.

These assertions are supported by a couple of explanations—that off the boat in Korean is the same as being born, that coming to New York means starting a new life in a new country. Kang's focus is not just on his immigrant status, however, but on what New York seemed to offer that no other place could. Kang uses elaborate metaphorical language to express this view: ". . . that magic city on rock yet ungrounded, nervous, flowing, million-hued as a dream, became, throughout the years I am recording, the vast mechanical incubator of me."

If we examine this image briefly, we can see how Kang's exposition of the central idea—the nature of New York and its significance to his own development—is packed into one sentence. His language is poetic and deliberately contradictory; New York is both a city on rock and a place that is as yet ungrounded; it's nervous and multicolored, a great organism, but it is also a machine, an incubator. And since an incubator keeps newborn babies alive until they're well enough to manage on their own, this metaphor also reinforces Kang's previous image of coming to New York to be reborn.

In the latter part of the essay, the exposition turns more toward what New York has to offer. Kang names the economic possibilities—"opportunity, enterprise, prosperity, success" and the fact that New York is America's best monument to the machine age—a reference that goes back to the incubator metaphor and forward to the final paragraph.

But having drawn contrasts throughout this essay between Korea and New York, Kang returns to that idea by contrasting the "little grass-roofed, hill-wrapped village" that he was born in with New York's architecture. Like the earlier metaphor, which describes New York as simultaneously an organism and a machine, the metaphor here describes skyscrapers as concrete blocks "with crowns as delicate as pinnacled ice."

This kind of exposition is deliberately poetic, piled with language and metaphor, imagery and simile. What makes it work is that these expository techniques are an expression of the main idea in the essay—that New York is attractive to Kang because it is so full of energy, variety, and possibility. Kang's idea of New York and the words he uses to describe it are full of the same nervous energy, and through them he communicates both the unruliness of the city and the sense of liberation it gives him. This is an expository essay in which the writer's language is profoundly in tune with his thesis.

Analytical Essays   Most students are familiar with essays analyzing texts. They have written essays responding to literature and focusing on characters, images, or historical and philosophical contexts for the text. In analyzing argumentative or persuasive texts, students focus more on the ways in which the elements of a text work together to create an argument. They may focus on the contribution of imagery to evoke appeals to emotions, or they might evaluate the ways in which persuasive language sways a reader to adopt a certain point of view. They also examine the underlying assumptions and premises in a text and evaluate the logic of the conclusion drawn from those premises.

An example of an essay analyzing a persuasive text that is also a literary work is student writer Chris Countryman's essay on the Langston Hughes poem "Let America Be America Again" in Chapter 6. Let's take a look at his thesis statement:

> In his poem "Let America be America Again" Langston Hughes uses evocative language and structural techniques to help emphasize the separation he feels underclass Americans experience in a country they helped create.

In this thesis statement, we see the topic, the focus, and the direction of his analysis: Countryman will focus on the ways in which language and poetic structure convey the theme and argument—that certain groups of people whose contributions helped create America have been kept from full participation in their society. We recommend turning to Chapter 6 to this poem and the full essay for an excellent example of textual analysis.

Note that Countryman's essay is not simply a catalog of words and poetic structures in the poem; it is, rather, an examination of the ways in which these strategies contribute to Hughes's argument. An analysis of a text must be in service of a thesis—an assertion you make about the text or its argument. Such an essay, like other essays, needs an introduction to help orient the reader, as well as a logical organization to help the reader stay with the argument. Some organizational strategies range from following the order of the text to adopting a global-to-local focus (overall impression to specifics).

Less commonly, you may have been asked to analyze an image, in the form of an advertisement or painting. As noted in Chapter 2, a number of predominantly visual texts can be persuasive. Much of the information we now receive incorporates images with text—from war propaganda to political cartoons to the nightly news to the majority of Web pages. Increasingly, scholars and writers are grappling with the notion of "visual rhetoric," or the ways in which the visual elements of a text convey information or stance. As with textual rhetoric, visual rhetoric incorporates the rhetorical situation of audience and purpose. As with textual analysis, you will need to tease apart and analyze (1) any text accompanying the image; (2) the elements of the image; and (3) the ways in which these elements and the accompanying text put forth assertions, rely on assumptions, and draw conclusions.

In keeping with our practice of encouraging you to "read" visuals for their rhetoric, audience, purpose, and techniques, we present an essay by student Erica Heiman. Here she analyzes a poster that turned a famous American patriotic image—that of Uncle Sam saying "I Want

You"—into a statement of protest. First, examine the classic James Montgomery Flagg poster of Uncle Sam, made famous in the World War I era recruiting posters.

Now examine the contrasting image and Heiman's analysis.

❊❊ *I Want Out*

ERICA HEIMAN

Propaganda posters do not always encourage patriotic action; in times of protest, propaganda posters may carry messages of antipatriotism and ask for an end to action. The Vietnam War was one such event in America's history, when many questioned the validity of U.S.

involvement in the conflict, especially in light of the huge numbers of casualties the war was creating and had been for more than five years. This image, produced in 1971 by an organization that called itself the Committee to Help Unsell the War, depicts the familiar icon of Uncle Sam. Uncle Sam in this poster is represented similarly to the way in which he was depicted in a famous World War I recruiting poster, with which the audience of the poster was no doubt familiar. This Uncle Sam, however, is tattered and pathetic, reaching out to the viewer and hoping for a helping hand. The poster acts on two levels to encourage protest: it creates sympathy for the tortured, tattered old man, letting the viewer presume the same fate for his/her loved ones in Vietnam; and, by perverting a classic American icon, it suggests that our intervention in Vietnam corrupts the classic ideals of dignity and freedom that America holds sacred.

This antiwar image catches the viewer's attention in much the same way as the original pro-war poster did earlier in the century. The image is confrontational and personalized, addressing the viewer directly with an appeal. To avoid responding to an appeal of this sort would seem an affront to the old man, who is asking a personal favor. The staring eyes of the figure seem to follow the viewer, and disconcert her enough to prevent her from walking by the poster without glancing at it.

Though this poster and its predecessor both evoke emotional responses in the viewer, the emotions that each one hopes to conjure up are quite different. Instead of the dignified, fatherly image with which the World War I poster presented potential enlistees, this one portrays Uncle Sam as a torn and tattered pathetic individual who needs a handout. The old Uncle Sam, in his stern glory, invokes in the viewers a sense of responsibility and pride. He calls on them to take action and mobilize themselves in the name of American integrity and freedom. This new, battered Uncle Sam asks for his viewers' pity. Their action depends not on their own sense of pride or responsibility in themselves and their country, but on compassion for this bedraggled old man.

The poster stirs this pity for Uncle Sam so that the viewer will suppose the same fate for the entire American army, which had been fighting in Vietnam for over five years. In addition to representing the army as a whole, Uncle Sam can also quickly become any soldier, any son or husband, in the mind of an American viewer. This poster, then, targets those with family and friends in Vietnam, fighting until their bodies give out and they reach out their hands to beg for help. And in addition to representing the soldiers beloved by the viewers of this poster, the poster gives a face to those whom they have never met. By representing an army with one face, this image personalizes the suffering of an entire army, and makes it easier to sympathize with its plight.

In addition to asking viewers to reexamine what is happening to America's army halfway across the world, this poster asks them to reexamine the values that they endorse by supporting the war effort. Uncle Sam, a symbol inspiring American patriotism and pride, has deteriorated drastically, and the strong, spirited slogan "I Want You" has become a wailing "I Want Out." This perversion of such a classic American icon indicates that present U.S. policy is a corruption of the classic American ideals that Uncle Sam represents. The Vietnam War was an extremely controversial conflict: Many called into question the validity of U.S. involvement in a country on the other side of the world because of a clash in ideology. War protestors saw U.S. involvement in the war as putting limits on people's freedoms, an act very much at odds with presumed American ideals. The "I Want Out" poster is taking this antiwar standpoint. It presents the contrast between classic American ideals and the ideals represented by the Vietnam War as the contrast between the old representation of Uncle Sam and the new, pathetic one. The poster asks the viewer to protest the war in order to uphold American dignity and idealism.

Uncle Sam represents both a person and a concept in this Vietnam War protest poster. As a person, he is a soldier, injured and tired, stirring the viewer's sympathy. As a concept, he is American idealism, and his deterioration appeals to the viewer's system of values. In this way, this 1971 propaganda poster stirs the audience's sympathies and convictions in encouraging an end to the war.

Heiman organized her essay as follows: She began by challenging the conventional role of propaganda posters in encouraging patriotism. This approach provides a context for both the role of the poster in general and the specific role of this poster in protest. She provides additional context for this particular poster and the context for protest in her reference to the Vietnam War. She includes the provenance of the poster to provide context regarding the poster's author and alludes to its roots in the 1917 version of the poster. She ends this background information with her thesis statement to orient the reader to the aspects of the poster that she will discuss in her essay.

The next paragraph discusses the overall impression that the poster conveys to its audience. She then contrasts the two posters in terms of the emotional impact on the audience. The next paragraph analyzes the way in which the poster extends its emotional impact from the "bedraggled old man" of the poster to American fighting men in general and family members and friends in particular. Heiman then steps back to reflect on the poster's assertions: that viewers should reevaluate their support for the war; that the patriotic fervor of the traditional Uncle Sam has been perverted in U.S. policy in Vietnam; and that protesting the war will in fact uphold the earlier, idealistic and dignified image of Uncle Sam. Heiman concludes her essay by placing this American icon in its context as representing both individuals damaged by the war and the concept of American idealism.

Other analytical essays in this text include "Building Beliefs" by Daniel McKenzie (Chapter 7) and "Propaganda in FDR's 'Pearl Harbor Address'" by Neil A. Van Os (Chapter 10). Examining these essays can help you to develop your own range of strategies to construct analytical essays on textual and visual arguments.

Argumentative Essays   Although the prewriting and organizing suggestions described earlier should prove helpful in developing an argumentative essay, some writers prefer to conceptualize their more persuasive essays a bit differently, envisioning the argument as a more engaged and interactive process than writing exposition. Further, you will at times be engaged in arguments that are not assigned exercises or responses to texts or discussion questions, but rather evolve out of circumstances within and outside of your academic studies.

For most argument assignments, you will need to argue a point of view or propose a course of action. You may be assigned a topic, or you may be able to select one on the basis of your interests or observations. There are argument assignments in this text; check the end of selection and end of chapter assignments. You could consider writing an argument about something practical and close to home. Such topics might include campus residence regulations, gender studies/distribution requirements, theme residence halls, need-blind admission, scholarships for athletes/musicians/others, alcohol policy, or early admissions. You could write a letter to the campus newspaper or another newspaper or write a guest editorial, whether you choose a subject close to home or one with broad implications. Alternatively, you could write a letter directly to an administrator on campus, such as an academic or a student affairs dean. Student Mike Hipolito wrote his argumentative essay in Chapter 7, "Harvey Milk High School," in response to criticism about the controversial New York high school.

You could also consider a literary topic—*Huckleberry Finn* is/is not a great work or should/should not be required reading in high school courses, for example. Or you could write about something philosophical or political—U.S. troops should/should not pursue further military action without support from allies; the United States should trade with Cuba, pay reparations to Guatemala, negotiate with North Korea, and the like. In any event, make sure your topic is substantial enough to merit your effort and the reader's time. Beware of entirely idiosyncratic arguments that matter to you and no one else. (For example, most instructors and peers would probably rather not read arguments about why you and your friend should become "more involved.")

Limit your topic appropriately for the length of the assignment: you're better off focusing on the topic and dealing with it in depth than staying general and floundering around in superficialities. Finally, consider doing your readers the kindness of avoiding the usual litany (abortion, capital punishment) unless you feel that you have something unique to add to the discussion.

If you select a current event, make sure that your argument is your own and not an editorial writer's, although certainly you would be wise to consider the key arguments offered in various periodicals. In summary, you might draw from literature, from science or social science, from public policy, from experience and personal interests, from philosophy, and from the assignments in this text. Aim for a topic that challenges you but that is feasible in the time and space allowed.

Many students' arguments have one fatal flaw: they do not discuss the opposing or alternative views. Remember that traditional argument assumes an opposition; if there were no opposition or alternative view, there would be no need to argue. You should bring up the most compelling arguments on the other side, because assuredly your audience will be thinking of them anyway. When you bring them up yourself, you are, first of all, appealing to ethos and demonstrating that you have faith in your own position—enough to face the other side. This action gives you more credibility. Further, you are often able to refute those opposing arguments by demonstrating why they are faulty (in premises, in logic) or by bringing up even more convincing arguments and evidence to the contrary. But even if you cannot refute opposing views and must concede them, you have established yourself as a rhetor who is reasonable, fair-minded, and able to consider other views.

Use the appeals and evidence that seem appropriate to the topic and the audience at hand (and you might consider indicating your audience, perhaps in a footnote if it is not apparent from the context and content). You may decide that appeals to ethos and logos are the most powerful, but do not underestimate appeals to pathos if they suit your rhetorical situation.

In any case, you should follow these guidelines for a good essay:

- Get in step with the reader (intro).
- Focus the core topic of the essay (thesis).
- Develop and support that thesis (body of essay) with focused paragraphs (clear topic idea for each) that address and develop the subtopics of the essay.
- Leave your readers with a memorable conclusion that puts the issue in a larger context or leaves the reader with a thought-provoking image or statement that provides a sense of closure.

Writers have different approaches to organizing their essays. Some prefer a very rough outline of the major sections or large chunks of the essay, indicating the purpose of each section. Such an approach might have a rough organization as follows for an inductive essay:

Context

Prevailing view/beliefs/interpretations

Problems with current view

Your alternative view, supported by evidence

The larger conclusion/context, adjusted to take into account a revised view of context, text, or problem

Other writers prefer to envision the argument's structure as a thesis statement with an argumentative edge that captures the central claim or core assertion, with major subclaims or premises then supporting the thesis by serving as topic sentences. These subclaims are, in turn, supported by evidence, either reasons or examples or both. A basic outline, then, would consist of thesis statement and topic sentences supporting the thesis. Some of those topic sentences will be introducing or stating alternative or opposing views—counterclaims to your core assertion/thesis. The body of those paragraphs would then concede or refute the counterclaim.

You may outline your essay in a number of ways, and there is no perfect formula, but consider adapting one of the following structures:

Deductive/Direct Organization: Intro, State Your Point/Thesis and Then Provide

A	B
key supporting arguments	key supporting points
key opposing arguments	opposing point / rebuttal
rebuttal	opposing point / rebuttal (etc.)
conclusion	conclusion

Or, with an Inductive/Indirect Organization

A	B
intro	intro
opposing view	opposing view / rebuttal
opposing view	opposing view / rebuttal
opposing view	opposing view / rebuttal
rebuttal	

Thesis and Additional Support Not Covered in the Rebuttals

conclusion	conclusion

Although the sample outline indicates that you will be dealing with "opposing views," often the views are not diametrically opposed, but rather are simply different ways to approach the problem or topic—alternative views rather than opposites. Again, the crucial element here is anticipating and dealing with alternatives or objections to your point of view and your key assertions.

There are, as noted, variations on these approaches, but the point is to be mindful of organization and to select the best organization for your topic. For example, if your topic is controversial or your thesis is likely to meet with opposition, you may get a fairer hearing if you can dispatch a few opposing arguments or concerns before stating your position.

The conclusion is your last chance to make your points with the reader: Don't raise any new issues except, perhaps, to forecast a potential effect or result if your plan is/is not followed. Leave your reader with a thought-provoking point, a reinforcement of your theme or core issue (but don't be repetitious!), or a striking image or memorable statement. You could look at a few editorials in the newspapers to see what you find effective yourself as a critical reader.

Pay special attention to language, and maintain a reasonable tone throughout the argument. If you engage in the written equivalent of ranting and raving, your reader will react the way you do when you experience someone verbally ranting and raving at you. Watch out for patronizing or irritating language ("well obviously," etc.), which not only looks down on your audience but also reveals just how one-sided your argument is.

Know your readers! Unless you have designated a specific audience, think of your reader as an educated generalist who may not know the particular arguments or jargon of your topic. You'll need to communicate clearly without patronizing or offending your audience. Remember that you are writing an essay, not giving a speech, and you will need to adjust your style accordingly. For example, directly addressing the reader—"Look, if everyone contributed just $1 a day"—might be workable in a speech, but the rhetorical situation of the written argument calls for a less colloquial style. Further, to persuade effectively, you will need to understand your reader if you want your reader to identify with you or if you want to appeal to common values or concerns. You will also need to consider your reader to figure out the best organization for your argument.

A clear argumentative essay can be powerful. Professor Cornel West, a philosopher who was formerly the head of African American Studies at Princeton and is currently at Harvard, writes in the following essay about a controversial topic—affirmative action—and lays out a series of argumentative points as part of a larger philosophical question.

✳✳✳ *Affirmative Action in Context*

CORNEL WEST

Today's affirmative action policy is not the appropriate starting point for a substantive debate on affirmative action. Instead, we must begin with the larger historical and moral context of the recent controversy. Why was the policy established in the first place? What were the alternatives? Who questioned its operation, and when? How did it come about that a civil rights initiative in the 1960s is viewed by many as a civil rights violation in the 1990s? Whose civil rights are we talking about? Is there a difference between a right and an expectation? What are the limits of affirmative action? What would the consequences be if affirmative action disappeared in America?

The Aim of Affirmative Action

The vicious legacy of white supremacy—institutionalized in housing, education, health care, employment, and social life—served as the historical context for the civil rights movement in the late 1950s and 1960s. Affirmative action was a *weak* response to this legacy. It constituted an imperfect policy conceded by a powerful political, business, and educational establishment in light of the pressures of organized citizens and the disturbances of angry unorganized ones.

The fundamental aim of affirmative action was to put a significant dent in the tightly controlled networks of privileged white male citizens who monopolized the good jobs and influential positions in American society. Just as Catholics and Jews had earlier challenged the white Anglo-Saxon Protestant monopoly of such jobs and positions, in the 1960s blacks and women did also. Yet since the historical gravity of race and gender outweighs that of religion and ethnicity in American society, the federal government had to step in to facilitate black and female entry into the U.S. mainstream and malestream. This national spectacle could not but prove costly under later, more hostile circumstances.

The initial debate focused on the relative lack of fairness, merit, and public interest displayed by the prevailing systems of employment and education, principally owing to arbitrary racist and sexist exclusion. In the 1960s, class-based affirmative action was not seriously considered, primarily because it could easily have been implemented in such a way as to perpetuate exclusion, especially given a labor movement replete with racism and sexism. Both Democratic and Republican administrations supported affirmative action as the painful way of trying to create a multiracial democracy in which women and people of color were not second-class citizens. Initially, affirmative action was opposed by hard-line conservatives, usually the same ones who opposed the civil rights movement led by Dr. Martin Luther King, Jr. Yet the pragmatic liberals and conservatives prevailed.

The Neoconservative Opposition

The rise of the neoconservatives unsettled this fragile consensus. By affirming the principle of equality of opportunity yet trashing any mechanism that claimed to go beyond merit, neoconservatives drove a wedge between civil rights and affirmative action. By claiming that meritocratic judgments trump egalitarian efforts to produce tangible results, neoconservatives cast affirmative action policies as multiracial reverse racism and the major cause of racial divisiveness and low black self-esteem in the workplace and colleges.

Yet even this major intellectual and ideological assault did not produce a wholesale abandonment of affirmative action on behalf of business, political, and educational elites. The major factor that escalated the drive against affirmative action was the shrinking job possibilities—along with stagnating and declining wages—that were squeezing the white middle class. Unfortunately, conservative leaders seized this moment to begin to more vociferously scapegoat affirmative action, and to seek its weakening or elimination.

Their first move was to define affirmative action as a program for "unqualified" women and, especially, black people. Their second move was to cast affirmative action as "un-American," a quota system for groups rather than a merit system for individuals. The third move was to claim that anti-discrimination laws are enough, given the decline or end of racism among employers. The latest move has been to soothe the agonized consciences of liberals and conservatives by trying to show that black people are genetically behind whites in intelligence; hence, nothing can be done.

The popularity—distinct from the rationality—of these moves has created a climate in which proponents of affirmative action are on the defensive. Even those of us who admit the excesses of some affirmative action programs—and therefore call for correcting, not eliminating, them—give aid and comfort to our adversaries. This reality reveals just how far the debate has moved in the direction of the neoconservative and conservative perceptions in the country. It also discloses that it is far beyond weak policies like affirmative action to confront the legacies of white supremacy and corporate power in the United States—legacies visible in unemployment and under-employment, unaffordable health care and inadequate child care, dilapidated housing and decrepit schools for millions of Americans, disproportionately people of color, women, and children.

The idea that affirmative action violates the rights of fellow citizens confuses a right with an expectation. We all have a right to be seriously and fairly considered for a job or position. But calculations of merit, institutional benefit, and social utility produce the results. In the past, those who were never even considered had their rights violated; in the present, those who are seriously and fairly considered yet still not selected do not have their rights violated but rather had their expectations frustrated.

For example, if Harvard College receives more than ten thousand applications for fourteen hundred slots in the freshman class and roughly four thousand meet the basic qualifications, how does one select the "worthy" ones? Six thousand applicants are already fairly eliminated. Yet twenty-six hundred still will not make it. When considerations of factors other than merit are involved, such as whether candidates are the sons or daughters of alumni, come from diverse regions of the country, or are athletes, no one objects. But when racial diversity is involved, the opponents of affirmative action yell foul play. Yet each class at Harvard remains about 5 to 7% black—far from a black takeover. And affirmative action bears the blame for racial anxiety and division on campus in such an atmosphere. In short, neoconservatives and conservatives fail to see the subtle (and not-so-subtle) white supremacist sensibilities behind their "color-blind" perspectives on affirmative action.

The Limits of Affirmative Action

Yet it would be myopic of progressives to make a fetish of affirmative action. As desirable as those policies are—an insight held fast by much of corporate America except at the almost lily-white senior management levels—they will never ameliorate the plight and predicament of poor people of color. More drastic and redistributive measures are needed in order to address their situations, measures that challenge the maldistribution of wealth and power and that will trigger cultural renewal and personal hope.

If affirmative action disappears from the American scene, many blacks will still excel and succeed. But the larger signal that sends will be lethal for the country. It is a signal that white supremacy now has one less constraint and black people have one more reason to lose trust in the promise of American democracy.

In examining West's argument, it is a good idea to start with the title, because "Affirmative Action in Context" suggests a historical and/or social perspective that is crucial to his organizational sense. This perspective is borne out by the first two sentences:

> Today's affirmative action policy is not the appropriate starting point for a substantive debate on affirmative action. Instead, we must begin with the larger historical and moral context of the recent controversy.

What West then proceeds to do is divide his argument into three distinct sections: The Aim of Affirmative Action, The Neoconservative Opposition, and The Limits of Affirmative Action. In the first part, he explains the birth of affirmative action as a weak response to the legacy of white supremacy, an effort supported by pragmatic liberals and conservatives as a way of facilitating "black and female entry into the U.S. mainstream and malestream." In the second and longest part of the essay, West describes how neoconservative opponents of affirmative action transformed the argument from one about social justice to a referendum on reverse racism and the hiring of unqualified women and blacks. In the final section, he asserts that affirmative action is not the answer to everything; it is too mild to affect the lives of poor people of color, but it's better than nothing, and destroying it would give black people "one more reason to lose trust in the promise of American democracy."

This summary indicates the progression of West's contextual argument, from the distant to the more recent past to the present and the future. That chronological approach is helpful in developing momentum for the whole essay, and it is one that you may find useful in your own work. But West does something else as well. Within each section he makes specific assertions that form the backbone of his argument. For example, in the main second section, he numbers three separate attacks on affirmative action. Then he moves to the moral question of redressing past wrongs through current social action, and he explains the distinction between having one's rights violated and one's expectations disappointed. He follows that with a good example of induction; many worthy students do not get into Harvard; no one objects to special consideration for athletes, children of alumni, and so on; neoconservatives do object, however, to special consideration for blacks. Conclusion: neoconservatives who insist that they are "color-blind" in fact fail to recognize their own racially based sensibilities.

The culmination of West's argumentation is as much a moral as a logical construction, but it also helps bring us as readers back to the opening page of the essay. He says that the end of affirmative action will eliminate one more constraint on white supremacy. White supremacy is also the subject of his first section, The Aim of Affirmative

Action. By repeating the phrase at the end, West suggests that though a lot of time may have passed since the heyday of white supremacy, the actual situation may be more static than one would have thought. In effect, he refutes the arguments in favor of ending affirmative action, appeals to his readers' logic, applies inductive reasoning, and finishes with a moral warning. His essay is a compendium of well-wrought rhetorical strategies. You don't have to use all of them, but you might want to refer back to this essay when you are thinking about and preparing your own argument, implicitly or explicitly refuting someone else's point of view, or searching for a structure to hold your argument in hand.

We close this chapter with one more sample essay, this one by student writer Kris Andeen, whose assignment was to analyze a visual image, a painting by the famous American illustrator Norman Rockwell. We chose this essay not only because it gives you one more example of how to analyze visual rhetoric and to read a picture like a text, but also because we wanted you to see how a student starting from scratch goes through the entire process of completing such a project. This selection includes Kris Andeen's prewriting, his planning, draft, final revision, and reflection. We hope that this complete record of one student's efforts will give you both encouragement and additional tools to help with your own work.

Kris's assignment for his writing class was to find a visual argument and analyze it. He browsed through some books containing World War I and II era posters at the school library and selected "Hasten the Home-coming—Buy Victory Bonds" by Norman Rockwell. He made a color photocopy of the poster to attach to the submitted essay. Then he brainstormed a list of his first impressions of the poster, jotting them all down as they came to him. He could also have searched the Web and downloaded an appropriate image, taking care to cite his source appropriately.

Next, he reviewed what he had learned about Aristotle's appeals—to ethos, pathos, and logos—and examined the poster with those elements in mind, generating more material on the poster. The outline that follows organized these impressions:

"Hasten the Homecoming—Buy Victory Bonds," USA, 1939–1945.
Norman Rockwell painting, originally for *Saturday Evening Post*

I.   First Impressions
  A. First thing which draws the eye is red line: "Buy Victory Bonds."
    1. This makes sense since it is most important part of the poster.
  B. After one's eyes have seen red "Buy Victory Bonds," the eyes are next taken to the red sweater of the mother who is reaching out to her son.
    1. Her eyes point toward her son, which is next place viewer's eyes look.

Norman Rockwell, "Hasten the Homecoming. Buy Victory Bonds." Poster. © 1943. Norman Rockwell Family Trust. Photo courtesy of the Franklin D. Roosevelt Library.

C. After viewer has seen son, he/she begins to see the rest of the picture, but by this point, a central association has been made in the viewer's mind: "Buy victory bonds, and the men will come home."

1. Rest of picture reveals 16 faces witnessing the soldier's return—17, if you count the dog!!
2. All faces are smiling (with exception of one), which associates happiness with the return of the soldier.
3. Obviously, this is not a mansion, but a lower-class, more common American home. Therefore, the ad will appeal to a large percentage of the American population.
4. It appears as though some previous problems with the roof are being repaired.
5. There also appear to be light shining down on the scene from the upper right-hand corner of the picture as if it is just coming out of the clouds.

II. Appeals

A. Appeals to Ethos

1. The family portrayed in the poster represents the common American family of the time.
   a. excited, motherly figure
   b. Pops is smoking a pipe
   c. lots of kids (neighborhood too)
   d. Sparky, the dog
2. The scene represents the common American neighborhood.
   a. After depression ('30s), people still living in lower-class homes.
   b. Clothes dried on clothesline.
   c. The classic American sweetheart is waiting for soldier-boy just around the corner.
3. The headlines for the poster, "Hasten the Homecoming—Buy Victory Bonds," are printed in red and blue against a white background → red, white, and blue → patriotism, nationalism.

B. Appeals to Pathos

1. If you did not have any children/family members in the war, this poster still might make you feel sorry for those with loved ones at war, so you might be convinced to buy victory bonds to bring your neighbor's son home. Neighbors *are* shown in the picture, with smiles on their faces.
2. If you were a wealthy American, you might feel sorry for lower-class citizens upon seeing this poster, and thus be convinced to buy victory bonds.

C. Appeals to Logos

1. As earlier stated, this poster seems to suggest that if one were to buy victory bonds, then the men of the war could come

home faster, thus bringing happy smiles, repairs, and bright
sunshine.

III. Audience

I believe this poster can be aimed at three types of people: families
with relatives fighting in the war, neighbors of people fighting in
the war and their families, and wealthy citizens who feel sorry for
lower-class families with relatives in the war.

After putting the project aside for a day or two, Kris tried to compose a draft that was based on his working outline. He considered and reconsidered his dominant impression or thesis—the main assertion or inference he would make on the basis of his material—so that he would be able to focus the essay and make sure it stayed on track. Kris identified this as his dominant point: "the poster's strength lay in its ability to identify with the common American."

After reviewing the biographical notes on Rockwell in the book of posters and in a reference book on American biographies, Kris drafted some background information for the introduction to provide context and help prepare the reader to listen to his analysis. The introduction led smoothly into the thesis for this draft. For the draft, Kris didn't use all the material he had generated; the assignment was to write a two- to three-page analysis of a visual argument, and he had generated enough material for a longer paper. Once he developed his thesis around the notion of identifying with the common person, he was able to determine what to keep and what to let go. The first body paragraph focuses on Rockwell's use of the family in the poster; he then expands his point to involve the neighborhood; he then shifts to broader American attitudes, values, and desire for an end to the war. All paragraphs stay focused on the theme of appeals to the common American. The draft that follows includes some comments from both an instructor and a peer.

Kris Andeen
English 1D5
10/1/97
Draft

The Common American

Norman Rockwell's work represents a hallmark of the American

You ordinarily need a noun after "this" to avoid reference errors.

dream. His paintings during the early half of this century are known for

great background

portraying the common American. The U.S. government recognized

this and used one of his cover paintings for *The Saturday Evening Post*

Andeen 2

in a poster encouraging financial support for World War II. Although

Yes, the thesis can be placed at end of intro to lead into essay.

Rockwell probably wasn't commissioned by the U.S. government to

paint this picture, it served the government's purposes quite well. The

the poster's? Or the other way works because Americans can identify w/the scene

poster's strength lies in its ability to identify with the common Ameri- *portrayed?*

can. Indeed, Rockwell was so skilled at depicting the people of the

time, that his painting could have been used for any of a number of *move to end of essay?*

causes and still have been successful.

check w.c.

The first way which this poster appeals to the common American

dominant? *rephrase?*

is through the family, the most dominating figure of which (in this

painting) is the mother. Thanks to her bright red sweater, Mom stands

out as the first figure that catches the viewer's eye. Traditionally, she

represents the passionate, caring head of the family, just as she is por-

trayed here with her arms outstretched. She is also shown as a white

person (as is the whole neighborhood) as white people represented the

largest racial percentage of the nation's population. Also seen on the

front porch is Dad, who appears to have just gotten out of his recliner,

pipe still in hand. Again, this fits the classic image we have of the fa-

therly figure who rests after a day at work in his recliner with his pipe

and slippers. And of course, the American family is not a small one—

whom

indeed, there are plenty of children about, some of which may be as-

sumed are siblings. But Rockwell doesn't stop at human figures—Sparky,

the dog, plays a crucial role in the classic American family, and he too

can be seen running anxiously towards) the returning soldier

Andeen 3

Another way in which Rockwell is able to identify with the people

vague   of the time is to associate with the neighborhood. In this painting, the

neighborhood plays an even larger role than the family. So what did

the common American neighborhood look like from 1939 to 1945?

One must remember that during this time, not only was the U.S. at war,

Usually capitalized

but it was still recovering from the great depression. A very large per-

unclear sentence

centage of the population lived in the city and inner-city housing

wasn't any more beautiful then than it is now. The brick house, the

clotheslines, the garbage-ridden street, the sweetheart around the cor-

ner, the hordes of frolicking children (they weren't inside playing Nin-

He's also dealing with class issues.)
Victory Bonds are not just for the wealthy, etc.

tendo or surfing the Web back then), the repairman on the roof, and

even the faded paint on the porch all contribute in providing an arche-

Needed?

typal image of the urban American neighborhood. *(*Once again,*)* Rock-

well has identified with the American population by meticulously

allegorizing the American home.

One last key theme in identifying with American is happiness and

Check w.c.—needed? most precise?

an odium for war. The American people don't like to be active in wars.

There are many reasons for this; increased stress on the household,

Could use, such as . . . or a colon. But the semicolon won't work here.

possible increase on the price of imports, and the threat of attack. But

most of all, Americans are troubled by the absence of loved ones who

may or may not return after the war. With the return of the soldier in

Avoid shifts to 2nd person point of view

Rockwell's painting we see a number of happy connotations. For one,

Write out numbers up to 99 (a convention).

there are 16 smiling faces in the picture, and that's if you don't count

Sparky. We also see (consciously or unconsciously) green leaves

emerging from the tree which otherwise appears not to have any fo- *great*
details

liage. This͝ suggests Springtime and a new happiness. Another sugges-

tion of such happiness is that while most of the scene appears to be

very dark, with the exception of Mom's clothesline, there appears to be

a bright light shining down from the upper right-hand corner of the pic-

ture. This implies the sun breaking through the clouds of wartime, an-
Transition? Needed?

other concept which America most certainly welcomes. So once again,
Ref?

Rockwell has identified with the American through its desire for an end

to the war and the return of happy times.

Happy times are just what the American public wanted. Norman

Rockwell was aware of this͝ and by incorporating such values into his

painting he was able to identify with the nation. His abilities in relating
Resource? (See if you want the connotation

to the nation's people made him a valuable tool for the U.S. govern- *that "tool"*
provides.)

ment. The power of such identification in art could just as well have

been used to rouse the country in a cultural diversity campaign. If Mom
for example

were stretching her arms out to a newly arrived Japanese family͒, then

the same concepts of identification would work in promoting the ac-

ceptance of the Japanese culture. Indeed, Rockwell's work, with its na-

tionalistic morals and commonplace subjects, provides an excellent ex- *Good*
analysis

ample of the power of ethos appeals.

To revise this essay, Kris chose to keep the focus that he developed
in this draft, so his work was primarily geared toward crafting

smoother transitions and effective prose. He had already incorporated evidence from the "text," or image, to support his assertions; indeed, in an inductive process, he had generated his evidence and then used inferences from that evidence to make a point. In the essay, the inferences are structured as topic sentences, which are then, in turn, supported by the evidence, examples, and images from the poster.

Kris's draft went through two reviews before final submission, including one peer review. Because this essay was written early in the term, peers were not yet well skilled in providing substantial feedback, so much of the peers' suggestions focused on word choice or mechanics. The instructor's suggestions targeted focus and placement of the thesis (end of introduction or end of essay), selection of evidence to support topic ideas, and some matters of style that needed attention (inappropriate transitions, word choice). Kris also chose to change his title from "The Common American" to "End of the Tunnel," because the artist's strategy of identification with the common man or woman was, in fact, a means to a larger end—expressing the persuasive message that the end of the war is near and that the troops will be home even sooner if we all do our part and buy Victory Bonds. The title ties in well with the conclusion, where Kris amplifies this point.

Kris's final essay, while not perfect, is an excellent example of how a writer analyzes, selects, focuses, and organizes material to develop a coherent expository essay on a visual argument. Kris made particular choices and used a particular approach in doing the analysis and writing the essay. You could take the same image and come up with a very different essay, because your own ideas, creativity, ability to analyze, interests, and skill would determine the outcome.

Kris Andeen
English 1D5
Revision

End of the Tunnel

Norman Rockwell's art represents a hallmark of the American dream. His paintings in the early half of this century are known for portraying the common American and his/her struggles and joys in this society. The U.S. government recognized Rockwell's talent, and in 1939 they used one of his cover paintings for *The Saturday Evening Post* in a poster encouraging financial support for World War II.

Although Rockwell wasn't commissioned by the U.S. government to paint this picture, it served the government's purposes quite well. The poster's persuasive strength lay in the ease with which the common American could identify with the scene portrayed.

The first way in which this poster appealed to the common American was through the family. The most dominant figure of the family, in this painting, is the mother. Thanks to her brilliant red sweater, Mom stands out as the first figure who catches the viewer's eye. Traditionally, she represents the passionate, caring head of the family, just as she is portrayed here with her arms outstretched. She is also shown as a white person (as is the whole neighborhood) since white people represented the largest racial percentage of the nation's population. Also seen on the front porch is Dad, who appears to have just gotten out of his recliner, pipe still in hand. Rockwell's painting fits the classic image we have of the fatherly figure who rests after a day at work in his recliner with his pipe and slippers. And of course, the American family is not a small one—indeed, there are plenty of children about, some of whom may be assumed are siblings. But Rockwell doesn't stop at human figures—Sparky, the dog, plays a crucial role in the classic American family, and he too can be seen running anxiously toward the returning soldier.

Another way in which Rockwell was able to identify with the people of the time was to associate his painting with the American neighborhood. In this painting, the neighborhood plays an even larger role than the family. So what did the common American neighborhood look like from 1939 to 1945? One must remember that during this time the U.S. was not only at war, but it was still recovering from the Great Depression. A large percentage of the population lived in the city, and inner-city housing wasn't any more beautiful then than it is now. The brick apartment building, the clotheslines, the garbage-ridden street, the sweetheart around the corner, the hordes of frolicking children (they weren't inside playing Nintendo or surfing the Web), the repairman on the roof, and even the faded paint on the porch all contribute in providing an archetypal image of the urban American neighborhood. In a sense, Rockwell has painted his audience's neighborhood, providing a mirror in which they may see themselves.

One last key theme in identifying with America is happiness and a repugnance for war. The American people don't like to be active in wars. There are many reasons for this isolationist mindset, such as increased stress on the household, possible increase on the price of imports, and the threat of attack. But most of all, Americans are troubled by the absence of loved ones who may or may not return after the war. With the return of the soldier in Rockwell's painting we see a number of happy connotations. For one, there are *sixteen* smiling faces in the picture, and that's if you don't count Sparky. We also see (consciously or subconsciously) green leaves emerging from the tree which otherwise appears barren. This emerging foliage suggests Springtime and a new happiness. Another suggestion of such happiness is that while the lighting in most of the scene is very dark (with the exception of Mom's clothesline), there appears to be a bright light shining down from the upper right-hand corner of the picture. Such illumination implies the sun breaking through the clouds of wartime, another concept which America most certainly welcomes. Subconsciously, these hints of joy suggest a light at the end of the tunnel, a tunnel of war and depression which all Americans were anxious to exit.

An end to the tunnel is just what the American public wanted. Norman Rockwell was aware of this desire and by incorporating such values into his painting he was able to identify with the nation. The power of such identification in Rockwell's art is so strong that it could have been used successfully to support any number of causes. For example, if Mom were stretching her arms out to a newly arrived Japanese family, then the same concepts of identification would work in promoting the acceptance of the Japanese culture. Indeed, Rockwell's work, with its nationalistic morals and commonplace subjects, provides an excellent example of the power of ethos appeals.

Kris wrote the following reflection on how he went about completing his essay assignment:

> Our assignment was to choose an advertisement and write about the different ways in which it appealed to its audience. We weren't restricted to war ads, but I was familiar with war ads since we had been analyzing them in class. So I went to the library and looked up books about war advertising. There were quite a few books, each filled with full-color war ads. I checked out a few of the books and chose three possible posters to write about. Then I wrote possible hypotheses for each and reasoned that the Rockwell poster had the strongest, most supportable thesis.
>
> Since my thesis focused on Rockwell's remarkable appeals to ethos, I wrote down every aspect of the scene that was common to the American family. My list was long, and with such a list of supporting images, writing the essay itself wasn't very difficult. My outline was basic. The first paragraph would be my lead-in, with some background on Rockwell and the thesis. Each paragraph of the body would cite different aspects of the poster and their relation to the common American. The closing paragraph would wrap up my argument, restating the thesis.
>
> As far as revision went, I read back through my essay to check for fluency in tone and clear progression of thought. Transitions were important and I was careful to use varied transitions where necessary. My professor also read through the rough draft and made some suggestions. For example, she cited my continual use (near the end of each paragraph) of the phrase "once again," or "again we see . . ." I had been using these types of phrases to wrap up each paragraph and tie the paragraphs back to the thesis. However, the use of "again" was repetitive and unoriginal, and I was over-relying on these words to make connections between my points. We were able to rephrase each of these instances, creating a more diverse paragraph structure.
>
> Finally, after making all of my own revisions and those that my professor suggested in our conference, I subjected my prose to my class peers. My peers and their reactions were valuable since they provided me with different, fresh feedback. Then I revised my paper for style and mechanics one more time and submitted the essay.

4

❋❋❋

Research

Integrating Research into Writing

College is a community of scholars. The academic community develops and transmits scholarly opinion, research findings, and reports in papers, books, lectures, Web sites, and, in some cases, computer programs. Being part of that community entails pursuing the ongoing and exciting enterprise known as research. As you begin to conduct research, you take part in worldwide conversations and construction of knowledge. As you see how to integrate research into your writing and writing into your research, you learn to set other ideas and evidence next to your own and to draw connections between them.

A writer who invites other voices into the text must strive to represent their views fairly, to credit them appropriately, and to manage these multiple voices in such a way that she remains the author of this particular paper and the dominant voice in it. The experts can support her, but she must make the core proposal and maintain control of the flow of conversation. She must also take responsibility for everything in the paper and must stand behind her core assertion, her key supporting points, and the evidence she includes.

Researched essays sometimes get a poor reputation for being long, dry exercises in library treasure hunts or fussy documentation styles. To maintain this view is to miss one of the most exciting aspects of the academic community: learning to think, read, write, and contribute as a scholar. As you learn to conduct and carry out research, to use the library, to communicate with other scholars, you claim membership in the community and also equip yourself to become a thoughtful, contributing member of society.

Research activities are complex and recursive processes. As in writing an essay, you start with an idea—maybe from reading or through class discussion, or perhaps from an assigned topic. You discuss, read, review, take notes, and in the process integrate what you are learning with what you already know. You determine what you know enough about and what you need to learn more about—and that "learning more about" is one of the main reasons you do research. During the process of research, it may be useful to employ some of the prompts and questions included in the earlier section on techniques for developing essays to help you think about, focus, structure, and develop your paper. Generally your process of writing researched essays will entail the steps of prewriting, close reading, note taking, organizing ideas, drafting, and revising.

Before proceeding, it may be useful to look at the role of research in expository and argumentative essays. Remember that they are different parts of a continuum, with exposition developing an assertion that is not highly controversial and argument developing an assertion with an argumentative edge.

Expository essays can be based on your own experience, observations, reflections, interpretations of readings, and the like. They are used to explain, and although they convey a point of view and develop an assertion, their goal is not necessarily to change beliefs or behavior. Sometimes you will research a subject to add credibility to the assertions you make in your expository essay; you will analyze a development, a historical process, the causes of a situation, the potential effects of some event. You might research the history of jazz or different drafts of a novel, or convey the history or the background of some event or issue. Expository essays in the humanities might include materials from the text to support an interpretation; essays in the sciences and social sciences generally incorporate evidence acceptable in their disciplines to support their assertions, whether that evidence is statistics or observations. The point of the evidence is generally to suggest how the assertion or conclusion was obtained and to support the writer's interpretations.

In an *argumentative essay,* you need to be concerned with the skeptical reader who asks, "Who says so?" and "Why should I believe it?" To answer the first question, you bring in reinforcements in the form of expert opinion and testimony to back up any claims. Although your voice needs to remain dominant in the essay, the authority of the experts you quote adds support to your argument. To answer the second question, you turn to evidence—examples, observations, statistics, or whatever other data are respected in the discipline.

An argumentative essay that integrates outside research is still similar to one that does not in that its goal is to persuade people to change their minds—about the ramifications of European settlement of the American continent, or the behavior of an ethnic group toward other Americans, or support of educational or public policy. For example, Susan Faludi's essay in Chapter 7 offers substantial evidence to support her argumentative thesis that there is a backlash against the modest gains that American women have made. In deciding the land-mark case *Brown v. Board of Education* (Chapter 9), the Supreme Court used a sociologist's report to help decide the case.

Research has an important place in both expository and argumen-tative essays, but special caution must be exercised in argumentative essay research. As you browse through potential sources, it may be tempting to fall prey to "selective attention," a situation in which you look for evidence that supports your view and avoid materials that contradict it. Remember that you must consider opposing views; simi-larly, in researching controversial or argumentative topics, you need to consider material that contradicts your hypothesis or your belief. Such open-mindedness will help you develop sound scholarly re-search methods and ultimately will strengthen your paper by demon-strating that you have researched alternatives to your belief or proposal. Dealing with contradictory evidence in your essay will ap-peal to ethos by ensuring readers that you have a broad background in the topic, that you are not trying to slant the evidence in your favor, and that your argument is strong and well supported enough to with-stand contrary evidence. In any case, your readers will already be con-sidering opposing views; your willingness to acknowledge those views will only strengthen your case.

Beginning the Process

Begin by selecting the general topic area and developing a re-search question. If you have been assigned a topic, determine some as-pect of it that interests you and that you can develop fully in the time and space allowed. If you choose your own topic, be guided by your interests but also by the limits of time and paper length; having the freedom to choose a topic often entails a more careful assessment of what you can manage. Additional concerns about topic selection for a documented essay include selecting a subject about which you can find enough materials with the resources available to you; also, since you will likely spend considerable time with your topic, you should find a subject that genuinely engages your interest. Finally, remember your role as a contributing member of the academic community; don't bother researching something that is obvious or a foregone conclusion. And consider researching subjects about which you can truly con-tribute: legislative research that serves the public interest, for example, or environmental research that can help your community or school make informed decisions about policy.

An underappreciated aspect of research papers, especially in first-year courses, is developing a research question. When you identify a question to which you truly want to find some answers, you are more likely to be interested in your topic and to keep an open mind as you research. For example, "Was the Civil War truly about economic issues?" or "What stereotypes have remained constant through different stages in American history?" are both much more likely to help you focus and develop a topic than if you say to yourself, "Maybe I can write about the Civil War or about prejudice." A research question can guide your research, help you to develop a working thesis, and prevent you from floundering around in a sea of readings, papers, notes, and miscellaneous unfocused ideas.

You will also need to establish a schedule. Determine the due dates for your paper and any intermediate due dates for parts of the paper during the research process. Often instructors establish checkpoints by which time you will have established a research question, tentative thesis, preliminary research, a working bibliography, an annotated bibliography, a working outline and revised thesis statement, a draft, peer reviews, and a revision. If you have not received such guidelines, make your own, and stick to the schedule. It is too easy to let big projects slide in the face of daily competing demands for your time and interest. The results of waiting too long to start include finding that most of the best sources have been checked out, that you don't have time to do careful research, and that you are fresh out of ideas late in the night before the draft is due.

As with any writing project, consider the audience. Understanding the audience is crucial in making decisions about the subject and focus of the researched essay. If you are writing about literature in a composition class, you are in the position of being a generalist writing to an expert in the field. Your audience knows more about the topic than you do, but you bring with you new insights on the topic and unique responses to the texts you are interpreting. You may also uncover unique connections between sources and new insights in recent critical interpretations. In that same composition class, when you research particular topics of interest that are not literary topics, you will probably become the expert on the topic at hand. You will then have to be particularly aware of your readers' backgrounds and assumptions about your topic.

When you write as an expert to other experts, as you do when you are advancing in your chosen major or discipline, you have the advantage of a common language and a common understanding of the core concepts of the discipline. If you are writing papers for your courses, you will still be writing to specialists who know more than you do in the discipline, but you will have less explaining of terminology to do and can draw on shared assumptions and background knowledge.

Let us say that you are interested in physics or astronomy—in string theory or dark matter in the universe or nanotechnology. Your interest in the topic may carry you through the extensive technical research that will be needed, but if you are writing the essay in response to an open assignment in your writing class, the additional task remains of translating concepts and technical jargon for an audience of writing-class peers and instructor. Such a writing situation is not restricted to writing courses; scientists and scholars frequently must translate the concepts of their work either to publish in general periodicals or to write grant proposals to outside funding sources who may be highly educated but unfamiliar with the particulars of the scientist's work.

Gathering Information

In addition to thinking about the functions of research and researched essays in college, you should consider expanding your sense of sources. Probably in high school, you used books, articles, and Web sites as sources for papers, and these remain excellent choices; but in the academic community, other sources now become necessary and helpful. For example, your college faculty includes experts in various fields and disciplines; plan to visit them to obtain their expert opinions on issues related to your research. Faculty are away from time to time, so plan ahead; call the department and find out who in the field is knowledgeable about the issue in question. Then ask for that professor's office hours and call to schedule an appointment. If this person has written articles or books, try to read something before your visit, or to at least be aware of it, so that you can ask informed questions and can use the time to best advantage. It is often difficult for students to work up the nerve to speak to their professors outside of class, but in fact they choose their field because it interests them, and very few faculty will not be willing to discuss with you what they are so involved in themselves. Experts in business, schools, and industry are other people you can interview for information about topics you might be researching. Other members of the community can help as well. If you are doing oral histories, for example, as Studs Terkel does (Chapter 8), you will be interviewing people to find out their stories or their attitudes about some part of their lives.

To assemble background information about your topic, ask yourself some questions about what you know. Where did you first learn about the topic? Do you have class materials or notes? Do you know people who can serve as resources? And finally, how will you start your library search strategy?

The first part of your search for information should help you to develop a brief overview of the topic: important names, dates, and terminology associated with the topic; related subjects and terms to use for searching for articles; and a list of potential sources for information. After collecting a basic list of core terms and key words, you are ready to search in more depth.

Using On-line Resources in Research

You have probably already used the World Wide Web, perhaps using Google or another search engine, to conduct a preliminary search of your general topic area, or perhaps just to look around for some promising topic ideas. Even though the library has been the traditional starting point in research for generations past, libraries are not just about books—they are about information. Because historically we have been accustomed to using books and periodicals as the primary means of transmitting knowledge, we sometimes think that on-line resources represent different categories of information and require entirely different research strategies. Although there are some special approaches to utilizing Internet-based resources, they, like the library, essentially represent the storage, indexing, retrieval, and dissemination of information. It is therefore not surprising that libraries have invested heavily in ways to access on-line resources beyond the physical boundaries of the traditional library system. A key difference between on-line and more traditional "hard copy" resources, however, is the speed of transmission of information.

When you search the World Wide Web, for example, you can start a search, refine it, click on a topic area, click on the title of a linked page, and generally zip around all kinds of resources in a matter of minutes. Links between related topics are often already in place, and you can explore several closely related areas, explore your own topic in depth, save your places with "bookmarks," print out materials, get bibliographies—accomplish in a matter of moments what would have been a painstaking, time-intensive process.

A second key feature of Web-based research, mentioned earlier, is the linking of information. Find the Purdue Writing Center site, for example (an excellent resource for writers), and in moments you have access to all kinds of related sites, including the Library of Congress and the different rooms and the displays currently featured. Any number of sites related to writing and research are accessible from the initial page, and often different sites will lead you to other interesting, related ones. And many sites have information not easily available in most libraries. If you wanted to investigate traditional music of an American Indian tribe, for example, you could likely find a site with a sample recording and background information.

Access to a wide range of information, however, does not guarantee accuracy or even a truly representative sampling of knowledge on a given topic. Although a selection of library books may be limited— librarians can't buy every book printed—researching on-line creates the opposite problem. Your desktop can be overloaded with all kinds of on-line information, some of which may be authoritative and the rest questionable. The time you save in physically going from place to place in the library, the reference room, the bookshelves, back to the catalog for another search, and the like, should be devoted to evaluating on-line sources. Nearly anyone can create a Web page and post information. You have to use your scholarly skills, as well as common sense, in determining the credibility of such sources. The Library of Congress Web site, for example, has tremendous authority behind it, whereas Joe Zook's Cool Disco Revival may not (then again, it may have recordings of popular disco tunes or a top-ten list of disco hits, and if you are researching popular culture, you went to the right place after all). But if you are just starting to inform yourself about a topic, you can start browsing and learn what the principal divisions or elements of your topic are and then follow your interest and the available links.

Linking on the Web is not an exact science, however, and it is important not to overrely on the links; they are someone else's idea of how topics should be connected. Use links to interesting Web pages to inform yourself in a general area of knowledge, but only as part of a larger, thoughtful research strategy. And when you have ten thousand "hits" for your search, it's time to reconsider your focus.

Strategies for Internet Research

Internet-based sources include indexes similar to those that have existed in print for some time. Reference sources include Web-based dictionaries, encyclopedias, almanacs, quotations, resources for questions, people locators, and medical/legal reference sites. A number of sites are devoted to news and have counterparts in print and other media: the *New York Times, Times of London, Chicago Tribune, Irish Times,* and *San Jose Mercury News* are examples. Most of the Internet-accessed indexes that students are likely to use now have a Web interface for access on-line.

Search Engines   You are likely to begin your search by using a search engine, or a mechanism for retrieving and sorting information from the Web. As of this writing, a list of search engines for the Web includes the popular Google, Yahoo, Ask Jeeves, Excite, Go.com, GoTo, HotBot, Infoseek, Lycos, MetaCrawler, and Web Crawler. You would access them from your home page, and in fact your computer may open to one of these pages as a default. Some sample addresses include *http://www.altavista.com/, http://www.excite.com/,* and *http://www.yahoo.com/.*

Different search engines have different options that may be helpful—some permit you to limit the language of the search (e.g., English), and others let you specify other parameters such as specific dates or let you ask questions. One way to start a search is to review the search engine's index. This process would be most helpful when you have a general category of interest (environment or health, for example) but have not yet defined or identified a specific area of interest (geothermal energy in the Philippines, or stem cell research, for example). In browsing the list of categories, you may find a more focused area of interest to pursue.

Many searches, though, begin by indicating a key word or words, hitting the search or "go" button, and waiting to see how many and what kind of "hits" you got. Often a frustration is that you get either a vast array of Web sites too numerous to evaluate effectively or a collection of sites just off the topic enough to be of little value. A way to focus your search is to use Boolean searching. In Boolean searching, named for mathematician George Boole, you add related terms to limit the type and number of Web sites returned in your search. Boolean searches use the words "and," "or," and "not," as well as quotes and parentheses, to indicate terms to be considered together while searching. These terms may be adapted by various search engines, so experiment with a few basic searches, trying out different terms to see how they work.

Evaluating Web-Based Information   Because Web-based materials have not been through the winnowing process of peer-reviewed journals, librarian selection, or publisher review, you will need to be particularly critical in your evaluation of Web sources. Here are several guidelines:

• Author: One criterion to consider is authorship and authority. Who is the author? What are his or her credentials? Affiliations? Is the publisher also the author? Is an organization the author? Are any organizational affiliations acknowledged? Are any affiliations likely to bias the information in unacknowledged ways? Who pays for the site? If there is advertising, can it be readily distinguished from the ostensible content of the site? Has there been a review process?

• Purpose: What is the purpose of the site? Information? Instruction? Advocacy? Entertainment? Sales? Creating or maintaining a community of users? An entry point to other sites?

• Quality of content: Can the information be verified as accurate? Is it credible? Is it current, with date of site's creation, date the information was placed, and date that the site was last updated visible? Are there links to other sites? Is there a Web creator to access for comments and questions? How does the information on this site compare with other sites and other media on this topic?

Following are some examples of Web sites that might be useful in researching themes related to American cultures:

*http://nativeamculture.about.com/culture/nativeamculture/mbody.htm
(Native American culture)*

*http://afroamculture.about.com/culture/afroamculture/mbody.htm
(African American culture)*

*http://www.newton.mec.edu/Angier/DimSum/chinadimsumaconnection
.html (Chinese American culture)*

*http://www.dla.utexas.edu/depts/ams/Jazz/Jazz.html (an on-line journal
on jazz scholarship published by the University of Texas)*

*http://www.library.yale.edu/pubstation/databases/chicano.html (Chicano
database)*

*http://www.library.yale.edu/pubstation/databases/hlas.html (handbook of
Latin American studies)*

*http://www.soci.swt.edu/areas/europeanbib.htm (multicultural relations:
bibliographies: European Americans)*

*http://www.soci.swt.edu/areas/multicltrlinks.htm (multicultural relations
links)*

Finally, a caution: ownership of text can get especially murky on the Web. Text is easily uploaded, downloaded, modified, integrated, and otherwise manipulated and shaped. You still bear the responsibility of ethical scholarship: When you quote, quote exactly and give credit. When you summarize or integrate information, particularly if it is unique in content or phrasing, credit the source. If you are ever tempted to do the unthinkable and to lift a paper or part of a paper off the Web, or to overrely on a source for an assignment, remember this: your instructor and classmates have access to the Web just as you do. A sobering lesson at our institution occurred when two students both plagiarized the same paper copied from a Web site. But these reminders should be beside the point: as a scholar and a thinker, you need to do your own original thinking and writing. Sources will help you think through and then build your own arguments—not argue in your place while you tag along for the ride.

Keep in mind, then, good sense, critical thinking skills, and traditional research techniques, and let them guide you through the maze of networked information.

Using Library Sources

Library sources, both print and other media, will probably serve as your core materials for research, so it is important to get to know your library system. You have probably already used reference materials and library books to find information you needed; you may be less familiar with alternatives—electronic media, for example, including on-line, or networked, researching capabilities and CD-ROMs, which store large amounts of information and are updated frequently. Familiarize yourself with such data-gathering resources as soon as possible, because they will become more and more prominent in the future. Ask your instructor or a librarian for class or individual instruction on using them. Some public libraries now have such sources to search for magazine articles; generally, they are "user friendly" and entail only punching a few clearly marked buttons.

Materials in the library fall into three categories. *Primary sources* are original materials, such as interviews, survey data, oral histories, photographs, posters, advertisements, paintings, and literary works. What constitutes a primary resource depends on the field and context, but generally they are the raw data about which others may write or which they may interpret. Examples of primary sources in this book are *Keep within Compass* and the writings of Frederick Douglass. Student writer John Wu used statistical evidence as a primary source in his research paper (Chapter 7).

Secondary sources are materials written *about* the primary sources: authors describe, interpret, or otherwise integrate primary sources into their writings. Langston Hughes's poem "Let America Be America Again" (Chapter 6) is an example of a primary source. Chris Countryman's essay analyzing the poem is a secondary source. A student analyzing propaganda materials could use both primary materials, such as posters, and secondary materials to develop an analytical or argumentative essay about techniques of propaganda.

Tertiary sources are third-level materials, such as bibliographies, which list collections of both primary and secondary sources. *The Mexican American: A Selected and Annotated Bibliography* is a tertiary source.

The sources you need will vary depending on the research stage. Initially, general sources, such as general or specialized encyclopedias, can provide an overview of the topic and identify the core concepts and issues. Encyclopedias range from the general, such as *Encyclopaedia Britannica,* to the specialized, such as encyclopedias of music, religion, social science, and the like. Encyclopedias and specialized dictionaries are shelved in the reference sections of the library, and they generally are listed in on-line catalogs as well. While you are doing basic general information gathering, look up your topic's key words in the Library of Congress Subject Headings reference guide, which should be available in the reference room as well. As on-line searches for materials become more and more important in conducting research, it is essential that you have a good working list of key words with which to conduct your searches. For example, people researching Latino studies may need to use key words such as *ethnic identity, Cuban Americans,* or *Puerto Rico—U.S.*

Once you have general background information, you can start digging for additional, more focused materials. Compile a list of selec-

✳✳✳ *Victory Liberty Loan* (1919)

HOWARD CHANDLER CHRISTY

See the headnote and discussion questions for this poster on pages 126–128.

Plate I

Edward Hopper (1882–1967), "Office in a Small City," 1953. Oil on canvas, H. 28 in. W. 40 in. Signed (lower left) Edward Hopper. The Metropolitan Museum of Art, George A. Hearn Fund, 1953. (53.183)

✾✾✾ *Office in a Small City* (1953)

EDWARD HOPPER

See the headnote and discussion questions for this painting on pages 221–222.

Plate II

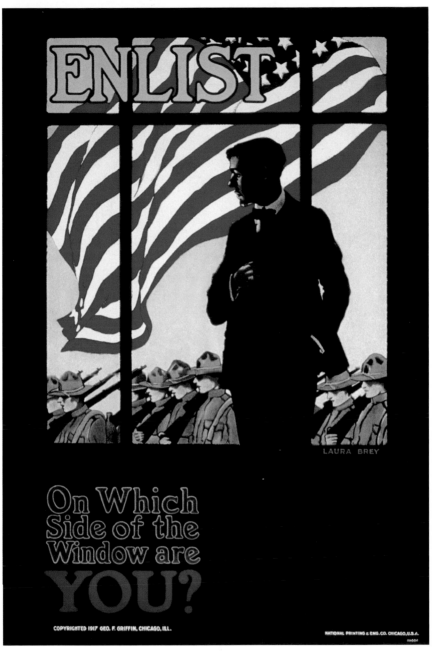

Poster Collection, Hoover Institution Archives.

❊❊❊ *Enlist: On Which Side of the Window Are YOU?* (1917)

See the headnote and discussion questions for this poster on page 259.

Plate III

❀❀❀ Destroy This Mad Brute (1917)

H. R. HOPPS

See the headnote and discussion questions for this poster on pages 471–473.

Plate IV

✺✺✺ *The Last of the Buffalo* (1889)

ALBERT BIERSTADT

See the headnote and discussion questions for this painting on pages 546–549.

Plate V

✵✵✵ *"Indian Belle" crate label* (ca. 1920)

See the headnote and discussion questions for this crate label on pages 566–568.

Plate VI

tions in books, academic journals, and general interest magazines to help you find more detailed information.

To find books on your topic, consult either the card catalog or whatever on-line computer catalog your institution or local library uses. Start with the list of key words, and browse for titles that look interesting. Consider both general and more specific levels of your topic, and pay special attention to any bibliographies or books that indicate that they include bibliographies.

To find articles, search periodical indexes in both print and media forms. You are probably familiar with the *Reader's Guide to Periodical Literature*, but you may not yet have used specialized indexes. Some important ones are the *Humanities Index, Social Science Index, General Science Index, Alternative Press Index, Index to Black Periodicals, Women's Studies Abstracts, Historical Abstracts, MLA Bibliography, PAIS International, Psych Abstracts*, and, for general information, a newspaper index such as *The New York Times Index*.

The electronic media include both general and specific magazine and journal indexes as well as reference sources. Lexis-Nexis, as one example, provides full texts of articles in business, general news, and law. Specialized sources you may have access to include *Bibliography of Native North Americans, EconLit, PsychLit, Art Index*, and the on-line *Oxford English Dictionary*, as well as duplication of print versions of *MLA Bibliography* and *Historical Abstracts*.

In addition to the general reference and research sources already outlined, your library may have some specialized sources for research on American themes. Following are some of the possible categories of specialized references and some examples of the kinds of material you may be able to find to help you investigate your subject.

General Sources for American Themes

American Writers before 1800

American Writers

American Drama Criticism: Interpretations, 1890–1977

MLA International Bibliography

American Humanities Index

The Democracy Reader: Classic and Modern Speeches, Essays, Poems, Declarations, and Documents on Freedom and Human Rights

The Bill of Rights: A Documentary History

Encyclopedia of the American Constitution

Documentary History of the Modern Civil Rights Movement

Slavery in the Courtroom: Annotated Bibliography of Cases

Black Slavery in the Americas

The American Civil Liberties Union: An Annotated Bibliography

Social Reform and Reaction in America: An Annotated Bibliography

Women's Rights Movement in the United States

Encyclopedia of the American Constitution

Index on Censorship

The Anthropology of War: A Bibliography

Encyclopedia of Military History

Peace Research Abstracts Journal

American Public Opinion Index

American Public Opinion Data

Public Opinion, 1935–1946

The Gallup Poll: Public Opinion (annual)

An American Profile: Opinions and Behavior, 1972–1989

Public Opinion Polls and Survey Research: Selective Annotated Bibliography of U.S. Guides and Studies from the 1980s

Statistical Abstracts of the United States (from the U.S. Census Bureau)

Historical Statistics of the United States: Colonial Times to 1970

Social Indicators III: Selected Data and Social Conditions and Trends in the United States

American Statistics Index

The Official Washington Post *Index*

Immigration and Ethnicity: A Guide to Information Sources

Statistical Abstracts of the United States

We the People: An Atlas of America's Ethnic Diversity

America: History and Life

Film Studies

The American Film Industry: A Historical Dictionary

The Film Encyclopedia

Blacks in American Films and Television

The Hispanic Image on the Silver Screen: An Interpretive Filmography from Silents

Contemporary Theatre, Film and Television

Who's Who in American Film

Film Study: An Analytical Bibliography

The New Film Index: A Bibliography of Magazine Articles in English, 1930–1970

Ethnic and Racial Images in American Film and Television: Historical Essays and Bibliography

Blacks in Film and Television: A Pan-African Bibliography of Films, Filmmakers, and Performers

Film Literature Index

New York Times *Film Reviews*

Film Review Index

Index to Critical Reviews

African American Studies

Some key words for searching: Afro-Americans—Race-Identity; Afro-American Press; Afro-Americans—History; Black Power—United States; Civil Rights—United States; School Integration—United States.

The African American Encyclopedia

Dictionary of Afro-American Slavery

Encyclopedia of Black America

Encyclopedia of Southern Culture

Notable Black American Women

Black Women in America

The Harlem Renaissance: A Historical Dictionary

The Negro Almanac: A Reference Work on the Afro-American into Sound, 1898–1935

Women of Color and Southern Women: A Bibliography of Social Science Research

Afro-American Folk Culture

Afro-American History

Afro-American Reference: An Annotated Bibliography of Selected Resources

Black Adolescence: Current Issues and Annotated Bibliography

Black American Writers: Bibliographical Essays

The Black Family in the United States

Black Rhetoric: A Guide to Afro-American Communication

Index to Black Periodicals

Latino Studies

Some key words for searching: Mexican Americans—Ethnic Identity; Hispanic Americans—Ethnic Identity; Cuban Americans; Mexican American Women; Migrant Agricultural Laborers; Puerto Ricans—U.S.

Chicano Literature: A Reference Guide

Dictionary of Mexican American History

Bibliografía Chicana: A Guide to Information Sources

A Bibliography of Criticism of Contemporary Chicano Literature

Bibliography of Mexican American History

Chicano Anthology Index: A Comprehensive Author, Title, and Subject Index to Chicano Anthologies, 1965–1987

The Chicana Studies Index: Twenty Years of Gender Research, 1972–1991

Latinos in the United States: A Historical Bibliography

The Mexican American: A Selected and Annotated Bibliography

Mexican American Biographies: A Historical Dictionary

Statistical Handbook on U.S. Hispanics

The Chicano Index

Latin American Studies

Native American Studies

The Library of Congress term for the aboriginal peoples of the Western Hemisphere, including the Inuit, is *Indians.* The Western Hemisphere is divided into regions: North America, Mexico, Central America, West Indies, and South America. Works on Indians of a particular region are listed as, for example, *Indians of North America.* Individual tribal names are used as appropriate, such as *Navaho Indians* or *Choctaw Indians.* Other key words include Western Algonquin Indians; Athapascan Indians; Caddoan Indians; Eskimos; Mound-builders; Ojibwa Indians; Piegan Indians; Shoshoni Indians; Tinne Indians; United States—Civilization—Indian influences.

Atlas of Ancient America

Atlas of the North American Indian

A Concise Dictionary of Indian Tribes of North America

Dictionary of Daily Life of Indians of the Americas

Encyclopedia of Native American Religions: An Introduction

Encyclopedia of Native American Tribes

Handbook of the American Frontier: Four Centuries of Indian-White Relationships

Handbook of North American Indians

Native American Almanac: A Portrait of Native America Today

American Indian Women: A Guide to Research

Native American Folklore, 1879–1979: An Annotated Bibliography

Native North Americans: Crime, Conflict, and Criminal Justice: A Research Bibliography

Southwest Native American Arts and Material Culture: A Guide to Research

Bibliography of Native North Americans on Disc (on CD-ROM)

Who Was Who in Native American History: Indians and Non-Indians from Early Contacts Through 1900

Native Women: A Statistical Overview

Reports of the American Indian Family History Project

Statistical Record of Native North Americans

Nations Within a Nation: Historical Statistics of American Indians

Asian American Studies

The Library of Congress uses *Asian American,* but other headings include the following: American Literature—Asian American Authors; Chinese Americans; East Indians; Filipino Americans; Filipinos in the United States; Hawaiians; Japanese Americans; Korean Americans; Oceanian Americans; Pacific Islander Americans; Vietnamese Americans.

Asian-Americans Information Directory

The Chinese in America, 1920–1973

The Filipinos in America, 1898–1974

The Koreans in America, 1882–1974

Dictionary of Asian American History

Japanese American History: An A to Z Reference from 1868 to the Present

Harvard Encyclopedia of American Ethnic Groups

Refugees in the United States

Asian American Literature: An Annotated Bibliography

The Asian American Media Reference Guide, 2d ed.

Asian American Studies: An Annotated Bibliography and Research Guide

A Comprehensive Bibliography for the Study of American Minorities

Images of Color: A Guide to Media from and for Asian, Black, Latino and Native American Communities

Immigrant Women in the United States: A Selectively Annotated Multidisciplinary Bibliography

Pacific/Asian American Research

A Selected Bibliography on the Asians in America

South Asians in North America: An Annotated and Selected Bibliography (covers 1900–1986)

Biographical Sources

Chinese American Portraits: Personal Histories, 1828–1988

Who's Who Among Asian Americans

Statistical Record of Asian Americans

A number of sources already listed can also be good sources for information on Asian Americans.

Focusing the Search

Once you have found a general overview of your subject and a list of potential sources, deepen your search for materials. Many of the general and bibliographical sources are in the reference area of your library or can be accessed on-line; your next step will probably be to collect some important books and periodical articles in the field.

In some fields, books will be your most important sources; a scholarly book has the advantage of being an in-depth examination of some issue or element in the field. A periodical, on the other hand, by virtue of the recurrent issuing of the material, offers less in-depth but more current information.

Books are generally spread out through the library storage system in what are commonly called *stacks*. Sometimes the stacks are closed, and you need to request books you want from the circulation desk. If stacks at your library are open, you can browse the shelves in your subject area. If the book you tracked down in a bibliography isn't available, perhaps another interesting book is. Or perhaps other nearby books on the shelves look helpful. You should plan on taking some time in the stacks and in perusing tables of contents, introductory chapters, and bibliographies of books in the area of your topic.

Working with Sources

As you assemble general, preliminary, and increasingly special-ized sources, you will need to keep track of your materials, both the original sources and your notes on them. Few experiences in academia are more frustrating than finding an excellent piece of information or an idea and then losing track of where you located it. Different writers approach notes and note taking in different ways.

First, you have to determine what you are looking for when you read sources. In addition to keeping in mind the general advice of-fered in Chapter 1 for reading critically, pay special attention to the following questions when critiquing sources:

1. What is the theme? What is the author's purpose in writing? Who are the intended audiences? What are the author's assumptions? Do you share those assumptions? Do the author's assumptions or emphasis indicate bias?

2. What is the overall idea the author develops? What is the pri-mary organizing plan (cause-effect, problem-solution, definition, process)?

3. Is the evidence presented clearly? Is it persuasive? Do the author's conclusions logically follow from the evidence?

4. How does the selection connect with other readings? Does it pro-vide information on other sources? Does it provide an example of a point made in another source? Does it contradict another source? Are there points of comparison or contrast with another source? What common threads run through the sources?

Taking Notes   As a fellow scholar in the academic community, you are expected not to take your sources at face value but to chal-lenge and question them, to assess critically the merit of their argu-ments and the logic of their conclusions.

Be an active, assertive reader. Question information as you read it; argue with the text. If you own the book or if you are using photo-copies, make extensive marginal notes. Otherwise, use note cards, computer "note cards," or notepaper to keep track of your informa-tion. Try to use a medium for taking notes that allows you to sort the notes by topic as you collect more information.

As you take notes, write down not only the information itself but also key words, phrases, reactions to points the author makes, critical arguments and comments, and reactions you may have. *But take great care to keep track of exactly what information comes from the sources and which comments are your own reflections on the source.* When information or ideas appear in a number of sources (usually three or more), most writers will consider it common knowledge in the field and will not document the source. Until you have researched enough to know what will need citing, however, you should keep track of the sources in your notes.

There are three different types of notes we generally use to record our research of sources: summaries, paraphrase, and direct quotation. *Summaries* of information from the source help you to make sure you have digested the material and help you to translate the information into your own words. They pull out the key ideas of a source. *Paraphrases* are a kind of running commentary or translation of the original source; they capture essentially all of the material in the original. Paraphrase is a frequent suspect in plagiarism, the unacknowledged use of the ideas or phrases of others. The difference between summary and paraphrase can be seen in the following example, based on an excerpt from "The Gettysburg Address."

Original

Four score and seven years ago our fathers brought forth on this continent, a new nation, conceived in Liberty, and dedicated to the proposition that all men are created equal.

Now we are engaged in a great civil war, testing whether that nation, or any nation so conceived and so dedicated, can long endure. We are met on a great battlefield of that war. We have come to dedicate a portion of that field as a final resting-place for those who here gave their lives that that nation might live. It is altogether fitting and proper that we should do this.

Summary

Eighty-seven years ago a country was founded on the principles of freedom and equality. We are now involved in a war that will test whether the nation and those principles will survive. Appropriately, we gather on a battlefield of that war to dedicate a cemetery for those who died here fighting for the nation's survival.

Paraphrase

Eighty-seven years ago the founding fathers created on the American continent a new country, born in freedom and committed to the ideal that everyone is created equal.

We are now involved in a large-scale civil war that will determine if a nation with such ideals and such a purpose can last. We meet at the site of one of the great battles of that war, and we are here to dedicate part of the battlefield as a cemetery for those who died here to save the nation. It is appropriate that we do so.

Direct quotations *must* be taken down exactly as written and put inside quotation marks. They should be saved for those occasions when the quotation so perfectly captures a concept, idea, or image that it would require a great deal more time and space to say the same thing that would have much less impact. Direct quotations, too, need to be carefully documented. Sometimes you can summarize an author's point and then put key or specialized words into quotations. If you use only parts of a quotation by an author, be sure to use ellipses—three spaced dots—to indicate that you have left material out; be careful not to change the author's intended meaning. For a quotation within a quotation, use single quotation marks; if the author quotes someone else you want to quote directly, your citation would say, for example, "(Pritchard, qtd. in Garcia 32)." Keep careful track of who says what in your sources so that you can quote accurately.

Avoiding Plagiarism Plagiarism is the unacknowledged use of the ideas or words of others. Whether accidental or intentional, plagiarism is a serious offense. To avoid plagiarism, you should follow these general guidelines.

Cite your sources in the following cases: an original idea from a source, whether you summarize it, paraphrase it, or quote it directly; factual information that is not common knowledge; any exact wording or unique phrasing taken from a source.

There is no need to cite when material is considered common knowledge; that is, it appears in a number of sources or can be verified by agreed-on measurement or criteria. How many sources must it appear in? Some scholars suggest a minimum of three sources; others say five. We have found that if the material is general background information and occurs in three sources or more, it can safely be considered common knowledge. But if you are writing about some scientific findings and it is relevant that a number of scientists duplicated certain results, then you would be better off citing even a large number of studies, as the confirmation of some findings by others is crucial to the information's credibility. Again, you need to develop judgment about audience, purpose, and subject as you make such decisions. Too many citations can interrupt the flow of your paper or give the impression that the sources' voices are taking over your paper, but when in doubt, it is better to cite rather than not.

Plagiarism is essentially the passing off of the ideas or words of others as your own. The most common instances of punishable plagiarism in colleges now seem to be misappropriation of other people's computer work—codes, solutions, and so on—and the purchase of essays off the Web. In a sense these are easy cases—it is hard not to know that you're plagiarizing when you pay $25.00 for someone else's essay and turn it in with your name on it. But since plagiarism also covers the failure to do something—to not give credit to someone whose ideas you are using, to leave out a citation on a piece of information because you're just using a bit and not quoting—try to think of what you would feel if the you were the person whose brain work was being appropriated. That technique will probably give you a pretty good idea of what you shouldn't do to somebody else. Keep in mind the spirit of the law, and you will be guided by it as you make specific decisions about particular pieces of information in your essay.

Writing Drafts

As you collect information, review notes, and sift through ideas and evidence, connections should begin to form in your mind, and responses to your initial research question begin to suggest themselves. You can foster this process by reviewing notes as you collect new information, determining where the new sources fit with the material you already know. Take time at regular intervals to free write about your topic, either in a journal or in scheduled bursts of free writing at the computer after a research session.

Some writers find it helpful to take notes from different sources and then to begin to sort them by subtopic; or go back to their research question and divide the question into smaller questions; or review the working hypothesis, refine it, and divide it into categories. For example, a paper on the myth of the model minority could focus on the family ethos of work, the glass ceiling in corporations, the different patterns of immigration from Asia, the relative economic and educational status of each group, and so on. Sometimes a diagram or flowchart helps, with lines and circles connecting various parts of the material. Whatever your method, try to begin lining up the general elements of the material.

Consider the kinds of supporting assertions you can make on the basis of your evidence; review your tentative thesis or hypothesis and refine it, if needed, according to your findings. Review your supporting assertions in light of your refined thesis. Those supporting assertions can become your topic ideas. Line up those supporting assertions in the order in which your reader needs to hear them and in an order that links up one point to the next. Then draft a working outline that is based on the assertions you have identified, work through the material to find the support for your assertions, and write a rough draft. At this stage, you are primarily interested in getting the basic structure down. Although you should keep track of where your information is coming from, don't worry too much about the specifics of documentation or style: "(Smith 21)" or "(Smith teaching article p. 21)" in some form is sufficient at this stage, but try to keep track of article and page number. Checking spelling and worrying about specifics of grammar are tasks for a later stage of writing. Just get your core argument down. Save your file often if you are working on the computer! If you are writing out or typing your draft, photocopy it as you write large parts of it to guard against losing your work.

Documentation

When you converse in the academic community, you generally need to use the conventions of the various disciplines to communicate ideas and research findings. As you begin to think of yourself as a part of the scholarly community, you will see how citation forms work as a kind of shorthand that permits scholars to share their findings with others in the national and international academic communities and that helps those scholars follow up on each other's work. The cooperative nature of research may help explain the very specific formats used in different disciplines. In the social sciences, for example, the date of a research study is crucial, so the American Psychological Association (APA) format puts the date right after the author's name. In humanities fields, on the other hand, where the date of the findings is less important, the Modern Language Association (MLA) format for in-text citations contains a name or book title and page number. In the "Works Cited" list as well, the date comes last.

You may have been instructed to use a particular documentation style. An excellent resource is the MLA's Web site or an alternative such as *www.wisc.edu/writing/Handbook/DocMLA*. Your instructor may provide guidance, or you can use a style book. Both MLA and APA have style books. Some examples of style manuals in other disciplines include *Council of Biology Editors Style Manual: A Guide for Authors, Editors, and Publishers; A Manual for Authors of Mathematical Papers;* and *Style Manual for Guidance in the Preparation of Papers.* In addition to using the resources indicated at the end of this section, you could do a Google search to find any number of sites with documentation guidelines. With electronic sources and reference techniques evolving rapidly, the Web itself may be your best source for examples of the current and appropriate style in citing sources. We have included several of the resources at the end of this section.

Most composition courses suggest following either the MLA or APA style. If you have a choice and you know you are interested in humanities or social science, you may want to start using the format you are likely to use in future classes and to buy the appropriate manual. Following are the general guidelines for documenting your essays and citing your sources.

How to Document Sources   Most disciplines are moving toward parenthetical within-text citation, and that is the style we will use here. In APA style, supply the last name of the author(s) and the year of publication: (Garcia & Collins, 1988). In MLA style, if you are referring to a work by an author, cite the author's name and a page number: (Garcia 38). Note that in MLA style, you don't need a comma or "p." to indicate the page number. If Garcia's name or book or article title is implied in the context, you can simply use the page number (38) as the reference. If you are citing two works by Garcia, you can use a brief title of the work (Messages 28) to indicate to the reader which work this particular quotation comes from. Look at the documented student essays in this book for samples; John Wu (Chapter 7) documented his essay in correct MLA style. If you have substantive notes or "asides" to the reader, you can include those as footnotes or endnotes. If you use endnotes, place them at the end of the paper, but before your list of references.

References/Works Cited   Within the general guidelines for documentation, there are specific forms that should be followed for different types of sources. A "Works Cited" list is now commonly used with MLA style; it contains only the references actually cited in the paper. The APA style uses a "References" list with all relevant readings that may have influenced the paper.

Sample Documentation   The following lists provide samples of common works that you will use. Note that underlining may be substituted for italics if you are writing by hand or on a typewriter.

A book by one author

> *MLA:*   Sowell, Thomas. <u>Ethnic America</u>. New York: Basic Books, 1981.
> *APA:*   Sowell, T. (1981). *Ethnic America.* New York: Basic Books.

A book by two authors

> *MLA:*   Neesom, Lisa, and George Madera. <u>Early American Art</u>. Englewood Cliffs: Prentice-Hall, 1955.
> *APA:*   Neesom, M., & Madera, G. (1955). *Early American art.* Englewood Cliffs, NJ: Prentice-Hall.

A book by three authors

> *MLA:*   Lewis, Peter, A. J. McGee, and Martin Washington. <u>American Folk Art</u>. 3rd ed. New York: McGraw-Hill, 1993.
> *APA:*   Lewis, P., McGee, A. J., & Washington, M. (1993). *American folk art* (3rd ed.). New York: McGraw-Hill.

A book with more than three authors

> *MLA:*   Isselbacher, Kurt J., et al. <u>Harrison's Principles of Internal Medicine</u>. 9th ed. New York: McGraw-Hill, 1980.
> *APA:*   Isselbacher, K. J., Adams, D. A., Braunwald, E., Petersdorf, R. G., Wilson, J. D. (1980). *Harrison's principles of internal medicine* (9th ed.). New York: McGraw-Hill.

The edited work of an author

> *MLA:*   Hawthorne, Nathaniel. <u>The Portable Hawthorne</u>. Ed. Malcolm Cowley. New York: Viking, 1969.
>
> *APA:*   Hawthorne, N. (1969). *The portable Hawthorne.* (M. Cowley, Ed.). New York: Viking Press.

A work in an anthology

> *MLA:*   Hawthorne, Nathaniel. "Young Goodman Brown." <u>Heritage of American Literature</u>. Ed. James E. Miller, Jr., with Kathleen Farley. Vol. 1. New York: Harcourt Brace, 1991. 1413–21.
>
> *APA:*   Hawthorne, N. (1991). Young Goodman Brown. In J. E. Miller, Jr. (Ed.), *Heritage of American literature: Vol. 1* (pp. 1413–1421). New York: Harcourt Brace.

A work in translation

> *MLA:*   Pushkin, Aleksander. <u>Eugene Onegin</u>. Trans. Vladimir Nabokov. 4 vols. New York: Bollingen Foundation, 1964.
>
> *APA:*   Pushkin, A. (1964). *Eugene Onegin* (Vols. 1–4). (V. Nabokov, Trans.). New York: Bollingen Foundation.

An article in a journal with separate pagination for each issue

> *MLA:*   Budd, Matthew A. "Human Suffering: Road to Illness or Gateway to Learning?" <u>Advances: The Journal of Mind-Body Health</u> 3 (Summer 1993): 28–35.
>
> *APA:*   Budd, M. A. (1993, Summer). Human suffering: Road to illness or gateway to learning? *Advances: The Journal of Mind-Body Health, 3,* 28–35.

An article in a journal with continuous pagination

> *MLA:*   Frey, Olivia. "Beyond Literary Darwinism: Women's Voices and Critical Discourse." <u>College English</u> 52 (1990): 507–26.
>
> *APA:*   Frey, O. (1990). Beyond literary Darwinism: Women's voices and critical discourse. *College English, 52,* 507–526.

An unsigned newspaper article or editorial

> *MLA:*   "Small Companies Earn Big Honors." <u>San Francisco Examiner</u> 20 May 1994: B1.
>
> *APA:*   Small companies earn big honors. (1994, May 20). *San Francisco Examiner,* p. B1.

A signed newspaper article or editorial

> *MLA:*   Ulrich, Allan. "Variations on a Gould-en Theme." <u>San Francisco Examiner</u> 20 May 1994: C1.

> APA: Ulrich, A. (1994, May 20). Variations on a Gould-en theme. *San Francisco Examiner*, p. C1.

A public document

> MLA: United States Department of Health and Human Services, Administration for Children, Youth and Families, Children's Bureau. <u>Child Welfare Strategies in the Coming Years</u>. Washington: Office of Human Development Services, 1978.
>
> APA: U.S. Department of Health and Human Services, Administration for Children, Youth and Families, Children's Bureau. (1978). *Child welfare strategies in the coming years*. Washington: Office of Human Development Services.

A film

> MLA: <u>Judgment at Nuremberg</u>. Stanley Kramer, dir. United Artists, 1961.
>
> APA: Kramer, S. (Director). (1961). *Judgment at Nuremberg* [Film]. United Artists.

A lecture

> MLA: Rebholz, Ronald. "Shakespeare and the Power of an Idea." Centennial Lecture Series. Stanford U. 23 Sept. 1991.
>
> APA: Rebholz, Ronald. (1991, September 23). *Shakespeare and the power of an idea*. Lecture presented at the Centennial Lecture Series, Stanford University.

An interview

> MLA: Garcia, Juana. Personal interview. 3 Dec. 1993.
> APA: Garcia, J. (1993, December 3). [Interview].

A computer program

> MLA: Watters, Ann. <u>The Art of Persuasion</u>. Vers. 1.0. Computer software, CD-ROM. Focus Interactive, 1995.
>
> APA: Watters, A. (1995). *The art of persuasion* [Computer software]. Menlo Park, CA: Focus Interactive.

Legal cases

> Plessy v. Ferguson, 163 U.S. 537 (1896).

(Note: Both the MLA and APA follow the style set forth in *A Uniform System of Citation*, 15th edition, published by the Harvard Law Review Association in 1991.)

Internet and World Wide Web Sources

Standards are gradually emerging for Internet and World Wide Web resources. The functional rule remains: Provide for the reader sufficient information to document your results and to guide your reader to the same source. Insofar as possible, include author, title, date of publication of source, date you accessed it, and URL or means of access.

Examples of Web Site Citations in MLA and APA

The MLA does not publish its documentation style guidelines but does offer an informative frequently asked questions section which you can find on this site:

MLA *http://www.mla.org/style*

Some other sites offer excellent guidelines:

http://memorial.library.wisc.edu/citing.htm#MLA
http://www.westwords.com/guffey/mla.html
APA http://www.apastyle.org/elecref.html

Additional sites on APA style are available through search.
Purdue University has excellent resources on writing as well as documentation:

http://owl.english.purdue.edu/handouts/research/r mla.html
http://owl.english.purdue.edu/handouts/research/r apa.html

Helpful Web Sites

Google Search Engine
http://www.google.com

Purdue On-line Writing Lab
http://owl.english.purdue.edu/

Virtual Learning Resources Center
http://www.virtuallrc.com/

5

Identities

Whom do you visualize when you hear the term *American?* Do you identify a specific gender, race, occupation, or age that you consider typical? Do you see a white male banker? A Native American high school student? A family of migrant farmers? A Chinese American factory worker? All of these people can be American citizens, of course, but is there one that seems *more* typically American to you than the others?

America is a confluence of cultures: American Indians who have lived here for millennia; European and Asian immigrants who came here in search of a better life; people of African descent brought by force. Over time, these cultures have mingled and evolved into something new and recognizably American. How do all of these disparate identities come together to form an American identity?

In understanding American identities, we need to come to terms with unity and division, with separateness and common ground. The question "What do we mean by 'American'?" encompasses a host of related questions: Is there a distinctly American identity? Is there one overriding, generalized American culture? Or are there only disparate subcultures that form strategic alliances for survival? Should we retain the old metaphor of the melting pot, into which various cultures are tossed, melted down, and pulled out as generic Americans? If so, what are the characteristics of that generic American? If we reject the metaphor of the melting pot, what should we use as a more fitting metaphor: A mosaic? A puzzle? A salad bowl?

In addition, we increasingly are asking what America is in the larger context: What is our place in history? In the global community? In what ways is the American identity unique? In what respects does it resemble other powerful world powers that preceded it? What can the world's only superpower learn from the lessons of history?

Identity has always been a difficult question nagging the collective American mind. We wonder how much we have in common besides living in the same country. We argue about a common culture, a shared set of values—whether there is one, whether we should try to cobble one together, whether we should try to revise one that has been thrust upon us or simply evolved. We debate whether it is more important for Americans of a particular ethnic, racial, or cultural heritage to celebrate that history or to feel part of mainstream America—or whether both can coexist.

The question of who is an American is clearly important on a personal level as each of us comes to terms with who we are. But it is also a pressing political issue because citizenship, government entitlements, voting rights, job protection, civil liberties, and every other advantage or opportunity that America offers depend ultimately on whether a person is considered a true American.

American Identities through History

As long as there has been an America, Americans have wondered and argued about who they were. The dominant issues and topics have shifted over time, but the same concerns have surfaced time and time again. All of the authors in this chapter have taken part in the debate about Americans and American identities, about individuality and cohesion, on personal, political, and geopolitical levels.

One of the first issues was whether there was—or could be—a unified American identity at all. Before the American Revolution, European settlers typically thought of themselves as residents of their own colonies and subjects of European monarchs, not as part of a unified new nation. In the 1750s, however, with the French and Indian War looming, Benjamin Franklin and others began calling for a union of the colonies for mutual protection. Franklin's lithograph *Join, or Die* is a graphic representation of the advantages of such unity: self-preservation rather than destruction.

After the Revolution, when political unity had been established, observers began offering assessments of the American character and culture, based almost exclusively on the Anglo-Americans of the Northeast and Eastern seaboard. Alexis de Tocqueville attempts to define the American character by describing the political and social history of its most dominant group, and he identifies that group as English settlers, especially in New England. The approach that he takes—seeing the English character as the origin of true American culture—is one that almost all succeeding writers have had to address.

Although Tocqueville and other historians at the time focused on the British ancestry of mainstream America, many other cultures were contributing to the American identity. Over the course of the nineteenth century, the American population became more and more diverse: Irish fleeing famine; Jews and Catholics fleeing religious persecution; and Italians, Swedes, Chinese, Russians, and others seeking jobs and opportunities. How were all these people—whose looks, languages, and actions were generally quite different from the dominant Anglo culture—to be incorporated into the American identity?

These immigrants generally favored assimilation. After arriving in America, each group found itself faced with further hardship and discrimination because they were so easily identified as "foreign." Their desire to succeed became a desire to escape the unwanted attention of other groups, to merge with mainstream American culture. The dominant ideal became that of the melting pot, with foreign differences melted away and identical Americans rolling off the assembly line.

At one time or another, every foreign element or influence associated with new immigrants was considered suspect. But when America was faced with an outside enemy, all Americans were considered acceptable, regardless of their heritage. Propagandistic posters from World War I such as *Americans All! Victory Liberty Loan* proudly present a diverse but united America.

One name often missing even from a picture of multicultural America is a recognizable Native American. European immigrant groups were not, of course, writing their history on a blank page. For countless generations, Native Americans had identified themselves with the American land. In "What the Indian Means to America," Luther Standing Bear articulates the argument that the true American is the Indian, identified with the essence of the American continent. Another group struggling in the early twentieth century to be recognized as full-fledged Americans were African Americans. Because the American identity had always been defined in terms of whites, African Americans were, as Ralph Ellison pointed out, invisible. In the Prologue to *Invisible Man*, Ellison uses the metaphor of invisibility to explore how the prevailing definition of *American* has kept some groups dominant and others excluded.

By the mid–twentieth century, the melting pot ideal was falling into disfavor. Clearly, not all Americans had been accounted for, and those who had been were beginning to challenge the value of assimilation. Critic Kenneth Burke suggests, "If men were not apart from one another, there would be no need for the rhetorician to proclaim their unity." John F. Kennedy, elected president in 1960, sought to unite the divided nation by proclaiming its unity. In his inaugural address, he defines a new American identity based on the nation's role in the international scene and its presumed unity of purpose. In recent decades, many writers have focused on forging a coherent personal identity as Americans living within a cultural mosaic. Some commentators, such as historian and educator Arthur Schlesinger, Jr., suggest that recognition of America's ethnic subcultures have gone too far. In his essay "The Cult of Ethnicity," he argues that the traditional American values of integration and assimilation have been rejected to the detriment of society.

Jean Wakatsuki Houston takes a more personal perspective in her speech "A Tapestry of Hope," making a strong case, without insult or accusation, for the strength to be found in America's diversity. In "Chicana," the chapter's student essay, student writer Martha Serrano argues for her right to define her own identity, choosing a label that accurately reflects her heritage.

In times of crisis and threat, a drive for unity may, temporarily at least, suppress its plurality and diversity. A pivotal reading in this chapter focuses on the relationship between America's diversity of perspectives and America's strength as a nation. In "Disunited We Stand," published several weeks after 9/11, Richard Rodriguez asserts, as does Houston, that it is difference that can most profoundly illustrate our founding values.

In a visible response to 9/11 and the economic problems that followed, the poster "America: Open for Business" draws together the threads of patriotism, unity, and consumerism in this unique poster, characterizing shopping as a patriotic response to outside threat and echoing the approach for *Victory Liberty Loan* earlier in this chapter.

Scholars and commentators have written extensively about America's identity in a global context, particularly following 9/11. In an essay published in 2002, "In Praise of American Empire," self-identified conservative commentator Dinesh D'Souza argues that America exerts an overwhelmingly positive force in the world. In contrast, author Kevin Phillips offers a cautionary essay. In "Hegemony, Hubris, and Overreach," he places America's current political stance in historical context, comparing the U.S. of the twenty-first century to the great empires of the past that considered themselves invincible and eventually reached beyond their grasp.

Our final selection is the film *Bowling for Columbine,* filmmaker Michael Moore's documentary exploration of American culture as it concerns the media, gun ownership, and a climate of fear.

As you read and reflect on the selections that follow, consider not only your own personal identity and cultural origins but also the social and political implications of your identity and that of others as you begin to take part in the obligations and privileges of citizenship: open debate, difference of opinion, and the need to take a stand on important issues. Ask yourself the questions that the readings pose: Who is an American? Who is entitled to what America has to offer? What are our common bonds, our goals, our ethics and beliefs as a society?

✳✳✳ *Join, or Die* (1754)

BENJAMIN FRANKLIN

Benjamin Franklin (1706–1790), American statesman, author, printer, inventor, was apprenticed at age twelve to his brother, a printer, and in 1723 went to Philadelphia, where he eventually set up his own paper and published Poor Richard's Almanac. *Franklin was active throughout the American Revolution and was a signer of the Declaration of Independence. "Join, or Die," considered the first American cartoon, was Franklin's contribution to the debate about unity among the colonies as the French and Indian War approached. Franklin was the delegate from Pennsylvania as seven colonies sent representatives to negotiate with the Iroquois Nation, but his argument for a union of colonies with "one general government" for common defense would serve in other crises as well. To make his point, Franklin draws upon a myth that is familiar to his audience: a cut-up snake that is reassembled before sundown will come back to life.*

For Journals

Some created images, such as the American flag or the Statue of Liberty, evoke a sense of America for many people. What images from nature, whether plant or animal, embody your sense of America?

For Discussion

1. What is the primary argument of the cartoon? What does Franklin want the audience to do? Why? What are the advantages of an image that may convey fear to its adversaries?

2. Woodcuts with a moral or lesson combining text and a visual image date back centuries. What are some advantages of making an argument in both word and image? What audiences would an author hope to reach in this way?

3. What are some of the advantages of visual argument over text, especially a simple design, as in this cartoon? Consider your own responses to other visual images, such as cartoons and advertisements, as well as the response you would expect of Franklin's contemporaries. Reflect in particular on the images that have come to symbolize America in the post 9/11 era.

4. Mid-twentieth-century audiences may find the image of a snake threatening or disturbing, but what of the largely agrarian American population of the mid–eighteenth century? Do you suspect that they had a similar response? Why might Franklin have wanted to identify the united colonies as a dangerous creature? Consider the use of other, similar slogans in early U.S. history, such as "don't tread on me," frequently accompanying an image of a coiled snake.

5. If a separated snake can unite its parts before sundown and survive, to what symbolic, political sundown is Franklin drawing an analogy?

6. What identity does Franklin foresee for the colonies? In what ways is this identity a precursor to other identities for America?

For Writing

1. Look through some newspapers, especially in the editorial pages, and select a political cartoon dealing with some aspect of American identity (foreign policy or immigration, for example). Analyze the allusions or references in the cartoon that readers need to know in order to understand the point of it. Will audiences fifty, one hundred, or two hundred years from now understand the cartoon you have selected? Why, or why not?

2. Research some aspect of American history or politics at the beginning of the twentieth century by looking at cartoons from the era— during an election, for example. You could review old newspapers or look at a cartoon collection at the library. Alternatively, browse through old newspapers or magazines, and see what you can infer about the social or political debates of the times. To what extent do you understand the allusions or jokes? Why do you think this is so? Write up your findings in an analytical essay; if possible, include photocopies of the cartoons you analyze.

3. Research the imagery of the snake in American political history, considering both colonial-era accounts, such as the writings of

Benjamin Franklin, and contemporary commentary, such as Chris Matthews's *American Beyond our Grandest Notions.*

✖✖ *Origin of the Anglo-Americans* (1839)

ALEXIS DE TOCQUEVILLE

Count Alexis [Charles Henri Maurice Clerel] de Tocqueville (1805–1859), magistrate and political observer, held a number of positions in the French government. His observations of and writings on the workings of democracy in the United States, based on an extended visit to America, comprise the well-known work Democracy in America (De la démocratie en Amérique), *from which the following selection is excerpted. Written between 1835 and 1839, this work is considered a landmark study of American institutions and is often quoted to this day. It is valuable in studying both historical and contemporary aspects of American cultures.*

After the birth of a human being, his early years are obscurely spent in the toils or pleasures of childhood. As he grows up, the world receives him, when his manhood begins, and he enters into contact with his fellows. He is then studied for the first time, and it is imagined that the germ of the vices and the virtues of his maturer years is then formed. This, if I am not mistaken, is a great error. We must begin higher up; we must watch the infant in his mother's arms; we must see the first images which the external world casts upon the dark mirror of his mind, the first occurrences which he witnesses; we must hear the first words which awaken the sleeping powers of thought, and stand by his earliest efforts,—if we would understand the prejudices, the habits, and the passions which will rule his life. The entire man is, so to speak, to be seen in the cradle of the child.

The growth of nations presents something analogous to this; they all bear some marks of their origin. The circumstances that accompanied their birth and contributed to their development affect the whole term of their being. If we were able to go back to the elements of states, and to examine the oldest monuments of their history, I doubt not that we should discover in them the primal cause of the prejudices, the habits, the ruling passions, and, in short, of all that constitutes what is called the national character. We should there find the explanation of certain customs which now seem at variance with the prevailing manners; of such laws as conflict with established principles; and of such incoherent opinions as are here and there to be met with in society, like those fragments of broken chains which we sometimes see hanging from the vaults of an old edifice, and supporting nothing. This might explain the destinies of certain nations which seem borne on by an unknown force to ends of which they themselves are ignorant. But hitherto facts have been wanting to researches of this kind: the spirit of inquiry has only come upon communities in their latter days; and when they at length contemplated their origin, time had already obscured it, or ignorance and pride adorned it with truth-concealing fables.

America is the only country in which it has been possible to witness the natural and tranquil growth of society, and where the influence exercised on the future condition of states by their origin is clearly distinguishable. . . . America, consequently, exhibits in the broad light of day the phenomena which the ignorance or rudeness of earlier ages conceals from our researches. Near enough to the time when the states of America were founded, to be accurately acquainted with their elements, and sufficiently removed from that period to judge of some of their results, the men of our own day seem destined to see further than their predecessors into the series of human events. Providence has given us a torch which our forefathers did not possess, and has allowed us to discern fundamental causes in the history of the world which the obscurity of the past concealed from them. If we carefully examine the social and political state of America, after having studied its history, we shall remain perfectly convinced that not an opinion, not a custom, not a law, I may even say not an event, is upon record which the origin of that people will not explain. The readers of this book will find in the present chapter the germ of all that is to follow, and the key to almost the whole work.

The emigrants who came at different periods to occupy the territory now covered by the American Union differed from each other in many respects; their aim was not the same, and they governed themselves on different principles. These men had, however, certain features in common, and they were all placed in an analogous situation. The tie of language is, perhaps, the strongest and the most durable that can unite mankind. All the emigrants spoke the same tongue; they were all offsets from the same people. Born in a country which had been agitated for centuries by the struggles of faction, and in which all parties had been obliged in their turn to place themselves under the protection of the laws, their political education had been perfected in this rude school; and they were more conversant with the notions of right, and the principles of true freedom, than the greater part of their European contemporaries. At the period of the first emigrations, the township system, that fruitful germ of free institutions, was deeply rooted in the habits of the English; and with it the doctrine of the sovereignty of the people had been introduced into the bosom of the monarchy of the house of Tudor. . . .

Another remark, to which we shall hereafter have occasion to 5 recur, is applicable not only to the English, but to . . . all the Europeans who successively established themselves in the New World. All these European colonies contained the elements, if not the development, of a complete democracy. Two causes led to this result. It may be said generally, that on leaving the mother country the emigrants had, in general, no notion of superiority one over another. The happy and the powerful do not go into exile, and there are no surer guaranties of equality among men than poverty and misfortune. It happened, however, on several occasions, that persons of rank were driven to America by political and religious quarrels. Laws were made to establish a gradation of ranks; but it was soon found that the soil of America was opposed to a territorial aristocracy. To bring that refractory land into cultivation, the constant and interested exertions of the owner himself were necessary; and when the ground was prepared, its produce was found to be insufficient to enrich a proprietor and a farmer at the same time. This land was then naturally broken up into small portions, which the proprietor cultivated for himself. Land is the basis of an aristocracy, which clings to the soil that supports it; for it is not by privileges alone, nor by birth, but by landed property handed down from generation to generation, that an aristocracy is constituted. A nation may present immense fortunes and extreme wretchedness; but unless those fortunes are territorial, there is no true aristocracy, but simply the class of the rich and that of the poor.

All the British colonies had then a great degree of family likeness at the epoch of their settlement. All of them, from their beginning, seemed destined to witness the growth, not of the aristocratic liberty of their mother country, but of that freedom of the middle and lower orders of which the history of the world had as yet furnished no complete example. In this general uniformity, however, several striking differences were discernible, which it is necessary to point out. Two branches may be distinguished in the great Anglo-American family, which have hitherto grown up without entirely commingling; the one in the South, the other in the North.

Virginia received the first English colony; the emigrants took possession of it in 1607. The idea that mines of gold and silver are the sources of national wealth was at that time singularly prevalent in Europe; a fatal delusion, which has done more to impoverish the European nations who adopted it, and has cost more lives in America, than the united influence of war and bad laws. The men sent to Virginia were seekers of gold, adventurers without resources and without character, whose turbulent and restless spirit endangered the infant colony, and rendered its progress uncertain. Artisans and agriculturists arrived afterwards; and, although they were a more moral and orderly race of men, they were hardly in any respect above the level of the inferior classes in England. No lofty views, no spiritual conception, presided over the foundation of these new settlements. The colony was scarcely established when slavery was introduced; this was the capital fact which was to exercise an immense influence on the character, the laws and the whole future of the South. Slavery . . . dishonors labor; it introduces idleness into society, and with idleness, ignorance and pride, luxury and distress. It enervates the powers of the mind, and benumbs the activity of man. The influence of slavery, united to the English character, explains the manners and the social condition of the Southern States.

In the North, the same English character . . . received totally different colors. Here . . . the two or three main ideas which now constitute the basis of the social theory of the United States were first combined. . . . They now extend their influence . . . over the whole American world. The civilization of New England has been like a beacon lit upon a hill, which, after it has diffused its warmth immediately around it, also tinges the distant horizon with its glow. . . .

The settlers who established themselves on the shores of New England all belonged to the more independent classes of their native country. Their union on the soil of America at once presented the singular phenomenon of a society containing neither lords nor common people, and we may almost say, neither rich nor poor. These men possessed, in proportion to their number, a greater mass of intelligence than is to be found in any European nation of our own time. All, perhaps without a single exception, had received a good education, and many of them were known in Europe for their talents and their acquirements. The other colonies had been founded by adventurers without families; the emigrants of New England brought with them the best elements of order and morality; they landed on the desert coast accompanied by their wives and children. But what especially distinguished them from all others was the aim of their undertaking. They had not been obliged by necessity to leave their country; the social position they abandoned was one to be regretted, and their means of subsistence were certain. . . . In facing the inevitable sufferings of exile, their object was the triumph of an idea.

The emigrants, or, as they deservedly styled themselves, the Pilgrims, belonged to that English sect the austerity of whose principles had acquired for them the name of Puritans. Puritanism was not merely a religious doctrine, but it corresponded in many points with the most absolute democratic and republican theories. It was this tendency which had aroused its most dangerous adversaries. Persecuted by the government of the mother country, and disgusted by the habits of a society which the rigor of their own principles condemned, the Puritans went forth to seek some rude and unfrequented part of the world, where they could live according to their own opinions, and worship God in freedom. . . . Puritanism . . . was scarcely less a political than a religious doctrine. No sooner had the emigrants landed on the barren coast . . . than it was their first care to constitute a society, by subscribing the [Mayflower Compact]:

"In the name of God. Amen. We, whose names are underwritten, the loyal subjects of our dread Sovereign Lord King James, &s, &c., Having undertaken for the glory of God, and advancement of the Christian Faith, and the honour of our King and country, a voyage to plant the first colony in the northern parts of Virginia; Do by these presents solemnly and mutually, in the presence of God and one another, covenant and combine ourselves together into a civil body politick, for our better ordering and preservation, and furtherance of the ends aforesaid: and by virtue hereof do enact, constitute, and frame such just and equal laws, ordinances, acts, constitutions, and offices, from time to time, as shall be thought most meet and convenient for the general good of the Colony: unto which we promise all due submission and obedience. . . ."

This happened in 1620, and from that time forwards the emigration went on. The religious and political passions which ravaged the British empire during the whole reign of Charles I drove fresh crowds of sectarians every year to the shores of America. In England, the stronghold of Puritanism continued to be in the middle classes; and it was from the middle classes that most of the emigrants came. The population of New England increased rapidly; and whilst the hierarchy of rank despotically classed the inhabitants of the mother country, the colony approximated more and more the novel spectacle of a community homogeneous in all its parts. A democracy, more perfect than antiquity had dared to dream of, started in full size and panoply from the midst of an ancient feudal society.

For Journals

Whom do you think of as the first Americans?

For Discussion

1. Why do you think Tocqueville frames his study of America and Americans using the analogy of studying the child to know the man? How does this image illuminate and clarify his purpose?

2. To what in the Anglo Americans' history does Tocqueville attribute their knowledge of the principles of freedom? Are you persuaded by his conclusion? Do you think his contemporaries would have been?

3. How does Tocqueville characterize New England and the Puritans? Pay special attention to the passages he cites to illuminate "the spirit of these pious adventurers." What conclusions does he draw from his evidence? Do you think his contemporary audience would

have been convinced? Are you convinced of the Puritans' character on
the basis of the passage he cites?

4. According to Tocqueville, what effects does slavery have on a society in general? What do you infer from his remark "The influence of
slavery, united to the English character, explains the manners and the
social condition of the Southern states"?

5. Tocqueville writes in paragraph 4, "The tie of language is, perhaps, the strongest and the most durable that can unite mankind."
What assumption is he making about language and culture? How
does this approach to culture define "American"? Do you agree with
his assumption and with this definition? How do you think his contemporaries would have reacted to his assertion?

For Writing

1. Drawing from your discussions in response to discussion items 3
and 4, write an essay in which you compare and contrast Tocqueville's
treatment of North and South and the American identities that developed in each region. Which identity do you find more clearly articulated? Which assertions are more persuasive? Do you find his
generalizations merited, considering the evidence he offers? How is
your assessment of his argument biased by your own cultural or geographical identity?

2. Tocqueville's discussion of a common language has had strong re-
verberations in recent debates over "English only" in schools and over
policies establishing English as the official language of the United
States. Research one of these issues, checking recent journal, newspaper, and magazine indexes for both educational journals and popular
magazines, as well as books, so that you have up-to-date information.
Develop a thesis about the topic, and support it with well-reasoned arguments based on evidence from your research.

✳✳✳ *Victory Liberty Loan* (1919)

HOWARD CHANDLER CHRISTY

> *World War I began in Europe in 1914, and the United States entered the war in*
> *1917. In the year and a half following the U.S. declaration of war, civilian efforts to*
> *support the war included some $18 billion in war-bond purchases. War bonds, or*
> *funds through which consumers lent money to the government at a modest interest*
> *rate, helped finance war matériel without harsh increases in federal income taxes; to*
> *some extent, bonds were said to help deal with currency inflation that can ensue when*
> *there are few consumer goods to buy. Of more importance, though, Americans were*

also persuaded to "buy into" the war through purchasing bonds. William Gibbs McAdoo, who was then secretary of the Treasury, wrote: "We went directly to the people, and that means to everybody—to business men, workmen, farmers, bankers, millionaires, school-teachers, laborers. We capitalized on the profound impulse called patriotism. It is the quality of coherence that holds a nation together; it is one of the deepest and most powerful of human motives." Artists such as Christy were commissioned to create posters to advertise the bonds, while film stars and others appeared at rallies to urge people to buy bonds—and to support the war. This particular design was quite successful both during and for some time after the war. (See Color Plate I for a color image of this poster.)

For Journals

What visual symbols remind you of America? What kinds of symbols appeal to your sense of patriotism?

For Discussion

1.   What draws your eye when you first look at the poster? What are the poster's most prominent features? What did the artist want the viewer to see and feel first? Why?

2.   Is the clothing of the female figure in the poster what you expect for its era? How would you account for her style of dress?

3.   What do the wreath, the gold star, and the honor roll symbolize? (In what other contexts have you seen these symbols?) The woman is literally draping herself in the American flag. What do her posture and gestures suggest?

4.   Read the list of names under the heading "Honor Roll" carefully. What do you notice? What point is the artist trying to make?

5.   Who do you think was the intended audience for this poster?

For Writing

1.   Compare and contrast the assumptions about the American identity evident in this poster with the assertions about identity in other chapter readings. Are the assumptions similar or different? Explain your assessment.

2.   Select a modern advertisement that tries to appeal to Americans with a variety of ethnic heritages. Write an essay analyzing the choice of persuasive strategies in the ad and their effectiveness.

3.   If you were asked to provide a poster or flyer to appeal to patriotism, what design choices would you make? Try to design such a poster or flyer (you may want to take an existing one and give it a patriotic edge), writing out the text and sketching the images you would use. Write an essay explaining your choices.

❊❊❊ *What the Indian Means to America* (1933)

LUTHER STANDING BEAR

Luther Standing Bear (1868–1947), a member of a Teton Sioux tribe, attended the government Indian school at Carlyle, Pennsylvania, and later worked in jobs ranging from storekeeper to minister to performer in Buffalo Bill's Wild West Show. Having lived during and observed firsthand the forcible removal of Native Americans to reservations during the rapid expansion of the West, Standing Bear found the government practices untenable. His views are set out in My People the Sioux *(1928),* My Indian Boyhood *(1931),* Stories of the Sioux *(1934), and* Land of the Spotted Eagle *(1933), from which the following selection is excerpted. In this essay, Standing Bear identifies the American Indian as the one who truly understands the American lands.*

The feathered and blanketed figure of the American Indian has come to symbolize the American continent. He is the man who through centuries has been moulded and sculpted by the same hand that shaped its mountains, forests, and plains, and marked the course of its rivers.

The American Indian is of the soil, whether it be the region of forests, plains, pueblos, or mesas. He fits into the landscape, for the hand that fashioned the continent also fashioned the man for his surroundings. He once grew as naturally as the wild sunflowers; he belongs just as the buffalo belonged.

With a physique that fitted, the man developed fitting skills—crafts which today are called American. And the body had a soul, also formed and moulded by the same master hand of harmony. Out of the Indian approach to existence there came a great freedom—an intense and absorbing love for nature; a respect for life; enriching faith in a Supreme Power; and principles of truth, honesty, generosity, equity, and brotherhood as a guide to mundane relations. . . .

The white man does not understand the Indian for the reason that he does not understand America. He is too far removed from its formative processes. The roots of the tree of his life have not yet grasped the rock and soil. The white man is still troubled with primitive fears; he still has in his consciousness the perils of this frontier continent, some of its fastnesses not yet having yielded to his questing footsteps and inquiring eyes. He shudders still with the memory of the loss of his forefathers upon its scorching deserts and forbidding mountaintops. The man from Europe is still a foreigner and an alien. And he still hates the man who questioned his path across the continent.

But in the Indian the spirit of the land is still vested; it will be until 5 other men are able to divine and meet its rhythm. Men must be born and reborn to belong. Their bodies must be formed of the dust of their forefathers' bones.

The attempted transformation of the Indian by the white man and the chaos that has resulted are but the fruits of the white man's disobedience of a fundamental and spiritual law. The pressure that has been brought to bear upon the native people, since the cessation of armed conflict, in the attempt to force conformity of custom and habit has caused a reaction more destructive than war, and the injury has not only affected the Indian, but has extended to the white population as well. Tyranny, stupidity, and lack of vision have brought about the situation now alluded to as the "Indian Problem."

There is, I insist, no Indian problem as created by the Indian himself. Every problem that exists today in regard to the native population is due to the white man's cast of mind, which is unable, at least reluctant, to seek understanding and achieve adjustment in a new and a significant environment into which it has so recently come.

The white man excused his presence here by saying that he has been guided by the will of his God; and in so saying absolved himself of all responsibility for his appearance in a land occupied by other men.

Then, too, his law was a written law; his divine decalogue reposed in a book. And what better proof that his advent into this country and his subsequent acts were the result of divine will! He brought the Word! There ensued a blind worship of written history, of books, of the written word, that has denuded the spoken word of its power and sacredness. The written word became established as a criterion of the superior man—a symbol of emotional fineness. The man who could write his name on a piece of paper, whether or not he possessed the spiritual fineness to honor those words in speech, was by some miraculous formula a more highly developed and sensitized person than the one who had never had a pen in hand, but whose spoken word was inviolable and whose sense of honor and truth was paramount. With false reasoning was the quality of human character measured by man's ability to make with an implement a mark upon paper. But granting this mode of reasoning be correct and just, then where are to be placed the thousands of illiterate whites who are unable to read and write? Are they, too, "savages"? Is not humanness a matter of heart and mind, and is it not evident in the form of relationship with men? Is not kindness more powerful than arrogance; and truth more powerful than the sword?

True, the white man brought great change. But the varied fruits of 10 his civilization, though highly colored and inviting, are sickening and deadening. And if it be the part of civilization to maim, rob, and thwart, then what is progress? . . .

After subjugation, after dispossession, there was cast the last abuse upon the people who so entirely resented their wrongs and punishments, and that was the stamping and labeling of them as savages. To make this label stick has been the task of the white race and the greatest salve that it has been able to apply to its sore and troubled conscience now hardened through the habitual practice of injustice.

But all the years of calling the Indian a savage has never made him one; all the denial of his virtues has never taken them from him; and the very resistance he has made to save the things inalienably his has been his saving strength—that which will stand him in need when justice does make its belated appearance and he undertakes rehabilitation.

All sorts of feeble excuses are heard for the continued subjection of the Indian. One of the most common is that he is not yet ready to accept the society of the white man—that he is not yet ready to mingle as a social entity.

This, I maintain, is beside the question. The matter is not one of making over the external Indian into the likeness of the white race—a process detrimental to both races. Who can say that the white man's way is better for the Indian? Where resides the human judgment with the competence to weigh and value Indian ideals and spiritual concepts; or substitute for them other values?

Then, has the white man's social order been so harmonious and ideal as to merit the respect of the Indian, and for that matter the thinking class of the white race? Is it wise to urge upon the Indian a foreign social form? Let none but the Indian answer! 15

Rather, let the white brother face about and cast his mental eye upon a new angle of vision. Let him look upon the Indian world as a human world; then let him see to it that human rights be accorded to the Indians. And this for the purpose of retaining for his own order of society a measure of humanity. . . .

The spiritual health and existence of the Indian was maintained by song, magic, ritual, dance, symbolism, oratory (or council), design, handicraft, and folk-story.

Manifestly, to check or thwart this expression is to bring about spiritual decline. And it is in this condition of decline that the Indian people are today. There is but a feeble effort among the Sioux to keep alive their traditional songs and dances, while among other tribes there is but a half-hearted attempt to offset the influence of the Government school and at the same time recover from the crushing and stifling regime of the Indian Bureau.

One has but to speak of Indian verse to receive uncomprehending and unbelieving glances. Yet the Indian loved verse and into this mode of expression went his deepest feelings. Only a few ardent and advanced students seem interested; nevertheless, they have given in book form enough Indian translations to set forth the character and quality of Indian verse.

Oratory receives a little better understanding on the part of the white public, owing to the fact that oratorical complications include those of Indian orators. 20

Hard as it seemingly is for the white man's ear to sense the differences, Indian songs are as varied as the many emotions which inspire them, for no two of them are alike. For instance, the Song of Victory is spirited and the notes high and remindful of an unrestrained hunter or warrior riding exultantly over the prairies. On the other hand, the song of the *Cano unye* is solemn and full of urge, for it is meant to inspire the young men to deeds of valor. Then there are the songs of death and the spiritual songs which are connected with the ceremony of initiation. These are full of the spirit of praise and worship, and so strong are some of these invocations that the very air seems as if surcharged with the presence of the Big Holy.

The Indian loved to worship. From birth to death he revered his surroundings. He considered himself born in the luxurious lap of Mother Earth and no place was to him humble. There was nothing between him and the Big Holy. The contact was immediate and personal, and the blessings of Wakan Tanka flowed over the Indian like rain showered from the sky. Wakan Tanka was not aloof, apart, and ever seeking to quell evil forces. He did not punish the animals and the birds, and likewise He did not punish man. He was not a punishing God. For there was never a question as to the supremacy of an evil power over and above the power of Good. There was but one ruling power, and that was *Good.*

Of course, none but an adoring one could dance for days with his face to the sacred sun, and that time is all but done. We cannot have back the days of the buffalo and the beaver; we cannot win back our clean blood-stream and superb health, and we can never again expect the beautiful *rapport* we once had with Nature. The springs and lakes have dried and the mountains are bare of forests. The plow has changed the face of the world. Wi-wila is dead! No more may we heal our sick and comfort our dying with a strength founded on faith, for even the animals now fear us, and fear supplants faith.

And the Indian wants to dance! It is his way of expressing devotion, of communing with unseen power, and in keeping his tribal identity. When the Lakota heart was filled with high emotion, he danced. When he felt the benediction of the warming rays of the sun, he danced. When his blood ran hot with success of the hunt or chase, he danced. When his heart was filled with pity for the orphan, the lonely father, or bereaved mother, he danced. All the joys and exaltations of life, all his gratefulness and thankfulness, all his acknowledgments of the mysterious power that guided life, and all his aspirations for a better life, culminated in one great dance—the Sun Dance.

When the Indian has forgotten the music of his forefathers, when 25 the sound of the tomtom is no more, when noisy jazz has drowned the melody of the flute, he will be a dead Indian. When the memory of his heroes are no longer told in story, and he forsakes the beautiful white buckskin for factory shoddy, he will be dead. When from him has been taken all that is his, all that he has visioned in nature, all that has come to him from infinite sources, he then, truly, will be a dead Indian. His spirit will be gone, and though he walk crowded streets, he will, in truth, be—*dead!*

But all this must not perish; it must live, to the end that America shall be educated no longer to regard native production of whatever tribe—folk-story, basketry, pottery, dance, song, poetry—as curios, and native artists as curiosities. For who but the man indigenous to the soil could produce its song, story, and folk-tale; who but the man who loved the dust beneath his feet could shape it and put it into undying, ceramic form; who but he who loved the reeds that grew beside still waters, and the damp roots of shrub and tree, could save it from seasonal death, and with almost superhuman patience weave it into enduring objects of beauty—into timeless art!

Regarding the "civilization" that has been thrust upon me since the days of reservation, it has not added one whit to my sense of justice; to my reverence for the rights of life; to my love for truth, honesty, and generosity; nor to my faith in Wakan Tanka—God of the Lakotas. For after all the great religions have been preached and expounded, or have been revealed by brilliant scholars, or have been written in books and embellished in fine language with finer covers, man—all man—is still confronted with the Great Mystery.

So if today I had a young mind to direct, to start on the journey of life, and I was faced with the duty of choosing between the natural way of my forefathers and that of the white man's present way of civilization, I would, for its welfare, unhesitatingly set that child's feet in the path of my forefathers. I would raise him to be an Indian!

For Journals

What do you know about the relationship between American Indians and the land?

For Discussion

1. How does Standing Bear establish the argument that the American Indian is not only the true symbol but also the essence of the American continent? In what ways do the American Indian and the land share an identity?

2. Standing Bear contrasts the American Indians and the whites in terms of their relationship with the land. What does he mean when he asserts that "in the Indian the spirit of the land is still vested"? How can others inherit that spirit?

3. According to Standing Bear, in what ways are whites foreigners in America? What kind of assimilation do white people need to undergo so as not to be aliens? How is this process similar to and different from other kinds of assimilation with which you are familiar?

4. How have the pressure and "conformity of custom" injured both American Indians and whites?

5. How do whites justify their presence in America and their subjugation of Indians? How does the author refute these arguments? Standing Bear published this selection in 1933 as part of a larger work. How do you think his audiences responded to the initial arguments of whites and to Standing Bear's refutation? How do you respond?

For Writing

1. Write an essay summarizing Standing Bear's definition of a true American and then either offer support for or refute his position.

2. Some Native American tribes, as a result of the legality of gambling on their lands and exemptions from some taxes, have seen greatly increased revenues and economic and political power. Research the impact of gaming on American Indians tribes, perhaps focusing on increased influence in politics in California and other states. You could examine, for example, political advertising using this issue to promote, or discredit, particular candidates in the 2003 recall election, or the ways in which this issue is represented in the popular media.

3. Research the Trail of Tears, the establishing of the reservation system, or some other specific issue in the history of Indian-white relations in America, and write a documented essay explaining the issue or event. Alternatively, investigate the current status of the relationship between one or more of the Native American nations and the U.S. government, focusing on the degree to which Indian-white relations have, or have not, changed since the publication of Standing Bear's books in the late 1920s and early 1930s.

❈❈❈ *Prologue to* Invisible Man (1947)

RALPH ELLISON

Born in Oklahoma in 1914 and educated at the Tuskegee Institute in Alabama, Ralph Ellison established his considerable reputation with his first and only novel, Invisible Man, *originally published in 1947 and reprinted numerous times since, most recently in 1990. This selection from the Prologue is typical of Ellison's lyrical and unflinching portrayal of black identity in American society, an identity the novelist has fleshed out more fully in collections of essays such as* Shadow and Act *(1964) and* Going to the Territory *(1986). Ellison lectured at Yale, Columbia, and New York Universities, and remains a dominant figure on the American literary landscape even after his death in 1994.*

I am an invisible man. No, I am not a spook like those who haunted Edgar Allan Poe; nor am I one of your Hollywood-movie ectoplasms. I am a man of substance, of flesh and bone, fiber and liquids—and I might even be said to possess a mind. I am invisible, understand, simply because people refuse to see me. Like the bodiless heads you see sometimes in circus sideshows, it is as though I have been surrounded by mirrors of hard, distorting glass. When they approach me they see only my surroundings, themselves, or figments of their imagination—indeed, everything and anything except me.

Nor is my invisibility exactly a matter of a biochemical accident to my epidermis. That invisibility to which I refer occurs because of a peculiar disposition of the eyes of those with whom I come in contact. A matter of the construction of their *inner* eyes, those eyes with which they look through their physical eyes upon reality. I am not complaining, nor am I protesting either. It is sometimes advantageous to be unseen, although it is most often rather wearing on the nerves. Then too, you're constantly being bumped against by those of poor vision. Or again, you often doubt if you really exist. You wonder whether you aren't simply a phantom in other people's minds. Say, a figure in a nightmare which the sleeper tries with all his strength to destroy. It's when you feel like this that, out of resentment, you begin to bump people back. And, let me confess, you feel that way most of the time. You ache with the need to convince yourself that you do exist in the real world, that you're a part of all the sound and anguish, and you strike out with your fists, you curse and you swear to make them recognize you. And, alas, it's seldom successful.

One night I accidentally bumped into a man, and perhaps because of the near darkness he saw me and called me an insulting name. I sprang at him, seized his coat lapels and demanded that he apologize. He was a tall blond man, and as my face came close to his he looked insolently out of his blue eyes and cursed me, his breath hot in my face as he struggled. I pulled his chin down sharp upon the crown of my head, butting him as I had seen the West Indians do, and I felt his flesh tear and the blood gush out, and I yelled, "Apologize! Apologize!" But he continued to curse and struggle, and I butted him again and again until he went down heavily, on his knees, profusely bleeding. I kicked him repeatedly, in a frenzy because he still uttered insults though his lips were frothy with blood. Oh yes, I kicked him! And in my outrage I got out my knife and prepared to slit his throat, right there beneath the lamplight in the deserted street, holding him in the collar with one hand, and opening the knife with my teeth—when it occurred to me that the man had not *seen* me, actually; that he, as far as he knew, was in the midst of a walking nightmare! And I stopped the blade, slicing the air as I pushed him away, letting him fall back to the street. I stared at him hard as the lights of a car stabbed through the darkness. He lay there, moaning on the asphalt; a man almost killed by a phantom. It unnerved me. I was both disgusted and ashamed. I was like a drunken man myself, wavering about on weakened legs. Then I was amused: Something in this man's thick head had sprung out and beaten him within an inch of his life. I began to laugh at this crazy discovery. Would he have awakened at the point of death? Would Death himself have freed him for wakeful living? But I didn't linger. I ran away into the dark, laughing so hard I feared I might rupture myself. The next day I saw his picture in the *Daily News,* beneath a caption stating that he had been "mugged." Poor fool, poor blind fool, I thought with sincere compassion, mugged by an invisible man!

Most of the time (although I do not choose as I once did to deny the violence of my days by ignoring it) I am not so overtly violent. I remember that I am invisible and walk softly so as not to awaken the sleeping ones. Sometimes it is best not to awaken them; there are few things in the world as dangerous as sleepwalkers. I learned in time though that it is possible to carry on a fight against them without their realizing it. For instance, I have been carrying on a fight with Monopolated Light & Power for some time now. I use their service and pay them nothing at all, and they don't know it. Oh, they suspect that power is being drained off, but they don't know where. All they know is that according to the master meter back there in their power station a hell of a lot of free current is disappearing somewhere into the jungle of Harlem. The joke, of course, is that I don't live in Harlem but in a border area. Several years ago (before I discovered the advantages of being invisible) I went through the routine process of buying service and paying their outrageous rates. But no more. I gave up all that, along with my apartment, and my old way of life: That way based upon the fallacious assumption that I, like other men, was visible. Now, aware of my invisibility, I live rent-free in a building rented strictly to whites, in a section of the basement that was shut off and forgotten during the nineteenth century, which I discovered when I was trying to escape in the night from Ras the Destroyer. But that's getting too far ahead of the story, almost to the end, although the end is in the beginning and lies far ahead.

The point now is that I found a home—or a hole in the ground, as 5 you will. Now don't jump to any conclusion that because I call my home a "hole" it is damp and cold like a grave; there are cold holes and warm holes. Mine is a warm hole. And remember, a bear retires to his hole for the winter and lives until spring; then he comes strolling out like the Easter chick breaking from its shell. I say all this to assure you that it is incorrect to assume that, because I'm invisible and live in a hole, I am dead. I am neither dead nor in a state of suspended animation. Call me Jack-the-Bear, for I am in a state of hibernation.

My hole is warm and full of light. Yes, *full* of light. I doubt if there is a brighter spot in all New York than this hole of mine, and I do not exclude Broadway. Or the Empire State Building on a photographer's dream night. But that is taking advantage of you. Those two spots are among the darkest of our whole civilization—pardon me, our whole *culture* (an important distinction, I've heard)—which might sound like a hoax, or a contradiction, but that (by contradiction, I mean) is how the world moves: Not like an arrow, but a boomerang. (Beware of those who speak of the *spiral* of history; they are preparing a boomerang. Keep a steel helmet handy.) I know; I have been boomeranged across my head so much that I now can see the darkness of lightness. And I love light. Perhaps you'll think it strange that an invisible man should need light, desire light, love light. But maybe it is exactly because I *am* invisible. Light confirms my reality, gives birth to my form. A beautiful girl once told me of a recurring nightmare in which she lay in the center of a large dark room and felt her face expand until it filled the whole room, becoming a formless mass while her eyes ran in bilious jelly up the chimney. And so it is with me. Without light I am not only invisible, but formless as well; and to be unaware of one's form is to live a death. I myself, after existing some twenty years, did not become alive until I discovered my invisibility.

For Journals

Are there groups of people in your community—ethnic minorities, older people, people with apparent or invisible disabilities—whom you rarely notice?

For Discussion

1.   How is the notion of invisibility developed in this selection? Why do you think Ellison uses the idea of invisibility? What associations does it have? What could a person do—or not do—if invisible?

2.   The speaker notes that he found a home, a "hole in the ground," literally in a basement of a building restricted to whites. What is significant about his living in such a place? What is special, literally and metaphorically, about the light and power company?

3.   In what sense is the invisible man's identity related to and developed by how others see him? Consider his growing awareness of being invisible, the incident with the blond stranger, and his relationship with the power company.

4. In an introduction to *Invisible Man* that accompanied an edition printed in 1981, Ellison writes, "My task was one of revealing the human universals hidden within the plight of one who was both black and an American." What do you infer from this selection about the plight of those who live with this double identity? How effectively do you think Ellison appealed to readers to understand the universals—to identify or empathize with the speaker in this narrative?

For Writing

1. Write an essay discussing the effects of others' perceptions on developing one's own identity, whether in terms of ethnicity, race, culture, nationality, physical abilities, or age. You could develop this assignment as a personal essay; alternatively, you could investigate and incorporate recent research on the subject, found in psychology or sociology books and journals.

2. Ellison wrote that his task in *Invisible Man* was to deal with "the sheer rhetorical challenge involved in communicating across our barriers of race and religion, class, color, and region—barriers which consist of the many strategies of division that were designed, and still function, to prevent what would otherwise have been a more or less natural recognition of the reality of blackness." How does he cope with the rhetorical challenges—obstacles to persuasion—he mentions here? In what ways do his metaphor of invisibility and the voice and tone of the speaker serve to meet those challenges? How does he appeal to ethos?

❅❅❅ *Inaugural Address* (1961)

JOHN F. KENNEDY

John Fitzgerald Kennedy (1917–1963) was born in Brookline, Massachusetts, and graduated from Harvard University. He served as a torpedo boat commander in the Pacific during World War II and received both the Navy Medal and the Purple Heart for his service. For his book Profiles in Courage *(1956) Kennedy won the Pulitzer Prize, and after a career in Congress he became the youngest elected and first Roman Catholic president. His administration was cut tragically short when rifle fire from an assassin in Dallas, Texas, ended his life in 1963. Kennedy's famous inaugural address exemplifies the youth, vitality, and vision of a generation and remains a classic of American rhetoric.*

We observe today not a victory of party but a celebration of freedom—symbolizing an end as well as a beginning, signifying renewal as well as change. For I have sworn before you and Almighty God the same solemn oath our forebears prescribed nearly a century and three-quarters ago.

The world is very different now. For man holds in his mortal hands the power to abolish all forms of human poverty and all forms of human life. And yet the same revolutionary beliefs for which our forebears fought are still at issue around the globe: the belief that the rights of man come not from the generosity of the state but from the hand of God.

We dare not forget today that we are the heirs of that first revolution. Let the word go forth from this time and place, to friend and foe alike, that the torch has been passed to a new generation of Americans—born in this century, tempered by war, disciplined by a hard and bitter peace, proud of our ancient heritage—and unwilling to witness or permit the slow undoing of those human rights to which this nation has always been committed, and to which we are committed today at home and around the world.

Let every nation know, whether it wishes us well or ill, that we shall pay any price, bear any burden, meet any hardship, support any friend, oppose any foe to assure the survival and the success of liberty.

This much we pledge—and more. 5

To those old allies whose cultural and spiritual origins we share, we pledge the loyalty of faithful friends. United, there is little we can not do in a host of cooperative ventures. Divided, there is little we can do—for we dare not meet a powerful challenge at odds and split asunder.

To those new states whom we welcome to the ranks of the free, we pledge our word that one form of colonial control shall not have passed away merely to be replaced by a far more iron tyranny. We shall not always expect to find them supporting our view. But we shall always hope to find them strongly supporting their own freedom—and to remember that, in the past, those who foolishly sought power by riding the back of the tiger ended up inside.

To those people in the huts and villages of half the globe struggling to break the bonds of mass misery, we pledge our best efforts to help them help themselves, for whatever period is required—not because the Communists may be doing it, not because we seek their votes, but because it is right. If a free society cannot help the many who are poor, it cannot save the few who are rich.

To our sister republics south of the border, we offer a special pledge: to convert our good words into good deeds—in a new alliance for progress—to assist free men and free governments in casting off the chains of poverty. But this peaceful revolution of hope cannot become the prey of hostile powers. Let all our neighbors know that we shall join with them to oppose aggression or subversion anywhere in the Americas. And let every other power know that this hemisphere intends to remain the master of its own house.

To that world assembly of sovereign states, the United Nations, 10 our last best hope in an age where the instruments of war have far outpaced the instruments of peace, we renew our pledge of support—to prevent it from becoming merely a forum for invective, to strengthen its shield of the new and the weak, and to enlarge the area in which its writ may run.

Finally, to those nations who would make themselves our adversary, we offer not a pledge but a request: that both sides begin anew the quest for peace, before the dark powers of destruction unleashed by science engulf all humanity in planned or accidental self-destruction.

We dare not tempt them with weakness. For only when our arms are sufficient beyond doubt can we be certain beyond doubt that they will never be employed.

But neither can two great and powerful groups of nations take comfort from our present course—both sides overburdened by the cost of modern weapons, both rightly alarmed by the steady spread of the deadly atom, yet both racing to alter that uncertain balance of terror that stays the hand of mankind's final war.

So let us begin anew, remembering on both sides that civility is not a sign of weakness, and sincerity is always subject to proof. Let us never negotiate out of fear. But let us never fear to negotiate.

Let both sides explore what problems unite us instead of belabor- 15 ing those problems which divide us.

Let both sides, for the first time, formulate serious and precise proposals for the inspection and control of arms—and bring the absolute power to destroy other nations under the absolute control of all nations.

Let both sides seek to invoke the wonders of science instead of its terrors. Together let us explore the stars, conquer the deserts, eradicate disease, tap the ocean depths, and encourage the arts and commerce.

Let both sides unite to heed in all corners of the earth the command of Isaiah—to "undo the heavy burdens . . . [and] let the oppressed go free."

And if a beachhead of cooperation may push back the jungle of suspicion, let both sides join in creating a new endeavor, not a new balance of power, but a new world of law, where the strong are just and the weak secure and the peace preserved.

All this will not be finished in the first one hundred days. Nor will it 20 be finished in the first one thousand days, nor in the life of this administration, nor even perhaps in our lifetime on this planet. But let us begin.

In your hands, my fellow citizens, more than mine, will rest the final success or failure of our course. Since this country was founded, each generation of Americans has been summoned to give testimony to its national loyalty. The graves of young Americans who answered the call to service surround the globe.

Now the trumpet summons us again—not as a call to bear arms, though arms we need; not as a call to battle, though embattled we are— but a call to bear the burden of a long twilight struggle, year in and year out, "rejoicing in hope, patient in tribulation," a struggle against the common enemies of man: tyranny, poverty, disease, and war itself.

Can we forge against these enemies a grand and global alliance, north and south, east and west, that can assure a more fruitful life for all mankind? Will you join in that historic effort?

In the long history of the world, only a few generations have been granted the role of defending freedom in its hour of maximum danger. I do not shrink from this responsibility—I welcome it. I do not believe that any of us would exchange places with any other people or any other generation. The energy, the faith, the devotion which we bring to this endeavor will light our country and all who serve it—and the glow from that fire can truly light the world.

And so, my fellow Americans: Ask not what your country can do 25 for you—ask what you can do for your country.

My fellow citizens of the world: Ask not what America will do for you, but what together we can do for the freedom of man.

Finally, whether you are citizens of America or citizens of the world, ask of us here the same high standards of strength and sacrifice which we ask of you. With a good conscience our only sure reward, with history the final judge of our deeds, let us go forth to lead the land we love, asking His blessing and His help, but knowing that here on earth God's work must truly be our own.

For Journals

What have you learned, from people older than you or from the media, about the Kennedy administration? What images, expressions, and values come to mind?

For Discussion

1.   Identify the audience for and the purpose of an inaugural address. What special demands do they place on the speaker? Kennedy was not only the youngest and first-ever Catholic president elected; he also won by an exceedingly narrow margin. What additional demands did he need to meet? What strategies did he use to meet these demands? Was he successful?

2.   How does Kennedy define his generation? How does he link these definitions to the goals of his administration?

3. What rhetorical strategies does Kennedy use to unite his audience and evoke a sense of shared purpose? Focus specifically on word choice and on literary or biblical allusions in the speech. How do you think most people in Kennedy's audience reacted, either consciously or unconsciously, to his words? What appeals to ethos, pathos, and logos does he make, and which type of appeal predominates? Do you think such a speech would be suitable for an audience of your contemporaries? Why, or why not?

4. Study the themes of the address. What do you infer about how Americans at that time defined their role in international affairs? In what ways does their identity rest on a contrast to the Soviet Union?

5. Kennedy draws a particular portrait of America and Americans. Write out or discuss in your own words the visions, goals, and ideas either suggested by or articulated in the speech.

For Writing

1. Choose a topic from one of the prominent issues of the early 1960s—civil rights, space exploration, communism, youth culture, rock music, free speech, or something else—to explore. Develop a research question; then collect information by reading books and essays on the topic and also by finding and evaluating magazines, newspapers, television shows, radio broadcasts, and music lyrics or albums of the time that were written on the topic. Try to interview people who were young adults at the time. Develop your findings into a presentation to share with your peers.

2. Communicating clearly through a speech is different from communicating through writing. Good public speakers must take advantage of word choice, strong organization, parallelism, rhythm, and other elements of style to make their points. In other words, they take many features of good prose and accentuate them. Write an essay analyzing the use of one or more of these stylistic features in Kennedy's address. Try to show how the president used stylistic devices to emphasize his themes.

❈❈❈ *The Cult of Ethnicity* (1991)

ARTHUR M. SCHLESINGER, JR.

Arthur M. Schlesinger, Jr. (1917–), educator and historian, is well known for his service during the Kennedy and Johnson administrations. His books, which have earned him awards such as the Pulitzer Prize and National Book Award, include The Age of Jackson *(1945),* The Age of Roosevelt *(1957, 1959, 1960),* A Thousand

Days: John F. Kennedy in the White House *(1965),* Robert Kennedy and His Times *(1978), and, more recently,* The Disuniting of America *(1992). The following essay appeared in* Time *magazine.*

The history of the world has been in great part the history of the mixing of peoples. Modern communication and transport accelerate mass migrations from one continent to another. Ethnic and racial diversity is more than ever a salient fact of the age.

But what happens when people of different origins, speaking different languages and professing different religions, inhabit the same locality and live under the same political sovereignty? Ethnic and racial conflict—far more than ideological conflict—is the explosive problem of our times.

On every side today ethnicity is breaking up nations. The Soviet Union, India, Yugoslavia, Ethiopia, are all in crisis. Ethnic tensions disturb and divide Sri Lanka, Burma, Indonesia, Iraq, Cyprus, Nigeria, Angola, Lebanon, Guyana, Trinidad—you name it. Even nations as stable and civilized as Britain and France, Belgium and Spain, face growing ethnic troubles. Is there any large multiethnic state that can be made to work?

The answer to that question has been, until recently, the United States. "No other nation," Margaret Thatcher has said, "has so successfully combined people of different races and nations within a single culture." How have Americans succeeded in pulling off this almost unprecedented trick?

We have always been a multiethnic country. Hector St. John de 5 Crèvecoeur, who came from France in the 18th century, marveled at the astonishing diversity of the settlers—"a mixture of English, Scotch, Irish, French, Dutch, Germans and Swedes . . . this promiscuous breed." He propounded a famous question: "What then is the American, this new man?" And he gave a famous answer: "Here individuals of all nations are melted into a new race of men." *E pluribus unum.*

The U.S. escaped the divisiveness of a multiethnic society by a brilliant solution: the creation of a brand-new national identity. The point of America was not to preserve old cultures but to forge a new, American culture. "By an intermixture with our people," President George Washington told Vice President John Adams, immigrants will "get assimilated to our customs, measures and laws: in a word, soon become one people." This was the ideal that a century later Israel Zangwill crystallized in the title of his popular 1908 play *The Melting Pot.* And no institution was more potent in molding Crèvecoeur's "promiscuous breed" into Washington's "one people" than the American public school.

The new American nationality was inescapably English in language, ideas and institutions. The pot did not melt everybody, not even all the white immigrants; deeply bred racism put black Americans, yellow Americans, red Americans and brown Americans well outside the pale. Still, the infusion of other stocks, even of nonwhite stocks, and the experience of the New World reconfigured the British legacy and made the U.S., as we all know, a very different country from Britain.

In the 20th century, new immigration laws altered the composition of the American people, and a cult of ethnicity erupted both among non-Anglo whites and among nonwhite minorities. This had many healthy consequences. The American culture at last began to give shamefully overdue recognition to the achievements of groups subordinated and spurned during the high noon of Anglo dominance, and it began to acknowledge the great swirling world beyond Europe. Americans acquired a more complex and invigorating sense of their world—and of themselves.

But, pressed too far, the cult of ethnicity has unhealthy consequences. It gives rise, for example, to the conception of the U.S. as a nation composed not of individuals making their own choices but of inviolable ethnic and racial groups. It rejects the historic American goals of assimilation and integration.

And, in an excess of zeal, well-intentioned people seek to transform   10 our system of education from a means of creating "one people" into a means of promoting, celebrating and perpetuating separate ethnic origins and identities. The balance is shifting from *unum* to *pluribus.*

That is the issue that lies behind the hullabaloo over "multiculturalism" and "political correctness," the attack on the "Eurocentric" curriculum and the rise of the notion that history and literature should be taught not as disciplines but as therapies whose function is to raise minority self-esteem. Group separatism crystallizes the differences, magnifies tensions, intensifies hostilities. Europe—the unique source of the liberating ideas of democracy, civil liberties and human rights—is portrayed as the root of all evil, and non-European cultures, their own many crimes deleted, are presented as the means of redemption.

I don't want to sound apocalyptic about these developments. Education is always in ferment, and a good thing too. The situation in our universities, I am confident, will soon right itself. But the impact of separatist pressures on our public schools is more troubling. If a Kleagle of the Ku Klux Klan wanted to use the schools to disable and handicap black Americans, he could hardly come up with anything more effective than the "Afrocentric" curriculum. And if separatist tendencies go unchecked, the result can only be the fragmentation, resegregation and tribalization of American life.

I remain optimistic. My impression is that the historic forces driving toward "one people" have not lost their power. The eruption of ethnicity is, I believe, a rather superficial enthusiasm stirred by romantic ideologues on the one hand and by unscrupulous con men on the other: self-appointed spokesmen whose claim to represent their minority groups is carelessly accepted by the media. Most American-born members of minority groups, white or nonwhite, see themselves primarily as Americans rather than primarily as members of one or another ethnic group. A notable indicator today is the rate of intermarriage across ethnic lines, across religious lines, even (increasingly) across racial lines. "We Americans," said Theodore Roosevelt, "are children of the crucible."

The growing diversity of the American population makes the quest for unifying ideals and a common culture all the more urgent. In a world savagely rent by ethnic and racial antagonisms, the U.S. must continue as an example of how a highly differentiated society holds itself together.

For Journals

What are your beliefs about what makes someone "American"?

For Discussion

1. What does Schlesinger mean by "the cult of ethnicity"? Do you agree with his definition? What is his assertion about it? What evidence does he offer for support? What counterpoints does he neglect?

2. The author suggests that a focus on ethnicity, if "pressed too far," results in rejecting assimiliation and integration. Do you agree that rejecting these historic goals is unhealthy? How do you think that the author defines "too far"? How should a society determine when the focus on ethnicity, at the expense of assimilation, has gone too far?

3. Set up a debate in your whole class, with half the class taking the "assimilation" perspective and half the class arguing for recognizing ethnic diversity. Have someone keep track of the main points made by each side, on the board or overhead projector. Then, evaluate the merit and persuasiveness of arguments made on each side. (This activity could also be carried out in small groups.)

4. Do you agree with the author's assertion that "most American-born members of minority groups, white or nonwhite, see themselves primarily as American rather than primarily as members of one or another ethnic group"? Discuss, providing evidence to support your view.

For Writing

1. Using material developed in discussion item 3, write a response to Schlesinger, arguing in favor of maintaining unique ethnic cultural

traditions and groups in American society. Be sure to respond to his main points as you shape your own argument.

2. If you agree with Schlesinger, write an argument that takes the same stand and responds to Schlesinger's likely critics, again using material generated in discussion item 3 as a starting point.

3. How would one of the other authors in this chapter respond to Schlesinger? Create an imaginary dialogue between Schlesinger and Ellison, Standing Bear, or Serrano, debating one or more of the key points raised in this essay.

✽✽✽ A Tapestry of Hope
America's Strength Was, Is, and Will Be Its Diversity (1994)

JEANNE WAKATSUKI HOUSTON

Jeanne Wakatsuki Houston (1934–) was born in Los Angeles and lived in Santa Monica with her family until the Japanese attack on Pearl Harbor on December 7, 1941; her father was a fisherman. After the attack, President Roosevelt signed an order (see Chapter 10, "War and the Enemy") that led to the internment of many thousands of Japanese Americans in camps on the grounds that they might prove disloyal. They did not, but they lost their homes and livelihoods; the Wakatsukis were forced to spend three and a half years in a camp called Manzanar, in the Owens Valley in California. In 1973, Wakatsuki Houston and her husband, writer James Houston, wrote what became the most famous Japanese American memoir of the internment camps, Farewell to Manzanar. *The following speech was delivered by Wakatsuki Houston at the graduation ceremonies at De Anza College in California in June 1994.*

Many years ago—43 to be exact—when I stood on the ground where De Anza College now stands, I looked out onto lush orchards, fragrant with blossoms in springtime and ladened with plump fruit in summer. I viewed acres of foliage carpeting the earth with green—patches of beans, tomatoes, and squash, and long furrows of strawberries, glistening red under their leafy canopies. In those days I knew this area well, for I had spent several summers picking those berries at a large strawberry ranch called Esperanza, located not far from here. Esperanza, the Spanish word for "hope," was farmed by Japanese families in partnership with the Driscoll brothers. They were sharecroppers. My father sharecropped with the Driscolls at another ranch in South County from 1951 to 1955.

In 1945 when our family re-entered society after three and a half years of incarceration at Manzanar, a concentration camp for Japanese-Americans during World War II, my father's fishing license was revoked. It forced him to seek a livelihood outside a successful pre-war fishing occupation.

Starting at economic zero, at age 59 he seized the opportunity to begin again and brought his family to San Jose from Southern California to farm strawberries. Although my father had been in this country for more than 35 years, and his family, including my mother, had been born here, we arrived at this luscious valley like new immigrants, refugees from another world.

Why do I tell you this? I tell you this because when I picked those berries I never dreamed I would be speaking at a college that someday would rise up within view of where I knelt in the dirt. It was beyond my imagination. But here I am sharing with you some thoughts and insights I have accrued since those days in the strawberry fields more than 40 years ago.

As Santa Clara Valley's landscape has changed, so has its con- 5 sciousness. I'm not going to lecture about how tough it was then to be Asian, to be poor, and to be a woman. But I would like to say a few words to remind us how we have changed, how things are different— especially in attitudes toward ethnic diversity.

When I was growing up in the '50s, being "American" and acceptable into mainstream society meant one had to assimilate, melt into one great pot where the broth was predominantly Anglo-European flavored.

No one talked about the concept of cultural diversity as a mosaic or as a tapestry of multi-colored threads that when woven together created a vibrantly rich and textured fabric. "Real Americans" were white. People of color had to think and act "white" to prove their "Americanness." And while I was growing up after the war, muted by the internment experience, it never occurred to me to question this attitude.

Not even when I was told I should not continue with a journalism major at San Jose State because I was "Oriental" and a female. There were no jobs in the field. So I changed my major to social welfare. And when I was told again by the head of Juvenile Probation Services that they could not hire me as a probation officer because the community was not "ready" for "Orientals," I did not protest—although I had been educated enough by then to know it was wrong. But that was the '50s.

Equal opportunity laws were non-existent. I remained silent, returning to the safety zone of invisibility and "don't make waves" mentality.

Rediscovering Our Histories

Then in the '60s, the Black Power movement changed forever the 10 way racial and ethnic minorities thought of themselves. Black leaders led us to rediscover our cultural backgrounds and our histories. We rediscovered our participation in and our contributions to the development of this country, and with this recognition came a sense of pride and identity.

For the first time in U.S. history, an awareness of values inherent in America's sub-cultures rose into public consciousness. We began to see that when individuals have a strong sense of identity, of pride in one's heritage, this sense of self-worth strengthens the larger society. Not only were attitudes changing in the dominant culture, but also subgroups themselves began to recognize that America is a land of immigrants, and that all immigrants had a hand in developing it.

Thirty years ago, the word "immigrant" seemed reserved for people of color, individuals from the Third World. Today, this still seems to be the prevailing myth. I hear so often the comment, "America is becoming so multi-cultural with all this immigration from Asia and south of the border." Some people are surprised or mystified or threatened by this idea that the country is becoming so diverse, when in fact, it always has been.

From the moment Portuguese and Italian sailors landed in the New World to mingle with indigenous peoples in what we now call the West Indies, America began its cross-cultural heritage. And up North, more than 500 indigenous tribes, speaking as many different languages, for centuries had lived on this vast and fertile continent.

Ethnicity is not the exclusive property of people of color. We all have ethnicity. We are descendants of individuals from China, Ireland, Ethiopia, Vietnam, El Salvador, Canada—to name a few. Ideally, Americans should not have a problem with identity; we must realize there is no need to "wanna-be ethnic"—because, in fact, we all are.

"The World Is Watching"

I would like to share an experience I had two years ago when I 15 was in Japan. I met a Japanese man, a visionary who founded a grass-roots movement called "the Sweet Potato Movement." It was a calling back to the land from the cities, the dense urban areas he referred to as the "fourth world."

He surprised me with this comment, "The world is watching America deal with its diversity. For the Japanese, America is the role model for democracy. We may be strong economically, but we need your country to lead us in human rights and values. You must succeed if democracy is to succeed around the world."

He was one of many Japanese I met who saw multi-culturalism as a pivotal test for America's democratic ideals.

I like to view our diversity as a metaphor, a microcosm of the macrocosm of a world of nations. I like to see America as a great experiment, a laboratory for testing ideals—the big test today being tolerance and cooperation. If we can't get along in our own communities because of our cultural differences, how can we expect nations around the world to co-exist peacefully?

One of our greatest challenges is to embrace our differences while seeking out the common bonds that hold us together. What are those bonds? What are those threads, the warp in the loom that sets the pattern for who we are as Americans? For me, those threads are the ideals of freedom, equality, opportunity, justice. I also include the human qualities of gratitude, generosity, curiosity and love. Those threads together provide the strength and foundation around which our individual cultural differences weave, making each and every one of us unique and interesting Americans.

As I noted earlier, there was a major shift in perception to reach 20 the point of agreement that we are, indeed, a multi-cultural society, that we began with diversity. But there is a difference between cultural diversity and cross-cultural understanding. They are not synonymous. The great opportunity now is to seek out ways to enhance cross-cultural understanding and not fall back on separatism and attitudes of "our tribe against theirs."

The Search for Scapegoats

Today, in a time of economic crisis, there are those in our political leadership who are all too ready to find scapegoats.

More and more, it seems, those scapegoats are immigrants. The voices of fear echo daily on the front pages of newspapers, in our television broadcasts: "They are different from us. They have no idea of democracy and freedom. They won't speak our language and they keep to themselves."

Those are the words used today to describe the newest Americans. How many of us who lived through the racism and internment of Japanese-Americans during World War II remember what it was like to have those words directed against one innocent group?

In 1942, we had no one to speak up for us. But after the war, empowered by the Civil Rights movement of the '60s, Japanese-Americans began a 10-year drive for redress from our government. It culminated with the passage of the Civil Liberties Act of 1988, which officially apologized for the internment.

Japanese-Americans were vindicated in the eyes of history. But 25 this victory was not for Japanese-Americans alone. It was a great victory for all Americans, for it proved our Constitution is not just a piece of parchment under glass in the National Archives. It is a living, vital contract that binds us all together as Americans.

And if that contract is broken—as it was in 1942—it is not just the rights of individuals that are threatened, but the very fabric of this nation. And we know that the fabric is woven from threads representing many different groups. If one of those threads is cut, stretched out of proportion, or bleached of color, the design becomes listless and in danger of unraveling.

I began this talk with a memory, a powerful memory, which should underline one of the ironic possibilities of living in America. Who knows what the future holds for any of us? But whatever measure of success we have achieved is because we own a certain capacity. That capacity is hope.

When I was a teenager picking strawberries on that ranch, so appropriately named "Esperanza," I did not have vision. I could not envision the future I have today. Yet, I did have an unexplainable pull to fulfill some possibility, some unknown challenge. I now know that urge to fulfill was hope, a submerged belief in my own power, in the possibility I could accomplish "something."

Today I salute the accomplishments of all people and their faith— their faith in themselves and thus, in a future for this country.

For Journals

Do you believe that there is strength in cultural diversity? Why, or why not?

For Discussion

1. Graduation speeches tend to exhort the graduates to action, but they have a reputation for being rather long and dry. Imagine yourself in the audience listening to this speech. How do you think you would have reacted, and why? What strategies does Houston use in this speech to keep her audience's attention and to enable them to follow her points? Consider language, paragraphing, and other rhetorical strategies you have studied.

2. Houston begins her speech with a memory, an anecdote, to lead into her argument. How effective do you find this strategy? What other introductions might Houston have used? Do you think that they would be more, or less, effective than the speech as given?

3. What strategies does the author use to identify with her audience? To what beliefs and values does she appeal? To what emotions?

For Writing

1. Using material developed in response to the discussion questions as a starting point, write an essay analyzing the persuasive strategies in this speech.

2. Houston writes, "Ethnicity is not the exclusive property of people of color. We all have ethnicity." Write an essay exploring your own ethnicity identity. Draw upon memories, stories, family history, oral histories, or outside research to develop and support your dominant theme.

Chicana (1994)

MARTHA SERRANO

Martha Serrano grew up in Los Angeles. In her adolescent years she was a member of a gang, but she dropped out of it to concentrate on high school studies. A recent college graduate, she plans to attend law school and work on behalf of her people. As part of a first-year writing course, Serrano wrote the essay that follows in response to writing assignment 1 at the end of this chapter.

Don't call me Hispanic. Don't call me Latina. Don't call me Mexican. Don't call me Mexican American. I want to be called Chicana. I am *mestiza*—indigenous and Spanish. My heritage is struggle and strength. I join my strength and struggle to that of my *hermanas,* my sisters. I am a woman of *Aztlan,* the southwestern United States. I don't want to be called Hispanic because I don't want people to tell me who I am and where I come from.

Most, if not all, of the people who call me Hispanic do not know that "Hispanic" is a term imposed on Americans of Latin descent by federal regulators, unprepared educators, and merchants who want our money but not us. In the mid 1970s, the U.S. Census Bureau first admitted that its 1970 census had seriously undercounted persons of Latin American descent in the United States. Under pressure from Latino activists to avoid a repetition of that mistake in the 1980 head count, the bureau searched for an all-encompassing word to describe the diverse assortment of Latin Americans living in this country: Mexican Americans and Mexican citizens, Puerto Ricans and Cuban Americans, and "other Hispanics" was the Census Bureau's solution.

The term "Hispanic" denies my cultural heritage. However, a Chicana is both Hispanic and Indian. For the Chicana, her world has been shaped by historical forces beyond the barrio and this country. My ancestors are the *conquistadores* and the conquered indigenous people of 1492. Our vanquished heritage has always haunted us and has been ignored by American historians.

The term "Chicana" is linked to my indigenous past. The roots of the word date back to the conquest of *El Valle de México.* Back then, Mexico was pronounced "meshico." The Spaniards had no letter or sound in their alphabet for the Nahuatl "sh" or hard "j" so they put an "x" in its place. In Meshico, "Mejico" became "Mexico" and "Tejas," "Texas." Mexico's Catholicism (which came from the encounter between Spaniards and Native Americans), and its food, art, and customs manifest Indian presence. Moreover, the Mexican dialect of Spanish, used to create world-famous prose and poetry, is influenced by Aztec words.

The first *mestizos* were born of Spanish soldiers and indigenous 5 maidens. This scorned underclass was called Meshicanos and evolved to shicanos, Chicanos. Culturally, in the past, the word "Chicano" was a pejorative, class-bound adjective. Latinos used to associate the word "Chicano" with violent gangsters who had nothing better to do but hang out in the street and cause trouble. Now, however, it is the root idea of a new cultural identity for my people. It reveals a growing solidarity and the development of a common social praxis. Today, the widespread use of the word signals a rebirth of pride and confidence. It embodies an ancient truth: "Man is never closer to his true self as when he is close to his community."

All Chicanos agree that being Chicano/a is more than being an American of Mexican descent; it is a way of thinking. It means being politically and culturally aware. It means knowing who you are and where you came from. It means being proud of your ethnic background and history. Most important of all, it means resisting assimilation into American mainstream society. Chicanos fight for self-determination and tackle issues facing the Chicano community. Chicanos struggle for the betterment of *La Raza,* the people.

Chicanos are *mestizos,* or the blending of two races and cultures. No matter what our differences may be, all Chicanos believe that education, especially higher education, leads to progress and the development of our community. We believe that once our people get educated, we can go to our own lawyers, doctors, architects, engineers, and others to help build a stronger and united Chicano community. However, we believe that education must contribute to the formation of a complete man or woman who truly values life and freedom. I am Chicana!

For Journals

Are there particular ways in which people categorize you that you dislike? What do you know about the origins of these labels?

For Discussion

1. Do your intellect and emotion respond in the same way to Serrano's argument? If not, how do your reactions conflict? Do you find her introduction effective? Explain your answer.

2. What connections is Serrano making between the term "Chicana" and cultural identity? What is the connection between the individual, and community, and culture in forming identity?

3. Serrano describes the history of the terms "Chicana" and "Hispanic" to support her view that the former is the better term for her identity and her people. Are you persuaded by the information she provides? Could she offer other arguments to support her view?

4. Serrano rejects the term "Hispanic" as one imposed by others. Should people be able to name and define their own ethnicity and culture as they wish?

5. Serrano writes of resisting assimilation; some of the other readings in this chapter, however, assume that assimilation is good. Working in groups or pairs in class, argue that being American does or does not entail assimilation into mainstream American society. In the process, try to come up with a working definition of assimilation for contemporary Americans.

For Writing

1. Compare and contrast Serrano's idea of cultural identity with Ellison's on Rodriguez's (this chapter). Alternatively, construct a dialogue between Serrano and Jeanne Wakatsuki Houston on claiming a cultural identity.

2. Analyze the ways in which exposure to others of your ethnic group or national origin has, or has not, helped you form an identity.

❈❈❈ *America: Open for Business* (2001)

CRAIG FRAZER, CITY OF SAN FRANCISCO

This image, along with the "United We Stand" flag posters, pervaded some American communities following the 9/11 attacks and other threats to public safety in late 2001. This poster was sponsored by the San Francisco city government in response to the economic downturn following 9/11 and was distributed throughout business and shopping areas, largely through the Chambers of Commerce; and in some cases, it was hand-delivered by the mayor and city supervisors. This design, by artist Craig Frazer, ingeniously combines motifs such as a patriotic flag and a symbol of business and consumerism.

For Journals

Reflect on the most compelling images you remember in the aftermath of 9/11.

For Discussion

1. Analyze the poster's elements, composition, and appeals to ethos, pathos, and logos. What is its message? How persuasively does it convey that message? How does this poster convey a particular image of American culture? What are the pros and cons of emphasizing shopping in this poster?

2. How do the composition, the design, the symbolism, and the argument compare with other posters you observed following 9/11?

3. How do you think societies unfriendly to the United States might interpret the image?

For Writing

1. Research and, if possible, collect or copy samples of patriotic posters used in your community or distributed on the Internet, and bring them to class to analyze themes, arguments, and appeals. Then in a collaborative writing project, being mindful of copyright laws and fair use, develop a Web site for this collection, annotating the images to include the location at which the poster was observed or obtained and an analysis of the image's persuasive appeals. Consider linking your Web page to a larger archival or library collection, perhaps through your campus library or information center.

2. Research the history of American images from early colonial days to the present; consider focusing on depictions of the American flag or on images that dominate American media in times of war or other crisis.

❋❋❋ *Disunited We Stand* (2001)

RICHARD RODRIGUEZ

Richard Rodriguez, the son of Mexican-American immigrants, was born in California and graduated from Stanford University, later earning an M.A. at Columbia University. He was enrolled in the doctoral program in English literature at the University of California at Berkeley, where he was awarded a Fulbright scholarship; he then studied in London. As a child, Rodriguez arrived at a Catholic grammar school knowing some fifty English words and was encouraged to speak English rather than his native Spanish at home; he later reflected on the experience of assimilation, particularly in his book The Hunger of Memory: The Education of Richard Rodriguez *(1982). His other books include* Days of Obligation: A Letter to My Mexican Father *(1992). His most recent books include* King's Highway *(1999) and* Movements *(1999). Currently Rodriguez works as a writer and an editor for the Pacific News Service, in addition to providing commentary for broadcast media such as PBS. The following essay was published through the Pacific News Service shortly after 9/11.*

In peace time, America is the most original nation in the world. We are the maddest, most inventive; truly a splendid disorder are we. When America goes to war, we become a nation like any other.

Nowadays, I turn on TV and hear Americans gamely stumbling through the national anthem. At an intersection yesterday, I saw a Lexus carrying a socialite alongside a pickup with a kid who was absorbing the thump-thump-thump of rap music—both cars wearing the stars and stripes.

Everywhere I walk in San Francisco, in shop windows, signs of uniform size, identical lettering, proclaim: UNITED WE STAND.

Odd. I had always assumed the reverse: That the strength of America derives from our variety and disparate opinions. Which is to say: DISUNITED WE STAND.

In today's nation of wartime unity, television comedians, newspa- 5
per columnists, Berkeley politicians and everyday loonies—indeed, anyone who might voice an eccentric opinion about Sept. 11 and our government's response—have been called down by their fellow Americans as unpatriotic.

Immediately after Sept. 11, I found it dismaying that opinion turned so uniform. And it was not until I began to hear dissenting voices—opinions I didn't necessarily share—that I knew the America I recognized had survived.

Meanwhile, from his cave emerges Osama bin Laden, a medieval villain, fondling a microphone, to describe the United States as a "Jewish-Christian alliance."

America, of course, is no such thing. America is the Enlightenment's daughter, a nation that someone like bin Laden cannot comprehend. America was created as a secular country. Which is why, today, a Buddhist, pagan, Methodist and Hindu live side by side.

In my opinion, President Bush was not only shrewd but authentically patriotic in his insistence that Muslims should be regarded by their neighbors as true Americans. Treating Muslims as Americans at this moment of history is not magnanimous, but an act essential to our nation's meaning.

My Mexican immigrant father, I remember, was never less than 10
grateful for the economic freedom of America; never wasted a moment of nostalgia for the country he had left behind. But my father was confused by the variety of America.

"There is truly no unity here; this is not a real country," my father used to remark. Coming from a Mexican village of continuity, my father found metropolitan America a puzzle.

But from the first, I was seduced by America, enchanted by the idea that a nation could be organized, disorganized around the first-person, singular pronoun.

The history of America I read was the history of a young country extending, too slowly and painfully at times, but certainly extending, the definition of "the American," decade after decade. It was a marvel to me and the source of my greatest love of this country—the way the country enlarged with every facet, every religion and race and tongue and recipe. America became the jewel of civilization.

Wartime is not the best time to see this America. In wartime, Americans are merely united; the country defines itself by what it must exclude and resist.

When I was a boy in the 1950s, I remember hearing adults talk   15 nostalgically about the way the country had been united a decade earlier. Americans in World War II had been galvanized by a sense of a shared enemy, a common purpose. "You wouldn't believe it," a neighbor lady said to me.

But in the peacetime America of the 1950s, America was drawing new worlds to itself—drawing my Mexican family to itself, even while the country was finding its meaning in its disunion.

By the late 1950s, rock 'n' roll jack-hammered a channel we named the "generation gap." And Americans of every age sped along newly constructed interstates, trying to get as far as possible from in-laws and the inner city. And my neighbor lady was getting a divorce.

I sing the American parade in peacetime: the Chinese teenager with earphones; the Russian woman in a sparkling sweater, the blue-suited Big Deal chattering into her cell phone; the tattoos and the shorts; the big bellies; the prim; the rabbinical; the anarchic.

It is true that the chaos of America can leave us melancholic and lonely. The pace and frenzied desires of our lives often leave us, more than any other people on Earth, addicted to sexual titillation, celebrity (the glamour of the oversized ego) and drugs, "recreational" and not.

There are days, I admit, when the fury of America—the determi-   20 nation of each driver to pull ahead—seems a madness and leaves me feeling that America is the thinnest culture in the world, barely a "nation."

But from the American respect for individualism would also come our nation's great originality and creativity. American culture is the mass culture of the world, because the world is hungry for an idea of itself larger than a single creed, nation or color.

This is, of course, why the religious fundamentalist, the nationalist and the tribalist must hate America.

It is nothing for me to hate in return. I loathe bin Laden—may his tribe decrease. I resent him most because he has taken away my America at peace, at frenzy, and has replaced it with a nation of uniform opinion and too little sense of its greatness.

I cannot imagine a more patriotic insult America could offer bin Laden than to become as divided in wartime as we are divided in peace.

For Journals

What are your views on American unity as it relates to 9/11?

For Discussion

1.   According to Rodriguez, diversity—of culture, of opinion—is central to American strength. Does Rodriguez support his view convincingly? Why, or why not?

2.   Rodriguez asserts that after 9/11, public opinion became uniform. Do you agree with this assessment? Do you agree with the author that dissent and divergent viewpoints are crucial? If so, how would you respond to opposing views?

3.   Does the author adequately respond to critics who would argue with his benign assessment of American culture? Do you agree that "the world is hungry for an idea of itself larger than a single creed, nation or color"?

4.   The author notes that in wartime America, as in other countries, people are united by a common enemy. Do you agree with this view? Has it been the case regarding the wars in Afghanistan and in Iraq?

5.   Do you agree with Rodriguez that America has become "the jewel of civilization," encompassing a range of religions and races? Why, or why not?

For Writing

1.   Write a brief reflection on your assessment of American unity post-9/11, perhaps focusing on the question of unity and the expression of that unity.

2.   Write a response to Rodriguez, arguing that unity in wartime is essential and is not the time for dissent. Alternatively, write an essay agreeing with Rodriguez that diversity is essential, but use different arguments to support your view.

3.   Research the home front during World War I or II. Was the response similar to the events after 9/11? Or was it closer to the response to the Korean and Vietnam wars?

4.   Compare and contrast Rodriquez's arguments regarding the benefits of diversity with the Houston essay in this chapter.

✻✻✻ In Praise of American Empire (2002)

DINESH D'SOUZA

Dinesh D'Souza (1961–) was born in Bombay, India, and is a self-identified con-
servative whose works focus on controversial areas such as race relations and ethnic
identity. He graduated Phi Beta Kappa from Dartmouth College in 1983 and previ-
ously served as senior domestic policy analyst in the Reagan White House from 1987
to 1988. Currently a fellow at the Hoover Institution in Palo Alto, California,
D'Souza most recently published What's So Great about America *(2002) and had*
previously published Illiberal Education *(1991);* The End of Racism *(1995);*
Ronald Reagan: How an Ordinary Man Became an Extraordinary Leader
(1997); and The Virtue of Prosperity: Finding Values in an Age of Techno-
Affluence *(2000). The following essay, which appeared in the* Christian Science Monitor, *ultimately asserts, "If this be the workings of empire, let us have more of it."*

America has become an empire, a fact that Americans are reluctant to admit and that critics of the United States regard with great
alarm.

Since the end of the cold war, the US has exercised an unparalleled
and largely unrivaled influence throughout the world—economically,
politically, culturally, and militarily. Critics of America, at home and
abroad, are right to worry about how US power is being used.

The critics charge that America is no different from other rapa-
cious empires that have trampled the continents in previous centuries.
Within the universities, intellectuals speak of American policies as
"neo-imperialist," because they promote the goals of empire while es-
chewing the term.

America talks about lofty ideals, the critics say, but in reality it
pursues its naked self-interest. In the Gulf War, for example, America's leaders asserted they were fighting for human rights, but in truth
they were fighting to protect US access to oil. The critics point to past
US support for dictators like Anastasio Somoza in Nicaragua, Augusto
Pinochet in Chile, Ferdinand Marcos in the Philippines, and the Shah
of Iran as evidence that Americans don't really care about democratic
ideals.

Even now the US supports unelected regimes in Pakistan, Egypt, 5
and Saudi Arabia. No wonder, the critics say, so many people around
the world are anti-American and some even resort to terrorism to
lash out.

Are the critics right? They are correct to note the extent of American influence, but wrong to suggest that the US is no different from
such colonial powers as the British, French, and Spanish that once
dominated the world. Those empires—like the Islamic, Mongol, and

Chinese empires—were sustained primarily by force. The British ruled my native country of India with some 100,000 troops.

US domination is not sustained primarily by force. True, America has bases in the Middle East and Far East, and it can intervene militarily just about anywhere in the world.

But the real power of America extends far beyond its military capabilities. Walk into a hotel in Barbados or Bombay and the bellhop is whistling the theme from "Titanic." African boys in remote villages wear baseball caps. Millions of people around the globe want to move to America. Countless people are drawn to America's technology, freedom, and way of life.

Some critics sneer that these aspirations are short-sighted. Perhaps they are right. People may be wrong to want the American lifestyle, and may not foresee its disadvantages, but at least they are seeking it voluntarily.

What about the occasions, though, when America does exercise 10 military power? Here we can hardly deny the critics' allegation that the US acts to promote its self-interest. Even so, Americans can feel immensely proud of how often their country has served their interests while simultaneously promoting noble ideals and the welfare of others. Yes, America fought the Gulf War in part to protect its oil interests, but it also fought to liberate the Kuwaitis from Iraqi invasion.

But what about long-lasting US backing for dictators, like Somoza, Pinochet, Marcos, and the shah? It should be noted that, in each case, the US eventually turned against their regimes and aided in their ouster.

In Chile and the Philippines, the outcome was favorable: The Pinochet and Marcos regimes were replaced by democratic governments that endure. In Nicaragua and Iran, however, one form of tyranny gave way to another.

These outcomes highlight a foreign-policy staple, the principle of the lesser evil. This means that one should not pursue a thing that seems good if it is likely to result in something worse. A second implication is that one is usually justified in allying with a bad guy to oppose a regime that is worse. A classic example was the American alliance with Stalin to defeat Hitler.

Thus, many US actions that support tin-pot dictators become defensible. Remember, America was fighting a cold war. If one accepts that the Soviet Union was indeed an "evil empire," then the US was right to attach more importance to Marcos and Pinochet's anti-Soviet position than to their autocratic thuggery.

Now the cold war is over, so why does America support despotic 15 regimes like those of Pervez Musharraf in Pakistan, Hosni Mubarak in Egypt, and the royal family in Saudi Arabia? Again, examine the practical alternative to those regimes.

Unfortunately there do not seem to be viable liberal, democratic parties in the Middle East. The alternative to Mr. Mubarak and the Saudi royal family appears to be Islamic fundamentalists of the bin Laden stripe. Faced with the choice between "uncompromising medievals" and "corrupt moderns," America must side with the corrupt.

Remember, also, the larger context. America is the most magnanimous imperial power ever. After leveling Japan and Germany during World War II, the US rebuilt them. For the most part, America is an abstaining superpower. It shows no real interest in conquering the rest of the world, even though it can. On occasion, the US intervenes in Grenada or Haiti or Bosnia, but it never stays to rule them.

Moreover, when America does get into a war, it is supremely careful to avoid targeting civilians. Even as US bombs destroyed the infrastructure of the Taliban, American planes dropped rations of food to avert hardship and starvation of Afghan civilians. What other country does such things?

Jeane Kirkpatrick once said that "Americans need to face the truth about themselves, no matter how pleasant it is." The reason many Americans don't feel this way is that they judge themselves by a higher standard. Thus if the Chinese, the Arabs, or the sub-Saharan Africans slaughter 10,000 of their own people, the world utters a collective sigh and resumes normal business.

By contrast, if America, in the middle of a war, accidentally bombs 20 a school and kills 200 civilians, there is an uproar and an investigation. All of this demonstrates America's evident moral superiority.

If this be the workings of empire, let us have more of it.

For Journals

Do you think of America as an empire? Why, or why not? How do you define the word?

For Discussion

1.   What connotations does the word *empire* have? Do you believe it is a positive or negative characterization of America?

2.   Outline the author's argument, noting in particular his placement of thesis, support, and refutation. How effective is this organizational plan in view of his topic and his stance on the topic? Why might the author have chosen this structure?

3.   D'Souza's paragraphs often lead with an opposing point and then respond to that point. What are the pros and cons of this arrangement? What are the advantages and disadvantages of his relatively short paragraphs, especially in a newspaper column?

4. Which of the opposing points is most effectively refuted? Which refutation do you find less convincing? Do you accept the "lesser evil" argument he uses? Do you think that D'Souza accurately summarizes the arguments he plans to refute? Why do you think he attributes some of the arguments to intellectuals? Does he bring up the most widely held opposing views? Do you detect any logical fallacies in his argument? If so, identify them.

5. D'Souza cites a choice between "uncompromising medievals" and "corrupt moderns," and asserts that America has no choice but to side with the corrupt moderns. Does he prove this case, or could this assertion be a false dilemma? Is there any middle ground with regard to this position?

6. Compare and contrast D'Souza's and Phillips's (this chapter) arguments regarding America as an empire. Which persuasive appeals are most prominent in each? How does each provide support and refute opposing views? Do the writers equally well establish their authority and credibility?

For Writing

1. Drawing on your response to for discussion item 6, write an essay comparing the arguments by D'Souza and Phillips, paying particular attention to one or two key elements, such as use of evidence or refutation.

2. Write a response to D'Souza, either refuting his position or several of his arguments, or agreeing with his view but offering different evidence. Alternatively, write an essay analyzing D'Souza'a argument. Focus particularly on his appeals to logic. Does he construct a sound argument? Do you detect fallacies?

3. Research some of the historical events D'Souza refers to in this essay, either in America's past or in other countries' histories. For example, you could research the role of the British in the history of India, or twentieth-century conflicts in Central America.

✿✿✿ *Hegemony, Hubris, and Overreach* (2003)

KEVIN PHILLIPS

Author and political analyst Kevin Phillips is the former editor-publisher of The American Political Report, a contributing columnist for the Los Angeles Times *and the* Wall Street Journal, *and a regular commentator for National Public Radio. He was a commentator for CBS-TV News at the 1984, 1988, and 1992 Democratic and Republican national conventions. Phillips's books include* The Emerging Republican Majority *(1969),* The Politics of Rich and Poor *(1990),* The Cousins Wars *(1999), and* Wealth and Democracy: A Political History of the American Rich

(2002) in which he explores the relationship between politics and wealth. Some review-ers of his work have called him a "modern Thomas Paine." The essay that follows, for which he also drew on his book Wealth and Democracy, *was written for inclusion in* The Iraq War Reader *(2003).*

Let us leave for the news analysts and cameras the short-term con-sequences of deploying the United States military to establish a *de facto* U.S. protectorate or sphere of influence in the region between the Per-sian Gulf, the Caspian Sea and the Khyber Pass. This inquiry is aimed at a less-discussed subject: the long-term effects on a leading world economic power of hubris and overreach in the projection of its power as a hegemon.*

To put things in plain English, I am talking about the past pow-ers—Britain most recently, Holland back when New York was New Amsterdam, and Hapsburg Spain when hidalgos named Coronado, DeSoto and Ponce De Leon were crisscrossing what is now the United States—and how they ruined their economies by going one or two wars too far. Given the present levels of U.S. individual, corporate, na-tional and international debts and payments imbalances, there is good reason to worry about a similar fate for the United States developing over the next ten or twenty years.

The hubris of the Bush White House and cabinet hardly needs elaboration. Satisfaction with the republic of yesteryear is no longer enough, and talk of empire is open in Washington. Unfortunately, this cockiness also has precedents: the arrogance of Edwardian Britain, the smugness of Holland's bankers to the world, the military hauteur of the Great Armada and the crack Castilian regiments.

Readers unfamiliar with the commercial and economic circum-stances of the three can glean the attitudes, if not the cold statistics, from the following displays of pride. A late 16th century Spaniard ob-served, "Let London manufacture those fine fabrics . . . Holland her chambrays, Florence her cloth; the Indies their beaver and vicuna; Milan her broaches; India and Flanders their linens . . . so long as our capital can enjoy them. The only thing it proves is that all nations train journeymen for Madrid and that Madrid is the queen of parliaments, for all the world serves her, and she serves nobody."

The most conspicuous Dutch boast was expressed in the imagery 5 decorating the exterior of the great Amsterdam town hall begun in the glory year of 1648, which showed that city receiving the tributes of four continents—Europe, Africa, Asia, and America—while a Dutch Atlas, unaided, supported the globe on his back.

---

*Editor's Note: *Hegemon,* one who exercises hegemony, or the holding of predominant influence over a state, country, or region; to some it indicates not only influence but also domination.

In Britain, economist W. S. Jevons caught the assurance of the Victorian Era: "The plains of North America and Russia are our cornfields: Chicago and Odessa are our granaries; Canada and the Baltic are our timber forests, Australia contains our sheep farms, and in Argentina and on the Western prairies of North America are our herds of oxen: Peru sends her silver, and the gold of South Africa and Australia flows to London; the Hindus and Chinese grow tea for us, and our coffee, sugar and spice plantations are all in the Indies, Spain and France are our vineyards, and the Mediterranean our fruit garden."

Not any longer, of course. Today's over-extended empire has its seat in Washington, where happy-talk economists write similar speeches for treasury officials and Sun Belt congressmen. But let us now return to the premise of this analysis: that nothing matches war for undoing a leading economic power that is decades past its absolute global zenith (1945–50 for us) yet is at the peak of its glorious self-perception and elite sense of global entitlement.

The 9/11 terrorist attack on the United States produced a proper and effective retaliation in Afghanistan. There is less to be said for the metamorphosis of that response into a broader ambition to subdue, dominate and reshape an area that stretches northwest from the Persian Gulf to the Caucasus and eastward to Afghanistan and Central Asia. History may describe the Balkans as a burial ground of great power ambition, but the geopolitical lessons of this part of the world have been just as brutal for would-be hegemons from Alexander the Great to Russia and Britain.

Early military results are not a reliable long-term yardstick. From European Macedonia, Alexander got as far as present-day Pakistan, Hitler almost made it to the oil-rich Caucasus in 1942, and Russian and British troops held Kabul, Afghanistan, for a number of years during their respective attempts to subdue it. Thus the irony: military success in 2003 could be a long-term minus, while defeat could have aspects of a silver lining.

The Spanish, Dutch and British experiences with war and over- 10 reach are instructive. Fifteen years ago, Yale Professor Paul Kennedy offered lessons that are still just as relevant today about the succession of mistakes made by Spain at its peak. The costly failure of the Great Armada sent against England in 1588 was followed by the royal bankruptcy of 1596. Next, the deepening decline in gold and silver shipments from the new world made an economic disaster out of Spain's lengthy, draining military embroilment in Europe's Thirty Years War (1618–1648). By the time the war ended, the nation's hegemony in Europe was over and its economy a shambles.

It is not generally realized how far-flung was the global reach of the Dutch, whose new maritime nation succeeded Hapsburg Spain as the leading world economic power of the 17th century. At its peak in the middle of the century, the de facto empire of the Dutch Republic stretched from stations in Japan to control of Manhattan, from the Spice Islands of current-day Indonesia to Africa's Cape of Good Hope, the Caribbean and territories adjacent to Brazil.

In retrospect, the Dutch, who were already beginning to lose some territory in the 1660s and 1670s, overreached in 1688 when William of Orange, their hereditary ruler, also took the crown of England. The result was a war with France that wound up, a few intermissions notwithstanding, lasting almost a quarter of a century. By the time the Dutch emerged from the military and economic stress of that encounter, they had dissipated their onetime naval and commercial hegemony, lost vital markets, industries and more overseas possessions, and taken on enough wartime debt to double interest rates. Within a few decades, the only clear leadership they retained was in one aspect of finance—lending to foreign rulers and governments.

The chronology of British decline is more recent and better remembered. The zenith in Britain's share of world manufacturing and trade came in the 1850s and 1860s, but the man in the street did not feel the change in the tides of world industry until the 1890s and 1900s. For Britain's aristocracy and financiers, the peak of overseas investment and imperial splendor and hubris did not come until the 1900–1914 period. The Boer War of 1899–1901 had brought some military burdens and unexpected budget demands, but concerns about these were quickly pushed aside by Kipling's cultural nationalism and the battleship race with Germany.

Some forty years have passed since a hit show "Oh What a Lovely War" opened in London, but the title, and the words and music, are as evocative and appropriate today as they were then. The great conflict that was to be remembered as "the deluge" began in August 1914 with the cheers of a huge crowd in Trafalgar Square. In an intermediate stage, it was hailed as "the war to end all wars." What it ended instead was Britain's status as the leading world economic power. Even before 1914, the United States had moved ahead of Britain in manufacturing, and the First World War put New York on a level with London as an international financial center. Now, all of a sudden, the United States had become the global lender, Britain the borrower required to sell assets. World War Two, of course, completed the process. By 1947–48, the British people were living under food rationing more suited to a loser than victor, and Britain maintained its financial footing only with the assistance of the U.S. Treasury Department.

Do these Hapsburg, Dutch and British examples hold out a warning to the United States? I think so. America's first war with Iraq in 1991 was actually a money-making proposition because Washington   15 was able to pass the hat to other members of the coalition, including Japan and Saudi Arabia. Many billions were raised this way. Of course, that was when we had a true coalition of the fiscally willing.

The possibilities discussed for 2003, by contrast, carried a steep price tag. The estimates for U.S. military outlays ranged between $50 and $200 billion. The rewards-cum-compensation offered to allies varied from $5 to 15 billion for Turkey down to relative peanuts for the *borscht* republics of Eastern Europe counting on weapons overhauls and marching-around money in return for their war endorsements. The occupation and rebuilding of Iraq was down for another $75 billion. All of this, moreover, presumed that nothing much would go wrong militarily.

The trouble is that things can go wrong *economically* even if, initially at least, they don't go wrong *militarily*. Gaining a *de facto* protectorate over such a large unstable region could turn out to be less an opportunity—to gain hegemony over Iraqi resources, expand regional oil production and lower prices—than a potential burden. Despite the difficulty in making comparisons across centuries, there is a chance that such a role could begin the U.S. equivalent of the Hapsburg, Dutch and British draining experiences of 1618–1648, 1688–1713 and 1914–1945.

Certainly the current context of U.S. indebtedness argues for caution, but one gets the sense that either the favorable petroleum calculus dominates or the supply-side theorists manning the economic battlements in Washington simply cannot stand to let the prospect of possibly limitless deficits interrupt a reverie. The extent to which debt and interest burdens were part of what choked Spain, the Netherlands and Britain in their days becomes all the more relevant when one considers that the United States is already the world's leading debtor, to the tune of some $2 trillion. The economic hubris displayed here could turn out to match the geopolitical and military hauteur.

Actually, it probably already has. The federal budget deficit is already returning to the dollar levels that worried policymakers during the 1990–1991 confrontation with Iraq. Worse, because the United States manufactures and produces less and less of what it physically requires, the U.S. current account deficit is now closing in on $500 billion a year, roughly 5% of Gross Domestic Product.

Borrowing on this level is only sustainable when foreigners want 20 to invest in U.S. stocks, bonds, property or industry on a very large scale and when they have faith in the valuation of the U.S. dollar and the wisdom of U.S. leadership. If they turn sour on the U.S., there is the potential—no one can set the odds—for an economic disaster. The U.S. is already within fumbling distance of the record British current account deficit—in the 6–7% range—that prevailed in 1947–48 when Britain, for all practical purposes, was on a financial respirator.

Recent policies of the United States—from doctrines of pre-emptive war to insults exchanged with European allies and actions that often appear to reflect an anti-Muslim bias—have dissipated much of the international goodwill extended after 9/11 and created a new global surge of anti-Americanism that clearly adds to the threat. International support for the United States in matters of economics and in its efforts to control of global terrorism has never been more important, but military hubris and geopolitical chutzpah verging on unilateralism may put such support in jeopardy.

The United States is not *sui generis*. God does not march under the American flag. We may come to regret pretending otherwise.

For Journals

What comparisons do you make between contemporary America and other powerful societies in history such as the British Empire or the Hapsburg dynasty?

For Discussion

1. In the opening paragraph, what is the writer's stance toward the topic? What voice, or sense of the author, comes through in the language? What approach to the topic does the introduction forecast?

2. Examine the form and structure of the essay. Identify the author's thesis and main supporting points. What is the current American policy under discussion, and how does Phillips contextualize this policy by drawing connections to other historical events? How does the author use transitions to link points, draw parallels, develop ideas, introduce contrasting information, or anticipate opposing views?

3. How does the author differentiate between military and economic success and failure? How does this distinction enter into his argument?

4. Does Phillips convincingly argue his case? Do you accept the premise that we should consider current U.S. policy in light of earlier historical examples? Do you find his examples relevant enough and parallel enough to support his central premise?

For Writing

1. Compare and contrast Phillips's thesis with that of Dinesh D'Souza earlier in this chapter with regard to the idea of American empire.

2. Research one of the examples included in this essay, such as British or Dutch political and economic power, or economic conditions following World War I or II. Assess to what degree Phillips's thesis is supported by your research.

3. Assess the current state of postwar Iraq, focusing on reconstruction, U.S. troop presence, policy in the region, or oil and economic fallout from the war. Document your results, and share them with peers in an oral report or presentation as well as in your researched essay. Consider a group project in which you and your classmates research different aspects of current U.S. policy or military action in Iraq or Afghanistan and in which you combine your findings and present them on a Web page.

⚘⚘ *Film: Bowling for Columbine* (2002)

MICHAEL MOORE

Michael Moore was born in Flint, Michigan, where his father and most of his relatives worked in General Motors automobile factories. Moore was elected to the local school board at 18 and later founded and edited The Flint Voice *(later* The Michigan Voice)*. He was a commentator on National Public Radio and briefly worked at* Mother Jones *magazine before writing, producing, directing, and narrating* Roger and Me *(1989), an ironic film focusing on the effects of factory closings on the town and people of Flint. In 2002, Moore produced the documentary* Bowling for Columbine, *an ironic examination of American media and gun-obsessed culture.*

For Journals

This film contains both serious and ironically comic elements. Write a journal entry reflecting on your emotional response to the film and to its subject matter.

For Discussion

1. Comment on the techniques of narrative in the film, exploring, for example, the ways in which the filmmaker juxtaposes music, images, situations, and narrative. How do these techniques contribute to the film's persuasiveness?

2. How pervasive is irony in the film? Give examples, considering such scenes or examples as the bank, the fundraiser, the Kosovo bombings, and the Lockheed Martin plant.

3. Which image, scene, or point did you find most compelling? Why? Cite material from the film to support your view.

4. What appeals to ethos, logos, and pathos pervade the film? How does the author establish authority?

5. Although the film is often described as examining America's gun obsession, what other themes or points are prominent? What is the relevance of the "culture of fear" to other points discussed in the film?

For Writing

1.   Take a specific example or scene from the film and analyze it, particularly in the ways that it illustrates a larger point or theme in the film. How does the scene implicitly or explicitly convey a point?

2.   Write a review of the film for your school paper, your class, or a friend. Would you recommend it? Why, or why not? In your review, remember to introduce the topic, develop a dominant impression or core assertion, and then briefly summarize the plot before analyzing the film's strengths and weaknesses.

Chapter Writing Assignments

1.   Write a memoir, a narrative, or an autobiography that conveys a sense of your personal identity as an American and what the term *American* means to you. Review the readings by Ellison, Standing Bear, Serrano, and Rodriguez to find ways in which these authors developed their self-definition or search for identity. Be sure to determine a specific focus or claim about your identity rather than stringing together examples or anecdotes without a persuasive intent.

2.   Investigate past or contemporary issues in immigration policy. Examine how people are defined as American citizens, who is a citizen automatically and who must apply, what kinds of restrictions are in place, whether different categories of immigrants are able to enter in higher numbers, and why. Some research questions you might consider include the following: What kinds of immigrants does American policy favor? How can definitions be used to favor particular groups? In what ways have policies changed over the years? Present your thesis and findings in an essay that documents this research.

3.   Imagine that you are an advertising copywriter who has been asked to create a public relations campaign for a political candidate that defines the best that America and Americans have to offer. The audience is a group of U.S. citizens. Sketch out your strategy, propose it to your client, and argue that your strategy will be effective.

Alternatively, design a campaign for a U.S. tourism organization that will target an overseas audience from a country or region you designate. It might be interesting, for example, to devise a campaign encouraging citizens of countries of the former Soviet Union to visit the United States.

4.   In recent years, scholars, activists, and students have been discussing the notion of "identity politics"—or the belief that people from nondominant cultures should define themselves rather than have

identities imposed on them by others. Martha Serrano's essay is an example of the kinds of debate revolving around conflicts between how people identify themselves and how others define them. Research this concept in recent periodicals, and write an essay explaining the concept to your classmates or other peer group. Alternatively, argue for a redefinition of an ethnic group or culture with which you identify.

5. Browse non-U.S. Web sites, and research either the attitudes toward and characterization of America or Americans, or compare and contrast divergent accounts of a prominent event or news story, examining American and non-U.S. Web sites. If you do not speak a foreign language, locate an English-language version of a site, or use an English-speaking nation's site, such as from Australia, Ireland, Canada, or Britain, being mindful of historical and political alliances and their influence on the point of view.

6. Locate a non-U.S. travel book describing America, Americans, and travel to the United States. Analyze the assumptions about Americans and American cultures evident in the book.

Web Sites for Further Exploration

Library of Congress
http://www.loc.gov/

Ellis Island (Immigration)
http://www.ellisisland.com

The Tocqueville Connection (French/American News and Analysis)
http://www.ttc.org/aboutocq.htm

Pacific News Service
http://news.pacificnews.org/news/

National Archives and Records Administration
http://www.archives.gov/index.html

Asian American Resources
http://www.ai.mit.edu/people/irie/aar/

6

✽✽✽

American Dreams

T he selections in this chapter revolve around the most familiar but elusive expression of the American national character, the American dream. It is an expression that turns up everywhere in our culture; open any newspaper or watch any news program, and you will probably find more samples like these:

- An African American banker helps provide mortgages to minority applicants. The headline of the newspaper story is "The American Dream"; the subtitle is "Doing Well by Doing Good."
- Three promising navy officers, a woman and two men, are killed in a double murder and suicide. The news story focuses on the poignancy of the loss by pointing out that all three officers were on the way to achieving the American dream.
- A teenage television actor becomes wealthy and famous; a television magazine program reporting on his newfound stardom calls it an example of achieving the American dream.

As these examples show, the American dream is so well established—both as an expression and as an idea—that no one feels the need to define it; however, no one seems to agree on exactly what it means. Perhaps the closest we can come is to say that the American dream represents both what Americans believe themselves entitled to and what they believe themselves capable of. In other words, it is the promise inherent in the idea of America itself.

The idea of America actually began with a mistake; Renaissance Europeans in search of a route to the East Indies stumbled on it. As the famous naval historian Samuel Eliot Morrison remarked, they spent the next fifty years trying to get around it or through it. Actually finding such a continent, even by accident, had exciting and unsettling impact on the European imagination. As a result, early European dreams about America reflected a curious combination of fantasy and science

171

fiction. Writers who had never been to America described Native Americans with feathers sprouting from their feet, precious stones growing out of their chests, heads that grew from below their shoulders, no government, no private property, a taste for cannibalism, and a life span of 150 years.

Of course the reality was very different, and dreams changed, from the discovery of golden cities to the acquisition of land for farming. But two early elements were fixed—that America represented the possibility of prosperity and that whoever came here could make a new start.

From the beginning, then, the American dream has existed as a series of evolving promises and discrepancies, of continuous conflicts and renewed possibilities for achievement, and of the tension between faith in a glorious promise and the more difficult task of making that promise come true under less-than-ideal conditions. These contradictions are elements in a three-hundred-year debate that continues to this day, because, although most Americans believe in the American dream, there is much disagreement on its particulars. We argue about what the dream consists of—money, social equality, power, success, democratic ideals; we argue about the means to achieve it—hard work, luck, aggressiveness, drive or the will to succeed at any cost; we argue about who is entitled to it—long-term residents, new immigrants, everyone, or just the lucky few. And finally, we argue over how much each person is entitled to—the complete fulfillment of his or her dream, or just the right to compete?

American Dreams through History

The selections in this chapter reflect reality and myth, coexisting contradictions, disappointing experience, and renewed optimism in pursuing the American dream. The built-in paradox of the dream is that everyone thinks he or she knows what it is, but it remains fuzzy around the edges, even unstable, and needs to stay that way to suit changing aspirations. Some of the factors that contributed to it are still discernable, though: apparently limitless natural resources; an economics of relatively unfettered capitalism; the Protestant biblical metaphor that identified the arrival of the English in the American wilderness with the arrival of the children of Israel in the Promised Land or the land of milk and honey; the early importation of Africans as a slave labor force; a social mobility for whites such as existed nowhere else; and a belief that in a new place far from a constrained European caste system, arrivals could forget their pasts, create new lives, and gain the material wealth that was determined in Europe more by class and inheritance than by initiative.

Our first two selections are by men who lived some portion of the American dream so completely and in such an extreme fashion that they left a permanent mark on our consciousness, even though hardly anyone can duplicate their experiences. The first and more famous is Benjamin Franklin. If any one American can be said to have codified the most common parameters of the American dream, he's it. The most popular and least understood of the founding fathers, he is associated in the public mind with kite flying and electricity; with the slogans of one of his many spokespersons, Poor Richard ("Early to bed and early to rise, makes a man healthy, wealthy and wise; a stitch in time saves nine," etc.); and with making a lot of money. But he was in fact a genius and a polymorph, an enormous contributor to pure science, applied science, diplomacy, languages, business, and public service. His great talent for friendship and an ability to laugh at himself were as crucial to his ability to improve communities as his belief in the possibilities of individual achievement, and his *Autobiography* is still the model for all subsequent American success stories. Our first selection contains its most famous scene, seventeen-year-old Franklin's arrival in Philadelphia. Walking down the wharf, eating a roll, and looking around him, he enters American history. For him, and for his young country, anything seems possible.

The second exceptional embodiment of the dream, that part of it which is associated with the poor man who attains great wealth, is Andrew Carnegie, one of the most interesting and complex of the nineteenth-century entrepreneurs. These men—who tended not to be the first explorers or woodsmen, but more likely fur traders like Jacob Astor, businessmen, ship builders—factory owners, and railroad builders—had enormous energy and often considerable ruthlessness—characteristics that would be perfectly at home on Wall Street in the 1990s. They made their fortunes expanding, developing, and often stealing access to the country's resources, industrial power, and technological possibilities. Carnegie was unusal both in the poverty of his background and in the stupendous power he came to exercise. Arriving in the United States as a poverty-stricken Scottish immigrant of twelve, he made a huge fortune in coal and railroads. What was different about him was an apparent conflict between his drive to succeed on an unparalleled scale and an inheritance of social activism that he got from his immediate family, who had experienced discrimination and displacement in Scotland. The result was that on the one hand, Carnegie was extremely rich, and on the other hand, he felt the need to address wealth as a burden and a responsibility as well as a privilege. Later in his life he devoted himself to philanthropic activities—establishing free libraries, the school that became Carnegie-Mellon, and the Carnegie Endowment for Peace, among others. In his famous essay "Wealth," excerpted in this chapter, he proposes the rather unusual

idea that the best thing rich men can do for themselves and their children is to give away all their money. The closest contemporary American figure to Carnegie in terms of the decision to devote a vast
acquired fortune to good causes and foundation grants seems to be
Microsoft founder Bill Gates, but Gates was raised in very comfortable
circumstances and seems unburdened by Carnegie's sense of guilt.

Of course, for most immigrants, who might have known
Carnegie's name but who lived, for all practical purposes, in a parallel
universe, making the step from poverty to working-class existence, or
especially into the middle class, was complicated, commonplace, and
traumatic. The Spanish, Engish, and French immigrants of the seventeenth and eighteenth centuries had been succeeded by immigrants
from Ireland, Germany, China, and eastern and southern Europe, and
later by people from Central and South America and southeastern
Asia. The pattern that dominated their arrivals in America involved a
continual, often painful effort to find a community, get a job, overcome the prejudices and hatreds of whoever had preceeded them,
maybe learn enough English to manage, and try to give their children
a step up—to education, or at least some kind of employment. Chinese
Americans, who came to escape political turmoil at home, worked in
the Gold Rush. They had the extra burden of struggling not only
against the usual stresses but also against especially harsh and bla-
tantly exclusionary anti-Chinese laws to which they were subject. Sui
Sin Far was half-Anglo and half-Chinese and therefore blessed or
cursed with a unique perspective. In "In the Land of the Free," she examines the results of miscommunication and differing cultural values
in an encounter between a young Chinese immigrant mother and the
well-meaning but uncomprehending American woman who disrupts
her life, and that of her child, with tragic consequences.

The dream remained equally elusive for some of the people who
had lived in America the longest. Langston Hughes, the African
American poet, writer, and leader in the great cultural explosion of the
Harlem Renaissance in the 1920s, repeatedly questioned why the
dream of success and equality that was so clear in theory remained so
inaccessible in practice to so many. Both angry and hopeful, he wrote a
series of poems, including "Let America Be America Again," in which
he underlined the contradictions between the dream of opportunity
and fulfillment and a much grimmer reality, between what America
held out as a promise and what it delivered. As an African American,
he became a voice not only for his own ancestors and comtemporaries
but also for all the Americans he saw as dispossessed, and for the
dream he believed in, evidence to the contrary.

A decade after Hughes wrote so hopefully about the possibilities
of a new American rebirth, however, the country was in the midst of
the Great Depression, an economic disaster so enormous that it made

an indelible impression on those who lived through it. Fifteen million people were out of work. The poor got poorer, and, more than at any other time in our history, the middle class, the primary carriers of belief in the rewards of work and the inevitability of success, found themselves unemployed. The savings of a lifetime disappeared when banks failed; frugality and honesty were not rewarded; and confidence in one's ability to mold the future was destroyed.

Margaret Bourke-White, a famous photographer for *Life* and *Time* magazines, took many pictures of Americans coping with the terrors of the Depression; one of her best photos, the ironically titled "There's No Way like the American Way," captures an image of poor people juxtaposed with an image of a rich, secure America that seems utterly distant from their experience.

America didn't fully recover from the Great Depression until the beginning of World War II, when the need for war matériel put factories on overtime and created an immense need for laborers. As soon as the war ended and the men returned home, though, traditional roles reasserted themselves. Women were rerouted out of the defense plants and back into domestic life with a vengeance. Magazines like *Woman's Day* emphasized not their lost earning power but their ability to make a good tuna casserole. Men, on the other hand, were expected to provide more and more material proof of their own success at the office: the split-level ranch house in the suburbs, the healthy 2.3 children, and an ever-changing model of American-made car. But understandably, that was what returning soldiers wanted: jobs, marriage, children, a home, a good job. The late 1940s and the 1950s were a time of economic growth for many Americans, who found themselves moving from lower-class to middle-class life, owning property, working in secure blue-collar jobs with good benefits or white-collar office jobs, going to college on the G.I. Bill, and building the life their parents never had.

However, while millions of Americans enthusiastically pursued the vision of suburban fulfillment, African Americans, as usual, were still largely excluded from the new prosperity. African American soldiers who fought for their country in World War II returned to find that jobs, houses, and good education were as difficult to come by as ever. There were some changes. President Truman had desegregated the armed forces in 1948 by executive order, and a Supreme Court case the same year overturned a real estate transaction in which a clause called a restrictive covenant could forbid selling to someone of a particular color or religion. But in 1951, Jim Crow was still the only way of life in the South, and African American migration to the big northern and midwestern cities had shifted rather than eliminated a struggle to survive. Langston Hughes, ever sensitive and responsive to the situation, made his discontent explicit in a short, powerful, and angry poem, "Harlem," which forms a kind of psychological companion piece to "Let America Be America Again." By now the dream of diverse populations finding common cause in their mutual political and economic disenfranchisement has been replaced by a grim impatience.

But the nobler sense of possibility that Hughes had articulated in his poetry never completely disappeared. It was the ethical underpinning of the civil rights movement, and in 1963, thirty years after Hughes made his plea for a renewed commitment to the American dream, Martin Luther King, Jr., made the most famous American speech of the twentieth century: the partly extemporaneous address at the Lincoln Memorial, "I Have a Dream." At the time, southern blacks could not share a water fountain, a beach, a bus seat, a schoolroom, or a voting booth with southern whites; in fact, they couldn't vote at all. King, a believer in the power of nonviolent resistance, had already led a successful bus boycott in Montgomery, Alabama, and a long series of marches, demonstrations, and sit-ins at ordinary places like lunch counters; he had been arrested by southern sheriffs and was the frequent recipient of death threats. But a huge civil rights march in Washington, D.C., gave him the opportunity to address a larger American audience and to locate civil rights at the political center of the American dream, to make one the expression of the other.

These two strains of the American dream—the ideals of opportunity and achievement based on character, perseverance, and fairness, versus the charms of getting rich quick, winning or borrowing money, and keeping ahead of, rather than even with, the Joneses—continue to dominate contemporary American life. Jacob Weisberg, the editor of an on-line magazine, explores in "United Shareholders of America" the debilitating effects of stock market madness on middle-class Americans. He sees the passion for betting one's future on rising stock prices as yet another instance of how short Americans' memories are; not only have they forgotten the causes of the Great Depression, but also they still think that they can circumvent the less glamorous paths to the dream, like saving money, by engaging in what is effectively a different kind of sweepstakes.

On a somewhat more hopeful note, urban studies expert Witold Rybczynski visits a new community, Celebration, which attempts to reinvigorate the American sense of community while accommodating it to the computer age, in effect seeking the best of the past and the present. The fact that "Tomorrowland," as he calls it, was built by the Disney Corporation raises interesting issues about how much the American dream owes to both nostalgia and self-perpetuated mythology.

If Rybczynski sees Celebration as at least an attempt at creating an idealized American community, David Putnam sees the deterioration of social networks and community support in this country as the most serious of the last twenty years. In "Bowling Alone" he examines the falling away of civic responsibility and involvement, what he calls "social capital," and he challenges us to reweave our sense of self—in our neighborhoods, with friends, and with a sense of the public welfare that registers more than our material well-being.

As a visual representaton of Putnam's point, we have Edward Hopper's painting "Office in a Small City," one of Hopper's most beautiful and sympathetic renditions of isolation and alienation in his beloved urban landscape.

In the next two readings, two other writers establish their own particular connections to the American dream by reinvigorating its past. First, in his essay on "Let America Be America Again," student Chris Countryman, analyzing the poem seventy years after Hughes wrote it, proves how eloquent the voice of a poet can be, shaping lines and stanzas, and arguing that the best way for the American dream to be realized is for America to return to its first, best promises. Then Clayborne Carson, Professor of History and Editor-in-Chief of the Martin Luther King Papers Project at Stanford University, looks back forty years at the hot August day in 1963 when he was a teenager and his father took him to the Washington Mall to hear Dr. King speak. Whatever remains unfulfilled about King's dream, it is probably impossible to calculate all the social capital that it generated, but in "The March—40 years later," Professor Carson recaptures the beginning of what would turn out to be for him his life's work. Like Putnam, he believes in a sense of history that is reflective and constructive, but not nostalgic.

Our last reading, is Jon Gertner's article "The Futile Pursuit of Happiness," and, as the title suggests, it questions whether Americans have ever really known what makes them feel good to begin with. Research results suggest that getting what we want, at least materially, doesn't make us as happy as we thought it would in the long term. This is a somewhat disconcerting counterweight to the idea that the more we buy, the better we feel. But it is not entirely a bleak assessment. As one of the researchers suggests, Americans live in hope, and that characteristic, too, is part of the American dream.

Finally, *Citizen Kane,* probably the most highly regarded American film ever made, traces the life of the fabulously wealthy Charles Foster Kane, who has brilliance and money and power to spare but who turns out to have both too much and too little of everything. Neither a Franklin nor a Carnegie, but with aspirations towards both, he gives the dream a gloriously dramatic form and an almost tragic resonance.

All selections in this chapter, separated as they are by time and distance, speak to us in distinct and recognizable American voices. In Chapter 5, you read about Americans trying to establish their identities by defining, for themselves as much as for anyone else, who an

American is. This chapter's selections continue that process by trying to express what Americans want and what they feel are their unique opportunities; the selections appeal to a common sense of possibility that both shapes our ambitions and survives our experience.

✳✳✳ FROM *The Autobiography* (1771)

BENJAMIN FRANKLIN

Benjamin Franklin (1706–1790) had established himself as a printer, writer, and public servant in Philadelphia, the biggest city in the colonies, by the time he was twenty-four years old. He was able to retire at forty-two and spend the rest of his life in service to science, philanthropy, and the young country he helped to found. He also found time to teach himself several languages, start America's first lending library and first fire department, invent the Franklin stove and bifocals, and lay the basis for the American Philosophical Society and the University of Pennsylvania. A hugely successful American representative in France and an early supporter of the abolition of slavery, he wrote of himself with a characteristic mixture of objectivity and self-mockery.

My brother had, in 1720 or 21, begun to print a newspaper. It was the second that appeared in America, and was called the *New England Courant.* The only one before it was the *Boston News-Letter.* I remember his being dissuaded by some of his friends from the undertaking, as not likely to succeed, one newspaper being, in their judgment, enough for America. At this time (1771) there are not less than five-and-twenty. He went on, however, with the undertaking, and after having worked in composing the types and printing off the sheets, I was employed to carry the papers through the streets to the customers.

He had some ingenious men among his friends, who amused themselves by writing little pieces for this paper, which gained it credit and made it more in demand, and these gentlemen often visited us. Hearing their conversations, and their accounts of the approbation their papers were received with, I was excited to try my hand among them; but, being still a boy, and suspecting that my brother would object to printing anything of mine in his paper if he knew it to be mine, I contrived to disguise my hand and, writing an anonymous paper, I put it in at night under the door of the printing-house. It was found in the morning and communicated to his writing friends when they called in as usual. They read it, commented on it in my hearing, and I had the exquisite pleasure of finding it met with their approbation, and that, in their different guesses at the author, none were named but men of some character among us for learning and ingenuity. I suppose now that I was rather lucky in my judges, and that perhaps they were not really so very good ones as I then esteemed them.

Encouraged, however, by this, I wrote and conveyed in the same way to the press several more papers which were equally approved; and I kept my secret till my small fund of sense for such performances was pretty well exhausted, and then I discovered it, when I began to be considered a little more by my brother's acquaintance, and in a manner that did not quite please him, as he thought, probably with reason, that it tended to make me too vain. And perhaps this might be one occasion of the differences that we began to have about this time. Though a brother, he considered himself as my master, and me as his apprentice, and accordingly expected the same services from me as he would from another, while I thought he demeaned me too much in some he required of me, who from a brother expected more indulgence. Our disputes were often brought before our father, and I fancy I was either generally in the right, or else a better pleader, be cause the judgment was generally in my favor. But my brother was passionate, and had often beaten me, which I took extremely amiss; and, thinking my apprenticeship very tedious, I was continually wishing for some opportunity or shortening it, which at length offered in a manner unexpected.

One of the pieces in our newspaper on some political point, which I have now forgotten, gave offense to the Assembly. He was taken up, censured, and imprisoned for a month, by the speaker's warrant, I suppose because he would not discover his author. I too was taken up and examined before the council; but, though I did not give them any satisfaction, they contented themselves with admonishing me, and dismissed me, considering me, perhaps, as an apprentice who was bound to keep his master's secrets.

During my brother's confinement, which I resented a good deal, 5 notwithstanding our private differences, I had the management of the paper; and I made bold to give our rulers some rubs in it, which my brother took very kindly, while others began to consider me in an unfavorable light, as a young genius that had a turn for libeling and satire. My brother's discharge was accompanied with an order of the House (a very odd one), that "James Franklin should no longer print the paper called the *New England Courant.*"

There was a consultation held in our printing-house among his friends what he should do in this case. Some proposed to evade the order by changing the name of the paper; but my brother seeing inconveniences in that, it was finally concluded on as a better way to let it be printed for the future under the name of *Benjamin Franklin,* and to avoid the censure of the Assembly, that might fall on him as still printing it by his apprentice, the contrivance was that my old indenture should be returned to me, with a full discharge on the back of it, to be shown on occasion; but to secure to him the benefit of my service, I was to sign new indentures for the remainder of the term, which were to be kept private. A very flimsy scheme it was; however, it was immediately executed, and the paper went on accordingly under my name for several months.

At length, a fresh difference arising between my brother and me, I took upon me to assert my freedom, presuming that he would not venture to produce the new indentures. It was not fair in me to take this advantage, and this I therefore reckon one of the first errata of my life; but the unfairness of it weighed little with me when under the impression of resentment for the blows his passion too often urged him to bestow upon me, though he was otherwise not an ill-natured man; perhaps I was too saucy and provoking.

When he found I would leave him, he took care to prevent my getting employment in any other printing-house of the town, by going round and speaking to every master, who accordingly refused to give me work. I then thought of going to New York, as the nearest place where there was a printer; and I was rather inclined to leave Boston when I reflected that I had already made myself a little obnoxious to the governing party, and, from the arbitrary proceedings of the Assembly in my brother's case, it was likely I might, if I stayed, soon bring myself into scrapes; and father, that my indiscreet disputations about religion began to make me pointed at with horror by good people as an infidel or atheist. I determined on the point, but my father now siding with my brother, I was sensible that, if I attempted to go openly, means would be used to prevent me. My friend Collins, therefore, undertook to manage a little for me. He agreed with the captain of a New York sloop for my passage, under the notion of my being a young acquaintance of his, that had got a naughty girl with child, whose friends would compel me to marry her, and therefore I could not appear or come away publicly. So I sold some of my books to raise a little money, was taken on board privately, and as we had a fair wind, in three days I found myself in New York, near three hundred miles from home, a boy of but seventeen, without the least recommendation to, or knowledge of, any person in the place, and with very little money in my pocket.

My inclinations for the sea were by this time worn out, or I might now have gratified them. But, having a trade, and supposing myself a pretty good workman, I offered my service to the printer in the place, old Mr. William Bradford, who had been the first printer in Pennsylvania, but removed from thence upon the quarrel of George Keith. He could give me no employment, having little to do and help enough already; but, says he, "My son at Philadelphia has lately lost his principal hand, Aquila Rose, by death; if you go thither, I believe he may employ you." Philadelphia was one hundred miles further; I set out, however, in a boat for Amboy, leaving my chest and things to follow me round by sea.

In crossing the bay, we met with a squall that tore our rotten sails 10
to pieces, prevented our getting into the Kill, and drove us upon Long
Island. In our way, a drunken Dutchman, who was a passenger too,
fell overboard; when he was sinking, I reached through the water to
his shock pate, and drew him up, so that we got him in again. His
ducking sobered him a little, and he went to sleep, taking first out of
his pocket a book, which he desired I would dry for him. It proved to
be my old favorite author, Bunyan's *Pilgrim's Progress*, in Dutch, finely
printed on good paper, with copper cuts, a dress better than I had ever
seen it wear in its own language. I have since found that it has been
translated into most of the languages of Europe, and suppose it has
been more generally read than any other book, except perhaps the
Bible. Honest John was the first that I know of who mixed narration
and dialogue, a method of writing very engaging to the reader, who in
the most interesting parts finds himself, as it were, brought into the
company and present at the discourse. Defoe in his *Crusoe*, his *Moll
Flanders, Religious Courtship, Family Instructor*, and other pieces, had
imitated it with success; and Richardson has done the same in his
Pamela, etc.

When we drew near the island, we found it was at a place where
there could be no landing, there being a great surf on the stony beach.
So we dropped anchor, and swung round towards the shore. Some
people came down to the water edge and hallowed to us, as we did to
them; but the wind was so high, and the surf so loud, that we could
not hear so as to understand each other. There were canoes on the
shore, and we made signs, and hallowed that they should fetch us; but
they either did not understand us, or thought it impracticable, so they
went away, and night coming on, we had no remedy but to wait till
the wind should abate; and in the mean time the boatman and I concluded to sleep if we could; and so crowded into the scuttle, with the
Dutchman, who was still wet, and the spray, beating over the head of
our boat, leaked through to us, so that we were soon almost as wet as
he. In this manner we lay all night, with very little rest; but, the wind
abating the next day, we made a shift to reach Amboy before night,
having been thirty hours on the water, without victuals or any drink
but a bottle of filthy rum, the water we sailed on being salt.*** In the
morning, crossing the ferry, I proceeded on my journey on foot, having fifty miles to Burlington, where I was told I should find boats that
would carry me the rest of the way to Philadelphia.***

I have been the more particular in this description of my journey,
and shall be so of my first entry into that city, that you may in your
mind compare such unlikely beginning with the figure I have since
made there. I was in my working dress, my best clothes being to come
round by sea. I was dirty from my journey; my pockets were stuffed
out with shirts and stockings; I knew no soul nor where to look for

lodging. I was fatigued with traveling, rowing, and want of rest; I was very hungry; and my whole stock of cash consisted of a Dutch dollar and about a shilling in copper. The latter I gave the people of the boat for my passage, who at first refused it, on account of my rowing; but I insisted on their taking it, a man being sometimes more generous when he has but a little money than when he had plenty, perhaps through fear of being thought to have but little.

Then I walked up the street, gazing about, till near the market-house. I met a boy with bread. I had made many a meal on bread, and, inquiring where he got it, I went immediately to the baker's he directed me to, in Second Street, and asked for biscuit, intending such as we had in Boston; but they, it seems, were not made in Philadelphia. Then I asked for a three-penny loaf, and was told they had none such. So, not considering or knowing the difference of money, and the greater cheapness nor the names of his bread, I bade him give me three-penny-worth of any sort. He gave me, accordingly, three great puffy rolls. I was surprised at the quantity, but took it, and, having no room in my pockets, walked off with a roll under each arm, and eating the other. Thus I went up Market Street as far as Fourth Street, passing by the door of Mr. Read, my future wife's father; when she, standing at the door, saw me, and thought I made, as I certainly did, a most awkward, ridiculous appearance. Then I turned and went down Chestnut Street and part of Walnut Street, eating my roll all the way, and, coming round, found myself again at Market Street wharf, near the boat I came in, to which I went for a draught of the river water; and, being filled with one of my rolls, gave the other two to a woman and her child that came down the river in the boat with us, and were waiting to go farther.

Thus refreshed, I walked again up the street, which by this time had many clean-dressed people in it, who were all walking the same way. I joined them, and thereby was led into the great meetinghouse of the Quakers near the market. I sat down among them, and, after looking round awhile and hearing nothing said, being very drowsy through labor and want of rest the preceding night, I fell fast asleep, and continued so till the meeting broke up, when one was kind enough to rouse me. This was, therefore, the first house I was in, or slept in, in Philadelphia.

For Journals

If you were making a film of Franklin's entry into Philadelphia, whom would you cast as Franklin? Remember that we are talking about a confident, brilliant, and somewhat brash seventeen-year-old, not the cliché of an older man flying a kite.

For Discussion

1. Franklin describes with great relish what he looked like when he landed in Philadelphia, how his future wife laughed at him, and how absurd he must have appeared as he walked around munching on a roll and looking at everything. Why is this a precious memory to him, and what kinds of appeals does it make to us as readers?

2. The whole trip that Franklin made from Boston to Philadelphia fits into a kind of story called the bildungsroman, a story of growing up in which a young man comes of age. In the course of this excerpt, what does Franklin learn about himself and about making his way in the world?

3. Given that nobody else came close to accomplishing what Franklin did, why is he the model for success in this country? Wouldn't somebody more ordinary be more of a plausible model than a genius who excelled at almost everything?

For Writing

1. Write a rhetorical analysis of Franklin's entry into the Philadelphia scene. Break the scene into two or three parts whose turning points you identify. Within each of those parts, these are some possibilities to consider: What words and phrases does he use most effectively to convey his excitement? Given that he was really a spectator, how does he make himself the center of that big city scene? Even within this short passage, which sentences really stand out to you? And what do they tell you about the image he creates here? What shifts in Franklin's emotional state can you identify from the time he leaves until Quakers take him in? And at what points does he make comments that reveal to you that he is consciously setting a scene with ramifications for the future rather than just recalling a great moment in his youth? Use the text sparingly here, but it is your best evidence. You can even analyze individual sentences in which the shift in mood reflects a shift in Franklin's experience. Finally, you can examine this passage as a spiritual and geographical journey that changed him.

2. Write an essay about an event in your own life that you consider your entry into adulthood or your first encounter with a wider frame of reference than the one you grew up in. You can model it rhetorically on Franklin's continuous fighting with his brother and his objection to his brother's authority over him, or on his entrance into Philadelphia. The first experience is one of conflict, which leads to a kind of rebellion, and the second experience gives a sense of doors opening and opportunities, even if they are are still ill-defined; the second part also shows Franklin finding what he didn't have in Boston—not family, but a place where for the first time he knew he was at home.

3. Everyone starts out with clichés about Franklin: that he's the same person as Poor Richard, whose Almanac was full of good practical advice; that he had a dozen illegitimate children; that he flew a kite and discovered electricity; and so on. Go to the Smithsonian Institution home page or the Franklin biographies by Clark, or better yet, by Isaacson, to find more accurate information about Franklin. Write an essay in which you either debunk some of the most common misconceptions or illuminate something he actually did: wrote elaborate practical jokes, some of which were taken as truth for years afterwards; was a very early abolitionist, largely because of his acquaintance with the Quaker community in Philadelphia; got the gunpowder that revolutionary soldiers needed through his scientific friendship with the great French chemist Lavoisiere; had a troubled and bitter relationship with his own son, who favored the British during the Revolution; and had the eighteenth-century equivalent of rock star status in France when he was a diplomat there.

❃❃❃ *Wealth* (1889)

ANDREW CARNEGIE

Andrew Carnegie (1835–1919) emigrated from Scotland to the United States. He began his career as a weaver like his father, but then he became a telegraph messenger boy and eventually a telegraph operator and superintendent. He made his fortune in railroads, communications, and steel; he sold his interest to J. P. Morgan in 1901 for $250 million. When he retired from public life, he dedicated much of his fortune to establishing institutions for the public good, including Carnegie Tech (later Carnegie-Mellon University), Carnegie Hall, the Carnegie Foundation, the Carnegie Endowment for Peace, and libraries in many towns and cities in the United States and Britain. Most of his writings concern the importance of preserving and maintaining world peace, but he also wrote about business and money.

There are but three modes in which surplus wealth can be disposed of. It can be left to the families of the decedents; or it can be bequeathed for public purposes; or, finally, it can be administered during their lives by its possessors. . . . [T]he question which forces itself upon thoughtful men in all lands is: Why should men leave great fortunes to their children? If this is done from affection, is it not misguided affection? Observation teaches that, generally speaking, it is not well for the children that they should be so burdened. Neither is it well for the state. Beyond providing for the wife and daughters moderate sources of income, and very moderate allowances indeed, if any, for the sons, men may well hesitate, for it is no longer questionable that great sums bequeathed oftener work more for the injury than for the good of the recipients. Wise men will soon conclude that, for the best interests of the members of their families and of the state, such bequests are an improper use of their means. . . .

As to the second mode, that of leaving wealth at death for public uses, it may be said that this is only a means for the disposal of wealth, provided a man is content to wait until he is dead before it becomes of much good in the world. . . .

There remains, then, only one mode of using great fortunes; but in this we have the true antidote for the temporary unequal distribution of wealth. . . .

This, then, is held to be the duty of the man of Wealth: First, to set an example of modest, unostentatious living, shunning display or extravagance; to provide moderately for the legitimate wants of those dependent upon him; and after doing so to consider all surplus revenues which come to him simply as trust funds. . . . [T]he man of wealth thus becoming the mere agent and trustee for his poorer brethren, bringing to their service his superior wisdom, experience, and ability to administer, doing for them better than they would or could do for themselves. . . .

In bestowing charity, the main consideration should be to help 5 those who will help themselves; to provide part of the means by which those who desire to improve may do so; to give those who desire to rise the aids by which they may rise; to assist, but rarely or never to do all. Neither the individual nor the race is improved by alms-giving. Those worthy of assistance, except in rare cases, seldom require assistance. The really valuable men of the race never do, except in cases of accident or sudden change. . . .

The rich man is thus almost restricted to following the examples of Peter Cooper, Enoch Pratt of Baltimore, Mr. Pratt of Brooklyn, Senator Stanford, and others, who know that the best means of benefiting the community is to place within its reach the ladders upon which the aspiring can rise—parks, and means of recreation, by which men are helped in body and mind; works of art, certain to give pleasure and improve the public taste, and public institutions of various kinds, which will improve the general condition of the people;—in this manner returning their surplus wealth to the mass of their fellows in the forms best calculated to do them lasting good.

Thus is the problem of Rich and Poor to be solved. The laws of accumulation will be left free; the laws of distribution free. Individualism will continue, but the millionaire will be but a trustee for the poor; intrusted for a season with a great part of the increased wealth of the community, but administering it for the community far better than it could or would have done for itself. The best minds will thus have reached a stage in the development of the race in which it is clearly seen that there is no mode of disposing of surplus wealth creditable to thoughtful and earnest men into whose hands it flows save by using it year by year for the general good. . . . "The man who dies thus rich dies disgraced."

Such, in my opinion, is the true Gospel concerning Wealth, obedience to which is destined some day to solve the problem of the Rich and the Poor, and to bring "Peace on earth, among men Good-Will."

For Journals

Do you think that there is such a thing as having too much money? Why, or why not?

For Discussion

1. Describe what you think your standard of living is. What markers do you use to decide if someone is lower-class, middle-class, or upper-class?

2. F. Scott Fitzgerald once wrote that "The very rich are different from you and me," and Hemingway responded rather snidely that they have more money. Aside from the obvious, what according to Carnegie—and according to you—are the special responsibilities and burdens that come with a great deal of money?

3. How do you respond to Carnegie's argument that a great fortune in the hands of a few people can do society more good than a little money spread around among many people? How can a man who started with nothing argue that it is better for only a few people to have a lot of money?

For Writing

1. Carnegie gives three possible models for how great American wealth should be distributed: rich people could leave it to their children; they could leave money in their wills for public purposes; or they could spend their money philanthropically during their lifetimes. Assume that you have found yourself in control of a great deal of money—and that you have already gratified your personal whims and those of your family. Write an essay arguing in favor of one of Carnegie's suggestions. Find specific examples of what kinds of projects you would like to see supported (world health is nice, but check the Web site for the World Health Organization, or the United Nations, or Doctors Without Borders, or the Carnegie Foundation, and see what they actually spend their funds, on to get some ideas).

2. Bill Gates, the founder of Microsoft and the man who is as rich today as Carnegie was in his time, has started a foundation that has already given away billions of dollars. Use the Web and/or library sources to see what Gates has said about what he and his wife intend to do with their money, and why. Write an essay in which you compare Gates's ideas about how to deal with enormous wealth with those of Carnegie. Identify the assumptions they have in common, if any, and the points on which they differ. Whose approach would you favor?

3. Write a persuasive essay about your own attitude toward money. You will want to avoid platitudes like "The best things in life are free," so give examples. It is also important to avoid logical errors in what is for Americans a somewhat emotional subject. Here are some issues to consider: Are you extravagant? Cheap? Do you or your family save money or argue over it? What do you like to spend money on? What attitudes toward money did you grow up with? When you have children, what would you tell them, and how would you teach them to regard money appropriately? Is it important to you to eventually make a lot of money and to live in a certain social and economic class? Respond to two or three of these examples, or establish your own questions about money with your teacher's agreement.

✹✹ *In the Land of the Free* (ca. 1900)

SUI SIN FAR

Sui Sin Far (1865–1914) was the Chinese name of the daughter of an English father and a Chinese mother; her English name was Edith Eaton. She is the first Asian American whose fiction was published in the United States. This story is from a collection, Mrs. Spring Fragrance, *published in 1912.*

1

"See, Little One—the hills in the morning sun. There is thy home for years to come. It is very beautiful and thou wilt be very happy there."

The Little One looked up into his mother's face in perfect faith. He was engaged in the pleasant occupation of sucking a sweetmeat; but that did not prevent him from gurgling responsively.

"Yes, my olive bud; there is where thy father is making a fortune for thee. Thy father! O, wilt thou not be glad to behold his dear face. 'Twas for thee I left him."

The Little One ducked his chin sympathetically against his mother's knee. She lifted him on to her lap. He was two years old, a round, dimple-cheeked boy with bright brown eyes and a sturdy little frame.

"Ah! Ah! Ah! Ooh! Ooh! Ooh!" puffed he, mocking a tugboat 5
steaming by.

San Francisco's waterfront was lined with ships and steamers,
while other craft, large and small, including a couple of white trans-
ports from the Philippines, lay at anchor here and there off shore. It
was some time before the *Eastern Queen* could get docked, and even
after that was accomplished, a lone Chinaman who had been waiting
on the wharf for an hour was detained that much longer by men with
the initials U.S.C. on their caps, before he could board the steamer and
welcome his wife and child.

"This is thy son," announced the happy Lae Choo.

Hom Hing lifted the child, felt of his little body and limbs, gazed
into his face with proud and joyous eyes; then turned inquiringly to a
customs officer at his elbow.

"That's a fine boy you have there," said the man. "Where was he
born?"

"In China," answered Hom Hing, swinging the Little One on his 10
right shoulder, preparatory to leading his wife off the steamer.

"Ever been to America before?"

"No, not he," answered the father with a happy laugh.

The customs officer beckoned to another.

"This little fellow," said he, "is visiting America for the first time."

The other customs officer stroked his chin reflectively.   15

"Good day," said Hom Hing.

"Wait!" commanded one of the officers. "You cannot go just yet."

"What more now?" asked Hom Hing.

"I'm afraid," said the customs officer, "that we cannot allow the
boy to go ashore. There is nothing in the papers that you have shown
us—your wife's papers and your own—having any bearing upon the
child."

"There was no child when the papers were made out," returned 20
Hom Hing. He spoke calmly; but there was apprehension in his eyes
and in his tightening grip on his son.

"What is it? What is it?" quavered Lae Choo, who understood a
little English.

The second customs officer regarded her pityingly.

"I don't like this part of the business," he muttered.

The first officer turned to Hom Hing and in an official tone of
voice, said:

"Seeing that the boy has no certificate entitling him to admission 25
to this country you will have to leave him with us."

"Leave my boy!" exclaimed Hom Hing.

"Yes; he will be well taken care of, and just as soon as we can hear
from Washington he will be handed over to you."

"But," protested Hom Hing, "he is my son."

"We have no proof," answered the man with a shrug of his shoulders; "and even if so we cannot let him pass without orders from the Government."

"He is my son," reiterated Hom Hing, slowly and solemnly. "I am   30 a Chinese merchant and have been in business in San Francisco for many years. When my wife told to me one morning that she dreamed of a green tree with spreading branches and one beautiful red flower growing thereon, I answered her that I wished my son to be born in our country, and for her to prepare to go to China. My wife complied with my wish. After my son was born my mother fell sick and my wife nursed and cared for her; then my father, too, fell sick, and my wife also nursed and cared for him. For twenty moons my wife care for and nurse the old people, and when they die they bless her and my son, and I sent for her to return to me. I had no fear of trouble. I was a Chinese merchant and my son was my son."

"Very good, Hom Hing," replied the first officer. "Nevertheless, we take your son."

"No, you not take him; he my son too."

It was Lae Choo. Snatching the child from his father's arms she held and covered him with her own.

The officers conferred for a few moments; then one drew Hom Hing aside and spoke in his ear.

Resignedly Hom Hing bowed his head, then approached his wife.   35 "'Tis the law," said he, speaking in Chinese, "and 'twill be but for a little while—until tomorrow's sun arises."

"You, too," reproached Lae Choo in a voice eloquent with pain. But accustomed to obedience she yielded the boy to her husband, who in turn delivered him to the first officer. The Little One protested lustily against the transfer; but his mother covered her face with her sleeve and his father silently led her away. Thus was the law of the land complied with.

2

Day was breaking. Lae Choo, who had been awake all night, dressed herself, then awoke her husband.

"'Tis the morn," she cried. "Go, bring our son."

The man rubbed his eyes and arose upon his elbow so that he could see out of the window. A pale star was visible in the sky. The petals of a lily in a bowl on the windowsill were unfurled.

"'Tis not yet time," said he, laying his head down again.   40

"Not yet time. Ah, all the time that I lived before yesterday is not so much as the time that has been since my Little One was taken from me."

The mother threw herself down beside the bed and covered her face.

Hom Hing turned on the light, and touching his wife's bowed head with a sympathetic hand inquired if she had slept.

"Slept!" she echoed, weepingly. "Ah, how could I close my eyes with my arms empty of the little body that has filled them every night for more than twenty moons! You do not know—man—what it is to miss the feel of the little fingers and the little toes and the soft round limbs of your little one. Even in the darkness his darling eyes used to shine up to mine, and often have I fallen into slumber with his pretty babble at my ear. And now, I see him not; I touch him not; I hear him not. My baby, my little fat one!"

"Now! Now! Now!" consoled Hom Hing, patting his wife's shoul- 45 der reassuringly; "there is no need to grieve so; he will soon gladden you again. There cannot be any law that would keep a child from its mother!"

Lae Choo dried her tears.

"You are right, my husband," she meekly murmured. She arose and stepped about the apartment, setting things to rights. The box of presents she had brought for her California friends had been opened the evening before; and silks, embroideries, carved ivories, ornamental lacquer-ware, brasses, camphorwood boxes, fans, and chinaware were scattered around in confused heaps. In the midst of unpacking the thought of her child in the hands of strangers had overpowered her, and she had left everything to crawl into bed and weep.

Having arranged her gifts in order she stepped out on to the deep balcony.

The star had faded from view and there were bright streaks in the western sky. Lae Choo looked down the street and around. Beneath the flat occupied by her and her husband were quarters for a number of bachelor Chinamen, and she could hear them from where she stood, taking their early morning breakfast. Below their dining-room was her husband's grocery store. Across the way was a large restaurant. Last night it had been resplendent with gay colored lanterns and the sound of music. The rejoicings over "the completion of the moon," by Quong Sum's firstborn, had been long and loud, and had caused her to tie a handkerchief over her ears. She, a bereaved mother, had it not in her heart to rejoice with other parents. This morning the place was more in accord with her mood. It was still and quiet. The revellers had dispersed or were asleep.

A roly-poly woman in black sateen, with long pendant earrings in 50 her ears, looked up from the street below and waved her a smiling greeting. It was her old neighbor, Kuie Hoe, the wife of the gold embosser, Mark Sing. With her was a little boy in a yellow jacket and lavender pantaloons. Lae Choo remembered him as a baby. She used to like to play with him in those days when she had no child of her own. What a long time ago that seemed! She caught her breath in a sigh, and laughed instead.

"Why are you so merry?" called her husband from within.

"Because my Little One is coming home," answered Lae Choo. "I am a happy mother—a happy mother."

She pattered into the room with a smile on her face.

The noon hour had arrived. The rice was steaming in the bowls and a fragrant dish of chicken and bamboo shoots was awaiting Hom Hing. Not for one moment had Lae Choo paused to rest during the morning hours; her activity had been ceaseless. Every now and again, however, she had raised her eyes to the gilded clock on the curiously carved mantelpiece. Once, she had exclaimed:

"Why so long, oh! why so long?" Then, apostrophizing herself: 55 "Lae Choo, be happy. The Little One is coming! The Little One is coming!" Several times she burst into tears, and several times she laughed aloud.

Hom Hing entered the room; his arms hung down by his side.

"The Little One!" shrieked Lae Choo.

"They bid me call tomorrow."

With a moan the mother sank to the floor.

The noon hour passed. The dinner remained on the table.   60

3

The winter rains were over: the spring had come to California, flushing the hills with green and causing an ever-changing pageant of flowers to pass over them. But there was no spring in Lae Choo's heart, for the Little One remained away from her arms. He was being kept in a mission. White women were caring for him, and though for one full moon he had pined for his mother and refused to be comforted he was now apparently happy and contented. Five moons or five months had gone by since the day he had passed with Lae Choo through the Golden Gate; but the great Government at Washington still delayed sending the answer which would return him to his parents.

Hom Hing was disconsolately rolling up and down the balls in his abacus box when a keen-faced young man stepped into his store.

"What news?" asked the Chinese merchant.

"This!" The young man brought forth a typewritten letter. Hom Hing read the words:

"Re Chinese child, alleged to be the son of Hom Hing, Chinese 65 merchant, doing business at 425 Clay Street, San Francisco.

"Same will have attention as soon as possible."

Hom Hing returned the letter, and without a word continued his manipulation of the counting machine.

"Have you anything to say?" asked the young man.

"Nothing. They have sent the same letter fifteen times before. Have you not yourself showed it to me?"

"True!" The young man eyed the Chinese merchant furtively. He 70 had a proposition to make and was pondering whether or not the time was opportune.

"How is your wife?" he inquired solicitously—and diplomatically.

Hom Hing shook his head mournfully.

"She seems less every day," he replied. "Her food she takes only when I bid her and her tears fall continually. She finds no pleasure in dress or flowers and cares not to see her friends. Her eyes stare all night. I think before another moon she will pass into the land of the spirits."

"No!" exclaimed the young man, genuinely startled.

"If the boy not come home I lose my wife sure," continued Hom 75 Hing with bitter sadness.

"It's not right," cried the young man indignantly. Then he made his proposition.

The Chinese father's eyes brightened exceedingly.

"Will I like you to go to Washington and make them give you the paper to restore my son?" cried he. "How can you ask when you know my heart's desire?"

"Then," said the young fellow, "I will start next week. I am anxious to see this thing through if only for the sake of your wife's peace of mind."

"I will call her. To hear what you think to do will make her glad," 80 said Hom Hing.

He called a message to Lae Choo upstairs through a tube in the wall.

In a few moments she appeared, listless, wan, and hollow-eyed; but when her husband told her the young lawyer's suggestion she became electrified; her form straightened, her eyes glistened; the color flushed to her cheeks.

"Oh," she cried, turning to James Clancy. "You are a hundred man good!"

The young man felt somewhat embarrassed; his eyes shifted a little under the intense gaze of the Chinese mother.

"Well, we must get your boy for you," he responded. "Of 85 course"—turning to Hom Hing—"it will cost a little money. You can't get fellows to hurry the Government for you without gold in your pocket."

Hom Hing stared blankly for a moment. Then: "How much do you want, Mr. Clancy?" he asked quietly.

"Well, I will need at least five hundred to start with."

Hom Hing cleared his throat.

"I think I told to you the time I last paid you for writing letters for me and seeing the Custom boss here that nearly all I had was gone!"

"Oh well then we won't talk about it, old fellow. It won't harm the boy to stay where he is, and your wife may get over it all right."

"What that you say?" quavered Lae Choo.

James Clancy looked out of the window.

"He says," explained Hom Hing in English, "that to get our boy we have to have much money."

"Money! Oh, yes."

Lae Choo nodded her head.

"I have not got the money to give him."

For a moment Lae Choo gazed wonderingly from one face to the other; then, comprehension dawning upon her, with swift anger, pointing to the lawyer, she cried: "You not one hundred man good; you just common white man."

"Yes, ma'am," returned James Clancy, bowing and smiling ironically.

Hom Hing pushed his wife behind him and addressed the lawyer again: "I might try," said he, "to raise something; but five hundred—it is not possible."

"What about four?"

"I tell you I have next to nothing left and my friends are not rich."

"Very well!"

The lawyer moved leisurely toward the door, pausing on its threshold to light a cigarette.

"Stop, white man; white man, stop!"

Lae Choo, panting and terrified, had started forward and now stood beside him, clutching his sleeve excitedly.

"You say you can go to get paper to bring my Little One to me if Hom Hing give you five hundred dollars?"

The lawyer nodded carelessly; his eyes were intent upon the cigarette which would not take the fire from the match.

"Then you go get paper. If Hom Hing not can give you five hundred dollars—I give you perhaps what more that much."

She slipped a heavy gold bracelet from her wrist and held it out to the man. Mechanically he took it.

"I go get more!"

She scurried away, disappearing behind the door through which she had come.

"Oh, look here, I can't accept this," said James Clancy, walking back to Hom Hing and laying down the bracelet before him.

"It's all right," said Hom Hing, seriously, "pure China gold. My wife's parent give it to her when we married."

"But I can't take it anyway," protested the young man.

"It is all same as money. And you want money to go to Washing- 115
ton," replied Hom Hing in a matter-of-fact manner.

"See, my jade earrings—my gold buttons—my hairpins—my
comb of pearl and my rings—one, two, three, four, five rings; very
good—very good—all same much money. I give them all to you. You
take and bring me paper for my Little One."

Lae Choo piled up her jewels before the lawyer.

Hom Hing laid a restraining hand upon her shoulder. "Not all, my
wife," he said in Chinese. He selected a ring—his gift to Lae Choo
when she dreamed of the tree with the red flower. The rest of the jewels he pushed toward the white man.

"Take them and sell them," said he. "They will pay your fare to
Washington and bring you back with the paper."

For one moment James Clancy hesitated. He was not a sentimental 120
man; but something within him arose against accepting such payment
for his services.

"They are good, good," pleadingly asserted Lae Choo, seeing his
hesitation.

Whereupon he seized the jewels, thrust them into his coat pocket,
and walked rapidly away from the store.

4

Lae Choo followed after the missionary woman through the mission nursery school. Her heart was beating so high with happiness
that she could scarcely breathe. The paper had come at last—the precious paper which gave Hom Hing and his wife the right to the possession of their own child. It was ten months now since he had been
taken from them—ten months since the sun had ceased to shine for
Lae Choo.

The room was filled with children—most of them wee tots, but
none so wee as her own. The mission woman talked as she walked.
She told Lae Choo that little Kim, as he had been named by the school,
was the pet of the place, and that his little tricks and ways amused and
delighted every one. He had been rather difficult to manage at first
and had cried much for his mother; "but children so soon forget, and
after a month he seemed quite at home and played around as bright
and happy as a bird."

"Yes," responded Lae Choo. "Oh, yes, yes!"   125

But she did not hear what was said to her. She was walking in a
maze of anticipatory joy.

"Wait here, please," said the mission woman, placing Lae Choo in
a chair. "The very youngest ones are having their breakfast."

She withdrew for a moment—it seemed like an hour to the mother—then she reappeared leading by the hand a little boy dressed in blue cotton overalls and white-soled shoes. The little boy's face was round and dimpled and his eyes were very bright.

"Little One, ah, my Little One!" cried Lae Choo.

She fell on her knees and stretched her hungry arms toward her son.   130

But the Little One shrunk from her and tried to hide himself in the folds of the white woman's skirt.

"Go 'way, go 'way!" he bade his mother.

For Journals

There's an idea of America as a melting pot and another of America as a tossed salad; which one do you think better describes the mix of cultures in this country?

For Discussion

1.   In the first sentence of this story, Lae Choo, arriving in San Francisco with her infant son, expresses her dream for his future in America: "See, Little One—the hills in the morning sun. There is thy home for years to come. It is very beautiful and thou wilt be very happy there." But in fact, in each of the four parts of this story, dreams are derailed, if not destroyed. What are these dreams, whose are they, and how are they changed by circumstances?

2.   How does the involvement of white Americans in the lives of Hom Hing, Lae Choo, and their child highlight cultural differences between the Chinese and the white American characters? What assumptions about family, progress, civilization, Christianity, or Americanization do you yourself start with in deciding whether these involvements have positive or negative consequences?

3.   What do you think are Lae Choo's hopes for her son? What do you think the missionary lady wants for him? On the basis of what you've read in this story, whose path do you think the child is likely to follow?

4.   Is the title of the story ironic or literal? If you were going to give it another title, what would you call it?

For Writing

1.   Rewrite the last scene in this story, when Lae Choo finally gets her son back, but with the missionary lady as the narrator. To find evidence for your version, reread the last scene, and look at the various exchanges: between Lae Choo and the missionary lady, Lae Choo and

her son, and the son and the missionary lady. Include the actual dialogue that Sui Sin Far used, and work it into your version.

2. Write a rhetorical analysis of the way the reader is led to sympathize with Lae Choo. Don't retell the story; focus instead on the language and on the appeals it makes to us. Although there are certainly adjectives and adverbs that are significant, you will have more material if you select one or two passages, or a scene with dialogue, and read them very closely indeed to see how one sentence is helped by those before and after it, where the turning points are, and where the author seems to identify most with the emotions that Lae Choo experiences. Here are some possibilities: Lae Choo's response to the lawyer; the last scene; and the early part of the story before the child is taken away.

3. Research and write a report on one of the following topics: the cultural life in San Francisco's Chinatown at the turn of the century; the anti-Chinese immigration laws, including the prohibition of marriage; the role of Chinese laborers in building the transcontinental railroad; the prevalence of Chinese medicine and the unavailability of American health care in Chinatown; the way the Chinese in America were portrayed around 1900 in American newspapers, such as the *New York Times* and the *San Francisco Chronicle,* and in tabloids, such as the *Police Gazette* (see Chapter 11).

✵✵ *Let America Be America Again* (1938)

LANGSTON HUGHES

Langston Hughes (1902–1967) was one of the premier figures of the Harlem Renaissance—that jubilant outpouring of black art and culture in New York City in the 1920s. Hughes uses the rhythms of jazz, blues, and gospel music to celebrate and probe the role of black people in American society. His collections of verse include The Dream Keeper *(1932),* The Way of White Folks *(1934),* Shakespeare in Harlem *(1941), and* Montage of a Dream Deferred *(1951).*

Let America be America again.
Let it be the dream it used to be.
Let it be the pioneer on the plain
Seeking a home where he himself is free.

(America never was America to me.)   5

Let America be the dream the dreamers dreamed—
Let it be that great strong land of love
Where never kings connive nor tyrants scheme
That any man be crushed by one above.

(It never was America to me.)   10

O, let my land be a land where Liberty
Is crowned with no false patriotic wreath,
But opportunity is real, and life is free,
Equality is in the air we breathe.

(There's never been equality for me,   15
Nor freedom in this "homeland of the free.")

Say who are you that mumbles in the dark?
And who are you that draws your veil across the stars?

I am the poor white, fooled and pushed apart,
I am the red man driven from the land.   20
I am the refugee clutching the hope I seek—
But finding only the same old stupid plan

Of dog eat dog, of mighty crush the weak.
I am the Negro, "problem" to you all.
I am the people, humble, hungry, mean—   25
Hungry yet today despite the dream.
Beaten yet today—O, Pioneers!
I am the man who never got ahead,
The poorest worker bartered through the years.
Yet I'm the one who dreamt our basic dream   30
In that Old World while still a serf of kings,
Who dreamt a dream so strong, so brave, so true,
That even yet its mighty daring sings
In every brick and stone, in every furrow turned
That's made America the land it has become.   35
O, I'm the man who sailed those early seas
In search of what I meant to be my home—
For I'm the one who left dark Ireland's shore,
And Poland's plain, and England's grassy lea,
And torn from Black Africa's strand I came   40
To build a "homeland of the free."

The free?
Who said the free? Not me?
Surely not me? The millions on relief today?
The millions who have nothing for our pay   45
For all the dreams we've dreamed
And all the songs we've sung
And all the hopes we've held

And all the flags we've hung,
The millions who have nothing for our pay—   50
Except the dream we keep alive today.

O, let America be America again—
The land that never has been yet—
And yet must be—the land where every man is free.
The land that's mine—the poor man's, Indian's, Negro's,   55
  ME—
Who made America,
Whose sweat and blood, whose faith and pain,
Whose hand at the foundry, whose plow in the rain,
Must bring back our mighty dream again.

O, yes,   60
I say it plain,
America never was America to me,
And yet I swear this oath—
America will be!

For Journals

What do you know about the America of the 1930s and the Great
Depression? What do you think they have to do with the subject of
the poem?

For Discussion

1.   With whom, or with what, does Hughes identify the America that
is "the dream it used to be" (line 2)? In the first three stanzas, which
examples of the dream does he celebrate?

2.   Beginning with line 52, Hughes gives examples of the people he
thinks of as the real source of the American dream, a dream that must
be "the poor man's, Indian's, Negro's, ME" (line 55) in order to be valid.
How can this viewpoint coexist with the idea of an America exemplified
by the founding fathers, including Benjamin Franklin (see Chapter 8)?

3.   Analyze the poem as an argument. What are the two sides? What
are they fighting over? What points does each side make? Where does
the poem "turn"? How would you describe the tone of the speaker?
Optimistic? Cheerful? Bitter? What do you consider the most persuasive part of the poem?

4.   What does it mean for America to be America again, as the title
says, if it never was in the first place? Since the population of America
is almost all descended from people who came from somewhere else,
including all the nationalities Hughes mentions, is there any evidence

in the poem to support the possibility of change? Where would it come from?

5. Considering how much of the American dream revolves around success, how do you respond to the fact that Hughes identifies the dream with examples of people who are not successful—"I am the man who never got ahead, / The poorest worker bartered through the years" (lines 28–29)? Do you think he is distorting the definition of the dream, or redefining it? Why?

For Writing

1. Write an essay that provides a persuasive answer to the following questions: If the people who originated the American dream are left out of it, what about the dream is still worthwhile to them? Why do they still want it? Read several newspaper or magazine articles about the problems and attitudes that prospective immigrants to America currently encounter. Support your essay with examples and, if possible, with actual quotations from immigrants about their desires to come to this country.

2. Hughes was active as a writer both during and after the Harlem Renaissance. Research and write an essay on one of the following: the historical and social background for the Harlem Renaissance; the work of any of the artists, musicians, and writers involved in the Renaissance, for example, Jean Toomer, Zora Neale Hurston, Duke Ellington, Richard Wright, Countee Cullen, or Lou Jones; the history of the Cotton Club and the entertainers who worked there; the story of the Apollo Theater; or other work by Langston Hughes, including his great collection of short stories, *The Best of Simple.*

❋❋❋ *There's No Way like the American Way* (1937)

MARGARET BOURKE-WHITE

Margaret Bourke-White (1904–1971) was a photojournalist who covered major news stories for Life *magazine when that publication was home to the world's best photographers. As well as the work she did on the Great Depression, she is famous for her photographs of the invasion of Russia in World War II and the liberation of concentration camps.*

One of Bourke-White's most famous photographs is this picture of Americans in 1937, during the Great Depression, standing in line at an emergency relief station in the aftermath of an Ohio flood that killed hundreds of people and left thousands of others homeless.

For Journals

What do you know about the Great Depression of the 1930s? Was anyone in your family affected by it?

For Discussion

1. From looking at this photo, what would you say was the image of the ideal American family in 1937? How is that image affected by the fact that in 1937 the Depression was in full force, with roughly 15 million Americans out of work?

2. There are two verbal assertions in this photograph, both of them slogans on the billboard. How does the rest of the photograph, including the line of people, support or refute those statements?

3. How do you suppose that the people in the line would respond to the billboard behind them? What is your response to the billboard?

4. The composition of a great photograph is never accidental. Since the line of people was longer than the billboard, what do you think were Bourke-White's reasons for taking a photograph of those particular people under that particular billboard? Would it have a different impact if the flood victims were white? Is their color or their economic situation more important?

5. If you had to translate this photo into a verbal assertion about life in America in 1937, what would it be? What details of the photograph would you choose to support your statement?

For Writing

1. Today America still has problems of homelessness and unemployment. Look in recent newspapers or magazines for a picture or pictures of homeless or unemployed Americans. Write a reflective essay in which you consider the following: whether you could imagine yourself or your family in a similar situation and whether your choice of your major in school is affected by your concerns for the future.

2. Bourke-White took this photograph from a particular point of view. Using back copies of magazines, contemporary magazines, or books of photographs, find an American photograph from a historic event—for example, the Civil War, the Great Depression, one of the world wars, a political assassination, the civil rights struggle in the South, a presidential campaign—in which the photographer makes a judgment about the event through the image. Research the background of the event to be sure you understand the historical context. Then write an essay in which you respond to the following questions: What is the photo's impact on you? Has the meaning of the photo changed over time? What biases or values or assumptions do you think that the photographer is expressing? What details in the photograph support your assertions?

✻✻✻ *Harlem* (1951)

LANGSTON HUGHES

This poem, written more than a decade after "Let America Be America Again," poses a very different set of questions and answers.

What happens to a dream deferred?

Does it dry up
like a raisin in the sun?
Or fester like a sore—
And then run?   5
Does it stink like rotten meat?
Or crust and sugar over—
like a syrupy sweet?

Maybe it just sags
like a heavy load.   10

Or does it explode?

For Journals

To what social or political issues might this poem be applicable today?

For Discussion

1. "Let America Be America Again" is distinguished, among other reasons, by Hughes's ability to incorporate a large number of voices in a kind of symphonic poetry. Whose voice or voices do you think are speaking in this poem?

2. This poem has only eleven short lines, but they include five different questions. Paraphrase each of those questions. What mood or moods do you think are suggested by such verbal terms as "dries up," "festers," "stinks," "crusts over," or "sags"?

3. Why do you think that Hughes separates the last line from the rest of the questions in the poem?

For Writing

1. Write an essay answering question 2 in the discussion section. Besides paraphrasing the questions that Hughes asks, assess how each verb he chooses suggests a slightly different mood, what the turning points in the poem are, and who the voice or voices belong to. Alternatively, look at another of Hughes's poems as a subject for analysis, particularly for his use of language and diction—for example, "Theme for English B" or "Brass Spitoons."

✻✻✻ I Have a Dream (1963)

MARTIN LUTHER KING, JR.

Martin Luther King, Jr. (1929–1968), was the leader of the nonviolent civil rights struggle. A minister from a family of ministers, he became a public figure while still in his twenties when he led a bus boycott in Montgomery, Alabama. Frequently threatened or arrested, he was the main organizer of sit-ins and marches in segregated southern towns and cities, particularly Birmingham, Alabama, in 1963. That summer he addressed a huge audience of civil rights workers who had marched in protest in Washington, D.C. His speech, delivered from the steps of the Lincoln Memorial, is one of the most famous of the century. King received the Nobel Peace Prize in 1964, the youngest person ever to do so. He was assassinated in Memphis, Tennessee, in 1968.

Five score years ago, a great American, in whose symbolic shadow we stand, signed the Emancipation Proclamation. This momentous decree came as a great beacon light of hope to millions of Negro slaves who had been seared in the flames of withering injustice. It came as a joyous daybreak to end the long night of captivity.

But one hundred years later, we must face the tragic fact that the Negro is still not free. One hundred years later, the life of the Negro is still sadly crippled by the manacles of segregation and the chains of discrimination. One hundred years later, the Negro lives on a lonely island of poverty in the midst of a vast ocean of material prosperity. One hundred years later, the Negro is still languishing in the corners of American society and finds himself an exile in his own land. So we have come here today to dramatize an appalling condition.

In a sense we have come to our nation's Capitol to cash a check. When the architects of our republic wrote the magnificent words of the Constitution and the Declaration of Independence, they were signing a promissory note to which every American was to fall heir. This note was a promise that all men would be guaranteed the unalienable rights of life, liberty, and the pursuit of happiness.

It is obvious today that America has defaulted on this promissory note insofar as her citizens of color are concerned. Instead of honoring this sacred obligation, America has given the Negro people a bad check; a check which has come back marked "insufficient funds." But we refuse to believe that the bank of justice is bankrupt. We refuse to believe that there are insufficient funds in the great vaults of opportunity of this nation. So we have come to cash this check—a check that will give us upon demand the riches of freedom and the security of justice. We have also come to this hallowed spot to remind America of the fierce urgency of *now*. This is no time to engage in the luxury of cooling off or to take the tranquilizing drug of gradualism. *Now* is the time to make real the promises of Democracy. *Now* is the time to rise from the dark and desolate valley of segregation to the sunlit path of racial justice. *Now* is the time to open the doors of opportunity to all of God's children. *Now* is the time to lift our nation from the quicksands of racial injustice to the solid rock of brotherhood.

It would be fatal for the nation to overlook the urgency of the mo-   5
ment and to underestimate the determination of the Negro. This sweltering summer of the Negro's legitimate discontent will not pass until there is an invigorating autumn of freedom and equality. 1963 is not an end, but a beginning. Those who hope that the Negro needed to blow off steam and will now be content will have a rude awakening if the nation returns to business as usual. There will be neither rest nor tranquility in America until the Negro is granted his citizenship rights. The whirlwinds of revolt will continue to shake the foundations of our nation until the bright day of justice emerges.

But there is something I must say to my people who stand on the warm threshold which leads into the palace of justice. In the process of gaining our rightful place we must not be guilty of wrongful deeds. Let us not seek to satisfy our thirst for freedom by drinking from the cup of bitterness and hatred. We must forever conduct our struggle on the high plane of dignity and discipline. We must not allow our creative protest to degenerate into physical violence. Again and again we must rise to the majestic heights of meeting physical force with soul force. The marvelous new militancy which has engulfed the Negro community must not lead us to a distrust of all white people, for many of our white brothers, as evidenced by their presence here today, have come to realize that their destiny is tied up with our destiny and their freedom is inextricably bound to our freedom. We cannot walk alone.

And as we walk, we must make the pledge that we shall march ahead. We cannot turn back. There are those who are asking the devotees of civil rights, "When will you be satisfied?" We can never be satisfied as long as the Negro is the victim of the unspeakable horrors of police brutality. We can never be satisfied as long as our bodies, heavy with the fatigue of travel, cannot gain lodging in the motels of the highways and the hotels of the cities. We cannot be satisfied as long as the Negro's basic mobility is from a smaller ghetto to a larger one. We can never be satisfied as long as a Negro in Mississippi cannot vote and a Negro in New York believes he has nothing for which to vote. No, no, we are not satisfied, and we will not be satisfied until justice rolls down like waters and righteousness like a mighty stream.

I am not unmindful that some of you have come here out of great trials and tribulations. Some of you have come fresh from narrow jail cells. Some of you have come from areas where your quest for freedom left you battered by the storms of persecution and staggered by the winds of police brutality. You have been the veterans of creative suffering. Continue to work with the faith that unearned suffering is redemptive.

Go back to Mississippi, go back to Alabama, go back to South Carolina, go back to Georgia, go back to Louisiana, go back to the slums and ghettoes of our northern cities, knowing that somehow this situation can and will be changed. Let us not wallow in the valley of despair.

I say to you today, my friends, that in spite of the difficulties and 10
frustrations of the moment I still have a dream. It is a dream deeply rooted in the American dream.

I have a dream that one day this nation will rise up and live out the true meaning of its creed: "We hold these truths to be self-evident; that all men are created equal."

I have a dream that one day on the red hills of Georgia the sons of former slaves and the sons of former slaveowners will be able to sit down together at the table of brotherhood.

I have a dream that the state of Mississippi, a desert state sweltering with the heat of injustice and oppression, will be transformed into an oasis of freedom and justice.

I have a dream that my four little children will one day live in a nation where they will not be judged by the color of their skin but by the content of their character.

I have a dream today. 15

I have a dream that the state of Alabama, whose governor's lips are presently dripping with the words of interposition and nullification, will be transformed into a situation where little black boys and black girls will be able to join hands with little white boys and white girls and walk together as sisters and brothers.

I have a dream today.

I have a dream that one day every valley shall be exalted, every hill and mountain shall be made low, the rough places will be made plain, and the crooked places will be made straight, and the glory of the Lord shall be revealed, and all flesh shall see it together.

This is our hope. This is the faith with which I return to the South. With this faith we will be able to hew out of the mountain of despair a stone of hope. With this faith we will be able to transform the jangling discords of our nation into a beautiful symphony of brotherhood. With this faith we will be able to work together, to pray together, to struggle together, to go to jail together, to stand up for freedom together, knowing that we will be free one day.

This will be the day when all of God's children will be able to sing 20 with new meaning.

> My country, 'tis of thee
> Sweet land of liberty,
>   Of thee I sing:
> Land where my fathers died,
> Land of the pilgrims' pride,
> From every mountainside
>   Let freedom ring.

And if America is to be a great nation this must become true. So let freedom ring from the prodigious hilltops of New Hampshire. Let freedom ring from the mighty mountains of New York. Let freedom ring from the heightening Alleghenies of Pennsylvania!

Let freedom ring from the snowcapped Rockies of Colorado!

Let freedom ring from the curvaceous peaks of California!

But not only that; let freedom ring from Stone Mountain of Georgia!

Let freedom ring from Lookout Mountain of Tennessee!   25

Let freedom ring from every hill and molehill of Mississippi. From every mountainside, let freedom ring.

When we let freedom ring, when we let it ring from every village and every hamlet, from every state and every city, we will be able to speed up that day when all of God's children, black men and white men, Jews and Gentiles, Protestants and Catholics, will be able to join hands and sing in the words of the old Negro spiritual, "Free at last! free at last! thank God almighty, we are free at last!"

For Journals

What have you heard or read about the civil rights movement? About Martin Luther King, Jr.? If you have seen film or newsreels of the struggle between civil rights advocates and segregationists, how did you react to them?

For Discussion

1. What is King trying to convince African Americans they should do about segregation? What is he trying to convince white Americans to do?

2. King gave this speech at the Lincoln Memorial. Aside from the obvious location, why does he begin with a line reminiscent of the beginning of Lincoln's Gettysburg Address, "Four score and seven years ago"? What associations might he be trying to raise in the minds of his audience?

3. In order to identify the consequences of racial injustice in American life, King uses both unusual figures of speech, like the promissory note of equality (paragraph 3), and examples of the effects of prejudice in ordinary life, like not being able to get into a hotel (paragraph 7). Look for some more examples of both unusual language and ordinary experience. What do you think he gains from using both kinds of examples? How do the two together help make his argument more persuasive?

4. King says his dream is deeply rooted in the American dream. But he also uses Judeo-Christian references that are part of his background as a minister. Divide the speech into sections based on these two themes; with two of your peers, look through the speech for examples of religious and biblical language and for references to the American dream. What values or ideas are expressed in those examples, as you see it?

5. King addresses the frustrated dreams of African Americans in the civil rights movement who thought progress was too slow and the irritation of northerners who thought it was too fast. Look at the section of the speech starting with, "We have also come to this hallowed spot to remind America of the fierce urgency of *now*" (the middle of paragraph 4). What examples does he use to address each group? Which examples advocate patience, and which ones express determination? Do you recognize the sources of any of his metaphorical examples?

6. The video of King's speech is available in many college libraries. If it is in yours, watch it in class. If not, read the speech out loud in class. In the last and most famous part of the speech, King begins paragraphs with the words "I have a dream," and then "Let freedom ring." What kinds of fulfillment does he dream about in these passages? You might want to paraphrase his language to see how many kinds of dreams he evokes here.

For Writing

1. King gave this speech in the summer of 1963. Using contemporary newspaper and magazine reports and at least one biography of King or a history of the civil rights movement (Taylor Branch's *Parting the*

Waters is a good example), write a researched paper on the circum-stances that preceded the march. Here are some points to include: Who was against it? Why were there fears about what would happen at the march? What was the response of the audience? The press? What was the aftermath? Did people who heard King's speech talk about their own dreams for America in response?

2.   This speech is remarkable for the number of other texts it borrows from, rephrases, or uses for its own purposes—the Bible, the Declaration of Independence, the Gettysburg Address, Shakespeare, spirituals, and others. Write an essay in which you identify at least three examples of these borrowed texts, and explain why you think that King picked them, what point they were used to make, and how persuasive you think they are. Then try to come up with examples of contemporary texts or songs that you would borrow from if you were delivering this speech today.

❆❆ *Tomorrowland* (1997)

WITOLD RYBCZYNSKI

Witold Rybczynski (1943–), the Martin and Margy Myerson Professor of Ur-banism at the University of Pennsylvania, has written in-depth, thoughtful works on urban architecture, housing, and the uses of technology. His books include Taming the Tiger *(1983),* Looking Around: A Journey Through Architecture *(1993), and* City Life *(1995). This selection is an article he wrote in 1997 for the* New Yorker.

Famous firsts are recorded by sports statisticians, academic jour-nals, and the Guinness Book. Everyday firsts are not. I've never heard of a statue to the suburbanite who sprinted through the first mall, or to the person who punched into the first ATM. I have these thoughts while I'm standing in front of 931 Jasmine Street. It is unlikely that there will ever be a commemorative plaque here, but perhaps there should be. The building itself, while attractive, is unremarkable. It is a one-story house of a type that is not uncommon in the South. The hipped roof extends over a deep front veranda. The walls are clap-board; the double-hung windows are shuttered. There is a U-Haul van in the driveway. I'm standing on the sidewalk watching Larry Haber move into his new home. He is a good sport and pauses so that I can take a photograph. Larry and his wife, Terri, and their two young chil-dren are the first residents of an unusual town: a town that is being built by an organization whose chief business is storytelling and make-believe—the Walt Disney Company.

It was Walt himself who had the idea of building a town. Exactly thirty years ago, he announced that he was going to create a showcase for advanced technology—a kind of urban laboratory. It would be called EPCOT, for Experimental Prototype Community of Tomorrow, and it would be an actual community. But Disney died before he could realize his vision of a city of the future, and his successors were unable to reconcile his coercive brand of social engineering with the demands of American home buyers. When EPCOT finally opened, in 1982, it did feature futuristic technology, but there were no residents. It was a theme park.

EPCOT is situated in Walt Disney World, on the enormous tract of land—twenty-eight thousand acres—that Disney owns outside Orlando, in central Florida. There are two other theme parks there—the Magic Kingdom and the Disney-MGM Studios—and a fourth, Disney's Animal Kingdom, is slated to open in 1998. Even so, about a third of the land remained unused. The idea of building a residential community had lingered on in the Disney Company's corporate memory, and when a master plan was being prepared under the aegis of the current C.E.O., Michael Eisner, it was determined that it was finally time to implement Walt's vision. There were also practical considerations: highway access to the theme parks and various wetlands restrictions made residential use attractive. "At that point, we could have gone in any direction," says Disney's Tom Lewis, who oversaw planning during the first five years of the project. "It could have been a second-home community or a resort or a retirement village. Instead, we decided that it would be a place where families would have their primary residences. We wanted it to be a real town."

The notion that Disney World could be a setting for real life will strike most people as improbable. Yet the town promises not only to be real but to be a model for others to follow. Celebration, as it is called, is not a theme park. It is an unincorporated town under the rule of Osceola County. There will be a school, a health campus, and an office park. Planned recreational facilities include a golf course, a lake, and miles of walking trails and bike paths. The town center will have restaurants, shops, offices, a supermarket, a bank, a small inn, and a cinema. When Celebration is completed, in ten or fifteen years, it could have as many as twenty thousand inhabitants. It is the most comprehensively planned new town since Columbia, Maryland, and Reston, Virginia, were built, in the mid-sixties. . . .

You would look in vain for manifestations of any of the current 5 vogues in high-fashion architecture. There is no free-form deconstructivism here, no corrugated-metal high tech. Instead, there are gable roofs with dormers, bay windows and porches, balustrades and columns. Like all houses built commercially in the United States today, these houses favor distinctly traditional styles. The Habers' house, on Jasmine Street, is an example of Coastal, which is a loose interpretation of the type of house that was built in the South Carolina low country. It is a style characterized by deep one- or two-story porches, high ceilings, full-length windows, and first floors raised off the ground. Coastal is one of six—and only six—architectural styles permissible in Celebration; the others are Classical, Victorian, Colonial Revival, Mediterranean, and French. The six styles are defined in a pattern book, which insures that the builders achieve a degree of architectural clarity that is missing in most builder homes. Unusual, too, is Celebration's approach to parking. Alleys running behind the houses give access to garages in the rear, and many of these garages have rooms above them. Larry Haber has built a suite for his mother-in-law above his garage. . . .

The downtown buildings are owned by Disney and are leased to retail tenants. But there is no Banana Republic here. Instead of major national chains, Disney has chosen only local and regional shops and restaurants. The intention is to attract the public by creating an experience different from that found in a typical shopping mall, Don Killoren told me. Though a downtown like Celebration's, with but a single landlord, does resemble a shopping mall, there is one crucial difference here: this is a commercial area where people will also live. . . .

A lively downtown, apartments above shops, front porches, houses close to the street, and out-of-sight garages all add up to an old-fashioned sort of place. But there is more to Celebration than nostalgia and tradition. What families like the Habers really want—what most Americans really want—has less to do with architecture and urban design than with good schools, health care, safe neighborhoods, and a sense of community. "We understand that community is not something that we can engineer," I was assured by Todd Mansfield, who is an executive vice-president of Disney Imagineeering, the division that oversees the design and construction of all the company's enterprises. "But we think that it's something we can foster." Despite Disney's reputation for obsessively leaving nothing to chance, fostering has not meant controlling. The Celebration school (kindergarten through twelfth grade) will be owned and operated not by Disney but by the Osceola County School District. The school will open next year and will eventually serve about fourteen hundred students—from the surrounding county as well as from the town. What is unusual about the school, apart from pedagogical innovations, is that it's in the center of the town. Children will be able to walk and bike to class. This fall will see the opening of the Teaching Academy, a teacher-training facility that is owned by Disney, run by Disney and Stetson University, and housed in a handsome building designed by William Rawn, who is also the architect of the school.

The health campus, now under construction on the outskirts of town, is a large facility belonging to Florida Hospital and including outpatient surgery, advanced diagnostics, primary-care physicians, and a fitness center. A fibre-optic network will eventually link both the school and the health facility to individual homes. This is just the sort of technological innovation that Walt Disney imagined would be the cornerstone of life in the future. But Michael Eisner's Celebration is actually the opposite of Walt Disney's urban vision. Walt Disney imagined a world in which problems would be solved by science and technology. Celebration puts technology in the background and concentrates on putting in place the less tangible civic infrastructure that is a prerequisite for community. Home buyers agree to be governed by their own homeowners' association and by a set of restrictive deed covenants whose purpose is to strike a balance between individual freedom and communal responsibility. You can park your cars in front of your house, for example, but no more than two cars. You can sublet your house—or your garage apartment—but you can't lease individual rooms. You can hold a garage sale, but only once a year. Writers and artists can work out of their homes, but not dentists—unless they live in the "home business district," where professional offices are allowed. A real sense of community can't develop in a vacuum, however, and Disney seems to have gone out of its way to insure that Celebration will not become a hermetic place. It is neither walled nor gated, unlike many recent master-planned communities. None of the streets are private. Policing is by the county sheriff's office, not by hired security guards (although the homeowners' association may hire additional security if it chooses to). The golf course, designed by the Robert Trent Joneses—father and son—is a public daily-fee facility, not a private club.

Yet, in spite of these efforts to make Celebration open to the outside world, much of the public assumes—or, at least, hopes—that a Disney town will be a perfect town. "It's one of my fears," says Todd Mansfield, who is himself going to build a house in Celebration. "We have people who have purchased houses who think they're moving to Utopia. We keep having to remind them that we can't provide safeguards for all the ills of society. We will have everything that happens in any community." He's right. I'm confident that despite the advanced Honeywell security systems there will be break-ins. Despite the fibreoptic networks, there will be children with learning problems. Despite the state-of-the-art medical technology, there will be sickness. And, despite the sociable appearance of the front porches, there will be neighborly disputes. If there weren't, Celebration would not be the real place that Disney says it will become. . . .

For Journals

When you see the name Disney, what immediate associations come to your mind? How many of them come from your childhood?

For Discussion

1. Since Celebration looks like a traditional community, why does Rybczynski call the article "Tomorrowland"? Why not "Yester-dayland"?

2. Look up the meaning of the word *nostalgia* in the dictionary. In what ways does Celebration play upon that concept? Why?

3. What assumptions about the idea of a Disney town did Rybczynski have when he came to see Celebration? Find examples of them in the text. What assumptions did you start with?

4. When you finished reading this article, were you convinced that Celebration was in fact as close as possible to an ideal community? Why would or wouldn't you want to live there?

5. Since early in this century, most Americans have lived in cities. What, if any, features of Celebration could be adapted to improve city living?

For Writing

1. Write an essay in which you set forth your idea of a dream community—its appearance, its size, its neighborhoods, its values, and the kinds of people who would live there.

2. Listen to the Disney song "Tomorrowland," and write an essay in which you compare the world described in the lyrics with the community described in Rybczynski's article.

3. There's a long history of both writing about ideal communities and attempting to establish them: Plato's *Republic,* Thomas More's *Utopia,* and various real-life experiments. Research and write a paper on one of the following American attempts to set up the perfect place to live: Brook Farm, the Oneida Community, the Shakers, or the effort in Colorado to form a self-sustaining community within a bubble.

✳✳ *United Shareholders of America* (1998)

JACOB WEISBERG

Jacob Weisberg is the chief political correspondent for the on-line magazine Slate. This article is from an issue of the Sunday New York Times *devoted entirely to Americans and their relationship to money.*

. . . With half the country in the market, the gap is no longer just between those with incomes going up and those with stagnant incomes. It's between those with a steadily escalating net worth multiplying in the market and those who have little prospect of building any net worth. It makes the separation between haves and have-nots seem more like a division between will-always-haves and won't-ever-haves.

The market creates a powerful argument for ignoring inequality. It does so not just by highlighting the self-interest of the investing majority but also by fostering political values based on the market. At a basic level, Wall Street is drawing the majority of Americans into a very different idea of citizenship and a very different experience of democracy than the one the country had long been familiar with.

There are superficial similarities between political democracy and shareholder democracy. Shareholders elect management to run a company in their interest. If management fails, the majority of owners can vote them out. But a publicly held company is a democracy without any care for equality. Shareholders have voting rights, but they do not all have the same rights. Voting power is proportionate to one's ownership stake. In a corporation, the majority owners owe no special obligation to the minority. To expend resources on the interests of nonshareholders—by analogy the nation or society as a whole—would be a breach of fiduciary responsibility.

As Alexander Hamilton noted, economic institutions do teach civic lessons, and the experience of voting one's shares as opposed to voting one's conscience has affected the mind-set and the rhetoric of American politics. Ronald Reagan was the first to pose a challenge to an incumbent President in terms of narrow, personal self-interest. "Are you better off now than you were four years ago?" he asked in 1980, implying that voters should assess management's performance in quantitative terms. The citizen's position in relation to the country is increasingly referred to as an ownership stake—the view taken by the C.E.O. candidate Ross Perot in 1992. Results overwhelm questions of democratic legitimacy. . . .

The shareholder-citizen in whose image politics is being remade is 5 not a new player on the American stage. In fact, he is the reincarnation of an old character. The new ideal of the financially autonomous individual, who manages his own investments so as not to be dependent on government, the community or institutions, embodies the eternal American aspiration to individualism and self-sufficiency. Investing man is a successor to the Jeffersonian ideal of the yeoman farmer, whose ability to satisfy his own modest needs was taken as an underpinning of democratic health.

But the contemporary shareholder-citizen is at the same time an impoverished embodiment of that ideal, concentrating on material aspects of independence while largely excluding the experience of community and cultivation of civic virtue. An idea of material sufficiency that might have seemed appropriate just a few years ago has been supplanted by an ever-rising standard of how much is necessary for true happiness. Rather than fostering the kind of democratic citizen who can be trusted to govern, as Jefferson's ideal did, the market ideal of citizenship is about developing the means to withdraw from unsatisfactory common institutions—public schools, the Social Security system, even the need to work. The explicit version of this ideology, libertarianism, has been gaining adherents and credibility in recent years. It is the political philosophy fostered by the stock market.

The citizen-investor serves his fellow citizens badly by his inclination to withdraw from the community. He tends to serve himself badly as well. He does so by focusing his pursuit of happiness on something that very seldom makes people happy in the way they expect it to.

A hundred years ago, during another popular spasm of enthusiasm for investment, a President was more likely to remind the country of this human truth than to indulge its fascination with the market. In his 1893 Fourth of July proclamation, President Grover Cleveland warned the nation to "guard against the sordid struggle for unearned wealth" and to "hold fast to the American idea that work is honorable and economy a virtue." He viewed getting rich in the stock market as a dismal aspiration, not just for America but for Americans.

For Journals

How do you expect to provide for yourself financially when you leave school?

For Discussion

1. How does using language reminiscent of the Declaration of Independence or phrases with political overtones—like "citizen-investor"—strengthen Weisberg's argument against the get-rich quick mentality?

2. Weisberg's definition of the American dream is a middle-class standard of living for all. How would your personal definition of the American dream compare with his? With the definition of your parents? Your friends?

For Writing

1. Go to the library or a magazine stand, and find one or two articles that have advice about money—making it, saving it, losing it, managing with very little of it—as their subject. Write an essay in which you consider the following questions: What assumptions, explicit or implicit, does the writer make about Americans and their attitude toward money? What are the strongest and weakest points the writer makes, and why? Does the author make any connections between money and the achievement or destruction of the American dream? If so, what are they?

2. Write an essay on an incident from your own life that you think best illustrates your attitude toward money and toward the issues of responsibility, selfishness, and involvement that Weisberg raises. As objectively as possible, analyze your own relationship to money and what you think it can and cannot do for you.

❀❀ FROM *Bowling Alone* (2000)

ROBERT D. PUTNAM

Robert Putnam is the author of several books on American community, including Democracies in Flux: The Evolution of Social Capital in Contemporary Society *(2002) and* Better Together: Restoring the American Community *(2003).*

"To everything there is a season, and a time for every purpose under the heaven," sang the Hebrew poet in Ecclesiastes. When Pete Seeger put that ancient maxim to folk music in the 1960s, it was, perhaps, a season for Americans to unravel fetters of intrusive togetherness. As we enter a new century, however, it is now past time to begin to reweave the fabric of our communities.

At the outset of our inquiry I noted that most Americans today feel vaguely and uncomfortably disconnected. It seemed to many as the twentieth century closed, just as it did to the young Walter Lippmann at the century's opening, that "we have changed our environment more quickly than we know how to change ourselves." We tell pollsters that we wish we lived in a more civil, more trustworthy, more collectively caring community. The evidence from our inquiry shows that this longing is not simply nostalgia or "false consciousness." Americans are *right* that the bonds of our communities have withered, and we are *right* to fear that this transformation has very real costs. The challenge for us, however, as it was for our predecessors moving from the Gilded Age into the Progressive Era, is not to grieve over social change, but in guide it.

Creating (or re-creating) social capital is no simple task. It would be eased by a palpable national crisis, like war or depression or natural

---

I want to thank Tom Sander for help in preparing this chapter.

disaster, but for better *and* for worse, America at the dawn of the new century faces no such galvanizing crisis. The ebbing of community over the last several decades has been silent and deceptive. We notice its effects in the strained interstices of our private lives and in the degradation of our public life, but the most serious consequences are reminiscent of the old parlor puzzle: "What's missing from this picture?" Weakened social capital is manifest in the things that have vanished almost unnoticed—neighborhood parties and get-togethers with friends, the unreflective kindness of strangers, the shared pursuit of the public good rather than a solitary quest for private goods. Naming this problem is an essential first step toward confronting it, just as labeling "the environment" allowed Americans to hear the silent spring and naming what Betty Friedan called "the problem that has no name" enabled women to articulate what was wrong with their lives.

Naming our problem, however—and even gauging its dimensions, diagnosing its origins, and assessing its implications, as I have sought to do in this book—is but a preliminary to the tougher challenge. In a world irrevocably changed, a world in which most women are employed, markets global, individuals and firms mobile, entertainment electronic, technology accelerating, and major war (thankfully) absent, how can we nevertheless replenish our stocks of social capital? Like most social issues, this one has two faces—one institutional and one individual. To use the convenient market metaphor, we need to address both the *supply* of opportunities for civic engagement and the *demand* for those opportunities.

Just as did our predecessors in the Progressive Era, we need to create new structures and policies (public and private) to facilitate renewed civic engagement. As I shall explain in more detail in a moment, leaders and activists in every sphere of American life must seek innovative ways to respond to the eroding effectiveness of the civic institutions and practices that we inherited. At the same time we need to fortify our resolve as individuals to reconnect, for we must overcome a familiar paradox of collective action. Even if I privately would prefer a more vibrant community, I cannot accomplish that goal on my own—it's not a meeting, after all, if only I show up, and it's not a club if I'm the only member. It is tempting to retreat to private pleasures that I *can* achieve on my own. But in so doing, I make it even harder for you to solve your version of the same problem. Actions by individuals are not sufficient to restore community, but they *are* necessary.

So our challenge is to restore American community for the twenty-first century through both collective and individual initiative. I recognize the impossibility of proclaiming any panacea for our nation's problems of civic disengagement. On the other hand, because of my experience in spearheading in recent years a concerted nationwide conversation modeled on the intensive interchange among scholars and practitioners in the Progressive Era, I am optimistic that, working together, Americans today can once again be as civically creative as our Progressive forebears. These deliberations, the "Saguaro Seminar: Civic Engagement in America," brought together thinkers and doers from many diverse American communities to shape questions and seek answers. The ensuing discussions have informed my suggestions in this chapter in many ways. The group's objectives have been, first, to make Americans more aware of the collective significance of the myriad minute decisions that we make daily to invest—or disinvest—in social capital and, second, to spark the civic imaginations of our fellow citizens to discover and invent new ways of connecting socially that fit our changed lives.

Figuring out how to renew our stock of social capital is a task for a nation and a decade, not a single scholar, or even a single group. Commurutarian scholar-activists, such as Amitai Etzioni and William Galston, have long labored in this vineyard. My intention in this chapter is modest—to identify key facets of the challenge ahead, by sketching briefly six spheres that deserve special attention from aspiring social capitalists: youth and schools; the workplace, urban and metropolitan design; religion; arts and culture; and politics and government. For each, by offering some suggestions of my own, I seek to provoke the reader's own imagination in the hope that together we can produce something even more creative and powerful.

Philosophers from Aristotle and Rousseau to William James and John Dewey have begun discussions of civics with the education of youth. They have pondered the essential virtues and skills and knowledge and habits of democratic citizens and how to instill them. That starting point is especially appropriate for reformers today, for the single most important cause of our current plight is a pervasive and continuing generational decline in almost all forms of civic engagement. Today's youth did not initiate the erosion of Americans' social capital—their parents did—and it is the obligation of Americans of all ages to help rekindle civic engagement among the generation that will come of age in the early years of the twenty-first century.

So I set before America's parents, educators, and, above all, America's young adults the following challenge: *Let us find ways to ensure that by 2010 the level of civic engagement among Americans then coming of age in all parts of our society will match that of their grandparents when they were that same age, and that at the same time bridging social capital will be substantially greater than it was in their grandparents' era.* One specific test of our success will be whether we can restore electoral turnout to that of the 1960s, but our goal must be to increase participation and deliberation in other, more substantive and fine-grained ways, too—

from team sports to choirs and from organized altruism to grassroots social movements.

The means to achieve these goals in the early twenty-first century, 10 and the new forms of connectedness that will mark our success, will almost surely be different from those of the mid–twentieth century. For this reason, success will require the sensibility and skills of Gen X and their successors, even more than of baby boomers and their elders. Nevertheless, some "old-fashioned" ideas are relevant. Take civics education, for example. We know that knowledge about public affairs and practice in everyday civic skills are prerequisites for effective participation. We know, too, that the "civics report card" issued by the U.S. Department of Education for American elementary and high school students at the end of the twentieth century was disappointing. So improved civics education in school should be part of our strategy—not just "how a bill becomes a law," but "How can I participate effectively in the public life of my community?" Imagine for example, the civic lessons that could be imparted by a teacher in South Central Los Angeles, working with students to *effect* public change that her students think is important, like getting lights for a neighborhood basketball court.

We know other strategies that will work, too. A mounting body of evidence confirms that community service programs really do strengthen the civic muscles of participants, especially if the service is meaningful, regular, and woven into the fabric of the school curriculum. Episodic service has little effect, and it is hard to imagine that baby-sitting and janitorial work—the two most frequent types of "community service" nationwide, according to one 1997 study—have much favorable effect. On the other hand, well-designed service learning programs (the emerging evidence suggests) improve civic knowledge, enhance citizen efficacy, increase social responsibility and self-esteem, teach skills of cooperation and leadership, and may even (one study suggests) reduce racism. Interestingly, voluntary programs seem to work as well as mandatory ones. Volunteering in one's youth is, as we noted in chapter 7, among the strongest predictors of adult volunteering. Intergenerational mentoring, too, can serve civic ends, as in Boston's Citizen Schools program, which enables adult volunteers to work with youth on tangible after-school projects, like story-writing or Web site building.

Participation in extracurricular activities (both school linked and independent) is another proven means to increase civic and social involvement in later life. In fact, participation in high school music groups, athletic teams, service clubs, and the like is among the strongest precursors of adult participation, even when we compare demographically matched groups. From a civic point of view, extracurricular activities are anything but "frills," yet funding for them was decimated during the 1980s and 1990s. Reversing that perverse development would be a good start toward our goal of youthful reengagement by 2010. Finally, we know that smaller schools encourage more active involvement in extracurricular activity than big schools— more students in smaller schools have an opportunity to play trombone or left tackle or King Lear. Smaller schools, like smaller towns, generate higher expectations for mutual reciprocity and collective action. So deconcentrating megaschools or creating smaller "schools within schools" will almost surely produce civic dividends.

Our efforts to increase social participation among youth must not be limited to schooling. Though it is not yet easy to see what the Internet-age equivalent of 4-H or settlement houses might be, we ought to bestow an annual Jane Addams Award on the Gen X'er or Gen Y'er who comes up with the best idea. What we need is not civic broccoli—good for you but unappealing—but an updated version of Scouting's ingenious combination of values and fun. I challenge those who came of age in the civically dispiriting last decade of the twentieth century to invent powerful and enticing ways of increasing civic engagement among their younger brothers and sisters who will come of age in the first decade of the twenty-first century.

For Journals

What public service do you do, if any? What social networks do you belong to?

For Discussion

1. Respond to Putnam's assertion that today most Americans feel vaguely and uncomfortably disconnected. You can't speak for all Americans, but what arguments can you make for or against this proposition from your own experience and that of people close to you? Is it a generalization? What evidence do you have from you own experience on one side or the other?

2. Putnam defines social capital elsewhere in his book as social networks and reciprocity: ". . . your Sunday school class, the regulars who play poker on your commuter train, your college roommates, the civic organization to which you belong, the Internet chat group in which you participate, and the network of professional acquaintances recorded in your address book." Given this list, what other examples from your community would you offer as evidence of social capital?

3. Putnam says that the erosion of civic responsibility began not with today's youth but with their parents. What evidence do you have to argue for or against this proposition? Do your parents participate in any regular kind of volunteer work?

4. It is a crucial part of Putnam's argument that any discussion of civic participation has to begin with the education of youth. What would be your recommendations to improve the participation of young people in community-building activities?

5. Putnam suggests that there ought to be an award for the Gen X'er who comes up with the Internet idea that best approximates other kinds of social capital. Given that the Internet both enables people to contact each other and makes it possible for them to do so without ever being in the same room, or even the same country, how could it possibly be an instrument for building involvement?

6. Putnam wrote this book just before September 11 but after the Oklahoma bombings. If he is correct, one goad to your grandparents' sense of civic responsibility was that they had to cope with disasters like the Depression and World War II. What, if anything, do you think that the Oklahoma bombings and 9/11 have done to increase your own desire to be active in your community?

For Writing

1. Given Putnam's challenge to ". . . find ways to ensure that by 2010 the level of civil engagement will match that of their grandparents when they were the same age," collaborate with one to three other members of your class to write a proposal—with priorities, goals, and a budget—to accomplish one civic-minded activity that you are not presently engaged in: for example, volunteering for a blood drive or cancer 10k run, and tutoring in reading or math or basketball at a local elementary school.

2. Putnam keeps referring to the Progressive Era (largely the period of Theodore Roosevelt's and Woodrow Wilson's presidencies in the early twentieth century) as a time when new social structures and policies were created and civic engagement renewed. Research and write up one of those new structures and policies, such as the development of the national parks system or the successful movement to get for women the right to vote. Alternatively, research one of the individuals who was responsible for investigations that prompted some of the changes, like muckraking writer Ida Tarbell and her work on corruption in Standard Oil, or Upton Sinclair and his writing on contamination in the meat-packing industry, or John Muir and his successful efforts on behalf of Yosemite.

3. Create an ad campaign for a civic-minded activity that you support. Develop a short questionnaire about how effective the ad is, and ask the other members of your class to fill it out. Follow up with a report on what you did and what response there was to the materials.

❀❀❀ Office in a Small City (1953)

EDWARD HOPPER

Edward Hopper (1882–1967) studied in Paris, lived in New York, and devoted most of his work to the city as the great subject for modern painting. He often painted ordinary city dwellers who seem alone, whether in an office, a diner, a coffee shop, or the like, but he treated them with enormous respect and dignity as well as sympathy. (See Color Plate II for a color image of this painting.)

Edward Hopper (1882–1967), "Office in a Small City," 1953. Oil on canvas, H. 28 in. W. 40 in. Signed (lower left) Edward Hopper. The Metropolitan Museum of Art, George A. Hearn Fund, 1953. (53.183)

For Journals

New York is the quintessential modern metropolis; what kinds of images of this city come to your mind?

For Discussion

1. Edward Hopper painted many scenes of individuals in the city; what kind of daily office life do you imagine for the man in the painting? What adjectives would you use to describe him—self-contained, lonely, exposed, relaxed? Look closely at the picture, and however you choose to describe him, use details from the painting to explain your choices.

2. With your classmates each contributing a sentence, make up a story about the life, work, and/or thoughts of the person in this picture.

3. You have the black-and-white version of the picture, but the color version is also in this book. What difference does the presence of colors make? Do they change the mood or emotional effect, or do they stay the same?

For Writing

1. Look up another of Hopper's classic city paintings, like *Nighthawks* (people at a counter in a diner) or *Automat* (a woman having a cup of coffee by herself), and write a paper in which you analyze the painting for the following: the way the figures do or do not connect with each other—where they are in the picture; what or whom they are looking at; how much we can see of their faces; what their mood is; and what Hopper does to establish that mood through their body language, the setting, and the colors he chooses.

2. When Hopper studied in Paris, he was especially fascinated by the clear vision of the French painter Manet, who, among his other subjects, painted a lot of Paris city life. Look at one of Manet's paintings that involves someone alone in a city, either with no other people around or with no connection to the other people in the picture, and write an essay in which you compare that picture with this painting of Hopper's. You don't need to be an art expert to do this—you're looking for detail, composition of the figures, and the way loneliness can be portrayed through anonymous city dwellers.

❊❊❊ *Structured Appeal: Let America Be America Again* (1997)

CHRIS COUNTRYMAN

Chris Countryman is a college student from California who wrote this essay as part of his second-quarter writing class. His assignment was to analyze a persuasive text, and he chose this Langston Hughes poem from his course text.

Not all arguments come in the form of emotional speeches or legalistic essays: cartoons, newspaper articles, and even photographs can persuade as well, and sometimes much more efficiently. Poetry exemplifies this type of argumentation. Because many forms of verse follow a less restrictive format than the typical essay, poets have much more freedom to arrange elements of structure to enhance the argumentative nature of a work. In his poem "Let America Be America Again" Langston Hughes uses evocative language and structural techniques to help emphasize the separation he feels underclass Americans experience in a country they helped create.

From the beginning Hughes crafts the structure of his poem to match the nature of his thesis. The first section of his poem alternates between four-line stanzas and short sentences in parentheses. The use of these two stylistically different forms creates individual voices which present the division Hughes sees in American society. Hughes's word choice enhances this contrast. In the opening lines Hughes chooses slow, balanced sentences: "Let America be America again. / Let it be the dream it used to be. / Let it be the pioneer on the plain / Seeking a home where he himself is free" (lines 1–4). These lines resound with confidence and grandeur, and evoke a powerful patriotic image of the rugged frontiersman representing America in search of a land to claim in the name of freedom. Hughes contrasts this formal stanza with a short, much more personal line set off in parentheses: "(America never was America to me)" (line 5). Several techniques come into play here. The line's physical separation from the narrative highlights to the separation in viewpoint, and the enclosure in parentheses suggests an unequal relationship and differing viewpoints, the dominant majority's American dream and the submissive minority's American reality. Hughes's parenthetical interjection mimics the structure of the first line, but in replacing "again" in line 1 with "to me" he shifts the focus from past glory to present, and very personal, isolation.

The second and third verse paragraphs, up through line 10, follow the same pattern. Again, the first stanza employs highly connotative words in balanced structures, including the repetition of "dream" in the first line and the images of conniving kings and scheming tyrants (lines 6, 8). By repeating the formula of four-line stanza followed by interjection, Hughes creates a dialogue emphasizing the fact that all of these paragraphs address the same subject, America's deviation from the ideal. Hughes's formatting changes and word choice, however, give each speaker an entirely different message. One voice calls for a return to past greatness, the other claims that greatness never existed.

As the poem progresses Hughes alters his word choice and structure in order to bring about a reversal in this dialogue. After the short couplet in italics Hughes's speakers switch roles: the previously parenthetical voice gains new strength and the old narrator fades away. Hughes now indicates forcefulness by printing the second voice in normal text. In the stanza starting at line 19 Hughes has his second voice imitate the first, employing the same type of balanced sentence structure but with a twist. Instead of "America" he substitutes "I," emphasizing the isolation of the underprivileged from their own country.

In the next section Hughes concentrates on the collective iden- 5
tity, history, and struggle of the various groups that compose the
American underclass, and his choice of imagery and structure reflects this move toward unity. Having established the stereotypical
vision of the American foundation experience in his earlier stanzas,
Hughes falls back on these emotionally charged images to retell
American history in terms of the role of currently underprivileged
minorities. Now the Negroes, poor whites, and red men are the "Pioneers"; it is they who are the "serf[s] of kings" (lines 19–31). Hughes
also returns to images and phrases from earlier in the poem. The
modern-day victims of America "dreamt our basic dream" and built
a "homeland of the free" (lines 30, 41). Hughes inserts more parallel
constructions near the end of the paragraph to emphasize the shared
trials of the true American pioneers: ". . . all the dreams we've
dreamed / And all the songs we've sung / And all the hopes we've
held / And all the flags we've hung" (lines 46–49). In addition the
structure of the poem as a whole changes to reflect Hughes's argumentative tactic. Instead of individual stanzas, Hughes casts this section of the poem in a single unified paragraph, mirroring the unified
cause of Hughes's unsung American patriots.

In many ways poetry as an argumentative form bears a closer re-
semblance to photography or other artwork than to essays. While
structural concerns certainly occupy an essay's author, the incredible
flexibility of poetry allows the poet to balance phrases and order stanzas much like a photographer might arrange objects in a scene to create a certain effect. Poetry also relies heavily on visual language.
Although poetic arguments may tend toward emotional appeals, they
are no less valid than pathos appeals in essays, and can be much more
effective. Certainly in Hughes's "Let America Be America Again"
these images, combined with a carefully planned structure, create a
powerful, and ultimately convincing, argument.

For Journals

Do you read poetry on your own? Do you think of it as a vehicle for
intellectual expression?

For Discussion

1.   What is Countryman's thesis about the use of poetry or other
forms of art to make an argument or appeal?

2.   Countryman does a very close reading of this poem to explain
how the argument is constructed. What are the crucial voices and dialogues in the poem? What points of view do they express?

3. Given the different voices, how do the historical references to pioneers help structure the unity achieved at the end of the poem between various excluded groups like poor white, black, and red Americans?

4. How persuasive is Countryman's point that poetry resembles photography? What other arts do you think can pose an argument in the way that poetry can?

For Writing

1. "Let America Be America Again" was one of a series of poems Hughes wrote about his disappointment and hope for the realization of his country's potential. Pick another poem from the series, and apply Countryman's analytical structure to it: What appeal is Hughes making in the poem? How many different voices can you find, and what points of view can you identify? Pay attention to individual words, especially pronouns, to help establish the various voices. Finally, be sure to look for the argument that the language of the poem conveys, and rephrase it in your own words.

❀❀❀ *Looking Back at the March—* *40 Years Later* (2003)

CLAYBORNE CARSON

Clayborne Carson is a Professor of History at Stanford University and the Editor-in-Chief of the Martin Luther King Papers Project.

It has been 40 years since the March on Washington for Jobs and Freedom divided my life into unequal parts. Not much of historical importance happened to me during the first 19 years. Afterward, my life merged with history.

I'd just completed my first year at the University of New Mexico, and it was my first civil rights demonstration. Suddenly, there were more black people around me than I'd ever seen in my life. Having hitched a ride to Washington from a student conference in Indiana, I stood alone in the crowd, trying to make sense of it all.

Stokely Carmichael, whom I met at the conference, had derided the march, urging me instead to join him and other student activists in civil rights rallies in Cambridge, Md., and Greenwood, Miss. For me, however, joining the march was the most radical thing I had ever done. I was not yet ready to be arrested or join Stokely in the brashly militant Student Nonviolent Coordinating Committee (SNCC).

But my knowledge of SNCC shaped how I experienced the march. I listened intently when SNCC Chairman John Lewis—today a U.S. representative but then the youngest speaker on the program—cautioned the crowd at the Lincoln Memorial that "we have nothing to be proud of," reminded us that many of "our brothers" were unable to attend the march "for they are receiving starvation wages" and declared that the Kennedy administration's civil rights bill was "too little and too late."

Lewis' speech presaged the gulf that would soon divide youthful 5 SNCC radicals from more moderate civil rights leaders such as Martin Luther King Jr. But that afternoon, as everyone eagerly awaited King's concluding address, there were few signs of disunity. I had often read about King but, like many in the crowd, had never before heard him speak.

Though we were tired at the end of a long, hot summer day, King didn't disappoint us. In the years since then, I've listened to the "I Have a Dream" speech too many times to remember what I felt the first time. But I knew immediately that King was special—a speaker capable of expressing our best thoughts about why we were there. He reminded us that the movement was not just about the transitory goals of deaegregation and voting rights but about the enduring ideals of justice.

After the march, my life went in directions that I could not have imagined. King was a distant, revered figure on a podium then, but just two decades later I would become the editor of his papers. I would teach civil rights history to students at Stanford who were not yet born at the time of the march—a time where their university had no black professors and no African American history courses.

Although I never met King, I came to know his family. I also came to know—and write about—Carmichael and many other activists who were closer to my age, and they have shaped my understanding of the 1963 march and the civil rights movement. They taught me that the movement was about more than King, about more than marches and oratory and even about more than civil rights.

King would not be honored with a national holiday if not for Rosa Parks, E.D. Nixon, Jo Ann Robinson and the many others who made possible the success of the Montgomery, Ala., bus boycott. He would not be the subject of the comprehensive edition of the King Papers that my staff and I are preparing at Stanford if not for the youthful demonstrators in Birmingham, Ala., who braved dogs and fire hoses to snatch victory from defeat. The measure of King's greatness was that he stood out in a forest of tall trees.

The March on Washington was a turning point in my life and in 10 the African American freedom struggle, but it symbolized much more. During a century of human rights struggles, there would be moments of despair when even King realized that his Dream of 1963 was turning into a nightmare. In one of his last sermons, he lamented "the fact that our dreams are not fulfilled."

Yet 40 years later, the march remains an inspiring day of hope for those of us who were there. In the long, continuing, worldwide struggle for social justice, it was one of those exceptional moments when injustice seemed outnumbered if not subdued.

For Journals

What would you consider your single most life-changing experience?

For Discussion

1.   What do you think Carson means when he says that for the first nineteen years of his life, nothing much happened, and then his life merged with history?

2.   How does Carson explain the effect of SNCC and Lewis on the way he experienced the march?

3.   Carson says that like a lot of people in the crowd, he had never actually heard King speak before. What about King's words was so effective as far as Carson was concerned?

4.   Why does Carson mention other civil rights activists such as Rosa Parks, E. D. Dixon, Stokely Carmichael, and John Lewis? What do you think he wants you to learn from his mentioning other people besides King himself?

For Writing

1.   John Lewis is now a member of Congress, but in his early twenties he was one of the organizers of the attempt to register black voters in the South in 1964, which was a very dangerous undertaking. Research and write a paper about the summer of 1964, focusing on Lewis or on the killings of three civil rights workers, on local black activists who took civil rights workers into their homes, on press coverage of that summer, or on another topic approved by your teacher. You can concentrate on an individual personality; on political causes and effects; on how ordinary people, white and black, reacted; on the violence that occurred; and so on.

2.   Research and write a paper on the press and television coverage of King's speech. The *New York Times, Time, Newsweek,* the *Washington Post, Life* magazine, *Look* magazine, and every other major publication had coverage. You can get the *Times* on-line with full text. Pick out one or two articles, and write an essay in which you compare the reporter's coverage with Carson's experience. You might consider the differences between the reporter's writing about a public event and Carson's writing as an individual affected by what he saw and heard, but that is only one possible approach.

✿✿✿ *The Futile Search for Happiness* (2003)

JON GERTNER

Jon Gertner is a staff writer for Money Magazine.

If Daniel Gilbert is right, then you are wrong. That is to say, if Daniel Gilbert is right, then you are wrong to believe that a new car will make you as happy as you imagine. You are wrong to believe that a new kitchen will make you happy for as long as you imagine. You are wrong to think that you will be more unhappy with a big single setback (a broken wrist, a broken heart) than with a lesser chronic one (a trick knee, a tense marriage). You are wrong to assume that job failure will be crushing. You are wrong to expect that a death in the family will leave you bereft for year upon year, forever and ever. You are even wrong to reckon that a cheeseburger you order in a restaurant—this week, next week, a year from now, it doesn't really matter when—will definitely hit the spot. That's because when it comes to predicting exactly how you will feel in the future, you are most likely wrong.

A professor in Harvard's department of psychology, Gilbert likes to tell people that he studies happiness. But it would be more precise to say that Gilbert—along with the psychologist Tim Wilson of the University of Virginia, the economist George Loewenstein of Carnegie-Mellon and the psychologist (and Nobel laureate in economics) Daniel Kahneman of Princeton—has taken the lead in studying a specific type of emotional and behavioral prediction. In the past few years, these four men have begun to question the decision-making process that shapes our sense of well-being; how do we predict what will make us happy or unhappy—and then how do we feel after the actual experience? For example, how do we suppose we'll feel if our favorite college football team wins or loses, and then how do we really feel a few days after the game? How do we predict we'll feel about purchasing jewelry, having children, buying a big house or being rich? And then how do we regard the outcomes? According to this small corps of academics, almost all actions—the decision to buy jewelry, have kids, buy the big house or work exhaustively for a fatter pay-check—are based on our predictions of the emotional consequences of these events.

Until recently, this was uncharted territory. How we forecast our feelings, and whether those predictions match our future emotional states, had never been the stuff of laboratory research. But in scores of experiments, Gilbert, Wilson, Kahneman and Loewenstein have made a slew of observations and conclusions that undermine a number of fundamental assumptions: namely, that we humans understand what we want and are adept at improving our well-being—that we are good at maximizing our utility, in the jargon of traditional economics. Further, their work on prediction raises some unsettling and somewhat more personal questions. To understand affective forecasting, as Gilbert has termed these studies, is to wonder if everything you have ever thought about life choices, and about happiness, has been at the least somewhat naïve and, at worst, greatly mistaken.

The problem, as Gilbert and company have come to discover, is that we falter when it comes to imagining how we will feel about something in the future. It isn't that we get the big things wrong. We know we will experience visits to Le Cirque and to the periodontist differently; we can accurately predict that we'd rather be stuck in Montauk than in a Midtown elevator. What Gilbert has found, however, is that we overestimate the intensity and the duration of our emotional reactions—our "affect"—to future events. In other words, we might believe that a new BMW will make life perfect. But it will almost certainly be less exciting than we anticipated; nor will it excite us for as long as predicted. The vast majority of Gilbert's test participants through the years have consistently made just these sorts of errors both in the laboratory and in real-life situations. And whether Gilbert's subjects were trying to predict how they would feel in the future about a plate of spaghetti with meat sauce, the defeat of a preferred political candidate or romantic rejection seemed not to matter. On average, bad events proved less intense and more transient than rest participants predicted. Good events proved less intense and briefer as well. Gilbert and his collaborator Tim Wilson call the gap between what we predict and what we ultimately experience the "impact bias"—"impact" meaning the errors we make in estimating both the intensity and duration of our emotions and "bias" our tendency to err. The phrase characterizes how we experience the dimming excitement over not just a BMW but also over any object or event that we presume will make us happy. Would a 20 percent raise or winning the lottery result in a contented life: You may predict it will, but almost surely it won't turn out that way. And a new plasma television? You may have high hopes, but the impact bias suggests that it will almost certainly be less cool, and in a shorter time, than you imagine. Worse,

Gilbert has noted that these mistakes of expectation can lead directly to mistakes in choosing what we think will give us pleasure. He calls this "miswanting."

"The average person says, 'I know I'll be happier with a Porsche 5 than a Chevy,'" Gilbert explains. "'Or with Linda rather than Rosalyn. Or as a doctor rather than as a plumber.' That seems very clear to people. The problem is, I can't get into medical school or afford the Porsche. So for the average person, the obstacle between them and happiness is actually *getting* the futures that they desire. But what our research shows—not just ours, but Loewenstein's and Kahneman's—is that the real problem is figuring out which of those futures is going to have the high payoff and is really going to make you happy.

"You know, the Stones said, 'You can't always get what you want,'" Gilbert adds. "I don't think that's the problem. The problem is you can't always *know* what you want." . . .

Gilbert's papers on affective forecasting began to appear in the late 1990's, but the idea to study happiness and emotional prediction actually came to him on a sunny afternoon in October 1992, just as he and his friend Jonathan Jay Koehler sat down for lunch outside the psychology building at the University of Texas at Austin, where both men were teaching at the time, Gilbert was uninspired about his studies and says he felt despair about his failing marriage. And as he launched into a discussion of his personal life, he swerved to ask why economists focus on the financial aspects of decision making rather than the emotional ones. Koehler recalls, "Gilbert said something like: 'It all seems so small. It isn't really about money; it's about happiness. Isn't that what everybody wants to know when we make a decision?'" For a moment, Gilbert forgot his troubles, and two more questions came to him. Do we even know what makes us happy? And if it's difficult to figure out what makes us happy in the moment, how can we predict what will make us happy in the future? . . .

"People ask why I study happiness," Gilbert says, "and I say, 'Why study anything else?' It's the holy grail. We're studying the thing that all human action is directed toward."

One experiment of Gilbert's had students in a photography class at Harvard choose two favorite pictures from among those they had just taken and then relinquish one to the teacher. Some students were told their choices were permanent; others were told they could exchange their prints after several days. As it turned out, those who had time to change their minds were less pleased with their decisions than those whose choices were irrevocable.

Much of Gilbert's research is in this vein. Another recent study 10 asked whether transit riders in Boston who narrowly missed then trains experienced the self-blame that people tend to predict they'll feel in this situation. (They did not.) And a paper waiting to be published, "The Peculiar Longevity of Things Not So Bad," examines why we expect that bigger problems will always dwarf minor annoyances. "When really bad things happen to us, we defend against them," Gilbert explains. "People, of course, predict the exact opposite. If you ask, 'What would you rather have, a broken leg or a trick knee?' they'd probably say, 'Trick knee.' And yet, if your goal is to accumulate maximum happiness over your lifetime, you just made the wrong choice. A trick knee is a bad thing to have."

All of these studies establish the links between prediction, decision making and well-being. The photography experiment challenges our common assumption that we would be happier with the option to change our minds when in fact we're happier with closure. The transit experiment demonstrates that we tend to err in estimating our regret over missed opportunities. The "things not so bad" work shows our failure to imagine how grievously irritations compromise our satisfaction. Our emotional defenses snap into action when it comes to a divorce or a disease but not for lesser problems. We fix the leaky roof on our house, but over the long haul, the broken screen door we never mend adds up to more frustration.

Gilbert does not believe all forecasting mistakes lead to similar results; a death in the family, a new gym membership and a new husband are not the same, but in how they affect our well-being they are similar. "Our research simply says that whether it's the thing that matters or the thing that doesn't, both of them matter less than you think they will," he says. "Things that happen to you or that you buy or own—as much as you think they make a difference to your happiness, you're wrong by a certain amount. You're overestimating how much of a difference they make. None of them make the difference you think. And that's true of positive and negative events." . . .

"We're very, very nervous about overapplying the research," Loewenstein says. "Just because we figure out that X makes people happy and they're choosing Y, we don't want to impose X on them. I have a discomfort with paternalism and with using the results coming out of our field to impose decisions on people."

Still, Gilbert and Loewenstein can't contain the personal and philosophical questions raised by their work. After talking with both men, I found it hard not to wonder about my own predictions at every turn. At times it seemed like knowing the secret to some parlor trick that was nonetheless very difficult to pull off—when I ogled a new car at the Honda dealership as I waited for a new muffler on my '92 Accord, for instance, or as my daughter's fever spiked one evening and I imagined something terrible, and then something more terrible thereafter. With some difficulty, I could observe my mind overshooting the mark, zooming past accuracy toward the sublime or the tragic. It was tempting to want to try to think about the future more moderately. But it seemed nearly impossible as well.

To Loewenstein, who is especially attendant to the friction be-   15
tween his emotional and deliberative processes, a life without forecasting errors would most likely be a better, happier life. "If you had a
deep understanding of the impact bias and you acted on it, which is
not always that easy to do, you would tend to invest your resources in
the things that would make you happy," he says. This might mean
taking more time with friends instead of more time for making money.
He also adds that a better understanding of the empathy gap—those
hot and cold states we all find ourselves in on frequent occasions—
could save people from making regrettable decisions in moments of
courage or craving.

Gilbert seems optimistic about using the work in terms of improving "institutional judgment"—how we spend health care dollars, for
example—but less sanguine about using it to improve our personal
judgment. He admits that he has taken some of his research to heart;
for instance, his work on what he calls the psychological immune system has led him to believe that he would be able to adapt to even the
worst turn of events. In addition, he says that he now takes more
chances in life, a fact corroborated in at least one aspect by his research
partner Tim Wilson, who says that driving with Gilbert in Boston is a
terrifying, white-knuckle experience. "But I should have learned many
more lessons from my research than I actually have," Gilbert admits.
"I'm getting married in the spring because this woman is going to
make me happy forever, and I know it." At this, Gilbert laughs, a sudden, booming laugh that fills his Cambridge office. He seems to find it
funny not because it's untrue, but because nothing could be more true.
This is how he feels. "I don't think I want to give up all these motivations," he says, "that belief that there's the good and there's the bad
and that this is a contest to try to get one and avoid the other, I don't
think. I want to learn too much from my research in that sense."

Even so, Gilbert is currently working on a complex experiment in
which he has made affective forecasting errors "go away." In this test,
Gilbert's team asks members of Group A to estimate how they'll feel if
they receive negative personality feedback. The impact bias kicks in, of
course, and they mostly predict they'll feel terrible, when in fact they
end up feeling O.K. But if Gilbert shows Group B that others have gotten the same feedback and felt O.K. afterward, then its members predict they'll feel O.K. as well. The impact bias disappears, and the
participants in Group B make accurate predictions.

This is exciting to Gilbert. But at the same time, it's not a technique he wants to shape into a self-help book, or one that he even

imagines could be practically implemented. "Hope and fear are enduring features of the human experience," he says, "and it is unlikely that people are going to abandon them anytime soon just because some psychologist told them they should." In fact, in his recent writings, he has wondered whether forecasting errors might somehow serve a larger functional purpose he doesn't yet understand. If he could wave a wand tomorrow and eliminate all affective-forecasting errors, I ask, would he? "The benefits of not making this error would seem to be that you get a little more happiness," he says. "When choosing between two jobs, you wouldn't sweat as much because you'd say: 'You know, I'll be happy in both. I'll adapt to either circumstance pretty well, so there's no use in killing myself for the next week.' But maybe our caricatures of the future—these overinflated assessments of how good or bad things will be—maybe it's these illusory assessments that keep us moving in one direction over the other. Maybe we don't want a society of people who shrug and say, 'It won't really make a difference.'

"Maybe it's important for there to be carrots and sticks in the world, even if they are illusions," he adds. "They keep us moving towards carrots and away from sticks."

For Journals

What does the title refer to, and why did Gertner change it?

For Discussion

1. How do you define the pursuit of happiness for yourself?

2. Gilbert says that happiness is important to study because it is what all human action is directed toward. Do you agree or disagree? Why? Do you think that Americans are more likely to feel that happiness is a justifiable goal?

3. If you were going to spend a lot of money on something, or to marry someone, and you could find out for sure if the decision that the marriage would not make you happy in the long run, would you want to know? Why, or why not?

4. How does Gilbert define "miswanting"?

5. Money can't buy happiness, as a rule, but studies have shown that a great deal of money, like a big lottery ticket or a big inheritance, can make people feel better. Why do you think it doesn't work that way for less remarkable events, like getting a car you want or even suffering a romantic rejection?

For Writing

1. Write a reflective essay based on discussion question number 3, focusing especially on what you think you would lose or gain if you knew in advance that you were going to be less satisfied in the long run than you anticipated. What factors would you balance? Are there circumstances in which you would do or buy what you wanted anyway? Are there benefits to not knowing?

2. Write an argumentative essay in which you take sides for or against Gilbert's statement that although the Rolling Stones said, "You can't always get what you want," the real problem is that you can't always know what you want.

3. The article gives some examples of research that Gilbert has done with his students, with transit riders in Boston, and so forth. He says that people actually deal much better with major problems because our emotional defenses snap into action to protect us when big problems arise, but minor annoyances can lead to more frustration. Write an essay in which you agree or disagree with him on this point, and give examples based on your own experiences and observations of major problems and minor annoyances, and the way that you or those you know react to them.

❊❊❊ *Film: Citizen Kane* (1941)

Produced by RKO Radio Pictures; a Mercury production; director/producer/star, Orson Welles; screenplay, Herman J. Mankiewicz, Orson Welles (120 minutes).

Charles Foster Kane, a fabulously rich publisher, dies in Xanadu, the castle that he built. The last thing he says is "Rosebud." A curious reporter starts by trying to find out what the word means and ends up trying to find out what made Kane tick. Through flashbacks and the reporter's success in tracking down Kane's former best friend, his ex-wife, and people who used to work for him, we see the financial rise and the psychogical and spiritual fall of a man who had everything.

For Journals

What do you think is the best American movie?

For Discussion

1. Is Charles Foster Kane the hero or the villain of this film? How else can you characterize him?

2. How does the relationship between Kane and his closest friend change over the course of their lives? The relationship between Kane and his first wife? His second wife?

3. Why does Kane invest so much in trying to make his wife an opera star even though she doesn't have the voice for singing opera?

4. What do you think Kane values most? What does he lose?

5. There has been endless discussion of this point, but what do you think Rosebud represents to Charles Foster Kane?

For Writing

1. The cowriter and director of the film, Orson Welles, was also the star, and at the time he was only twenty-five years old. He had already gained national attention by doing a radio program about a Martian invasion that was so realistic that it terrified million of people. He never made another film as good as *Citizen Kane,* and he had a reputation in Hollywood for being over budget; however, other actors and filmmakers have always admired him enormously. Research one phase of Welles's career, and focus, for example, on the making of *Citizen Kane,* Welles's association with the Mercury Theater, his radio broadcast, his reputation as a genius, or his starring role in the great espionage film *The Third Man.* There is a considerable bibliography on him, including biographies and conversations, and several books about the movie.

2. This is the most highly praised American film of all time and is routinely listed at the top of critics' lists, but since everyone has copied it, it is difficult to appreciate just how revolutionary it is. But it is full of scenes exhibiting Welles' genius as a director and a technical innovator. For example, in one episode in the movie, the trajectory of Kane's entire first marriage is done in a series of scenes—without dialogue—at the same breakfast table. There is also the big party that Kane throws after hiring all a competitor's reporters; his first meeting with his second wife; her disastrous singing career; the scene in which he tries to keep her from leaving him, and so on. Pick a scene or episode you think was particularly interesting, and analyze it. Here are some possible angles of approach: Welles's creative use of light and shadow to underline character or to create a sense of place (consult the definitions in Chapter 2, but you don't need to use any technical vocabulary to describe what he is doing); the turning points in a scene, including what just preceeded it and what immediately followed it; or a scene in which you see Kane at his best or at his worst, or a scene that you think is especially characteristic of what his fatal flaws are.

Chapter Writing Assignments

1. Find an advertisement in a magazine or newspaper that uses examples of American symbols directly (for example, advertising U.S. savings bonds by showing the emblem of the American bald eagle) or indirectly (e.g., savings bank using Benjamin Franklin's portrait as a logo, or a jeans company that embroiders an American flag on the pocket). There are many such examples; you also might want to look at CD covers and movie advertisements. Write an analysis of the ad in which you consider the following questions: Who is the audience? Why do you think that the advertiser included an example of American symbolism in the ad? Why was the particular example chosen? How effective is that example in conveying American values? How successful or unsuccessful do you think this approach is?

2. The selections in this chapter each express some element of the American dream. Write an essay in which you argue for your own idea of what the American dream means—both what you think it means to most Americans and what it means to you. How do you see the American dream in members of your family? In yourself? What elements are crucial to it? Because you are dealing with a broad idea, it is especially important to include specific examples of what you believe the dream to be and how it manifests itself in you and your family. Do not confine yourself to generalizations like "My parents want me to have a better life than they have." Use your examples to explain their lives, including disappointments or worries, and to show what you really dream of for yourself.

3. Langston Hughes was vitally interested in the promise of the American dream and in the importance of making it accessible to all Americans. With his work in mind, listen to and read the lyrics of contemporary songs, including rap lyrics, that talk about American dreams and nightmares. Write an analytical essay in which you discuss the vision of American life, especially urban life, set forth in these songs, including what they say about dreams for the future. Cite examples from the lyrics to support your assertions. You can use Hughes as a point of comparison if you want to.

4. Imagine that you have to explain the American dream to an English-speaking visitor from another country and that you have to compose a popular culture curriculum featuring contemporary materials that would make the dream clearer to a stranger. Prepare a list of examples for this visitor that are drawn from each of the following categories: four movies to see; two to four musicians to listen to; two works of fiction and two works of nonfiction to read; and two magazines to read. After each selection, write a paragraph explaining why this particular example says something about the American dream, and what that is.

5. Go to the newsstand or your library and pick up the following: one issue of what is usually known as a women's magazine (*Family Circle, Ladies' Home Journal,* and so on), one issue of a magazine addressed to different women's interests (*Cosmopolitan, Mademoiselle,* and so on), and one issue of a magazine addressed largely to men (*GQ, Esquire,* and so on). Be sure that the magazines you choose have *at least one article apiece* on the home (entertaining at home, decorating the home, cooking for friends or family, spending time with children at home, and so on). Write an essay comparing the images of house and home that you find in these publications. What dreams of American home life do you think they advertise? Do the dreams of home revealed in articles in a men's magazine differ from those in the articles for women? If so, in what ways? Are any of the articles more informative than others? If they include photographs, how do the illustrations support the articles' points of view and persuade readers to accept them?

6. Choosing any two or three of the selections in this chapter, write an essay in which you explain what you think the pursuit of happiness would constitute for them. For example, you could write about one of Langston Hughes poems, Putnam's assertion that we need to get more civically and communally involved, Gilbert's idea that we have to live our lives even though we're often wrong about what we want, or Charles Foster Kane's ambitions.

Web Sites for Further Exploration

Andrew Carnegie
www.furman.edu/~benson/docs/carnegie.htm
wwsw.carnegie.org/sub/about/biography.html

Sui Sin Far
www.english.upenn.edu.sui sin far

Langston Hughes
http://www.pbs.org/wnet/ihas/poet/hughes.html
http://www.csustan.edu/english/reuben/pal/chap9/hughes.html#books

Martin Luther King, Jr.
http://www.stanford.edu/group/King/
http://thekingcenter.com/

Witold Rybczynski
www.wharton.upenn.edu/faculty/rybczyn.html

Jacob Weisberg
www.ojr.org/ojr/business/1056570358.php

Robert Putnam
www.bowlingalone.com/
www.ksg.harvard.edu/saguaro/putnam.html

Citizen Kane
www.imdb.com/title/tt0033467/

7

✻✻✻

Images of Gender
and Family

At the core of American identities and American dreams lies the
family. Whether a colonial-era farm household, an immigrant extended family, a native clan or tribe, an urban domestic partnership,
or a suburban nuclear family, families serve as a connection between
the individual and the outside world. The individual's identity, his or
her dreams, in large part depend on the family of origin or a family of
choice. The individual is shaped through beliefs, values, and assumptions that the family holds about the world and that are based on the
family members' experiences and collective memory. The family itself, in turn, derives its value from the social, cultural, political, and
philosophical assumptions and beliefs and the economic needs of the
larger culture.

Questions about the family are pervasive in contemporary American society: What is the "definition" of a family? Who can belong to a
family? What are appropriate gender roles within families? What restraints does the concept of family place on women? On men? On children? What happens to a society in which the nuclear family is no
longer the dominant configuration? What are "family values"? Are
they positive beliefs and aspirations that optimize growth and diversity for all, or narrow-minded strictures and intolerances that seek to
shut out differences of approach or opinion, or something in between?
The debates over these issues have become increasingly rancorous.

And yet this kind of conflict is not new. The history of American society is one of uneasy inequality between men and women.
Revolutionary-era rhetoric depended heavily on a philosophy that
was based on equality and on political rights, but those concepts applied to men only, white men at that. Industrialization brought with it
not only manufacturing jobs and manufactured goods but also exploitation of children for labor. World War I saw tremendous support
for the war effort and for social services from women, but although
women finally gained the vote in 1920, they received few additional

rights thereafter. World War II brought new and demanding jobs for women to support the war effort, but as soon as the men returned from war, society's need to employ these men and to increase social stability issued a new message to women: go home, stay home, and raise children. The civil rights and women's movements of the sixties and seventies brought attention to gross civil injustices, but the Equal Rights Amendment failed to pass. Women have made some strides in business and government, but cries from the media, to politicians, to the religious right have declared that feminism and women's liberation have brought women in particular and society in general nothing but grief.

Despite this inequality of the sexes, the idea of the stable American family—and, concomitantly, a stable American society—has been with us for a long time. Recent debates note the "decline" of the family and blame societal ills on a perceived lack of family stability. But to some degree we have idealized the family of the past. The current divorce rate is 50 percent of first marriages within forty years, but in the colonial era, marriages averaged only twelve years or less because of the death of one spouse. We deplore the numbers of absentee parents, but up to half of all colonial-era children lost at least one parent before the age of twenty-one, and before the 1920s, divorced fathers had no legal obligation to pay child support. We are rightfully concerned about problems in educating youth, but in the 1940s fewer than half of the students entering high school were able to finish. We mourn the death of the extended family, yet children are now more likely than at any earlier time in our history to have living grandparents and to be in contact with them. Many factories in the nineteenth century employed children under the age of eleven; and during the early industrial period, from 1850 to 1885, children worked at home, in tenement sweatshops, in the fields, in mines and mills. Domestic workers supported middle-class nurturing and mothering, but their own children frequently served as maids or garment workers. During the years of the Great Depression, in the 1930s, families united for their own collective survival, but incompatible people who were stuck together in this manner, with few resources and little hope, would sometimes produce phenomena all too familiar in other eras: withdrawn or violent men; exhausted, overextended women; and children with no resources with which to face the future.

Gender and Family in American History

Early recorded history of the colonies and the Revolution suggests that even though the United States was founded on principles of equality, women either were invisible or were assumed to absorb the political views of their husbands or male relatives, just as their husbands were able to absorb their property upon marriage. They were expected to support economic embargoes against Britain and to supply provisions and support for the war, and they could be tried for treason during the Revolution. Men were expected to carry out the public duties of government and commerce. Some early Republicans and philosophers may have noticed the contradictions in promoting arguments about equal rights while restricting those rights to male landowners, but few questioned assumptions that women's work should be restricted to the home (though in the largely rural society, work at home was substantial). Women's sphere was the domestic arena; men participated in and ruled the public domain, and debated affairs of state. One way to cope with this dichotomy was to state that the two realms were different but equal. As we examine this discussion, we will question just how equal those realms truly were, both in actuality and in perception.

The first selection in the chapter, the etching *Keep within Compass*, comes from the early post–Revolutionary period and taps into the notion of dual spheres for men and women. As such, it is part of a long-standing tradition of defining women's roles by circumscribing them and fostering a desire for stability. One change that did result from the Revolution, however, was that divorce was slightly easier for women to obtain, which may help explain why the etching contrasts the contented "virtuous woman" with images of what can happen to her if she steps outside her role. For a far more graphic example of the consequences that befell one young woman who was victimized for failing to stay within traditional lines of demarcation, read the dissent of Judge Wilner in *Rusk v. State*. This late-twentieth-century case makes a somewhat frightening companion piece to *Keep within Compass*.

In the nineteenth century, little challenged the assumptions of the twin spheres of domesticity and public realm, though domestic life, particularly in rural areas, certainly entailed labor, since families generally produced their own food and household goods and sometimes bartered for other needed commodities. Industrialization brought with it goods produced outside the home or farm, and along with increasing industry came the need for cheap labor. Immigrants, women, and children became part of that massive workforce. In the mid–nineteenth century, as household production decreased, wage labor and professional occupations developed, giving rise to an increasing middle class. Upper- and middle-class women could maintain a role focused on domesticity while men earned the family income, but the cost was borne by the laborers, often slaves and other men, women, and children, in mills, fields, and factories.

Some of the realities of slave life, particularly for women, pervade the next selection, "African American Women: Life in Bondage." In this reading, Gail Collins, contemporary writer and *New York Times* editorial page editor, weaves personal narrative, statistics, quotations, and historical accounts from this earlier era to convey the harrowing daily lives and often tragic family circumstances, as well as the strengths and resilience, of African American women and their families.

Addressing the status of women from a position that evoked both dominant culture with regard to race and subculture with regard to gender, Mary Garrett Hay anticipated the suffrage movement in her 1903 essay "The Political Woman," focusing on women's potential contributions to American politics and society.

The second decade of the twentieth century saw worldwide turmoil brought about by World War I and social turmoil as U.S. women agitated for the vote, which they finally obtained in 1920. In a society in which women were assumed to carry on the emotional, sentimental, and moral needs of society as men pursued individualistic and public pursuits, women were to give love and nurturing freely, uncontaminated by the market forces of the newly industrialized society.

In addition to their role as breadwinners, men were assumed to be strong heroes and the protectors of women and children. War-era rhetoric and propaganda in particular appealed to manly attributes such as physical strength and a muscular build.

The World War I recruiting poster included in this chapter, "Enlist: On Which Side of the Window Are YOU?" makes a graphic statement about proper spheres for men and women, goading the male viewer into taking his rightful place in the public domain by using shame as a persuasive technique.

In the years that followed the civil rights and free speech movements of the 1960s, the women's movement increasingly argued for equality for women in society, especially in the home and workplace. Progress was slow, and even within liberal or left-wing social and political movements, such as the Student Nonviolent Coordinating Committee, male leaders typically assigned women to clerical or support duties rather than to leadership roles. Increasing numbers of women in the workplace, relative to the postwar era of the 1950s and early 1960s, brought changes in the stable (to some, but stultifying to others) nuclear family. Long-standing assumptions that the nuclear family is the core of American communities underlie much of mainstream culture and affect how some Americans perceive cultures that differ from mainstream family values.

Assumptions also run deep about what is and is not appropriate behavior, particularly in women. As noted earlier, we begin this chapter with an eighteenth-century etching exhorting women to stay in their place. Almost two hundred years later, in a famous "date rape" legal case, *Rusk v. State,* we see that if a woman doesn't "keep to her place," she is in essence putting herself in harm's way. Judge Wilner, the author of the minority opinion included in this chapter, articulates some of these assumptions as he argues against overturning the conviction of the rapist in this case. Ultimately the conviction was reinstated, but the case represents a sobering look at the assumptions and values that we take with us into policy and legal arenas.

In the late 1980s and early 1990s, on the heels of the social changes of the previous two decades, gay and lesbian rights movements further challenged the concept and value of the heterosexual nuclear family; moreover, they brought the debate over homosexual marriages into the open. Thomas Stoddard, attorney and gay rights leader, argues that "Marriage Is a Fundamental Right" and that same-gender marriages are a civil rights issue. Attorney Bruce Fein's essay, "Reserve Marriage for Heterosexuals," cites legal precedent, as does Stoddard's, but also draws on our fears for children and our beliefs about two-parent families to make Fein's case. Since Stoddard and Fein made their respective arguments, the Supreme Court has overturned one of the keystones of Fein's argument, the *Bowers* case. Writing for the majority of the Court, Justice Anthony M. Kennedy asserts that Texas's antisodomy law "was not correct when it was decided, and it is not correct today. It ought not to remain binding precedent. *Bowers v. Hardwick* should be and now is overruled." He added that the law "furthers no legitimate state interest which can justify its intrusion into the personal and private life of the individual." This discussion continues with the 2004 gay marriage challenges in state and local jurisdictions, in the presidential election, and in the courts.

The post–civil rights movement era also shows increasing concern over the needs of children. Some 20 percent of children still grow up in poverty, abuse, and neglect; some are born addicted to drugs and alcohol. In one battle for children's rights being fought through the courts, child advocates are arguing for increased legal rights for young people. An adult who has worked on behalf of children's rights for years, child advocate and Children's Defense Fund founder Marian Wright Edelman, explains the values, assumptions, and beliefs that led her to her life's work on behalf of children. Edelman's essay, "A Family Legacy," describes the family and extended family of community from which she learned the values of hard work, discipline, doing for others, and repaying the privileges of intellectual and material gifts by serving the community. In the next reading, Dr. Mary Pipher, author of *Reviving Ophelia: Saving the Selves of Adolescent Girls*, asks us to consider why young girls in our culture feel the need to stifle their voices, their energy, their creativity, and to ponder a corollary to this process—the incidence of depression, eating disorders, addictions, and suicide attempts. These young girls existing in a difficult culture are, she suggests, "Saplings in the Storm," and our society needs to look long and hard at what we are doing to them.

Not only girls, but also young boys are being acculturated in ways that do not promote either their growth or a healthy society, suggests authors Daniel J. Kinglon and Michael Thompson. In fact, we rear our young men in "The Culture of Cruelty," a culture without security either for the bullied or for the bully, a culture that, in the schoolyards and the hallways and the locker room, is not all that far removed from the fictional world of William Golding's *Lord of the Flies*.

From the assumptions in primary sources such as *Keep within Compass* and *Rusk v. State*, to expert opinion in secondary sources by Pipher as well as Kindlon and Thompson, we see values and beliefs that both define and absorb their time and culture. Assumptions about power, sexuality, and violence have evolved, as have notions of men's rights over wives and families and of the rights of the less powerful to protection from society and the law. In a selection from her book *No Turning Back*, in a chapter entitled "Gender and Violence," historian Estelle Freedman contextualizes the issues of sexual harassment and domestic violence, considering both the first sexual harassment legal case as well as battered women's syndrome and divergent feminist views on these issues.

Although some marginalized groups within American society sometimes appear to have resolved problems that others find perplexing, easy generalizations can flatten out layers of complexity. The final reading in the chapter, student writer Mike Hipolito's essay "Got Harvey Milk?: Supporting the Mission of a New York City High School," focuses on the controversial "gay high school" recently in the news. Commentators argue that such separatism is inappropriate and may be counterproductive, but Hipolito asserts that discrimination and harassment of gay youth, not to mention the high suicide rate, make a school like Harvey Milk vital.

This chapter's film selection, *Mi Familia* (*My Family*), reflects in a visual medium the assumptions, values, and conflicts of a multigenerational Mexican American family coping with the differing assumptions, values, and conflicts of the dominant culture.

✻✻✻ *Keep within Compass* (ca. 1790)

A metaphor that surfaces decade after decade in conveying social worlds is that of the circle, or in some cases, the three-dimensional sphere. Sometimes referring to a social class, other times to occupations, the image is frequently used, from the late eighteenth century through the twentieth century, to describe the designated and circumscribed roles for men and women: men's world of greater economic, industrial, and political society, and women's world of the home.

"Keep within Compass," England, 1785–1805. Graphic on laid paper, H. 9.310 cm. Courtesy, Winterthur Museum.

For Journals

Write about what you imagine to be the daily life of eighteenth-century American women: women of means, with landed or wealthy families, and women without family or financial support.

For Discussion

1. What is your overall impression of the etching? What draws your eye? What is emphasized? Why do you think that the etching was drawn to create this impression and this emphasis? Relative to the entire circle, how much space is allotted to the virtuous woman?

2. Who are the intended audiences? Do different elements of the etching appeal to different audiences? To different audience concerns?

3. Why do you think that the artist used a compass to make his point? In the late eighteenth century, who would have been likely to wield a compass? Who, then, would be setting the limits on women?

4. Analyze the etching as a moral lesson or argument with supporting subtopics and evidence, including the smaller pictures and the additional printed messages. Write out a text outline of the argument. What is inside the compass? What are "good" women supposed to do? What is outside the compass? What are women not supposed to do? Is this what you would expect?

5. Why is it important that a woman be "a crown to her husband"? Do you think that the authors of this etching would expect a man to be a crown to his wife? What associations does the crown bring to mind?

6. In what ways might the assumptions apparent in this etching be relevant today? Do you see any connections between this two-hundred-year-old image and arguments about date rape today? (See the legal augments regarding the noted "date rape" case later in this chapter.)

For Writing

1. In what ways are gender roles still restricted today? Draw a contemporary version of this etching for men or for women. Then write an essay explaining your diagram.

2. Argue that women are no longer restricted by gender roles—or that men are more restricted in their choices and behavior than women are.

3. Do research in art or literature of the American colonial period to examine the role of women or home life. Examine art books from your library, primary materials such as diaries if they are available, or secondary sources about the period. What do you conclude about women's or men's role in the home or in society during this period? Write a documented essay reporting your conclusions.

❈❈❈ *African American Women: Life in Bondage* (2003)

GAIL COLLINS

Gail Collins is the first woman editorial-page editor at the New York Times. *She previously worked as a columnist for the op-ed page of the* Times *as well as for the* New York Daily News *and* New York Newsday. *She also served as a member of the* Times *editorial board. Collins has also published* Scorpion Tongues: Gossip, Celebrity, and American Politics *(1998). The selection that follows is from her comprehensive book on American womanhood entitled* America's Women: Dolls, Drudges, Helpmates, and Heroines *(2003). In the following selection, Collins turns her attention to some of the women of color in American history, describing their daily lives and drawing from first-person accounts as well as historical and statistical evidence.*

"The Women Were the Pluckiest"

Most American slaves came from West Africa, where women frequently worked as both farmers and merchants. In fact, outsiders had the impression that the women did pretty much everything that needed to be done. "They are the ones who work the fields, and plant the crops, and the houses in which they live, even though small, are clean and bright," wrote a Portuguese man who lived in West Africa in the late seventeenth century. Perhaps their usefulness was one of the reasons that white slave traders found it easier to acquire male captives. "Women are scarce," reported the English captain of a slave ship that arrived in the colonies with three men for every woman.

A slave ship took anywhere from three weeks to three months to cross the Atlantic from West Africa. By various estimates, somewhere between one-sixth and two-thirds of the Africans died along the way. Suicides were common. One ship, acquiring slaves in Angola, was preparing for departure when eighteen of the women flung themselves into the ocean. The men spent the voyage chained together in the hold, packed so tight they could not sit upright, lying in their own body wastes. Sometimes the women fared better and were allowed to spend time on deck with the children. Occasionally, they used their liberty to help stage rebellions. In 1721, an African woman stole weapons and served as lookout for two male slaves who attempted to take over the slave ship *Robert*. On another boat in 1785, the captain said he had been attacked by a group of women who tried to toss him overboard. When they were overpowered, some of the women threw themselves to their death down the hatchway, and others starved themselves. Edward Manning, a sailor on an American slave ship, had a low opinion of the male Africans his ship picked up. "The women were the pluckiest," he said, "and had they all been of that sex we should probably have had a mutiny on board before the ship had been at sea two weeks."

When the slave ships arrived in America, the new country seemed so strange to the captives that some were convinced they had been taken by cannibals and were doomed to be eaten. Most of the early slaves faced lives of terrible isolation—only one in ten wound up in households with other Africans to talk to. Some embarked on a lifetime of passive resistance. Samuel Hall, a former slave, remembered that his mother, who had been captured in Liberia, "would never work after she was sold into slavery but pined away, never even learning the language of the people of this country."

"I Never See How My Mammy Stand Such Hard Work"

The first African Americans were free, and there were always sizable communities of free blacks in towns along the Atlantic seaboard. By the late 1700s in the North, black women had begun starting schools and organizing clubs that sponsored social welfare programs. Katy Ferguson, who became the nation's first black female educator, was herself illiterate but possessed a determination to help New York City's poor children. Ferguson, a slave whose own children had died in infancy, purchased her freedom in 1793. She used the money she made by catering parties for wealthy white families to establish New York's first Sunday school and classes in reading and writing. She also offered adoption services for homeless children, white and black, taking forty-eight of those waifs into her own home.

But soon the bulk of the American black population was com- 5 posed of slaves in the southern states. By the mid-nineteenth century, there were nearly 4 million. The vast majority, including about 80 percent of the women, worked in the fields, plowing, hoeing, planting and picking crops. They worked up to fourteen hours a day, and perhaps sixteen hours at harvest time. The women did the same jobs as the men, using heavy iron tools to hoe and in some cases steering the bulky wooden plows, controlling the mules or oxen that pulled them. The elderly, children, and pregnant women were put on "trash gangs" that did weeding and cleaning chores. Those were the only work units that female slaves were ever chosen to lead.

Slave owners expected women to do three-quarters of the fieldwork a man could do, but some did much more. At a time when a reasonably productive male slave picked about 200 pounds of cotton a day, Susan Mabry of Virginia could pick 400 to 500. Some plantation records list a female slave as the best picker. But even though both sexes worked together in the fields, the men did not share much in the family housework. "The women plowed just like the men," remembered former slave Henry Baker. "On Wednesday night they had to wash and after they washed they had to cook supper. The next morning they would get up with the men and they had to cook breakfast before they went to the field and had to cook [the noon meal] at the same time and take it with them." Men hunted for game and tilled the family garden, but even small boys were generally excused from cooking, cleaning, or washing chores.

In addition to the fieldwork, many planters required women to do a quota of spinning or weaving before they went to bed. They worked as a group, with the children helping to card the wool. Bob Ellis, whose mother was head spinner on a Virginia plantation, said that as the other slaves worked, she walked around checking progress, singing "Keep your eyes on the sun. See how she run. Don't let her catch you with your work undone." The point, Ellis said, was to make the women finish before dark because it was "mighty hard handling that cotton thread by firelight." Fannie Moore held the light for her mother to see while she made quilts. Sometimes, she said, her mother sewed through the night: "I never see how my mammy stand such hard work."

During her working life, a female slave spent much of her time pregnant, and most owners put a high value on good "breeders," Thomas Jefferson wrote: "A child raised every two years is of more profit than the crop of the best laboring man . . . what she produces is an addition to capital." The *Plantation Manual* advised readers to encourage reproduction by giving every woman "with six children alive" all their Saturdays off. Major Wallon, a plantation owner, offered every new mother a calico dress and a silver dollar. More important than the presents to many young women was the fact that if they became pregnant, they were much less likely to be sold away, from their husbands and relatives.

"I Want to Be in Heaven Sitting Down"

On large plantations, only a small percentage of slaves worked as house servants. Although those jobs seemed on the surface to be more pleasant and higher in prestige, many women tried to avoid them, and some deliberately failed at their house chores in order to get back into the fields. Their impulses were similar to the ones that made young white women prefer even the more unpleasant types of factory work to domestic service. Housework meant being under the close watch of a mistress who had high expectations when it came to her family's comfort, and who might not know how to give clear directions. House slaves had no downtime—even their meals had to be grabbed on the run. When white people were in the room, they had to remain standing.

(A spiritual from the era says, "I want to be in heaven sitting down.") Residents of the Big House even expected slaves to sleep at the foot of their beds, in case they wanted something during the night. Angelina Grimke said she knew of a black woman who had been married eleven years "and yet has never been allowed to sleep out of her mistress's chamber." The image of the slave lying at the foot of the bed like a dog sometimes was extended further. Some slaves reported that, as children, they were encouraged to sit under the table during dinner and beg scraps from their mistress.

Slaves were not permitted to learn to read or write. "If Marse catch   10 a paper in your hand he sure whip you," recalled Ellen Betts, a former slave in Louisiana. "Marse don't allow no bright niggers around. If they act bright he sure sell them quick. He always say: 'Book learning don't raise no good sugarcane.'" Owners also feared, with some justification, that slaves who became literate would forge passes that allowed their friends and relatives to escape. But despite all the obstacles, about 5 percent of the slaves learned how to read anyway. Some were taught by their owners. Others simply listened while their master's children learned their ABCs, and taught themselves. The idea of educating African Americans was so threatening in the South that even white women who taught free black children were sometimes arrested and a literate slave caught teaching others would generally be sold as punishment. Milla Granson learned to read from her master's children in Kentucky and then instructed other slaves. When she was sold to Mississippi, she taught in the middle of the night, and slaves who had worked all day in the field—and, if they were women, spent several more hours spinning thread—sat up half the night, struggling to learn.

"It Was Freedom Before She Come out of That Cave"

When female slaves were whipped, they were often stripped to the waist and tied to a tree, or from a rafter in the barn. Pregnant women were beaten, too. "They'd dig a hole in the ground and put their stomach in the hole and then beat them," recounted Anne Clark, a former slave. A woman's husband and children were helpless. "Husbands always went to the woods when they know the wives was due for a whipping," remembered Jordan Johnson. "But in the field they dare not leave. Had to stay there, not daring even [to] look like they didn't like it." Once, Johnson said, a slave named Annie Jones was working in the same field with her husband while she was far along in a pregnancy. When she made a mistake and chopped down some young cotton plants, the overseer beat her until she fell to the ground screaming. "And Charlie he just stood there hearing his wife scream and staring at the sky, not daring to look at her or even say a word."

Leah Garrett remembered one man who hid his wife in the woods when she was threatened with a beating. "He carried her to a cave and hauled pine straw and put [it] in there for her to sleep on," she said. "He fixed that cave up just like a house for her, put a stove in there and run the pipe out through the ground into a swamp. . . . He sealed the house with pine logs, made beds and tables out of pine poles, and they lived in this cave seven years. During this time they had three children . . . and they was wild." Her husband, who stayed on the plantation, brought the woman food, Garrett said, and "it was freedom before she come out of that cave for good."

That kind of active resistance was rare. Slaves who endured repeated beatings often responded much like battered wives or abused children. They lost confidence, became dependent on the judgments of others, and sometimes identified with the very people who abused them. Salomon Oliver, whose mother was beaten to death by white overseers, concluded that she might have deserved it: "I guess sometimes she took advantage and tried to do things that maybe wasn't right."

"We Made the Gals Hoops out of Grapevines"

In the 1930s, Violet Guntharpe, an elderly South Carolinian, remembered being courted by her future husband when she was a fifteen-year-old slave. "I glance at him one day at the pigpen when I was slopping the hogs. I say, 'Mr. Guntharpe, you follows me night and morning to this pigpen; do you happen to be in love with one of those pigs?' . . . Thad didn't say nothing but just grin. Him took the slop bucket out of my hand and look at it, all round it, put it upside down on the ground, and set me on it. . . . Us carry on foolishness about the little boar shoat pig and the little sow pig, then I squeal with laughter. The slop bucket tipple over and I lost my seat. That ever remain the happiest minute of my eighty-two years."

Under slavery, African Americans led desperately constricted and 15 frequently brutal existences. But ordinary life went on as well. For most, the average day was filled with couplings and quarreling, friendship and feuds, moments of silliness, acts of selfishness, and gestures of incredible kindness. They carved out their own worlds as best they could.

Plantation slaves typically lived in one-room cabins. Some were substantial, with plank floors raised well above the ground and solid chimneys. But many were as small as ten feet square, with dirt floors and no windows. Although some former slaves reminisced about the sturdy furniture their fathers made for the cabins, and visitors sometimes reported seeing homes that were well appointed and decorated with painted china or wall hangings, most had little but mattresses made of straw or moss, and some pots for cooking. Slaves often had plots of land where they gardened, although the work had to be done, as one recalled, "on moonlight nights and on a Saturday evening." Although visitors to Southern plantations often commented on the unwashed bodies and soiled clothes of the house servants, Southerners seldom said anything about their slaves' hygiene, and they may have regarded cleanliness as something reserved to the upper class. (When Fanny Kemble urged her husband's slaves to tidy their houses, they protested—probably with some accuracy—that they were already as clean as poor white households.) Certainly a woman who had spent twelve hours in the field and a few more spinning thread wouldn't want to do much heavy-duty scrubbing. But according to the oral histories taken from ex-slaves in the 1930s, many mothers struggled to wash the family clothes every weekend, and women told how, as young girls, they kept their best dress pressed with flowers and herbs so it would smell nice. A white Georgian recalled seeing, on Saturday nights, the roads filled with male slaves on their way to visit wives on other plantations, "each pedestrian or horseman bearing his bag of soiled clothes."

Women often obtained calico to make a special dress for parties and church—some owners doled out calico dresses to reward good performance, and it was one of the first things slave women bought if they made money by selling garden produce. Red, which was reserved for royalty in some parts of Africa, was a favorite color. "Sunday clothes was dyed red for the gals. . . . We made the gals hoops out of grapevines. They give us a dime, if they had one, for a set of hoops," recalled Gus Feaster of South Carolina. To stiffen their petticoats, girls starched them with hominy and water. Slaves tended to dress more carefully for church than the poor whites, and if they had to walk a long way to service, they carried their shoes to keep them clean.

Half the Southern slaves worked for small farmers, who lived in houses only slightly more impressive than the slave cabins on large plantations. White women on small Southern farms worked exceedingly hard, and when a farmer became prosperous enough to acquire a slave, his first purchase was often a woman to help his wife. "That sure was hard living there," recalled Mary Lindsay, who was the only slave of a poor white blacksmith. "I have to get up at three o'clock sometimes so I have time to water the horses and slop the hogs and feed the chickens and milk the cows, and then get back to the house and get the breakfast." A former slave in Nashville whose master hired her out to a working-class family said that she was required "to nurse, cook, chop in the fields, chop wood, bring water, wash, iron and in general just do everything." She was six years old at the time.

Besides the multitudinous chores, the lone slave was cut off from the community that was the one great source of comfort and support in a world where she was regarded as something less than fully human by the whites. Katie Phoenix, who was sold as a little girl to a solitary woman who had no other slaves, said she had no idea that she was a child until her mistress's granddaughter came for a visit. "I thought I was just littler, but as old as grown-ups. I didn't know people had grown up from children," she said.

Christmas was the biggest holiday of the year. "Slaves lived just 20 for Christmas to come round," said Fannie Berry. "Start getting ready the first snowfall. Commence to saving nuts and apples, fixing up party clothes, snitching lace and beads from the big house. General celebrating time, you see, because husbands is coming home and families is getting united again. Husbands hurry on home to see the new babies. Everybody happy." On regular Saturday nights there were dances in the slave quarters or gatherings of young people who played kissing games. "Used to go over to the Saunders place for dancing," said Fannie Berry. "Must have been a hundred slaves over there, and they always had the best dances. . . . Gals always tried to fix up for partying, even if they ain't got nothing but a piece of ribbon to tie in their hair." Courtship rituals were much like those of other working-class Americans. Girls concerned themselves with their hair and dresses. "All week they wear the hair rolled up with cotton," said Amos Lincoln of Charleston. "Sunday come, they comb the hair out fine." Like white girls of the era, the young slaves felt eating in public was unladylike, and they ate at home before they went out to dinner. Men initiated a romantic pursuit, but the chain of approval necessary for courting a slave girl was more arduous than that of an upper-class heiress. "Couldn't spring up, grab a mule and ride to the next plantation without a pass," explained Andy Marion, a former slave who remembered the difficulties for men who couldn't find a desirable partner on their own plantation. "Suppose you get your master's consent to go? Look here, the girl's master's got to consent, the gal got to consent, the gal's daddy got to consent, the gal's mammy got to consent. It was a hell of a way!"

"A Chance Here That Women Have Nowhere Else"

It was not unusual for unwed girls to get pregnant, but they generally were married soon after, frequently to their child's father. Most slave communities did not think that premarital sex was immoral, although they vigorously disapproved of adultery. Slave women, the well-to-do Virginian Mary Chesnut wrote somewhat enviously, "have a chance here that women have nowhere else. They can redeem themselves—the 'impropers' can. They can marry decently and nothing is remembered against these colored ladies." This attitude toward premarital sex was probably carried from Africa, where a woman who had demonstrated her fertility was seen as a more valuable marriage partner than an untested virgin. But as African Americans converted to Christianity, the standards for sexual behavior changed in some communities. Priscilla McCullough, who had been a slave in Darien, Georgia, said that sexually active girls were sometimes "put on the banjo. . . . When they play that night they sing about that girl and they tell all about her. That's putting on the banjo. Then everybody know and that girl she better change."

Slaves were not allowed to marry legally, but they almost always celebrated their union with a ceremony. Many preferred religious services—as many as two-fifths of the Episcopalian weddings in the Confederate states in the year before the war involved slaves. But the ministers never said "what God has joined together, let no man put asunder." The white owner could sunder a marriage with the wave of a pen, and in the eyes of the law, slaves could no more marry than they could go to court, own property, or control their children's fate. One black preacher in Kentucky, in a stroke of realism, told his brides and grooms that they were married "until death or distance do you part."

Sometimes an owner underwrote the wedding of a favored slave, including a feast for the entire plantation. "We was married on the front porch of the big house," recalled Temple Durham, a former slave in North Carolina. " . . . Miss Betsy had Georgianna, the cook, to bake a big wedding cake all iced up white as snow with a bride and groom standing in the middle holding hands. . . . I had on a white dress, white shoes and long white gloves that come to my elbow, and Miss Betsy done made me a wedding veil out of a white net window curtain. When she played the wedding march on the piano, me and Exter marched down the walk and up on the porch to the altar Miss Betsy done fixed. . . . Exter done made me a wedding ring. He made it out of a big red button with his pocket knife. He done cut it so round and polished it so smooth that it looked like a red satin ribbon tied around my finger." Temple and her husband retired to a cabin that had been fixed up for the wedding night, but the next day he had to return to his own plantation. "But he come back every Saturday night," she said. "We had 11 children."

On plantations where the white people were not interested in their slaves' personal affairs, the bride and groom could seek out a wise elder, usually a woman, to perform the ceremony. Often, husband and wife sealed their union by jumping over a broomstick—a ritual that some poor southern whites followed as well. "Didn't have to ask Marsa or nothing," said Caroline Johnson Harris. "Just go to Aunt Sue and tell her you want to get married." When Harris and her intended went, Aunt Sue sent them home to think hard about it. "After two days Mose and I went back and say we done thought about it and still want to get married. Then she called all the slaves after tasks to pray for the union that God was gonna make. Pray we stay together and have lots of children and none of them get sold away from the parents. Then she lay a broomstick across the sill of the house we gonna live in and join our hands together. Before we step over it she asked us once more if we was sure we wanted to get married. Of course we say yes. Then she say, 'In the eyes of Jesus step into Holy land of matrimony.' When we step across the broomstick, we was married."

Most slaves married and stayed married to the same person all 25 their lives. But husbands were often a fleeting presence, living on another plantation, arriving on Saturday night and leaving the next evening. Hannah Chapman remembered that her father sometimes snuck an extra visit during the week. "Us would gather round him and crawl up in his lap, tickled slap to death, but he give us these pleasures at a painful risk," she said. Sometimes her father was discovered by the "patrollers"—working-class whites who made extra money watching for slaves who were out at night without permission. When the patrollers caught her father, Chapman said, "us would track him the next day by the blood stains." In a sense, slave families were matriarchies in which the women were the only stable element. But fathers often made heroic efforts to stay involved in their children's lives. Mattie Jackson, a slave raised in Georgia, said her father and mother originally lived on neighboring plantations. When her mother's owner moved twenty miles away, her father continued his weekly visits "walking the distance every Saturday evening and returning Sunday evening." Charles Ingram ran away from his master and was living and working as a free man when his wife died and his sons were sold to Texas. Ingram gave himself up and voluntarily resumed life as a slave in order to take care of them.

For Journals

What do you expect to hear in a historical account of life for African American women early in U.S. history?

For Discussion

1. Do an informal writing exercise in response to this selection, freewriting or brainstorming a list of your reactions and observations. Then, discuss your responses with other classmates who also share their responses. What themes emerge? What surprised you in responses or in the selection itself? How do responses compare and differ? Do you have observations about the ways in which gender, ethnicity, class, or region of origin influence responses?

2. What themes do you discern in the selection itself? What images of women from any race or class during this time period emerge? What images of daily life?

3. Assess the evidence offered in this selection: narrative and personal report, quotations, statistics, description. Which types of evidence do you find most persuasive, and why?

For Writing

1. Using discussion question number 1 as a starting point, write a personal reflection on your response to this selection. Then, step back and analyze the ways in which your identity, especially with regard to gender, race, class, and region, provides a context for your response.

2. Research the lives of men or women, of African, European, Asian American, or Native American descent, during the time frame discussed in this selection. Focus on a particular aspect of this topic that interests you—daily life, political influence, types of work or duties at work, and relationships with regard to gender and within familes.

3. Using resources such as written slave narratives available through your library or through the Web (URLs for access to Library of Congress slave narratives and women's history provided at the end of this chapter), locate and read some first-person accounts related to the material in this selection. Either evaluate Collins's use of this type of source to support the larger chapter theme, or more fully research the primary sources that you encounter, and draw your own inferences from your evidence. Write up and document your findings in an essay.

✵✵✵ *The Political Woman* (1903)

MARY GARRETT HAY

Mary Garrett Hay, an organizer of the National Women's Suffrage Association, wrote the following essay for a column entitled "The American Woman" that appeared in Harper's Weekly. *In this opinion piece, she makes a case for women's involvement in political affairs, drawing on analogies to a woman's role in the home as well as on principles and values that she believed would appeal to her readership.*

It seems to me that it should be every woman 's ideal to be equally independent with her brother-man in all practical competition. So far, she is not permitted to encourage this ideal. Surely the government of the State is no less important to her than the government of her own home, and as she has the controlling voice in the management of her home, why not a political voice in the government of the State and nation? Those women who do interest themselves in the political life of the country certainly idealize political conditions, because ambition to hold office, or individual honors, are not alarming considerations of these women. When the American woman in her political endeavors strives to establish ideals of citizenship, she does so without the purpose of gratifying personal ambition. Furthermore, the political woman is not so partisan in her activities as a man, because she aims at political equality with him, to bring about better conditions in that which is to her but a larger home of principles—the State and national government.

All practical ideals are being influenced and brought about in American life today by the emancipation of woman. She has broken the chains of conventional prejudice against her activity, and in social, educational, and commercial matters meets men on an equal footing. All this is, of course, contributing to her ultimate success in achieving this last important scheme of idealization, her recognition in the State and national government.

This is the last state of her emancipation to be secured. There are good and sufficient reasons why a woman should be deeply interested in the political life of the country.

Who is more vitally affected by the local municipal government of a town and city than the woman? Isn't her own particular government of the home dependent upon the broader details of the municipality? Are not the life and health of her home dependent upon a good water-supply, for instance, good police service, efficient transportation facilities, and numerous other daily obligations?

To carry this argument into State politics, who else but the woman 5 is most affected by legislation in regard to the liquor laws, for example—in legislation governing the State penal and charitable institutions, in all laws affecting small children, the sweat-shop system, and so forth?

In national politics who is more interested than the woman in the laws made by Congress? In she not concerned in the question of polygamy? And, another problem, as personal in its influence upon her as this, is she not interested in the political complications that bring upon her the penalties of war?

Is there any single phase of political life that a woman's ideals could not improve? It seems to me that the study of politics furnishes women with the highest ideals obtainable. I believe that the germ of this political ideal is instinctively in every woman, for she is the mother, and she it is who instils into both her boys and her girls the ideals of citizenship.

Isn't it the woman who in the schoolroom prepares the boys and girls to go out into the world and become useful citizens? And yet, when the boy becomes a man, he turns away from his mother and his teacher, and seeks political advice from his father or some other man. Why does he do this? Because the man is part of the body politic and the woman is not. Still, that boy owes to his mother and teacher his good or bad tendency in citizenship.

So long as women are ruled out of the body politic, morality will never be fully represented. Since women can offer a higher percent of morality and certainly an equal amount of intelligence with men, it shows that women will help to make the world better and more ideal.

For Journals

In reflecting on a time in American history when women were not able to vote, consider what you think would have been the arguments for keeping the status quo and the arguments for extending voting rights to women.

For Discussion

1. Reflect on the rhetorical situation—the audience and purpose—for this essay. Who seems to be the intended audience? To what values and beliefs does the writer appeal? What is the main point? What assertions and what type of evidence does the writer offer to support her view?

2. Examine the style and structure of the essay. Pay particular attention to coordination, or the balancing of equal grammatical and thematic units, and parallelism. Analyze other rhetorical elements as well, such as the order of examples—municipal, state, and national government—and the use of rhetorical questions.

3. Does Hay respond to potential objections to her argument? If so, what are they, and how does she respond? If not, what might be objections to her point of view?

For Writing

1. Research the history of the women's suffrage movement. Consider focusing on the National Women's Suffrage Association, for which Hay served as an organizer, or on some of the early leaders of this movement. Other potential areas of interest could include issues related to race, class, or immigrant status.

2. Write a response to Hay in the form of a follow-up letter to the editor of *Harper's Weekly*, either endorsing her overall point but offering different support, or proposing an alternative view.

❋❋❋ *Enlist: On Which Side of the Window Are YOU?* (1917)

This American poster (see page 260), based on an earlier British poster, uses an approach that differs from the positive appeals to ethos and pathos that characterize many other war recruitment posters. You may want to review Chapter 2 for additional information on posters as a medium of persuasion. (See Color Plate III for a color image of this poster.)

For Journals

Do you believe that men and women have an equal responsibility to participate in military service?

For Discussion

1. Examine the elements of the poster. What first catches your eye? What next? Is the man inside the window confined in any way? Where does he seem to belong? What is the argument of the poster? What are the appeals used to persuade the audience? How do light and shading affect the message?

2. Look closely at the man, his appearance, and his posture; then look at the soldiers. What differences do you notice? What is implied by those differences?

3. Compare and contrast this image to that of *Keep within Compass*. What do you infer about a woman's proper role? What is, conversely, a man's proper sphere? In what ways did women's and men's roles change, or remain constant, between 1790 and 1917? In what ways have they changed, and in what ways remained constant, since 1917?

For Writing

1. Review all the war-era images in this book. What are the common themes and appeals? How do their strategies differ? Select two posters, and write an essay comparing and contrasting them. Alternatively, select some other focus—appeals to ethos, for example—and develop an essay, drawing evidence from the posters.

2. Using books of posters, a library collection, or a museum brochure, research other war-era posters. You might look for particular ways in which the posters portray "the enemy" or particular kinds of appeals in posters from different countries.

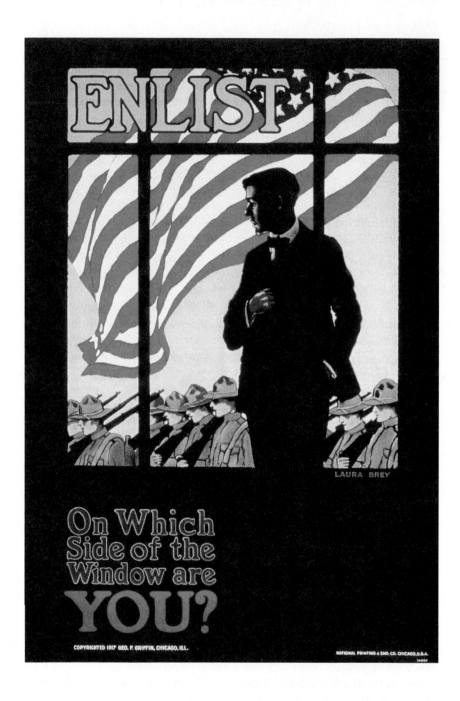

✻✻ *More Help for Busy Mothers* (1925)

THE LADIES HOME JOURNAL

According to a contemporary fact sheet supplied by The Ladies Home Journal, *this magazine, still in publication, reaches some eight million women readers each month, describing a typical reader as someone who "is a major influence on purchase decisions, inside and outside her home." This advertisement (see page 262) appeared on a full page and in color; an equivalent display today would cost close to two-hundred-thousand dollars. Named for its founder, Alfred C. Fuller, who started his business in 1906, the company for decades employed "Fuller Brush Men" (and sometimes women) as door-to-door salespersons who brought in and demonstrated their brush products to homemakers; these salespeople were a suburban fixture for decades, and the company, still in business, has since branched out into chemicals and other products.*

For Journals

Reflect on your assumptions about housework and homemaking in your grandparents' day, your parents', and your own.

For Discussion

1. Identify and analyze both the layout and the text of this advertisement and its appeals to ethos, logos, and pathos. Why do you think that the authors chose the appeals they did choose? Which seems likely to have been most effective? What arguments does the advertisement make? Do you detect logical fallacies?

2. What assumptions about gender, family, and women's status and role are evident? Which gender, race, and class does the ad target?

For Writing

1. Drawing from discussion question number 1, write an analytical essay assessing the advertisement's persuasive appeals; consider focusing on a particular type of appeal, and use evidence from the ad to support your view.

2. Research attitudes about women, domestic labor, child care, and race and class in this era. Consider referring to Gail Collins's book *America's Women: 400 Years of Dolls, Drudges, Helpmates, and Heroines,* from which an earlier selection in this chapter is drawn.

3. In *Satisfaction Guaranteed,* her book on American consumerism, Susan Strasser says that Americans had to be trained to want products

and to believe that they needed them, so that they would go out and spend money on consumer goods. On the basis of your own observations and experience, do you agree or disagree with Strasser? Develop your argument into an essay supported by examples and details that you have observed or experienced.

❋❋❋ *Rusk v. State*

Court of Special Appeals of Maryland, 406 A. 2d 624 (1979)

JUDGE WILNER

This legal opinion comes from the second of three parts in a court proceeding. In the first part, Mr. Rusk was convicted of rape and sentenced to ten years in prison. In the second part, he appealed for his conviction to be overturned, and he won. Judge Wilner served on the appeals court panel that heard Mr. Rusk's request, but unlike the majority of the court, he felt that Mr. Rusk's original sentence was correct. In the minority opinion presented here, he explains why he thinks that Mr. Rusk was in fact guilty of rape. (In the third phase, Mr. Rusk's victim appealed for his conviction to be reinstated, and the court agreed, relying for its decision on Wilner's reasoning in this earlier appeal.)

Wilner, Judge, dissenting.

With the deepest respect for the generally superior wisdom of my colleagues who authored or endorsed the majority Opinion, but with the equally profound conviction that, in this case, they have made a serious mistake, I record this dissent. . . .

Md. Annot. Code art. 27, § 463(a) considers three types of conduct as constituting second degree rape. We are concerned only with the first: a person is guilty of rape in the second degree if he (1) engages in vaginal intercourse with another person, (2) by force or threat of force, (3) against the will, and (4) without the consent of the other person. There is no real question here as to the first, third, or fourth elements of the crime. The evidence was certainly sufficient to show that appellant had vaginal intercourse with the victim, and that such act was against her will and without her consent. The point at issue is whether it was accomplished by force or threat of force; and I think that in viewing the evidence, that point should remain ever clear. *Consent is not the issue here, only whether there was sufficient evidence of force or the threat of force.*

Unfortunately, courts, including in the present case a majority of this one, often tend to confuse these two elements—force and lack of consent—and to think of them as one. They are not. They mean, and require, different things. See *State v. Studham*, 572 P.2d 700 (Utah, 1977). What seems to cause the confusion—what, indeed, has become a common denominator of both elements—is the notion that the victim must actively resist the attack upon her. If she fails to offer sufficient resistance (sufficient to the satisfaction of the judge), a court is entitled, or at least presumes the entitlement, to find that there was no force or threat of force, or that the act was not against her will, or that

she actually consented to it, or some unarticulated combination or syn-
thesis of these elements that leads to the ultimate conclusion that the
victim was not raped. Thus it is that the focus is almost entirely on the
extent of resistance—the victim's acts, rather than those of her as-
sailant. Attention is directed not to the wrongful stimulus, but to the
victim's reactions to it. Right or wrong, that seems to be the current
state of the Maryland law; and, notwithstanding its uniqueness in the
criminal law, and its illogic, until changed by statute or the Court of
Appeals, I accept it as binding.

But what is required of a woman being attacked or in danger of at- 5
tack? How much resistance must she offer? Where is that line to be
drawn between requiring that she either risk serious physical harm,
perhaps death, on the one hand, or be termed a willing partner on the
other? Some answers are given in *Hazel* v. *State,* 221 Md. 464, 157 A.2d
922 (1960), although, as in so many cases, they were stated in the context of both the requirement of force and the lack of consent. The Court
said, at pp. 469, 470, 157 A.2d at p. 925:

"Force is an essential element of the crime and to justify a conviction, the evidence must warrant a conclusion either that the victim resisted and her resistance was overcome by force or that she was
prevented from resisting by threats to her safety. But no particular
amount of force, either actual or constructive, is required to constitute
rape. Necessarily that fact must depend upon the prevailing circumstances. As in this case force may exist without violence. *If the acts and
threats of the defendant were reasonably calculated to create in the mind of
the victim—having regard to the circumstances in which she was placed—a
real apprehension, due to fear, of imminent bodily harm, serious enough to
impair or overcome her will to resist, then such acts and threats are the equivalent of force. . . .*

"With respect to the presence or absence of the element of consent,
it is true, of course, that however reluctantly given, consent to the act
at any time prior to penetration deprives the subsequent intercourse of
its criminal character. *There is, however, a wide difference between consent
and a submission to the act. Consent may involve submission, but submission
does not necessarily imply consent. Furthermore, submission to a compelling
force, or as a result of being put in fear, is not consent. . . .*

"The authorities are by no means in accord as to what degree of resistance is necessary to establish the absence of consent. However, the
generally accepted doctrine seems to be that a female—who was conscious and possessed of her natural, mental and physical powers when
the attack took place—must have resisted to the extent of her ability at
the time, unless it appears that she was overcome by numbers or was
so terrified by threats as to overpower her will to resist. . . . Since resistance is necessarily relative, the presence or absence of it must depend
on the facts and circumstances in each case. . . . *But the real test, which*

must be recognized in all cases, is whether the assault was committed without the consent and against the will of the prosecuting witness.

"The kind of fear which would render resistance by a woman unnecessary to support a conviction of rape includes, but is not necessarily limited to, a fear of death or serious bodily harm, or a fear so extreme as to preclude resistance, or a fear which would well nigh render her mind incapable of continuing to resist, or a fear that so overpowers her that she does not dare resist." (Citations omitted.) (Emphasis supplied.)

From these pronouncements in Hazel, this Court has articulated what the majority refers to as a "rule of reason"—i.e., that "where the victim's story could not be corroborated by wounds, bruises or disordered clothing, the lack of consent could be shown by fear based upon reasonable apprehension." *Winegan* v. *State,* 10 Md.App. 196, 200, 268 A.2d 585, 588 (1970); *Goldberg* v. *State,* 41 Md.App. 58, 395 A.2d 1213 (1979). *As so phrased,* I do not consider this to be a rule of reason at all; it is highly unreasonable, and again mixes the element of consent with that of force. But what I do accept is what the Court of Appeals said in *Hazel:* (1) if the acts and threats of the defendant were reasonably calculated to create in the mind of the victim—having regard to the circumstances in which she was placed—a real apprehension, due to fear, of imminent bodily harm, serious enough to impair or overcome her will to resist, then such acts and threats are the equivalent of force; (2) submission is not the equivalent of consent; and (3) the real test is whether the assault was committed without the consent and against the will of the prosecuting witness.[1]

Upon this basis, the evidence against appellant must be considered. Judge Thompson recounts most, but not quite all, of the victim's story. The victim—I'll call her Pat—attended a high school reunion. She had arranged to meet her girlfriend Terry there. The reunion was over at 9:00, and Terry asked Pat to accompany her to Fell's Point.[2] Pat had gone to Fell's Point with Terry on a few prior occasions, explaining in court: "I've never met anybody [there] I've gone out with. I met people in general, talking in conversation, most of the time people that Terry knew, not that I have gone down there, and met people as dates." She agreed to go, but first called her mother, who was babysitting with Pat's two-year-old son, to tell her that she was going with Terry to Fell's Point, and that she would not be home late. It was just after 9:00 when Pat and Terry, in their separate cars, left for Fell's Point, alone.[3]

They went to a place called Helen's and had one drink. They stayed an hour or so and then walked down to another place (where they had another drink), stayed about a half hour there, and went to a third place. Up to that point, Pat conversed only with Terry, and did not strike up any other acquaintanceships. Pat and Terry were standing against a wall when appellant came over and said hello to Terry, who was conversing with someone else at the time. Appellant then began to talk with Pat. They were both separated, they both had young children; and they spoke about those things. Pat said that she had been ready to leave when appellant came on the scene, and that she only talked with him for five or ten minutes. It was then about midnight. Pat had to get up with her baby in the morning and did not want to stay out late.

Terry wasn't ready to leave. As Pat was preparing to go, appellant asked if she would drop him off on her way home.[4] She agreed because she thought he was a friend of Terry's. She told him, however, as they walked to her car, "I'm just giving a ride home, you know, as a friend, not anything to be, you know, thought of other than a ride." He agreed to that condition.

Pat was completely unfamiliar with appellant's neighborhood. She had no idea where she was. When she pulled up to where appellant said he lived, she put the car in park, but left the engine running. She said to appellant, "Well, here, you know, you are home." Appellant then asked Pat to come up with him and she refused. He persisted in his request, as did she in her refusal. She told him that even if she wanted to come up, she dared not do so. She was separated and it might cause marital problems for her. Finally, he reached over, turned off the ignition, took her keys, got out of the car, came around to her side, opened the door, and said to her, "Now, will you come up?"

It was at this point that Pat followed appellant to his apartment, 15 and it is at this point that the majority of this Court begins to substitute its judgment for that of the trial court and jury. We know nothing about Pat and appellant. We don't know how big they are, what they look like, what their life experiences have been. We don't know if appellant is larger or smaller than she, stronger or weaker. We don't know what the inflection was in his voice as he dangled her car keys in front of her. We can't tell whether this was in a jocular vein or a truly threatening one. We have no idea what his mannerisms were. The trial judge and the jury could discern some of these things, of course, because they could observe the two people in court and could listen to what they said and how they said it. But all we know is that, between midnight and 1:00 A.M., in a neighborhood that was strange to Pat, appellant took her car keys, demanded that she accompany him, and most assuredly implied that unless she did so, at the very least, she might be stranded.

Now, let us interrupt the tale for a minute and consider the situation. Pat did not honk the horn; she did not scream; she did not try to run away. Why, she was asked. "I was scared. I didn't think at the time what to do." Later, on cross-examination: "At that point, because I was scared, because he had my car keys. I didn't know what to do. I was someplace I didn't even know where I was. It was in the city. I didn't know whether to run. I really didn't think, at that point, what to do. Now, I know that I should have blown the horn. I should have run. There were a million things I could have done. I was scared, at that point, and I didn't do any of them." What, counsel asked, was she afraid of? "Him," she replied. What was she scared that he was going to do? "Rape me, but I didn't say that. It was the way he looked at me, and said, 'Come on up, come on up;' and when he took the keys, I knew that was wrong. I just didn't say, are you going to rape me."

So Pat accompanied appellant to his apartment. As Judge Thompson points out, appellant left her in his apartment for a few minutes.[5] Although there was evidence of a telephone in the room, Pat said that, at the time, she didn't notice one. When appellant returned, he turned off the light and sat on the bed. Pat was in a chair. She testified: "I asked him if I could leave, that I wanted to go home, and I didn't want to come up. I said, 'Now, I came up. Can I go?'" Appellant, who, of course, still had her keys, said that he wanted her to stay. He told her to get on the bed with him, and, in fact, took her arms and pulled her on to the bed. He then started to undress her; he removed her blouse and bra and unzipped her pants. At his direction, she removed his clothes. She then said:

> "I was still begging him to please let, you know, let me leave. I said, 'you can get a lot of other girls down there, for what you want,' and he just kept saying, 'no;' and then I was really scared, because I can't describe, you know, what was said. It was more the look in his eyes; and I said, at that point—I didn't know what to say; and I said, 'If I do what you want, will you let me go without killing me?' Because I didn't know, at that point, what he was going to do; and I started to cry; and when I did, he put his hands on my throat, and started lightly to choke me; and I said, 'If I do what you want, will you let me go?' And he said, yes, and at that time, I proceeded to do what he wanted me to."

He "made me perform oral sex, and then sexual intercourse." Following that:

> "I asked him if I could leave now, and he said, 'Yes'; and I got up and got dressed; and he got up and got dressed; and he walked me to my car, and asked if he could see me again; and I said, 'Yes'; and he asked me for my telephone number; and I said, 'No, I'll see you down Fell's Point sometime,' just so I could leave."[6]

At this point, appellant returned her car keys and escorted her to her car. She then drove off:

> "I stopped at a gas station, that I believe was Amoco or Exon (sic), and went to the ladies' room. From there I drove home. I don't know—I don't know if I rode around for a while or not; but I know I went home, pretty much straight home and pulled up and parked the car.

"I was just going to go home, and not say anything."
Q. "Why?"
A. *"Because I didn't want to go through what I'm going through now."*
Q. "What, in fact, did you do then?"
A. "I sat in the car, thinking about it a while, and I thought I wondered what would happen if I hadn't of done what he wanted me to do. So I thought the right thing to do was to go report it, and I went from there to Hillendale to find a police car." (Emphasis supplied.)

How does the majority Opinion view these events? It starts by noting that Pat was a 21-year-old mother who was separated from her husband but not yet divorced, as though that had some significance. To me, it has none, except perhaps (when coupled with the further characterization that Pat and Terry had gone "bar hopping") to indicate an underlying suspicion, for which there is absolutely no support in the record, that Pat was somehow "on the make." Even more alarming, and unwarranted, however, is the majority's analysis of Pat's initial reflections on whether to report what had happened. Ignoring completely her statement that she "didn't want to go through what I'm going through now," the majority, in footnote 1, cavalierly and without any foundation whatever, says: [20]

"If, in quiet contemplation after the act, she had to wonder what would have happened, her submission on the side of prudence seems hardly justified. Indeed, if she had to wonder afterward, how can a fact finder reasonably conclude that she was justifiably in fear sufficient to overcome her will to resist, at the time." (Emphasis in the original.)

It is this type of reasoning—if indeed "reasoning" is the right word for it—that is particularly distressing. The concern expressed by Pat, made even more real by the majority Opinion of this Court, is one that is common among rape victims, and largely accounts for the fact that most incidents of forcible rape go unreported by the victim. See *F.B.I. Uniform Crime Reports* (1978), p. 14; *Report of Task Force on Rape Control,* Baltimore County (1975); *The Treatment of Rape Victims in the Metropolitan Washington Area,* Metropolitan Washington Council of Governments (1976), p. 4. See also *Rape and Its Victims: A Report for Citizens, Health Facilities, and Criminal Justice Agencies,* LEAA (1975). If appellant had desired, and Pat had given, her wallet instead of her body, there would be no question about appellant's guilt of robbery. Taking the car keys under those circumstances would certainly have supplied the requisite threat of force or violence and negated the element of consent. No one would seriously contend that because she failed to raise a hue and cry she had consented to the theft of her money. Why then is such life-threatening action necessary when it is her personal dignity that is being stolen?

Notes

1. Other courts have stated the rule this way: A rape victim is not required to do more than her age, strength, surrounding facts and all attending circumstances make it reasonable for her to do to manifest her opposition. See *Dinkens* v. *State*, 92 Nev. 74, 546 P.2d 228 (1976); *State* v. *Studham*, 572 P.2d 700 (Utah 1977). See also *Schrum* v. *Com.*, 219 Va. 168, 246, S.E.2d 893 (1978). [Author's note]

2. Fell's Point is an old section of Baltimore City adjacent to the harbor. It has been extensively renovated as part of urban renewal and, among refurbished homes and shops, hosts a number of cafes and discotheques. It is part of the City's night scene. [Author's note]

3. Pat said that Terry and she lived at opposite ends of town and that Fell's Point was sort of midway between their respective homes. [Author's note]

4. Her testimony about this, on cross-examination, was: "I said I was leaving. I said, excuse me. It's nice meeting you; but I'm getting ready to leave; and he said, 'which way are you going,' and I told him; at that time, he said, 'Would you mind giving me a lift?'" [Author's note]

5. On direct examination, she twice said that he left the room "for a minute" after telling her to sit down. On cross-examination, she said she couldn't remember how long he was gone, but, at counsel's suggestion, said that it was not longer than five minutes. [Author's note]

6. Pat explained this last comment further: "I didn't know what else to say. I had no intention of meeting him again." [Author's note]

For Journals

What is your understanding of the crime of rape? What are your biases or attitudes toward survivors of rape?

For Discussion

1. Much of Judge Wilner's argument rests on a clear definition. What is the subject of his definition? What kinds of evidence does he use to substantiate his definition? Which kind is most effective?

2. Judge Wilner recounts, from the majority opinion, the story of "Pat," the woman who was raped by a man she had met in a bar. Why do you think he did so? What attitude toward her story did he have? What do you infer was the attitude toward Pat's story of the majority justices (who overturned the rape conviction)? Do you discern any arguments or assumptions in this case that are surfacing in more recent legal proceedings, such as in the Kobe Bryant case?

3. Examine the etching *Keep within Compass* presented earlier in this chapter. Do you sense any connection between the values and attitudes conveyed in the etching and in this court case? Explain. You could look, for example, at Judge Wilner's comment about the selection of details in the majority opinion, such as that "Pat" was a 21-year-old mother who was separated but not divorced and had gone "bar-hopping" with a friend.

For Writing

1. Judge Wilner's argument refutes the majority opinion in *Rusk v. State.* Using discussion item 3 as a starting point, examine the assumptions held by the majority and opposing views, perhaps comparing and contrasting them with the message of the etching.

2. Research the other arguments in this case: the majority opinion in *Rusk v. State,* and the arguments in the *State v. Rusk* (the original conviction). You could select one argument to analyze in depth, examining types of appeals, use of evidence, or arguments. Or select one particular type of appeal (such as appeal to ethos), and examine the ways in which it is used in the series of arguments.

❋❋❋ *Marriage Is a Fundamental Right* (1989)

THOMAS STODDARD

Thomas Stoddard (1948–) is an attorney and serves as executive director of the Lambda Defense and Education Fund, a gay rights organization. He is the author of The Rights of Gay People *(1983) and frequently speaks out on gay civil rights issues. In the essay that follows, which first appeared in the* New York Times, *Stoddard argues on behalf of a controversial but fundamental issue: the rights of same-gender couples to marry, a topic surfacing often in contemporary public debate, particularly since the recent* Lawrence v. Texas *Supreme Court ruling regarding the right to privacy.*

"In sickness and in health; 'til death do us part." With those words, millions of people each year are married, a public affirmation of a private bond that both society and the newlyweds hope will endure. Yet for nearly four years, Karen Thompson was denied the company of the one person to whom she had pledged life-long devotion.

Her partner is a woman, Sharon Kowalski, and their home state of Minnesota, like every other in the United States, refuses to permit same-sex marriages.

Karen Thompson and Sharon Kowalski are spouses in every respect except the legal. They exchanged vows and rings. They lived together until November 13, 1983—when Kowalski, as the result of an automobile accident, was rendered unable to walk and barely able to speak.

Thompson sought a ruling granting her guardianship over her partner, but Kowalski's parents opposed the petition and obtained sole guardianship. They then moved Kowalski to a nursing home 300 miles away from Thompson and forbade all visits between the two women.

In February 1989, in the wake of a reevaluation of Kowalski's 5 mental competence, Thompson was permitted to visit her partner again. But that prolonged injustice and anguish inflicted on both women hold a moral for everyone.

Marriage, the Supreme Court declared in 1967 in *Loving v. Virginia*, is "one of the basic civil rights of man" (and, presumably, of woman as well). The freedom to marry, said the Court, is "essential to the orderly pursuit of happiness."

Marriage is far more than a symbolic state. It can be the key to survival—emotional and financial. Marriage triggers a universe of rights, privileges and presumptions. In every jurisdiction in this country, a married person can share in a spouse's estate even when there is no will. She typically has access to the group insurance and pension programs offered by the spouse's employer, and she enjoys tax advantages.

The decision whether or not to marry belongs properly to individuals, not to the government. While marriage historically has required a male and a female partner, history alone cannot sanctify injustice.

If tradition were the only measure, most states still would limit matrimony to partners of the same race. As recently as 1967, before the Supreme Court declared in *Loving* that miscegenation statutes are unconstitutional, sixteen states still prohibited marriages between a white person and a black person. When all the excuses were stripped away, it was clear that the only purpose of those laws was to maintain white supremacy.

Those who argue against reforming the marriage statutes because   10
they believe that same-sex marriage would be "anti-family" overlook the obvious: Marriage creates families and promotes social stability. In an increasingly loveless world, those who wish to commit themselves to a relationship founded upon devotion should be encouraged, not scorned. Government has no legitimate interest in how that love is expressed.

And it can no longer be argued—if it ever could—that marriage is fundamentally a procreative unit. Otherwise, states would forbid marriage between those who, by reason of age or infertility, cannot have children, as well as those who elect not to.

The case of Sharon Kowalski and Karen Thompson demonstrates that sanctimonious illusions can lead directly to the suffering of others. Denied the right to marry, these women were left to the whims and prejudices of others, and of the law.

It is time for the marriage statutes to incorporate fully the concept of equal protection of the law by extending to the many millions of gay Americans the right to marry.

For Journals

Freewrite for five or ten minutes on your assumptions about or biases toward same-gender marriages or domestic partnerships. Have they changed in view of recent civic and court debates?

For Discussion

1. Why do you think that Stoddard begins with an anecdote? Why do you think his example focuses on women? On the issue of caring for sick loved ones? How does this strategy shift the focus of the debate?

2. How does Stoddard's introductory strategy counter his readers' assumptions about the issue of gay marriage?

3. Stoddard's assertion is that same-gender marriage is not antifamily, as some have charged, but rather profamily. Does he adequately counter the antifamily arguments? Does he adequately support his assertions that same-gender marriage "creates families and promotes social stability" (paragraph 10)? In what ways is he transforming traditional definitions of family to do so?

4. What appeals to values and beliefs does Stoddard make? What appeals to emotion? To logic? Which do you find most persuasive?

5. Although this essay was first published in the *New York Times*, a newspaper with a general rather than legal audience, Stoddard (who is an attorney) is comfortable citing legal precedent to support his argument. Do you think that his evidence is convincing to a diverse audience? Stoddard's article was later reprinted in the *Journal of the American Bar Association*. Do you think that that audience is more, or less, likely to accept the arguments he makes?

For Writing

1. Write a rebuttal to Stoddard, arguing with the specific points he makes, challenging his assumptions or premises, and making any additional points to support the opposing view. You may develop your argument using appeals to ethos, pathos, or logos, or appeals to values and authority, to emotion and empathy, to logic and evidence. (See Chapter 2, on appeals to ethos, pathos, and logos.) Or you may wish to integrate evidence from outside sources into your arguments. If you do, be sure to read about both sides of the issue and to use your evidence to represent the opposing views fairly and ethically and in accord with the author's intended meaning. (See Chapter 4, "Research," for additional information on research.)

2. With a peer or in groups, write a dialogue between two people debating this topic or another controversial social issue. Then exchange dialogues with another peer or group. Evaluate the assumptions, premises, and appeals used in the dialogues. Summarize your findings, and share them with your class.

❋❋❋ Reserve Marriage for Heterosexuals (1990)

BRUCE FEIN

Bruce Fein, an attorney living in Washington, D.C., is the author of Significant Decisions of the Supreme Court *(1979–1980). He has contributed articles to the* National Review *and the* American Legion Magazine. *Fein's article first appeared in the* Journal of the American Bar Association, *which also reprinted the preceding selection by Thomas Stoddard. Note that the recent Supreme Court ruling in* Lawrence v. Texas *(2003) overturned the decision in* Bowers, *cited in Fein's argument.*

Authorizing the marriage of homosexuals, like sanctioning polygamy, would be unenlightened social policy. The law should reserve the celebration of marriage vows for monogamous male-female attachments to further the goal of psychologically, emotionally and educationally balanced offspring.

As Justice Oliver Wendell Holmes noted, the life of the law has not been logic, it has been experience. Experience confirms that child development is skewed, scarred or retarded when either a father or mother is absent in the household.

In the area of adoption, married couples are favored over singles. The recent preferences for joint child-custody decrees in divorce proceedings tacitly acknowledge the desirability of child intimacies with both a mother and father.

As Supreme Court Justice Byron White recognized in *Taylor v. Louisiana (1975):* "[T]he two sexes are not fungible; a community made up exclusively of one is different from a community of both; the subtle interplay of influence one on the other is among the imponderables" (quoting from *Ballard v. United States*).

A child receives incalculable benefits in the maturing process by 5 the joint instruction, consolation, oversight and love of a father and mother—benefits that are unavailable in homosexuals' households. The child enjoys the opportunity to understand and respect both sexes in a uniquely intimate climate. The likelihood of gender prejudice is thus reduced, an exceptionally worthy social objective.

The law should encourage male-female marriage vows over homosexual attachments in the interests of physically, mentally, and psychologically healthy children, the nation's most valuable asset.

Crowning homosexual relationships with the solemnity of legal marriage would wrongly send social cues that male-female marriages are not preferable. And there is no constitutional right to homosexual marriage since homosexual sodomy can be criminalized. See *Bowers v. Hardwick* (1986).

The fact that some traditional marriages end in fractious divorce, yield no offspring, or result in families with mistreated children does not discredit limiting marriage to monogamous female-male relationships. Anti-polygamy laws are instructive. They seek to discourage female docility, male autocracy, and intra-family rancor and jealousies that are promoted by polygamous marriages. That some might not exhibit such deplorable characteristics is no reason for their repeal or a finding of constitutional infirmity.

To deny the right of homosexual marriage is not an argument for limiting other rights to gays, because of community animosity or vengeance. These are unacceptable policy motivations if law is to be civilized.

Several states and localities protect homosexuals against discrimination in employment or housing. In New York, a state law confers on a homosexual the rent-control benefits of a deceased partner. Other jurisdictions have eschewed special legal rights for homosexuals, and the military excludes them. Experience will adjudge which of the varied legal approaches to homosexual rights has been the most enlightened. 10

Sober debate over homosexual rights is in short supply. The subject challenges deep-rooted and passionately held images of manhood, womanhood and parenthood, and evokes sublimated fears of community ostracism or degradation.

Each legal issue regarding homosexuality should be examined discretely with the recognition that time has upset many fighting faiths and with the goal of balancing indiviudal liberty against community interests. With regard to homosexual marriage, that balance is negative.

For Journals

Freewrite for five to ten minutes on the assumptions about marriage that you had as a child and now have as an adult. How do children fit into the image you have in mind?

For Discussion

1. What kinds of appeals does Fein make? Consider particularly his core assertion: that children will suffer from same-gender marriages. What assumptions about the purpose of marriage does his argument rest on? Is the argument that children are the key consideration in marriage laws one that would be as persuasive to general audiences as Fein believes it will be to lawyers?

2. In addition to citing legal cases, Fein cites authorities such as Oliver Wendell Holmes. But he then states that "experience confirms that child development is skewed, scarred or retarded when either a father or mother is absent in the household" (paragraph 2). Are you persuaded by his citing of "experience"? If not, what additional evidence could he offer that might be more convincing? Does the fact that *Bowers* has been overturned affect your response to Fein's argument?

3. Fein's overall organizational pattern is direct: he asserts and then supports. How might writing for an audience of lawyers have dictated this pattern? Would it have been equally effective writing for a general audience?

4. Fein also argues by making an analogy to polygamous marriages. How convincing is the analogy? How appropriate is it to the argument?

5. Fein differentiates and separates this issue from other civil rights issues. Do you accept his premise that marriage rights differ fundamentally from other civil rights?

6. Examine the logic of Fein's arguments, such as the one in paragraph 7. It may be helpful to outline the premises and conclusion for each argument he makes. Which of his arguments stand up to the analysis? Which ones are weak? Which ones could be strengthened with evidence?

For Writing

1. Write a letter of rebuttal to Fein. Use a different approach and different arguments from those that Thomas Stoddard (this chapter) uses in "Marriage Is a Fundamental Right." Keep in mind the biases and assumptions you wrote about in your journal assignment for the Stoddard article.

2. Compare and contrast Fein's and Stoddard's arguments, focusing on the effectiveness of their appeals, their use of evidence, and their patterns of development. Which argument makes more appeals to emotion? To logic? To traditions, values, beliefs? Keeping in mind your own biases and attitudes toward the topic, which argument seems more sound?

3. How might the mayor of San Francisco or President Bush respond to Fein or Stoddard?

❊❊❊ *A Family Legacy* (1992)

MARIAN WRIGHT EDELMAN

Marian Wright Edelman (1939–), attorney and founding president of the Children's Defense Fund, is one of five children of a Baptist minister. She graduated from Spelman College, a historically black institution, and Yale Law School; she was the first woman to pass the state bar exam in Mississippi. Edelman has spent her professional life as an activist for disadvantaged Americans, especially children. She has received many honors and awards, and her writings include Children out of School in America *(1974),* Black and White Children in America *(1980), and* Families in Peril: An Agenda for Social Change *(1987). The essay that follows is the first chapter of her book* The Measure of Our Success: A Letter to My Children and Yours.

South Carolina is my home state and I am the aunt, granddaughter, daughter, and sister of Baptist ministers. Service was as essential a part of my upbringing as eating and sleeping and going to school. The church was a hub of Black children's social existence, and caring Black adults were buffers against the segregated and hostile outside world that told us we weren't important. But our parents said it wasn't so, our teachers said it wasn't so, and our preachers said it wasn't so. The message of my racially segregated childhood was clear: let no man or woman look down on you, and look down on no man or woman.

We couldn't play in public playgrounds or sit at drugstore lunch counters and order a Coke, so Daddy built a playground and canteen behind the church. In fact, whenever he saw a need, he tried to respond. There were no Black homes for the aged in Bennettsville, so he began one across the street for which he and Mama and we children cooked and served and cleaned. And we children learned that it was our responsibility to take care of elderly family members and neighbors, and that everyone was our neighbor. My mother carried on the home after Daddy died, and my brother Julian has carried it on to this day behind our church since our mother's death in 1984.

Finding another child in my room or a pair of my shoes gone was far from unusual, and twelve foster children followed my sister and me and three brothers as we left home.

Child-rearing and parental work were inseparable. I went everywhere with my parents and was under the watchful eye of members of the congregation and community who were my extended parents. They kept me when my parents went out of town, they reported on and chided me when I strayed from the straight and narrow of community expectations, and they basked in and supported my achievements when I did well. Doing well, they made clear, meant high academic achievement, playing piano in Sunday school or singing or participating in other church activities, being helpful to somebody, displaying good manners (which is nothing more than consideration toward others), and reading. My sister Olive reminded me recently that the only time our father would not give us a chore ("Can't you find something constructive to do?" was his most common refrain) was when we were reading. So we all read a lot! We learned early what our parents and extended community "parents" valued. Children were taught—not by sermonizing, but by personal example— that nothing was too lowly to do. I remember a debate my parents had when I was eight or nine as to whether I was too young to go with my older brother, Harry, to help clean the bed and bedsores of a very sick, poor woman. I went and learned just how much the smallest helping hands and kindness can mean to a person in need.

The ugly external voices of my small-town, segregated childhood 5 (as a very young child I remember standing and hearing former South Carolina Senator James Byrnes railing on the local courthouse lawn about how Black children would never go to school with whites) were tempered by the internal voices of parental and community expectation and pride. My father and I waited anxiously for the *Brown* v. *Board of Education* decision in 1954. We talked about it and what it would mean for my future and for the future of millions of other Black children. He died the week before *Brown* was decided. But I and other children lucky enough to have caring and courageous parents and other adult role models were able, in later years, to walk through the new and heavy doors that *Brown* slowly and painfully opened—doors that some are trying to close again today.

The adults in our churches and community made children feel valued and important. They took time and paid attention to us. They struggled to find ways to keep us busy. And while life was often hard and resources scarce, we always knew who we were and that the measure of our worth was inside our heads and hearts and not outside in our possessions or on our backs. We were told that the world had a lot of problems; that Black people had an extra lot of problems, but that we were able and obligated to struggle and change them; that being poor was no excuse for not achieving; and that extra intellectual and material gifts brought with them the privilege and responsibility of sharing with others less fortunate. In sum, we learned that service is the rent we pay for living. It is the very purpose of life and not something you do in your spare time.

When my mother died, an old white man in my hometown of Bennettsville asked me what I do. In a flash I realized that in my work at the Children's Defense Fund I do exactly what my parents did—just on a different scale. My brother preached a wonderful sermon at Mama's funeral, but the best tribute was the presence in the back pew of the town drunk, whom an observer said he could not remember coming to church in many years.

The legacies that parents and church and teachers left to my generation of Black children were priceless but not material: a living faith reflected in daily service, the discipline of hard work and stick-to-itness, and a capacity to struggle in the face of adversity. Giving up and "burnout" were not part of the language of my elders—you got up every morning and you did what you had to do and you got up every time you fell down and tried as many times as you had to get it done right. They had grit. They valued family life, family rituals, and tried to be and to expose us to good role models. Role models were of two kinds: those who achieved in the outside world (like Marian Anderson, my namesake) and those who didn't have a whole lot of education or fancy clothes but who taught us by the special grace of their lives the message of Christ and Tolstoy and Gandhi and Heschel and Dorothy Day and Romero and King that the Kingdom of God was within—in what you are, not what you have. I still hope I can be half as good as Black church and community elders like Miz Lucy Mc-Queen, Miz Tee Kelly, and Miz Kate Winston, extraordinary women who were kind and patient and loving with children and others and who, when I went to Spelman College, sent me shoeboxes with chicken and biscuits and greasy dollar bills.

It never occurred to any Wright child that we were not going to college or were not expected to share what we learned and earned with the less fortunate. I was forty years old before I figured out, thanks to my brother Harry's superior insight, that my Daddy often responded to our requests for money by saying he didn't have any change because he really didn't have any rather than because he had nothing smaller than a twenty dollar bill.

I was fourteen years old the night my Daddy died. He had holes in his shoes but two children out of college, one in college, another in divinity school, and a vision he was able to convey to me as he lay dying in an ambulance that I, a young Black girl, could be and do anything; that race and gender are shadows; and that character, self-discipline, determination, attitude, and service are the substance of life.

I have always believed that I could help change the world because I have been lucky to have adults around me who did—in small and large ways. Most were people of simple grace who understood what Walker Percy wrote: You can get all As and still flunk life.

Life was not easy back in the 1940s and 1950s in rural South Carolina for many parents and grandparents. We buried children who died from poverty (and I can't stand it that we still do). Little Johnny Harrington, three houses down from my church parsonage, stepped on and died from a nail because his grandmother had no doctor to advise her, nor the money to pay for health care. (Half of all low-income urban children under two are still not fully immunized against preventable childhood diseases like tetanus and polio and measles.) My classmate, Henry Munnerlyn, broke his neck when he jumped off the bridge into the town creek because only white children were allowed in the public swimming pool. I later heard that the creek where Blacks swam and fished was the hospital sewage outlet. (Today thousands of Black children in our cities and rural areas are losing their lives to cocaine and heroin and alcohol and gang violence because they don't have enough constructive outlets.) The migrant family who collided with a truck on the highway near my home and the ambulance driver

10

who refused to take them to the hospital because they were Black still live in my mind every time I hear about babies who die or are handicapped from birth when they are turned away from hospitals in emergencies or their mothers are turned away in labor because they have no health insurance and cannot pay pre-admission deposits to enter a hospital. I and my brothers and sister might have lost hope—as so many young people today have lost hope—except for the stable, caring, attentive adults in our family, school, congregation, civic and political life who struggled with and for us against the obstacles we faced and provided us positive alternatives and the sense of possibility we needed.

At Spelman College in Atlanta, I found my Daddy and Mama's values about taking responsibility for your own learning and growth reinforced in the daily (except Saturday) chapel service. Daily chapel attendance was compulsory and enforced by the threat of points taken off one's earned grade average as a result of truancy. For all my rebellion then, I remember now far more from the chapel speakers who came to talk to us about life and the purpose of education than from any class. And during my tenure as chairwoman of Spelman's board, I advocated reinstitution of some compulsory assemblies (monthly, not daily!) so our young women would have to hear what we adults think is important.

Many of my mentors and role models, such as Dr. Benjamin Mays, then president of Morehouse College, Whitney Young, dean of the School of Social Work at Atlanta University and later National Urban League head, M. Carl Holman, a professor at Clark College, later head of the National Urban Coalition, Dr. Howard Thurman, dean of the Chapel at Boston University, and Dr. King, all conveyed the same message as they spoke in Sisters Chapel at Spelman: education is for improving the lives of others and for leaving your community and world better than you found it. Other important influences during my Spelman years—Ella Baker, Septima Clark, Howard Zinn, Charles E. Merrill, Jr., and Samuel Dubois Cook—stretched my vision of the future and of one person's ability to help shape it. I'm still trying to live up to their teachings and to the examples of the extraordinary ordinary people whom I had the privilege to serve and learn from after law school during my civil rights sojourn in Mississippi between 1963 and 1968.

Fannie Lou Hamer, Amzie Moore, Winson and Dovie Hudson, Mae   15 Bertha Carter, school desegregation and voting rights pioneers in Mississippi, and Unita Blackwell, who rose from sharecropper to mayor of rural Mayersville, Mississippi—and countless courageous men and women who gave their voices and homes and lives to get the right to vote and to secure for their children a better life than they had—guide and inspire me still. Those largely unknown and usually unlettered people of courage and commitment, along with my parents, remind me each day to keep trying and to let my little light shine, as Mrs. Hamer sang and did through her inspiring life. In a D.C. neighborhood church, I recently saw a banner that reminded me "there is not enough darkness in the world to snuff out the light of even one small candle."

I have always felt extraordinarily blessed to live in the times I have. As a child and as an adult—as a Black woman—I have had to struggle to understand the world around me. Most Americans remember Dr. King as a great leader. I do too. But I also remember him as someone able to admit how often he was afraid and unsure about his next step. But faith prevailed over fear and uncertainty and fatigue and depression. It was his human vulnerability and his ability to rise above it that I most remember. In this, he was not different from many Black adults whose credo has been to make "a way out of no way."

The Children's Defense Fund was conceived in the cauldron of Mississippi's summer project of 1964 and in the Head Start battles of 1965, where both the great need for and limits of local action were apparent. As a private civil rights lawyer, I learned that I could have only limited, albeit important, impact on meeting epidemic family and child needs in that poor state without coherent national policy and investment strategies to complement community empowerment strategies. I also learned that critical civil and political rights would not mean much to a hungry, homeless, illiterate child and family if they lacked the social and economic means to exercise them. And so children—my own and other people's—became the passion of my personal and professional life. For it is they who are God's presence, promise, and hope for humankind.

For Journals

How do you think that American families measure their success? What kinds of achievements or possessions are often used to measure success?

For Discussion

1.   The subtitle of Edelman's book, of which this selection is the first chapter, is "A Letter to My Children and Yours." Why do you believe that Edelman is addressing her remarks to these audiences? How do the audiences shape her message?

2.   Edelman and the children of her community grew up knowing that they were valued and important. How did the adults of the community transmit these beliefs? What were the adults' expectations of the children? What did the children assume about their role in the community?

3.   Edelman writes of the legacies from her family and community—of service, of doing for others, and of making the most of intellectual

and material gifts. How have such legacies changed her life? How have they influenced her work?

4. Edelman concludes, "Service is the rent we pay for living" (paragraph 6). What are the assumptions on which she bases this statement?

5. Edelman's community served as an extended family in supporting her and other children. In what ways was her upbringing like, and unlike, that of children growing up in the 1980s and 1990s? What has changed for the better? For the worse? What has not changed?

6. Edelman writes that her father died with "holes in his shoes but two children out of college, one in college, another in divinity school, and a vision" (paragraph 10). How does Edelman's measure of her father's success compare with, and contrast to, statements of family values and beliefs evident in other readings in this book? (Look, for example, at Martin Luther King, Jr.'s, "I Have a Dream," in Chapter 6, and at "Bricklayer's Boy," in Chapter 8.)

For Writing

1. Write an essay examining and explaining the values and beliefs with which you were raised. What did you learn about your role in the family? In the community? What were the expectations of your parents and any extended family you have? You could focus on education, community involvement, music, or some other aspect of your youth.

2. Research a current issue in children's rights—for example, health care, legal protection, or issues of abuse. In addition to drawing on books, periodicals, and government documents, try to interview people in your community who work on behalf of children in the area you are researching. What are the controversies? Write up your research in a documented essay.

3. Write a letter to the children you have or expect to have, or to nieces or nephews or other relatives. Explain to them the legacies that you grew up with and that you hope you will pass on to them.

✼✼✼ *Saplings in the Storm* (1994)

MARY PIPHER

Mary Pipher, Ph.D., is a clinical psychologist in private practice in Lincoln, Nebraska. She teaches part-time at the University of Nebraska Wesleyan University. Dr. Pipher is also a commentator for Nebraska Public Radio. This selection is from her book Reviving Ophelia: Saving the Selves of Adolescent Girls.

When my cousin Polly was a girl, she was energy in motion. She danced, did cartwheels and splits, played football, basketball and baseball with the neighborhood boys, wrestled with my brothers, biked, climbed trees and rode horses. She was as lithe and as resilient as a willow branch and as unrestrained as a lion cub. Polly talked as much as she moved. She yelled out orders and advice, shrieked for joy when she won a bet or heard a good joke, laughed with her mouth wide open, argued with kids and grown-ups and insulted her foes in the language of a construction worker.

We formed the Marauders, a secret club that met over her garage. Polly was the Tom Sawyer of the club. She planned the initiations, led the spying expeditions and hikes to haunted houses. She showed us the rituals to become blood "brothers" and taught us card tricks and how to smoke.

Then Polly had her first period and started junior high. She tried to keep up her old ways, but she was called a tomboy and chided for not acting more ladylike. She was excluded by her boy pals and by the girls, who were moving into makeup and romances.

This left Polly confused and shaky. She had temper tantrums and withdrew from both the boys' and girls' groups. Later she quieted down and reentered as Becky Thatcher. She wore stylish clothes and watched from the sidelines as the boys acted and spoke. Once again she was accepted and popular. She glided smoothly through our small society. No one spoke of the changes or mourned the loss of our town's most dynamic citizen. I was the only one who felt that a tragedy had transpired.

Girls in what Freud called the latency period, roughly age six or 5 seven through puberty, are anything but latent. I think of my daughter Sara during those years—performing chemistry experiments and magic tricks, playing her violin, starring in her own plays, rescuing wild animals and biking all over town. I think of her friend Tamara, who wrote a 300-page novel the summer of her sixth-grade year. I remember myself, reading every children's book in the library of my town. One week I planned to be a great doctor like Albert Schweitzer. The next week I wanted to write like Louisa May Alcott or dance in Paris like Isadora Duncan. I have never since had as much confidence or ambition.

Most preadolescent girls are marvelous company because they are interested in everything—sports, nature, people, music and books. Almost all the heroines of girls' literature come from this age group—Anne of Green Gables, Heidi, Pippi Longstocking and Caddie Woodlawn. Girls this age bake pies, solve mysteries and go on quests. They can take care of themselves and are not yet burdened with caring for others. They have a brief respite from the female role and can be tomboys, a word that conveys courage, competency and irreverence.

They can be androgynous, having the ability to act adaptively in any situation regardless of gender role constraints. An androgynous person can comfort a baby or change a tire, cook a meal or chair a meeting. Research has shown that, since they are free to act without worrying if their behavior is feminine or masculine, androgynous adults are the most well adjusted.

Girls between seven and eleven rarely come to therapy. They don't need it. I can count on my fingers the girls this age whom I have seen: Coreen, who was physically abused; Anna, whose parents were divorcing; and Brenda, whose father killed himself. These girls were courageous and resilient. Brenda said, "If my father didn't want to stick around, that's his loss." Coreen and Anna were angry, not at themselves, but rather at the grown-ups, who they felt were making mistakes. It's amazing how little help these girls needed from me to heal and move on.

A horticulturist told me a revealing story. She led a tour of junior-high girls who were attending a math and science fair on her campus. She showed them side oats grama, bluestem, Indian grass and trees— redbud, maple, walnut and willow. The younger girls interrupted each other with their questions and tumbled forward to see, touch and smell everything. The older girls, the ninth-graders, were different. They hung back. They didn't touch plants or shout out questions. They stood primly to the side, looking bored and even a little disgusted by the enthusiasm of their younger classmates. My friend asked herself, What's happened to these girls? What's gone wrong? She told me, "I wanted to shake them, to say, 'Wake up, come back. Is anybody home at your house?'"

Recently I sat sunning on a bench outside my favorite ice-cream 10 store. A mother and her teenage daughter stopped in front of me and waited for the light to change. I heard the mother say, "You have got to stop blackmailing your father and me. Every time you don't get what you want, you tell us that you want to run away from home or kill yourself. What's happened to you? You used to be able to handle not getting your way."

The daughter stared straight ahead, barely acknowledging her mother's words. The light changed. I licked my ice-cream cone. Another mother approached the same light with her preadolescent daughter in tow. They were holding hands. The daughter said to her mother, "This is fun. Let's do this all afternoon."

Something dramatic happens to girls in early adolescence. Just as planes and ships disappear mysteriously into the Bermuda Triangle, so do the selves of girls go down in droves. They crash and burn in a social and developmental Bermuda Triangle. In early adolescence, studies show that girls' IQ scores drop and their math and science scores plummet. They lose their resiliency and optimism and become less curious and inclined to take risks. They lose their assertive, energetic and "tomboyish" personalities and become more deferential, self-critical and depressed. They report great unhappiness with their own bodies.

Psychology documents but does not explain the crashes. Girls who rushed to drink in experiences in enormous gulps sit quietly in the corner. Writers such as Sylvia Plath, Margaret Atwood and Olive Schreiner have described the wreckage. Diderot, in writing to his young friend Sophie Volland, described his observations harshly: "You all die at 15."

Fairy tales capture the essence of this phenomenon. Young women eat poisoned apples or prick their fingers with poisoned needles and fall asleep for a hundred years. They wander away from home, encounter great dangers, are rescued by princes and are transformed into passive and docile creatures.

The story of Ophelia, from Shakespeare's Hamlet, shows the destructive forces that affect young women. As a girl, Ophelia is happy and free, but with adolescence she loses herself. When she falls in love with Hamlet, she lives only for his approval. She has no inner direction; rather she struggles to meet the demands of Hamlet and her father. Her value is determined utterly by their approval. Ophelia is torn apart by her efforts to please. When Hamlet spurns her because she is an obedient daughter, she goes mad with grief. Dressed in elegant clothes that weigh her down, she drowns in a stream filled with flowers. 15

Girls know they are losing themselves. One girl said, "Everything good in me died in junior high." Wholeness is shattered by the chaos of adolescence. Girls become fragmented, their selves split into mysterious contradictions. They are sensitive and tenderhearted, mean and competitive, superficial and idealistic. They are confident in the morning and overwhelmed with anxiety by nightfall. They rush through their days with wild energy and then collapse into lethargy. They try on new roles every week—this week the good student, next week the delinquent and the next, the artist. And they expect their families to keep up with these changes.

My clients in early adolescence are elusive and slow to trust adults. They are easily offended by a glance, a clearing of the throat, a silence, a lack of sufficient enthusiasm or a sentence that doesn't meet their immediate needs. Their voices have gone underground—their speech is more tentative and less articulate. Their moods swing widely. One week they love their world and their families, the next they are critical of everyone. Much of their behavior is unreadable. Their problems are complicated and metaphorical—eating disorders, school phobias and self-inflicted injuries. I need to ask again and again in a dozen different ways, "What are you trying to tell me?"

Michelle, for example, was a beautiful, intelligent seventeen-year-old. Her mother brought her in after she became pregnant for the third time in three years. I tried to talk about why this was happening. She smiled a Mona Lisa smile to all my questions. "No, I don't care all that much for sex." "No, I didn't plan this. It just happened." When Michelle left a session, I felt like I'd been talking in the wrong language to someone far away.

Holly was another mystery. She was shy, soft-spoken and slow-moving, pretty under all her makeup and teased red hair. She was a Prince fan and wore only purple. Her father brought her in after a suicide attempt. She wouldn't study, do chores, join any school activities or find a job. Holly answered questions in patient, polite monosyllables. She really talked only when the topic was Prince. For several weeks we talked about him. She played me his tapes. Prince somehow spoke for her and to her.

Gail burned and cut herself when she was unhappy. Dressed in 20 black, thin as a straw, she sat silently before me, her hair a mess, her ears, lips and nose all pierced with rings. She spoke about Bosnia and the hole in the ozone layer and asked me if I liked rave music. When I asked about her life, she fingered her earrings and sat silently.

My clients are not different from girls who are not seen in therapy. I teach at a small liberal arts college and the young women in my classes have essentially the same experiences as my therapy clients. One student worried about her best friend who'd been sexually assaulted. Another student missed class after being beaten by her boyfriend. Another asked what she should do about crank calls from a man threatening to rape her. When stressed, another student stabbed her hand with paper clips until she drew blood. Many students have wanted advice on eating disorders.

After I speak at high schools, girls approach me to say that they have been raped, or they want to run away from home, or that they have a friend who is anorexic or alcoholic. At first all this trauma surprised me. Now I expect it.

Psychology has a long history of ignoring girls this age. Until recently adolescent girls haven't been studied by academics, and they have long baffled therapists. Because they are secretive with adults and full of contradictions, they are difficult to study. So much is happening internally that's not communicated on the surface.

Simone de Beauvoir believed adolescence is when girls realize that men have the power and that their only power comes from consenting to become submissive adored objects. They do not suffer from the penis envy Freud postulated, but from power envy.

She described the Bermuda Triangle this way: Girls who were the 25 subjects of their own lives became the objects of others' lives. "Young girls slowly bury their childhood, put away their independent and imperious selves and submissively enter adult existence." Adolescent girls experience a conflict between their autonomous selves and their need to be feminine, between their status as human beings and their vocation as females. De Beauvoir says, "Girls stop being and start seeming."

Girls become "female impersonators" who fit their whole selves into small, crowded spaces. Vibrant, confident girls become shy, doubting young women. Girls stop thinking, "Who am I? What do I want?" and start thinking, "What must I do to please others?"

This gap between girls' true selves and cultural prescriptions for what is properly female creates enormous problems. To paraphrase a Stevie Smith poem about swimming in the sea, "they are not waving, they are drowning." And just when they most need help, they are unable to take their parents' hands.

Olive Schreiner wrote of her experiences as a young girl in *The Story of an African Farm*. "The world tells us what we are to be and shapes us by the ends it sets before us. To men it says, work. To us, it says, seem. The less a woman has in her head the lighter she is for carrying." She described the finishing school that she attended in this way: "It was a machine for condensing the soul into the smallest possible area. I have seen some souls so compressed that they would have filled a small thimble."

Margaret Mead believed that the ideal culture is one in which there is a place for every human gift. By her standards, our Western culture is far from ideal for women. So many gifts are unused and unappreciated. So many voices are stilled. Stendhal wrote: "All geniuses born women are lost to the public good."

Alice Miller wrote of the pressures on some young children to [30] deny their true selves and assume false selves to please their parents. *Reviving Ophelia* suggests that adolescent girls experience a similar pressure to split into true and false selves, but this time the pressure comes not from parents but from the culture. Adolescence is when girls experience social pressure to put aside their authentic selves and to display only a small portion of their gifts.

This pressure disorients and depresses most girls. They sense the pressure to be someone they are not. They fight back, but they are fighting a "problem with no name." One girl put it this way: "I'm a perfectly good carrot that everyone is trying to turn into a rose. As a carrot, I have good color and a nice leafy top. When I'm carved into a rose, I turn brown and wither."

Adolescent girls are saplings in a hurricane. They are young and vulnerable trees that the winds blow with gale strength. Three factors make young women vulnerable to the hurricane. One is their development level. Everything is changing—body shape, hormones, skin and hair. Calmness is replaced by anxiety. Their way of thinking is changing. Far below the surface they are struggling with the most basic of human questions: What is my place in the universe, what is my meaning?

Second, American culture has always smacked girls on the head in early adolescence. This is when they move into a broader culture that is rife with girl-hurting "isms," such as sexism, capitalism and lookism, which is the evaluation of a person solely on the basis of appearance.

Third, American girls are expected to distance from parents just at the time when they most need their support. As they struggle with countless new pressures, they must relinquish the protection and closeness they've felt with their families in childhood. They turn to their none-too-constant peers for support.

Parents know only too well that something is happening to their 35 daughters. Calm, considerate daughters grow moody, demanding and distant. Girls who loved to talk are sullen and secretive. Girls who liked to hug now bristle when touched. Mothers complain that they can do nothing right in the eyes of their daughters. Involved fathers bemoan their sudden banishment from their daughters' lives. But few parents realize how universal their experiences are. Their daughters are entering a new land, a dangerous place that parents can scarcely comprehend. Just when they most need a home base, they cut themselves loose without radio communications.

Most parents of adolescent girls have the goal of keeping their daughters safe while they grow up and explore the world. The parents' job is to protect. The daughters' job is to explore. Always these different tasks have created tension in parent-daughter relationships, but now it's even harder. Generally parents are more protective of their daughters than is corporate America. Parents aren't trying to make money off their daughters by selling them designer jeans or cigarettes, they just want them to be well adjusted. They don't see their daughters as sex objects or consumers but as real people with talents and interests. But daughters turn away from their parents as they enter the new land. They befriend their peers, who are their fellow inhabitants of the strange country and who share a common language and set of customs. They often embrace the junk values of mass culture.

This turning away from parents is partly for developmental reasons. Early adolescence is a time of physical and psychological change, self-absorption, preoccupation with peer approval and identity formation. It's a time when girls focus inward on their own fascinating changes.

It's partly for cultural reasons. In America we define adulthood as a moving away from families into broader culture. Adolescence is the time for cutting bonds and breaking free. Adolescents may claim great independence from parents, but they are aware and ashamed of their parents' smallest deviation from the norm. They don't like to be seen with them and find their imperfections upsetting. A mother's haircut or a father's joke can ruin their day. Teenagers are furious at parents who say the wrong things or do not respond with perfect answers. Adolescents claim not to hear their parents, but with their friends they discuss endlessly all parental attitudes. With amazing acuity, they sense nuances, doubt, shades of ambiguity, discrepancy and hypocrisy.

Adolescents still have some of the magical thinking of childhood and believe that parents have the power to keep them safe and happy. They blame their parents for their misery, yet they make a point of not telling their parents how they think and feel; they have secrets, so things can get crazy. For example, girls who are raped may not tell their parents. Instead, they become hostile and rebellious. Parents bring girls in because of their anger and out-of-control behavior. When I hear about this unexplainable anger, I ask about rape. Ironically, their parents should have known about the danger and been more protective; afterward, they should have sensed the pain and helped.

Most parents feel like failures during this time. They feel shut out, 40 impotent and misunderstood. They often attribute the difficulties of this time to their daughters and their own failings. They don't understand that these problems go with the developmental stage, the culture and the times.

Parents experience an enormous sense of loss when their girls enter this new land. They miss the daughters who sang in the kitchen, who read them school papers, who accompanied them on fishing trips and to ball games. They miss the daughters who liked to bake cookies, play Pictionary and be kissed goodnight. In place of their lively, affectionate daughters they have changelings—new girls who are sadder, angrier and more complicated. Everyone is grieving.

Fortunately adolescence is time-limited. By late high school most girls are stronger and the winds are dying down. Some of the worst problems—cliques, a total focus on looks and struggles with parents—are on the wane. But the way girls handle the problems of adolescence can have implications for their adult lives. Without some help, the loss of wholeness, self-confidence and self-direction can last well into adulthood. Many adult clients struggle with the same issues that overwhelmed them as adolescent girls. Thirty-year-old accountants and realtors, forty-year-old homemakers and doctors, and thirty-five-year-old nurses and schoolteachers ask the same questions and struggle with the same problems as their teenage daughters.

Even sadder are the women who are not struggling, who have forgotten that they have selves worth defending. They have repressed the pain of their adolescence, the betrayals of self in order to be pleasing. These women come to therapy with the goal of becoming even more pleasing to others. They come to lose weight, to save their marriages or to rescue their children. When I ask them about their own needs, they are confused by the question.

Most women struggled alone with the trauma of adolescence and have led decades of adult life with their adolescent experiences unexamined. The lessons learned in adolescence are forgotten and their memories of pain are minimized. They come into therapy because their marriage is in trouble, or they hate their job, or their own daughter is giving them fits. Maybe their daughter's pain awakens their own pain. Some are depressed or chemically addicted or have stress-related illnesses—ulcers, colitis, migraines or psoriasis. Many have tried to be perfect women and failed. Even though they followed the rules and did as they were told, the world has not rewarded them. They feel angry and betrayed. They feel miserable and taken for granted, used rather than loved.

Women often know how everyone in their family thinks and feels 45 except themselves. They are great at balancing the needs of their coworkers, husbands, children and friends, but they forget to put themselves into the equation. They struggle with adolescent questions still unresolved: How important are looks and popularity? How do I care for myself and not be selfish? How can I be honest and still be loved? How can I achieve and not threaten others? How can I be sexual and not a sex object? How can I be responsive but not responsible for everyone?

As we talk, the years fall away. We are back in junior high with the cliques, the shame, the embarrassment about bodies, the desire to be accepted and the doubts about ability. So many adult women think they are stupid and ugly. Many feel guilty if they take time for themselves. They do not express anger or ask for help.

We talk about childhood—what the woman was like at ten and at fifteen. We piece together a picture of childhood lost. We review her own particular story, her own time in the hurricane. Memories flood in. Often there are tears, angry outbursts, sadness for what has been lost. So much time has been wasted pretending to be who others wanted. But also, there's a new energy that comes from making connections, from choosing awareness over denial and from the telling of secrets.

We work now, twenty years behind schedule. We reestablish each woman as the subject of her life, not as the object of others' lives. We answer Freud's patronizing question "What do women want?" Each woman wants something different and particular and yet each woman wants the same thing—to be who she truly is, to become who she can become.

Many women regain their preadolescent authenticity with menopause. Because they are no longer beautiful objects occupied primarily with caring for others, they are free once again to become the subjects of their own lives. They become more confident, self-directed and energetic. Margaret Mead noticed this phenomenon in cultures all over the world and called it "pmz," postmenopausal zest. She noted that some cultures revere these older women. Others burn them at the stake.

Before I studied psychology, I studied cultural anthropology. I 50
have always been interested in that place where culture and individual psychology intersect, in why cultures create certain personalities
and not others, in how they pull for certain strengths in their members, in how certain talents are utilized while others atrophy from lack
of attention. I'm interested in the role cultures play in the development
of individual pathology.

For a student of culture and personality, adolescence is fascinating. It's an extraordinary time when individual, developmental and
cultural factors combine in ways that shape adulthood. It's a time of
marked internal development and massive cultural indoctrination.

I want to try in this book to connect each girl's story with larger
cultural issues—to examine the intersection of the personal and the
political. It's a murky place; the personal and political are intertwined
in all of our lives. Our minds, which are shaped by the society in
which we live, can oppress us. And yet our minds can also analyze
and work to change the culture.

An analysis of the culture cannot ignore individual differences in
women. Some women blossom and grow under the most hostile conditions while others wither after the smallest storms. And yet we are more
alike than different in the issues that face us. The important question is,
Under what conditions do most young women flower and grow?

Adolescent clients intrigue me as they struggle to sort themselves
out. But I wouldn't have written this book had it not been for these last
few years when my office has been filled with girls—girls with eating
disorders, alcohol problems, posttraumatic stress reactions to sexual or
physical assaults, sexually transmitted diseases (STDs), self-inflicted
injuries and strange phobias, and girls who have tried to kill themselves or run away. A health department survey showed that 40 percent of all girls in my midwestern city considered suicide last year.
The Centers for Disease Control in Atlanta reports that the suicide rate
among children age ten to fourteen rose 75 percent between 1979 and
1988. Something dramatic is happening to adolescent girls in America,
something unnoticed by those not on the front lines.

At first I was surprised that girls were having more trouble now. 55
After all, we have had a consciousness-raising women's movement
since the sixties. Women are working in traditionally male professions
and going out for sports. Some fathers help with the housework and
child care. It seems that these changes would count for something.
And of course they do, but in some ways the progress is confusing.
The Equal Rights Amendment was not ratified, feminism is a pejorative term to many people and, while some women have high-powered
jobs, most women work hard for low wages and do most of the "second shift" work. The lip service paid to equality makes the reality of
discrimination even more confusing.

Many of the pressures girls have always faced are intensified in the 1990s. Many things contribute to this intensification: more divorced families, chemical addictions, casual sex and violence against women. Because of the media, which Clarence Page calls "electronic wallpaper," girls all live in one big town—a sleazy, dangerous tinsel town with lots of liquor stores and few protected spaces. Increasingly women have been sexualized and objectified, their bodies marketed to sell tractors and toothpaste. Soft- and hard-core pornography are everywhere. Sexual and physical assaults on girls are at an all-time high. Now girls are more vulnerable and fearful, more likely to have been traumatized and less free to roam about alone. This combination of old stresses and new is poison for our young women.

Parents have unprecedented stress as well. For the last half-century, parents worried about their sixteen-year-old daughters driving, but now, in a time of drive-by shootings and car-jackings, parents can be panicked. Parents have always worried about their daughters' sexual behavior, but now, in a time of date rapes, herpes and AIDS, they can be sex-phobic. Traditionally parents have wondered what their teens were doing, but now teens are much more likely to be doing things that can get them killed.

This book will tell stories from the front lines. It's about girls because I know about girls. I was one, I see them in therapy, I have a teenage daughter and I teach primarily young women. I am not writing about boys because I have had limited experience with them. I'm not saying that girls and boys are radically different, only that they have different experiences.

I am saying that girls are having more trouble now than they had thirty years ago, when I was a girl, and more trouble than even ten years ago. Something new is happening. Adolescence has always been hard, but it's harder now because of cultural changes in the last decade. The protected place in space and time that we once called childhood has grown shorter. There is an African saying, "It takes a village to raise a child." Most girls no longer have a village.

Parents, teachers, counselors and nurses see that girls are in trou- 60 ble, but they do not realize how universal and extreme the suffering is. This book is an attempt to share what I have seen and heard. It's a hurricane warning, a message to the culture that something important is happening. This is a National Weather Service bulletin from the storm center.

For Journals

Think back to what your life was like when you were ten years old, then at age fifteen. In what ways did you change the way you thought of yourself? Of your role as a young woman or young man?

For Discussion

1. What is the "storm" that the author writes about? Who are the "saplings"?

2. Pipher quotes the writer Diderot as saying to a young woman, "You all die at 15." What do you think Diderot means? Do you agree or disagree? Cite examples from the text, or from your own observation or experience, to support your view.

3. The author integrates several different types of evidence—specific cases, literary examples, assertions, and authority—to support her key assertions. Which do you find most persuasive, and why?

For Writing

1. Using your journal writing as a starting point, write a reflective essay on your own passage into adolescence. Use a specific anecdote or examples to illustrate your essay.

2. Research rites of passage for adolescence in American cultures or in other countries and cultures. Be sure to focus your topic so that you can develop the paper well in the space available.

3. Write a response to Pipher. If you agree with her, provide a case example that supports her view. If you disagree, offer convincing evidence that refutes her assertion.

✿✿✿ *"The Culture of Cruelty,"* FROM Raising Cain: Protecting the Emotional Life of Boys (2000)

DANIEL J. KINDLON AND MICHAEL THOMPSON

Daniel J. Kindlon is a researcher and a psychology professor at Harvard as well as a psychologist specializing in adolescent boys. Michael Thompson is a child psychologist and staff psychologist at an all-boys school. They have more than thirty-five years of combined experience working with boys and their families. The following selection is a chapter from their larger work on male adolescence in America. You may wish to consider it a companion reading to "Saplings in the Storm," a selection about girls' adolescence that appeared earlier in this chapter.

> Cruelty and fear shake hands together.
> —HONORÉ DE BALZAC

Almost every man has boyhood memories of camaraderie and a coming-of-age story to tell. Maybe it's about a friend, or his gang of friends, and the memorable times they spent together—riding bikes, shooting hoops, going to movies, or just "hanging out." Or maybe his story isn't about friends but about an event, a moment as vivid in memory as on the day it happened years ago. These are the stories men like to tell.

There are other coming-of-age stories that men don't tell so eagerly or won't tell at all, even years later, because the emotional pain of the experience remains as deeply disturbing as on the day it happened when they were ten or twelve or fourteen. These are stories of boy cruelty—of domination, humiliation, fear, and betrayal—that most women never hear and most men and boys are reluctant or unable to share even with one another.

Beginning around age ten, as a boy approaches puberty, normal cognitive development makes him more aware of himself and his place in the group and raises the stakes in the many diverse competitions that consume boys: who is stronger, who is more attractive to girls, who gets better grades, who is a better basketball player, who is richer and has better things, and who can get the upper hand in teasing verbal combat. A boy's eagerness for autonomy, the fact that he now receives less teacher supervision, and his desire to cut loose from his parents' influence make him a willing recruit into the peer culture. At the same time, the group demands conformity and holds him up to ridicule for any failure to conform. Whether it is the TV shows he watches, the books he reads, the shoes he wears, the color of his socks, the length of his shorts, the cut of his hair, the sound of his laugh, or the length of his stride, anything a boy says or does that's different can and will be used against him. The physical changes of this age, in height, musculature, voice, and facial hair, for insistence, only add to a boy's self-consciousness. Almost all boys hide their hurt because to admit it appears weak. And they all look to make preemptive strikes when possible—to divert attention from themselves and onto others. In this psychological war no boys are truly protected, and there are no real "winners."

Boys are desperate for role models as they head into this uncertain age, and in most cases the dominant image of masculinity is one that requires strength and stoicism. Among themselves boys engage in continuous psychological warfare. Older boys pick on younger boys—dominating them by virtue of their greater size—and younger boys mimic them, creating an environment that pits the strong against the weak, the popular against the unpopular, the power brokers against the powerless, and the conformity-driven "boy pack" against the boy who fails in any way to conform with pack expectations.

The headmistress of an East Coast boarding school wrote to us to 5 share her concerns about cruel teasing that had become especially virulent among the boys at the school, going beyond the garden-variety insults and name-calling to more subtle psychological "pranks" that showed a disturbing undercurrent of emotional cruelty.

One incident had occurred one afternoon in the common room of the dormitory, when an eleventh-grade boy, flanked by somber-faced friends, pretended to be distraught and in emotional shock about the death of his father. Another boy approached him to console him, sincerely believing the boy was in the saddest of circumstances. After stringing the caring boy along for several minutes, the boy confessed the ruse—his parents were alive and well—and with the joke splendidly revealed, he and his friends had a good laugh. The compassionate boy was made a laughing-stock and felt foolish and angry at the trick. And he learned his lesson: he wouldn't be so quick with compassion the next time around.

Other troubling incidents she described could have come from any school or neighborhood in America where young adolescent boys gather:

On one unpopular boy's birthday, a number of boys sang "Happy Birthday" to him but pretended to forget his name. When it was clear that he was embarrassed, they apologized, then brought out his cake—a block of ice covered with frosting.

In the school gym locker room, some boys urinated on other boys' belongings or into their shampoo bottles. There were incidents of "nipple twisting," painful and humiliating to the victim. Boys mooned one another or mooned and rubbed themselves against boys targeted for harassment. Boys left used condoms or trash on other boys' clothes or in their lockers.

Neither the victim nor his friends generally report these incidents to teachers, for the most part because they know the acts are so intimate and so obviously hurtful that any teacher or parent would disapprove and there would be penalties to pay; the repercussions could be worse than the original incident. Showing the hurt also would be an admission of defeat and would only heighten a boy's vulnerability to new waves of scorn and attack. Every boy knows this. Why would a boy sit uncomfortably through an entire afternoon of classes rather than set foot in the boys' rest room to relieve himself, as one of our students confided he often did? Because an open row of urinals is an invitation to humiliation. All it takes is a quick push on the back, and a boy knocked off balance is left with wet pants and endless ridicule. Not only the aggressor will tease; any other boys who see or hear of the incident will, too. They will taunt him with it and whisper and snicker about it until someone more humiliated is pushed to the forefront.

We consulted at a school where the members of the lacrosse team periodically would take two small ninth-grade boys out to a field and force them to fight each other. If they resisted, said the bigger boys, the rest of the team would beat them up anyway. And so these smaller boys would fight, and the older boys would videotape it and show it around school.

Despite collegial appearances, all boys live with fear in this culture of cruelty. They also adhere to its code, and are loyal to its tenets even though they may not feel as if they fit in, because they view it as an inevitable test of their manliness.

With every lesson in dominance, fear, and betrayal, a boy is tutored away from trust, empathy, and relationship.[1] This is what boys lose to the culture of cruelty. What they learn instead is emotional guardedness, the wariness with which so many men approach relationships for the rest of their lives.

This is a culture that offers no security. Some boys are more frequently targeted than others, some more often lead the assaults, but all boys know they are vulnerable. As a self-possessed and popular boy confided: "Everybody thinks you've got it so easy when you're on top, but being on top just means that you have to worry all the time about slipping or somebody gaining on you. All it takes is one mistake or a bad day, and all sorts of people are waiting to take you down." For a boy not so high in the pecking order, life can be brutal—physically and psychologically—when the whim of the pack turns against him or, worse, turns a humiliated boy against himself, resulting in serious emotional problems, suicide, or violence. Boys who are under constant pressure to assert power or be labeled a weakling are more likely to level cruelty at others with little recognition of, or regard for, its emotional impact. Boys are cruel, in part because they are afraid, and their need to defend against that fear is ironclad.

Colin, an insightful eleventh grader, reflects on his experiences in 15 the seventh grade: "You get into a habit of saying stuff to people, and it gets to a point where you don't even think about what you're saying anymore—like 'You're a dork'—and then it happens so much, it gets worse and worse, and then it's just like another word, like 'and' or 'I,' and you don't think of it as a word that can hurt somebody. I don't think you see the consequences of it. When you punch somebody in the eye, you see that they get a black eye, but when you and thirty other people call somebody a loser ten times day, you don't see the kid having low self-esteem or being hurt by it. You might see it if he cried or something, but then that's only like pouring fuel on the fire: everybody goes after him for crying."

We are realistic. We know that powerful influences shape the culture of cruelty and perpetuate it. To the extent that the period of puberty and early adolescence is for all kids a time of radical change, self-definition, and emotional insecurity, it is to some degree inevitable that boys will become rivals, friends, enemies.[2] But just as one boy's careless taunt can inflict a lasting wound on another boy, so can even a few boys change the climate dramatically with their decision to resist joining in the teasing or to stand up for a boy under attack. If the culture of cruelty thrives on boys' fears of vulnerability, then the challenge is to replace their fears with a greater understanding of their own emotional struggle and in so doing diminish their need for cruelty and their tolerance of it.

Michael with Seventh-Grade Boys: Learning to Talk ... but Not Too Much

The principal of a suburban middle school asks me to meet with two sections of seventh-grade boys for an hour. She says there is a lot of teasing among the boys, and she's hoping that conversation will be more effective without girls present.

The meeting takes place in a dark classroom in the late afternoon. All the boys—about forty of them—are sitting at desks with their huge book bags on the floor beside them. It is quite a sight, these boys with their fresh, open faces. They look so handsome, so adultlike, and yet they are not.

The boys arrange themselves in groups immediately upon entering the room, while some boys keep to themselves, and some hug the wall. There is always a center group, very close together, that conveys a sense of power and popularity. "You are going to hear from us," their position tells me. I cannot exactly explain the underlying theory of power seating in a school, but I know it when I see it. Within seconds it's clear which boys want to be the center of attention, which boys are going to compete for my time, which boys want to dominate the conversation, and which boys are going to be on the margins.

I begin by asking them why boys tease one another. To them it's a 20 dumb question. Because it's funny, says one, everyone knows that. The joke is right there, the stupid behavior is obvious; someone has to point it out. Then I ask them what the most painful moment—emotionally speaking—has been for them in school. There is an uncomfortable silence as the boys glance around the room at one another and shift in their chairs. A boy starts to describe an athletic injury, and I remind him that we are talking about hurt feelings. Someone describes having dropped a test tube filled with a smelly mixture in science lab, and how everyone started to tease him about being a klutz. Another boy says he used to get made fun of because he wore braces.

Then Steven, one of the boys sitting alone and against the wall, begins to talk about being regularly tormented on the bus, having his books grabbed out of his backpack, his papers scattered, and how all the kids laugh when he goes to pick them up. The tone of his voice signals us all that his pain is recent and deep. The discomfort in the room is palpable. His tormentors are here, and he is telling their "secret" to a "stranger."

What is most unnerving to the boys, however, is the emotion in Steven's voice. He has taken the wraps off; this is real. Boys start to squirm or giggle; a few nudge one another. Little noises arise from around the room. I can tell that Steven knows he is breaking the code of silence but doesn't care; he has my attention, and he is going to tell his story.

I am torn, because as a psychologist, I want to encourage this self-disclosure, but Steven has opened himself up for a whole new round of teasing. He is not reading the cues. If he goes on this way, exposing his vulnerabilities, the group will gang up on him. I want to help Steven speak his truth without having him become the victim, the "Piggy" of the group, like the classic vulnerable boy in William Golding's *Lord of the Flies.*

"Piggy" is the classic scapegoat in the literature of boy cruelty, the overweight boy in *Lord of the Flies.* In the novel, shipwrecked school-boys, ranging in age from six to thirteen, struggle to maintain civilization and democracy but ultimately fail, succumbing to crueler impulses to shame and punish each other. Even the most fair-minded leader among the boys is, at some point, drawn into the pack's frenzied taunting of Piggy, the pudgy, bespectacled picture of vulnerability and the voice of reason. Finally, as the mob of boys grows restless in a violent swell of discord about duty assignments, Piggy cries out for calm deliberation, and he is killed.

In many schools the book is a standard part of the curriculum in 25 seventh- and eighth-grade English classes. For the girls it is a powerful piece of fiction about the human potential for cruelty. For the boys the story is real: it's as close as the crowded hall between classes or the locker room before gym period. It accurately captures their own, only slightly more civilized world. It is a place every man has been. A boy lives that story, too, aware every day that the group could turn on him in a flash, that every moment holds the "Piggy" potential, and that, if he is targeted, it will be almost impossible for anyone—even a friend—to stand up with him against the crowd. Except in the most violent communities, most boys don't face the potential of physical annihilation so much as they experience a marginalization—being made to feel worthless or virtually nonexistent—that can be emotionally debilitating.

I stop Steven and thank him for his contribution. He starts to speak on two later occasions in the meeting, and when I see the other boys becoming scornful, I close him down. I will seek him out, either directly or through the middle school principal, and find some time to speak with him privately.

Striving for Masculinity: In Search
of the Big Impossible

It is normal for a child to seek the respect or appreciation of peers. Friendship provides affection, intimacy, and reliable alliance. From either a friend or the group, you can get practical assistance, nurturance, companionship, and enhancement of worth. What only a group can provide is a sense of inclusion, which all children crave.

For boys on the cusp of adolescence, this desire to fit in is supercharged by their developing gender identity need to establish themselves as successful males. In the Eastern Highlands of Papua, New Guinea, the Fox Indians call manhood the "Big Impossible."[3] What an appropriate name for manhood, which in so many cultures is recognized only after a rite of passage that tests the mettle of a boy against the fire of cultural expectations. Inherent in this thinking is the idea that to be a real man requires something more than simple anatomical maleness, that a boy must rise to a performance challenge that will earn him his manly status. When masculinity is defined as an achievement, then manhood becomes "a prize to be won or wrested through struggle" and a "precarious or artificial state," as David Gilmore notes in *Manhood in the Making.*

Yet performance-based masculine identity is virtually impossible to achieve in any lasting way. "You're only as good as your last game," they say in baseball. Boys understand this message on a personal level. In the boys' world, you can never, ever be satisfied with your performance. You have to prove yourself anew, continuously. This unending quest to fit in, to be cool, inevitably pits boys against one another—and against the men in their lives as well. In this psychologically competitive male environment, part of proving yourself is to belittle others.

A boy lives in a narrowly defined world of developing masculinity in which everything he does or thinks is judged on the basis of the strength or weakness it represents: you are either strong and worthwhile, or weak and worthless. He must also be willing to fight. Even if you have never fought, and never intend to fight, you have to pretend to yourself that you can and will. A respected boy is someone who can "handle himself," as one nonviolent fifteen-year-old put it, which he said meant mentally taking the measure of another boy and assessing whether you could beat him up if you had to.

A common debate in many households is how to counsel a boy who is being harassed by bullies. Mothers take the position that "violence doesn't solve anything"; fathers have no qualms about telling a ten-year-old son to "punch out" the jerk, acknowledging that the punch might not get rid of the bully—but that that isn't the point. Walking away from tormentors is a sign of weakness, and the lasting feeling of cowardice is greater punishment than any blow.

Boys not only feel the pressure to appear masculine, but they feel that, in doing so, they must be clearly not feminine—perhaps even antifeminine—and so they consciously and deliberately attack in others and in themselves traits that might possibly be defined as feminine. This includes tenderness, empathy, compassion, and any show of emotional vulnerability. Whether these pressures produce a street fighter or not, they impose a standard for masculinity that all boys accept and use to judge themselves.

Howard, a teacher from a family of teachers, confided a story from his own youth, when his parents sent him to a camp in Vermont famous for its manly traditions. Every Friday night there was an "American Indian" ceremony by the campfire. All of the older boys, who had "passed the test," dressed up as "braves" and marched down to the campfire in single file. All of the younger boys were "squaws," who marched down at the end of the line with blankets over their heads. A boy remained a squaw until he had passed the "test," which involved singing a complicated "Indian" song filled with unfamiliar words.

Because of his nervousness, Howard could not learn the words to the song. Even so, each Friday night he stood up and tried to sing it, in front of the group, in front of all the "braves," and each time he tried, he failed. For that entire first summer, every Friday night he had to wear the blanket again and be a "squaw."

To be labeled a girl—a "squaw"—is the most humiliating thing 35 that can happen to a boy. To have the "honor" of manhood withheld from him because he could not memorize the words to a camp song added further insult to Howard's injury. In a life distinguished by a wealth of experience and accomplishments, Howard still carries this memory with him as one of the most unremittingly cruel and humiliating experiences of his life.

Notes

1. Alferi, T., D. N. Ruble, and E. T. Higgins. "Gender Stereotypes during Adolescence: Developmental Changes and the Transition to Junior High School." *Developmental Psychology* 32 (1996): 1129–37.

2. Anthony, E. *American Manhood: Transformation in Masculinity from the Revolution to the Modern Era.* New York: Basic Books, 1993.

3. Faludi, Susan. "The Naked Citadel." *The New Yorker,* September 5, 1994, 62–81.

For Journals

Write about a time around puberty when you became acutely aware of social expectations about your gender role.

For Discussion

1. From your experience or observation, does this selection accurately represent struggles of late childhood and early adolescence for boys and young men? Why, or why not? How does the knowledge that the authors are psychologists affect your view of their authority on this topic?

2. Do you agree with the authors that "the dominant image of masculinity is one that requires strength and stoicism"? Do the authors suggest positive as well as negative outcomes from this culture? Do you believe that there are positive as well as negative aspects to this image? Discuss.

3. The authors suggest that "a greater understanding of their own emotional struggle" will diminish boys' need for and tolerance of cruelty. Would you agree? Why, or why not?

4. The authors note different approaches in dealing with bullies—with mothers frequently suggesting that "violence doesn't solve anything" and fathers telling boys to "punch out the jerk." Do the authors appear to side with one or the other approach? Do you? Develop a class discussion on this topic with several class members observing and tracking the discussion. Then analyze the arguments made in terms of the gender of the discussants. What themes or patterns emerge, if any?

For Writing

1. Write a response to the authors, either agreeing with their point of view or refuting it. Support your response with personal experience or observation.

2. Analyze the premises, evidence, and conclusions of the authors. What points are strongest? Which evidence is most persuasive? Compare, for example, the authors' unsupported premises and those backed by case histories or anecdotal evidence.

3. Integrate this selection as a secondary source, and revisit the William Golding novel *Lord of the Flies*. How does this reading inform your interpretation of the novel?

4. Compare and contrast this selection with the Pipher selection on adolescent girls. What common themes emerge? What striking contrasts do you find?

✖✖✖ Expanding the Definition: Sexual Harassment and Domestic Violence (2002)

ESTELLE B. FREEDMAN

Estelle B. Freedman, a U.S. historian specializing in women's history and feminist studies, is a professor of history and cofounder of the Program in Feminist Studies at Stanford University, where she has received numerous teaching awards. Freedman graduated from Barnard College and holds a Ph.D. from Columbia University. She has written extensively about the history of women in the United States. Freedman authored two award-winning studies: Their Sisters' Keepers: Women's Prison Reform in America, 1830–1930 *(1981), and* Maternal Justice: Miriam Van Waters and the Female Reform Tradition *(1996). She also coauthored* Intimate Matters: A History of Sexuality in America *(1997). The following selection is from her 2002 book,* No Turning Back: The History of Feminism and the Future of Women.

Feminists have named all forms of unwanted sexual and physical acts as a source of gender inequality, including behaviors once taken for granted as woman's lot to suffer. In 1974, for example, Carmita Wood, a U.S. wage-earning mother of four, resigned from her job after her supervisor made repeated sexual advances toward her. In her claim for unemployment benefits, she used the phrase "sexual harassment." Courts had never ruled on this concept, but at least half of all working women had experienced it. The phrase would soon come to national and then international attention. In 1979 feminist legal theorist Catharine MacKinnon argued in *The Sexual Harassment of Working Women* that sexual pressures on women workers enforced women's economic disadvantage in the labor market. Sexual harassment, she held, was therefore a form of sex discrimination prohibited under Title VII of the U.S. Civil Rights Act of 1964. Serving as cocounsel before the U.S. Supreme Court, MacKinnon contributed to a 1986 ruling that made sexual harassment illegal in the United States. The court's narrow ruling, however, permitted a woman's speech or dress to be cited as relevant "sexual provocation."

In her book MacKinnon identified two ways in which the imposition of unwanted sexual requirements in the context of a relationship of unequal power could disadvantage women at work or in school. The first, quid pro quo, involved the promise of some form of advancement, such as a job, a raise, or better grades, in exchange for sex. The second, a hostile work environment, meant that sexual advances made the workplace or classroom unbearable, even if the worker refused the advances and no exchange of favors occured. Both forms left psychological scars and undermined job or academic performance. While women who have advanced professionally can also harass their subordinates, as many as 90 percent of reported cases involve male workers who use sexual language and gestures to harass women. According to MacKinnon, sexual harassment is not simply about sex; rather, it rests at the intersection of the economic and the sexual control of women. Harassment often dissuades women from persisting in higher-paying blue-collar or managerial jobs or in professional education.

Like women who report rape, those who name sexual harassment often face disbelief and questioning about their sexual histories, as former Equal Employment Opportunity Commission employee Anita Hill learned in 1991 when she testified about harassment at the confirmation hearings for Supreme Court Justice nominee Clarence Thomas. Commentators discredited her testimony because she had remained in her job despite the offensive behavior of her supervisor, even though Hill explained that she had feared retribution in her career if she revealed his unwanted advances and crude comments. Moreover, her status as a single African American woman made his behavior seem acceptable to some.

Anita Hill's painful testimony riveted the American public and the hostile response of male legislators unleashed a powerful female political force. African American women organized a defense of Hill in the press; after the hearings, sexual harassment complaints increased by 50 percent at the EEOC; membership in the National Organization for Women surged the following year; and 1992 became known as the Year of the Woman in U.S. politics, with 117 women candidates for congress. During the 1990s more women took employers and schools to court for not controlling sexual harassment, with major victories won by U.S. workers at Mitsubishi Motors and by public school students in Georgia and Texas who demanded protection from harassment by peers or teachers.

Tolerance for sexual harassment has declined outside the United 5 States as well. In 1989, for example, Spain outlawed sexual harassment, while lawyers in Japan organized a hotline for women workers who felt they had been harassed. By the end of the 1990s countries such as Israel, Korea, and Venezuela had outlawed the practice, and the Indian Supreme Court ruled that sexual harassment violated a woman's right not only when manifested by physical touching but also through verbal offenses. As with rape, legal reform could achieve only limited progress toward changing cultural practices. Feminists have insisted on broader measures, including educational workshops for teachers and managers to explain the costs of inappropriate sexual advances and the procedures for complaining of them.

While institutions struggle to change practices that once intimidated women, feminists have disagreed about the extent and importance of sexual harassment. Some fear that highlighting sex as the source of a hostile work environment could produce a climate that constrains free speech about sexuality in the name of protecting women. For instance, a teacher or worker could elicit charges of sexual harassment for discussing sex in any form. In addition, the law itself is vulnerable to abuse through false charges. In the "he said/she said" scenarios, one party claims that the other either misunderstood or misrepresented the encounter, finding hostile intent in allegedly innocent behaviors. Like the controversy over date rape, the line between sexual play and sexual harassment creates a blurred legal and ethical space that fosters dissent among feminists. Most can agree, however, that learning to communicate clearly about sexual desire and respect for women's right to say no are common goals.

Domestic Violence

Sexual harassment occurs in public work and educational settings, so it is subject to antidiscrimination laws. In contrast, violence against women in the home has long been protected by the privacy accorded to the family and the implicit right permitted to husbands to rule over their wives and children. Behind closed doors, battery, verbal abuse, and life-threatening assaults take place regularly. "I can't remember a time when my mother wasn't physically abused by my father," a woman recalled in 1991. "I learned at an early age," another woman wrote, "that a man has the right to beat his wife and if he abstains, she should be grateful."

In patriarchal cultures, husbands had the right to chastise their wives physically. From the Greeks through the Reformation, European husbands ruled over their wives and children and could correct them, as St. Augustine wrote, "by word or blow." The "rule of thumb" in Anglo-American law held that a husband could beat his wife as long as he used a stick that was no thicker than his thumb. The legitimacy of the practice persisted in the English-speaking world even after courts began to reject the legality of wife beating in the 1800s. In other cultures, husbands meted out physical punishment of wives, whether in China (where mothers-in-law also beat daughters-in-law), Africa, or the Middle East.

Early European feminists challenged the right of husbands to punish their wives. In England, Harriet Martineau and John Stuart Mill fought for the right to divorce in part so that wives could leave abusive husbands. In the United States social purity reformers and the Women's Christian Temperance Union blamed liquor for making men brutish husbands. Historian Elizabeth Pleck has shown that by the 1890s women's organizations provided social services, encouraged victims to bring charges in court, and established the first safe houses for abused wives. By the twentieth century a new legal concept of marital cruelty provided grounds for divorce. For mothers, however, it was difficult to apply these grounds if divorce left women either without custody of their children or economically unable to support them.

Although abuse of wives in Europe and the Americas has been 10 publicly portrayed as a lower-class phenomenon, estimates of its incidence reveal a more extensive social problem. At the end of the twentieth century, each year between 10 and 20 percent of North American women were beaten by a man with whom they had an intimate relationship. One-fourth to one-half of all North American women could expect to experience domestic violence at some point in their lives. In the United States a woman is battered every fifteen seconds, and domestic violence is a major cause of injuries to women, including one-third of their murders. The Federal Bureau of Investigation notes that four women die every day in the United States from domestic assaults. In one Canadian study 62 percent of the murderers of women had been their intimate partners. One-third of all U.S. calls for police assistance concern domestic violence, yet until recently no police training existed and police departments typically advised officers not to interfere with private family matters. For years a "stitch rule" held that perpetrators should be charged with a crime only if the violence required stitches.

Internationally, the figures are equally disturbing. A 1985 survey in Thailand found that 50 percent of respondents had experienced domestic abuse. While the figures emphasized lower-class violence, they probably reflected underreporting among other social groups. United Nations figures for the proportion of adult women who had been physically assaulted by an intimate partner ranged in 1995 from about one-fourth in northern Europe and some Latin American countries, such as Chile, to three-fourths of the lower-caste women in Indian villages. An Egyptian study found that domestic violence was the major reason women were treated for physical trauma. Unique forms of family violence lead to injury and death in India. Dowry deaths and dowry burnings refer to the harassment of a wife who is either pressured to commit suicide or murdered so that her husband's family can extract and keep her dowry, the price paid at marriage. During the 1980s one or two women were burned to death a day in each of several Indian cities. Estimates during the 1990s ranged from five thousand to fifteen thousand Indian women killed annually in dowry-related incidents.

Contemporary feminists analyze domestic violence as a problem shared by women across class, race, and national lines. While social science studies show that patterns of abuse are passed from parents to children in families of any background, feminists move beyond a purely psychological argument based on family dynamics. Rather, they emphasize the economic problem of female dependency as a contributing factor to domestic violence. As Zimbabwe's deputy health minister, Tsungirirai Hungwe, explains, "Those leaving violent relationships often have limited options to support themselves and their children, and face poverty and isolation. Each year, a number of women try to commit suicide to escape such difficult situations." A survey of Thai women found that those who worked in the low-paid informal sector and those who considered divorce a stigma for their families often remained in abusive relationships. Women who cannot be economically self-supporting may become trapped in cycles of "learned helplessness." Most battered women in North America are homemakers, many of whom have internalized blame for a husband's violence. When a wife depends on her husband for economic support she may feel both financially and psychologically dependent. Whether in Africa, India, Iran, or the United States, women who feel trapped within their families fear that they may be beaten or killed if they attempt to leave.

Throughout the world feminists have responded to domestic violence by naming the problem, providing services, and empowering women to claim their rights. In India protest marches began in 1979 to call attention to dowry burnings, making the once-personal issue a public one. Refusing the stories that deaths by fire were suicides, Indian women rallied with signs reading Down with Dowry. They also demanded police investigations and pressed for laws to punish cruelty to wives. In Latin America Brazilian women formed the Committee on Violence Against Women, which became the most active feminist organization in the country at the end of the 1970s. After a series of murders of Brazilian women, feminists staged public demonstrations that paralleled the Take Back the Night marches that protested rape.

Along with protests and services feminists insist on adequate police protection from domestic violence. Pop singer Tracy Chapman captured well the way law enforcement once handled domestic disputes: "The police always come too late if they come at all." In 1976 feminist lawyers brought a class action suit against the Oakland, California, police department because of its weak response to calls about domestic violence. A court settlement required special training for officers who intervene in domestic disputes. By 1986 almost half of the large urban police departments in the United States had adopted the policy of arresting perpetrators of domestic violence, compared to only 10 percent just two years earlier. Laws mandating the arrest of batterers have also become more common—twenty-six U.S. states had enacted them by 1994. The process of obtaining a judicial restraining order against an abusive partner has been simplified in the United States, and hospitals have also changed their responses. Since the American Medical Association declared the physical abuse of women a major health issue in 1991, emergency room staff have become more sensitive to the signs of domestic abuse.

International movements to protect women from abuse and to 15 prosecute batterers expanded rapidly after 1980. Between 1985 and 1995 a hundred special police stations for women opened in Brazil, with feminist monitoring so that women could report violence and find their way to shelters. Women's courts hear cases of abuse in the Indian capital, New Delhi. In 1995 the Association of Women's Organizations in Jamaica succeeded in obtaining the passage of the Domestic Violence Act, which allows courts to remove abusive partners.

Feminists around the world have established shelters for battered women. First founded in England, the movement spread internationally after 1970. By 1990 there were over 1,250 shelters in the United States and Canada. The Women's Shelter Programme in Bangkok, founded in the 1980s, serves poor women in a neighborhood where up to half of them had been attacked by husbands. Some of these women fought back; some had killed their attackers. The founders of the shelter recognized that "the issue of battered women is not merely one of 'bad Karma' or a private matter of each individual woman. We see it as a problem embedded in our social structure, which neglects the fundamental rights of women." In response they provided a temporary refuge from abuse, group therapy for residents, and a campaign to raise public consciousness "of battered wives as another form of violence which any woman, regardless of status or class, can fall prey to." Run by volunteers who have survived abuse themselves, the Ambassador One-Stop Drop-in Advice Centre in England, established in 1998, provides a range of services to women fleeing domestic violence. In both Great Britain and the United States law enforcement agencies sometimes cooperate with shelters, directing women to them when they report abuse. By the 1990s specialized agencies reached out to immigrants. South Asian women living in the United States had organized shelters in New York, New Jersey, and California.

Most of these shelters rely on private funding, although some governments have provided help. The Netherlands, for example, subsidized forty-eight shelters in the 1990s, while Spain offered a toll-free hotline advising women about shelters. To fund its shelter, one city used a marriage license tax, while in the Basque area of Spain, battered women receive a "salary" to encourage them to leave their abusers. In 1994 the U.S. Violence Against Women Act provided funding for grants to shelters, as well as for research on violence and its prevention. Despite conservative opposition, the funding was renewed in 2000. Much of the funding for shelters continues to be raised by the feminist community, however. In the United States young women take wilderness hikes to raise funds for the Elizabeth Stone House in Boston, founded in 1974. In California a shelter solicits funds by sending

Mother's Day cards created by children who reside there with their mothers.

Shelters offer a variety of services, including a safe house (a location kept secret from an abusive husband), group therapy, child care, and legal counseling to let women know their rights and options. In some cases consciousness-raising or support groups are critical elements. As one woman explained, the shelter helped her forget her husband and her fears. "They listened when I told my story . . . I felt safe." As in the cases of rape and incest, part of the resistance to violence is to break down silence and isolation.

Shelters and restraining orders cannot always protect women, some of whom have been murdered while under court protection. Fear of continued abuse has driven some women to strike back. A large proportion of women serving prison sentences for murder in the United States have killed their batterers, often in self-defense. Lawyers have turned to the psychological theory of "battered woman syndrome" to explain why these women remained in abusive relationships to the point that they became violent themselves.

Women can be violent against partners or children as well as in re- 20 sponse to abusive husbands. Studies of violence suggest that those who feel most entitled to social power are most likely to use violence to achieve or enforce it. Since power, not simply masculinity, produces violence, the solution is not just for women to achieve greater power. Rather, as theorists such as Nancy Hartsock have argued, feminists must reexamine the very concept of power. One kind of power, self-determination, is critical to full citizenship in democratic societies; another form, power over others, can legitimate violence as a means to enforce it. Thus, for African American feminist bell hooks, "Feminist efforts to end male violence against women must be expanded into a movement to end all forms of violence."

For Journals

What is your understanding of the terms "sexual harassment" and "domestic violence"?

For Discussion

1. Identify the definitions of sexual harassment and domestic violence stated or implied in this selection. To what degree do they coincide with your own definition? Exchange definitions with other class members, either in the whole class or in groups. If you do not agree with the definitions from the selection, see whether you can develop definitions in your groups and compare notes. If you found it difficult to do so, why do you think that problem occurred?

2. From what you have read in this selection, why do you think that sexual harassment occurs? What are some of the divergent opinions regarding sexual harassment among feminists?

3. Compare and contrast the social science/psychological explanation for domestic violence, which focuses on parent-child relationships and modeling, with a feminist approach, which looks to issues of economics and dependency. Which do you find more persuasive? Why? What other explanations might clarify this issue?

For Writing

1. Check out Freedman's book, and read the full chapter on "Gender and Violence" in which this selection appears. Write an essay that draws on Freedman's book to contextualize this selection—for example, the connections between rape, sexual harassment, and domestic violence, or the issues of power.

2. Reread the *Rusk v. State of Maryland* case, and view the *Keep within Compass* etching earlier in this chapter. What common themes do you discern? Write an essay exploring one of these themes.

3. Read comtemporary news accounts or legal proceedings regarding a case of sexual harassment, domestic violence, or sexual assault; then write an essay analyzing the assumptions, inferences, or historical context evident in one or more of these accounts.

❋❋ *Got Harvey Milk?: Supporting the Mission of a New York City High School* (2003)

MIKE HIPOLITO

Mike Hipolito is a college student from Huntington Beach, California, majoring in psychology and biological sciences. He is also an active member of his university's Pilipino American Student Union and LGBTQ Center, two organizations that aim to educate the college community about Pilipino culture and queer issues, respectively. He plans to become a psychiatrist to help represent and treat ethnic and sexual minorities, especially those who suffer from psychological disorders that are related to their oppression as a marginalized population. Hipolito originally heard of the Harvey Milk High School controversy through the media. He decided to write this paper to persuade Americans to support the expansion of the New York City public high school in order to promote safety and equal education for gay youth.

America's gay-friendly summer of 2003 catapulted gays and lesbians into the national spotlight like never before. In June, the U.S.

Supreme Court struck down anti-sodomy laws in Texas in a landmark decision that would protect the personal privacy of gays. In the 2004 Presidential race, Democratic front-runner Howard Dean announced that he would support civil unions for gay people. On the cable network, the premiere of two gay reality shows, "Boy Meets Boy" and "Queer Eye for the Straight Guy," featured positive interactions between homosexuals and heterosexuals in romantic and social settings.

Although these recent advancements are a step forward toward awareness and toward equality of rights, gays still suffer from daily discrimination that has very serious consequences. These effects are especially visible in gay youth. According to a survey conducted by the Sexual Information and Education Council of the United States, forty percent of gay youth do not feel safe at their respective high schools. Many report being mistreated, ridiculed, and harassed by their heterosexual peers. Moreover, the survey reports that gay youth are three times more likely to commit suicide than their straight counterparts (*http://www.hmi.org*). To address such concerns, in 1985 New York City opened Harvey Milk High School (HMHS) with the mission of providing a safe environment for gay adolescents to pursue education. Recently, the New York Board of Education approved a $3.2 million expansion to increase the school's enrollment from 50 to 170 students at the beginning of the 2003 school year. Opponents to the expansion claim that the school worsens the situation by segregating students and limiting the youths' perspective of the larger community. Advocates, however, argue that gay youth require the focused attention because they constitute such a marginalized population. By protecting gay youth from harassment and equipping them with skills to survive in the mainstream, Harvey Milk High School serves as a keystone in the ongoing pursuit of safety and equal education for gay youth.

Although opponents of the high school expansion decry the school for promoting segregation, a school designed to recognize the challenges of the gay community is the only place for these students to regain ground. HMHS addresses the sensitive needs of the gay population and offers appropriate career programs and psychological counseling. Their curriculum also focuses on the importance of combating injustices. This educational policy of targeting underrepresented groups is already adopted by other nationally-renowned educational institutions. Some examples include historically-black universities such as Howard and Morehouse, and all-women colleges such as Wellesley and Vassar. These schools intend to protect minority populations from dangerous environments that would interfere with learning—not intentionally separate them from certain groups.

Even though this educational approach seems unorthodox, the credibility and resources of HMHS are comparable to most New York

City public high schools. In order to adhere to the guidelines set by the state's Department of Education, Harvey Milk High School is accredited and requires satisfactory completion of the New York State Regents Exams. Students benefit from a host of after-school programs, various career-planning resources, and a competitive student/faculty ratio. These offerings combined with high academic standards have led to the school's current 95% graduation rate and 60% college acceptance rate. According to a 2001 study conducted by the Manhattan Institute for Policy Research, New York State's public high school graduation rate only reaches 70%. Like its neighboring peers, HMHS emphasizes the importance of seeking higher education and preparing for a suitable career.

Despite the school's academic success, critics contend that the high 5 school demographics are not representative of the typical population, which inhibits optimal social functioning of gay youth with people of various backgrounds. Although the school mainly targets gay youth who seek a tolerant educational environment, students still learn about issues that face people with different life histories. Furthermore, Harvey Milk High School has a non-discriminatory policy that recognizes diversity in sexual orientation, ethnicity, gender, and religion. Heterosexual students may enroll and benefit from the resources provided at HMHS, while contributing their ideas and talents to the student body. The school's emphasis on healthy youth development, programs on arts and culture, and college/career planning prepares students to network with people who have an array of interests.

Despite the spate of controversy and possible stigma attached to a "gay high school," students at Harvey Milk High School take advantage of the unique opportunity to learn in an environment free of verbal harassment or physical abuse. At HMHS, gay and lesbian youth do not need to choose either safety or education but can treasure both. By providing safe instruction and individual support, Harvey Milk High School eases a gay adolescent's transition into adulthood and reinstates youth displaced in a homophobic society. Most importantly, students can finally reconcile sexual orientation with the life they envision for themselves in the larger world, where Harvey Milk High School promises to be the beacon that guides their once dim and harrowing path to higher education.

For Journals

What are your views on high schools that focus on serving the needs of groups within the larger society—such as single-gender high schools, or schools focusing on the needs of certain ethnic or cultural groups?

For Discussion

1. Locate Hipolito's thesis statement, and then put it in your own words. What are the key arguments pro and con? How effective does he refute opposing views? What type of evidence is most persuasive?

2. Do you agree or disagree with the author? If you agree, what other arguments would you offer to support your view? If you disagree, how would you refute his arguments? What additional support would you offer to support your own view?

For Writing

1. Explore Hipolito's argument in view of "The Culture of Cruelty" in this chapter. Does the Kindlon and Thompson selection offer support or refutation for Hipolito's thesis? Write an essay discussing Hipolito's essay in view of the larger cultural context for this high school and for adolescence.

2. Write a response to Hipolito, either agreeing with him but citing different supporting arguments and evidence, or disagreeing with him and offering reasons and examples to support your view.

3. Research the social science literature to learn about the pros and cons of high schools aimed toward serving the needs of certain students or groups, such as the Kamehameha Schools in Hawaii and the same-gender religious schools or American Indian schools.

✳✳✳ *Film: Mi Familia (My Family)* (1995)

Directed by Gregory Nava, with Jimmy Smits, Esai Morales. New Line Cinema. 126 minutes. This film's subject is the story and struggles of the three-generation Sanchez family, seen through the eyes of the eldest son, a writer. The narrative includes the father's journey on foot from Mexico to California in the 1920s, a brother's tragic death in the 1950s, and social and economic struggles in contemporary America.

For Journals

Do you have expectations or images that come to mind regarding a film about a Mexican American family? If you are Mexican American, what themes or issues do you think are likely to appear in this film?

For Discussion

1.   In what ways is the Sanchez family similar to your own family? In what ways is it different?

2.   The film begins, and ends, with images of the bridges connecting East Los Angeles with Los Angeles. What is the significance of those bridges? What do they mean to the members of the Sanchez family?

3.   Jose Sanchez comes to California to find a relative who was born in California "when it was still Mexico." Discuss the political implications of this situation in terms of people who are, and who are not, considered "American."

4.   Mrs. Sanchez suffers extreme difficulties in order to be reunited with her husband and children. Discuss the ways in which this element of the film, or another particular example, conveys values and beliefs about family.

5.   Compare and contrast the values and beliefs that the parents and children have about work and money.

For Writing

1.   Write a review of this film for your campus newspaper, or write a letter to a friend urging him or her to see the film (or not). If you are unfamiliar with the genre of film reviews, read several from your local newspaper. The review captures reader interest, makes a claim about the film's merit or lack thereof, and usually briefly summarizes the film in a way that does not give away the plot or any surprises. The reader should be able to make an informed decision about viewing the film based on your review.

2.   Select one scene in the film, and write about how it illuminates a larger theme or idea that the film as a whole suggests (for example, the father's journey, the mother's river crossing, the wedding scene, one of the scenes in which a new romantic partner is introduced to the family).

3.   Research and write a documented essay about one of the actual or historical events or situations referred to in the film, such as forced relocation of American citizens who "looked Mexican" during the Great Depression of the 1930s.

Chapter Writing Assignments

1.   Select a reading in this chapter, and diagram the assumptions on which it rests. Put the main point in a box at the top of the page, and then draw boxes and connecting lines showing the supporting as-

sumptions and reasons. How do you think the writer knew which assumptions to state explicitly and which ones would be understood or automatically accepted by the audience?

2. Examine a piece of artwork or other visual image that appears in another chapter in this book. Articulate the implicit and explicit assumptions and values on which it is based, and write an essay analyzing what such assumptions tell us about the audiences for which the image was intended.

3. Develop your own argument on the subject of women's or men's proper role in society, on same-gender domestic partnerships, on interracial adoption, or on some other social issue of concern to you. Exchange essays with a peer, preferably one who has taken an opposing view or has written on a different subject. Write refutations of each other's essays, and turn in both originals and refutations. Did you find yourselves refuting primarily the assumptions, the reasons, the conclusions drawn, or some of each part of the argument in equal amounts?

4. Examine your own values and beliefs about family and gender. Do some private freewriting, reflecting on how you have come to hold those values. What are your assumptions about family life? The work ethic? Dating roles? Parental roles? Friendship between genders? Marriage or partnership roles? Write a reflective essay exploring the process through which you have come to hold these particular beliefs.

5. Interview your parents or grandparents or other people of their generations; ask them about the expectations they grew up with about dating, gender roles, or family and parental duties. Do they still hold those assumptions? What do they think of current customs? Write an essay summarizing your findings, and share it with other class members. Alternatively, compare the assumptions held by the people you interviewed with those you hold, and analyze the similarities and differences.

6. In a group, and if everyone is willing to share, put up butcher paper around the classroom and have everyone write his or her name, ethnic background, parents' and grandparents' occupations, and any sayings, proverbs, legacies (ideas they've passed down to you or possessions that represent these ideas). After everyone has finished, silently review the material, looking for connections, themes, values, or assumptions that emerge. Discuss them as a class, or write up your reflections to consider in private or to share.

7. Design a flyer to inform an audience about an issue regarding family or gender. Write an essay explaining your design, focusing on the assumptions you made about your audience and the premises on which your flyer is based.

Web Sites for Further Exploration

American Woman Suffrage Timeline

http://womenshistory.about.com/library/weekly/aa031600a.htm

International Women's Suffrage Timeline

http://womenshistory.about.com/library/weekly/aa091600a.htm

The Statue of Liberty–Ellis Island Foundation, Inc. "The Immigrant Experience"

http://www.ellisisland.org/Immexp/indexframe.asp?

African Studies Center

http://www.sas.upenn.edu/African_Studies/Home_Page/GIF_Images.html

American Women: Gateway to Library of Congress Resources for the Study of Women's History and Culture in the United States

http://lcweb2.loc.gov/ammem/awhhtml/

Women's News

http://www.womensenews.org/

Lawrence v. Texas (2003) Supreme Court Ruling

http://caselaw.lp.findlaw.com/scripts/getcase.pl?court=US&vol=000&invol=02-102

8

※※※

Work and Play

The relationship of Americans to work is one of the most complicated dynamics in our culture. The ethics of worth, beliefs about
wealth and the importance of money, and ways of measuring success
for ourselves and others all come into the discussion. Work, like religion, family, the American dream, and other deeply rooted beliefs, is
closely identified with who we are, how we value ourselves, and how
we in turn are valued, or not valued, by society.

Americans believe that everyone deserves at least the chance to be
successful; perhaps that's how most would interpret the Declaration of
Independence's guarantee of the pursuit of happiness. But they have
never agreed on how success is to be achieved or measured, and they
are torn between the Protestant work ethic—a belief in hard work and
diligence rewarded by middle-class prosperity—and the fantasy of
wealth gained without any work, through the blind luck of buying a
winning lottery ticket or marrying the boss's only child.

Between those two extremes, Americans have historically entertained a variety of beliefs about work, some of them mutually inconsistent. The Calvinist theology that prevailed in early New England
included the belief that God chooses to save some unworthy souls as a
sign of infinite mercy; these fortunate few are called the elect. Gradually that austere tenet of faith came to include an assumption that
someone living the comfortable life must be doing it with God's help;
thus, outward success was viewed as proof of good work habits and
God's favor. Calvinism has long since ceased to dominate our country's religious life, but the connection of high pay, status, and success
with personal self-worth has remained embedded in American culture
and consciousness.

Industrialization, especially after the Civil War, brought factory
jobs and long hours. The fortunate few—the elect of industrial
America—were known as the robber barons. Many of these railroad,
mine, and factory owners came from poor or ordinary backgrounds
and went on to make inconceivably vast amounts of money. Poorer
Americans both resented and worshipped them; low pay and terrible

working conditions were the reality for most Americans, and their highest goal was to become middle-class. But secretly they dreamed that perhaps their children would do better—much better.

Part of the reward system for doing better and entering the middle class was the opportunity to enjoy a privilege that was once reserved for the rich—leisure time in which to engage in a pleasurable activity such as a sport or a craft, to be a spectator at professional sports events, to go to the theater or to a musical performance, or even to travel. Well-off Victorian America offered baseball, tennis, boating, parlor games and card games, and bicycling. For the very poor, of course, leisure was still a rare luxury, but some sports, such as baseball and boxing, were more generally available to everyone. Baseball was probably the most democratized sport of all, played before the Civil War, spread by prisoners on both sides during the Civil War, played in cities, by immigrants as well as native-born Americans, by blacks as well as whites. However, when baseball, like other American institutions, embraced segregation in the late nineteenth century, it established what would eventually become a truism about sports in America—they represented a microcosm of the country as a whole, and, in this case, a tragic reflection of inequalities in other areas of American life.

Baseball was significant in another way too. It became the first American sport to turn into a business, and big business at that. Eventually, other sports that were originally strictly amateur—football and basketball, for example—followed its lead. College stars went on to play on professional teams, with salaries, owners, fans, local pride, local economies, and a lot of money at stake. The area of athletics that remained amateur the longest (that is, with no real money involved) was women's college sports. Many of them—track and field, field hockey, softball—still draw women for the love of the sport alone. But others—women's tennis, golf, and particularly basketball—now imitate men's sports in the sense that the best college athletes can now join professional tours or leagues. At the same time, the Olympics highlight sports in which women are particularly well established, such as gymnastics and figure skating, and a gold medal means endorsements and high salaries, not to mention product advertisements, celebrity, and pictures of the champion emblazoned on Wheaties boxes.

These changes certainly signal a definite move toward equality and recognition that great women athletes are as interesting, if not more interesting, to watch than men. But these opportunities are not an unalloyed blessing: now some women athletes experience the problems of commercialization and overmarketing that were previously the preserve of men alone. Whether women's sports handle those problems any differently remains to be seen.

The most significant American writing about work and play is both a response to and a reflection of the values behind them and the national experience that shaped them. The selections in this chapter sample a spectrum of those values, examine various kinds of work and play, and offer possibilities for combining the two. They also raise related issues: the tenuousness of life in this country for those who lack paying work or whose work is unfulfilling and poorly paid; the corruption of the amateur ideal by the reality of sports finances; the questionable status of women in a culture in which husbands work outside and supply the paychecks, and wives work at home but do not earn money; the significance of work and money as satisfying, non-gendered activities; and the benefits of athletic competition and the dangers of completely commercialized sports. Finally, this chapter raises the question of balance—between work and play, between amateur and professional, between the lives of working men and women, between Americans' faith in the redeeming possibilities of work as well as their desire to escape it.

Work and Play through History

The selections in this chapter revolve around two areas: work and play. Work-related issues include needing a job, having a job and getting the most out of it, looking for job security, or dealing with the trauma of losing it. Play includes both sports and a less determinate but valuable category called leisure—the time and the freedom to choose a night out, a vacation, a stay at home, or nothing at all.

Benjamin Franklin worked at many jobs in his lifetime—some for money, some for science, some for public service—but his overall brilliance makes it difficult to know where his work ended and his play began. In the first selection, taken from the *Autobiography*, we see him embark on one of his oddest self-improvement programs: he decided as a young man to make a list of his faults and work on them one at a time until he reached moral perfection, which he thought would take a few weeks. The ridiculousness of the enterprise was not lost on him.

In another part of the *Autobiography*, Franklin reports on a widow who proved infinitely more successful at running a business than was her husband. Franklin's conclusion—that women should be educated about money, accounting, and business transactions—was far ahead of its time, and it fell on deaf ears. But it found an echo, more than a century later, in the groundbreaking work of Charlotte Perkins Gilman, who knew from personal experience what it meant to have no control over one's finances, and therefore one's independence; what it meant to be a well-brought-up Victorian woman suffocated by conventions and restrictions. She wrote a remarkable story, "The Yellow Wallpaper," about a young mother who has a breakdown that is exacerbated by the condescending and wrong-headed ministrations of her doctor and husband. Gilman's understanding of what it meant for married women to have no legal or financial independence led to her innovative study *Women and Economics,* which is excerpted here. It made her the first professional American woman economist.

As a member of the middle class, Gilman never suffered from grinding poverty, but she understood the economic extremities that brought it about. The working conditions of early-twentieth-century American factories were poor in almost every conceivable way—ventilation, pay, hours. In 1911, the Triangle Waist Factory in New York caught fire, and because the doors were locked, 143 young women, mostly Italian and Jewish immigrants, either burned to death or jumped from windows as horrified passersby watched. In general, the newest immigrants took jobs that no one else wanted, but the worst jobs went to African American women, who suffered from racial prejudice as well as the usual constraints of low educational levels and poverty. A 1922 photograph showing young black women stripping tobacco leaves and working without backrests is an indication of how bad conditions were for uneducated working women in general, and black women in particular. Of course, during the Depression the middle class was unemployed too, and shocked to find that it had no financial cushion to fall back on because the banks that were the repositories of its holdings had failed. It took World War II, with its enormous need to convert factories for war materiel, to bring the country close to full employment.

One side effect of the war boom was that millions of women who had never expected to work outside the home suddenly found themselves recruited for well-paying jobs, often in factories vacated by the men who had joined the armed forces. For the first time, many found themselves in business, earning money and feeling successful in ways that had traditionally been reserved for men. A photograph of three unnamed women workers at a defense plant in San Diego is a study in determined achievement and a sense of enormous pride. But as the war ended and the men got their jobs back, many women went back into the home, and the new iconography of female success was not Rosie the Riveter but the happy homemaker. So as a companion piece to the photo of the defense plant workers is a 1950s advertisement for a new stove, with a very dressed-up housewife pointing to it as though it were one of her children.

What also begins to appear in the 1950s and to grow continuously thereafter is the woman in the dual roles of wife/mother/housekeeper and income earner. Buying all those appliances cost money, buying the little house in the large subdivision cost money. Even if a woman was still single, she no longer stayed at home but got herself a job, at least until she got married. If she had some marketable skills, like typing or shorthand, which she could be trained for rather cheaply in secretarial school, she could get a clerical job in an office, almost always working for a male boss. Our next reading, "Office Politics," explains how the femininization of office work gave women more prestige than factory jobs even if it didn't pay them much money.

Journalist and interviewer Studs Terkel, who is, in his own way, a historian of American culture, carved out a special place for himself in the history of American working people by writing a best-selling book, *Working,* in which all kinds of Americans, from celebrities to unknown citizens, just talk to him about what they do for a living and how they feel about it. The interview with Mr. Bates, a stonemason, depicts a man at the fortunate end of the work spectrum, who has spent his whole life at a job that he loves and that gives him great pride and satisfaction. His delight in his craft, his sense of having made something lasting, is almost as palpable as the stone with which he works. So is his understanding that he may be the last of his breed. No doubt Benjamin Franklin, who so enjoyed seeing anyone do a job well, especially a craftsman, would have enjoyed Mr. Bates enormously.

Reporter Alfred Lubrano, on the other hand, raises a further issue of work satisfaction and complicates it with a question: what happens when a blue-collar father, like Mr. Bates, raises a son who, thanks to education, rises into the middle class and the world of white-collar work and values? Lubrano recognizes the darker side of the work ethic, but he is also an example of how contemporary writers continue to reevaluate that ethic in the light of their own experience. Lubrano can neither deny nor escape the cost to familial intimacy and comfort when a son succeeds at a kind of work his father cannot share.

A completely different perspective on work comes from Barbara Ehrenreich, a well-known chronicler of American women's life experience. In her book *Nickled and Dimed: On Not Getting By in America,* she reports on her decision to take a series of minimum-wage jobs—waitress, cleaner, saleswoman at Wal-Mart, etc.—and actually try to live on the proceeds in order to find out how poorer women manage. The selection here is from her baptism by fire on her first job, waitressing at two different Florida restaurants whose names have been changed to protect everyone.

One final work selection is the bridge to the rest of the chapter, which deals with issues arising from the one area of American life in which work and play are supposed to coincide: the world of amateur sports. For sports historian Leonard Koppett, ethics, or the lack of it, is a central issue now that the classic American reward for work—money—has intruded into the supposedly amateur life of college sports teams. The result, according to Koppett, is hypocrisy. Colleges insist that they observe the division between work and play in their athletic programs, but in truth student/athletes get paid under the table, and amateurism becomes a byword for corruption

Student Katie Norris, in another argumentative essay, explores some of the physical and psychological dangers confronting adolescent

female athletes, and she suggests some solutions. And veteran sports-
writer C. W. Nevius carries Koppett's argument about the unacknowledged professionalization of amateur sports to its logical if grotesque
conclusion by examining children's sports. In a series of articles for the
San Francisco Chronicle, Nevius wrote about Little League, Pop Warner,
gymnastics, hockey, and other venues. In this selection, he examines
how the obsessive parents and ill-tempered coaches of children's
teams contribute to an atmosphere of competition and violence that
would be excessive at a professional football game and that completely violates the notion of child's play.

Our final readings are about amateur athletics and the complications of measuring resources, finding the means to win, and finding a
way just to compete on literal and metaphorical level playing field. In
Gigs, a book about how people earn their livings—a kind of contemporary tribute to Terkel's *Working*—an anonymous high school basketball coach speaks with amazing frankness about winning, recruiting,
and whether or not knowing the rules makes a difference. The last two
readings in this chapter are about Title IX, the law that made possible
the development of women's sports on an amateur level comparable
to men's. The current controversy about Title IX and who is entitled to
what is given a retrospective look on its thirtieth anniversary by two
former Olympic champions, Dan Gable and Mary Hogshead-Makar.

Finally the film *Jerry Maguire,* a comedy about a seeming contradiction in terms—the moral rebirth of a sports agent—provokes another look at the sports/work/ethics dilemma, as well as a witty
reminder that all honest work has dignity, and that doing a job honestly and well may be the hardest work of all.

✻✻✻ FROM *The Autobiography* (1771)

BENJAMIN FRANKLIN

*Benjamin Franklin (1706–1790). What follows is one of his early experiments—
personal rather than scientific—whose failure he managed to learn from. (See Chapter 6
for a fuller inventory of Franklin's infinitely varied life).*

. . . I now open'd a little Stationer's Shop. I had in it Blanks of all
Sorts the correctest that ever appear'd among us, being assisted in that
by my Friend Brientnal; I had also Paper, Parchment, Chapmen's Books,
&c. One Whitemash a Compositor I had known in London, an excellent
Workman now came to me & work'd with me constantly & diligently,
and I took an Apprentice the Son of Aquila Rose. I began now gradually
to pay off the Debt I was under. . . . In order to secure my Credit and
Character as a Tradesman, I took care not only to be in *Reality* Industri-

ous & frugal, but to avoid all *Appearances* of the Contrary. I drest plainly; I was seen at no Places of idle Diversion; I never went out a-fishing or shooting; a Book, indeed, sometimes debauch'd me from my Work; but that was seldom, snug, & gave no Scandal: and to show that I was not above my Business, I sometimes brought home the Paper I purchas'd at the Stores, thro' the Streets on a Wheelbarrow. Thus being esteem'd an industrious thriving young Man, and paying duly for what I bought, the Merchants who imported Stationary solicited my Custom, others propos'd supplying me with Books, & I went on swimmingly. . . .

It was about this time that I conceiv'd the bold and arduous Project of arriving at moral Perfection. I wish'd to live without committing any Fault at any time; I would conquer all that either Natural Inclination, Custom, or Company might lead me into. As I knew, or thought I knew, what was right and wrong, I did not see why I might not *always* do the one and avoid the other. But I soon found I had undertaken a Task of more Difficulty than I had imagined: While my Care was employ'd in guarding against one Fault, I was often surpriz'd by another. . . .

The Precept of *Order* requiring that *every Part of my Business should have its allotted time,* one Page in my little Book contain'd the following Scheme of Employment for the Twenty-four Hours of a natural Day,

The Morning Question, What Good shall I do this Day?	5 6 7 8	Rise, wash, and address *Powerful Goodness;* contrive Day's Business and take the Resolution of the Day; prosecute the present Study: and breakfast —
	9 10 11	Work.
	12 1	Read, or overlook my Accounts, and dine.
	2 3 4 5	Work.
	6 7 8 9	Put Things in their Places, Supper, Musick, or Diversion, or Conversation, Examination of the Day.
Evening Question, What Good have I done to-day?	10 11 12 1 2 3 4	Sleep. —

. . . My Scheme of Order, gave me the most Trouble, and I found, that tho' it might be practicable where a Man's Business was such as to leave him the Disposition of his Time, that of a Journey-man Printer for instance, it was not possible to be exactly observ'd by a Master, who must mix with the World, and often receive People of Business at their own Hours.—*Order* too, with regard to Places for Things, Papers, &c. I found extreamly difficult to acquire. I had not been early accustomed to it, & having an exceeding good Memory, I was not so sensible of the Inconvenience attending Want of Method. This Article therefore cost me so much painful Attention & my Faults in it vex'd me so much, and I made so little Progress in Amendment, & had such frequent Relapses, that I was almost ready to give up the Attempt, and content my self with a faulty Character in that respect. . . . In Truth I found myself incorrigible with respect to *Order;* and now I am grown old, and my Memory bad, I feel very sensibly the want of it. But on the whole, tho' I never arrived at the Perfection I had been so ambitious of obtaining, but fell far short of it, yet I was by the Endeavour made a better and a happier Man that I otherwise should have been, if I had not attempted it.

For Journals

Do you think that Franklin would succeed in a business today if he were starting one? Would his skills still be useful?

For Discussion

1. How would you describe Franklin's work ethic? Why does he work hard? What does he get out of his efforts? What are his own assertions about work? Look for supporting evidence in the text—either quotations or accounts of his work experience.

2. Franklin was very open about promoting his reputation as a hardworking and industrious young man. He says, "In order to secure my Credit and Character as a Tradesman, I took care not only to be in *Reality* Industrious & frugal, but to avoid all *Appearances* of the Contrary." What relationship do you think there is between his public advertisement of his hard work and his private success? Could he have one without the other? If he did, would that make his achievements less valuable to him? To you?

3. How do you think that Franklin would have defined success? Would you define it differently? How much of Franklin's definition do you think has to do with money?

For Writing

1.   Write an essay about your own work ethic. Whatever assertions you make about what you think of work and why it is or isn't important to you, try to be aware of the assumptions you are basing your ideas on. Consider the following questions: How important is making money to you? Is that why you work? Would you work if you didn't need the money? What would you do instead? It might be interesting to make up a chart like Franklin's, using your own assessment of how your time should be divided up daily for you to get the most out of it.

2.   Starting with Franklin's *Autobiography*, research and write a paper on Philadelphia in the eighteenth century. Consider, for example, what people did for a living, what cultural institutions there were (aside from the ones that Franklin started himself), the role of the Quaker community, what food people ate, and what houses looked like and how they were furnished.

3.   Franklin was the most prolifically talented American of his time, with the possible exception of Thomas Jefferson. Write a paper in which you research one of the following topics: Franklin's inventions and their uses; his role as ambassador to France during the American Revolution and his celebrity status there; his other publications, including *Poor Richard's Almanac*; his contributions to the Declaration of Independence and the Constitutional Convention; his troubled relationship with his own son, who supported the British during the Revolution; his political satires; or his antislavery writings.

4.   Different audiences and people read the same text very differently. In his book *Studies in Classic American Literature* (1923), the twentieth-century English writer D. H. Lawrence detested Franklin and wrote of him:

> The perfectability of Man! The perfectability of the Ford car! The perfectability of which man? I am many men. Which of them are you going to perfect? I am not a mechanical contrivance. Education! Which of the various me's do you propose to educate, and which do you propose to suppress? . . . Old Daddy Franklin will tell you. He'll rig him up for you, the pattern American. . . . He knew what he was about, the sharp little man. He set up the first dummy American.

Write an essay comparing Lawrence's impression of Franklin with your own view of him, and use Franklin's text for examples. Consider these questions: What values, positive or negative, does Franklin represent to Lawrence? What does Lawrence seem to think that the American dream is? Do you think that one has to be an American to appreciate Franklin? Why, or why not?

✵✵ FROM *Women and Economics* (1898)

CHARLOTTE PERKINS GILMAN

Born in Hartford, Connecticut, in 1860, Charlotte Perkins Gilman supported herself as an artist, a teacher, and a governess before discovering her gift for writing. In the 1890s she escaped destitution by publishing short stories like "Similar Cases" and "The Yellow Wallpaper," the latter a harrowing fictionalization of her own experience of nervous breakdown. Women and Economics *appeared in 1898 and was hailed as the most important work of its kind since John Stuart Mill's* Subjugation of Women. *Gilman committed suicide in 1934 when she was terminally ill with breast cancer. She is recognized as one of the intellectual leaders of the women's movement in American history.*

What we do modifies us more than what is done to us. The freedom of expression has been more restricted in women than the freedom of impression, if that be possible. Something of the world she lived in she has seen from her barred windows. Some air has come through the purdah's[1] folds, some knowledge has filtered to her eager ears from the talk of men. Desdemona learned somewhat of Othello. Had she known more, she might have lived longer. But in the ever-growing human impulse to create, the power and will to make, to do, to express one's new spirit in new forms,—here she has been utterly debarred. She might work as she had worked from the beginning,—at the primitive labors of the household; but in the inevitable expansion of even those industries to professional levels we have striven to hold her back. To work with her own hands, for nothing, in direct body-service to her own family,—this has been permitted,—yes, compelled. But to be and to do anything further from this she has been forbidden. Her labor has not been limited in kind, but in degree. Whatever she has been allowed to do must be done in private and alone, the first-hand industries of savage times. . . .

It is painfully interesting to trace the gradual cumulative effect of these conditions upon women: first, the action of large natural laws, acting on her as they would act on any other animal; then the evolution of social customs and laws (with her position as the active cause), following the direction of mere physical forces, and adding heavily to them; then, with increasing civilization, the unbroken accumulation of precedent, burnt into each generation by the growing force of education, made lovely by art, holy by religion, desirable by habit; and, steadily acting from beneath, the unswerving pressure of economic ne-

---

[1]Purdah is the Hindu word for hiding or concealing women from strangers by means of a veil or a curtain.

cessity upon which the whole structure rested. These are strong modifying conditions indeed.

The process would have been even more effective and far less painful but for one important circumstance. Heredity has no Salic law.[2] Each girl child inherits from her father a certain increasing percentage of human development, human power, human tendency; and each boy as well inherits from his mother the increasing percentage of sex-development, sex-power, sex-tendency. The action of heredity has been to equalize what every tendency of environment and education made to differ. This has saved us from such a female as the gypsy moth. It has held up the woman, and held down the man. It has set iron bounds to our absurd effort to make a race with one sex a million years behind the other. But it has added terribly to the pain and difficulty of human life,—a difficulty and a pain that should have taught us long since that we were living on wrong lines. Each woman born, re-humanized by the current of race activity carried on by her father and re-womanized by her traditional position, has had to live over again in her own person the same process of restriction, repression, denial; the smothering "no" which crushed down all her human desires to create, to discover, to learn, to express, to advance. . . .

To the young man confronting life the world lies wide. Such powers as he has he may use, must use. If he chooses wrong at first, he may choose again, and yet again. Not effective or successful in one channel, he may do better in another. The growing, varied needs of all mankind call on him for the varied service in which he finds his growth. What he wants to be, he may strive to get. What he wants to get, he may strive to get. Wealth, power, social distinction, fame,— what he wants he can try for.

To the young woman confronting life there is the same world beyond, there are the same human energies and human desires and ambition within. But all that she may wish to have, all that she may wish to do, must come through a single channel and a single choice. Wealth, power, social distinction, fame,—not only these, but home and happiness, reputation, ease and pleasure, her bread and butter,— all must come to her through a small gold ring. This is a heavy pressure. It has accumulated behind her through heredity, and continued about her through environment. It has been subtly trained into her through education, till she herself has come to think it a right condition, and pours its influence upon her daughter with increasing impetus. Is it any wonder that women are oversexed? But for the constant inheritance from the more human male, we should have been queen

---

[2]Law prohibiting a woman from ascending a throne.

bees, indeed, long before this. But the daughter of the soldier and the sailor, of the artist, the inventor, the great merchant, has inherited in body and brain her share of his development in each generation, and so stayed somewhat human for all her femininity.

For Journals

What is your response to Gilman's first assertion: "What we do modifies us more than what is done to us" (paragraph 1)?

For Discussion

1.   According to Gilman, what different kinds of conditions have combined to make women dependent? Do you agree with her? If you do not, would you substitute other reasons to support her conclusion?

2.   How do you respond to Gilman's views on heredity and its consequences for creativity in both men and women? Identify her central assertion about heredity, and rephrase it in your own terms. Do you accept her reasoning? What evidence do you have, personal or otherwise, to support or deny it?

3.   What assertions does Gilman make about the effect of marriage on women's independence? Why is a gold wedding ring such a heavy burden to her? What do you think she would consider a successful woman's life?

4.   Gilman is talking about the situation of middle- and upper-middle-class Victorian women. How valid or invalid do you find her assertions about women, independence, and the need for work today? How do you think that women who work entirely in the home today feel about their independence or the value of their work?

5.   What is your evaluation of Gilman's belief that a young man confronting life can try for anything he wants, do any kind of work he wants, and keep getting new opportunities if the work he is doing doesn't suit him? Do you agree? Why, or why not?

6.   In her book on the history of American housework, *Never Done*, Susan Strasser writes, "When Charlotte Perkins Gilman described the food of her ideal future, she envisioned kitchenless houses; individuals and families would patronize establishments that served hot cooked food ready to eat, produced according to the industrial principles of the division of labor and economies of scale. Eighty years later her dream has come true at McDonald's." From what you have read of Gilman and what you know of McDonald's, how valid is Strasser's assertion?

For Writing

1. Write an essay in which you analyze a major compromise made by your mother, another female relative, a friend, or you for the sake of financial security. The choice can be personal or professional, and you can argue either for or against it, but, even if you disagree with the result, try to be objective. What reasons or assertions were given or assumed in making the trade-off? What values or beliefs supported it? What pressures, economic or otherwise, were brought to bear on the person who made the compromise?

2. Research and write a report to share with your peers about a Victorian American woman who found a way to combine work and marriage, or one who chose work over marriage (for example, political activists Susan B. Anthony and Carrie Chapman Catt, or writers such as Harriet Beecher Stowe, Louisa May Alcott, Kate Chopin, and Edith Wharton). Pay special attention to the economic and social obstacles these women had to struggle with in order to find fulfilling work.

☼☼☼ *Young Women Picking Tobacco Leaves* (1922)

ANONYMOUS

See the photo on page 328.

For Journals

What other documentary photographs or historical photographs have you seen? What made the greatest impression on you, and why?

For Discussion

1. With no other information except the picture itself, what can you deduce about the working conditions depicted in this photograph? Which details in this picture are the most persuasive in expressing the women's poverty?

2. Describe the contents of this photograph in detail. How would you describe the body language of the young woman at the forefront?

3. If this picture were in color instead of black and white, what colors do you think would predominate? What are the advantages of using only black and white for documentary pictures?

For Writing

1. Jacob Riis, Alfred Stieglitz, and other photographers who took pictures of workers in order to document the conditions under which they lived were interested in arousing public interest in the working lives of immigrants and other poor Americans. Write an essay in which you compare and contrast the picture here with another image of labor, either an old photo or a contemporary one. (The *New York Times* on-line has had many articles and pictures in the last several years on sweatshops on both coasts using illegal immigrants from Central America and China.) Examine how the figures are arranged, how the background (other people, objects, or interiors) is composed, and how those details contribute to the overall impression.

✻✻ *Three Women at a Parachute Plant in San Diego, California* (1940s)

RUSSELL LEE

See the photo on page 330.

For Journals

Have you known or had a single mother who had to support a family without another adult to earn a paycheck?

For Discussion

1. What is the ethnic mix of these women? What would you guess about their socioeconomic status?

2. What adjectives would you choose to describe the expressions on their faces? Why aren't these women smiling?

3. How does the poster behind the women fit with their demeanor?

4. Look ahead to the next ad, a 1950s stove with a smiling housewife, and discuss the differences. Some of them will be pretty obvious to you, but the more detail you get into, the more subtle they will become. You might want to work with a couple of people in your class to draw up two lists of what constitutes the distinctive look of both these ads.

For Writing

1. Write an essay based on discussion question number 4. These ads are culturally specific enough to give you a lot of material for comparison, particularly with regard to such issues as posture, clothing, and backdrop. When you identify these differences, consider using inductive reasoning to use those details as a basis for making some more general conclusions about changing attitudes toward work and women's place. There are other comparisons you can make among this photo, the stove ad, and other images in this book. Take a look at *Keep within Compass* in Chapter 5, on a women's proper sphere of activity, or the photograph of the young black woman earlier in this chapter. Take one of the other images, and examine it next to the defense plant photo or the ecstatic housewife with stove photo, and write a persuasive essay about these models for appropriate female behavior.

🌺🌺 *Advertisement of Wife and Her New Gibson Ultra 600 Electric Range* (1950s)

See the photo on page 332.

For Journals

What household appliance—such as a new computer of your own— would make you look as happy as the woman in this ad?

For Discussion

1. This advertisement portrays a woman showing off her wonderful new range. What observations can you make about her hair, her clothing, and what she has presumably been working at?

2. This woman looks extremely proud or, as Marilyn Yalom says in her book *The History of the Wife,* she is "an ecstatic housewife." What does she have to be ecstatic about? What wonders will her stove perform?

3. If you are a woman, what was your first reaction to this picture? If you are a man, what was your first reaction?

4. Research has shown that the more labor-saving devices a home has, the more time the homemaker expends on taking care of everything. If you were going to simplify your life by getting rid of any conveniences, what would they be, and why do you think you could do without them?

For Writing

1. Browsing the Internet, the back ads of magazines, or your junk mail, find one or two advertisements that promise to make some aspect of your ordinary life easier that you think are fake or bogus, and debunk them by analyzing their appeals, their language, and the product itself.

2. Write an analysis of the visual rhetoric of this ad. Consider the following: What is in the foreground, and what's in the background? How is the woman dressed in her kitchen? What is her body language in relation to the stove and its contents? What written information is there, where is it placed on the page, and why is it effective? Do you find the ad odd, endearing, old-fashioned?

3. Find a contemporary ad in a magazine for a kitchen or for a home appliance, and analyze its rhetoric as you did in the previous question, but using the older ad as a point of comparison. Identify details and specific elements in the ads just as you would sentences in a text.

Office Politics (1993)

ELLEN LUPTON

Ellen Lupton is the author of The Mechanical Bride, *a publication of the Cooper-Hewitt Museum of the Smithsonian Institution. The book is about American women, work, appliances and office equipment, and the cultural and social context in which they occur. What follows is a chapter from that book.*

Most modern clerical occupations, including secretary, typist, stenographer, and keypunch operator, are dominated by women. The design and use of mechanical objects, from telephones and typewriters to furniture engineered for efficiency and comfort, are central to the gendered organization of the modern office.

Prior to the 1880s, clerical work was a male occupation involving the writing and filing of letters, invoices, and other documents. A clerk was an entry-level employee who could entertain hopes of upward movement through a firm. As he advanced, a clerk earned a degree of decision-making authority and enjoyed considerable variety and personal autonomy within his daily activities. The term *secretary,* from the same root as *secret,* had carried cultural prestige since the Renaissance, referring to the confidant and deputy of a powerful figure. The feminization of this almost exclusively male world occurred with unprecedented speed at the close of the nineteenth century. By 1890, women held 60 percent of all typing and stenography jobs in the U.S.; by 1900, their share was 77 percent; by 1920, it was 90 percent. Rarely has a field of employment—especially one invested with social status—altered its identity so quickly from male to female.

Several factors contributed to the feminization of office work, including the rising *demand* for clerical employees (owing to the explosion of business communications), and the rising *supply* of educated women (owing to the expansion of public schooling and mass literacy). In a situation that was ripe for the admittance of female employees, the newness of the typewriter served as a wedge into the male domain of the office. Because typewriting was a job with no established sexual history, female typists were not perceived as displacing male clerks. Employers were socially discouraged from hiring women to do men's work, which would mean taking jobs away from fathers and husbands—whose employment was seen as necessary—and giving jobs to lower-paid daughters and wives—whose work was understood as the luxurious pursuit of "pin money." The keyboard, whose very *neutrality* first made it available to women, soon became a defining feature of feminized office work.

Through its newness as an object, the typewriter enabled managers to clear the table for the entrance of a new class of clerical workers with highly circumscribed roles to play. Whereas the traditional clerk often had been responsible for mentally *composing* as well as physically *writing* a text, workers in the mechanized office were assigned limited functions as stenographers (who captured an executive's spoken words in shorthand) and typists (who mechanically transcribed such words). The clerk's editorial role diminished as managers split the making of documents into two distinct phases: conception and production. The new system, which borrowed the division of labor from modern factories, saved the high-cost time and effort of managers, while a lower-paid crew of clerical workers generated a huge volume of legible, uniform documents.

In addition to accepting low wages, women offered a number of attractive qualities to employers, including their perceived docility and agility, their willingness to perform routine work, and their lack of career ambitions. Prior to the 1950s, native-born white women typically entered the work force for a brief period before marrying; this pattern discouraged them from expecting the same opportunities for advancement and benefits as men of their class. As historian Elyce Rotella has explained, the routinized modern office that emerged in the late nineteenth century needed large numbers of workers with general skills—transferable to any business—rather than specific skills acquired in relation to a given company. The generically qualified typist or stenographer could be trained in a high school business course or commercial school; the firm that hired her, having invested minimally in her training, thus could take full advantage of both the low wages commanded by women and the rapid turnover associated with their work.

In the 1910s and 1920s, the female office worker figured in popular literature and film as a new social type, an adventurer in the urban wilderness—the "flapper" of the 1920s often was a typist. By the 1930s, as historian Mary Kathleen Benét has written, the female clerical force was a familiar cultural fact: "the real novelty had gone from the working girl, and in any description of the office world, she was simply there—as irrevocable and uninteresting as the desks and the telephones." Because typing, stenography, and switchboard operating were thoroughly feminized, women were not pressured to give up these jobs to men during the Depression; many married women with unemployed husbands sought work in offices in the 1930s.

During World War II, women occupied male-defined jobs both in offices and in factories; although they were forced to surrender most of the Rosie-the-Riveter factory positions to returning vets after 1945, women were able to keep many of the lower-paying office jobs they had claimed during the war, including bookkeeping, which has become increasingly feminized since 1950. With the accelerating demand for clerical workers in the 1950s and 1960s, more married women, older women, and women from diverse ethnic and racial backgrounds pursued office jobs; meanwhile, the wages of clerical employees relative to other women workers gradually declined. While in 1890 a female typist earned 1.8 times as much as a female factory worker, this gap diminished between 1900 and 1930, as wages evened out across feminized occupations in teaching, manufacturing, and retail. Since World War II, routine clerical positions have paid much less than factory jobs.

Thus high wages have not been the main incentive for women to become clerical workers. As a site of cultural prestige, the office has been seen as a more appropriate setting than the factory or store for middle-class women; it can serve, in fact, to endow its occupants with a middle-class status. The design of business machines and their environments has shaped and expressed the social meaning of office work. Design has helped articulate the differences between employees occupying various levels of an organization and has linked the language of the office to other institutional vocabularies, such as the home and the factory. Design has molded the psychological, physical, and symbolic value of work in modern offices.

For Journals

Is there any job that you would refuse to take even if you needed the money and had the qualifications?

For Discussion

1. According to this article, what historical factors led to the decrease in significance in the role of the secretary?

2. In her book, *The Souls of a Skyscraper,* Lisa Fine says that between the 1870s and 1890s, "women's clerical positions posed a direct challenge to the commonly held belief that not only was the office a male space, but all sorts of urban settings—elevators, streetcars, restaurants, boarding houses—were inappropriate to women." What would the men have been worried about? What do you think they were trying to preserve by keeping women out of those places?

3. Why do you think that working in an office, as opposed to a factory, makes a job middle-class rather than working-class?

For Writing

1. According to the author, the design of business machines shows the differences between employees at different levels in an organization. Along with someone else from your class, ask for permission to interview female staff members at your school about the kind of work setup they have—computers, chairs, cubicle, etc. Alternatively, observe the design and physical layout in a couple of places at your school. Concentrate on the furnishings and work sites of the support staff—for example, clerical, administrative, reception. Write up a report in which you prioritize the best and the worst jobs in the office on the basis of your observations. You can include recommendations for improvement as well (see Chapter 2 on reports).

2. Write a persuasive article on what makes certain jobs have status in your eyes. You should pick jobs with which you are somewhat familiar, either because you have had them yourself or know someone well who has. Restrict yourself to three jobs at the most, and try to make selections that are at least somewhat on the same financial level, high or low, so that salary doesn't become the sole measure of status. If possible, try to think of jobs you admire that don't pay much.

FROM *Working* (1972)

STUDS TERKEL

Studs Terkel (1912–) grew up and still lives in Chicago. Having worked as a disc jockey and a sports commentator, among other jobs, he has for many years hosted a daily interview program, which is broadcast all over the country; for a writer to be interviewed by Mr. Terkel is considered a great honor. Mr. Terkel is the author of several books, including Division Street: America *(1967),* The Good War *(1984), and* Hard Times *(1970). All of them use interviews with Americans from all walks of life to reveal the effect of historic events, like the Great Depression and World War II, on the lives of individuals. The following selection is from his book about Americans and what they do for a living, called* Working *(1974).*

The Mason

Carl Murray Bates

We're in a tavern no more than thirty yards from the banks of the Ohio. Toward the far side of the river, Alcoa smokestacks belch forth: an uneasy coupling of a bucolic past and an industrial present. The waters are polluted, yet the jobs out there offer the townspeople their daily bread.

He is fifty-seven years old. He's a stonemason who has pursued his craft since he was seventeen. None of his three sons is in his trade.

As far as I know, masonry is older than carpentry, which goes clear back to Bible times. Stone mason goes back way *before* Bible time: the pyramids of Egypt, things of that sort. Anybody that starts to build anything stone, rock, or brick, start on the northeast corner. Because when they built King Solomon's Temple, they started on the northeast corner. To this day, you look at your courthouses, your big public buildings, you look at the cornerstone, when it was created, what year, it will be on the northeast corner. If I was gonna build a septic tank, I would start on the northeast corner. (Laugh.) Superstition, I suppose.

With stone we build just about anything. Stone is the oldest and best building material that ever was. Stone was being used even by the cavemen that put it together with mud. They built out of stone before they even used logs. He got him a cave, he built stone across the front. And he learned to use dirt, mud, to make the stones lay there without sliding around—which was the beginnings of mortar, which we still call mud. The Romans used mortar that's almost as good as we have today.

Everyone hears these things, they just don't remember 'em. But me being in the profession, when I hear something in that line, I remember it. Stone's my business. I, oh, sometimes talk to architects and engineers that have made a study and I pick up the stuff here and there.

Every piece of stone you pick up is different, the grain's a little different and this and that. It'll split one way and break the other. You pick up your stone and look at it and make an educated guess. It's a pretty good day layin' stone or brick. Not tiring. Anything you like to do isn't tiresome. It's hard work; stone is heavy. At the same time, you get interested in what you're doing and you usually fight the clock the other way. You're not lookin' for quittin'. You're wondering you haven't got enough done and it's almost quittin' time. (Laughs.) I ask the hod carrier what time it is and he says two thirty. I say, "Oh, my Lord, I was gonna get a whole lot more than this."

I pretty well work by myself. On houses, usually just one works. 5 I've got the hod carrier there, but most of the time I talk to myself, "I'll get my hammer and I'll knock the chip off there." (Laughs.) A good hod carrier is half your day. He won't work as hard as a poor one. He knows what to do and makes every move count makin' the mortar. It has to be so much water, so much sand. His skill is to see that you don't run out of anything. The hod carrier, he's above the laborer. He has a certain amount of prestige.

I think a laborer feels that he's the low man. Not so much that he works with his hands, it's that he's at the bottom of the scale. He always wants to get up to a skilled trade. Of course he'd make more money. The main thing is the common laborer—even the word *common* laborer—just sounds so common, he's at the bottom. Many that works with his hands takes pride in his work.

I get a lot of phone calls when I get home: how about showin' me how and I'll do it myself? I always wind up doin' it for 'em. (Laughs.) So I take a lot of pride in it and I do get, oh, I'd say, a lot of praise or whatever you want to call it. I don't suppose anybody, however much he's recognized, wouldn't like to be recognized a little more. I think I'm pretty well recognized.

One of my sons is an accountant and the other two are bankers. They're mathematicians, I suppose you'd call 'em that. Air-conditioned offices and all that. They always look at the house I build. They stop by and see me when I'm aworkin'. Always want me to come down and fix somethin' on their house, too. (Laughs.) They don't buy a house that I don't have to look at it first. Oh sure, I've got to crawl under it and look on the roof, you know. . . .

I can't seem to think of any young masons. So many of 'em before, the man lays stone and his son follows his footsteps. Right now the only one of these sons I can think of is about forty, fifty years old.

I started back in the Depression times when there wasn't any ap- 10 prenticeships. You just go out and if you could hold your job, that's it. I was just a kid then. Now I worked real hard and carried all the blocks I could. Then I'd get my trowel and I'd lay one or two. The second day the boss told me: I think you could lay enough blocks to earn you wages. So I guess I had only one day of apprenticeship. Usually it takes about three years of being a hod carrier to start. And it takes another ten or fifteen years to learn the skill.

I admired the men that we had at that time that were stonemasons. They knew their trade. So naturally I tried to pattern after them. There's been very little change in the work. Stone is still stone, mortar is still the same as it was fifty years ago. The style of stone has changed a little. We use a lot more, we call it golf. A stone as big as a baseball up to as big as a basketball. Just round balls and whatnot. We just fit 'em in the wall that way.

Automation has tried to get in the bricklayer. Set 'em with a crane. I've seen several put up that way. But you've always got in-between the windows and this and that. It just doesn't seem to pan out. We do have a power saw. We do have an electric power mix to mix the mortar, but the rest of it's done by hand as it always was.

In the old days they all seemed to want it cut out and smoothed. It's harder now because you have no way to use your tools. You have no way to use a string, you have no way to use a level or a plumb. You just have to look at it because it's so rough and many irregularities. You have to just back up and look at it.

All construction, there's always a certain amount of injuries. A scaffold will break and so on. But practically no real danger. All I ever did do was work on houses, so we don't get up very high—maybe two stories. Very seldom that any more. Most of 'em are one story. And so many of 'em use stone for a trim. They may go up four, five feet and then paneling or something. There's a lot of skinned fingers or you hit your finger with a hammer. Practically all stone is worked with hammers and chisels. I wouldn't call it dangerous at all.

Stone's my life. I daydream all the time, most times it's on stone. Oh, I'm gonna build me a stone cabin down on the Green River. I'm gonna build stone cabinets in the kitchen. That stone door's gonna be awful heavy and I don't know how to attach the hinges. I've got to figure out how to make a stone roof. That's the kind of thing. All my dreams, it seems like it's got to have a piece of rock mixed in it.

If I got some problem that's bothering me, I'll actually wake up in the night and think of it. I'll sit at the table and get a pencil and paper and go over it, makin' marks on paper or drawin' or however . . . this way or that way. Now I've got to work this and I've only got so much. Or they decided they want it that way when you already got it fixed this way. Anyone hates tearing his work down. It's all the same price but you still don't like to do it.

These fireplaces, you've got to figure how they'll throw out heat, the way you curve the fireboxes inside. You have to draw a line so they reflect heat. But if you throw out too much of a curve, you'll have them smoke. People in these fine houses don't want a puff of smoke coming out of the house.

The architect draws the picture and the plans, and the draftsman and the engineer, they help him. They figure the strength and so on. But when it comes to actually makin' the curves and doin' the work, you've got to do it with your hands. It comes right back to your hands.

When you get into stone, you're gettin' away from the prefabs, you're gettin' into the better homes. Usually at this day and age they'll start into sixty to seventy thousand and run up to about half a million. We've got one goin' now that's mighty close, three or four hundred thousand. That type of house is what we build.

The lumber is not near as good as it used to be. We have better fabricating material, such as plywood and sheet rock and things of that sort, but the lumber itself is definitely inferior. Thirty, forty years ago a house was almost entirely made of lumber, wood floors. . . .

Now they have vinyl, they have carpet, everything, and so on. The framework wood is getting to be of very poor quality.

But stone is still stone and the bricks are actually more uniform than they used to be. Originally they took a clay bank . . . I know a church been built that way. Went right on location, dug a hole in the ground and formed bricks with their hands. They made the bricks that built the building on the spot.

Now we've got modern kilns, modern heat, the temperature don't vary. They got better bricks now than they used to have. We've got machines that make brick, so they're made true. Where they used to, they were pretty rough. I'm buildin' a big fireplace now out of old brick. They run wide, long, and it's a headache. I've been two weeks on that one fireplace.

The toughest job I ever done was this house, a hundred years old plus. The lady wanted one room left just that way. And this doorway had to be closed. It had deteriorated and weathered for over a hundred years. The bricks was made out of broken pieces, none of 'em were straight. If you lay 'em crooked, it gets awful hard right there. You spend a lifetime tryin' to learn to lay bricks straight. And it took a half-day to measure with a spoon, to try to get the mortar to match. I'd have so much dirt, so much soot, so much lime, so when I got the recipe right I could make it in bigger quantity. Then I made it with a coffee cup. Half a cup of this, half a cup of that . . . I even used soot out of a chimney and sweepin's off the floor. I was two days layin' up a little doorway, mixin' the mortar and all. The boss told the lady it couldn't be done. I said, "Give me the time, I believe I can do it." I defy you to find where that door is right now. That's the best job I ever done.

There's not a house in this country that I haven't built that I don't look at every time I go by. (Laughs.) I can set here now and actually in my mind see so many that you wouldn't believe. If there's one stone in there crooked, I know where it's at and I'll never forget it. Maybe thirty years, I'll know a place where I should have took that stone out and redone it but I didn't. I still notice it. The people who live there might not notice it, but I notice it. I never pass that house that I don't think of it. I've got one house in mind right now. (Laughs.) That's the work of my hands. 'Cause you see, stone, you don't prepaint it, you don't camouflage it. It's there, just like I left it forty years ago.

I can't imagine a job where you go home and maybe go by a year 25 later and you don't know what you've done. My work, I can see what I did the first day I started. All my work is set right out there in the open and I can look at it as I go by. It's something I can see the rest of my life. Forty years ago, the first blocks I ever laid in my life, when I was seventeen years old. I never go through Eureka—a little town down there on the river—that I don't look thataway. It's always there.

Immortality as far as we're concerned. Nothin' in this world lasts forever, but did you know that stone—Bedford limestone, they claim—deteriorates one-sixteenth of an inch every hundred years? And it's around four or five inches for a house. So that's gettin' awful close. (Laughs.)

For Journals

What skills or knowledge of a craft do you have or would like to have?

For Discussion

1. Usually the word *professional* is used to describe jobs that require a college education or advanced degrees. Judging from the text of this interview, explain Mr. Bates's sense of pride in his job. In what ways is he a professional?

2. What do you think of the status hierarchy Mr. Bates sets up among levels of workers? Between him and his own sons, who have white-collar jobs?

3. How does Terkel's decision to call this interview "The Mason" instead of "Mr. Bates" establish his attitude toward Mr. Bates and his work? How does it affect your own attitude toward Mr. Bates?

4. Looking at the text, identify the assertions Mr. Bates makes to connect the history of masonry and the possibilities for achieving immortality. Are those possibilities affected by the fact that no young masons are following in his footsteps? Is that irrelevant? Why, or why not?

For Writing

1. In the excerpt from the *Autobiography* at the beginning of this chapter, Franklin talks about his work and going into business. Write an essay in which you compare Franklin's attitude toward work, pride in one's occupation, and ambition, with Mr. Bates's ideas on the same subjects, or on other work-related issues you find in the two texts. Use specific references and quotations from each to support your points.

2. Do an interview with someone whom you know who works hard at his or her job. Pick someone, inside or outside the home, whose work you admire or are curious about. If you can, use a tape recorder for accuracy, and show the person a copy of what you've written. Encourage this person to show you or tell you exactly what he or she does, how meaningful the work is or isn't, and what the most rewarding parts of it are. Be sure that whomever you interview understands that you are treating his or her work with respect.

✻✻✻ Bricklayer's Boy (1989)

ALFRED LUBRANO

Alfred Lubrano is a reporter for New York Newsday *and is a contributor to* Gentleman's Quarterly, *where this essay originally appeared. Lubrano frequently writes about personal relationships and family life. In the memoir that follows, he writes about the family and work values gained from his blue-collar upbringing and how they are, or are not, reconciled with his adult way of life.*

My father and I were college buddies back in the mid 1970s. While I was in class at Columbia, struggling with the esoterica du jour, he was on a bricklayer's scaffold not far up the street, working on a campus building.

Sometimes we'd hook up on the subway going home, he with his tools, I with my books. We didn't chat much about what went on during the day. My father wasn't interested in Dante, I wasn't up on arches. We'd share a *New York Post* and talk about the Mets.

My dad has built lots of places in New York City he can't get into: colleges, condos, office towers. He makes his living on the outside. Once the walls are up, a place takes on a different feel for him, as if he's not welcome anymore. It doesn't bother him, though. For my father, earning the dough that paid for my entrée into a fancy, bricked-in institution was satisfaction enough, a vicarious access.

We didn't know it then, but those days were the start of a branching off, a redefining of what it means to be a workingman in our family. Related by blood, we're separated by class, my father and I. Being the white-collar son of a blue-collar man means being the hinge on the door between two ways of life.

It's not so smooth jumping from Italian old-world style to U.S.   5
yuppie in a single generation. Despite the myth of mobility in America, the true rule, experts say, is rags to rags, riches to riches. According to Bucknell University economist and author Charles Sackrey, maybe 10 percent climb from the working to the professional class. My father has had a tough time accepting my decision to become a mere newspaper reporter, a field that pays just a little more than construction does. He wonders why I haven't cashed in on that multi-brick education and taken on some lawyer-lucrative job. After bricklaying for thirty years, my father promised himself I'd never pile bricks and blocks into walls for a living. He figured an education—genielike and benevolent—would somehow rocket me into the consecrated trajectory of the upwardly mobile, and load some serious loot into my pockets. What he didn't count on was his eldest son breaking blue-collar rule No. 1: Make as much money as you can, to pay for as good a life as you can get.

He'd tell me about it when I was nineteen, my collar already fading to white. I was the college boy who handed him the wrong wrench on help-around-the-house Saturdays. "You better make a lot of money," my blue-collar handy dad wryly warned me as we huddled in front of a disassembled dishwasher I had neither the inclination nor the aptitude to fix. "You're gonna need to hire someone to hammer a nail into a wall for you."

In 1980, after college and graduate school, I was offered my first job, on a now-dead daily paper in Columbus, Ohio. I broke the news in the kitchen, where all the family business is discussed. My mother wept as if it were Vietnam. My father had a few questions: "Ohio? Where the hell is Ohio?"

I said it's somewhere west of New York City, that it was like Pennsylvania, only more so. I told him I wanted to write, and these were the only people who'd take me.

"Why can't you get a good job that pays something, like in advertising in the city, and write on the side?"

"Advertising is lying," I said, smug and sanctimonious, ever the 10
unctuous undergraduate. "I wanna tell the truth."

"The truth?" the old man exploded, his face reddening as it does when he's up twenty stories in high wind. "What's truth?" I said it's real life, and writing about it would make me happy. "You're happy with your family," my father said, spilling blue-collar rule No. 2. "That's what makes you happy. After that, it all comes down to dollars and cents. What gives you comfort besides your family? Money, only money."

During the two weeks before I moved, he reminded me that newspaper journalism is a dying field, and I could do better. Then he pressed advertising again, though neither of us knew anything about it, except that you could work in Manhattan, the borough with the water-beading high gloss, the island polished clean by money. I couldn't explain myself, so I packed, unpopular and confused. No longer was I the good son who studied hard and fumbled endearingly with tools. I was hacking people off.

One night, though, my father brought home some heavy tape and that clear, plastic bubble stuff you pack your mother's second-string dishes in. "You probably couldn't do this right," my father said to me before he sealed the boxes and helped me take them to UPS. "This is what he wants," my father told my mother the day I left for Columbus in my grandfather's eleven-year-old gray Cadillac. "What are you gonna do?" After I said my good-byes, my father took me aside and pressed five $100 bills into my hands. "It's okay," he said over my weak protests. "Don't tell your mother."

When I broke the news about what the paper was paying me, my father suggested I get a part-time job to augment the income. "Maybe

you could drive a cab." Once, after I was chewed out by the city editor
for something trivial, I made the mistake of telling my father during a
visit home. "They pay you nothin', and they push you around too
much in that business," he told me, the rage building. "Next time, you
gotta grab the guy by the throat and tell him he's a big jerk."

"Dad, I can't talk to the boss like that."   15

"Tell him. You get results that way. Never take any shit." A few
years before, a guy didn't like the retaining wall my father and his
partner had built. They tore it down and did it again, but the guy still
bitched. My father's partner shoved the guy into the freshly laid
bricks. "Pay me off," my father said, and he and his partner took the
money and walked. Blue-collar guys have no patience for office politics and corporate bile-swallowing. Just pay me off and I'm gone.
Eventually, I moved on to a job in Cleveland, on a paper my father has
heard of. I think he looks on it as a sign of progress, because he hasn't
mentioned advertising for a while.

When he was my age, my father was already dug in with a trade, a
wife, two sons and a house in a neighborhood in Brooklyn not far
from where he was born. His workaday, family-centered life has been
very much in step with his immigrant father's. I sublet what the real-
estate people call a junior one-bedroom in a dormlike condo in a
Cleveland suburb. Unmarried and unconnected in an insouciant, per-
petual student kind of way, I rent movies during the week and feed
single women in restaurants on Saturday nights. My dad asks me
about my dates, but he goes crazy over the word "woman." "A girl,"
he corrects. "You went out with a girl. Don't say 'woman.' It sounds
like you're takin' out your grandmother."

I've often believed blue-collaring is the more genuine of lives, in
greater proximity to primordial manhood. My father is provider and
protector, concerned only with the basics: food and home, love and
progeny. He's also a generation closer to the heritage, a warmer spot
nearer the fire that forged and defined us. Does heat dissipate and
light fade further from the source? I live for my career, and frequently
feel lost and codeless, devoid of the blue-collar rules my father grew
up with. With no baby-boomer groomer to show me the way, I've
been choreographing my own tentative shuffle across the wax-shined
dance floor on the edge of the Great Middle Class, a different rhythm
in a whole new ballroom.

I'm sure it's tough on my father, too, because I don't know much
about bricklaying, either, except that it's hell on the body, a daily sacrifice. I idealized my dad as a kind of dawn-rising priest of labor, engaged in holy ritual. Up at five every day, my father has made a
religion of responsibility. My younger brother, a Wall Street white-collar
guy with the sense to make a decent salary, says he always felt safe

when he heard Dad stir before him, as if Pop were taming the day for us. My father, fifty-five years old, but expected to put out as if he were three decades stronger, slips on machine-washable vestments of khaki cotton without waking my mother. He goes into the kitchen and turns on the radio to catch the temperature. Bricklayers have an occupational need to know the weather. And because I am my father's son, I can recite the five-day forecast at any given moment.

My father isn't crazy about this life. He wanted to be a singer and 20 actor when he was young, but that was frivolous doodling to his Italian family, who expected money to be coming in, stoking the stove that kept hearth fires ablaze. Dreams simply were not energy-efficient. My dad learned a trade, as he was supposed to, and settled into a life of pre-scripted routing. He says he can't find the black-and-white publicity glossies he once had made.

Although I see my dad infrequently, my brother, who lives at home, is with the old man every day. Chris has a lot more blue-collar in him than I do, despite his management-level career; for a short time, he wanted to be a construction worker, but my parents persuaded him to go to Columbia. Once in a while he'll bag a lunch and, in a nice wool suit, meet my father at a construction site and share sandwiches of egg salad on semolina bread.

It was Chris who helped my dad most when my father tried to change his life several months ago. My dad wanted a civil-service bricklayer foreman's job that wouldn't be so physically demanding. There was a written test that included essay questions about construction work. My father hadn't done anything like it in forty years. Why the hell they needed bricklayers to write essays I have no idea, but my father sweated it out. Every morning before sunrise, Chris would be ironing a shirt, bleary-eyed, and my father would sit at the kitchen table and read aloud his practice essays on how to wash down a wall, or how to build a tricky corner. Chris would suggest words and approaches.

It was so hard for my dad. He had to take a Stanley Kaplan–like prep course in a junior high school three nights a week after work for six weeks. At class time, the outside men would come in, twenty-five construction workers squeezing themselves into little desks. Tough blue-collar guys armed with No. 2 pencils leaning over and scratching out their practice essays, cement in their hair, tar on their pants, their work boots too big and clumsy to fit under the desks.

"Is this what finals felt like?" my father would ask me on the phone when I pitched in to help long-distance. "Were you always this nervous?" I told him yes. I told him writing's always difficult. He thanked Chris and me for the coaching, for putting him through school this time. My father thinks he did okay, but he's still awaiting the test results. In the meantime, he takes life the blue-collar way, one brick at a time.

When we see each other these days, my father still asks how the 25 money is. Sometimes he reads my stories; usually he likes them, although he recently criticized one piece as being a bit sentimental: "Too schmaltzy," he said. Some psychologists say that the blue-white-collar gap between fathers and sons leads to alienation, but I tend to agree with Dr. Al Baraff, a clinical psychologist and director of the Men-Center in Washington, D.C. "The core of the relationship is based on emotional and hereditary traits," Baraff says. "Class [distinctions] just get added on. If it's a healthful relationship from when you're a kid, there's a respect back and forth that'll continue."

Nice of the doctor to explain, but I suppose I already knew that. Whatever is between my father and me, whatever keeps us talking and keeps us close, has nothing to do with work and economic class.

During one of my visits to Brooklyn not long ago, he and I were in the car, on our way to buy toiletries, one of my father's weekly routines. "You know, you're not as successful as you could be," he began, blue-collar blunt as usual. "You paid your dues in school. You deserve better restaurants, better clothes." Here we go, I thought, the same old stuff. I'm sure every family has five or six similar big issues that are replayed like well-worn videotapes. I wanted to fast-forward this thing when we stopped at a red light.

Just then my father turned to me, solemn and intense. His knees were aching and his back muscles were throbbing in clockable intervals that registered in his eyes. It was the end of a week of lifting fifty-pound blocks. "I envy you," he said quietly. "For a man to do something he likes and get paid for it—that's fantastic." He smiled at me before the light changed, and we drove on. To thank him for the understanding, I sprang for the deodorant and shampoo. For once, my father let me pay.

For Journals

What did you learn from your family, implicitly or explicitly, about class and money?

For Discussion

1. What is your response to the voice and tone of the essay? Do the author and his family seem like people you would like to meet? Do any of his family members have values that you share?

2. Lubrano directly addresses issues of class, comparing blue-collar and white-collar lifestyles. What does he suggest is typical of each lifestyle?

3.   The author mentions "blue-collar" rules. What do you think would be his "white-collar" rules? Do the "rules" lead to conflict in this family?

4.   The essay is full of rich language and metaphor. Select some of the more vivid metaphors, and discuss ways in which they underscore and reinforce Lubrano's assertions about values.

5.   What is the myth of mobility discussed in this essay? What is the connection of this myth to class values?

For Writing

1.   Develop your journal writing into a reflective essay on the ways in which your family taught you values, attitudes, and beliefs. You could focus on a specific area, such as work or education.

2.   Research and develop an expository essay on the myth of mobility and the notion of "rags to riches." Do you find evidence to support Lubrano's claim that the usual scenario is "rags to rags"?

❋❋❋ *Serving in Florida* (2000)

BARBARA EHRENREICH

Barbara Ehrenreich is the author several books, including For Her Own Good, *a history of advice, medical and otherwise, that's been given to American women.*

Mostly out of laziness, I decide to start my low-wage life in the town nearest to where I actually live, Key West, Florida, which with a population of about 25,000 is elbowing its way up to the status of a genuine city. The downside of familiarity, I soon realize, is that it's not easy to go from being a consumer, thoughtlessly throwing money around in exchange for groceries and movies and gas, to being a worker in the very same place. I am terrified, especially at the beginning, of being recognized by some friendly business owner or erstwhile neighbor and having to stammer out some explanation of my project. Happily, though, my fears turn out to be entirely unwarranted: during a month of poverty and toil, no one recognizes my face or my name, which goes unnoticed and for the most part unuttered. In this parallel universe where my father never got out of the mines and I never got through college, I am "baby," "honey," "blondie," and, most commonly, "girl."

My first task is to find a place to live. I figure that if I can earn $7 an hour—which, from the want ads, seems doable—I can afford to spend $500 on rent or maybe, with severe economies, $600 and still have $400 or $500 left over for food and gas. In the Key West area, this pretty much confines me to flophouses and trailer homes—like the one, a pleasing fifteen-minute drive from town, that has no air-conditioning, no screens, no fans, no television, and, by way of diversion, only the challenge of evading the landlord's Doberman pinscher. The big problem with this place, though, is the rent, which at $675 a month is well beyond my reach. All right, Key West is expensive. But so is New York City, or the Bay Area, or Jackson, Wyoming, or Telluride, or Boston, or any other place where tourists and the wealthy compete for living space with the people who clean their toilets and fry their hash browns. Still, it is a shock to realize that "trailer trash" has become, for me, a demographic category to aspire to.

So I decide to make the common trade-off between affordability and convenience and go for a $500-a-month "efficiency" thirty miles up a two-lane highway from the employment opportunities of Key West, meaning forty-five minutes if there's no road construction and I don't get caught behind some sun-dazed Canadian tourists. I hate the drive, along a roadside studded with white crosses commemorating the more effective head-on collisions, but it's a sweet little place—a cabin, more or less, set in the swampy backyard of the converted mobile home where my landlord, an affable TV repairman, lives with his bartender girlfriend. Anthropologically speaking, the trailer park would be preferable, but here I have a gleaming white floor and a firm mattress, and the few resident bugs are easily vanquished.

The next piece of business is to comb through the want ads and find a job. I rule out various occupations for one reason or another: hotel front-desk clerk, for example, which to my surprise is regarded as unskilled and pays only $6 or $7 an hour, gets eliminated because it involves standing in one spot for eight hours a day. Waitressing is also something I'd like to avoid, because I remember it leaving me bone-tired when I was eighteen, and I'm decades of varicosities and back pain beyond that now. Telemarketing, one of the first refuges of the suddenly indigent, can be dismissed on grounds of personality. This leaves certain supermarket jobs, such as deli clerk, or housekeeping in the hotels and guest houses, which pays about $7 and, I imagine, is not too different from what I've been doing part-time, in my own home, all my life.

So I put on what I take to be a respectable-looking outfit of ironed 5 Bermuda shorts and scooped-neck T-shirt and set out for a tour of the local hotels and supermarkets. Best Western, Econo Lodge, and HoJo's all let me fill out application forms, and these are, to my relief, mostly interested in whether I am a legal resident of the United States and have committed any felonies. My next stop is Winn-Dixie, the supermarket, which turns out to have a particularly onerous application process, featuring a twenty-minute "interview" by computer since,

apparently, no human on the premises is deemed capable of representing the corporate point of view. I am conducted to a large room
decorated with posters illustrating how to look "professional" (it helps
to be white and, if female, permed) and warning of the slick promises
that union organizers might try to tempt me with. The interview is
multiple-choice: Do I have anything, such as child care problems, that
might make it hard for me to get to work on time? Do I think safety on
the job is the responsibility of management? Then, popping up cun-
ningly out of the blue: How many dollars' worth of stolen goods have
I purchased in the last year? Would I turn in a fellow employee if I
caught him stealing? Finally, "Are you an honest person?"

Apparently I ace the interview, because I am told that all I have to
do is show up in some doctor's office tomorrow for a urine test. This
seems to be a fairly general rule: if you want to stack Cheerios boxes or
vacuum hotel rooms in chemically fascist America, you have to be
willing to squat down and pee in front of a health worker (who has no
doubt had to do the same thing herself.)[1] The wages Winn-Dixie is offering—$6 and a couple of dimes to start with—are not enough, I de-
cide, to compensate for this indignity.

I lunch at Wendy's, where $4.99 gets you unlimited refills at the
Mexican part of the Super bar, a comforting surfeit of refried beans
and cheese sauce. A teenage employee, seeing me studying the want
ads, kindly offers me an application form, which I fill out, though
here, too, the pay is just $6 and change an hour. Then it's off for a
round of the locally owned inns and guest houses in Key West's Old
Town, which is where all the serious sightseeing and guzzling goes
on, a couple of miles removed from the functional end of the island,
where the discount hotels make their homes. At The Palms, let's call it,
a bouncy manager actually takes me around to see the rooms and
meet the current housekeepers, who, I note with satisfaction, look
pretty much like me—faded ex-hippie types in shorts with long hair
pulled back in braids. Mostly, though, no one speaks to me or even
looks at me except to proffer an application form. At my last stop, a
palatial B & B, I wait twenty minutes to meet "Max," only to be told
that there are no jobs now but there should be one soon, since "nobody
lasts more than a couple weeks."

Three days go by like this and, to my chagrin, no one from the
approximately twenty places at which I've applied calls me for an

---

[1]Eighty-one percent of large employers now require preemployment drug testing, up
from 21 percent in 1987. Among all employers, the rate of testing is highest in the South. The
drug most likely to be detected—marijuana, which can be detected weeks after use—is also
the most innocuous, while heroin and cocaine are generally undetectable three days after use.
Alcohol, which clears the body within hours after ingestion, is not tested for.

interview. I had been vain enough to worry about coming across as too educated for the jobs I sought, but no one even seems interested in finding out how overqualified I am. Only later will I realize that the want ads are not a reliable measure of the actual jobs available at any particular time. They are, as I should have guessed from Max's comment, the employers' insurance policy against the relentless turnover of the low-wage workforce. Most of the big hotels run ads almost continually, if only to build a supply of applicants to replace the current workers as they drift away or are fired, so finding a job is just a matter of being in the right place at the right time and flexible enough to take whatever is being offered that day. This finally happens to me at one of the big discount chain hotels where I go, as usual, for housekeeping and am sent instead to try out as a waitress at the attached "family restaurant," a dismal spot looking out on a parking garage, which is featuring "Pollish sausage and BBQ sauce" on this 95-degree day. Phillip, the dapper young West Indian who introduces himself as the manager, interviews me with about as much enthusiasm as if he were a clerk processing me for Medicare, the principal questions being what shifts I can work and when I can start. I mutter about being woefully out of practice as a waitress, but he's already on to the uniform: I'm to show up tomorrow wearing black slacks and black shoes; he'll provide the rust-colored polo shirt with "Hearthside," as we'll call the place, embroidered on it, though I might want to wear my own shirt to get to work, ha ha. At the word *tomorrow*, something between fear and indignation rises in my chest. I want to say, "Thank you for your time, sir, but this is just an experiment, you know, not my actual life."

So begins my career at the Hearthside, where for two weeks I work from 2:00 till 10:00 P.M. for $2.43 an hour plus tips.[2] Employees are barred from using the front door, so I enter the first day through the kitchen, where a red-faced man with shoulder-length blond hair is throwing frozen steaks against the wall and yelling, "Fuck this shit!" "That's just Billy," explains Gail, the wiry middle-aged waitress who is assigned to train me. "He's on the rag again"—a condition occasioned, in this instance, by the fact that the cook on the morning shift had forgotten to thaw out the steaks. For the next eight hours, I run after the agile Gail, absorbing bits of instruction along with fragments of personal tragedy. All food must be trayed, and the reason she's so

[2]According to the Fair Labor Standards Act, employers are not required to pay "tipped employees," such as restaurant servers, more than $2.13 an hour in direct wages. However, if the sum of tips plus $2.13 an hour falls below the minimum wage, or $5.15 an hour, the employer is required to make up the difference. This fact was not mentioned by managers or otherwise publicized at either of the restaurants where I worked.

tired today is that she woke up in a cold sweat thinking of her boyfriend, who was killed a few months ago in a scuffle in an upstate prison. No refills on lemonade. . . .

At least Gail puts to rest any fears I had of appearing overquali- 10
fied. From the first day on, I find that of all the things that I have left behind, such as home and identity, what I miss the most is competence. Not that I have ever felt 100 percent competent in the writing business, where one day's success augurs nothing at all for the next. But in my writing life, I at least have some notion of *procedure:* do the research, make the outline, rough out a draft, etc. As a server, though, I am beset by requests as if by bees: more iced tea here, catsup over there, a to-go box for table 14, and where are the high chairs, anyway? Of the twenty-seven tables, up to six are usually mine at any time, though on slow afternoons or if Gail is off, I sometimes have the whole place to myself. There is the touch-screen computer-ordering system to master, which I suppose is meant to minimize server-cook contacts but in practice requires constant verbal fine-turning: "That's gravy on the mashed, OK? None on the meatloaf," and so forth. Plus, something I had forgotten in the years since I was eighteen: about a third of a server's job is "side work" invisible to customers—sweeping, scrubbing, slicing, refilling, and restocking. If it isn't all done, every little bit of it, you're going to face the 6:00 P.M. dinner rush defenseless and probably go down in flames. I screw up dozens of times at the beginning, sustained in my shame entirely by Gail's support— "It's OK, baby, everyone does that sometime"—because, to my total surprise and despite the scientific detachment I am doing my best to maintain, I *care.*

The whole thing would be a lot easier if I could just skate through it like Lily Tomlin in one of her waitress skits, but I was raised by the absurd Booker T. Washingtonian precept that says: If you're going to do something, do it well. In fact, "well" isn't good enough by half. Do it better than anyone has ever done it before. . . . As in most endeavors I have encountered in my life, "doing it better than anyone" is not a reasonable goal. Still, when I wake up at 4 A.M. in my own cold sweat, I am not thinking about the writing deadlines I'm neglecting; I'm thinking of the table where I screwed up the order and one of the kids didn't get his kiddie meal until the rest of the family had moved on to their Key lime pies. That's the other powerful motivation—the customers, or "patients," as I can't help thinking of them on account of the mysterious vulnerability that seems to have left them temporarily unable to feed themselves. After a few days at Hearthside, I feel the service ethic kick in like a shot of oxytocin, the nurturance hormone. The plurality of my customers are hardworking locals—truck drivers, construction workers, even housekeepers from the attached hotel—and I want them to have the closest to a "fine dining" experience that the grubby circumstances will allow. No "you guys" for me; everyone over twelve is "sir" or "ma'am." I ply them with iced tea and coffee refills; I return, midmeal, to inquire how everything is; I doll up their salads with chopped raw mushrooms, summer squash slices, or whatever bits of produce I can find that have survived their sojourn in the cold storage room mold-free.

There is Benny, for example, a short, tight-muscled sewer repairman who cannot even think of eating until he has absorbed a half hour of air-conditioning and ice water. We chat about hyperthermia and electrolytes until he is ready to order some finicky combination like soup of the day, garden salad, and a side of grits. There are the German tourists who are so touched by my pidgin *"Wilkommen"* and *"Ist alles gut?"* that they actually tip. (Europeans, no doubt spoiled by their trade union–ridden, high-wage welfare states, generally do not know that they are supposed to tip. Some restaurants, the Hearthside included, allow servers to "grat" their foreign customers, or add a tip to the bill. Since this amount is added before the customers have a chance to tip or not tip, the practice amounts to an automatic penalty for imperfect English.) There are the two dirt-smudged lesbians, just off from their shift, who are impressed enough by my suave handling of the fly in the piña colada that they take the time to praise me to Stu, the assistant manager. There's Sam, the kindly retired cop who has to plug up his tracheotomy hole with one finger in order to force the cigarette smoke into his lungs.

Sometimes I play with the fantasy that I am a princess who, in penance for some tiny transgression, has undertaken to feed each of her subjects by hand. But the nonprincesses working with me are just as indulgent, even when this means flouting management rules—as to, for example, the number of croutons that can go on a salad (six). "Put on all you want," Gail whispers, "as long as Stu isn't looking." She dips into her own tip money to buy biscuits and gravy for an out-of-work mechanic who's used up all his money on dental surgery, inspiring me to pick up the tab for his pie and milk. . . . At Hearthside, we utilize whatever bits of autonomy we have to ply our customers with the illicit calories that signal our love. It is our job as servers to assemble the salads and desserts, pour the dressings, and squirt the whipped cream. We also control the number of butter pats our customers get and the amount of sour cream on their baked potatoes. So if you wonder why Americans are so obese, consider the fact that waitresses both express their humanity and earn their tips through the covert distribution of fats.

Ten days into it, this is beginning to look like a livable lifestyle. I like Gail, who is "looking at fifty," agewise, but moves so fast she can alight in one place and then another without apparently being anywhere between. I clown around with Lionel, the teenage Haitian busboy, though we don't have much vocabulary in common, and loiter near the main sink to listen to the older Haitian dishwashers' musical Creole, which sounds, in their rich bass voices, like French on testosterone. I bond with Timmy, the fourteen-year-old white kid who buses at night, by telling him I don't like people putting their baby seats right on the tables: it makes the baby look too much like a side dish. He snickers delightedly and in return, on a slow night, starts telling me the plots of all the *Jaws* movies (which are perennial favorites in the shark-ridden Keys): "She looks around, and the water-skier isn't there anymore, then SNAP! The whole boat goes . . ."

I especially like Joan, the svelte fortyish hostess, who turns out to   15
be a militant feminist, pulling me aside one day to explain that "men run everything—we don't have a chance unless we stick together." Accordingly, she backs me up when I get overpowered on the floor, and in return I give her a chunk of my tips or stand guard while she sneaks off for an unauthorized cigarette break. We all admire her for standing up to Billy and telling him, after some of his usual nastiness about the female server class, to "shut the fuck up." I even warm up to Billy when, on a slow night and to make up for a particularly unwarranted attack on my abilities, or so I imagine, he tells me about his glory days as a young man at "coronary school" in Brooklyn, where he dated a knockout Puerto Rican chick—or do you say "culinary"?

I finish up every night at 10:00 or 10:30, depending on how much side work I've been able to get done during the shift, and cruise home to the tapes I snatched at random when I left my real home—Marianne Faithfull, Tracy Chapman, Enigma, King Sunny Adé, Violent Femmes—just drained enough for the music to set my cranium resonating, but hardly dead. Midnight snack is Wheat Thins and Monterey Jack, accompanied by cheap white wine on ice and whatever AMC has to offer. To bed by 1:30 or 2:00, up at 9:00 or 10:00, read for an hour while my uniform whirls around in the landlord's washing machine, and then it's another eight hours spent following Mao's central instruction, as laid out in the Little Red Book, which was: Serve the people.

For Journals

What's the absolutely worst job you ever had?

For Discussion

1. What effect does it have on your reading of Ehrenreich's story, if any, that she can quit whenever she wants and do something else?

2. Describe Ehrenreich's work ethic; how similar to or different from her coworkers' attitude is it? What does she learn from them?

3. What are the biggest surprises Ehrenreich encounters from the time she embarks on this adventure?

For Writing

1. Write an essay in which you compare Ehrenreich's work experience in this article with that of the stonemason, Mr. Bates, earlier in this chapter. Obviously Mr. Bates loves his job and gets paid a lot more, but what cultural or social factors separate Ehrenreich's waitress work from his stone work? What are her sources of satisfaction as opposed to his?

2. In another selection in this chapter, "Office Politics," Ellen Lupton says that the feminization of secretarial work also lowered its status. Using Lupton's comments as a basis, write an essay in which you analyze the feminization of waitressing as presented in Ehrenreich's article. For example, how much does gender play a role in the way she is treated? Is there any evidence of blue-collar men being treated better? How does Stu, her boss, use his authority? What bonds do the women workers form with each other?

3. If you have ever had a job serving the public—sales, working in a food store, waiting on people, cleaning tables—write a reflective essay on the experience, on the people you worked with, and on how you felt about the customers and your boss.

❊❊❊ FROM *Sports Illusion, Sports Reality* (1994)

LEONARD KOPPETT

Leonard Koppett (1926–2003) was a sports reporter for the New York Times *and the* New York Post. *The author of ten books about sports, he was one of this country's greatest experts on professional and amateur sports, as well as sports journalism. He was a member of the writers' division of both the Baseball Hall of Fame and the Basketball Hall of Fame.*

The Poison of Amateurism

One concept peculiar to sports deserves condemnation.

It is called *amateurism.* Amateurism has been pumping a poisonous hypocrisy through American society for more than a century, and continues to do so. Almost all the harmful effects of the sports establishment can be traced to this misnamed "ideal." And it's a virus that touches everyone everywhere, even those who have no apparent connection to sports.

Amateurism, as it has come to be defined and interpreted by the worldwide sports community, is evil *in principle.* That amateur "rules" are widely violated in practice is generally accepted, with a wink, or a sigh, or indignation, or indifference. And it is also well understood that tolerating these violations is hypocritical. What is rarely considered however, is that the amateur ideal—if perfectly observed and policed—is incompatible with any decent modern society, especially American society. In many twentieth-century cultures, it is simply an inapplicable term. In others, where its definition can be put into some sort of correspondence with reality, it reflects and promotes concepts those very societies renounce.

In short, amateurism doesn't work anywhere; if it did work, it would be a bad thing; and since it can't work and shouldn't, institutionalizing its respectability (through the American school system, primarily) corrupts the intellect as well as the ethical sense. . . . Why make such a designation as "amateur" in the first place? And why consider it a virtue?

In ordinary usage, *amateur,* as distinguished from *professional,* connotes less proficiency. As Tevye says about poverty in *Fiddler on the Roof,* it's no disgrace, but it's no great honor, either. When we speak of a musician (or any artist) as an amateur, we don't imply moral superiority, or even praise. We are explaining the artist's status, either as a justification for lack of skill or as something to marvel at, if the skill is of professional quality. Do you know of anyone who prefers to be treated by an amateur doctor? Or defended by an amateur lawyer, before an amateur judge?

Note, incidentally, that this demarcation has nothing to do with talent. Professionalism is the cultivation of a talent through time, training, and dedication. An amateur may actually be more talented, in native aptitude, than a polished professional, but he or she hasn't developed that talent to the same degree.

In sports, unlike the arts, medicine, or law, the activity consists of pitting one competitor against another, for the express purpose of finding out which one will win. It would make admirable sense, therefore, to ensure fair competition by grading the participants, so that only those of reasonably equal abilities are brought together. And that's exactly what's done with weight classes in boxing or wrestling, age designations in Little League, major-league and minor-league affiliations among professional teams, and varsity and intramural distinctions in schools.

But what is the essential ingredient in developing athletic talent to the highest, world-class levels of proficiency? Time. Time to train, practice, concentrate, and gain competitive experience. So it would make perfect sense to separate amateurs from professionals on the basis of time and effort devoted to becoming proficient. The term *professional* itself signifies someone who has completed a rigorous, accepted program of preparation, and who makes the practiced activity his chief occupation.

But that is not how sports amateurism is defined. It is defined exclusively in terms of *remuneration*. . . .

The concept of sports organization, which didn't exist before the 1800s, and evolved in the England of Queen Victoria, wasn't pointless in the culture of that time. That was a time when "gentlemen" still didn't soil their hands with "commerce," if they could help it; when hereditary privilege was still the backbone of social status; when work performed for pay was considered vaguely degrading, if sometimes necessary; when affiliation to club or caste or family was still considered more important than personal worth or eccentricity.

It was also a time when the facilities and leisure time for sports activity were generally unavailable to ordinary or working-class people. The golf course, the running oval, the polo field, the cricket ground, the newly designed tennis court were the provinces of the upper class. (The working-class game was football—soccer—and it became openly professional without much fuss, throughout Europe and soon throughout the world.)

But athletic games are mastered by muscle, determination, reflexes, and alertness—commodities not restricted to "nice" people. In fact, since the lower classes were so much more numerous and generally less inhibited, they could certainly overwhelm club members if they could compete under equal conditions for any extended period of time. So elevating the lack of remuneration to a symbol of moral purity was in tune with the social climate; and it was very, very convenient. In plain language, it kept the riff-raff out. For a while, that is.

At this point, someone is sure to ask about the ancient Greeks and their ideals. The ancient Olympics, which inspired the modern Games, had no cash prizes and were also our model for democracy and citizen participation, weren't they? No, they weren't. Ancient Greek "democracy," where it did exist briefly, was a slave-based society that supported a small upper layer of citizens. Professionalism was plentiful in the ancient Olympics, and prizes of great value were heaped upon winners by their communities. (Even at Olympia, the promoters knew how to avoid putting up expensive awards themselves.)

In any case, the social forces of mid-Victorianism had nothing to do with American life, even then. But the practices and frames of reference that became codified in the financial definition of amateurism were grafted onto American culture too.

The messages embedded in such concepts can be paraphrased 15 thus:

- Since athletic excellence can be achieved only through full-time application, and since tangible rewards for the fruits of this effort are forbidden, there must be something wrong with honest pay for honest work.

- Since superior achievement is honored but cannot be rewarded directly (as it can for the artist or the surgeon), and since part-time effort can't achieve the goal, it must be all right to accept sponsorship, openly or covertly.

- Since everyone has to eat, and since only the "authorities" can determine whether you have complied with rules only the independently wealthy could live up to, it must be proper to lie (at worst) or pervert logic (at best) and stay eligible.

But what if every single individual in America were a paragon of integrity, and lies and subterfuge did not exist? Would we want a system that restricts competition to amateurs drawn only from a leisure class? That brands compensation for honest work as somehow dirty? That cheats a performer of a decent share of the tangible rewards his performances generate for those authorities who sell tickets and television rights, have salaried staffs, and share profits with ancillary businesses?

We would not want it, and we don't have it. In practice, everyone sees that value is given for value received in amateur sports. The high school athlete is rewarded with college admission he might not get otherwise—a ticket to upward mobility. The college athlete gets a free ride (worth thousands of dollars a year) and is in a position to obtain advantageous postgraduate opportunities through alumni and publicity. . . .

By subscribing to this definition, uncritically, American society has been infected with a debilitating disease. The entire school system, which forms the backbone of America's athletic programs, insists on an amateur posture. But the high school football or basketball star is perfectly aware of the tangible reward he is playing for: a free college education. And the college player knows he is getting it. His coaches know. And his teachers. And the school administrators. And his parents and family. And his nonplaying classmates. And his out-of-school friends. And all the neighbors and local businessmen who congratulate him on his athletic success. And he knows they know. And they know he knows.

A more pervasive institutionalization of hypocrisy is hard to imagine, and it is at work every single day, in millions of cases. The lesson is inescapable: It is all right to do one thing while professing its opposite. It's not only all right, it is warmly endorsed and fostered by the leaders of society and all the authority figures who fashion a child's values: parents, clergy, teachers, and government officials.

If you accept the idea that remuneration is O.K. when it is prop- 20 erly disguised, you cripple your moral sensibilities. If you accept the disguises at face value and say they are not really remuneration, you cripple your capacity to think straight. And for three generations, *everyone* who has been to school in America, not just the athletes, has been exposed to this moral flabbiness and intellectual dishonesty. The athlete, at least, earns his keep by actual effort, but everyone else sees—and enjoys and profits from, in many cases—the hypocrisy that is being accepted.

None of this, please note, involves *violations* of the serpentine rules. Those also abound, come to the attention of millions, and are usually accepted. When, in some particular instance, punishment is inflicted and self-righteous horror is expressed, the rarity and quixotic nature of the incident merely heightens everyone's perception of injustice. The violations, which can't be kept secret from those who participate in them, even if they are never uncovered officially, compound the problem but don't alter its basic nature.

The problem is that upholding amateurism as an ideal in an industrialized world guarantees daily indoctrination in false values. Work *should* be rewarded. World-class athletic performance, for the entertainment of millions of paying customers, is *work*. A privileged leisure class which could afford to play just for the love of it, is what Western civilization has been rejecting for the last two hundred years, in capitalistic countries no less than in socialistic ones.

In reality, there are millions of true amateurs playing sports everywhere—but not in front of ticket-buying audiences, for the purpose of mass entertainment. It's the deliberate confusion of two distinct functions—play and entertainment—that does the damage.

Why, then, does modern democratic society cling to the old definition? Cheap labor. The professional is controlled by whoever pays him: he must perform when and where and how the employer decides. But before he agrees, he can command a high price for his services (that is, a significant fraction of the income he generates for the promoter). The amateur, on the other hand, is controlled by *eligibility*. And that can't be negotiated. It's completely in the hands of the promoter—the school, club, IOC,[1] or whatever. To stay eligible, the amateur must accept what's offered: scholarship, books, room, training table, expense money, free equipment, lionization, promises, or even

---

[1]International Olympic Committee.

the products of cheating. These awards are substantial in themselves, but they add up to a smaller fraction of the promoter's budget than negotiated fees would.

Just as it suits the socialist world to have a no-money definition of 25 amateurism imposed on market-exchange societies, it suits school and amateur-sports authorities to have the same definition imposed on the performers they "hire" so indirectly. You couldn't get away with that if you presented it openly. If nothing else, the antitrust laws would get in the way, but aside from that, the illusion of glamour, which draws spectators, would be tarnished by acknowledged cheapness.

So the package is wrapped in high-sounding morality. Amateurs are presented as "pure," "noble," "disinterested in profit," and "motivated by love of sport." Professionals are grubby, greedy, commerce-soiled mercenaries. And of course professionals must never, never, *never* be allowed to compete against amateurs, because they would show up the amateurs for what they really are—less proficient—and would destroy the amateurs' gate appeal.

There is only one appropriate word for such a system: *sick.*

For Journals

Do you participate or have you ever wanted to participate in any team or individual sports? Do you consider yourself a fan? Why, or why not?

For Discussion

1. *Poison* is a very strong word to use. How does it fit Koppett's argument as he makes his case that amateurism, as it is practiced in America, is both hypocritical and unethical? Is the use of such a strong word justified?

2. In another part of his book, Koppett suggests that in a modern, affluent, high-technology society, watching sports provides a vicarious and pleasurable thrill without any personal danger. Do you agree? What are other reasons for watching athletes compete, either as amateurs or as professionals?

3. Koppett says that any sport pursued as the work of a lifetime is in fact work and should be rewarded as such. Does that explain the enormous salaries that professional athletes get paid? What other factors can you think of?

4. If you had a chance to go to college on a full athletic scholarship, what arguments could you make to justify your position to a nonathlete who had to work twenty hours a week to qualify for an ordinary scholarship?

For Writing

1. The old definition of *amateur* is "one who participates and always has participated in sport as an avocation without material gain of any kind." On the basis of Koppett's article, write an essay in which you either argue in support of this definition or make up a definition of your own. Incorporate your own experience as a spectator or as a participant.

2. Elsewhere in his book, Koppett notices the tendency of many writers to use sports metaphors in writing about topics that have nothing to do with sports, such as in business or politics: for example, X can't get to first base with that customer; Hertz is number one; the candidates are going for the knockout punch in their debate. Find a newspaper or magazine article that uses this kind of language, and rewrite it in terms that do not refer to sports at all. Either omit those terms altogether, or substitute typical terminology or slang from a different field, such as the military. Then write an assessment of how the change in language affects the tone and overall effect of the article.

3. Research and write a paper on one of the following topics: the decision to allow professional athletes to compete in the Olympic Games; the salaries of professional athletes; charges of corruption or payoffs in the National Collegiate Athletic Association; charges that steroids and drug supplements are taken routinely by athletes who want to compete on the highest levels. For your sources, check newspaper and magazine articles, the work of sportswriters such as Koppett or Roger Angell, and, if you have access to it, the Internet.

✳✳✳ *Sports, Body Image, and the American Girl* (2000)

KATIE NORRIS

Katie Norris is a California college graduate.

In the 1980s, a generation after the passage of Title IX and several Olympics in which young female gymnasts and ice skaters became media stars, there was a noticeable increase in sports participation by women. The athletic ability of female athletes began to be recognized, and young girls were encouraged to become more active in the sports organizations in their communities and schools. Since then, women's athletic programs around the country have thrived and successfully proven themselves as a popular pastime of nearly one-half of all females in the United States. Many of them enrolled in dance classes or softball teams by the age of five.

Once a girl reaches high school, the intensity of her particular sport increases and demands more time, exertion, money, and ability. Trying to balance school, social life, adolescence, and a high level of athleticism is difficult for a teenage athlete, and as a result, many girls do not give their bodies appropriate attention. Because of the importance of staying healthy, all female athletes participating in high school sports should be given mandatory seminars to educate them about how to properly care for themselves, and to learn the connections between their emotional and physical well-being.

In high school, many female athletes resort to ways of enhancing their athletic performance that have nothing to do with hard work. Soccer players, softball players, volleyball players, and basketball players are among the athletes who often take steroids to increase the production of male hormones, which give women larger muscles that allow them to hit the ball harder, run faster, or kick farther. However, increasing testosterone in a teenage girl will dramatically affect her female hormones and damage her for the rest of her life. Educating young woman athletes about the effects of these drugs have could prevent their use in the future by other women athletes.

Eating disorders are also a common occurrence among female athletes in sports that require grace, flexibility, and agility. In the past decade, sports such as gymnastics, figure skating, and diving have been reporting an increase in the number of girls who have developed anorexia or bulimia. The less you weigh and the less body fat you have, the better, according to coaches and trainers. Young girls are often so pressured to conform to their coaches' expectations and social peer pressure that they feel they have no choice but to starve themselves or regurgitate their food. However, if they had a person to guide them and teach them the right way to stay in shape, the number of female athletes with eating disorders would decrease. Many girls are just not well informed of the dangers of eating disorders and the long-term health risks. Teaching female athletes from childhood on how to take care of their active bodies will prevent them from resorting to unhealthy habits.

Girls who learn about the dangers of eating disorders or un- 5 healthy diet supplements will spread the word to other female athletes, as well as to younger girls, older girls, siblings, parents, and friends. The girls who are knowledgeable about healthy eating habits could act as informal peer counselors to other young women who are in danger. Seminars in high schools on health and body image, for example, are just one of the many steps that should be taken to inform young girls on how to value themselves and their health.

People who oppose this view believe that because female athletes are so consumed with their sports they fall into the body image issues that consume almost every teenage girl. These critics believe that an athlete does not need to be told how to maintain her body because her sport maintains it for her. However each sport requires a certain body type. Dancers are supposed to be slender and lightweight; gymnasts and figure skaters are supposed to be tiny and thin. Sports magazines often feature female athletes who both excel in their sport and have these body types. Teenage female athletes who read these magazines look to these women as role models, and quickly become the ones who are most at risk to develop eating disorders.

Another opposing view is that bringing in an expert on healthy body image to present a lecture to the female athletes would cost too much money and take up too much time. Proponents of this view feel that public high schools have too many other academic and athletic issues to deal with and that an extra seminar would not be worth the time and money. But if adding an extra seminar means reaching just one person and preventing her from making unhealthy choices in their life, don't you think it's worth it? That's much more important than a few extra dollars that would have been spent on some new soccer balls. In any case, schools would have control over hiring and paying a speaker, and deciding when and for how long the speaker should meet with the athletes. The meetings could be after school for a few days or during a couple of practices one afternoon. The time is minimal compared with what girls would learn. The information would help them make wise, healthy choices in their daily lives, and also help other girls around them who may see them as role models, in much the same way that the young female school athletes see athletes in magazines as role models.

Some people believe that the coaches are the ones qualified to inform girls about how to take care of their bodies and educate the girls on sport-related body issues. Softball, soccer, volleyball, basketball, and rugby coaches should give suggestions for body toning, strength enhancing, and mind and body coordination supplements, and dance, figure skating, and swim coaches should give suggestions for good weight loss techniques. This is a possibility. However coaches do not have PhDs in medicine or psychology; they are coaches and only know so much. More importantly, the coaches themselves may be the ones demanding and encouraging female athletes to attain a certain body type that's supposed to help them succeed in competition, regardless of what the girls have to go through and regardless of the negative long-term effects. Athletes need an outside influence to inform them of all their options and explain to them what products and techniques are beneficial or dangerous. An expert in the field of body-image issues can provide information in an unbiased way and can also be easier for an athlete to talk to than the coach who already judges and criticizes her. She'd be more comfortable talking to an objective outsider.

Adolescent teenage girls in high school sports deal with new pressures in their lives every day. Body image is just one more thing that they have to deal with. For an athlete, maintaining the right build, weight, strength, and flexibility are essential for excelling in sports. However, reaching that physical condition can be difficult, frustrating, and ultimately dangerous. When these girls grow older, they carry with them the side effects and aftermaths of what they did to their bodies. Many girls never recover from eating disorders, no matter how much counseling and medical help they've received, and the drugs and hormones that some girls take can alter their estrogen levels for life, preventing them from having children, and sometimes causing organ damage. No girls want these outcomes, and they would not decide to destroy their bodies if they really understood the consequences. But because many female athletes are unaware of the consequences, they treat their bodies badly and will continue to use harmful substances and techniques to enhance their athletic ability, or at least the body type they've been taught to admire. Teaching these young women how to deal with body issues and showing them the best ways to stay healthy will prevent an increase in substance abuse and eating disorders, thus keeping the future women of America healthier and happier.

For Journals

Have you or anyone in your family ever played in sports, like Little League, the elementary school soccer or hockey team, Pop Warner football, or any other organized children's sports? If not, what kind of less official play did you have as a child?

For Discussion

1. Restate Norris's main arguments in favor of educating young women athletes about staying healthy. Which do you find the most convincing, and why?

2. Davis also gives two opposing viewpoints. Do they seem more or less convincing than Norris's own argument? Why? What additional points could you make to strengthen them?

3. State your own version of Norris's thesis. Then come up with your own opening paragraph.

4. Look at a few contemporary magazines that focus on women's athletics. Pick several photographs of young women athletes in different sports who look to you like the ideal for that sport. For example, a woman basketball player, soccer player, gymnast, figure

skater, rower, swimmer. How would you describe the differences among them? Which ones seem to you the most or least attractive and/or healthy?

For Writing

1.   No image of the American young woman has been as powerful, as persistent, or as adaptable as the Barbie doll. Either go to a toy store, or check out the Barbie doll Web site, and examine the range of Barbie dolls available, including any professional sports Barbies. Write a paper in which you compare the differing images of young womanhood represented. Use the dolls themselves—their clothing, their accessories, their physical structure—as evidence for your comparisons. Alternatively, use Bratz dolls as a comparison of body types and feminine ideals.

2.   Anorexia and bulimia are unusually common among first-year female college students, and there is a great deal of literature on the subject. Research and write a paper about the available information on those illnesses at your own or a different school. Possible sources include campus health professionals, journal articles, and health information handed out to entering students.

✳✳✳ The Cost of High Stakes on Little League Games (2000)

C. W. NEVIUS

C. W. Nevius is a veteran sports columnist at the San Francisco Chronicle. *The following is one of a series of articles on the increased violence and the loss of control on America's playing fields; it was published on December 11, 2000.*

When he was 10 years old, Joseph Matteucci had a coach for his Castro Valley Little League team who was a "screamer." Joseph's mother, Alexandra, had concerns, but as a single parent she wanted to encourage her son to meet and play with other kids, so she didn't complain.

Another parent did not hold back however. In the parking lot after a game, he confronted the coach about the yelling at his son. The coach got out of the car and began throwing punches. The father went down in the barrage and when his wife rushed out to aid him, the coach slugged her too.

Joseph Matteucci, sitting in the car, saw it all and burst into tears. He quit Little League the next day. Alexandra Matteucci was relieved. Thank God she'd gotten her son out of that violent environment.

Six years later Joseph was dead.

An innocent bystander, he stopped by a spring Little League game 5 for 16-year-old players to pick up a friend. A brawl broke out after the game, the result of excessive taunting from spectators. A player swung a bat at one of his tormentors, he ducked, and Matteucci was hit in the back of the head. He died in less than 24 hours.

Some might call that 1993 incident a fluke, but the reality is the tragedy on that Castro Valley playground had all the elements of what has become an ugly trend in youth sports.

Violence has become commonplace on the fields of play in America, and the formula is simple, direct and brutal. Taunting from the sidelines escalates, coaches and spectators fail to quell the rising tensions, umpires or referees can not control the situation, and finally, rage boils over.

"Before it was coaches helping the kids who were having trouble controlling their emotions," says Jim Thompson, director of Stanford's Positive Coaching Alliance. "Now it is, 'Let's provide leadership to help the coaches control the parents.'"

The incidents of enraged parents are so out of proportion that they sound absurd. Orlando Lago, an assistant coach with the Hollywood, Fla., All-Stars, broke the jaw of umpire Tom Dziedzinski after a disputed call at third base in a Connie Mack game between high school teams.

Last January, police were called to a gym in Kirkland, Washing- 10 ton, when a heated confrontation at a wrestling match became so violent that a coach head-butted a parent and broke his nose. The wrestlers were 6 years old.

And the most shocking display took place in Reading, Mass., last July when Thomas Junta, a parent, beat to death Michael Costin, a hockey coach, at an ice rink. Junta, who was furious because he felt that Costin was allowing rough play, beat the coach to unconsciousness as his children begged him to stop. Junta, 42, has pleaded not guilty to charges of manslaughter.

But those are just the headlines. Anyone who has been to a youth sports game lately knows the truth. Parents are out of control. They scream at their kids, yell at the officials, and, in more cases than anyone would like to admit, something troubling happens.

Worse, every indicator shows it is becoming more common. Bob Still, spokesman for the National Association of Sports Officials, says his organization gets "between one and three" reports of physical assaults on an official each week.

"These are what we would call assaults as defined by law," says Still, whose organization has been tracking the numbers for 25 years.

"The verbal attacks have always been there. But people acting out, coming on the field, there is a definite trend to more violence."

Kill the ump? It isn't so funny. Still says it has reached the point 15 that in 1998 his association began offering "assault insurance" to its 19,000 members. The policy pays medical bills, provides counseling, and offers legal advice as to how to prosecute attackers.

It doesn't take much imagination to project the short term result. Would you want to be a referee in this climate?

"Finding referees is the single most important thing we have to deal with right now," says Bob Maas, president of Pleasanton's highly competitive Ballistic United Soccer League. "You get out there, some parent yells at you, and you think, 'You know, I am missing the 49er game right now.'"

But the referee shortage is the symptom, not the problem. Fueled by unrealistic expectations and an unhealthy obsession with winning, parents have gone from cheerleaders to taskmasters. Having invested large sums in clinics and private instruction for their kids, anything but success is unacceptable.

Alexandra Matteucci, who now runs the Joseph Matteucci Foundation (*www.jmf4peace.org*), was speaking to a group in Los Angeles when she heard a recent example. A mother, watching her son in a baseball game for 12- to 15-year-olds, was furious when her son was taken out.

"She went out and sat on second base and refused to move until 20 they put her son back in," Matteucci said. "They didn't know what to do, so they put him back in the game."

That kind of acting out may have worked in that case, but how many kids want their parent to become a laughingstock? The yelling, the gestures, and the intense pressure can drive even avid athletes out of organized sports.

"I can't tell you how many times I have heard kids say, 'Shut up dad!'" says Danville's John Wondolowski, whose under-11 soccer team won the State Cup last spring.

When dad won't pipe down, the next step is off the field. Many kids drop sports—an estimated 70 percent quit before they reach the age of 12—but some also find another outlet. Skateboarders, mountain bikers, and surfers are just part of an emerging X Games generation. There are fewer rules, less structure, and—best of all—dad doesn't know the first thing about it.

"That's the protection," says Positive Coaching Alliance's Thompson. "No adults. It is not hyper competitive. Fifteen or 20 years ago adults didn't know anything about soccer. Now you've got guys who think they know all about it. My son is into surfing, skating, and snowboarding. His point was: Do I want to stand in line, wait to bat, and have the coach yell at me? Or do I want to sit out in the ocean?"

A kinder, gentler approach was the idea behind "Silent Sunday" 25 last October in a Cleveland suburb. Coaches and parents in the 217-team league were told not to yell at the players, not even to cheer good plays. Was it hard to break old habits? Well, some parents, afraid they couldn't resist the temptation, put duct tape over their mouths.

Another soccer coach turned the tables on his parents. He put them on the field for a practice and let the kids scream instructions at them as they scrambled to kick the ball. Reportedly, the parents were ready for the exercise to stop long before the kids.

Are those the only choices? Do kids either have to drop out of sports or duct tape their parents' mouths shut?

Well no, there are options, proposed by groups like Thompson's PSA and the Matteucci Foundation. It begins with what groups like Ballistic soccer calls "zero tolerance" for attacks on officials, but more than anything it involves changing perceptions for parents.

"After all," says Thompson, "when you go to a spelling bee, nobody screams at the officials. It isn't done."

"We turn our heads," says Still of the Association of Sports Offi- 30 cials. "We say, 'I'm going to let it go. It is no big deal. Bill is a good guy, he just lost it that one time.'"

That, says facilitators like Matteucci, has to stop. A clear ethics code must be established before the season begins and the parents must go over it. Expecting them to read a handout isn't enough. Matteucci advocates reading the code aloud before every game.

Second, parents who get out of control need to be told so, and in a way that makes it clear that they are out of step with the entire group. And, if the coach, or some of the other parents, cannot calm the transgressor down, enforce the rules and call a forfeit.

"Call the game," says Matteucci. "If we do, life goes on."

But most important, parents need to monitor their level of involvement with an eye toward scaling it down. Chances are, their son or daughter is not going to get a college scholarship, or appear on a Wheaties box. In 10 years, the best you can hope is that the kids still enjoy staying physically active and look back fondly on their sports career.

What's fun about sports if you don't win? Thompson recommends 35 changing the goal. He worked with a soccer team that was so outclassed that it lost every game. Instead of winning, or even scoring, the team decided to make its objective to get the ball over midfield five times in one game.

When they finally did it, cheers rang up and down their sideline, puzzling the opposing parents.

"They were asking, 'What are they so happy about?'" Thompson said. "Aren't we beating them by eight goals?"

Yes, but they were playing a different game.

For Journals

When you were a child, what famous people were you interested in, and why did you admire them? Were any of them athletes?

For Discussion

1. Nevius says that the two examples he gives of killings at ordinary kids' ball games are not as extreme as they might seem. What evidence does he use to support that claim?

2. What do you think is at stake for the adults in these confrontations, and what kinds of effects could their behavior have on the children?

3. Nevius relates the story of a mother who sat down on the baseball field when her son was taken out of the game and who refused to get up until he was put back in. What better ways would you suggest of dealing with this situation and of defusing the rage of other adult nonparticipants?

For Writing

Leonard Koppett writes about how the professionalization of big-time college sports has made the idea of the pure amateur a bad joke, and Norris writes about the pressures on young girls to conform to particular body types, even at a risk to their health. Write an essay in which you compare what you believe to be the risks to young people posed by the first two articles with the risks to the children in Nevius's article. Which group do you see as being in the most danger? Why? Who is likely, in your opinion, to suffer the most long-term effects? And finally, for whichever group—college athletes, adolescent women athletes, and children on sports teams—that you see the most significant consequences, suggest your own remedies. Be as creative as you like; just try to find your own ethical solutions, even partial ones, to this growing problem.

✳✳ *The High School Basketball Coach* (2000)

JOHN ROWE, MARISA ROWE, AND SABIN STREETER, EDITORS

This is an interview from the book Gigs, *a contemporary tribute to Studs Terkel's many books interviewing Americans, and most similarly, his book* Working, *which is the source of the interview with Mr. Bates earlier in this chapter.*

High School Basketball Coach

James R.

I teach history and I'm the head varsity basketball coach at a Catholic high school in Pennsylvania. Teaching goes with coaching— the hours coincide. When the school day is done, that's when you practice. I'm not certified to teach or anything like that, but anybody can teach. You've got the book there—you just read it the day before and you memorize it and you—teach it, you know? I mean I graduated from college and stuff, so it's not hard. It's fun actually, I like it a lot. But what I'm here for is the coaching. The basketball.

I'm twenty-five. I went to high school in this area. Just a couple of towns away. Played four years of basketball and finished as my school's all-time leading scorer. I was all-county and then I got a full scholarship to a Division II school, which is a step down from Division I, but still it was a pretty good program. I did real well my freshman year—I was the first guy off the bench—backup point guard. I averaged about eleven points, four assists. Then my sophomore year, I became ineligible because of grades so I had to sit out a season. I ended up with like nine hundred and sixty career points, so I would've broke a thousand if I'd played all four years. And my senior year, I finished top five in the country in assists.

I thought about playing pro ball. [Laughs] Sort of. I mean, my coach talked to me about trying to go play in Europe and stuff, but I really didn't want to go over there. And I didn't want to play semipro. It's funny, but what I wanted to do—I just always wanted to coach. I think it was because, growing up, the people that I was always around and close with were coaches and I looked at what they did and thought, you know, I just want to be like that.

So after I graduated college, I moved back home to my parents' house and I got a job as the JV basketball coach at a public school near here. I was there one year and we did pretty well. Then I got lucky. 'Cause the next fall, the head coach of the varsity at this school I'm at now quit in September, which is two months before the basketball season starts. He was sick and had to retire. So I applied for the job. And I got it. I was only twenty-three at the time, but it's all about, you know, this is a pretty serious basketball school. They knew me from playing around here and I guess they liked me. [Laughs]

I think the kids were very happy to get a younger coach. I can talk 5 to them about stuff. Like I know what's going on, I listen to all the same music they do, you know? At the same time, when we're on the court, everything I tell them to do they listen, because a lot of them, when they were younger, they saw me play. So they respect me basketball-wise, so it works out pretty good. I mean, who would you rather play for—some sixty- or seventy-year-old guy who's got his own philosophies built in from the 1940s, or a young guy who's got some new approaches, some sharp drills, and is into the same stuff you are and knows exactly what you're going through with all your high school problems, you know what I mean? Like, I'll know when a kid comes in and is having a bad practice because he just got in a fight with his girlfriend in the hallway. So I won't go nuts on him that he's playing bad. I'll just say to him, "Hey look, I know you got problems with your girl or whatever, but you gotta put that aside for this time." Stuff like that. And kids respond.

My first year we finished fifteen and six. And we had some good players—I started some sophomores over some seniors, actually, which didn't make the seniors happy at first, but we won with those sophomores. We had the school's best record in four years. And it was fun because it was my first year, and I was kind of like just learning new stuff, but we didn't win the league, and I was thinking to myself, we were fifteen and six, which to me is average. We came in second in the league. We didn't make the Jamboree, which is the county tournament, we didn't make that. And I was like, you know, fuck this. We're a Catholic school—we can go and get whoever we want.

Because we can recruit, sort of. I mean, as a Catholic school, a kid can come here from anywhere. So I said to myself, there's no reason we should ever be bad. And I didn't think these sophomores were that good. So this year, I was like, fuck this—I went out and got a foreign kid from Finland, who is friggin' *real* good. Six-foot-two guard. A junior. And he really made an impact. We were twenty and five. We won the league—and we won a county tournament game for the first time in the history of the school. And I won coach of the year for the league, and area coach of the year from the local sportswriters association. Youngest guy ever to do both. Twenty-four years old. . . .

I brought this other kid on too last year, another junior, this kid from Philly, he's like six foot three, a black kid—so we brought him over, too. And he started and he played great. He's a real good student, so he wasn't fitting in too well over where he came from, cause that's just a wacked-out inner-city school. So I talked to him a little bit about coming. And he was easy. I said, "Hey, you'll get an opportunity to play, you'll end up going to college to play basketball, we got contacts." And he was just like, "All right, I'm definitely coming." But he had no money either, because his family was dirt poor, and he lives with just his mother. So we got him two in-school scholarships, and that pays for half, and then this other alumni guy pays the other half of his tuition. The two scholarships are straight-up—he applied for them, and he's a good student, so he got them. But the alumni guy, that's, you know—I don't even know if that's illegal or not. I don't think it would be—why would that be illegal? It's just helping a kid out by paying for his school.

So, you know, I brought in these two guys, these ringers, and we won like crazy. The other players were fine with it because they just want to be awesome. They all work their ass off, so they didn't have any problem with that. I don't know how the parents reacted because I don't talk to any of them. Parents are fucked up. They are. Because, like, everyone thinks their son is an All-American, right? So they all just scream at me during the game. They all think their son should be playing all the time. So they're yelling at me, "Why you taking him out now?!" They're yelling at me all the time. They never look at it fairly. It's always their son, their son, their son. But think about it—my team was twenty and five—we won the league! Obviously the people that are playing are getting the job done.

Actually, one set of parents did complain about the ringers specifi-   10
cally—the mother said to me—'cause her son was one of the sophomores that started my first year and got benched this past year—she said, "They had a perfectly good team and now you came and you gotta bring these two new players," and this and that. I was just like, "Well, things happen." But I should've told her, "Yeah, well it's because your son can't get it done at the level that I want him to." That's what I felt like saying. [Laughs] "Tell your son to make a jump shot and I wouldn't have to bring in these kids from Finland."

The school, the administration, they know about these ringers. They know how I got them. Everybody knows, I mean, because the people in the office, when I was coming in before school started last year—they were joking, saying like, "When are the ringers starting?" So everyone knows, but what are you going to do? It's what you've got to do to win. And everybody comes to the games. The priests come to the games. Everybody. They all fuckin' like winning.

The public school coaches, they all hate us. Catholic schools playing against public schools. "It's no fair—you guys can recruit kids—" This and that. But I say, you know what? Give me your job, then. Because I think public schools should have the advantage—because they already have all the kids in their town, and if they would just take over their recreation programs and start the kids out when they're young, then they could have kick-ass teams every year. Just start making those kids good from the time they're in third grade. And then your teams will be good, they'll have played together for years, they won't ever want to leave your town, and you won't have to worry about it.

But that's not the way it goes. So they hate us. . . .

With Catholic schools, you're never gonna have that hometown loyalty, you know? You gotta recruit. So I'm recruiting all the time. I'll probably go every Sunday night during the season to the local rec league games to see the seventh- and eighth-graders play. Then I'll probably go to three or four other games on Saturdays, over in Philly. It's nice—you just sit there and watch the games. The one kid that I wanted from Philly this summer, we got. He'll be a freshman this year. For him, I'd go to his games, and then I invited him to our open gyms and he came, so that's how we got him. This kid Josh—he's gonna be fuckin' good. This tough, five-ten Spanish kid guard.

If I see a kid I like, first thing I do is try to find out who the parent 15 is, and talk to them first. I'll say, "Hey, I coach at so-and-so high school. Your son's a very good player." And they'll say thank you. And then you've got to be careful, you don't want to screw yourself. So you've gotta say like, "Are you considering sending him to a Catholic school?" And if they say no, then you've just got to be like, all right. But most of them say yeah, because—to be honest—they kind of like it that somebody's coddling them a little bit. That's what I find. And the kids love it. They act like you're a college recruiter.

You can't be overt. You're recruiting, but you can't say that you're doing it, and you've got to do it in a way that's like—like you can't . . . send a kid a letter or anything like that. That's off the deep end. It's like, you'll get in trouble, I think. Actually, I don't know what the rules are. I have no idea. I mean I'll go up to kids and tell them that they're good and that they should come to—like we had a kid at camp this week, he's going to be an eighth-grader. I was hanging out with him for two weeks, and I'm trying to get him to come to our school. Because he said he might go to this other private school near here. And the kid's good, so I told him straight out, "Fuck that—you ain't going there. You don't wanna go there." He's black, and I was like, "There's no black kids there. You'll be hanging out with all Jewish kids and stuff like that, but we've got Spanish broads at our school, and everything else." [Laughs]

These kids think that's cool—they're like, "Oh yeah, yeah, yeah!" Then they go home and keep saying to their parents, "I want to go to—" you know, my school. So it gets to a point where the parents agree to come check us out. Then we'll show 'em around, and we've got a kick-ass development director who they'll have an interview with, and she'll lay out all the academic stuff. Because I don't know anything like that.

The one thing the parents always ask me, and I should learn it so I could give them an answer, is, they say, "What is the average SAT score?" I've got no idea. We had a kid on our team that got like a 1060 like two years ago, so I just always bring that up. I just say, Well, we regularly have kids that are in the thousands on our team, like 1060, 1100." [Laughs] That seems to impress them.

It's tough, though, because if you get caught you're screwed. My athletic director here has warned me not to get caught. Repeatedly warned me. And I don't know what will happen if I do get caught, but I take him seriously. And I've never gotten caught. . . .

I'm just really into it, I guess. I'm into it all the time. Right now, in 20 the summer, I work at a basketball camp in Philly—I do that from nine to four every day. And then my team plays in summer leagues, so at night I'll run to our summer league game. I get home at like ten-thirty every night. I talk to people, and they're like, "You're fuckin' crazy," this and that. Because in the summer I don't get paid by the school—I get paid by the camp, a tiny bit, but I coach my team at night and on weekends for free. But that's what you've got to do for your team to be good. Some people are like, "I don't understand why you do that if you're not getting paid for it." But you can't look at it that way. You have to look at it like coaching is always a full-year, everyday thing, if you want to be good.

And you have to want to be good. You have to want to win. I don't know what the point of playing is if you don't want to win, I mean, people talk about playing for fun. But what's fun is winning, you know? You're not doing anybody a service by losing. The kids sure as shit don't want to lose.

I win. And I work my ass off to win. That's probably why, fucking, I don't even have a girlfriend. 'Cause it's like, during the season if I have an early practice, then at night, I go to a game, scout a team. Even if it was a team that we don't have on our schedule, I go scout them 'cause maybe we could play in the county tournament; or in the state tournament. And I won't have a chance to scout them later. So during the season, regardless, I'm not home until ten o'clock. Then during the spring, same thing. I coach track, and a lot of my guys run track, then we have summer league, either practice or games every night. Plus all the recruiting. So it's definitely a committed thing. It's my commitment. . . .

The thing is, if you're into it and you put the time into it, kids notice. One of my kids said to me one time this summer, "You know, you're here every night, and none of these other coaches are here every night." And he said, "That's why we all come every night, because we know you're here." So you might not think that they notice, but all kids notice that stuff. It's almost like you have to look at it like a player—there's that old motto that every athlete has heard a thousand times: "Every minute you're not practicing, your next opponent is." It's that way for a coach, too. Every minute you're not preparing for your next opponent, that opponent is preparing for you. That's the way I look at it. . . . I just love what I'm doing. So as of now I just think about it like, I love it, so as far as I'm concerned, this'll be it for—forever. I don't care. I love it.

For Journals

When you were in high school, did you follow any high school teams? Are they a major source of community interest where you live?

For Discussion

1. If you've ever been a member of a team, what was your experience with your coach? How different from or similar to James R. was your coach?

2. What attitudes toward winning do you see reflected in this interview, not only in the coach, but in the administration, the parents, the priests, and the other students?

3. The coach brings in two ringers to improve his team; is this practice unethical to you, or sensible? How does he rationalize it? Does it matter that the school administration is in on it?

4. Is it necessary for him to know the SAT scores or to be honest with the parents to be a good coach? How much do James R.'s devotion, energy, and commitment count toward his overall success?

5. Why do you think he loves his job so much?

For Writing

1. Write a comparative essay using this interview and Studs Terkel's interview with Mr. Bates, the stonemason. Clearly both men love their work, but what do they have in common? How do they see their futures? What are they proudest of? Since these are interviews, you can use direct quotes; pick ones that you think are not only good evidence but characteristic of each man.

2. If you have ever played on a high school team, write a narrative in which you describe your coach, your perceptions of how effective he or she was, and why, and what you learned from the relationship, positive or negative. Alternatively, if you have ever coached students in a sport or tutored them, evaluate yourself as a teacher.

3. Choose what you think are the coach's central assertions about his job, and in keeping with them, write an essay in which you assess what his work ethic is.

✻✻✻ *Title IX —Two Views*

Title IX was first enacted in 1972 and was strengthened in 1988, when Congress passed the Civil Rights Restoration Act, which prohibits any educational institutions that accept federal money from discriminating on the basis of sex. Title IX says that "No person in the United States shall, on the basis of sex, be excluded from participation in, be denied the benefits of, or be subjected to any discrimination under any education program or activity receiving Federal assistance."

⁂ *What to Do with Title IX* (2002)

DAN GABLE

Dan Gable was an Olympic and a world champion wrestler. He coached the Iowa wrestling team to fifteen NCAA championships, and he has also coached three United States Olympic teams.

As a father of daughters who have participated in college athletics, I'm committed to fairness for females in sports. But reform is needed to address a fundamental imbalance that has resulted from Title IX interpretation.

When some hear the word "reform," they instinctively fear for the gains women have made. But reform is not about gutting Title IX. It is not about football or basketball programs. It is not about money or scholarships (although a federal commission is addressing these issues).

It is about how Title IX is being interpreted, especially "proportionality," one of the standards of compliance, which states the percentage of a college's varsity male and female athletes must mirror the percentage of the college's enrollment. Colleges were forced to conclude long ago that attaining proportionality in their athletic programs is the only way to be safe from lawsuits they cannot win.

The resulting so-called quota has had a devastating impact on men's sports. For example, if a college with an equal number of men and women offered nonscholarship track programs for its men and women, you'd think the standard of equal opportunity would be satisfied. Yet, if 46 men came out while only 30 women were interested, Title IX interpretation says women could demand the difference be made up elsewhere, i.e., with the addition of a tennis team of 10 members and a golf team of six.

The college then would have the choice of cutting 16 almost cost- 5 less male track members (called "squad capping") or spending a significant amount of money to start additional women's teams. What do you think a cash-strapped college would do?

Since 1990, more than 400 men's programs have been dropped. Proportionality has been particularly destructive to programs at relatively low-budget NCAA D-II and D-III schools.

Let's keep Title IX but get rid of proportionality. Or at least improve the equity of its application so all athletes—men and women—will have a fair opportunity to participate.

The Issue: In January 2002, coaching associations representing college wrestling, gymnastics, swimming and track filed a lawsuit against the Department of Education challenging Title IX's proportionality standard, which is one of three ways to show compliance with Title IX.

Where it stands: The lawsuit is pending in U.S. District Court. Meanwhile, a 15-member presidential advisory committee—the Commission on Opportunity in Athletics—is weighing what changes, if any, are called for in the enforcement of Title IX. The commission voted recently not to recommend eliminating the proportionality standard, instead offering modifications on how to define it.

Where it's headed: On February 28, the commission will send its 10 final recommendations to U.S. Education Secretary Rod Paige (who named the committee). The Department of Education then will decide what action, if any, to take on the recommendations.

For Journals

If you have any friends on college sports teams, or if you are on a team yourself, what is your opinion about Title IX?

For Discussion

1. The most important words in Gable's article are "proportionality" and "reform." What does he understand those words to mean? This legal language is crucial to any discussion of Title IX, so look for it in the context in which it is used. Whether or not you agree with him, you will need to think in his terms to do this.

2. What would you say are the basic assumptions about men's and women's teams under Title IX that Gable brings to his argument? Work with two or three other students in your class for ten minutes, and pool your conclusions; then report them back to the rest of the class. Remember that you are trying to figure out not what he says when he writes the article but what beliefs he brings to this subject beforehand.

3. Gable gives an example of what he says could happen in a college that has an equal number of men and women who are offered nonscholarship track programs and that has an unequal number of interested participants of both sexes. Is this example convincing to you as evidence for his argument? If so, why? If not, how could it be improved?

4. Are there any grounds in the article for assuming that Gable's stance on Title IX is affected by the fact that his sport is wrestling rather than, say, basketball or football? Or do you think that his ideas would be valid regardless of the sport involved? Why?

5. What do you think that the coaching associations that brought the lawsuit against the Department of Education to challenge Title IX would see as the ideal outcome if they won?

For Writing

1.   If you have Internet access to gateway sites such as Expanded Academic or Premier Academic, or if you can find the WomensSports Foundation, look up Title IX. Pick two or three of the articles with contrasting or conflicting points of view whose texts are given in full, and then use them to decide what your own argument is for how Title IX should be interpreted. Be sure that you note the strongest points against your case and that you deal with them rather than ignore them. Be particularly careful to avoid errors of logic like hasty generalizations, straw man, and false dilemmas (see Chapter 2). On the other hand, if you find those or other logical errors in the articles that you disagree with, feel free to point them out.

2.   Research the legislative background of Title IX. It's a primary source, and it will give you the three tests for compliance with its requirements. Write an essay in which you explain the three prongs, why proportionality seems to be the one that gets all the attention, and what you think would be the fairest way of applying the law. You can use the Gable and Hogshead-Makar articles as evidence for whatever side you take, but be sure to take the opposing view fairly into account.

✳✳✳ *The Ongoing Battle over Title IX* (2002)

NANCY HOGSHEAD-MAKAR

Nancy Hogshead-Makar won three gold medals and one silver medal in swimming at the 1984 Olympics. She is a member of he International Swimming Hall of Fame and is the founding director of a legal advocacy center for women in sport that focuses on legal issues surrounding athletic opportunities in high school and colleges, equal pay for coaches, and sexual harassment. She is a professor of law at Florida Coastal School of Law.

Title IX of the Education Amendments of 1972, the Federal law mandating gender equity in education, is under legal attack by a group of wrestling coaches who contend that its enforcement in athletics operates as a "quota" that discriminates against men. In 2002, the National Wrestling Coaches Association sued the U.S. Department of Education, contending that men's teams are being dropped not for school budgetary reasons, but because of women's lack of interest in sports that keeps men from being able to participate in the numbers their sex demands. In response, the Department of Education created an Orwellian-sounding Commission on Opportunity in Athletics, which could have been named the "Commission to Justify Taking Opportunities from Women." This hand-picked commission, weighted heavily against Title IX, was established to eviscerate the law's interpretive regulations via an end run around the courts, Congress, and the will of the people.

Having fought Title IX baffles over the past two decades as an athlete and an attorney advocate, I naively thought that certain tired, old, discredited anti–Title IX arguments would die a natural death. They haven't. Title IX remains as important today as when it was first enacted during the Nixon Administration in 1972.

The arguments against Title IX in the current debate are well-worn, having been raised and rejected time and again since the law was passed. Essentially, foes attempt to argue that Title IX is a quota, that it amounts to affirmative action, and that it discriminates against men. When Congress passed the current regulations in 1975, no fewer than nine amendments were introduced that would have weakened the law. Throughout the 31 years of Title IX's existence, Congress has heard from the law's detractors repeatedly, but it expressly rejected every attempt to curb its effectiveness.

In the 1980s and 1990s, these same arguments were heard before Federal appellate courts across the country. Every Federal appeals court that has examined this issue has upheld the regulations and concluded that Title IX does not constitute reverse discrimination and is not a quota law. It is difficult to find greater unanimity of judicial opinion on any topic.

Finally, critics try to persuade the general public that Title IX is to 5 blame for all the ills of athletic departments and that the law is forcing the hand of athletic directors. In fact, seven of 10 adults who are familiar with Title IX think the law should be strengthened or left alone, according to a USA Today/CNN/Gallup poll. The same results were found in an NBC/WSJ poll, even when the question was asked in the manner most likely to evoke a negative response—whether the respondent approved of Title IX when "many schools and universities have had to cut back on resources for men's athletic programs and invest more in women's athletic programs to make the programs more equal." Support for current legal interpretations of Title IX has come from more than 100 national organizations, as well as from the Executive Committee of the National Collegiate Athletic Association.

Foes of the law often rest on the stereotypical and flawed belief that women are less interested in sports than men. They point out that women participate at lower rates as justification for providing them with fewer opportunities, but that only makes the case for Title IX. The data show that, as opportunities are created, women fill them. Fewer opportunities in athletics exist for women because of the persistent discrimination against them, not lack of interest. About 2,800,000 high school girls, or one out of every 2.5, are athletes, and roughly 170,000 women are participating at the collegiate level.

Let me make this personal. I would not have become a world-class swimmer without the opportunity as an 11-year-old to be in a swimming program in my community. I would not have earned a full college scholarship without a school offering me one. This is not a "chicken or egg" conundrum: Creating opportunities creates interest and participation.

Women's sports are only now starting to realize the promise of Title IX, a promise the Commission and others would renege upon. While women have moved to fill sports opportunities in dramatic fashion as schools have created them, Title IX still is needed to prevent and remedy the serious discrimination that exists against women in athletic departments.

According to a 2002 General Accounting Office (GAO) report, men's sports overall enjoy the overwhelming share of opportunities and resources and do not need special Federal civil rights laws of protect them. After 31 years of Title IX and despite women in Division I-A colleges representing 53% of the student body, women currently receive 41% of the opportunities to participate in sports, 43% of the total athletic scholarship dollars, 32% of recruiting dollars, and 36% of operating budgets. While some men's sports have declined, some women's sports have shown drops, too. Men's gymnastics has lost 56 collegiate programs; women's gymnastics has lost 100. Although some men's sports have declined, others have increased dramatically. True, 180 men's wrestling programs have been dropped, but 120 new men's soccer teams have been added. When all gains and losses were tallied, men's sports showed an overall gain in participation—both in the number of teams and number of participants. . . .

None of the proposals would reinstate any of the dropped 10 wrestling programs. When Title IX was weakened in the *Grove City v. Bell* decision in 1984, wrestling continued to lose opportunities at an even greater rate than it is currently. The Commission's proposals would simply allow universities to perpetuate the trend of shoveling money into men's football and basketball at the expense of women's sports—a result that Congress and the courts expressly have rejected time and again. Indeed, Title IX is designed to guard against just this sort of gender discrimination in athletic budgets and resource-allocation decisions.

Secretary of Education Roderick Paige then pledged to consider only "unanimous" recommendations, but his refusal to accept the minority report by making it part of the public record makes his pledge ring hollow. Commissioners Julie Foudy and Donna de Varona explicitly dissented from two of the recommendations to which they had initially agreed and expressed concerns about the wording and interpretation of others. Without considering the minority report, as well as the full views of other commissioners, none of whom were given an opportunity to vote on the final report, the Secretary cannot credibly claim to be determining where true unanimity lies. . . .

Advocates for men's and women's sports alike agree that opportunities to participate in sports yield much more than the substantial life-long health benefits of running around a field or swimming up and down a pool, maintaining that participation in sports is an important educational experience. A Nike shoe commercial in 1995 aimed at girls stated: "If you let me play, if you let me play sports, I will like myself more; I will have more self-confidence. If you let me play sports, if you let me play, I will be 60% less likely to get breast cancer; I will suffer less depression. If you let me play sports, I will be more likely to leave a man who beats me. If you let me play, I will be less likely to get pregnant before I want to. I will learn what it means to be strong, if you let me play." The male wrestlers also express the sentiment in their motto: "Wrestling: Training for the Rest of Your Life."

The purpose of Title IX is to make discrimination based on gender in education and athletics unlawful. It is not designed to protect sports or any particular men's or women's sport or team. Title IX does not prevent schools from abandoning the educational mission of athletics, and it cannot stop schools from deciding to drop a men's team or, indeed, its entire athletic department. It does not give pretext to schools that make indefensible decisions. The law is limited to providing boys and girls, men and women, with educational experiences equitably.

It has not taken long for people to see the Department's report for what it is—an attempt to circumvent the will of Congress, the courts, and the public. The latter overwhelmingly support Title IX. Like the emperor's new clothes, the Department's report is a transparent attempt to undermine the gains that women in sports are only starting to realize.

For Journals

Do you watch big-team sports like basketball and football? Have you ever gotten interested in any of the less famous ones, like fencing, lacrosse, or any intramural sport?

For Discussion

1.   The author refers in her article to the lawsuit brought by small sports teams against Title IX and supported by Dan Gable in the previous article. What evidence does Hogshead-Makar use to counteract Gable's belief that Title IX institutes a quota that hurts small men's team sports like wrestling?

2.   Why do you think that the author puts such emphasis on previous attacks on Title IX that have all been defeated. Since that is no guarantee of future success, why does she want that on the record?

3.   What specific appeals to logic and emotion does Hogshead-Makar make in this article? Which, to you, are the most convincing?

4.   Hogshead-Makar includes quite a bit of statistical evidence here; does that strengthen any of her points, in your mind? Is it extraneous? Would you find anecdotes about the experience of individual athletes or teams more convincing?

For Writing

1.   Relying entirely on Gable's and on Hogshead-Makar's texts that you have before you, write a paper in which you compare their arguments in terms of the following: background material; appeals to ethos, pathos, or logos (see Chapter 2); and convincing weight of the evidence. In the process of this evaluation, you will inevitably decide whether there are gaps in either argument, whether they address each other's strong points or ignore them, and whose case is better.

2.   If you had no opinion on Title IX to begin with, what is your opinion now? If you had ideas about it, did they change any? Write a reflective essay in which you explain where you started on this issue—anything form complete ignorance to strong feelings—and where you are now. Use individual points in each writer's article as support for your thinking.

3.   Both writers competed as amateurs and speak idealistically about the benefits of college athletics. Write a critical examination of the claims about sports benefits in either Title IX article, using Koppett's article about corruption in college athletics as a counterweight. Who would prefer Koppett's article, Gable or Hogshead-Makar? Would his argument apply no matter what sport was involved?

❀❀❀ *Film: Jerry Maguire* (1997)

Jerry Maguire is a film about a sports agent who, in a tired moment, writes an unexpectedly honest memorandum about how hypocritical and greedy his profession has become. As a result, he is fired by his employer and deserted by all but one of his clients—a mediocre football player who provides him with one last chance to truly help and inspire an athlete and redeem himself. (126 minutes)

For Journals

Does this film give you a higher or lower opinion of professional sports? What did you think before you saw this film, and on what were you basing your opinion?

For Discussion

1.   What image of sports agents does the film communicate, particularly in the scenes at the office after Jerry sends around his mission statement? What do you think a sports agent is supposed to do?

2.   Jerry Maguire can't express intimate feelings but is good at his job, and Rod Tidwell is good at personal intimacy but not so good at his job. What scenes in the film are crucial, in your opinion, to the gradual change in both men? How do they affect and help one another?

3.   In what ways does this film portray sports as a business? What and who are marketed? What does success mean in this context? Look for specific scenes or exchanges of dialogue to prove your point.

4.   The most famous line in this movie is "Show me the money!" But the end of the film is more sentimental than financial in impact. How well does the director lay the groundwork for this change? In what scenes does he prepare us to accept a kinder, gentler resolution of the problems that the movie raises? Where, in particular, do you see Jerry Maguire changing his behavior?

For Writing

1.   Watch the movie *Field of Dreams,* and write an essay in which you analyze at least two of the following issues: the pure pleasure of sport; baseball as the ultimate game of American mythology; nostalgia for an earlier America that we think was simpler than the America we now live in; the powers of memory; and impractical idealism versus cold business practices. Look for scenes in which these issues appear, and examine them for crucial dialogue or character development. Give specific examples from them as evidence for your conclusions.

2.   The salaries of major league sports figures are much higher, even for average professional athletes, than they were ten years ago. In fact, Rod Tidwell's successful bid for a higher salary from his team would no longer be considered a great deal. Research and write a paper explaining the causes and effects of the enormous jump in major league salaries in either baseball or football. To find a range of facts and opinions, check the writings of Leonard Koppett, Roger Noll, Harry Edwards, or any other sports expert who has written extensively about the issue. Also, use the Internet to locate other articles on this subject.

Chapter Writing Assignments

1. Why do people work? Or more specifically, why do you, or will you, work? After brainstorming, reading, discussing, and recollecting some of the points made in class and in your readings, develop a core assertion as to the meaning, value, or purpose of work—to people in your family, to people of a certain class, and to people of a certain ethnic culture or gender. Avoid vague generalizations. Focus on a specific assertion, and offer strong support for it.

2. Research advertisements or political cartoons from times gone by—from nineteenth-century publications to back issues of *Life* or other popular magazines from the 1940s. Analyze the values implied and the assertions made about work or play in the images. Alternatively, view one or two television comedies from the 1950s and 1960s, and analyze the values, assumptions, and assertions they convey, particularly those about work and gender, or play and gender.

Web Sites for Further Exploration

Benjamin Franklin

http://earlyamerica.com/lives/franklin/
www.pbs.org/benfranklin/

Charlotte Perkins Gilman

http://www.cortland.edu/gilman/

Studs Terkel

www.studsterkel.org/
www.grandtimes.com/studs.html

Alfred Lubrano

www.bhny.com/pow/POW011.html

Barbara Ehrenreich

www.well.com/user/srhodes/ehrenreich.html
www.nickelanddimed.net/

Leonard Koppett

www.baseballlibrary.com/baseballlibrary/
    ballplayers/K/Koppett_Leonard.stm
www.paloaltoonline.com/paw/paonline/
    news/2003_06_23.koppett23.shtml

Title IX

comp.internet.net-happenings

9

✢✢✢

Justice and Civil Liberties

Every morning, millions of American schoolchildren recite the pledge of allegiance to the flag, which ends, "With liberty and justice for all." That phrase refers to more people today than it has in the past; today it includes women, children, ethnic minorities, the aged, and the disabled. This is a country proudly self-conscious that its political system was established to be something new, that it offered a readjustment of rights and privileges more profound than anything that had ever been attempted before. As a result, standards and expectations for justice and civil liberties have always been higher here, at least in theory, than anywhere else.

Given our ideals, however, the fact that for 250 years African Americans were bought and sold like furniture could not be easily explained, nor could the denial of their civil rights into modern times. So, more often than not, a consideration of social justice in America starts with racial justice.

Many of the high and low points associated with racial justice involve attempts of whites to deny or to correct past wrongs, and the attempts of African Americans to claim the promise of liberty and the American dream from which they had been excluded. At times, individual leaders—like Frederick Douglass—have taken upon themselves the role of spokespersons and protest leaders. Their job has been simultaneously to educate white Americans about the everyday injustices in African American life and to organize their constituencies to effect change.

The fact that laws did not change quickly or that the laws did but attitudes did not, has led to a continuing and sometimes violent debate over what justice is, who is entitled to justice (and how much), and whether there is a way to compensate citizens for past wrongs. These issues raise profound questions for Americans about the depth of their commitment to ideals of freedom, opportunity, and political participation.

Race is not the only social struggle in America. As the definitions of justice and freedom became gradually more inclusive in the nineteenth century, one of the offshoots of the first struggle for civil rights was the increased consciousness in other segments of the population that they too were discriminated against. Foremost among these other groups were women—mostly white and middle-class—who began organizing for the right to vote. Many of them had been abolitionists, and they turned the self-confidence and political skills they had honed during the fight against slavery to the fight for universal suffrage.

In Victorian America, however, constrained expectations of women as domestic goddesses who knew their place (at home with husband and children) meant that most men and many women were horrified by the open political participation of women and criticized them for being disobedient, unfeminine, and threatening to the status quo. Like African Americans who demanded to be treated equally, the suffragists were viewed as unnatural and ungrateful deviants from the norm who had forgotten their traditional virtues of deference and meekness.

In recent decades the gay rights movement has gained considerable momentum, though its members too have often been castigated as deviants from the norm who should stay in their place and not demand equal rights. Although gays have essentially secured civil liberties in arenas such as housing and employment, the ongoing debate about their presence in the armed forces indicates that the struggle is not fully resolved.

Indeed, complete civil liberties for ethnic and sexual minorities and women are still a long way from being assured as the twenty-first century begins. Unpopular causes and new ideas frequently make audiences angry, and although we all demand the right to say what we want, we are better at defending the speech of people who agree with us than that of people we think are wrong, misguided, extreme, disloyal, or simply very different. Fortunately, however, at all points in our history, this country has been graced by the presence of Americans who have been willing to stand up—by themselves, if necessary—to defend the civil liberties in which they believed, particularly the freedoms of speech and press guaranteed by the First Amendment to the Constitution.

Justice and Civil Liberties through History

The writers and artists in this chapter all engaged in an ongoing argument in which the interpretations about the extent of civil liberties and the meaning of justice in America have varied wildly. The values in question were established first in the Declaration of Independence in 1776, then in the Constitution and the Bill of Rights in 1787, in the subsequent amendments to the Constitution, in two hundred years of legal decisions, in reform movements and political debates, in the trauma of a Civil War in which 618,000 Americans died at each other's hands, and in the words and lives of individuals who have made civil liberties and justice their personal business.

The men who dominated the American Revolution do not fit the popular image of revolutionaries. They were not poverty-stricken peasants revolting against an insensitive aristocracy but established, educated, and powerful men—plantation and slave owners, ship-builders, businessmen, doctors—whose earliest and even adult loyalties were to England. Over time, however, for a complex of reasons both political and economic, they had come to feel capable of managing their own government; finally, they began to think of themselves differently—as Americans. But if they were not radical in the traditional sense, their great contribution to political history, a representative democracy headed by an elected leader, was a radical political development; and its first major expression, the Declaration of Independence, is a remarkable document. Like the Constitution that followed it eleven years later, the Declaration is written with such foresight and flexibility that it has stretched to accommodate the needs of later generations and previously excluded constituencies. Much of subsequent American political argument refers back to it or to its promise. Whenever the subject of justice, equality, and civil liberties comes up, either the phrases of the Declaration or the spirit—or both—hover over the discussion. For example, in the years before the Civil War, issues of equality and freedom were slowly if inexorably working their way to the forefront of American political consciousness, and some Americans were more sensitive than others to the impossibility of supporting slavery in a growing democracy with continental ambitions. Among those Americans were Henry David Thoreau and Frederick Douglass. Examples of their work in this chapter are, to differing degrees, early warning signals for the conflagration of the coming Civil War. Henry David Thoreau had a direct sense of the evils of slavery, and he interpreted the Declaration not only as an ideal for collective rebellion against injustice but as an injunction to every single American to heed his or her conscience, even if that meant disobeying the government. Thoreau's most famous piece on dissent, *Civil Disobedience*, which first appeared in 1849, has been a prod to American complacency and self-satisfaction ever since.

Thoreau spoke publicly against slavery because he was an abolitionist—a member of the movement that campaigned for the immediate end to slavery. The abolitionist movement was considered a collection of radicals by most Northerners, and it was never a large movement, but like all other campaigns, it depended on good speakers to attract attention, audiences, and public support. Thoreau was not in the same class as Frederick Douglass as an orator—nobody was—although he was once called upon to substitute for Douglass at a meeting in Boston.

Douglass, a former slave and a brilliant activist and writer, also had a charismatic presence as a speaker. At a time when audiences went to hear great orators as a form of entertainment as well as education, Douglass could completely enthrall an audience for as much as two hours. He was not the only escaped slave who became an active speaker on the abolitionist circuit, but the combination of his own extraordinary story with his intelligence, his appearance, his voice, and his passionately articulated message about slavery made him the most sought-after and successful speaker. Even some white abolitionists were sometimes uneasy around a black man of such brilliance and independence. At one point it was actually suggested to him that he dumb down his diction on the grounds that it was too good to be believable as that of a former slave. His powerful intellect and emotion come through intensely in his 1851 Independence Day speech in Rochester, New York, in which he forcefully reminded his white audience of the meaninglessness of the phrase "all men are created equal" for Americans who were enslaved.

Once the Civil War was over, racial division remained, but the political energy that had previously been concentrated on the abolition of slavery began to find its way into other protest movements, particularly the movement for women's right to vote. The intellectual leader and spokesperson of the suffrage movement, Susan B. Anthony, gave her famous speech, "Women's Right to Vote," after she was arrested for trying to register to vote in a presidential election. Like Douglass, also a supporter of women's rights, she was adept at turning the language of the Declaration of Independence and the Constitution back on her audience to prove her point.

By 1896, all the southern states had passed segregation laws against African Americans for the explicit purpose of undoing the civil rights they had won as a result of the Civil War, especially the Thirteenth, Fourteenth, and Fifteenth Amendments to the Constitution, which ended slavery and granted equal protection under the law and the right to vote. The Supreme Court undermined those amendments when, in 1896, it sided with the state of Louisiana in a case called *Plessy v. Ferguson* and declared that black Americans who were forced to ride in separate train cars from whites were not being deprived of equal protection under the law. This is what became known as the "separate but equal" doctrine. Technically, the *Plessy* decision applied only to railroads, but its real effect was to institutionalize segregation in every area of southern public life: transportation, restaurants, beaches, churches, schools. The lone dissenter to the Court's ruling in

Plessy was Justice John Harlan, a former slave owner who foresaw the tragic consequences of the decision very clearly.

The Supreme Court's interpretation of any case becomes the law of the land, until or unless the law changes or the interpretation changes. In the case of *Plessy*, the worst effects of segregation continued to make themselves felt everywhere in the ordinary experience, the psyches, and the economic suffering of African Americans in the South.

Roughly half a century, two world wars, and a Depression after *Plessy*, Justice Harlan's lonely dissent was finally vindicated in what is probably the most famous Supreme Court decision of the twentieth century, *Brown v. Board of Education* (1954). In *Brown*, the Warren Court declared, in an unusual unanimous decision that the "separate but equal" standard approved in *Plessy* is a contradiction in terms. Like *Plessy*, *Brown* was technically about only one kind of public segregation—in this instance, public schools. Like *Plessy*, however, it had a domino effect: the outlawing of segregation of children at school began, slowly, to dismantle legalized segregation in the South.

One of the distinctive characteristics of the case is that the Court decided to consider the intangible effects of segregation on African American children. To that end, it considered the results of a study by a distinguished sociologist who had used black dolls and white dolls as indices of self-esteem when he interviewed young African American children in the South shortly before the case came up for judgment. Most of the children favored the white dolls as the good dolls over the black dolls. That was not a new development, though. Twenty years earlier, in the 1930s, during the worst days of segregation as well as the Depression, Eudora Welty, a white Mississippian who would go on to write some of the greatest short stories about the South, took a series of photographs for a federal government project in rural Mississippi. One of them is reproduced here: a photograph, called "Dolls," of two little African American girls, wearing their Sunday-best clothes and clutching two white dolls. In this picture Welty condenses the effects of the prejudice that the Supreme Court would eventually confront in legal terms into one understated but powerful image.

But resistance to integration was fierce, and change was irregular and slow, opposed at every step by southern legislatures, governors, sheriffs, and private citizens who met peaceful efforts to integrate public facilities with hatred and often violence. The medium through which most Americans became acquainted with southern segregation and the civil rights movement was television. Pictures of police turning water cannons or attack dogs on unarmed marchers, including elderly men and women, or on college students asking for service at a lunch counter or a drink of water at a fountain marked "WHITES ONLY," made a powerful impression on Americans who had never been south of the Mason-Dixon line and whose only image of the South probably came from watching *Gone with the Wind.*

Martin Luther King, Jr., the young Baptist minister from Atlanta who had already become the leading spokesman of the civil rights movement—sometimes to the irritation of other local leaders who resented how much of public attention was directed at him—was frequently arrested. During one incarceration in Birmingham, Alabama, King took the opportunity to respond to some of his critics, who had taken out an advertisement in the local paper criticizing him and his followers. Ironically, these particular opponents were not Ku Klux Klan members or other white supremacists but southern clergymen—and mostly black clergymen at that, who had reached a kind of unacknowledged accommodation with the status quo and were afraid that King's entrée would upset the apple cart. King's answer, "Letter from Birmingham Jail," not only attacked what he perceived as the failure of these clergymen to lead their flocks but also immediately became an unofficial primer for the ideology of nonviolent resistance.

In the 1970s and later, a whole new series of arguments about justice and individual rights arose: for or against the Vietnam War, a new wave of the feminist movement, sex education in schools, gays in the military. In "What Is Hate Speech?," attorney and gadfly Alan Dershowitz defends the right to obnoxious freedom of speech. Probably one of the most incendiary civil liberties issues to emerge in recent years is the question of what can and should be allowed on the Internet. Student Vickie Chiang addresses this problem through a really interesting prism: adults who want the Internet access in libraries filtered to protect children from pornographic or obscene Web sites come into conflict with the free exchange of ideas and the First Amendment. How can all of these needs and rights be protected? On a related and more clearly commercial Internet issue, "Whatever Will Be on the Internet Will be Free" explores downloading music from the Internet and its civil rights consequences. What both these articles really attempt to assess, though, is the conflict between a technology that has become necessary, laws that evolve much more slowly through courts and legislation, and the fact that our views on who is entitled to freedom of speech tend to depend on where we're standing.

Our film, *To Kill a Mockingbird,* is a southern woman's story of a classic southern horror—a black man in 1930s Alabama being unjustly accused of rape, and a white lawyer, Atticus Finch, who defends him. What makes this story different is that it is told through the eyes of Scout, Finch's eight-year-old daughter, whose child's directness enables her to observe a tragic situation that her elders are far too mired in traditional prejudices to see clearly.

As long as Americans continue to believe in the ideals of the Declaration of Independence and the Constitution, they will recognize, intermittently and with considerable discomfort, that justice and civil liberty are easy to support but hard to practice. The tension between equality and conformity, individuality and difference, can lead to prejudice. Americans do not always welcome the artists, writers, or political leaders who remind them of the American promise or of how much they have fallen short. The perpetually recurring question is how to make our potential actual, not once, but over and over again in the light of each generation's experience. Despite our frequent mistakes, overt cynicism, philosophical laziness, or failure of will, the underlying principles survive, independent of us yet depending on us to give them shape.

✵✵✵ *The Declaration of Independence* (1776)

THOMAS JEFFERSON

The author of the Declaration was thirty-two-year-old Thomas Jefferson (1743–1826), who could, in the words of a contemporary, "break a horse, play the violin, dance the minuet," and of whom the usually acerbic John Adams said, he had a "reputation for literature, science, and a happy talent of composition. His writings were remarkable for their felicity of expression." Jefferson was, in succession, a member of the Continental Congress, governor of Virginia, ambassador to France, the first secretary of state, vice president, and then president for two terms, during which he authorized the Louisiana Purchase, doubling the size of the United States. He founded the University of Virginia; designed it and his home, Monticello; and collected the books that formed the basis for the Library of Congress.

In 1962, when President Kennedy invited a group of Nobel Prize winners to dinner, he said that it was the greatest concentration of intellect in the White House since the evenings when Thomas Jefferson dined there alone. Jefferson died on July 4, 1826—fifty years to the day after the signing of the Declaration of Independence. In the text that follows, the underlined words and phrases were in the first draft but were removed in the final draft. The words and phrases in the margin are those that appeared in the final version.

A DECLARATION BY THE REPRESENTATIVES OF THE UNITED STATES OF AMERICA, IN GENERAL CONGRESS ASSEMBLED.

When in the course of human events, it becomes necessary for one people to dissolve the political bands which have connected them with another, and to assume among the powers of the earth the separate and equal station to which the laws of nature and of nature's God entitle them, a decent respect to the opinions of mankind requires that they should declare the causes which impel them to the separation.

We hold these truths to be self evident: that all men are created equal, that they are endowed by their Creator with <u>inherent and</u> un- certain alienable rights; that among these are life, liberty, and the pursuit of happiness; that to secure these rights, governments are instituted among men, deriving their just powers from the consent of the governed; that whenever any form of government becomes destructive of these ends, it is the right of the people to alter or to abolish it, and to institute new government, laying its foundation on such principles, and organizing its powers in such form, as to them shall seem most likely to effect their safety and happiness. Prudence, indeed, will dictate that governments long established should not be changed for light and transient causes; and accordingly all experience hath shown that mankind are more disposed to suffer while evils are sufferable, than to right themselves by abolishing the forms to which they are accustomed. But when a long train of abuses and usurpations, <u>begun at a distinguished period and</u> pursuing invariably the same object, evinces a design to reduce them under absolute despotism, it is their right, it is their duty to throw off such government, and to provide new guards for their future security. Such has been the patient sufferance of these colonies; and such is now the necessity which constrains them to <u>expunge</u> their former systems of government. The history of the present king of Great Britain is a history of <u>unremitting</u> injuries and usurpations, <u>among which appears no solitary fact to contradict the uniform tenor of the rest, but all have</u> in direct object the establishment of an absolute tyranny over these states. To prove this, let facts be submitted to a candid world <u>for the truth of which we pledge a faith yet unsullied by falsehood.</u>

alter

repeated

all having

He has refused his assent to laws the most wholesome and necessary for the public good.

He has forbidden his governors to pass laws of immediate and pressing importance, unless suspended in their operation till his assent should be obtained; and, when so suspended, he has utterly neglected to attend to them.

5

He has refused to pass other laws for the accommodation of large districts of people, unless those people would relinquish the right of representation in the legislature, a right inestimable to them, and formidable to tyrants only.

He has called together legislative bodies at places unusual, uncomfortable, and distant from the depository of their public records, for the sole purpose of fatiguing them into compliance with his measures.

He has dissolved representative houses repeatedly <u>and continually</u> for opposing with manly firmness his invasions on the rights of the people.

He has refused for a long time after such dissolutions to cause others to be elected, whereby the legislative powers, incapable of annihilation, have returned to the people at large for their exercise, the state remaining, in the meantime, exposed to all the dangers of invasion from without and convulsions within.

He has endeavored to prevent the population of these states: for   10
that purpose obstructing the laws for naturalization of foreigners, refusing to pass others to encourage their migrations hither, and raising
the conditions of new appropriations of lands.

He has <u>suffered</u> the administration of justice <u>totally to cease in</u>   obstructed
<u>some of these states</u> refusing his assent to laws for establishing judi-   by
ciary powers.

He has made <u>our</u> judges dependent on his will alone for the tenure
of their offices, and the amount and payment of their salaries.

He has erected a multitude of new offices, <u>by a self-assumed</u>
<u>power</u> and sent hither swarms of new officers to harass our people
and eat out their substance.

He has kept among us in times of peace standing armies <u>and ships</u>
<u>of war</u> without the consent of our legislatures.

He has affected to render the military independent of, and supe-   15
rior to, the civil power.

He has combined with others to subject us to a jurisdiction foreign
to our constitutions and unacknowledged by our laws, giving his assent to their acts of pretended legislation for quartering large bodies of
armed troops among us; for protecting them by a mock trial from punishment for any murders which they should commit on the inhabitants of these states; for cutting off our trade with all parts of the
world; for imposing taxes on us without our consent; for depriving us
[   ] of the benefits of trial by jury; for transporting us beyond seas   in many
to be tried for pretended offenses; for abolishing the free system of   cases
English laws in a neighboring province, establishing therein an arbi-   in many
trary government, and enlarging its boundaries, so as to render it at   cases
once an example and fit instrument for introducing the same absolute
rule into these <u>states;</u> for taking away our charters, abolishing our   colonies
most valuable laws, and altering fundamentally the forms of our governments; for suspending our own legislatures, and declaring themselves invested with power to legislate for us in all cases whatsoever.   by declaring

He has abdicated government here <u>withdrawing his governors,</u>   us out of his
<u>and declaring us out of his allegiance</u> and <u>protection.</u>   protection
   and waging

He has plundered our seas, ravaged our coasts, burnt our towns,   war against
and destroyed the lives of our people.   us

He is at this time transporting large armies of foreign mercenaries   scarcely paral-
to complete the works of death, desolation and tyranny already begun   leled in the
with circumstances of cruelty and perfidy [   ] unworthy the head   most bar-
of a civilized nation.   barous ages,
   and totally

He has constrained our fellow citizens taken captive on the high   20
seas, to bear arms, against their country, to become the executioners of
their friends and brethren, or to fall themselves by their hands.   excited domestic insur-

He has [   ] endeavored to bring on the inhabitants of our   rection among
frontiers, the merciless Indian savages, whose known rule of warfare   us, and has

is an undistinguished destruction of all ages, sexes and conditions <u>of existence.</u>

<u>He has incited treasonable insurrections of our fellow citizens, with the allurements of forfeiture and confiscation of our property.</u>

<u>He has waged cruel war against human nature itself, violating its most sacred rights of life and liberty in the persons of a distant people who never offended him, captivating and carrying them into slavery in another hemisphere, or to incur miserable death in their transportation thither. This piratical warfare, the opprobrium of</u> INFIDEL <u>powers, is the warfare of the</u> CHRISTIAN <u>king of Great Britain. Determined to keep open a market where</u> MEN <u>should be bought and sold, he has prostituted his negative for suppressing every legislative attempt to prohibit or to restrain this execrable commerce. And that this assemblage of horrors might want no fact of distinguished die, he is now exciting those very people to rise in arms among us, and to purchase that liberty of which he has deprived them, by murdering the people on whom he also obtruded them: thus paying off former crimes committed against the</u> LIBERTIES <u>of one people, with crimes which he urges them to commit against the</u> LIVES <u>of another.</u>

In every stage of these oppressions we have petitioned for redress in the most humble terms: our repeated petitions have been answered only by repeated injuries.

A prince whose character is thus marked by every act which may 25
define a tyrant is unfit to be the ruler of a [   ] people <u>who mean to</u> free
<u>be free. Future ages will scarcely believe that the hardiness of one man adventured, within the short compass of twelve years only, to lay a foundation so broad and so undisguised for tyranny over a people fostered and fixed in principles of freedom.</u>

Nor have we been wanting in attentions to our British brethren. We have warned them from time to time of attempts by their legislature to extend <u>a</u> jurisdiction over <u>these our states.</u> We have reminded an/unwar
them of the circumstances of our emigration and settlement here, <u>no</u> able/us
<u>one of which would warrant so strange a pretension: that these were effected at the expense of our own blood and treasure, unassisted by the wealth or the strength of Great Britain: that in constituting indeed our several forms of government, we had adopted one common king, thereby laying a foundation for perpetual league and amity with them: but that submission to their parliament was no part of our constitution, nor ever in idea, if history may be credited: and,</u> we [   ] ap- have and w
pealed to their native justice and magnanimity <u>as well as to</u> the ties of have conju
our common kindred to disavow these usurpations which <u>were likely</u> them
<u>to</u> interrupt our connection and correspondence. They too have been by/would
deaf to the voice of justice and of consanguinity, <u>and when occasions</u> evitably
<u>have been given them, by the regular course of their laws, of removing from their councils the disturbers of our harmony, they have, by their</u>

free election, reestablished them in power. At this very time too, they are permitting their chief magistrate to send over not only soldiers of our common blood, but Scotch and foreign mercenaries to invade and destroy us. These facts have given the last stab to agonizing affection, and manly spirit bids us to renounce forever these unfeeling brethren. We must endeavor to forget our former love for them, and hold them as we hold the rest of mankind, enemies in war, in peace friends. We might have been a free and a great people together; but a communication of grandeur and of freedom, it seems, is below their dignity. Be it so, since they will have it. The road to happiness and to glory is open to us, too. We will tread it apart from them, and acquiesce in the necessity which denounces our eternal separation [   ]!

We must therefore and hold them as we hold the rest of mankind enemies in war, in peace friends

We therefore the representatives of the United States of America in General Congress assembled, do in the name, and by the authority of the good people of these states reject and renounce all allegiance and subjection to the kings of Great Britain and all others who may hereafter claim by, through or under them; we utterly dissolve all political connection which may heretofore have subsisted between us and the people or parliament of Great Britain: and finally we do assert and declare these colonies to be free and independent states, and that as free and independent states, they have full power to levy war, conclude peace, contract alliances, establish commerce, and to do all other acts and things which independent states may of right do.

And for the support of this declaration, we mutually pledge to each other our lives, our fortunes, and our sacred honor.

We, therefore, the representatives of the United States of America in General Congress assembled, appealing to the supreme judge of the world for the rectitude of our intentions, do in the name, and by the authority of the good people of these colonies, solemnly publish and declare, that these united colonies are, and of right ought to be free and independent states; that they are absolved from all allegiance to the British crown, and that all political connection between them and the state of Great Britain is, and ought to be, totally dissolved; and that as free and independent states, they have full power to levy war, conclude peace, contract alliances, establish commerce, and to do all other acts and things which independent states may of right do.

And for the support of this declaration, with a firm reliance on the protection of divine providence, we mutually pledge to each other our lives, our fortunes, and our sacred honor.

30

For Journals

Is the content of the Declaration of Independence what you expected it would be? What parts of it, if any, were familiar to you?

For Discussion

1.   Read the entire Declaration out loud, with each person in the class reading part of it. Then do five minutes worth of freewriting. Using your freewriting as a basis, compare your thoughts about the Declaration with those of your peers.

2.   The Declaration was the justification for the idea of a democratic republic when no such republic had ever existed before. Working with someone else in your class, find three good examples of Jefferson's argument for the form of government he wants. What is the main point in each example? What is the supporting evidence? What is the conclusion?

3.   The two most famous phrases in the Declaration of Independence declare that "all men are created equal" and that we are endowed by our Creator with the rights to "life, liberty, and the pursuit of happiness." What do you think those particular phrases mean? What does it mean to be created equal? Equal in what way? Equal spiritually? Equal legally? Equal intellectually? How do you think that an American pursues happiness?

4.   Jefferson, who was trained as a lawyer, was accustomed to framing arguments. Reread the Declaration as though you were a member of a jury listening to a trial lawyer's closing statement on behalf of his client. How does Jefferson refute the ideas that George III is a just king and that Americans owe him their loyalty under any circumstances? What kind of evidence does he present about the injustices committed by the king and Great Britain to prove that Americans are entitled to decide on their own?

5.   Many Americans did not support the Revolution and remained loyal to the English government. What arguments do you think that they might have made to refute Jefferson's assertions? What holes would they have tried to find in his argument?

6.   What do you think Jefferson wanted an American audience to take away from the Declaration? What do you think he wanted a British audience to learn?

For Writing

1.   Look at the underlined phrases that were in the first version of the Declaration but were eliminated or changed in the final version; then examine the words in the margin that replaced them. For example, in the first draft, Jefferson included a long denunciation of slavery; in the final draft, it is taken out because the southern slaveholders would not vote for a document that included it. Write an essay in which you respond to the following: What changes were the most surprising to

you? Are there any cases in which you prefer the first version over the final one? Which ones do you think present a stronger argument against British injustice? Why?

2.   There were many lawyers among the founding fathers; yet although they all opposed British rule, at least one of them was willing to defend British soldiers in court in the name of justice and civil liberties. Research and write a documented paper on the story of how John Adams defended British soldiers accused of murdering five colonials during the Boston Massacre. Include his reasons for taking on the case, what the colonial community thought of Adams's decision, and your own reaction.

❈❈ FROM *Civil Disobedience* (1850)

HENRY DAVID THOREAU

Henry David Thoreau (1817–1862) spent almost his entire life in and around Concord, Massachusetts, and found there all the subject matter he needed. An ardent abolitionist, diarist, nature writer, and natural scientist, he challenged American materialism and complacency as no other writer has before or since. Always an individualist, he wrote his most famous book, Walden *(1854), while living alone for two years at Walden Pond, where he said that he could live a life of "simplicity, independence, magnanimity, trust." It was at Walden that he was arrested—willingly—and spent a night in jail for having refused to pay taxes supporting slavery and the Mexican-American War.* Civil Disobedience, *which explains Thoreau's theory of passive resistance, challenged his neighbors—and us—to examine our lives and our ethics, and to act.*

I heartily accept the motto—"That government is best which governs least"; and I should like to see it acted up to more rapidly and systematically. Carried out, it finally amounts to this, which also I believe,—"That government is best which governs not at all"; and when men are prepared for it, that will be the kind of government which they will have. Government is at best but an expedient; but most governments are usually, and all governments are sometimes, inexpedient. The objections which have been brought against a standing army, and they are many and weighty, and deserve to prevail, may also at last be brought against a standing government. The standing army is only an arm of the standing government. The government itself, which is only the mode which the people have chosen to execute their will, is equally liable to be abused and perverted before the people can act through it. Witness the present Mexican war, the work of comparatively a few individuals using the standing government as their tool; for, in the outset, the people would not have consented to this measure.

The American government,—what is it but a tradition, though a recent one, endeavoring to transmit itself unimpaired to posterity, but each instant losing some of its integrity? It has not the vitality and force of a single living man; for a single man can bend it to his will. It is a sort of wooden gun to the people themselves; and, if ever they should use it in earnest as a real one against each other, it will surely split. But it is not the less necessary for this; for the people must have some complicated machinery or other, and hear its din, to satisfy that idea of government which they have. Governments show thus how successfully men can be imposed on, even impose on themselves, for their own advantage. It is excellent, we must all allow; yet this government never of itself furthered any enterprise, but by the alacrity with which it got out of its way. *It* does not keep the country free. *It* does not settle the West. *It* does not educate. The character inherent in the American people has done all that has been accomplished; and it would have done somewhat more, if the government had not sometimes got in its way. For government is an expedient by which men would fain succeed in letting one another alone; and, as has been said, when it is most expedient, the governed are most let alone by it. Trade and commerce, if they were not made of india rubber, would never manage to bounce over the obstacles which legislators are continually putting in their way; and, if one were to judge these men wholly by the effects of their actions, and not partly by their intentions, they would deserve to be classed and punished with those mischievous persons who put obstructions on the railroads.

But, to speak practically and as a citizen, unlike those who call themselves no-government men, I ask for, not at once no government, but *at once* a better government. Let every man make known what kind of government would command his respect, and that will be one step toward obtaining it.

After all, the practical reason why, when the power is once in the hands of the people, a majority are permitted, and for a long period continue, to rule, is not because this seems fairest to the minority, but because they are physically the strongest. But a government in which the majority rule in all cases cannot be based on justice, even as far as men understand it. Can there not be a government in which majorities do not virtually decide right and wrong, but conscience?—in which majorities decide only those questions to which the rule of expediency is applicable? Must the citizen ever for a moment, or in the least degree, resign his conscience to the legislator? Why has every man a conscience, then? I think that we should be men first, and subjects afterward. It is not desirable to cultivate a respect for the law, so much as for the right. The only obligation which I have a right to assume, is to do at any time what I think right . . . .

How does it become a man to behave toward this American 5 government to-day? I answer that he cannot without disgrace be associated with it. I cannot for an instant recognize that political organization as *my* government which is the *slave's* government also.

All men recognize the right of revolution; that is, the right to refuse allegiance to and to resist the government, when its tyranny or its inefficiency are great and unendurable. But almost all say that such is not the case now. But such was the case, they think, in the Revolution of '75. If one were to tell me that this was a bad government because it taxed certain foreign commodities brought to its ports, it is most probable that I should not make an ado about it, for I can do without them; all machines have their friction; and possibly this does enough good to counterbalance the evil. At any rate, it is a great evil to make a stir about it. But when the friction comes to have its machine, and oppression and robbery are organized, I say, let us not have such a machine any longer. In other words, when a sixth of the population of a nation which has undertaken to be the refuge of liberty are slaves, and a whole country is unjustly overrun and conquered by a foreign army, and subject to military law, I think that it is not too soon for honest men to rebel and revolutionize. What makes this duty the more urgent is the fact, that the country so overrun is not our own, but ours is the invading army. . . .

Practically speaking, the opponents to a reform in Massachusetts are not a hundred thousand politicians at the South, but a hundred thousand merchants and farmers here, who are more interested in commerce and agriculture than they are in humanity, and are not prepared to do justice to the slave and to Mexico, *cost what it may.* I quarrel not with far-off foes, but with those who, near at home, co-operate with, and do the bidding of those far away, and without whom the latter would be harmless. We are accustomed to say, that the mass of men are unprepared; but improvement is slow, because the few are not materially wiser or better than the many. It is not so important that many should be as good as you, as that there be some absolute goodness somewhere; for that will leaven the whole lump. There are thousands who are *in opinion* opposed to slavery and to the war, who yet in effect do nothing to put an end to them; who, esteeming themselves children of Washington and Franklin, sit down with their hands in their pockets, and say that they know not what to do, and do nothing; who even postpone the question of freedom to the question of free-trade, and quietly read the prices-current along with the latest advices from Mexico, after dinner, and, it may be, fall asleep over them both. . . .

The American has dwindled into an Old Fellow,—one who may be known by the development of his organ of gregariousness, and a manifest lack of intellect and cheerful self-reliance; whose first and chief concern, on coming into the world, is to see that the alms-houses are in good repair; and, before yet he has lawfully donned the virile garb, to collect a fund for the support of the widows and orphans that may be; who, in short, ventures to live only by the aid of the mutual insurance company, which has promised to bury him decently. . . .

Unjust laws exist: shall we be content to obey them, or shall we endeavor to amend them, and obey them until we have succeeded, or shall we transgress them at once? Men generally, under such a government as this, think that they ought to wait until they have persuaded the majority to alter them. They think that, if they should resist, the remedy would be worse than the evil. But it is the fault of the government itself that the remedy *is* worse than the evil. *It* makes it worse. Why is it not more apt to anticipate and provide for reform? Why does it not cherish its wise minority? Why does it cry and resist before it is hurt? Why does it not encourage its citizens to be on the alert to point out its faults, and *do* better than it would have them? Why does it always crucify Christ, and excommunicate Copernicus and Luther, and pronounce Washington and Franklin rebels?. . . .

If the injustice is part of the necessary friction of the machine of government, let it go, let it go: perchance it will wear smooth,—certainly the machine will wear out. If the injustice has a spring, or a pulley, or a rope, or a crank, exclusively for itself, then perhaps you may consider whether the remedy will not be worse than the evil; but if it is of such a nature that it requires you to be the agent of injustice to another, then, I say, break the law. Let your life be a counter friction to stop the machine. What I have to do is to see, at any rate, that I do not lend myself to the wrong which I condemn. 10

As for adopting the ways which the State has provided for remedying the evil, I know not of such ways. They take too much time, and a man's life will be gone. I have other affairs to attend to. I came into this world, not chiefly to make this a good place to life [*sic*], but to live in it, be it good or bad. A man has not everything to do, but something; and because he cannot do *every thing*, it is not necessary that he should do *something* wrong. It is not my business to be petitioning the governor or the legislature any more than it is theirs to petition me; and if they should not hear my petition, what should I do then? But in this case the State has provided no way: its very Constitution is the evil. This may seem to be harsh and stubborn and unconciliatory; but it is to treat with the utmost kindness and consideration the only spirit that can appreciate or deserves it. So is all change for the better, like birth and death which convulse the body.

I do not hesitate to say, that those who call themselves abolitionists should at once effectually withdraw their support, both in person and property, from the government of Massachusetts, and not wait till they constitute a majority of one, before they suffer the right to prevail through them, I think that it is enough if they have God on their side, without waiting for that other one. Moreover, any man more right than his neighbors constitutes a majority of one already. . . .

Under a government which imprisons any unjustly, the true place for a just man is also in prison. The proper place to-day, the only place which Massachusetts has provided for her freer and less desponding spirits, is in her prisons, to be put out and locked out of the State by her own act, as they have already put themselves out by their principles. It is there that the fugitive slave, and the Mexican prisoner on parole, and the Indian come to plead the wrongs of his race, should find them; on that separate, but more free and honorable ground, where the State places those who are not *with* her, but *against* her,—the only house in a slave-state in which a free man can abide with honor. If any think that their influence would be lost there, and their voices no longer afflict the ear of the State, that they would not be as an enemy within its walls, they do not know by how much truth is stronger than error, nor how much more eloquently and effectively he can combat injustice who has experienced a little in his own person. Cast your whole vote, not a strip of paper merely, but your whole influence. A minority is powerless while it conforms to the majority; it is not even a minority then; but it is irresistible when it clogs by its whole weight. If the alternative is to keep all just men in prison, or give up war and slavery, the State will not hesitate which to choose. If a thousand men were not to pay their tax-bills this year, that would not be a violent and bloody measure, as it would be to pay them, and enable the State to commit violence and shed innocent blood. This is, in fact, the definition of a peaceable revolution, if any such is possible. If the tax-gatherer, or any other public officer, asks me, as one has done, "But what shall I do?" my answer is, "If you really wish to do anything, resign our office." When the subject has refused allegiance, and the officer has resigned his office, then the revolution is accomplished. But even suppose blood should flow. Is there not a sort of blood shed when the conscience is wounded? Through this wound a man's real manhood and immortality flow out, and he bleeds to an everlasting death. I see this blood flowing now. . . .

I have paid no poll-tax for six years. I was put into a jail once on this account, for one night; and, as I stood considering the walls of solid stone, two or three feet thick, the door of wood and iron, a foot thick, and the iron grating which strained the light, I could not help being struck with the foolishness of that institution which treated me as if I were mere flesh and blood and bones, to be locked up. I wondered that it should have concluded at length that this was the best use it could put me to, and had never thought to avail itself of my services in some way. I saw that, if there was a wall of stone between me and my townsmen, there was a still more difficult one to climb or break through, before they could get to be as free as I was. I did not for a moment feel confined, and the walls seemed a great waste of stone and mortar. I felt as if I alone of all my townsmen had paid my tax. They plainly did not know how to treat me, but behaved like persons who are underbred. In every threat and in every compliment there was a blunder; for they thought that my chief desire was to stand the other side of that stone wall. I could not but smile to see how industriously they locked the door on my meditations, which followed them out again without let or hindrance, and *they* were really all that was dangerous. As they could not reach me, they had resolved to punish my body; just as boys, if they cannot come at some person against whom they have a spite, will abuse his dog. I saw that the State was half-witted, that it was timid as a lone woman with her silver spoons, and that it did not know its friends from its foes, and I lost all my remaining respect for it, and pitied it.

Thus the State never intentionally confronts a man's sense, intel-   15
lectual or moral, but only his body, his senses. It is not armed with superior wit or honesty, but with superior physical strength. I was not born to be forced. I will breathe after my own fashion. Let us see who is the strongest. What force has a multitude? They only can force me who obey a higher law than I. They force me to become like themselves. I do not hear of *men* being *forced* to live this way or that by masses of men. What sort of life were that to live? When I meet a government which says to me, "Your money or your life," why should I be in haste to give it my money? It may be in a great strait, and not know what to do: I cannot help that. It must help itself; do as I do. It is not worth the while to snivel about it. I am not responsible for the successful working of the machinery of society. I am not the son of the engineer. I perceive that, when an acorn and a chestnut fall side by side, the one does not remain inert to make way for the other, but both obey their own laws, and spring and grow and flourish as best they can, till one, perchance, overshadows and destroys the other. If a plant cannot live according to its nature, it dies; and so a man. . . .

I do not wish to quarrel with any man or nation. I do not wish to split hairs, to make fine distinctions, or set myself up as better than my neighbors. I seek rather, I may say, even an excuse for conforming to the laws of the land. I am but too ready to conform to them. Indeed I have reason to suspect myself on this head; and each year, as the tax-gatherer comes round, I find myself disposed to review the acts and position of the general and state governments, and the spirit of the people, to discover a pretext for conformity. I believe that the State will soon be able to take all my work of this sort out of my hands, and then I shall be no better a patriot than my fellow-countrymen. Seen from a lower point of view, the Constitution, with all its faults, is very good; the law and the courts are very respectable; even this State and this American government are, in many respects, very admirable and rare things, to be thankful for, such as a great many have described them; but seen from a point of view a little higher, they are what I have described them; seen from a higher still, and the highest, who shall say that they are, or that they are worth looking at or thinking of at all?

However, the government does not concern me much, and I shall bestow the fewest possible thoughts on it. It is not many moments that I live under a government, even in this world. If a man is thought-free, fancy-free, imagination-free, that which *is not* never for a long time appearing *to be* to him, unwise rulers or reformers cannot fatally interrupt him. . . .

The authority of government, even such as I am willing to submit to,—for I will cheerfully obey those who know and can do better than I, and in many things even those who neither know nor can do so well,— is still an impure one: to be strictly just, it must have the sanction and consent of the governed. It can have no pure right over my person and property but what I concede to it. The progress from an absolute to a limited monarchy, from a limited monarchy to a democracy, is a progress toward a true respect for the individual. Is a democracy, such as we know it, the last improvement possible in government? Is it not possible to take a step further towards recognizing and organizing the rights of man? There will never be a really free and enlightened State, until the State comes to recognize the individual as a higher and independent power, from which all its own power and authority are derived, and treats him accordingly. I please myself with imagining a State at last which can afford to be just to all men, and to treat the individual with respect as a neighbor, which even would not think it inconsistent with its own repose, if a few were to live aloof from it, not meddling with it, nor embraced by it, who fulfilled all the duties of neighbors and fellowmen. A State which bore this kind of fruit, and suffered it to drop off as fast as it ripened, would prepare the way for a still more perfect and glorious State, which also I have imagined, but not yet anywhere seen.

For Journals

Thoreau states that the government which governs best is the one which governs least. What functions does he seem to think that government should stay out of? Which areas today would you want government to stay out of, and which do you think it should pursue more actively?

For Discussion

1. What is your response to Thoreau's ideas that an individual American following his or her conscience is a majority of one, and that fighting injustice by persuading the majority to change the law takes too long? What traditional ideas of good government and citizenship does he refute in these statements?

2. Thoreau says that the government does not keep the country free, that it does not settle the West, that it does not educate. In his opinion, then, what does it do?

3. Democracy is supposed to be governed by the rule of the majority, but Thoreau says that his only obligation is "to do what I think is right." How do you respond to this assertion? Do you think that the two principles—majority rule and individual conscience—are compatible or mutually incompatible? Why?

4. Thoreau refused to pay a poll tax as a protest against slavery and the war American was waging against Mexico. Do you find withholding taxes or going to jail reasonable ways of protesting injustice? If not, what would you say to refute Thoreau's belief in civil disobedience? Are there any principles for which you would be willing to break the law, go to jail, or otherwise practice civil disobedience yourself?

5. What does Thoreau think constitute the responsibilities of a good citizen? Why does he think that most Americans, even the ones opposed to slavery, are not truly good citizens?

6. How would the government function if everyone followed his or her conscience the way Thoreau did? Did you see him as an extremist? A patriot? Both?

For Writing

1. Write an essay in which you compose your own definition of patriotism. Be sure to identify the principles—political, personal, or ethical—on which your definition is based. You can refer to Thoreau, the Declaration, or any other readings, and either refute these arguments or draw on them to support your own views.

2. Read one of Thoreau's other works—for example, *Walden,* the diary of his two-year-long adventure of living alone and being self-sufficient; or *A Week on the Concord and Merrimack Rivers,* an account of his canoeing trip in the American wilderness. Write a review critiquing Thoreau's skill as a naturalist and an observer, and share the review with your peers; you should use secondary library sources (articles, biographies, and so on) if possible.

✯✯✯ *Independence Day Speech at Rochester* (1852)

FREDERICK DOUGLASS

At the time that Frederick Douglass gave this speech, he had been living in Rochester, New York, for several years and editing his abolitionist newspaper, the Northern Star. His autobiography had been published in 1845, after he escaped from slavery, and he subsequently spent two years in England lecturing and earning money to buy his freedom so that he could not be captured and returned to the South. He had a remarkable career as a diplomat, a civil rights leader before and after the Civil War, a marshal of the District of Columbia, an organizer of black combat units, a campaigner for women's rights, a newspaper editor, and a writer. He was asked to deliver the Fourth of July speech in Rochester in 1852. Fourth of July speeches were already an old American political tradition. Like parades and fireworks, the speeches on such occasions are usually celebratory, uncritical, and immediately forgettable. Douglass's speech, made nine years before the start of the Civil War, is the exception.

Fellow citizens, pardon me, allow me to ask, why am I called upon to speak here today? What have I, or those I represent, to do with your national independence? Are the great principles of political freedom and of natural justice, embodied in that Declaration of Independence, extended to us? and am I, therefore, called upon to bring our humble offering to the national altar, and to confess the benefits and express devout gratitude for the blessings resulting from your independence to us?

Would to God, both for your sakes and ours, that an affirmative answer could be truthfully returned to these questions! Then would my task be light, and my burden easy and delightful. For who is there so cold that a nation's sympathy could not warm him? Who so obdurate and dead to the claims of gratitude that would not thankfully acknowledge such priceless benefits? Who so stolid and selfish that would not give his voice to swell the hallelujahs of a nation's jubilee, when the chains of servitude had been torn from his limbs? I am not that man. In a case like that the dumb might eloquently speak and the "lame man leap as an hart."[1]

But such is not the state of the case. I say it with a sad sense of the disparity between us. I am not included within the pale of this glorious anniversary! Your high independence only reveals the immeasurable distance between us. The blessings in which you, this day, rejoice are not enjoyed in common. The rich inheritance of justice, liberty, prosperity, and independence bequeathed by your fathers is shared by you, not by me. The sunlight that brought light and healing to you has

---

[1]From the Bible, Isaiah 35:6.

brought stripes and death to me. This Fourth of July is yours, not mine. You may rejoice, I must mourn. To drag a man in fetters into the grand illuminated temple of liberty, and call upon him to join you in joyous anthems, were inhuman mockery and sacrilegious irony. Do you mean, citizens, to mock me by asking me to speak today? If so, there is a parallel to your conduct. And let me warn you that it is dangerous to copy the example of a nation whose crimes, towering up to heaven, were thrown down by the breath of the Almighty, burying that nation in irrevocable ruin! I can today take up the plaintive lament of a peeled and woe-smitten people![2]

"By the rivers of Babylon, there we sat down. Yea! we wept when we remembered Zion. We hanged our harps upon the willows in the midst thereof. For there, they that carried us away captive, required of us a song; and they who wasted us required of us mirth, saying, Sing us one of the songs of Zion. How can we sing the Lord's song in a strange land? If I forget thee, O Jerusalem, let my right hand forget her cunning. If I do not remember thee, let my tongue cleave to the roof of my mouth."[3]

Fellow citizens, above your national, tumultuous joy, I hear the   5 mournful wail of millions! whose chains, heavy and grievous yesterday, are, today, rendered more intolerable by the jubilee shouts that reach them. If I do forget, if I do not faithfully remember those bleeding children of sorrow this day, "may my right hand forget her cunning, and may my tongue cleave to the roof of my mouth"! To forget them, to pass lightly over their wrongs, and to chime in with the popular theme would be treason most scandalous and shocking, and would make me a reproach before God and the world. My subject, then, fellow citizens, is *American slavery.* I shall see this day and its popular characteristics from the slave's point of view. Standing there identified with the American bondman, making his wrongs mine. I do not hesitate to declare with all my soul that the character and conduct of this nation never looked blacker to me than on this Fourth of July! Whether we turn to the declarations of the past or to the professions of the present, the conduct of the nation seems equally hideous and revolting. America is false to the past, false to the present, and solemnly binds herself to be false to the future. Standing with God and the crushed and bleeding slave on this occasion, I will, in the name of humanity which is outraged, in the name of liberty which is fettered, in the name of the Constitution and the Bible which are disregarded and trampled upon, dare to call in question and to denounce, with all the emphasis I

---

[2]In 586 B.C.E, the near eastern kingdom of Babylon invaded Judea, burned the first temple in Jerusalem, and took the population into captivity.

[3]Psalm 137:1–6. This is the lament of the Judean exiles.

can command, everything that serves to perpetuate slavery—the great sin and shame of America! "I will not equivocate, I will not excuse"; I will use the severest language I can command; and yet not one word shall escape me that any man, whose judgment is not blinded by prejudice, or who is not at heart a slaveholder, shall not confess to be right and just.

But I fancy I hear someone of my audience say, "It is just in this circumstance that you and your brother abolitionists fail to make a favorable impression on the public mind. Would you argue more and denounce less, would you persuade more and rebuke less, your cause would be much more likely to succeed." But, I submit, where all is plain, there is nothing to be argued. What point in the antislavery creed would you have me argue? On what branch of the subject do the people of this country need light? Must I undertake to prove that the slave is a man? That point is conceded already. Nobody doubts it. The slaveholders themselves acknowledge it in the enactment of laws for their government. They acknowledge it when they punish disobedience on the part of the slave. There are seventy-two crimes in the state of Virginia which, if committed by a black man (no matter how ignorant he be), subject him to the punishment of death; while only two of the same crimes will subject a white man to the like punishment. What is this but the acknowledgment that the slave is a moral, intellectual, and responsible being? The manhood of the slave is conceded. It is admitted in the fact that the Southern statute books are covered with enactments forbidding, under severe fines and penalties, the teaching of the slave to read or to write. When you can point to any such laws in reference to the beasts of the field, then I may consent to argue the manhood of the slave. When the dogs in your streets, when the fowls of the air, when the cattle on your hills, when the fish of the sea and the reptiles that crawl shall be unable to distinguish the slave from a brute, then will I argue with you that the slave is a man!

For the present, it is enough to affirm the equal manhood of the Negro race. Is it not astonishing that, while we are plowing, planting, and reaping, using all kinds of mechanical tools, erecting houses, constructing bridges, building ships, working in metals of brass, iron, copper, silver, and gold; that, while we are reading, writing, and ciphering, acting as clerks, merchants, and secretaries, having among us lawyers, doctors, ministers, poets, authors, editors, orators, and teachers; that, while we are engaged in all manner of enterprises common to other men, digging gold in California, capturing the whale in the Pacific, feeding sheep and cattle on the hillside, living, moving, acting, thinking, planning, living in families as husbands, wives, and children, and, above all, confession and worshiping the Christian's God, and looking hopefully for life and immortality beyond the grave, we are called upon to prove that we are men!

Would you have me argue that man is entitled to liberty? That he is the rightful owner of his own body? You have already declared it. Must I argue the wrongfulness of slavery? Is that a question for republicans? Is it to be settled by the rules of logic and argumentation, as a matter beset with great difficulty, involving a doubtful application of the principle of justice, hard to be understood? How should I look today, in the presence of Americans, dividing and subdividing a discourse, to show that men have a natural right to freedom? speaking of it relatively and positively, negatively and affirmatively? To do so would be to make myself ridiculous and to offer an insult to your understanding. There is not a man beneath the canopy of heaven that does not know that slavery is wrong for him.

What, am I to argue that it is wrong to make men brutes, to rob them of their liberty, to work them without wages, to keep them ignorant of their relations to their fellow men, to beat them with sticks, to flay their flesh with the lash, to load their limbs with irons, to hunt them with dogs, to sell them at auction, to sunder their families, to knock out their teeth, to burn their flesh, to starve them into obedience and submission to their masters? Must I argue that a system thus marked with blood, and stained with pollution, is wrong? No! I will not. I have better employment for my time and strength than such arguments would imply.

What, then, remains to be argued? Is it that slavery is not divine;   10
that God did not establish it; that our doctors of divinity are mistaken? There is blasphemy in the thought. That which is inhuman cannot be divine! Who can reason on such a proposition? They that can may; I cannot. The time for such argument is past.

At a time like this, scorching iron, not convincing argument, is needed. O! had I the ability, and could I reach the nation's ear, I would today pour out a fiery stream of biting ridicule, blasting reproach, withering sarcasm, and stern rebuke. For it is not light that is needed, but fire; it is not the gentle shower, but thunder. We need the storm, the whirlwind, and the earthquake. The feeling of the nation must be quickened; the conscience of the nation must be roused; the propriety of the nation must be startled; the hypocrisy of the nation must be exposed; and its crimes against God and man must be proclaimed and denounced.

What, to the American slave, is your Fourth of July? I answer: a day that reveals to him, more than all other days in the year, the gross injustice and cruelty to which he is the constant victim. To him, your celebration is a sham; your boasted liberty, an unholy license; your national greatness, swelling vanity; your sounds of rejoicing are empty and heartless; your denunciation of tyrants, brass-fronted impudence; your shouts of liberty and equality, hollow mockery; your prayers and hymns, your sermons and thanksgivings, with all your religious parade and solemnity, are, to Him, mere bombast, fraud, deception, impiety, and hypocrisy—a thin veil to cover up crimes which would disgrace a nation of savages. There is not a nation of savages. There is not a nation on the earth guilty of practices more shocking and bloody than are the people of the United States at this very hour.

Go where you may, search where you will, roam through all the monarchies and despotisms of the Old World, travel through South America, search out every abuse, and when you have found the last, lay your facts by the side of the everyday practices of this nation, and you will say with me that, for revolting barbarity and shameless hypocrisy, America reigns without a rival.

For Journals

Was Independence Day an appropriate time for Douglass to make his speech? Why, or why not?

For Discussion

1.   What do you think were the expectations of Douglass's audience when he began his speech? At what point in the speech do you think he begins to move toward his real topic?

2.   Review Douglass's speech with one or two other people in your class, and identify the main points of his argument. (You might begin by identifying the crucial sentence in each paragraph.) What are his conclusions? What do you think he wants his audience to take away with them?

3.   Refutation in Douglass's case is not only logically precise but full of emotion. Where in this speech do you find examples of Douglass's anger? Irony? Sarcasm? To what purpose does he express these? How do they help him make his point?

4.   What evidence does Douglass accumulate to justify his conclusion that a slave is indeed a man? How would the argument be weaker without this proof? Are there any pieces of evidence that you would add?

5.   Which phrases does Douglass quote or paraphrase from the language of the Declaration of Independence? How does he make use of those quotations to support his argument against slavery and to refute the idea that he should be celebrating the Fourth of July?

6.   Douglass uses the technique of raising objections that his audience might bring up and then refuting them himself. Find two or three examples of this strategy. Why do you think he employs it? In what ways is it effective in strengthening his argument?

For Writing

1. Douglass revised his autobiography, *The Life and Times of Frederick Douglass,* three times, adding information each time. For example, the first version, written before the Civil War, gives very few details about the people who helped him escape from slavery because Douglass didn't want to jeopardize anyone. The last version of the book, written many years later, is much more explicit. Write a research paper in which you compare elements of one version with those of another— for example, Douglass's childhood, his experiences as a slave, his education, his escape, or his relations with the Auld family. Consider these questions: What did Douglass add about a certain episode? Which version do you think is more effective? How was your initial response to the injustices that Douglass fought against affected by reading the later version?

2. Following the pattern of Douglass's speech, write a speech, for delivery at a formal occasion, about a political or social cause that you believe in and that your audience may be hostile to or not enthusiastic about. Be sure to identify your audience—your parents, the people who came to your high school graduation, a historical figure (living or dead), or a friend or an acquaintance. Begin by making the conventional remarks expected on the occasion, and then focus on what you really want to speak about. Anticipate the objections of your audience, and then refute these objections.

❋❋❋ *Women's Right to Vote* (1873)

SUSAN B. ANTHONY

Susan B. Anthony (1820–1906) grew up in a Quaker family with strong abolitionist beliefs. A campaigner for women's rights even as a teenager, she was an early advocate of equal pay for women teachers and of coed education. At a time when women had almost no legal rights, she helped a bill through the New York legislature that gave women some control over their children and their earnings: both had previously been controlled by the husband. She supported the emancipation of slaves and was an active abolitionist, but devoted her life mainly to the fight for women's right to vote. In 1872, during a presidential election, she decided to test whether the Fourteenth Amendment to the Constitution—equal protection under the law—applied to women. She tried to register but was arrested and fined; the fine was never collected. This is the speech she gave to explain her views.

I stand before you under indictment for the alleged crime of having voted at the last presidential election, without having a lawful right to vote. It shall be my work this evening to prove to you that in thus doing, I not only committed no crime, but instead simply exercised my citizen's rights, guaranteed to me and all United States citizens by the National Constitution beyond the power of any State to deny.

Our democratic-republican government is based on the idea of the natural right of every individual member thereof to a voice and a vote in making and executing the laws. We assert the province of government to be to secure the people in the enjoyment of their inalienable rights. We throw to the winds the old dogma that government can give rights. No one denies that before governments were organized each individual possessed the right to protect his own life, liberty and property. When 100 to 1,000,000 people enter into a free government they do not barter away their natural rights; they simply pledge themselves to protect each other in the enjoyment of them through prescribed judicial and legislative tribunals. They agree to abandon the methods of brute force in the adjustment of their differences and adopt those of civilization. . . . The Declaration of Independence, the United States Constitution, the constitutions of the several States and the organic laws of the Territories, all alike propose to *protect* the people in the exercise of their God-given rights. Not one of them pretends to bestow rights.

> All men are created equal, and endowed by their Creator with certain inalienable rights. Among these are life, liberty and the pursuit of happiness. To secure these, governments are instituted among men, deriving their just powers from the consent of the governed.

Here is no shadow of government authority over rights, or exclusion of any class from their full and equal enjoyment. Here is pronounced the right of all men, and "consequently," as the Quaker preacher said, "of all women," to a voice in the government. And here, in this first paragraph of the Declaration, is the assertion of the natural right of all to the ballot; for how can "the consent of the governed" be given, if the right to vote be denied? . . . The women, dissatisfied as they are with this form of government, that enforces taxation without representation—that compels them to obey laws to which they never have given their consent—that imprisons and hangs them without a trial by a jury of their peers—that robs them, in marriage, of the custody of their own persons, wages, and children—are this half of the people who are left wholly at the mercy of the other half, in direct violation of the spirit and letter of the declarations of the framers of this government, every one of which was based on the immutable principle of equal rights to all. By these declarations, kings, popes, priests, aristocrats, all were alike dethroned and placed on a common level, politically, with the lowliest born subject or serf. By them, too, men, as such, were deprived of their divine right to rule and placed on a political level with women. By the practice of these declarations all class and caste distinctions would be abolished, and slave, serf, plebeian, wife, woman, all alike rise from their subject position to the broader platform of equality.

The preamble of the Federal Constitution says:

> We, the people of the United States, in order to form a more perfect union, establish justice, insure domestic tranquillity, provide for the common defence, promote the general welfare and secure the blessings of liberty to ourselves and our posterity, do ordain and establish this Constitution for the United States of America.

It was we, the people, not we, the white male citizens, nor we, the 5 male citizens; but we, the whole people, who formed this Union. We formed it not to give the blessings of liberty but to secure them; not to the half of ourselves and the half of our prosperity, but to the whole people—women as well as men. It is downright mockery to talk to women of their enjoyment of the blessings of liberty while they are denied the only means of securing them provided by this democratic-republican government—the ballot. . . .

When, in 1871, I asked [Senator Charles Sumner] to declare the power of the United States Constitution to protect women in their right to vote—as he had done for black men—he handed me a copy of all his speeches during that reconstruction period, and said:

> Put "sex" where I have "race" or "color," and you have here the best and strongest argument I can make for woman. There is not a doubt but women have the constitutional right to vote, and I will never vote for a Sixteenth Amendment to guarantee it to them. I voted for both the Fourteenth and Fifteenth under protest; would never have done it but for the pressing emergency of that hour; would have insisted that the power of the original Constitution to protect all citizens in the equal enjoyment of their rights should have been vindicated through the courts. But the newly-made freedmen had neither the intelligence, wealth nor time to await that slow process. Women do possess all these in an eminent degree, and I insist that they shall appeal to the courts and through them establish the powers of our American magna charta to protect every citizen of the republic.

But, friends, when in accordance with Senator Sumner's counsel I went to the ballot-box, last November, and exercised my citizen's right to vote, the courts did not wait for me to appeal to them—they appealed to me, and indicted me on the charge of having voted illegally. . . .

For any State to make sex a qualification, which must ever result in the disfranchisement of one entire half of the people, is to pass a bill of attainder, an ex post facto law, and is therefore a violation of the supreme law of the land. By it the blessings of liberty are forever withheld from women and their female posterity. For them, this government has no just powers derived from the consent of the governed. For them this government is not a democracy; it is not a republic. It is the most odious aristocracy ever established on the face of the globe. An oligarchy of wealth, where the rich govern the poor; an oligarchy of learning, where the educated govern the ignorant; or even an oligarchy of race, where the Saxon rules the African, might be endured; but this oligarchy of sex which makes father, brothers, husband, sons, the oligarchs over the mother and sisters, the wife and daughters of every household; which ordains all men sovereigns, all women subjects—carries discord and rebellion into every home of the nation. . . .

It is urged that the use of the masculine pronouns *he, his* and *him* in all the constitutions and laws, is proof that only men were meant to be included in their provisions. If you insist on this version of the letter of the law, we shall insist that you be consistent and accept the other horn of the dilemma, which would compel you to exempt women from taxation for the support of the government and from penalties for the violation of laws. There is no *she* or *her* or *hers* in the tax laws, and this is equally true of all the criminal laws.

Take for example, the civil rights law which I am charged with having violated; not only are all the pronouns in it masculine, but everybody knows that it was intended expressly to hinder the rebel men from voting. It reads, "If any person shall knowingly vote without *his* having a lawful right." . . . I insist if government officials may thus manipulate the pronouns to tax, fine, imprison and hang women, it is their duty to thus change them in order to protect us in our right to vote. . . . 10

Though the words persons, people, inhabitants, electors, citizens, are all used indiscriminately in the national and State constitutions, there was always a conflict of opinion, prior to the war, as to whether they were synonymous terms, but whatever room there was for doubt, under the old regime, the adoption of the Fourteenth Amendment settled that question forever in its first sentence:

> All persons born or naturalized in the United States, and subject to the jurisdiction thereof, are citizens of the United States, and of the State wherein they reside.

The second settles the equal status of all citizens:

> No State shall make or enforce any law which shall abridge the privileges or immunities of citizens of the United States; nor shall any State deprive any person of life, liberty or property without due process of law, or deny to any person within its jurisdiction the equal protection of the laws.

The only question left to be settled now is: Are women persons? I scarcely believe any of our opponents will have the hardihood to say they are not. Being persons, then, women are citizens, and no State has a right to make any new law, or to enforce any old law, which shall abridge their privileges or immunities. Hence, every discrimination against women in the constitutions and laws of the several States is today null and void, precisely as is every one against negroes.

Is the right to vote one of the privileges or immunities of citizens? I think the disfranchised ex-rebels and ex-State prisoners all will agree that it is not only one of them, but the one without which all the others are nothing. Seek first the kingdom of the ballot and all things else shall be added, is the political injunction. . . .

However much the doctors of the law may disagree as to whether 15 people and citizens, in the original Constitution, were one and the same, or whether the privileges and immunities in the Fourteenth Amendment include the right of suffrage, the question of the citizen's right to vote is forever settled by the Fifteenth Amendment. "The right of citizens of the United States to vote shall not be denied or abridged by the United States, or by any State, on account of race, color or previous condition of servitude." How can the State deny or abridge the right of the citizen, if the citizen does not possess it? There is no escape from the conclusion that to vote is the citizen's right, and the specifications of race, color or previous condition of servitude can in no way impair the force of that emphatic assertion that the citizen's right to vote shall not be denied or abridged. . . .

If, however, you will insist that the Fifteenth Amendment's emphatic interdiction against robbing United States citizens of their suffrage "on account of race, color or previous condition of servitude," is a recognition of the right of either the United States or any State to deprive them of the ballot for any or all other reasons, I will prove to you that the class of citizens for whom I now plead are, by all the principles of our government and many of the laws of the States, included under the term "previous conditions of servitude."

Consider first married women and their legal status. What is servitude? "The condition of a slave." What is a slave? "A person who is robbed of the proceeds of his labor; a person who is subject to the will of another." By the laws of Georgia, South Carolina and all the States of the South, the negro had no right to the custody and control of his person. He belonged to his master. If he were disobedient, the master had the right to use correction. If the negro did not like the correction and ran away, the master had the right to use coercion to bring him back. By the laws of almost every State in this Union today, North as well as South, the married woman has no right to the custody and control of her person. The wife belongs to the husband; and if she refuse obedience he may use moderate correction, and if she do not like his moderate correction and leave his "bed and board," the husband may use moderate coercion to bring her back. The little word "moderate," you see, is the saving clause for the wife, and would doubtless be over-stepped should her offended husband administer his correction with the "cat-o'-nine-tails," or accomplish his coercion with blood-hounds.

Again the slave had no right to the earnings of his hands, they be-longed to his master; no right to the custody of his children, they be-longed to his master; no right to sue or be sued, or to testify in the courts. If he committed a crime, it was the master who must sue or be sued. In many of the States there has been special legislation, giving married women the right to property inherited or received by bequest, or earned by the pursuit of any avocation outside the home; also giv-ing them the right to sue and be sued in matters pertaining to such separate property; but not a single State of this Union has ever secured the wife in the enjoyment of her right to equal ownership of the joint earnings of the marriage copartnership. And since, in the nature of things, the vast majority of married women never earn a dollar by work outside their families, or inherit a dollar from their fathers, it fol-lows that from the day of their marriage to the day of the death of their husbands not one of them ever has a dollar, except it shall please her husband to let her have it. . . .

Is anything further needed to prove woman's condition of servi-tude sufficient to entitle her to the guarantees of the Fifteenth Amend-ment? Is there a man who will not agree with me that to talk of freedom without the ballot is mockery to the women of this republic, precisely as New England's orator, Wendell Phillips, at the close of the late war declared it to be to the newly emancipated black man? I admit that, prior to the rebellion, by common consent, the right to enslave, as well as to disfranchise both native and foreign born persons, was con-ceded to the States. But the one grand principle settled by the war and the reconstruction legislation, is the supremacy of the national govern-ment to protect the citizens of the United States in their right to free-dom and the elective franchise, against any and every interference on the part of the several States; and again and again have the American people asserted the triumph of this principle by their overwhelming majorities for Lincoln and Grant.

The one issue of the last two presidential elections was whether 20 the Fourteenth and Fifteenth Amendments should be considered the irrevocable will of the people; and the decision was that they should be, and that it is not only the right, but the duty of the national govern-ment to protect all United States citizens in the full enjoyment and free exercise of their privileges and immunities against the attempt of any State to deny or abridge. . . .

It is upon this just interpretation of the United States Constitution that our National Woman Suffrage Association, which celebrates the twenty-fifth anniversary of the woman's rights movement next May in New York City, has based all its arguments and action since the passage of these amendments. We no longer petition legislature or Congress to give us the right to vote, but appeal to women everywhere to exercise their too long neglected "citizen's right." We appeal to the inspectors of election to receive the votes of all United States citizens, as it is their duty to do. We appeal to United States commissioners and marshals to arrest, as is their duty, the inspectors who reject the votes of United States citizens, and leave alone those who perform their duties and accept these votes. We ask the juries to return verdicts of "not guilty" in the cases of law-abiding United States citizens who cast their votes, and inspectors of election who receive and count them.

We ask the judges to render unprejudiced opinions of the law, and wherever there is room for doubt to give the benefit to the side of liberty and equal rights for women, remembering that, as Sumner says, "The true rule of interpretation under our National Constitution, especially since its amendments, is that anything *for* human rights is constitutional, everything *against* human rights unconstitutional." It is on this line that we propose to fight our battle for the ballot—peaceably but nevertheless persistently—until we achieve complete triumph and all United States citizens, men and women alike, are recognized as equals in the government.

For Journals

What was your reaction to the first sentence in Anthony's speech?

For Discussion

1.   Almost all men in Victorian America, and many women, thought that women should not have the right to vote. What would you guess the arguments were against women's suffrage? What would the opponents of suffrage have been worried about if women did secure the right to vote?

2.   How do Anthony's references to the language of the Declaration of Independence, the Constitution, and the Fourteenth and Fifteenth Amendments help her refute the belief that women should not be allowed to vote? Why do you think that she chooses those particular quotations?

3.   How does Anthony see the political condition of women in her own time as compared with the role of American men in the Revolution? As compared with the condition of former slaves? Considering your own knowledge, how valid do you find her comparisons?

4. Evaluate Anthony's argument that if laws refer only to "he" and "him," women shouldn't have to pay taxes to support the government or go to jail for breaking the law. What are the strengths and weaknesses of this argument? How would you make it stronger? What would Thoreau think of it?

5. Anthony argues that women are "persons" within the legal meaning stated by the Constitution. In an earlier selection in this chapter, Douglass argued that African Americans are men. Look back at Douglass's argument, and compare it with Anthony's. Do they argue in similar ways or differently? Do they make different appeals to their audiences? Why do they feel compelled to argue these points at all?

6. Like Douglass, Anthony poses questions in her argument and then refutes them. What do you think are the advantages or disadvantages of this strategy? Which of her own questions do you think she answers best? In her place, what other questions would you ask? How would you answer them?

For Writing

1. Write a paper in which you argue either for or against one of the following:

a. An American teenager today has as much right to emancipation from parental control as a married woman in Anthony's time had with respect to her husband's control.

b. Women should be allowed to serve in combat units in the armed forces.

c. The women's movement has become too aggressive and does more harm than good.

Whichever issue or side you take, follow Anthony's example in using the Constitution and the Declaration of Independence for your argument. Keep in mind what someone who disagrees with you would say, so that you can anticipate some of the serious objections and then refute them.

2. Using recent biographies of Anthony or *The Life and Works of Susan B. Anthony,* write a documented paper on one of the following topics:

a. The influence of her Quaker upbringing on her activism; her early fights for equal pay for women teachers.

b. Her support of emancipation during the Civil War.

c. Her refusal to support the vote for freed slaves because it did not include a vote for women.

d. The circumstances surrounding her attempt to register to vote and her subsequent arrest.

❋❋❋ *Plessy v. Ferguson* (1894)

U.S. SUPREME COURT

After the Civil War and Reconstruction, southern legislatures began passing Jim Crow laws, which instituted segregation against African Americans. In an earlier decision, the Court had repealed the Civil Rights Act of 1875, and the majority decision in Plessy *effectively made discrimination legal. Justice John Harlan, who had grown up as a slaveholder but who had become one of a long line of distinguished Supreme Court dissenters, was the only justice to vote against the decision.*

Majority Opinion (by Justice Henry Billings Brown)

Mr. Justice Brown, . . . delivered the opinion of the court.

This case turns upon the constitutionality of an Act of the general assembly of the state of Louisiana, passed in 1890, providing for separate railway carriages for the white and colored races.

The first section of the statute enacts "that all railway companies carrying passengers in their coaches in this state, shall provide equal but separate accommodations for the white, and colored races."

. . . [Plessy argued that he] was seven-eighths Caucasian and one-eighth African blood; that the mixture of colored blood was not discernible in him; and that he was entitled to every right, privilege, and immunity secured to citizens of the United States of the white race; and that, upon such theory, he took possession of a vacant seat in a coach where passengers of the white race were accommodated, and was ordered by the conductor to vacate said coach and take a seat in another, assigned to persons of the colored race, and, having refused to comply with such demand, he was forcibly ejected, with the aid of a police officer, and imprisoned in the parish jail to answer a charge of having violated the above act.

The constitutionality of this act is attacked upon the ground that it 5 conflicts both with the Thirteenth Amendment of the Constitution abolishing slavery, and the Fourteenth Amendment, which prohibits certain restrictive legislation on the part of the states.

1. That it does not conflict with the Thirteenth Amendment, which abolished slavery and involuntary servitude, except as a punishment for crime, is too clear for argument. Slavery implies involuntary servitude,—a state of bondage; the ownership of mankind as a chattel, or, at least, the control of the labor and services of one man for the benefit of another, and the absence of a legal right to the disposal of his own person, property, and services.

. . . "It would be running the slavery question into the ground," said Mr. Justice Bradley, "to make it apply to every act of discrimination which a person may see fit to make as to the guests he will entertain, or as to the people he will take into his coach or cab or car, or admit to his concert or theater, or deal with in other matters of intercourse or business."

A statute which implies merely a legal distinction between the white and colored races—a distinction which is founded in the color of the two races, and which must always exist so long as white men are distinguished from the other race by color—has no tendency to destroy the legal equality of the two races, or re-establish a state of involuntary servitude. . . .

2. By the Fourteenth Amendment, all persons born or naturalized in the United States, and subject to the jurisdiction thereof, are made citizens of the United States and of the state wherein they reside; and the states are forbidden from making or enforcing any law which . . . shall deprive any person of life, liberty, or property without due process of law, or deny to any person . . . equal protection of the laws.

The object of the Amendment was undoubtedly to enforce the absolute equality of the two races before the law, but in the nature of things, it could not have been intended to abolish distinctions based upon color, or to enforce social, as distinguished from political, equality, or a commingling of the two races upon terms unsatisfactory to either. Laws permitting, and even requiring, their separation, in places where they are liable to be brought into contact, do not necessarily imply the inferiority of either race to the other. . . . The most common instance of this is connected with the establishment of separate schools for white and colored children. . . . 10

So far, then, as a conflict with the Fourteenth Amendment is concerned, the case reduces itself to the question whether the statute of Louisiana is a reasonable regulation, and with respect to this there must necessarily be a large discretion on the part of the legislature. In determining the question of reasonableness, it is at liberty to act with reference to the established usages, customs, and traditions of the people, and with a view to the promotion of their comfort, and the preservation of the public peace and good order. Gauged by this standard, we cannot say that a law which authorizes or even requires the separation of the two races in public conveyances is unreasonable, or more obnoxious to the Fourteenth Amendment than the acts of Congress requiring separate schools for colored children in the District of Columbia, the constitutionality of which does not seem to have been questioned, or the corresponding acts of state legislatures.

We consider the underlying fallacy of the plaintiff's argument to consist in the assumption that the enforced separation of the two races stamps the colored race with a badge of inferiority. If this be so, it is not by reason of anything found in the act, but solely because the colored race chooses to put that construction upon it. The argument necessarily assumes that if, as has been more than once the case, and is not unlikely to be so again, the colored race should become the dominant power in the state legislature, and should enact a law in precisely similar terms, it would thereby relegate the white race to an inferior position. We imagine that the white race, at least, would not acquiesce in this assumption. The argument also assumes that social prejudices may be overcome by legislation, and that equal rights cannot be secured to the Negro except by an enforced commingling of the two races. We cannot accept this proposition. If the two races are to meet upon terms of social equality, it must be the result of natural affinities, a mutual appreciation of each other's merits, and a voluntary consent of individuals. . . . Legislation is powerless to eradicate racial instincts, or to abolish distinctions based upon physical differences, and the attempt to do so can only result in accentuating the difficulties of the present situation. If the civil and political rights of both races be equal, one cannot be inferior to the other civilly or politically. If one race be inferior to the other socially, the Constitution of the United States cannot put them upon the same plane.

Dissenting Opinion (by Justice John Harlan)

. . . In respect of civil rights common to all citizens, the Constitution of the United States does not, I think, permit any public authority to know the race of those entitled to be protected in the enjoyment of such rights. Every true man has pride of race, and under appropriate circumstances when the rights of others, his equals before the law, are not to be affected, it is his privilege to express such pride and to take such action based upon it as to him seems proper. But I deny that any legislative body or judicial tribunal may have regard to the race of citizens when the civil rights of those citizens are involved. Indeed, such legislation, as that here in question, is inconsistent not only with the equality of rights which pertains to citizenship, national and state, but with the personal liberty enjoyed by every one within the United States. . . .

The white race deems itself to be the dominant race in this country. And so it is, in prestige, in achievements, in education, in wealth and in power. So, I doubt not, it will continue to be for all time, if it remains true to its great heritage and holds fast to the principles of constitutional liberty. But in view of the Constitution, in the eye of the law, there is in this country no superior, dominant, ruling class of citizens. There is no caste here. Our Constitution is color-blind, and neither knows nor tolerates classes among citizens. In respect of civil rights, all citizens are equal before the law. The humblest is the peer of the most powerful. The law regards man as man, and takes no account of his surroundings or of his color when his civil rights as guaranteed by the supreme law of the land are involved. It is, therefore, to be regretted that this high tribunal, the final expositor of the fundamental law of the land, has reached the conclusion that it is competent for a State to regulate the enjoyment by citizens of their civil rights solely upon the basis of race. . . .

The arbitrary separation of citizens, on the basis of race, while they 15 are on a public highway, is a badge of servitude wholly inconsistent with the civil freedom and the equality before the law established by the Constitution. It cannot be justified upon any legal grounds.

If evils will result from the commingling of the two races upon public highways established for the benefit of all, they will be infinitely less than those that will surely come from state legislation regulating the enjoyment of civil rights upon the basis of race. We boast of the freedom enjoyed by our people above all other peoples. But it is difficult to reconcile that boast with a state of the law which, practically, puts the brand of servitude and degradation upon a large class of our fellow-citizens, our equals before the law. The thin disguise of "equal" accommodations for passengers in railroad coaches will not mislead anyone, nor atone for the wrong this day done.

For Journals

In your own words, what did the Court decide in this case? Who won? Who lost?

For Discussion

1.   Mr. Plessy argued that denying him the right to ride in the white railway carriage was a violation of the Thirteenth Amendment, which prohibits slavery, and the Fourteenth Amendment, which grants equal protection under the law. What reasons does Justice Brown give to refute Plessy's argument? Why does he think that the two amendments do not apply to this case?

2.   How does the Court define "separate but equal"?

3.   In the majority opinion, Justice Brown says that equality before the law doesn't have to mean social equality. Do you think that it is possible to be equal before the law but not in any other way? What is your definition of equality?

4.   How would you refute the Court's statement that if blacks felt inferior because they were forced to ride in a separate railway carriage, it was their fault because they chose to look at it that way?

5.   In his minority opinion, what does Justice Harlan think is the real meaning of the separate-but-equal laws as far as the future of black-white relations is concerned? What kinds of injustices does he foresee in a segregated South?

6. Why do you think that Harlan sees dangers to other minorities besides African Americans in the *Plessy* decision? What does he mean when he says that the decision would not mislead anyone and not atone for the wrong done? Do you agree with him?

For Writing

1. Research the term "Jim Crow." Write a documented paper in which you discuss what the origins of the term are and how Jim Crow laws affected the lives of southern blacks (give specific examples of segregation in everyday life). If you know someone who had firsthand experience with the Jim Crow laws, interview him or her for your paper.

2. Both Justice Harlan in *Plessy* and Thoreau in *Civil Disobedience* believed, with very different results, that legislation is not a good way to change people's behavior. Write an essay in which you argue for or against the proposition that injustice cannot be changed through legislation and that trying to eradicate differences through legislation can only make a situation worse. Focus your argument around an injustice you think needs changing. Use Thoreau, *Plessy*, or both to back up your assertions.

✷✷✷ *Dolls* (1935)

EUDORA WELTY

Eudora Welty (1909–2001) was born in Mississippi. She is most famous as a writer of novels and short stories, including Delta Wedding *(1946),* Golden Apples *(1949), and* Losing Battles *(1970); and she won the Pulitzer Prize for* The Optimist's Daughter *(1972). In her fiction, which is set in the South she knows so well, she often writes about familial conflicts and people who don't know themselves or those close to them as well as they should. In her photography, which also revolves mainly around Mississippi, she provides a compassionate and an extraordinarily perceptive record of the lives of ordinary people, particularly the poor southern blacks whose dignity she portrays and respects. This photograph is one of a series she took in the 1930s, when she was hired by the Works Progress Administration to interview poor people and to see how they coped with the additional burden of the Depression. Many of her greatest photographs, taken in the rural South, New York City, and Ireland, among other places, have been collected in a book called* Welty Photographs *(1989).*

For Journals

What is your most or least favorite childhood photograph of yourself? What does it remind you of?

For Discussion

1. Until recently, almost no dolls were manufactured with a skin color other than white. What do you think was the effect on the children in this picture of having only blond dolls to play with? Why would there be a connection between the toys and the way they see themselves?

2. This picture is usually called "Dolls." On the basis of your own first impressions of it, what new title would you give that would be more descriptive of its emotional impact? Why do you think that Welty did not pick a more emotional title?

3. A photograph can establish a point of view, make an argument, or assert a moral viewpoint. Welty said that her photographs were facts. She took this photograph when life in the South was completely segregated and southern blacks lacked the most basic civil rights. Looking at the details of this picture—the way that the girls hold the dolls, the girls' facial expressions, the background, how the children and the dolls are dressed, and so on—explain in your own words what Welty was trying to communicate in this picture and how well you think she succeeded.

For Writing

1. Bring to class a childhood photograph of yourself that brings back strong memories or a photograph of children from a magazine. Trade that photograph with one from someone else in class. Write an essay on the other person's photograph, analyzing it closely, as you did with Welty's photo. Make up a history for it: describe what mood it conveys, what happened just before and after the picture was taken, and so on. Use details from the photo as evidence for your interpretation. Then trade essays with your peer, and compare the results; write follow-up notes on how accurate or inaccurate your interpretations were.

2. Eudora Welty said that her photographs were facts. Select another photograph from her book, and write an essay in which you evaluate and compare it with "Dolls," in the light of Welty's statement. Do you think that she points a finger at injustice? Do you find her photos of black southern life under segregation objective? Sympathetic? Depressing? Refer directly to the photographs to support your argument.

❦❦❦ *Brown v. Board of Education* (1954)

U.S. SUPREME COURT

Brown v. Board of Education *is the landmark decision of the Supreme Court, under Chief Justice Earl Warren, in the twentieth century. Its official result was to declare segregation in public schools unconstitutional and to overturn the Plessy doctrine of "separate but equal" facilities. It followed on the heels of other cases that had outlawed segregation in professional schools. Its effect was to take away the legal underpinnings of segregation in all areas, and it began a process of dismantling segregation that has had a profound effect on American life.*

These cases come to us from the states of Kansas, South Carolina, Virginia, and Delaware. They are premised on different facts and different local conditions, but a common legal question justifies their consideration together in this consolidated opinion.

In each of the cases, minors of the Negro race, through their legal representatives, seek the aid of the courts in obtaining admission to the public schools of their community on a nonsegregated basis. In each instance, they have been denied admission to schools attended by white children under laws requiring or permitting segregation according to race. This segregation was alleged to deprive the plaintiffs of the equal protection of the laws under the Fourteenth Amendment. In each of the cases other than the Delaware case, a three-judge federal district court denied relief to the plaintiffs on the so-called "separate but equal" doctrine announced by this Court in *Plessy* v. *Ferguson*. . . . Under that doctrine, equality of treatment is accorded when the races are provided substantially equal facilities, even though these facilities be separate. . . .

The plaintiffs contend that segregated public schools are not "equal" and cannot be made "equal," and that hence they are deprived of the equal protection of the laws. Because of the obvious importance of the question presented, the Court took jurisdiction. . . .

There are findings below that the Negro and white schools involved have been equalized, or are being equalized, with respect to buildings, curricula, qualifications and salaries of teachers, and other "tangible" factors. Our decision, therefore, cannot turn on merely a comparison of these tangible factors in the Negro and white schools involved in each of the cases. We must look instead to the effect of segregation itself on public education.

In approaching this problem, we cannot turn the clock back to 5 1868 when the Amendment was adopted, or even to 1896 when *Plessy* v. *Ferguson* was written. We must consider public education in the light of its full development and its present place in American life throughout the nation. Only in this way can it be determined if segregation in public schools deprives these plaintiffs of the equal protection of the laws.

Today, education is perhaps the most important function of state and local governments. Compulsory school attendance laws and the great expenditures for education both demonstrate our recognition of the importance of education to our democratic society. It is required in the performance of our most basic public responsibilities, even service in the armed forces. It is the very foundation of good citizenship. Today it is a principal instrument in awakening the child to cultural values, in preparing him for later professional training, and in helping him to adjust normally to his environment. In these days, it is doubtful that any child may reasonably be expected to succeed in life if he is denied the opportunity of an education. Such an opportunity, where the state has undertaken to provide it, is a right which must be made available to all on equal terms.

We come then to the question presented: Does segregation of children in public schools solely on the basis of race, even though the physical facilities and other "tangible" factors may be equal, deprive the children of the minority group of equal educational opportunities? We believe that it does.

In *Sweatt* v. *Painter*, in finding that a segregated law school for Negroes could not provide them equal educational opportunities, this Court relied in large part on "those qualities which are incapable of objective measurement but which make for greatness in a law school." In *McLaurin* v. *Oklahoma State Regents*, . . . the Court, in requiring that a Negro admitted to a white graduate school be treated like all other students, again resorted to intangible considerations: ". . . his ability to study, to engage in discussions and exchange views with other students, and, in general, to learn his profession." Such considerations apply with added force to children in grade and high schools. To separate them from others of similar age and qualifications solely because of their race generates a feeling of inferiority as to their status in the community that may affect their hearts and minds in a way unlikely ever to be undone. The effect of this separation on their educational opportunities was well stated by a finding in the Kansas case by a court which nevertheless felt compelled to rule against the Negro plaintiffs:

> Segregation of white and colored children in public schools has a detrimental effect upon the colored children. The impact is greater when it has the sanction of the law; for the policy of separating the races is usually interpreted as denoting the inferiority of the Negro group. A sense of inferiority affects the motivation of a child to learn. Segregation with the sanction of law, therefore, has a tendency to retard the educational and mental development of Negro children and to deprive them of some of the benefits they would receive in a racially integrated school system.

Whatever may have been the extent of psychological knowledge at the time of *Plessy* v. *Ferguson*, this finding is amply supported by modern authority. Any language in *Plessy* v. *Ferguson* contrary to this finding is rejected.

We conclude that in the field of public education the doctrine of "separate but equal" has no place. Separate educational facilities are inherently unequal. Therefore, we hold that the plaintiffs and others similarly situated for whom the actions have been brought are, by reason of the segregation complained of, deprived of the equal protection of the laws guaranteed by the Fourteenth Amendment. . . .

For Journals

Summarize the decision in the case. In your own words, write what you think that the essence of the decision was.

For Discussion

1.   In American law, precedent—what has been determined in previous legal decisions—is very important, so refuting the ruling of *Plessy* after almost fifty years required considerable justification. How does the Warren Court in *Brown* get around the fact that *Plessy* had stood since it was declared good law in 1896?

2.   What are the Court's main points in its argument that education today and education right after the Civil War are so different that a new interpretation of *Plessy* is appropriate?

3.   Analyze what the Court says about the harmful effects of segregated schooling on black children. What injustice does the Court in *Brown* see in segregation that the Court in *Plessy* did not? Why wouldn't a school for black children do as good a job as an integrated school?

4.   The decision of a court is called a ruling. In refuting *Plessy*, the Warren Court made a ruling that separate public schools could not also be equal. Why did the Court think that separate but equal was a contradiction?

5.   If you had to pick the most crucial sentence, the assertion, the thesis, from this ruling, what would it be? Why?

6.   The Court says that if it only took into account "tangible" factors like buildings and curriculum for segregated schools, it would fail to see the situation in its entirety. What kinds of "intangibles" do you think that the Warren Court considered in reaching its decision in *Brown*? Are intangibles as good as evidence as tangibles like school buildings?

For Writing

1.   Research one of the following and, in a documented essay, discuss its significance for civil liberties in the United States:

a. The life and career of Thurgood Marshall, who argued *Brown* and later became solicitor general of the United States and then the first African American justice of the Supreme Court.

b. Marshall's strategy, as leading attorney for the NAACP, in challenging segregation through the courts instead of in state legislatures, and in picking elementary school education as the point of attack.

c. The significance of the precedents that were decided in the cases before *Brown* that are mentioned by Chief Justice Warren, especially *Sweatt v. Painter* and *McLaurin v. Oklahoma State Regents.*

2. Chief Justice Warren wrote that we must look at the intangibles to get a complete picture. Write an essay in which you compare the *Brown* decision and its use of intangible factors with either Douglass's Independence Day speech or Anthony's "Women's Right to Vote" speech. What tangible evidence and intangibles do the authors consider in arguing against injustice? Which category is more important to them? Which do you think is more important? Use examples from the selections as proof for your conclusions.

Letter from Birmingham Jail (1963)

MARTIN LUTHER KING, JR.

The strategy developed by the modern civil rights movement and its leader, the young Atlanta minister Martin Luther King, Jr. (see Chapter 4), was the policy of nonviolent resistance. Based on the teachings of the Bible, Mahatma Gandhi, and Thoreau, it revolved around peaceful marches, sit-ins at lunch counters, and economic boycotts of buses and businesses. In 1963, while leading demonstrations in Montgomery, Alabama, King was arrested. In jail he wrote a letter of justification and explanation addressed to eight southern clergymen who had issued a public statement objecting to the demonstrations that King led and to demonstrations as a method for dealing with racial problems. Both letters are reprinted here.

Clergymen's Letter

We the undersigned clergymen are among those who, in January, issued "An Appeal for Law and Order and Common Sense," in dealing with racial problems in Alabama. We expressed understanding that honest convictions in racial matters could properly be pursued in the courts, but urged that decisions of those courts should in the meantime be peacefully obeyed.

Since that time there had been some evidence of increased forbearance and a willingness to face facts. Responsible citizens have undertaken to work on various problems which cause racial friction and unrest. In Birmingham, recent public events have given indication that we all have opportunity for a new constructive and realistic approach to racial problems.

However, we are now confronted by a series of demonstrations by some of our Negro citizens, directed and led in part by outsiders. We recognize the natural impatience of people who feel that their hopes are slow in being realized. But we are convinced that these demonstrations are unwise and untimely.

We agree rather with certain local Negro leadership which has called for honest and open negotiation of racial issues in our area. And we believe this kind of facing of issues can best be accomplished by citizens of our own metropolitan area, white and Negro, meeting with their knowledge and experience of the local situation. All of us need to face that responsibility and find proper channels for its accomplishment.

Just as we formerly pointed out that "hatred and violence have 5 no sanction in our religious and political traditions," we also point out that such actions as incite to hatred and violence, however technically peaceful those actions may be, have not contributed to the resolution of our local problems. We do not believe that these days of new hope are days when extreme measures are justified in Birmingham.

We commend the community as a whole, and the local news media and the law enforcement officials in particular, on the calm manner in which these demonstrations have been handled. We urge the public to continue to show restraint should the demonstrations continue, and the law enforcement officials to remain calm and continue to protect our city from violence.

We further strongly urge our own Negro community to withdraw support from these demonstrations, and to unite locally in working peacefully for a better Birmingham. When rights are consistently denied, a cause should be pressed in the courts and in negotiations among local leaders, and not in the streets. We appeal to both our white and Negro citizenry to observe the principles of law and order and common sense.

Signed by:
C. C. J. *Carpenter,* D.D., LL.D., Bishop of Alabama
Joseph A. Durick, D.D., Auxiliary Bishop, Diocese of Mobile,
  Birmingham
Milton L. Grafman, Rabbi, Temple Emanu-El, Birmingham, Alabama
Paul Hardin, Bishop of the Alabama-West Florida Conference of the
  Methodist Church
Nolan B. Harmon, Bishop of the North Alabama Conference of the
  Methodist Church
George M. Murray, D.D., LL.D., Bishop Coadjutor, Episcopal Diocese of
  Alabama
Edward V. Ramage, Moderator, Synod of the Alabama Presbyterian
  Church in the United States
Earl Stallings, Pastor, First Baptist Church, Birmingham, Alabama

King's Letter

April 16, 1963

My Dear Fellow Clergymen:

While confined here in the Birmingham city jail, I came across your recent statement calling my present activities "unwise and untimely." Seldom do I pause to answer criticism of my work and ideas. If I sought to answer all the criticisms that cross my desk, my secretaries would have little time for anything other than such correspondence in the course of the day, and I would have no time for constructive work. But since I feel that you are men of genuine good will and that your criticisms are sincerely set forth, I want to try to answer your statement in what I hope will be patient and reasonable terms.

I think I should indicate why I am here in Birmingham, since you have been influenced by the view which argues against "outsiders coming in." I have the honor of serving as president of the Southern Christian Leadership Conference, an organization operating in every southern state, with headquarters in Atlanta, Georgia. We have some eighty-five affiliated organizations across the South, and one of them is the Alabama Christian Movement for Human Rights. Frequently we share staff, educational and financial resources with our affiliates. Several months ago the affiliate here in Birmingham asked us to be on call to engage in a nonviolent direct-action program if such were deemed necessary. We readily consented, and when the hour came we lived up to our promise. So I, along with several members of my staff, am here because I was invited here. I am here because I have organizational ties here.

But more basically, I am in Birmingham because injustice is here. 10 Just as the prophets of the eighth century B.C. left their villages and carried their "thus saith the Lord" far beyond the boundaries of their home towns, and just as the Apostle Paul left his village of Tarsus and carried the gospel of Jesus Christ to the far corners of the Greco-Roman world, so am I compelled to carry the gospel of freedom beyond my own home town. Like Paul, I must constantly respond to the Macedonian call for aid.

Moreover, I am cognizant of the interrelatedness of all communities and states. I cannot sit idly by in Atlanta and not be concerned about what happens in Birmingham. Injustice anywhere is a threat to justice everywhere. We are caught in an inescapable network of mutuality, tied in a single garment of destiny. Whatever affects one directly, affects all indirectly. Never again can we afford to live with the narrow, provincial "outside agitator" idea. Anyone who lives inside the United States can never be considered an outsider anywhere within its bounds.

You deplore the demonstrations taking place in Birmingham. But your statement, I am sorry to say, fails to express a similar concern for the conditions that brought about the demonstrations. I am sure that none of you would want to rest content with the superficial kind of social analysis that deals merely with effects and does not grapple with underlying causes. It is unfortunate that demonstrations are taking place in Birmingham, but it is even more unfortunate that the city's white power structure left the Negro community with no alternative.

In any nonviolent campaign there are four basic steps: collection of the facts to determine whether injustices exist; negotiation; self-purification; and direct action. We have gone through all these steps in Birmingham. There can be no gainsaying the fact that racial injustice engulfs this community. Birmingham is probably the most thoroughly segregated city in the United States. Its ugly record of brutality is widely known. Negroes have experienced grossly unjust treatment in the courts. There have been more unsolved bombings of Negro homes and churches in Birmingham than in any other city in the nation. These are the hard, brutal facts of the case. On the basis of these conditions, Negro leaders sought to negotiate with the city fathers. But the latter consistently refused to engage in good-faith negotiation.

Then, last September, came the opportunity to talk with leaders of Birmingham's economic community. In the course of the negotiations, certain promises were made by the merchants—for example, to remove the stores' humiliating racial signs. On the basis of these promises, the Reverend Fred Shuttlesworth and the leaders of the Alabama Christian Movement for Human Rights agreed to a moratorium on all demonstrations. As the weeks and months went by, we realized that we were the victims of a broken promise. A few signs, briefly removed, returned; the others remained.

As in so many past experiences, our hopes had been blasted, and the shadow of deep disappointment settled upon us. We had no alternative except to prepare for direct action, whereby we would present our very bodies as a means of laying our case before the conscience of the local and the national community. Mindful of the difficulties involved, we decided to undertake a process of self-purification. We began a series of workshops on nonviolence, and we repeatedly asked ourselves: "Are you able to accept blows without retaliating?" "Are you able to endure the ordeal of jail?" We decided to schedule our direct-action program for the Easter season, realizing that except for Christmas, this is the main shopping period of the year. Knowing that a strong economic-withdrawal program would be the by-product of direct action, we felt that this would be the best time to bring pressure to bear on the merchants for the needed change.

Then it occurred to us that Birmingham's mayoral election was coming up in March, and we speedily decided to postpone action until after election day. When we discovered that the Commissioner of Public Safety, Eugene "Bull" Connor, had piled up enough votes to be in the run-off, we decided again to postpone action until the day after the run-off so that the demonstrations could not be used to cloud the issues. Like many others, we waited to see Mr. Connor defeated, and to this end we endured postponement after postponement. Having aided in this community need, we felt that our direct-action program could be delayed no longer.

You may well ask: "Why direct action? Why sit-ins, marches and so forth? Isn't negotiation a better path?" You are quite right in calling for negotiation. Indeed, this is the very purpose of direct action. Nonviolent direct action seeks to create such a crisis and foster such a tension that a community which has constantly refused to negotiate is forced to confront the issue. It seeks so to dramatize the issue that it can no longer be ignored. My citing the creation of tension as part of the work of the nonviolent-resister may sound rather shocking. But I must confess that I am not afraid of the word "tension." I have earnestly opposed violent tension, but there is a type of constructive, nonviolent tension which is necessary for growth. Just as Socrates felt that it was necessary to create a tension in the mind so that individuals could rise from the bondage of myths and half-truths to the unfettered realm of creative analysis and objective appraisal, so must we see the need for nonviolent gadflies to create the kind of tension in society that will help men rise from the dark depths of prejudice and racism to the majestic heights of understanding and brotherhood.

The purpose of our direct-action program is to create a situation so crisis-packed that it will inevitably open the door to negotiation. I therefore concur with you in your call for negotiation. Too long has our beloved Southland been bogged down in a tragic effort to live in monologue rather than dialogue.

One of the basic points in your statement is that the action that I and my associates have taken in Birmingham is untimely. Some have asked: "Why didn't you give the new city administration time to act?" The only answer that I can give to this query is that the new Birmingham administration must be prodded about as much as the outgoing one, before it will act. We are sadly mistaken if we feel that the election of Albert Boutwell as mayor will bring the millennium to Birmingham. While Mr. Boutwell is a much more gentle person than Mr. Connor, they are both segregationists, dedicated to maintenance of the status quo. I have hope that Mr. Boutwell will be reasonable enough to see the futility of massive resistance to desegregation. But he will not see this without pressure from devotees of civil rights. My friends, I must say to you that we have not made a single gain in civil rights without determined legal and nonviolent pressure. Lamentably, it is an historical fact that privileged groups seldom give up their privileges voluntarily. Individuals may see the moral light and voluntarily give up their unjust posture; but, as Reinhold Niebuhr has reminded us, groups tend to be more immoral than individuals.

We know through painful experience that freedom is never volun- 20 tarily given by the oppressor; it must be demanded by the oppressed. Frankly, I have yet to engage in a direct-action campaign that was "well timed" in the view of those who have not suffered unduly from the disease of segregation. For years now I have heard the word "Wait!" It rings in the ear of every Negro with piercing familiarity. This "Wait" has almost always meant "Never." We must come to see, with one of our distinguished jurists, that "justice too long delayed is justice denied."

We have waited for more than three hundred forty years for our constitutional God-given rights. The nations of Asia and Africa are moving with jetlike speed toward gaining political independence, but we still creep at horse-and-buggy pace toward gaining a cup of coffee at a lunch counter. Perhaps it is easy for those who have never felt the stinging darts of segregation to say, "Wait." But when you have seen vicious mobs lynch your mothers and fathers at will and drown your sisters and brothers at whim; when you have seen hate-filled police-men curse, kick, and even kill your black brothers and sisters; when you see the vast majority of your twenty million Negro brothers smothering in an airtight cage of poverty in the midst of an affluent so-ciety; when you suddenly find your tongue twisted and your speech stammering as you seek to explain to your six-year-old daughter why she can't go to the public amusement park that has just been adver-tised on television, and see tears welling up in her eyes when she is told that Funtown is closed to colored children, and see ominous clouds of inferiority beginning to form in her little mental sky, and see her beginning to distort her personality by developing an unconscious bitterness toward white people; when you have to concoct an answer for a five-year-old son who is asking: "Daddy, why do white people treat colored people so mean?"; when you take a cross-country drive and find it necessary to sleep night after night in the uncomfortable corners of your automobile because no motel will accept you; when you are humiliated day in and day out by nagging signs reading "white" and "colored"; when your first name becomes "nigger," your middle name becomes "boy" (however old you are) and your last name becomes "John," and your wife and mother are never given the respected title "Mrs."; when you are harried by day and haunted by night by the fact that you are a Negro, living constantly at tiptoe stance, never quite knowing what to expect next, and are plagued with inner fears and outer resentments; when you are forever fighting a de-generating sense of "nobodiness"—then you will understand why we find it difficult to wait. There comes a time when the cup of endurance runs over, and men are no longer willing to be plunged into the abyss of despair. I hope, sirs, you can understand our legitimate and unavoidable impatience.

You express a great deal of anxiety over our willingness to break laws. This is certainly a legitimate concern. Since we so diligently urge people to obey the Supreme Court's decision of 1954 outlawing segregation in the public schools, at first glance it may seem rather paradoxical for us consciously to break laws. One may well ask: "How can you advocate breaking some laws and obeying others?" The answer lies in the fact that there are two types of laws: just and unjust. I would be the first to advocate obeying just laws. One has not only a legal but a moral responsibility to obey just laws. Conversely, one has a moral responsibility to disobey unjust laws. I would agree with St. Augustine that "an unjust law is no law at all."

Now, what is the difference between the two? How does one determine whether a law is just or unjust? A just law is a man-made code that squares with the moral law or the law of God. An unjust law is a code that is out of harmony with the moral law. To put it in the terms of St. Thomas Aquinas: An unjust law is a human law that is not rooted in eternal law and natural law. Any law that uplifts human personality is just. Any law that degrades human personality is unjust. All segregation statutes are unjust because segregation distorts the soul and damages the personality. It gives the segregator a false sense of superiority and the segregated a false sense of inferiority. Segregation, to use the terminology of the Jewish philosopher Martin Buber, substitutes an "I—it" relationship for an "I—thou" relationship and ends up relegating persons to the status of things. Hence, segregation is not only politically, economically and sociologically unsound, it is morally wrong and sinful. Paul Tillich has said that sin is separation. Is not segregation an existential expression of man's tragic separation, his awful estrangement, his terrible sinfulness? Thus it is that I can urge men to obey the 1954 decision of the Supreme Court, for it is morally right; and I can urge them to disobey segregation ordinances, for they are morally wrong.

Let us consider a more concrete example of just and unjust laws. An unjust law is a code that a numerical or power majority group compels a minority group to obey but does not make binding on itself. This is *difference* made legal. By the same token, a just law is a code that a majority compels a minority to follow and that it is willing to follow itself. This is *sameness* made legal.

Let me give another explanation. A law is unjust if it is inflicted on 25 a minority that, as a result of being denied the right to vote, had no part in enacting or devising the law. Who can say that the legislature of Alabama which set up that state's segregation laws was democratically elected? Throughout Alabama all sorts of devious methods are used to prevent Negroes from becoming registered voters, and there are some counties in which, even though Negroes constitute a majority of the population, not a single Negro is registered. Can any law enacted under such circumstances be considered democratically structured?

Sometimes a law is just on its face and unjust in its application. For instance, I have been arrested on a charge of parading without a permit. Now, there is nothing wrong in having an ordinance which requires a permit for a parade. But such an ordinance becomes unjust when it is used to maintain segregation and to deny citizens the First-Amendment privilege of peaceful assembly and protest.

I hope you are able to see the distinction I am trying to point out. In no sense do I advocate evading or defying the law, as would the rabid segregationist. That would lead to anarchy. One who breaks an unjust law must do so openly, lovingly, and with a willingness to accept the penalty. I submit that an individual who breaks a law that conscience tells him is unjust, and who willingly accepts the penalty of imprisonment in order to arouse the conscience of the community over its injustice, is in reality expressing the highest respect for law.

Of course, there is nothing new about this kind of civil disobedience. It was evidenced sublimely in the refusal of Shadrach, Meshach and Abednego to obey the laws of Nebuchadnezzar, on the ground that a higher moral law was at stake. It was practiced superbly by the early Christians, who were willing to face hungry lions and the excruciating pain of chopping blocks rather than submit to certain unjust laws of the Roman Empire. To a degree, academic freedom is a reality today because Socrates practiced civil disobedience. In our own nation, the Boston Tea Party represented a massive act of civil disobedience.

We should never forget that everything Adolf Hitler did in Germany was "legal" and everything the Hungarian freedom fighters did in Hungary was "illegal." It was "illegal" to aid and comfort a Jew in Hitler's Germany. Even so, I am sure that, had I lived in Germany at the time, I would have aided and comforted my Jewish brothers. If today I lived in a Communist country where certain principles dear to the Christian faith are suppressed I would openly advocate disobeying that country's antireligious laws.

I must make two honest confessions to you, my Christian and Jewish brothers. First, I must confess that over the past few years I have been gravely disappointed with the white moderate. I have almost reached the regrettable conclusion that the Negro's great stumbling block in his stride toward freedom is not the White Citizen's Counciler or the Ku Klux Klanner, but the white moderate, who is more devoted to "order" than to justice; who prefers a negative peace which is the presence of tension to a positive peace which is the presence of justice; who constantly says: "I agree with you in the goal you seek, but I cannot agree with your methods of direct action"; who paternalistically believes he can set the timetable for another man's freedom; who lives by a mythical concept of time and who constantly advises the Negro to wait for a "more convenient season." Shallow understanding from people of good will is more frustrating than absolute misunderstanding from people of ill will. Lukewarm acceptance is much more bewildering than outright rejection.

I had hoped that the white moderate would understand that law and order exist for the purpose of establishing justice and that when they fail in this purpose they become the dangerously structured dams that block the flow of social progress. I had hoped that the white moderate would understand that the present tension in the South is a necessary phase of the transition from an obnoxious negative peace, in which the Negro passively accepted his unjust plight, to a substantive and positive peace, in which all men will respect the dignity and worth of human personality. Actually, we who engage in nonviolent direct action are not the creators of tension. We merely bring to the surface the hidden tension that is already alive. We bring it out in the open, where it can be seen and dealt with. Like a boil that can never be cured so long as it is covered up but must be opened with all its ugliness to the natural medicines of air and light, injustice must be exposed, with all the tension its exposure creates, to the light of human conscience and the air of national opinion before it can be cured.

In your statement you assert that our actions, even though peaceful, must be condemned because they precipitate violence. But is this a logical assertion? Isn't this like condemning a robbed man because his possession of money precipitated the evil act of robbery? Isn't this like condemning Socrates because his unswerving commitment to truth and his philosophical inquiries precipitated the act by the misguided populace in which they made him drink hemlock? Isn't this like condemning Jesus because his unique God-consciousness and never-ceasing devotion to God's will precipitated the evil act of crucifixion? We must come to see that, as the federal courts have consistently affirmed, it is wrong to urge an individual to cease his efforts to gain his basic constitutional rights because the quest may precipitate violence. Society must protect the robbed and punish the robber.

I had also hoped that the white moderate would reject the myth concerning time in relation to the struggle for freedom. I have just received a letter from a white brother in Texas. He writes: "All Christians know that the colored people will receive equal rights eventually, but it is possible that you are in too great a religious hurry. It has taken Christianity almost two thousand years to accomplish what it has. The teachings of Christ take time to come to earth." Such an attitude stems from a tragic misconception of time, from the strangely irrational notion that there is something in the very flow of time that will inevitably cure all ills. Actually, time itself is neutral; it can be used either destructively or constructively. More and more I feel that the people of ill will have used time much more effectively than have the people of good will. We will have to repent in this generation not merely for the hateful words and actions of the bad people but for the appalling silence of the good people. Human progress never rolls in on wheels of inevitability; it comes through the tireless efforts of men willing to be co-workers with God, and without this hard work, time itself becomes an ally of the forces of social stagnation. We must use time creatively, in the knowledge that the time is always ripe to do right. Now is the time to make real the promise of democracy and transform our pending national elegy into a creative psalm of brotherhood. Now is the time to lift our national policy from the quicksand of racial injustice to the solid rock of human dignity.

You speak of our activity in Birmingham as extreme. At first I was rather disappointed that fellow clergymen would see my nonviolent efforts as those of an extremist. I began thinking about the fact that I stand in the middle of two opposing forces in the Negro community. One is a force of complacency, made up in part of Negroes who, as a result of long years of oppression, are so drained of self-respect and a sense of "somebodiness" that they have adjusted to segregation; and in part of a few middle-class Negroes who, because of a degree of academic and economic security and because in some ways they profit by segregation, have become insensitive to the problems of the masses. The other force is one of bitterness and hatred, and it comes perilously close to advocating violence. It is expressed in the various black nationalists groups that are springing up across the nation, the largest and best-known being Elijah Muhammad's Muslim movement. Nourished by the Negro's frustration over the continued existence of racial discrimination, this movement is made up of people who have lost faith in America, who have absolutely repudiated Christianity, and who have concluded that the white man is an incorrigible "devil."

I have tried to stand between these two forces, saying that we 35 need emulate neither the "do-nothingism" of the complacent nor the hatred and despair of the black nationalist. For there is the more excellent way of love and nonviolent protest. I am grateful to God that, through the influence of the Negro church, the way of nonviolence became an integral part of our struggle.

If this philosophy had not emerged, by now many streets of the South would, I am convinced, be flowing with blood. And I am further convinced that if our white brothers dismiss as "rabble-rousers" and "outside agitators" those of us who employ nonviolent direct action, and if they refuse to support our nonviolent efforts, millions of the Negroes will, out of frustration and despair, seek solace and security in black-nationalist ideologies—a development that would inevitably lead to a frightening racial nightmare.

Oppressed people cannot remain oppressed forever. The yearning for freedom eventually manifests itself, and that is what has happened to the American Negro. Something within has reminded him of his birthright of freedom, and something without has reminded him that it can be gained. Consciously or unconsciously, he has been caught up by the *Zeitgeist*, and with his black brothers of Africa and his brown and yellow brothers of Asia, South America and the Caribbean, the United States Negro is moving with a sense of great urgency toward the promised land of racial justice. If one recognizes this vital urge that has engulfed the Negro community, one should readily understand why public demonstrations are taking place. The Negro has many pent-up resentments and latent frustrations, and he must release them. So let him march; let him make prayer pilgrimages to the city hall; let him go on freedom rides—and try to understand why he must do so. If his repressed emotions are not released in nonviolent ways, they will seek expression through violence; this is not a threat but a fact of history. So I have not said to my people: "Get rid of your discontent." Rather, I have tried to say that this normal and healthy discontent can be channeled into the creative outlet of nonviolent direct action. And now this approach is being termed extremist.

But though I was initially disappointed at being categorized as an extremist, as I continued to think about the matter I gradually gained a measure of satisfaction from the label. Was not Jesus an extremist for love: "Love your enemies, bless them that curse you, do good to them that hate you, and pray for them which despitefully use you, and persecute you." Was not Amos an extremist for justice: "Let justice roll down like waters and righteousness like an ever-flowing stream." Was not Paul an extremist for the Christian gospel: "I bear in my body the makers of the Lord Jesus." Was not Martin Luther an extremist: "Here I stand; I cannot do otherwise, so help me God." And John Bunyan: "I will stay in jail to the end of my days before I make a butchery of my conscience." And Abraham Lincoln: "This nation cannot survive half slave and half free." And Thomas Jefferson: "We hold these truths to be self-evident, that all men are created equal. . . ." So the question is not whether we will be extremists, but what kind of extremists we will be. Will we be extremists for hate or for love? Will we be extremists for the preservation of injustice or for the extension of justice? In that dramatic scene on Calvary's hill three men were crucified. We must never forget that all three were crucified for the same crime—the crime of extremism. Two were extremists for immorality, and thus fell below their environment. The other, Jesus Christ, was an extremist for love, truth and goodness, and thereby rose above his environment. Perhaps the South, the nation and the world are in dire need of creative extremists.

I had hoped that the white moderate would see this need. Perhaps I was too optimistic; perhaps I expected too much. I suppose I should have realized that few members of the oppressor race can understand the deep groans and passionate yearnings of the oppressed race, and still fewer have the vision to see that injustice must be rooted out by strong, persistent and determined action. I am thankful, however, that some of our white brothers in the South have grasped the meaning of this social revolution and committed themselves to it. They are still all too few in quantity, but they are big in quality. Some—such as Ralph McGill, Lillian Smith, Harry Golden, James McBride Dabbs, Ann Braden and Sarah Patton Boyle—have written about our struggle in eloquent and prophetic terms. Others have marched with us down nameless streets of the South. They have languished in filthy, roach-infested jails, suffering the abuse and brutality of policemen who view them as "dirty nigger-lovers." Unlike so many of their moderate brothers and sisters, they have recognized the urgency of the moment and sensed the need for powerful "action" antidotes to combat the disease of segregation.

Let me take note of my other major disappointment. I have been 40 so greatly disappointed with the white church and its leadership. Of course, there are some notable exceptions. I am not unmindful of the fact that each of you has taken some significant stands on this issue. I commend you, Reverend Stallings, for your Christian stand on this past Sunday, in welcoming Negroes to your worship service on a non-segregated basis. I commend the Catholic leaders of this state for integrating Spring Hill College several years ago.

But despite these notable exceptions, I must honestly reiterate that I have been disappointed with the church. I do not say this as one of those negative critics who can always find something wrong with the church. I say this as a minister of the gospel, who loves the church; who was nurtured in its bosom; who has been sustained by its spiritual blessings and who will remain true to it as long as the cord of life shall lengthen.

When I was suddenly catapulted into the leadership of the bus protest in Montgomery, Alabama, a few years ago, I felt we would be supported by the white church. I felt that the white ministers, priests and rabbis of the South would be among our strongest allies. Instead, some have been outright opponents, refusing to understand the freedom movement and misrepresenting its leaders; all too many others have been more cautious than courageous and have remained silent behind the anesthetizing security of stained-glass windows.

In spite of my shattered dreams, I came to Birmingham with the hope that the white religious leadership of this community would see the justice of our cause and, with deep moral concern, would serve as the channel through which our just grievances could reach the power structure. I had hoped that each of you would understand. But again I have been disappointed.

I have heard numerous southern religious leaders admonish their worshipers to comply with a desegregation decision because it is the law, but I have longed to hear white ministers declare: "Follow this decree because integration is morally right and because the Negro is your brother." In the midst of blatant injustices inflicted upon the Negro, I have watched white churchmen stand on the sideline and mouth pious irrelevancies and sanctimonious trivialities. In the midst of a mighty struggle to rid our nation of racial and economic injustice, I have heard many ministers say: "Those are social issues, with which the gospel has no real concern." And I have watched many churches commit themselves to a completely otherworldly religion which makes a strange, un-Biblical distinction between body and soul, between the sacred and the secular.

I have traveled the length and breadth of Alabama, Mississippi 45 and all the other southern states. On sweltering summer days and crisp autumn mornings I have looked at the South's beautiful churches with their lofty spires pointing heavenward. I have beheld the impressive outlines of her massive religious-education buildings. Over and over I have found myself asking: "What kind of people worship here? Who is their God? Where were their voices when the lips of Governor Barnett dripped with words of interposition and nullification? Where were they when Governor Wallace gave a clarion call for defiance and hatred? Where were their voices of support when bruised and weary Negro men and women decided to rise from the dark dungeons of complacency to the bright hills of creative protest?"

Yes, these questions are still in my mind. In deep disappointment I have wept over the laxity of the church. But be assured that my tears have been tears of love. There can be no deep disappointment where there is not deep love. Yes, I love the church. How could I do otherwise? I am in the rather unique position of being the son, the grandson, and the great-grandson of preachers. Yes, I see the church as the body of Christ. But, oh! How we have blemished and scarred that body through social neglect and through fear of being nonconformists.

There was a time when the church was very powerful—in the time when the early Christians rejoiced at being deemed worthy to suffer for what they believed. In those days the church was not merely a thermometer that recorded the ideas and principles of popular opinion; it was a thermostat that transformed the mores of society. Whenever the early Christians entered a town, the people in power became disturbed and immediately sought to convict the Christians for being "disturbers of the peace" and "outside agitators." But the Christians pressed on, in the conviction that they were "a colony of heaven," called to obey God rather than man. Small in number, they were big in commitment. They were too God-intoxicated to be "astronomically in-timidated." By their effort and example they brought an end to such ancient evils as infanticide and gladiatorial contests.

Things are different now. So often the contemporary church is a weak, ineffectual voice with an uncertain sound. So often it is an archdefender of the status quo. Far from being disturbed by the pres-ence of the church, the power structure of the average community is consoled by the church's silent—and often even vocal—sanction of things as they are.

But the judgment of God is upon the church as never before. If today's church does not recapture the sacrificial spirit of the early church, it will lose its authenticity, forfeit the loyalty of millions, and be dismissed as an irrelevant social club with no meaning for the twentieth century. Every day I meet young people whose disappoint-ment with the church has turned into outright disgust.

Perhaps I have once again been too optimistic. Is organized reli-   50
gion too inextricably bound to the status quo to save our nation and the world? Perhaps I must turn my faith to the inner spiritual church, the church within the church, as the true *ekklesia* and the hope of the world. But again I am thankful to God that some noble souls from the ranks of organized religion have broken loose from the paralyzing chains of conformity and joined us as active partners in the struggle for freedom. They have left their secure congregations and walked the streets of Albany, Georgia, with us. They have gone down the high-ways of the South on tortuous rides for freedom. Yes, they have gone to jail with us. Some have been dismissed from their churches, have lost the support of their bishops and fellow ministers. But they have acted in the faith that right defeated is stronger than evil triumphant. Their witness has been the spiritual salt that has preserved the true meaning of the gospel in these troubled times. They have carved a tun-nel of hope through the dark mountain of disappointment.

I hope the church as a whole will meet the challenge of this deci-sive hour. But even if the church does not come to the aid of justice, I have no despair about the future. I have no fear about the outcome of our struggle in Birmingham, even if our motives are at present misun-derstood. We will reach the goal of freedom in Birmingham and all over the nation, because the goal of America is freedom. Abused and scorned though we may be, our destiny is tied up with America's des-tiny. Before the pilgrims landed at Plymouth, we were here. Before the pen of Jefferson etched the majestic words of the Declaration of Inde-pendence across the pages of history, we were here. For more than two centuries our forebears labored in this country without wages; they made cotton king; they built the homes of their masters while suffering gross injustice and shameful humiliation—and yet out of a bottomless vitality they continued to thrive and develop. If the inexpressible cruelties of slavery could not stop us, the opposition we now face will surely fail. We will win our freedom because the sacred heritage of our nation and the eternal will of God are embodied in our echoing demands.

Before closing I feel impelled to mention one other point in your statement that has troubled me profoundly. You warmly commended the Birmingham police force for keeping "order" and "preventing violence." I doubt that you would have so warmly commended the police force if you had seen its dogs sinking their teeth into unarmed, nonviolent Negroes. I doubt that you would so quickly commend the policemen if you were to observe their ugly and inhumane treatment of Negroes here in the city jail; if you were to watch them push and curse old Negro women and young Negro girls; if you were to see them slap and kick old Negro men and young boys; if you were to observe them, as they did on two occasions, refuse to give us food because we wanted to sing our grace together. I cannot join you in your praise of the Birmingham police department.

It is true that police have exercised a degree of discipline in handling the demonstrators. In this sense they have conducted themselves rather "nonviolently" in public. But for what purpose? To preserve the evil system of segregation. Over the past few years I have consistently preached that nonviolence demands that the means we use must be as pure as the ends we seek. I have tried to make clear that it is wrong to use immoral means to attain moral ends. But now I must affirm that it is just as wrong, or perhaps even more so, to use moral means to preserve immoral ends. Perhaps Mr. Connor and his policemen have been rather nonviolent in public, as was Chief Pritchett in Albany, Georgia, but they have used the moral means of nonviolence to maintain the immoral end of racial injustice. As T. S. Eliot has said: "The last temptation is the greatest treason: to do the right deed for the wrong reason."

I wish you had commended the Negro sit-inners and demonstrators of Birmingham for their sublime courage, their willingness to suffer and their amazing discipline in the midst of great provocation. One day the South will recognize its real heroes. They will be the James Merediths, with the noble sense of purpose that enables them to face jeering and hostile mobs, and with the agonizing loneliness that characterizes the life of the pioneer. They will be old, oppressed, battered Negro women, symbolized in a seventy-two-year-old woman in Montgomery, Alabama, who rose up with a sense of dignity and with her people decided not to ride segregated buses, and who responded with ungrammatical profundity to one who inquired about her weariness: "My feets is tired, but my soul is at rest." They will be the young high school and college students, the young ministers of the gospel and a host of their elders, courageously and nonviolently sitting in at lunch counters and willingly going to jail for conscience' sake. One day the South will know that when these disinherited children of God sat down at lunch counters, they were in reality standing up for what is best in the American dream and for the most sacred values in our Judaeo-Christian heritage, thereby bringing our nation back to those great wells of democracy which were dug deep by the founding fathers in their formulation of the Constitution and the Declaration of Independence.

Never before have I written so long a letter. I'm afraid it is much 55 too long to take your precious time. I can assure you that it would have been much shorter if I had been writing from a comfortable desk, but what else can one do when he is alone in a narrow jail cell, other than write long letters, think long thoughts and pray long prayers?

If I have said anything in this letter that overstates the truth and indicates an unreasonable impatience, I beg you to forgive me. If I have said anything that understates the truth and indicates my having a patience that allows me to settle for anything less than brotherhood, I beg God to forgive me.

I hope this letter finds you strong in faith. I also hope that circumstances will soon make it possible for me to meet each of you, not as an integrationist or a civil-rights leader but as a fellow clergyman and a Christian brother. Let us all hope that the dark clouds of racial prejudice will soon pass away and the deep fog of misunderstanding will be lifted from our fear-drenched communities, and in some not too distant tomorrow the radiant stars of love and brotherhood will shine over our great nation with all their scintillating beauty.

> Yours for the cause of Peace and Brotherhood
> MARTIN LUTHER KING, JR.

For Journals

What does King mean, in response to accusations that the civil rights demonstrations have not come to Birmingham at the right time, that he has "yet to engage in a direct-action campaign that was 'well timed'" (paragraph 20)?

For Discussion

1.   Why do you think that the black clergymen opposed to King were so worried about the civil rights activists? Since they were subject to the same prejudice as King, why wouldn't they join in the demonstrations themselves?

2.   How does King refute the accusations that he is an outsider in Birmingham?

3.   What is your response to King's argument that there are legitimate reasons for breaking the law if it is unjust? What are his criteria for deciding whether a law is unjust? What basis would you use to decide if a law is unjust?

4.   King says that one reason injustice is so powerful is not the actions of bad people but the "appalling silence of the good people" (paragraph 33). Do you think that he is right? What is the responsibility of ordinary people when faced with an evil in their society? Is it fair to expect them to behave with extraordinary bravery?

5.   Why do you think that it pleases King to be referred to by his religious opponents as an extremist?

6.   What do King's criticisms of the contemporary church tell you about what he thinks that the role an effective clergy should be in promoting justice in American society? How does King refute the idea that an uninvolved clergy is better than an active one? How does he make the transition from discussing unheroic clergy to heroic activists?

For Writing

1.   Write an essay or a speech on a public topic that makes you angry. Use Douglass and King as models. Be very explicit about who your audience is; you can choose to address any audience you want. State the point of view that you disagree with; then refute it. If you want, write your essay as a letter to the editor of a local newspaper; mail it to the newspaper for possible publication.

2.   Like Thoreau, King spent time in jail for his beliefs, although Thoreau was never in danger of being killed and King was. Review Thoreau's *Civil Disobedience*, and write an essay in which you discuss the way both men approach and implement political resistance. Include a consideration of the following questions: What is Thoreau's definition of nonviolent resistance, and how does it compare with King's? What does King owe Thoreau in the development of his own philosophy? How does each man argue for the need to sometimes go to jail?

✿✿✿ *What Is Hate Speech?* (1993)

ALAN M. DERSHOWITZ

Alan Dershowitz was the youngest person ever to become a professor of law at Harvard University. Professor Dershowitz has become famous for appeals on behalf of controversial clients, including Klaus von Bulow, accused of trying to murder his wealthy wife, and O. J. Simpson. The von Bulow case and Dershowitz's role in it were the basis of a movie called Reversal of Fortune, *and Dershowitz has written often and passionately, in such books as* The Advocate's Devil *(1994),* Reasonable Doubts: The O. J. Simpson Case and the Criminal Justice System *(1996), and* Just Revenge *(1999), about the importance of safeguarding civil liberties and constitutional freedoms. The following article appeared in the* San Francisco Chronicle *on July 22, 1993.*

A recent letter to the editor of the *Boston Herald* clearly illustrates why the Supreme Court was right on target in striking down hate speech laws as unconstitutional.

The writer argued that "abortion counseling" is a form of "hate speech," since it constitutes advocacy of "taking the life of a developing human child." This may sound like a bizarre application of the hate speech laws, but the writer has a point—if you believe that a fetus is "a developing human child."

An equally compelling point could be made by a feminist, who believes that a fetus is merely a temporary appendage to a woman's body, that Operation Rescue, by accusing young women who are seeking abortions of being murderers, is guilty of hate speech. Plainly, the concept of hate speech is in the mind and heart of the beholder. It is not capable of objective application, as evidenced by several other recent incidents.

A few years ago in Great Britain, a number of universities branded all Zionist speakers as hate mongers and racists, pointing to the now-repealed United Nations resolution equating Zionism with racism. In Israel, speakers from the Palestine Liberation Organization are branded as purveyors of hate and racism because of the PLO's unwillingness to recognize Israel. The late Rabbi Meir Kahane was also branded as hateful and racist because of his advocacy that Arabs be expelled from Israel.

To many women, pornography is hate speech; to many men, feminist put-downs of men—as sexists and rapists—is hate speech. To religious fundamentalists, atheism and blasphemy are forms of hate speech; to many atheists, fundamentalist attacks on atheism as immoral is hate speech. 5

To some African Americans, opposition to race-specific affirmative action is racist and hateful; to some whites, advocacy of race-specific affirmative action is reverse discrimination and thus a form of racism and hate. The *Boston Globe* recently accused Harvard Law School of "bigotry" because it hired faculty on the basis of academic criteria rather than race or gender.

To policemen, rap songs that advocate "cop-killing" are hate speech; to rap singers, Bill Clinton's condemnation of Sister Souljah constituted bigotry.

To many gays, homophobic speech is hateful; to some literal readers of the Bible, advocacy of a gay life style is a hateful abomination. To most Jews, Holocaust denial is hate speech; to those who deny the

Holocaust, any claim that Nazis engaged in genocide against the Jews is anti-German hate speech.

To some liberals, extreme reactionaries are hateful; to some reactionaries, extreme leftists are guilty of hate speech.

I could go on and on in demonstrating that there is no content- 10 neutral way of defining what constitutes hate speech.

Americans tend to feel very strongly about their opinions, especially if they involve race, religion, ethnicity, sexual preference and ideology. We often express our views with strong words, without concern for the sensibilities of others. We are an impolite people, when it comes to expressing our opinions on controversial issues. Ask the Europeans. They will tell you how "direct"—a euphemism for impolite or insensitive—Americans can be. It is part of our national character.

For that reason, among others, speech codes do not suit us as a people. We were brought up on the ditty that "sticks and stones may break our bones, but names will never harm us." Though names can hurt, it is part of our cultural mythology that we must all develop thick skins. The First Amendment is premised on a thick-skinned response to open debate, including name-calling, personal attacks and hate speech.

Asking an African American family to develop a thick skin when a cross is burned by a skinhead is asking an awful lot, and so is asking a Holocaust survivor to tolerate Nazi marchers in his neighborhood. But unless we make these demands, there will be no end to censorship. The speech-cops will have to be called any time anyone is deeply offended by what they see or hear.

And if a subjective feeling of being offended could trigger censorship, Americans would feel offended more easily.

We must encourage vibrant—yes, sometimes even impolite— 15 debate about issues that matter deeply to Americans. We must not curtail the way people argue about race, sex, religion and ideology.

Nor can we—in a society founded on the equal protection of the law—be selective about what constitutes hate speech or who has the power to censor if offended. If we were to grant that power to one group, we would have to grant it to all. There can be no affirmative action when it comes to censorship.

The only answer to offensive speech—if we are to preserve our traditional way of debate and discourse in this country—is a fully open marketplace of ideas in which hate speech is rejected on its own demerits, rather than censored by a benevolent big brother or sister.

For Journals

Which of the following Constitutional freedoms—freedom of speech, of the press, or of religion—do you value the most? Why?

For Discussion

1. Do you think that you or anyone close to you has engaged in what Dershowitz refers to as hate speech? Have you ever been the object of hate speech?

2. The "marketplace of ideas," in which Americans would have access to all varieties of political ideas, including those they find hateful, and would pick the ones they want, goes back to Supreme Court opinions written early in the twentieth century by two of the most famous Justices, Oliver Wendell Holmes and Louis Brandeis. What is appealing about this notion of Americans "shopping" and choosing among all kinds of speech? Should it still apply today—to the Internet, for example?

3. Given that judging what constitutes hate speech is so subjective, what are Dershowitz's reasons for arguing against speech codes that would spell out what kinds of speech are not to be allowed?

4. Would you be in favor of or opposed to your school's having a speech code to guard against various forms of hate speech? Why?

For Writing

1. Assume that you and one or two of your classmates have been assigned the job of coming up with a speech code for your school that would lay out what constitutes the boundaries of acceptable speech on campus, including e-mail between students. To help you with your research, you might check with other colleges in your area, or with the legal department in your school, to find out what regulations are in place, if any, about limits on student freedom of speech. Then come up with your own two to four pages on what rules should be applied at your school. Use some of the examples in Dershowitz's article as samples of what you would or wouldn't allow, or come up with your own examples. If your class is divided into several groups doing this assignment, you can share your research and still come up with different speech codes. And it would be interesting to compare codes, to see what one group, as opposed to another, found really objectionable. In any case, along with your rules, write out your reasons for your choices, so that other people in the class can understand how you arrived at your conclusions.

2. Watch the movie about Dershowitz, *Reversal of Fortune*, and write a review of it. Consider the working relationship between Dershowitz and Klaus von Bulow and the portrayal of Dershowitz—heroic/publicity-seeking/brilliant—and the way that he justifies helping such a generally disliked client. What rights does Dershowitz feel he is defending? If you were in serious trouble, would you want him to be your lawyer?

3.   There are many legal decisions on freedom of speech in general and hate speech in particular. Look up the category of hate speech in newspaper microfiche, on the Internet, or in a law library, and find a ruling you disagree with, or a news story about hate speech that you had a strong reaction to. Write an argumentative essay in which you give your own definition of hate speech; or use Dershowitz's ideas, and explain, in three or four major points, why your definition would lead to a better resolution of the case, redress an injustice, or provide citizens with more useful guidelines for recognizing or dealing with hate speech when it occurs.

✳✳✳ *Libraries, the Internet, and Freedom of Speech* (2000)

VICKI CHIANG

Vicki Chiang is a college graduate; she began writing about this topic when she was a senior in high school.

The turn of the century has brought perhaps one of the greatest technological resources this nation has ever seen. Just in the past few years the United States has experienced an Internet boom, and the number of homes and institutions that are connected to the "net" is growing at a rapid pace. With the growing popularity and accessibility of this technological tool comes a new dilemma: The Internet is an incredible forum for free speech, free thought, free expression, and free information. Yet it is precisely the accessible nature of the Internet that provides people with the opportunity to abuse it.

For example, while pornographic sites on the Internet are technically accessible only to persons over the age of eighteen, a minor may easily subvert this barrier by simply clicking "ok" when the dialogue box appears on the screen. Some parents and conservative groups are concerned about children having access to vulgar and obscene images, which would otherwise not be available to them, and thus they are calling for government-mandated censorship of the Internet. This policy would create a problem for government institutions, and, most specifically, public libraries. Libraries should provide freedom of information, but they are being pressured to install filtering programs onto their computers that would censor the Internet.

It is this writer's opinion that public libraries should not install filtering programs on their computers. This type of censorship is constitutionally unsound and would be more of a problem than a solution. For over two hundred years, we have respected the authority of the

Constitution. Why tear it down now? The censorship of the Internet in public libraries would be an infringement of the First Amendment. Our right to freedom of speech has allowed us to generate a great intellectual community where information and opinions flow freely. Censorship of the Internet, the "information superhighway," would not only severely limit this public resource, but it would also be a step backward for democracy. A precedent has been established in this nation that intellectual freedom is more important than the need to protect our minds. Justice John Paul Stevens of the Supreme Court agrees: "The interest in encouraging freedom of expression in a democratic society outweighs any theoretical but unproven benefit of censorship."

It is true that the Internet differs from the current resources found in the library (i.e., books, newspapers, articles, paintings, etc.) in a few fundamental areas. Obviously, libraries do not carry everything that is published in society; there is usually a committee that screens texts and decides which texts to add to its collection. While libraries do follow a policy of intellectual freedom, the committee will usually screen out works that are extremely vulgar and inappropriate. This intermediate screening process does not exist for the Internet. A person may access virtually anything with a click of the mouse. Nevertheless, the Library Bill of Rights is the only guide we currently have to deal with the dilemma of the unrestricted freedom of the Internet. Until there is a new system established, which is declared to be constitutionally valid in all aspects, we must follow the precedent set by the American Library Association. To censor the Internet now, simply because of a few worried parents, may jeopardize the right of free access to information for future generations. Clearly, the government cannot make a rash decision on this issue.

Even if censorship of the Internet were deemed constitutional, the 5 process would be ineffective in public libraries. Software filters are the current technology used to prevent users from accessing certain Web sites on the Internet. While the filters are intended to block obscene images or texts, they often end up blocking a much broader spectrum of speech. For example, filters that block based on key words would exclude poetry by Anne Sexton simply because the word "sex" is in her last name. There was an instance of the White House Web site being blocked because it contained the word "couple" when referring to the "First Couple."

Aside from the technical pitfalls, Internet filters would be inhibiting because the software installers program them. Unlike the library process mentioned earlier, where an established committee is given the responsibility to screen texts, an arbitrary software installer would program which key words and which sites the filter would block. One person, uneducated in the needs of the patrons of the library, would be deciding what information people could and could not access. The government, let alone a software installer, cannot determine what is appropriate and what is indecent for each person or community.

Images that are offensive to one group of people may be appreciated expressions of art to another, and vice-versa. As Wini Allard, city librarian at Santa Monica Public Library, puts it, "One person's porn is another person's art, and it's not for any of us to decide for another person." It would be democratically irresponsible to install software filters that are programmed by one subjective source onto computers that are used by hundreds of different people. Therefore, as a whole, the currently available filtering system is inadequate. Too much important information is blocked from people who truly need it, so that the harm of filters outweighs the benefit of preventing Internet abuse.

Ultimately, it is the parents' responsibility to monitor their children's appropriate use of the Internet. While it is true that protecting the innocence of our youth should be one of the nation's top priorities, it is also true that the rights of freedom of expression and freedom of information for all people should not be compromised. Unfortunately, today's filtering systems only offer libraries two choices: either they continue to have an unrestricted Internet policy which runs the risk of Internet abuse; or they install extremely restrictive filters to censor the Internet and limit information available to their users.

At this point, the first option is the better of the two. While installing filters nearly guarantees that some important information will be blocked, having an unrestricted Internet does not necessarily leave the door wide open for abuse. There will be parents and teachers there to censor the actions of their children. If adults argue that they absolutely need Internet filters to censor what their children are exposed to, then perhaps they need to focus on their parental responsibilities first. The Internet is the information superhighway, and despite the fact that some may abuse it, the Internet should be a freely accessible road for everyone.

For Journals

What dangers did your family try to protect you from when you were a child? Was there anything you were not allowed to watch on television or to read, or were there any video games you were not allowed to play?

For Discussion

1. The coming of the new technology has been referred to as the New American Revolution. How persuasive is this analogy to you? Are

there any specific ways in which you believe that the changes have been really revolutionary? How different would your life be without them?

2. Although the Constitution says that Congress shall make no laws abridging freedom of speech, in fact speech has never been entirely free, and obscenity is not protected on or off the Internet. The Supreme Court has defined obscenity as that which lacks any literary, artistic, political, or social value—a deliberately vague standard. Community value also have to be recognized. What standards do you think would be applied in your community or by you or your friends? As you need something by which to judge, pick an advertisement, cartoon, or photograph, and use it as a test case for your discussion.

3. If you surf the Net, would you recommend any restrictions on what you could have access to in terms of subject matter or content? On what your little brother or sister could have access to? What rights do you think are involved here? How much access, if any, would you be willing to give up permanently so that children couldn't be exposed to pornography?

4. The author, however, says that the best thing would be for parents to restrict how much time their kids could spend on the Internet. What do you think are the parameters of parental responsibility in this conflict?

For Writing

1. The Constitution says that Congress shall make no laws abridging freedom of speech, but that statement has always been interpreted so that some kinds of speech are protected and some aren't. For example, Justice Oliver Wendell Holmes said that no one has the right to yell "Fire!" in a crowded theater when there is no fire, just to see what would happen. Write an essay in which you argue the limits of freedom of speech or freedom of the press; use the argumentative points in this article or in the Lohr article that follows.

2. If you have access to the Internet, look up the category of Internet and freedom of speech. Pick an entry that has a view different from your own, and write an essay in which you argue against it. Start with your strongest point, and give examples to illustrate any general statements you make about free speech. For an example of a good legal argument, look at the first selection in this chapter, the Declaration of Independence, or at the Frederick Douglass or the Susan B. Anthony selections.

❀❀❀ In the Age of the Internet, Whatever Will Be Will Be Free (2003)

STEVE LOHR

This article first appeared in the New York Times.

The recording industry's long-running battle against online music piracy has come to resemble one of those whack-a-mole arcade games, where the player hammers one rubber rodent's head with a mallet only to see another pop up nearby. Conk one, and up pops another, and so on.

Three years ago, the music industry sued Napster, the first popular music file-sharing network on the Internet. That sent Napster reeling, but other networks for trading copyrighted music—KaZaA, Grokster, Morpheus and others—sprang up. Last week, in the latest swing of the hammer, the Recording Industry Association of America filed 261 lawsuits against individual file sharers, which will surely make some of their estimated 60 million compatriots think twice—for now. Earth Station Five, a company based in the West Bank, surfaced recently with claims of being at war with the industry association. It promises the latest in anonymous Internet file sharing. Its motto: "Resistance is futile."

Since Gutenberg's printing press, new technologies for creating, copying and distributing information have eroded the power of the people, or industries, in control of various media. In the last century, the pattern held true, for example, when recorded music became popular in the early 1900's, radio in the 1920's and cable television in recent years.

But the heritage and design of the Internet present a particularly disruptive technology. Today's global network had its origins in the research culture of academia with its ethos of freely sharing information. And by design, the Internet turns every user in every living room into a mass distributor of just about anything that can be digitized, including film, photography, the written word and, of course, music. Already, Hollywood is trying to curb the next frontier, film swapping. The inevitable advance of technology will make reading on digital tablets more convenient than reading on paper, so the publishers of books, magazines and newspapers have their worries as well. "Nobody is immune," observed Michael J. Wolf, managing partner in charge of the media practice at McKinsey & Company, a consulting firm.

"The cultural and technical principle embedded in today's Internet is that it is neutral in the sense that the people who use it have the 5 power to determine its use, not corporations or the network operators," said Jonathan Zittrain, a co-director of the Berkman Center for the Internet and Society at the Harvard Law School. "The plan for the Internet was to have no plan."

Linux is an operating system whose computer code is distributed freely over the Internet and is maintained and debugged by a loose-knit global community of programmers. Linux has become a genuine challenge to Microsoft because programmers around the world can see and modify the underlying source code—instead of jealously guarding it as a trade secret.

That concept of open-source is inseparable from the Internet, because it provides the vehicle for free exchange and widespread distribution—the same idea that is at the heart of file sharing and one that is spreading well beyond the the techies. A group, led by Lawrence Lessig, a professor at Stanford Law School, has established a "creative commons" project for collecting and putting creative works including music, film, photography and literature in the public domain, inspired by the open-source software model.

The Massachusetts Institute of Technology is posting the content of 500 of its courses online this fall, a project called OpenCourseWare. In Britain, a small group of artists and editors has set up a Web site for Jenny Everywhere, an increasingly popular open-source cartoon. Its only requirement is that any "Jenny" cartoon include its license, which states "others may use this property as they wish. All rights reversed."

What all this means for the future of intellectual property, and some businesses, is as unpredictable as the open-source revolution itself. In the music business, it seems remarkable that only a few believe the technology cannot be held in check.

One of those few is David Bowie. "I'm fully confident that copy- 10 right, for instance, will no longer exist in 10 years, and authorship and intellectual property is in for such a bashing," Mr. Bowie said in an interview last year. The future of the music industry, he suggests, is that songs are essentially advertisements and artists will have to make a living by performing on tour.

Others fear that, as the futility of technological fixes becomes clearer, the response may be onerous legal restrictions on the Internet and how people use it. "You don't want to break the kneecaps of the Internet to protect one relatively small industry, the recording business," Mr. Lessig, the Stanford professor, said.

William Fisher, a Harvard law professor, offers a solution for the recording industry's Internet challenge, and one that borrows from the past. When radio became popular in the 1920's and 1930's and began broadcasting copyrighted songs, the record companies, singers and bands protested. The answer was to have the radio stations pay the copyright holders and set up a measuring system so the largest payments went for the most popular songs.

In a book to be published next year, Mr. Fisher recommends placing a 15 percent tax on Internet access and a 15 percent tax on devices used for storing and copying music and movies like CD-burners, MP3 players and blank CD's.

The funds raised, he estimates, would be about $2.5 billion in 2004, roughly the projected amount the recording industry and Hollywood would lose to online piracy. The music business and Hollywood would get refunds based on what works were the most popular downloads.

"It's not perfect," Mr. Fisher admitted.   15

Still, it does represent what is not much in evidence today—some sort of middle ground that would compensate rights holders but also move with the march of technology and consumer behavior instead of merely trying to fight it.

"With music file sharing, you have a cultural norm that is being established by what is technologically possible," said Daniel Weitzner, a director at the Word Wide Web Consortium. "That is very hard to resist."

For Journals

If you were writing music as opposed to listening to it, would you expect to get royalties for your work?

For Discussion

1. Do you believe that people should be able to download anything they want from the Internet, including films? If not, where would you draw the line?

2. What are the fears of the music, film, and publishing businesses that the Internet inspires? Are those worries based on sound assumptions about how people use the Internet? About how you use it?

3. What is your opinion of the recommendation that starting next year, a 15 percent tax be placed on Internet services like storing and copying movies?

For Writing

1. Use the Internet to find other articles on music and movie piracy. A lot of articles will express strong feelings on the subject, so be sure to critically examine opinions on both sides to inform yourself of what the real issues are. Then write your own proposal for what you think would be a fair way to find what Lohr calls a middle ground that would compensate creative people without fighting the technology that's already here.

2. The author says that ever since printing was invented, technology has been eroding the power of the people in control of media, and he gives recorded music, radio, and cable as examples. Research the history of any of these three media, or a more contemporary one, like video games, TiVo, cd-burning, music downloading. Write an essay in which you do one of the following two things: One possibility is that you explain persuasively how the use of this technology has changed the way you enjoy your entertainment and your sense of control over it. Alternatively, you can write an argumentative essay about why you think whatever is on the Internet is fair game. In either case, you should give anecdotal evidence from your own experience, but you should also be able to draw some conclusions about how far you believe that your right to other people's expression extends.

✻✻✻ *Film: To Kill a Mockingbird* (1962)

A Pakula-Mulligan, Brentwood Productions picture; produced by Alan J. Pakula; directed by Robert Mulligan; screenplay by Horton Foote. Cast: Gregory Peck, Robert Duvall (130 minutes)

In 1960, a young writer named Harper Lee, who is a native of Alabama and who was educated at the state university there, published her first and only novel, To Kill a Mockingbird. *It became famous and has remained so ever since. The movie, which came out only two years later, revolves around two plots. In one, Atticus Finch, a much-respected white lawyer in a small Alabama town and a widower with two small children, takes on the defense of a black man, Tom Robinson, falsely accused of raping a white woman. At the same time, Finch's eight-year-old daughter Scout and her brother are fascinated by a recluse, Boo Radley, whose nearby house both attracts and terrifies them. It is Scout who is the narrator and unifying element of the story.*

For Journals

Explain what you think that the title of the movie means.

For Discussion

1. Look up Atticus in a biographical dictionary or an encyclopedia, and then decide how applicable the name is for this character.

2. What do you think are the narrative advantages of having us see both the segregated world of Alabama and the curiosity about Boo Radley from the perspective of a small child?

3. Watch Atticus's speech to the jury at Tom Robinson's trial; where do you see him taking into account the prejudice of his neighbors against a black defendant accused of a sex crime? How does he deal with the fact that the neighbors assume Tom is guilty because of his color?

4. Given the kind of society in which he lives, what does Atticus risk by taking on Tom's case? Does anyone else in the movie also take risks of some kind? Think of scenes in the film that provide evidence for what you say.

5. Do you consider this a movie about civil rights? If not, then what else?

For Writing

1. The most famous scene in the movie occurs when Atticus Finch sits in front of the sheriff's office with a loaded gun to keep vigilantes—his neighbors—from dragging Tom Robinson out of jail and lynching him, and Scout saves his life without realizing what she's done. Look at that scene carefully, and write your analysis of Scout's role: what she says; why it is unexpected in that context; what there is about her conversation with her neighbor in the Ku Klux Klan robes that is so important to the outcome of the scene; and why Atticus responds the way he does.

2. The time at which this novel is set precedes Dr. King's "I Have a Dream" speech by three years, and the Civil Rights Act by four years. At this point, southern blacks lived almost in as much of a segregated society as they did in the nineteenth century. Research and write up any one of the events to help you understand the milieu of the time: the Montgomery bus boycott in 1955; President Eisenhower's sending federal troops to escort high school students to Little Rock High School in 1957; and Governor George Wallace's opposition to the integration of the University of Alabama.

Chapter Writing Assignments

1. Write an analytical essay comparing Frederick Douglass's "Independence Day Speech" with Martin Luther King, Jr.'s, "Letter from Birmingham Jail." Consider the audience each man was addressing; the way in which each criticizes his audience and why; the sources of their anger; and how successful each one is at refuting the argument of his opponents. Do Douglass and King have any persuasive or argumentative points in common? Do they evoke in you similar or different responses?

2. Investigate some of the Victorian stereotypes about women's behavior, weakness, and dependence that Susan B. Anthony had to refute in her efforts to secure the vote. Use periodicals and books, but, if they are available at your library, also look at nineteenth-century women's magazines, etiquette books, and so on. Write an essay on your findings.

3. Visit the nearest federal, state, or city courthouse, and sit in on a trial for a couple of hours. Call or write the court clerk in advance so that you will know what kinds of trials are scheduled for that week and thus can pick a case that interests you. Family court and juvenile court, for example, deal in emotional issues that are both immediate and comprehensible. Take notes on what you see and hear: the behavior of the judge and attorneys, the demeanor of the defendants, and the issues being raised. Write a paper analyzing the experience: what you saw and learned, whether the trial was different from what you've learned to expect from television, and how effectively each attorney refuted the other's arguments.

4. Devise your own favorite example of American individualism's coming up against either government regulations or majority opinion—anything from whether the government can make you fight a war to whether it can force you to wear a helmet when you're riding a motorcycle. Write an argumentative paper in favor of your opinion, and include quotations or ideas from *Civil Disobedience* as support for your refutation.

5. During the Civil War, Frederick Douglass petitioned President Lincoln for the formation of black army units. Eventually the Fifty-Fourth Regiment was formed, and two of Douglass's sons fought in it. Write a documented research paper on the history of this unit or on Douglass's role in getting it established. Alternatively, compare the results of your research with the way the unit is developed in the film *Glory*. Does the film support or refute the version you found during your research? Why, or why not?

6. The U.S. armed forces remained officially segregated until President Truman integrated them by executive order in 1947. Research this decision, and write a paper on your findings. What were the arguments against integration? What ideas were advanced to refute them? What was the immediate reaction of the military? How was integration put into practice?

Web Sites for Further Exploration

Declaration of Independence
http://www.nara.gov/exhall/charters/declaration/dechist.html
http://memory.loc.gov/const/declar.html

Henry David Thoreau

http://www.walden.org/thoreau/

Frederick Douglass

http://www.pbs.org/wgbh/aia/part4/4h2927.html

Women in American History

http://search.eb.com/women/

Susan B. Anthony

www.susanbanthonyhouse.org/

Plessy v. Ferguson

http://www.watson.org/~lisa/blackhistory/contents.html
sinfo.state.gov/usa/infousa/facts/democrac/33.htm

Brown v. Board of Education

www.nationalcenter.org/brown.html
www.georgetown.edu/centers/woodstock/ report/r-fea34.htm

Eudora Welty

www.olemiss.edu/depts/english/ ms-writers/dir/welty_eudora/

Alan Dershowitz

www.law.harvard.edu/faculty/directory/facdir.php?id=12

10

✳✳✳

War and the Enemy

A s narrator Sam Keen notes in the introduction to the video *Faces of the Enemy*, "Before we make war, even before we make weapons, we make an idea of the enemy." As we make an image of the enemy, we clarify who we are and set ourselves in opposition to that enemy: we are good, they are evil; our cause is just, theirs is unjust; we are human, they are animals. There is a certain peace of mind accompanying that clarity: suicide rates may go down in wartime, people feel that they have a common purpose, citizens rally to the cause, gray tones disappear in an increasingly black-and-white world where there is a good side (us) and a bad side (them).

As we identify and characterize an enemy, we more clearly establish our own national identity. Our leaders then appeal to that identity in order to rally the nation to support the war effort. In encouraging the citizenry to identify with national goals and in vilifying the enemy, politicians and officials, and often private commercial interests, primarily use appeals to ethos and pathos. Appeals to *ethos* establish a sense of common values and ideals to which true Americans would subscribe; those wishing to be considered real Americans support the efforts identified as essential to the common good. Leaders can also appeal to ethos to establish their credibility and their sense of leadership and authority, to appear "presidential" and offer an image of stability and steadfastness in the face of potential chaos.

Appeals to *pathos* convince us to suffer for the common good. On the home front, such appeals urge us to support the war politically; to work in factories; to conserve petroleum products; to do without luxuries, and sometimes necessities; and to support the war effort in any way possible. Even more difficult can be the appeal to offer one's time and loss of independence and income through military service. Along with such service comes the risk of losing one's life, and appeals must be strong indeed to urge men and women to be prepared to give their lives for their country and the "American way of life." Appeals to

pathos and ethos can also contradict our declared values, as the Iraq
prison abuse photographs that surfaced in 2004 painfully illustrate.

War and the Enemy through History

Throughout recorded history on the American continent, conflicts
between economic forces, between cultures and ways of life, and between competing claims on the land have created divergent views
about whose rights to the land, to the resources, to political and economic power, should be superior. White settlements intruded on the
indigenous peoples of America, and European settlers from various
countries fought over land and resources.

Most notable in mainstream American history is the Revolutionary War against Britain. In the first selection, Thomas Paine writes persuasively about the kind of American who Americans would not want
to be—the "summer soldier and sunshine patriot"—and the kind with
whom they want to identify—"he whose heart is firm, and whose conscience approves his conduct, will pursue his principles unto death."
Intertwined with his appeals to support American independence in its
most desperate hour are his descriptions of the enemy, "A sottish, stupid, stubborn, worthless, brutish man." In setting up oppositions—of
supporting America or not, of courage or fear—Paine relies on parallel
phrasing and balanced sentences to outline and reinforce the choices
Americans will need to make.

Speaking about the Civil War—a war that many argue was primarily economic yet pitted "brother against brother"—Abraham Lincoln sought, in "The Gettysburg Address," not to divide but to unite,
by linking the themes of birth and death, the deaths of Gettysburg in
exchange for "a new birth of freedom." Lincoln predicted in his address that "the world will little note nor long remember what we say
here," but about that he was wrong: The world rightly sees "The
Gettysburg Address" as a perhaps unparalleled statement of the
poignance of war.

Just as each side in the Civil War saw itself as the rightful victor,
so do we frequently need to see ourselves as good and the other side
as bad; we need to avoid seeing the enemy as anything but dangerous
and worthy of extinction. Mark Twain, a sharp if humorous critic of
American society, lacerates the tendency to simplify the waging of war
in "The War Prayer," a short satirical piece countering piety with the
grim reminder that victory for one side brings with it defeat and
blighted lives for the other.

Two images, from two world wars, confirm common themes in
how we create enemies in the process of waging war. The 1917 World
War I era poster "Destroy This Mad Brute," epitomizes the practice of
imagining the enemy as animalistic and barbaric. The second image,
from World War II, shows the results of the enemy's barbarity; this

anti-Nazi poster, entitled *"Deliver Us from Evil,"* appeals to emotion and to values in order to move its audience not merely to buy bonds but also to sacrifice on behalf of the innocent victims of war, with whom they easily identify.

The act of asking Congress to declare war is probably the most solemn occasion at which a sitting president can speak, and President Franklin Delano Roosevelt's "Pearl Harbor Address" on December 8, 1941, after the bombings of Pearl Harbor and other bases on Oahu, Hawaii, is a prime example of a difficult rhetorical situation and the ways in which a nation's leader can use such an occasion to unite citizens against a common enemy. In asking for a formal declaration of war, Roosevelt's speech required appeals to patriotism and a strong characterization of a treacherous enemy.

Sometimes in creating an enemy, we see something of ourselves in the enemy and something of the enemy in ourselves. The two Vietnam War–era photographs included in this chapter illustrate contradictions of that war. In "Saigon Execution," Americans are brought painfully close to the actuality of the war and to the confusion about friends and enemies that characterized it. In "The Terror of War," war's most horrifying damage—to innocent children—challenged political arguments and domino theories of spreading communism and had a profound effect on Americans' perceptions of the war.

Simple, straightforward narratives of war hold their own compelling power as well and can teach us something memorable about suffering. Jacqueline Navarra Rhoads's narrative "Nurses in Vietnam" is a story of healing in the midst of massive casualties and the waging of war. Rhoads's account of her tour of duty in Vietnam also reminds us of the power of the personal voice in bringing the pain and tragedy of massive warfare to an individual level.

In a reading that serves as a useful secondary source for analysis of the war texts and imagery in this chapter, Paul Fussell's essay "Type-Casting," from his book *Wartime,* discusses the stereotypes pervasive in war, helping us to examine the ways in which we characterize both our enemies and ourselves. Drawing from Fussell and from other texts, Student Neil A. Van Os, examining the range of materials in this chapter, selected Roosevelt's "Pearl Harbor Address" as a way to explore the principles of persuasion and propaganda evident in those selections. Van Os asserts that Roosevelt's speech is effective in utilizing strategies of propaganda, a label we usually reserve for "the enemy's" rhetoric. But Van Os does what we recommend that you do as you read these selections: think critically and carefully about assumptions, purpose, imagery, language—about the arts of persuasion.

In analyzing the "Pearl Harbor Address," Van Os had the advantage of historical distance and perspective; readers of this text will have a far different experience as they apply their critical skills to the aftermath of 9/11. In assessing and critiquing George W. Bush's

September 20, 2001, "Address to Congress," students will need to be mindful of their own experiences, interpretations, and biases, even as they analyze appeals to ethos, pathos, and logos in Bush's first volley in the war on terrorism. Continuing with the metaphor of war, Pulitzer-Prize-wining journalist Thomas Friedman, in his essay "The Real War," identifies the real war as one that "can't be fought by armies alone. It has to be fought in schools, mosques, churches and synagogues, and can be defeated only with the help of imams, rabbis and priests."

In the last chapter text, journalist Kathleen LaCamera, in her essay "Listening to the Bad Guys," draws connections between perceptions of the enemy in the Northern Ireland conflict and more widespread and international conflict. As LaCamera writes, in a world filled with "conflict and terror" . . . it leaves us with a mandate to listen, particularly when we don't want to. Especially when the actions of those asking for our ear (and sometimes they do that with violence) repel or baffle or terrify us."

Our film for this chapter, *We Were Soldiers,* graphically represents a story from a more traditional war; but in a manner untraditional for many war films, it offers us a perspective of the other side, the "bad guys" in the Vietnam War, even as we identify with soldiers in battle on behalf of Americans half a world away.

Each of the selections in this chapter is an argument: to unite against a common threat; to renounce an enemy; to embrace a former enemy and "bind up the nation's wounds"; to unite as a people to defeat a treacherous foe; to challenge our assumptions about who our political friends and enemies are and about the role of violence in our culture. The arguments about the war, and about waging war, appeal to the ethics of Americans—to fair play, to leadership in the free world, to protecting the innocent—and to logic—to protecting American and allies' interests. They also appeal to pathos—to empathy for the weak and hurt, to manliness and virility, to hatred of the less-than-human enemy. The authors in this chapter are all highly attentive to the power of language and imagery to move people's emotions and to move them to action. The discussion after the reading selections will help you to analyze persuasive language in what you read, to develop persuasive strategies of language in your own writing, and to appreciate the power of language to unite and to divide.

As you read and reflect on the selections in this chapter, consider the changes, even over your own lifetime, that have created the context in which questions about war and violence must now be asked. In the last years of the twentieth century, given the changing world political order that has resulted from the breakup of the Soviet Union, Americans increasingly looked upon war—and this nation's role in establishing and maintaining world peace—with skepticism. At the onset of the twenty-first century, Americans rallied around the commander-in-chief following the attacks on their soil, but too soon many recalled the lesson of earlier conflict: more difficult than waging war is waging a lasting peace.

❀❀ These Are the Times That Try Men's Souls (1776)

THOMAS PAINE

Thomas Paine (1737–1809) came to America from England in 1774. A political radical and an active writer and supporter of the American Revolution, Paine worked in a variety of occupations and held several official posts in the colonies; but it is for his crusades on behalf of democratic principles and rights, both in America and abroad, that he is best remembered. Paine's writings include Common Sense *(1776),* The American Crisis *(1776–1783),* Public Good *(1780),* The Rights of Man *(1791–1792), and* The Age of Reason *(1794–1796), a book for which he was denounced as an atheist.* The American Crisis, *a series of sixteen pamphlets supporting the American Revolution, was widely distributed in the American colonies. The selection that follows is from the famous first pamphlet in the series, which was read to American troops on the eve of the Battle of Trenton by order of General Washington.*

These are the times that try men's souls. The summer soldier and the sunshine patriot will, in this crisis, shrink from the service of his country; but he that stands it NOW, deserves the love and thanks of man and woman. Tyranny, like hell, is not easily conquered: yet we have this consolation with us, that the harder the conflict, the more glorious the triumph. What we obtain too cheap, we esteem too lightly: 'tis dearness only that gives every thing its value. Heaven knows how to put a proper price upon its goods: and it would be strange indeed, if so celestial an article as FREEDOM should not be highly rated. Britain, with an army to enforce her tyranny, has declared that she has a right (*not only to* TAX) but "to BIND *us in* ALL CASES WHATSOEVER," and if being *bound in that manner*, is not slavery, then is there no such a thing as slavery upon earth. Even the expression is impious, for so unlimited a power can belong only to God. . . .

I have as little superstition in me as any man living, but my secret opinion has ever been, and still is, that God Almighty will not give up a people to military destruction, or leave them unsupportedly to perish, who have so earnestly and so repeatedly sought to avoid the calamities of war, by every decent method which wisdom could invent. Neither have I so much of the infidel in me, as to suppose that He has relinquished the government of the world, and given us up to the care of devils, and as I do not, I cannot see on what grounds the king of Britain can look up to Heaven for help against us: a common murderer, a highwayman, or a housebreaker, has as good a pretence as he. . . .

I call not upon a few, but upon all: not on *this* state or *that* state, but on *every* state; up and help us; lay your shoulders to the wheel; better have too much force than too little, when so great an object is at stake. Let it be told to the future world, that in the depth of winter, when nothing but hope and virtue could survive, that the city and the country, alarmed at one common danger, came forth to meet and to repulse it. Say not that thousands are gone, turn out your tens of thousands: throw not the burden of the day upon Providence, but *"show your faith by your works,"* that God may bless you. It matters not where you live, or what rank of life you hold, the evil or the blessing will reach you all. The far and the near, the home counties and the back, the rich and the poor, will suffer or rejoice alike. The heart that feels not now, is dead: the blood of his children will curse his cowardice, who shrinks back at a time when a little might have saved the whole, and made *them* happy. I love the man that can smile in trouble, that can gather strength from distress, and grow brave by reflection. 'Tis the business of little minds to shrink; but he whose heart is firm, and whose conscience approves his conduct, will pursue his principles unto death. My own line of reasoning is to myself as straight and clear as a ray of light. Not all the treasures of the world, so far as I believe, could have induced me to support an offensive war, for I think it murder; but if a thief breaks into my house, burns and destroys my property, and kills or threatens to kill me, or those that are in it, and to *"bind me in all cases whatsoever,"* to his absolute will, am I to suffer it? What signifies it to me, whether he who does it is a king or a common man; my countryman or not my countryman: whether it be done by an individual villain, or an army of them? If we reason to the root of things we shall find no difference: neither can any just cause be assigned why we should punish in the one case and pardon in the other. Let them call me rebel, and welcome, I feel no concern from it; but I should suffer the misery of devils, were I to make a whore of my soul by swearing allegiance to one whose character is that of a sottish, stupid, stubborn, worthless, brutish man. I conceive likewise a horrid idea in receiving mercy from a being, who at the last day shall be shrieking to the rocks and mountains to cover him, and fleeing with terror from the orphan, the widow, and the slain of America.

There are cases which cannot be overdone by language, and this is one. There are persons too who see not the full extent of the evil which threatens them, they solace themselves with hopes that the enemy, if they succeed, will be merciful. It is the madness of folly, to expect mercy from those who have refused to do justice; and even mercy, where conquest is the object, is only a trick of war; the cunning of the fox is as murderous as the violence of the wolf; and we ought to guard equally against both. . . .

I thank God that I fear not. I see no real cause for fear. I know our situation well, and can see the way out of it. . . . By perseverance and fortitude we have the prospect of a glorious issue: by cowardice and submission, the sad choice of a variety of evils—a ravaged country—a depopulated city—habitations without safety, and slavery without hope—our homes turned into barracks and bawdy-houses for Hessians, and a future race to provide for, whose fathers we shall doubt of. Look on this picture and weep over it! and if there yet remains one thoughtless wretch who believes it not, let him suffer it unlamented.

For Journals

Have you heard someone use the expression in the title of this selection? What did it mean to you? If you haven't heard it before, freewrite about your initial reactions to it.

For Discussion

1. A number of the phrases in this essay became well-known expressions over time. Which ones have you heard before? Did you know that they came from the Revolutionary War era? What did they mean to you when you first heard them? What emotions did they inspire in you?

2. How does Paine characterize the kind of Americans who will answer the call? In what ways does he appeal to his audience so that they will want to support the cause of independence?

3. How does Paine characterize the enemy? What evidence does he offer to support his characterization? Cite examples of vivid language and concrete images.

4. Paine develops his argument with parallelism, or grammatically similar phrases; and antithesis, or the setting up of a statement that begins with what is *not* true and then states what *is* true: for example, "I call not upon a few, but upon all." Identify specific examples of these and other stylistic strategies that you believe are particularly effective, and analyze what they contribute to the argument.

5. Compare this selection with the Franklin woodcut *Join, or Die* (Chapter 5), or with George W. Bush's speeches regarding Iraq or the war on terror. What common themes and appeals do you find?

For Writing

1. Using discussion question number 2 as a starting point, develop an essay on Paine's ideal heroic American.

2. Look up some of Paine's other pamphlets from *The American Crisis*. Study several selections, and write an essay analyzing the most common strategies of language in his writings.

✻✻✻ *The Gettysburg Address* (1863)

ABRAHAM LINCOLN

The son of a pioneer, Abraham Lincoln was born in Hodgesville, Kentucky, in 1809 and moved to Illinois in 1831. After brief experiences as a clerk, postmaster, and county surveyor, he studied law and was elected to the state legislature in 1834. A prominent member of the newly organized Republican Party, Lincoln became president on the eve of the Civil War. In 1862, after the Union victory at Antietam, Lincoln issued the Emancipation Proclamation freeing the slaves—the crowning achievement of an illustrious presidency. He delivered "The Gettysburg Address," one of his greatest speeches, at the dedication of the Gettysburg National Cemetery in 1863. Lincoln was assassinated by John Wilkes Booth in 1865, shortly after Robert E. Lee's surrender and the end of the Civil War.

Four score and seven years ago our fathers brought forth on this continent, a new nation, conceived in Liberty, and dedicated to the proposition that all men are created equal.

Now we are engaged in a great civil war, testing whether that nation, or any nation so conceived and so dedicated, can long endure. We are met on a great battlefield of that war. We have come to dedicate a portion of that field as a final resting-place for those who here gave their lives that that nation might live. It is altogether fitting and proper that we should do this.

But, in a larger sense, we cannot dedicate—we cannot consecrate—we cannot hallow—this ground. The brave men, living and dead, who struggled here have consecrated it, far above our poor power to add or detract. The world will little note, nor long remember, what we say here, but it can never forget what they did here. It is for us the living, rather, to be dedicated here to the unfinished work which they who fought here have thus far so nobly advanced. It is rather for us to be here dedicated to the great task remaining before us—that from these honored dead we take increased devotion to that cause for which they gave the last full measure of devotion; that we here highly resolve that these dead shall not have died in vain; that this nation, under God, shall have a new birth of freedom; and that government of the people, by the people, for the people, shall not perish from the earth.

For Journals

What phrases from "The Gettysburg Address" have you heard before? What did they mean to you when you first heard them?

For Discussion

1. After your first reading, do a slow, line-by-line reading out loud. Do you find that the address engages your intellect, or your emotions, or both? Discuss your answer.

2. Analyze what Lincoln leaves out of the speech as well as what he includes; for example, the address does not mention either slavery or the animosity between North and South. What is the effect of his careful selection of themes and words?

3. What key ideas does Lincoln evoke in the address? What images? How do they work together to support Lincoln's persuasive purpose?

4. In what ways does Lincoln weave the themes of birth and death? How does the style—the sentence structure, or syntax; the diction, or word choice—convey those themes?

5. The address is full of expressions we have heard in other contexts: for example, Martin Luther King, Jr.'s, "I Have a Dream" (Chapter 6) echoes its opening, and countless military funerals have repeated the phrase "last full measure of devotion." Author Garry Wills wrote, "Hemingway claimed that all modern American novels are the offspring of *Huckleberry Finn.* It is no greater exaggeration to say that all modern political prose descends from 'The Gettysburg Address.'" Discuss this assertion in view of the examples and other prose that you have heard or read that have sought to invoke "The Gettysburg Address."

For Writing

1. Do a close textual analysis of the address, considering sentence-level strategies as they relate to the larger theme or paradox of the address and to Lincoln's persuasive purpose in speaking. Consider the rhythm of the language, parallelism, pauses, and diction in your analysis.

2. Research the context of the Battle of Gettysburg or of the address itself, writing a documented essay that gives the reader an understanding of the significance of the battle and the context of the speech.

The War Prayer (1904–1905)

MARK TWAIN

Mark Twain (1835–1910) is the pen name of Samuel Clemens. He was born in Florida, Missouri, and explored a variety of jobs—printer, riverboat pilot, gold prospector—before discovering success as a writer with the publication of The Celebrated Jumping Frog of Calaveras County and Other Sketches *(1867) and* The Innocents Abroad *(1869). Twain established his reputation as a humorist through his classic novels* The Adventures of Tom Sawyer *(1876) and* The Adventures of Huckleberry Finn *(1885). Twain was always a critic of American society—*Huckleberry Finn *attacks racism, for example—but in later years he grew especially somber, even pessimistic. "The War Prayer" exemplifies the darker side of his satire.*

It was a time of great and exalting excitement. The country was up in arms, the war was on, in every breast burned the holy fire of patriotism; the drums were beating, the bands playing, the toy pistols popping, the bunched firecrackers hissing and spluttering; on every hand and far down the receding and fading spread of roofs and balconies a fluttering wilderness of flags flashed in the sun; daily the young volunteers marched down the wide avenue gay and fine in their new uniforms, the proud fathers and mothers and sisters and sweethearts cheering them with voices choked with happy emotion as they swung by; nightly the packed mass meetings listened, panting, to patriot oratory which stirred the deepest deeps of their hearts, and which they interrupted at briefest intervals with cyclones of applause, the tears running down their cheeks the while; in the churches the pastors preached devotion to flag and country, and invoked the God of Battles, beseeching His aid in our good cause in outpouring of fervid eloquence which moved every listener. It was indeed a glad and gracious time, and the half dozen rash spirits that ventured to disapprove of the war and cast a doubt upon its righteousness straightway got such a stern and angry warning that for their personal safety's sake they quickly shrank out of sight and offended no more in that way.

Sunday morning came—next day the battalions would leave for the front; the church was filled; the volunteers were there, their young faces alight with martial dreams—visions of the stern advance, the gathering momentum, the rushing charge, the flashing sabers, the flight of the foe, the tumult, the enveloping smoke, the fierce pursuit, the surrender!—them home from the war, bronzed heroes, welcomed, adored, submerged in golden seas of glory! With the volunteers sat their dear ones, proud, happy, and envied by the neighbors and friends who had no sons and brothers to send forth to the field of honor, there to win for the flag, or, failing, die the noblest of noble deaths. The service proceeded; a war chapter from the Old Testament was read; the first prayer was said; it was followed by an organ burst that shook the building, and with one impulse the house rose, with glowing eyes and beating hearts, and poured out that tremendous invocation—

> "God the all-terrible!   Thou who ordainest,
> Thunder thy clarion and lightning thy sword!"

Then came the "long" prayer. None could remember the like of it for passionate pleading and moving and beautiful language. The burden of its supplication was, that an ever-merciful and benignant Father of us all would watch over our noble young soldiers, and aid, comfort, and encourage them in their patriotic work; bless them, shield them in the day of battle and the hour of peril, bear them in His mighty hand, make them strong and confident, invincible in the bloody onset; help them to crush the foe, grant to them and to their flag and country imperishable honor and glory—

An aged stranger entered and moved with slow and noiseless step up the main aisle, his eyes fixed upon the minister, his long body clothed in a robe that reached to his feet, his head bare, his white hair descending in frothy cataract to his shoulders, his seamy face unnaturally pale, pale even to ghastliness. With all eyes following him and wondering, he made his silent way; without pausing, he ascended to the preacher's side and stood there, waiting. With shut lids the preacher, unconscious of his presence, continued his moving prayer, and at last finished it with the words, uttered in fervent appeal, "Bless our arms, grant us the victory, O Lord our God, Father and Protector of our land and flag!"

The stranger touched his arm, motioned him to step aside—which the startled minister did—and took his place. During some moments he surveyed the spellbound audience with solemn eyes, in which burned an uncanny light; then in a deep voice he said:

"I come from the Throne—bearing a message from Almighty 5 God!" The words smote the house with a shock; if the stranger perceived it he gave no attention. "He has heard the prayer of His servant your shepherd, and will grant it if such shall be your desire after I, His messenger, shall have explained to you its import—that is to say, its full import. For it is like unto many of the prayers of men, in that it asks for more than he who utters it is aware of—except he pause and think.

"God's servant and yours has prayed his prayer. Has he paused and taken thought? Is it one prayer? No, it is two—one uttered, the other not. Both have reached the ear of Him Who heareth all supplications, the spoken and the unspoken. Ponder this—keep it in mind. If you would beseech a blessing upon yourself, beware! lest without intent you invoke a curse upon a neighbor at the same time. If you pray for the blessing of rain upon your crop which needs it, by that act you are possibly praying for a curse upon some neighbor's crop which may not need rain and can be injured by it.

"You have heard your servant's prayer—the uttered part of it. I am commissioned of God to put into words the other part of it—that part which the pastor—and also you in your hearts—fervently prayed silently. And ignorantly and unthinkingly? God grant that it was so! You heard these words: 'Grant us the victory, O Lord our God!' That is sufficient. The *whole* of the uttered prayer is compact into those pregnant words. Elaborations were not necessary. When you have prayed for victory you have prayed for many unmentioned results which follow victory—*must* follow it, cannot help but follow it. Upon the listening spirit of God the Father fell also the unspoken part of the prayer. He commandeth me to put it into words. Listen!

"O Lord our Father, our young patriots, idols of our hearts, go forth to battle—be Thou near them! With them—in spirit—we also go forth from the sweet peace of our beloved firesides to smite the foe. O Lord our God, help us to tear their soldiers to bloody shreds with our shells; help us to cover their smiling fields with the pale forms of their patriot dead; help us to drown the thunder of the guns with the shrieks of their wounded, writhing in pain; help us to lay waste their humble homes with a hurricane of fire; help us to wring the hearts of their unoffending widows with unavailing grief; help us to turn them out roofless with their little children to wander unfriended the wastes of their desolated land in rags and hunger and thirst, sports of the sun flames of summer and the icy winds of winter, broken in spirit, worn with travail, imploring Thee for the refuge of the grave and denied it—for our sakes who adore Thee, Lord, blast their hopes, blight their lives, protract their bitter pilgrimage, make heavy their steps, water their way with their tears, stain the white snow with the blood of their wounded feet! We ask it, in the spirit of love, of Him Who is the Source of Love, and Who is the ever-faithful refuge and friend of all that are sore beset and seek His aid with humble and contrite hearts. Amen."

(After a pause) "Ye have prayed it: if ye still desire it, speak! The messenger of the Most High waits."

It was believed afterward that the man was a lunatic, because 10 there was no sense in what he said.

For Journals

Do you think of Mark Twain as a humorous writer? As a writer of satire or social commentary? Write about your expectations of this selection that are based on the title.

For Discussion

1. Examine the diction in the first two paragraphs. What tone and stance are established? Through which particular words and expressions?

2. What is your understanding of what the worshippers are praying for? Do you envision people on the other side of the conflict doing the same?

3. What does the messenger want the people in church to understand? How does he help them to do so? How does Twain convey to us the people's response to the message?

4. How does Twain show the irony of their prayer and their "spirit of love"? Examine the language, and cite specific examples that support your point.

5. How do you interpret the ending of the selection, particularly the last two sentences? How do you think that the people hearing the stranger would respond? Would the other side respond any differently?

6. What is Twain's persuasive purpose in writing this selection? Why do you think that he selected this genre and format for his purpose?

For Writing

1. Using discussion question number 4 as a starting point, develop an analytical essay examining the style of this selection and the strategies Twain uses to convey irony.

2. Write a contemporary war prayer that pertains to a geopolitical situation in the middle- to late-twentieth century. Irony is not an easy writing technique, so aim for a subtle effect; get feedback from peers, and revise your language carefully.

Destroy This Mad Brute (1917)

H. R. HOPPS

This World War I image (p. 472), which was developed and circulated in the United States, was recycled by the Germans, who used both its overall theme and its style, in World War II. It illuminates many of the principles discussed later in this chapter in Paul Fussell's examination of stereotyping by ethnicity and culture. (See Color Plate IV for a color image of this poster.)

For Journals

What stereotypes do you believe that you have of other ethnic groups who have been in conflict with the United States? How do you think that Americans are stereotyped?

For Discussion

1. Analyze the content and composition of this poster—the objects, the positioning, the accompanying text, and the overall dominant impression. What elements contribute to its overall effect?

2. Which persuasive appeals are most powerful? Why would those appeals have been used for this audience and purpose? Do you detect logical fallacies?

For Writing

1. Write an analytical essay discussing the ways in which this poster achieves its persuasive purpose. Be sure to include evidence from the image itself to support your view.

2. Using resources such as the National Archives Web site or collections of war posters, or even on-line auction sites, examine a number of posters from World War I and World War II; try to determine whether common themes emerge within each era, or across the two time periods, or across the cultures involved.

3. Using appropriate secondary sources such as Paul Fussell, in this chapter, write an essay in which you apply the principles in such a source to one of the images in this textbook or to another poster that you locate on the Web or elsewhere.

✻✻ *Deliver Us from Evil* (ca. 1940)

This poster (p. 474) reveals a number of typical strategies used by poster artists to invoke American desire to support the war effort in Europe during both world wars—in this case, World War II. As you examine this selection and other visual materials in the chapter, consider what types of appeals are being made and which audiences are being targeted.

For Journals

What could convince you to work toward a war effort, whether by joining the military or contributing money? What are the most compelling ways in which a writer or an artist could appeal to you?

For Discussion

1. What is your immediate emotional response to the image?

2. What draws your eye? What do the shades and shapes emphasize?

3. Of what ethnicity does the child seem to be? How does that affect the viewer's reaction to the image?

4. The headline is from a Christian prayer. What is the significance of using this allusion?

For Writing

1.   Using your journal entry as a starting point, if that would be help-ful, write an essay on the different types of strategies that poster artists could use to elicit different kinds of support (monetary, military) from different segments of American society in a time of war. Pay special at-tention to the kinds of images that you think would be most persuasive.

2.   Compare this poster with others (available on the Internet and in reference books) that use children to make their persuasive appeals, and write an essay focusing on these appeals.

✷✷✷ *Pearl Harbor Address* (1941)

FRANKLIN DELANO ROOSEVELT

Franklin Delano Roosevelt (1882–1945) was the thirty-second president of the United States and the only president ever elected to four consecutive terms in office. His innovative New Deal economic recovery plan guided America through the diffi-cult years of the Great Depression, and his cooperation with Winston Churchill helped secure an Allied victory in World War II. He died in Warm Springs, Georgia, in 1945, ironically, three weeks before the Nazi surrender. Roosevelt's address to the House of Representatives after the Japanese attack on Pearl Harbor in 1941, with such ringing phrases as "a date which will live in infamy," remains a classic call to action.

To the Congress of the United States: Yesterday, December 7, 1941—a date which will live in infamy—the United States of America was suddenly and deliberately attacked by naval and air forces of the Empire of Japan.

The United States was at peace with that nation and, at the solici-tation of Japan, was still in conversation with its government and its emperor looking toward the maintenance of peace in the Pacific. In-deed, one hour after Japanese air squadrons had commenced bombing in Oahu, the Japanese ambassador to the United States and his col-league delivered to the secretary of state a formal reply to a recent American message. While this reply stated that it seemed useless to continue the existing diplomatic negotiations, it contained no threat or hint of war or armed attack.

It will be recorded that the distance of Hawaii from Japan makes it obvious that the attack was deliberately planned many days or even weeks ago. During the intervening time the Japanese government had deliberately sought to deceive the United States by false statements and expressions of hope for continued peace.

The attack yesterday on the Hawaiian Islands has caused severe damage to American naval and military forces. I regret to tell you that very many American lives have been lost. In addition American ships have been reported torpedoed on the high seas between San Francisco and Honolulu.

Yesterday the Japanese government also launched an attack 5 against Malaya.

Last night Japanese forces attacked Hong Kong.

Last night Japanese forces attacked Guam.

Last night Japanese forces attacked the Philippine Islands.

Last night the Japanese attacked Wake Island.

This morning the Japanese attacked Midway Island.   10

Japan has, therefore, undertaken a surprise offensive extending throughout the Pacific area. The facts of yesterday speak for themselves. The people of the United States have already formed their opinions and well understand the implications to the very life and safety of our nation.

As commander in chief of the army and navy I have directed that all measures be taken for our defense.

Always will we remember the character of the onslaught against us.

No matter how long it may take us to overcome this premeditated invasion, the American people in their righteous might will win through to absolute victory.

I believe I interpret the will of the Congress and of the people 15 when I assert that we will not only defend ourselves to the uttermost but will make very certain that this form of treachery shall never endanger us again.

Hostilities exist. There is no blinking at the fact that our people, our territory, and our interests are in grave danger.

With confidence in our armed forces—with the unbounded determination of our people—we will gain the inevitable triumph—so help us God.

I ask that the Congress declare that since the unprovoked and dastardly attack by Japan on Sunday, December 7, 1941, a state of war has existed between the United States and the Japanese Empire.

For Journals

Have your parents or grandparents ever talked about World War II or what they did in the war? Write for a few minutes on what you know about the war.

For Discussion

1. Have you previously heard excerpts from this speech on television or radio? What was your reaction then? If you haven't heard the speech before, talk with people who heard the speech in 1941, and ask them about their reactions; share your findings with your peers, and compare accounts.

2. How does Roosevelt seek to unite Americans? What sense of identity does he evoke? What themes does he dwell upon? What ethos appeals does he make? What pathos appeals?

3. How does Roosevelt establish a sense of the enemy for his audience? What kinds of logos or other appeals does he use? How do syntax and diction reinforce the appeals? Look, for example, at his use of repetition in the series that opens "last night," at midspeech (paragraph 6).

4. Examine the second-to-last sentence: "With confidence. . . ." What effect does opening with a dependent phrase have on the emphasis in this sentence?

5. Compare and contrast the rhetorical demands of a presidential address calling for war with an inaugural address or other presidential speech. Which type of speech do you believe would be the more difficult to write? Why?

For Writing

1. Through library research or through taking oral histories, investigate reactions to this speech at the time it was given. You could examine newspaper commentaries and magazine articles and could interview older people about their memories of the occasion. In what ways were they affected, practically and emotionally, by the address? How did the journalistic accounts of the times view the speech? Write an essay summarizing your findings.

2. Write an essay discussing the ways in which Roosevelt seeks to write the American people and how he develops an image of the enemy in the speech. Pay special attention to Roosevelt's use of language, syntax, and repetition.

Saigon Execution (1969)

EDWARD T. ADAMS

The following photograph became one of the most famous images of the Vietnam War. Colonel Nguyen Ngoc Loan, South Vietnam's police chief, executes a Vietcong suspect in Saigon. The filmed version of this execution was shown on television all over the world. Adams's photograph won the Pulitzer Prize for News Photography in 1969.

For Journals

Describe the visual images that come to mind when you think of the Vietnam War.

For Discussion

1. Analyze the photograph. What is emphasized? Whose face is more visible, and how does that visibility affect how you react to the photograph? How are the respective figures dressed? Where are their hands? What do these details tell you about the relative power of each man? How do such elements of the photograph contribute to your logical, ethical, and emotional reactions to the image?

2. In what ways is this sort of event expected in wartime? In what ways is it surprising? Compare this photograph with some of the images from the Gulf War, the Afghanistan campaign, and the Iraq War. Are more recent photographs more shocking, less shocking, or about the same as this image?

3. What effects would this photograph have on Americans' perceptions of their "friends" and "enemies" during the war?

For Writing

1. What impact do you think that this photograph, and others like it, may have had on the American public and their perception of the Vietnam War?

2. Research the Vietnam War in pictures and photographs, and see whether you can discern changes over time in the ways in which the war was covered in the popular print media.

✸✸✸ The Terror of War (1973)

HUYNH CONG "NICK" UT

The following photograph, taken by Associated Press photographer Huynh Cong "Nick" Ut, brought with it the horrifying realization of the many civilian participants in, and victims of, the war in Vietnam. Napalm, a gel developed in World War II, was used widely in Vietnam in flame throwers and incendiary bombs; it burns hotly and rather slowly, and sticks to its target. The children pictured were apparently the victims of napalm bombs dropped by the South Vietnamese air force. This photograph won the Pulitzer Prize for News Photography in 1973.

For Journals

Think about the truism that a picture is worth a thousand words. Do you agree?

For Discussion

1. What are your immediate reactions to the photograph? Do you respond primarily on an emotional or intellectual level? What does your response tell you about the power of an image?

2. Examine the composition and content of the photograph. What is being conveyed? Do you find it more reportorial or persuasive? Of what might a viewer of this photograph be persuaded?

3. Who are the primary victims of war? To what extent do you think they are represented in war images? Do you think the image in the photograph is more, or less, persuasive than images of young American men on the battlefield? Explain.

4. Contrast this image with photographs of children that you may have seen during the more recent conflicts in the Middle East. Do you think that the more recent photographs and Internet access to them has influenced American policy or support for these recent wars?

For Writing

1. Write a report describing the event portrayed in this photograph, using precise, concrete language. Then, in view of your journal entry, analyze the relative power of visual images and language.

2. Talk with people who remember the Vietnam War, and ask them about whom they perceived as America's friends and enemies during that war. Analyze the ways in which this photograph confirms or contradicts what you learned from your interviewees.

3. Analyze a photograph or series of photographs from the war in Iraq and Afghanistan, and evaluate the image's persuasive appeals.

✳✳✳ *Nurses in Vietnam* (1987)

JACQUELINE NAVARRA RHOADS

Jacqueline Navarra Rhoads was born in 1948 in Albion, New York, resided for some time in San Antonio, Texas, and now lives in Albuquerque, New Mexico, where she is on the nursing faculty of the University of New Mexico. She served as an army nurse in Vietnam from 1970 to 1971, and spent most of her tour with the 18th Surgical Hospital in Quang Tri. Her personal account of her tour focuses the politically charged conflict on a personal level, dealing with both the pain and the exhilaration of her work and the long-term effects it has had on her life.

We arrived in Vietnam on April 26, 1970, right in the middle of a rocket attack. We were ordered off the plane and everyone was supposed to lay down on the ground. So here I am with my dress uniform, stockings, shoes, and skirt, and suddenly I'm lying down on a cement pavement at Tan Son Nhut wondering, "My God, what did I get myself into?" The noise was so deafening. The heat—I remember how hot it was. We eventually got inside this terminal building where there were all these guys waiting to get on the plane to go home. They were whooping it up, running around with signs saying things like: "Only one hour and thirty-five minutes left!" They saw us coming and one of them said, "Cheer up, the worst is yet to come." We stayed there sixteen hours before we could get out. When we got on the bus, all the windows were screened. I learned from the bus driver that this was to prevent the Vietnamese from throwing grenades in through the windows. I said, "But I thought the enemy was up north somewhere." He told me, "No, the enemy is all around you here. You never know who you're fighting."

My first assignment was in Phu Bai. I was there for thirty days because they needed some emergency room nurses there. Then I was transferred to the 18th Surgical Hospital in Quang Tri, just a few miles from the DMZ. They had just put a MUST (Medical Unit Self-Transportable) unit in there from Camp Evans and they needed operating and emergency room nurses right away. I was there the remainder of my tour.

I was a very young twenty-one. At St. Mary's School of Nursing in Rochester (New York), I kept these Army recruiting posters all over my room. There was a big push at that time for nurses, and we had recruiters coming to the school constantly from the time I started in 1966. I don't know what it was, I loved nursing so much. I always thought—I know it sounds crazy—but I wanted to do something for my country. I just had a feeling that being a nurse in the Army was what I wanted to do. And of course my uncles were all in the Army in World War II. There were nine brothers in my mother's family, and they all went into the Army within six months of each other.

Everyone thought I was crazy. I remember my mother saying, "Jacque, do you know what you're getting yourself into?" Of course, when you're young you have no fear.

I did basic training at Fort Sam Houston in San Antonio. My main 5 memory of that time is the parties, big parties. I never took basic training very seriously. It was only later I realized that I should have. What to do in case of a nuclear attack, what to do for chemical warfare, how to handle a weapon—these were things we laughed at. We went out to Camp Bullis and shot weapons, but as nurses we never thought that shooting a weapon was something we needed to know. True, we never had to fire weapons, but we had wounded who came in with weapons as splints, and they were loaded weapons. When that happened, I thought, "Why didn't I listen when they taught us how to take this weapon apart?" You know, an M-16 with a full magazine. We had a young guy come in, he had a grenade with the pin pulled wrapped in a handkerchief and stuffed into his fatigue pocket, a live grenade! I thought, "Gosh, if only I had listened."

I think the practice village out where we trained at Camp Bullis is still in existence. The bamboo sticks smeared with excrement, they were authentic. There was an instructor in black pajamas, camouflage makeup on his face. Well, we kind of laughed. We didn't take it seriously until we started seeing these kinds of injuries in Vietnam.

My first real exposure to the war came five days after I landed. It was at Phu Bai. We received twenty-five body bags in on this giant Chinook helicopter. You know, the Chinook is this great big helicopter, this two-blade deal that can carry one hundred to one hundred and fifty people. And this Chinook came in with twenty-five body bags aboard. One of the nurses' responsibilities was to look inside these body bags to determine cause of death. Of course, they couldn't release the doctors for such trivial work. What you had to do was open the bag, look inside and see what possibly could have killed this person, and then write down on the tag what you felt the cause of death was. It was so obvious most of the time. That's something I still have flashbacks about—unzipping those bags. It was my first exposure to maggots, something I had never seen before in my life.

One was a young guy who had had his face blown away, with hundreds of maggots eating away where his face used to be. Another one, he had his eyes wide open. He was staring up at me. I remember he had a large hole in his chest and I knew it was a gunshot wound or a grenade injury. It had blown his heart, his lungs, everything to shreds. He had nothing left but a rib cage. Evidently, they had lain out on the ground awhile before someone could get to them. The corpsmen were told to take care of the wounded first, instead of spending time getting the dead in the bags. There were GIs exposed to flame throwers or gas explosions. We used to call them "crispy critters" to keep from getting depressed. They'd come in and there would be nothing more than this shell of a person. That was a little easier to take, they didn't have a face. It could have been an animal's carcass for all you knew. But to have to go looking for the dog tags, to find the dog tags on a person, that bothered me. I remember the first time I looked in a body bag I shook so badly. One of the doctors was kind enough to help me through it, saying, "Come on, it's your duty and you're going to have to do this. It's just something that I'm going to help you through. It's just a dead person." It was such a close-knit group. We were considered the most beautiful women in the world. The guys treated us special. You could have been the ugliest woman in the world, but still you were treated special.

The mass-cal, that's mass-casualty situation, traditionally was any-thing more than ten or fifteen wounded. It was mass chaos, bordering on panic. There'd be a corpsman walking around saying, "Dust off just called and they're bringing in twenty-five wounded. Everybody get going." So we'd pull out all our supplies. The nurses would put extra tourniquets around their necks to get ready to clamp off blood vessels. The stretchers were all prepared, and we'd go down each row hanging IVs all plugged and ready to go. It was mass production. You'd start the IVs on those people where the doctor was able to say, "This one is saved, this one is saved." We put them in triage categories. The expec-tant ones were the ones who required too much care. We'd make them comfortable and allow them to die. I guess it was making us comfort-able too.

I remember this guy named Cliff, a triple amputee we once had. 10 He came in with mast-trousers on. Mast-trousers is an apparatus you inflate that puts pressure on the lower half of your body to allow ade-quate blood flow to your heart and brain. When Cliff came in, he was conscious, which was amazing. He looked like a stage dummy who'd been thrown haphazardly in a pile. One of his legs was up underneath his chin so that he was able to look down at the underside of his foot. His left arm was twisted behind his head in a horrible way. We couldn't even locate his second leg. He had stepped on a land mine. With his legs that bad, we knew there probably wasn't much backbone left. He was alive because of these trousers. The corpsman must have been right there when he got wounded. He had put him in this bag and inflated it. Cliff should have been dead.

It was really funny because he looked at two of us nurses there and said, "God, I think I've died and gone to heaven . . . a round-eye, an American, you look so beautiful." He was so concerned about the way he looked because of us standing there, "Gee, I must look a mess." But he was alert, he knew where he was. "Doc, take good care of me. I know my leg is pretty bad because I can see it, but take good care of me, doc." The docs couldn't put him in the expectant category and give him morphine to make him comfortable, because he was too alert. The docs had trouble letting go. So one of them finally said, "Well, let's get him into the operating room, deflate the bag, and let's get in there and see if we can't do something."

Well, we knew just by looking at him in that condition that he wasn't going to last, that as soon as we deflated the bag he'd bleed to death in a matter of seconds. Somehow, he knew it too. I remember I was getting blood prepared for him. He called me from across the room, "Jacque, come here quick." I went over to him and said, "What's the matter Cliff, what's wrong?" He said, "Just hold my hand and don't leave me." I said, "Why, Cliff? Are you in pain?" We always worried about pain, alleviating pain. We'd do anything to alleviate pain. He said, "I think I'm going to die and I don't want to be alone." So I stood there crying, with him holding my hand. And when we deflated the trousers, we lost him in seconds. We found no backbone, no lower part of his body. Really, he had been cut in half.

The leg that was folded underneath his neck was completely severed from his body. It was just there. The corpsmen had evidently bundled him together into the bag hoping maybe something would be there that was salvageable. And he just died. I remember he had blond hair, blue eyes—cute as a button. I had to take his body myself to graves registration. I just couldn't let him go alone. I just couldn't do that. I had to pry my hand away from his hand, because he had held on to my hand so tightly. I had to follow him to graves registration and put him in the bag myself. I couldn't let go of him. It was something I had to do.

Usually the expectants had massive head injuries. They were practically gone, they couldn't communicate with you. You were supposed to clean them up, call the chaplain. You did all that stuff, I guess, to make you feel as though you were helping them. To preserve their lives, you would've had to put them on a respirator and evac them to a neuro facility, which in our case would have been all the way to Da Nang, which was hours, miles away. I was an operating room nurse, but when there was a mass-cal, since there were only twelve of us, we'd be called into triage to work there. After that, I'd follow them into the operating room and help do the surgery. A lot of the shrapnel extractions we'd do ourselves, and a lot of the closures too. The docs would say, "Why don't you close? I got this next case in the next room." You didn't have to worry about it too much, if you got into trouble he'd be right there next door.

We wanted to save everyone. We had a lot of ARVNs (Army of 15 the Republic of Vietnam), we called them "Marvin the ARVN." We tried to take care of the Americans first, but we also had to take care of whoever needed care—period, whether he was a Vietnamese, a POW, or whatever. In fact, when we tried to save Cliff, they brought in the Vietnamese who had laid the mine. He had an amputation. He was bleedingly badly and had to be treated right away. And we saved him. I guess in my heart I felt angry about what happened.

We were short on anesthesia and supplies. And we were giving anesthesia to this POW, which made me angry because I thought, "What if—what happens if someone comes in like Cliff and we don't have any anesthesia left because we gave it all to this POW?" Again, because I was very strongly Catholic, as soon as I heard myself thinking this, I thought, "God, how can you think that? The tables could be turned, and what if it was Cliff in the POW's place, and how would I feel if he received no anesthesia simply because he was an enemy?" First of all, it shocked me and embarrassed me. It made me think,

"Gosh, I'm losing my values, what's happened to me?" I had been taught in nursing school to save everybody regardless of race, creed, color, ethnic background, whatever. Life is life. But suddenly I wasn't thinking that anymore. I was thinking, "I'm American, and they're the enemy. Kill the enemy and save the American."

Before I went to Vietnam, I was kind of bubbly, excited about life. I haven't changed that much really, I'm still that way. But back then, suddenly, I began questioning things, wondering about what we were doing there. I remember talking with the chaplain, saying, "What are we doing? For what purpose are we here?" We were training Vietnamese helicopter pilots to go out and pick up their wounded and take them to their hospitals. And we treated plenty of them at our hospitals, too. Yet when we'd call up and say, "We got a wounded soldier in Timbuktu," they'd say, "It's five o'clock and we don't fly at night." We had soldiers in the hospital shot by ten-year-old boys and girls. We had women who'd invite GIs to dinner—nice women—and they'd have someone come out from behind a curtain and shoot them all down dead. I mean, what kind of war was this?

The chaplain told me, "Hey Jacque, you can't condemn the American government. We can't say the American government is wrong to put us in this position here. We can't say, because there is so much we don't know." It was good advice at the time; it really helped me. I was thinking, "Here I am judging, and I'm saying what the heck are we doing here, look at all these lives lost, all these young boys and for what? And who am I to judge that? There has to be a reason." I guess I'm still trying to hold on to that belief, even though people laugh at me when I say it. They think I'm living in a dream world because I'm hoping there was a good reason.

I didn't really have much time to worry about right and wrong back then, because during these mass-calls we'd be up for thirty-six hours at a stretch. Nobody wanted to quit until the last surgery case was stabilized. By that time, we were emotionally and physically numb. You couldn't see clearly, you couldn't react. Sounds were distant. We kind of policed each other. When we saw each other reacting strangely or slowly, we'd say, "Hey, Jacque, get some sleep, someone will cover, go get some sleep." That's how close we were. That's how we coped with stress.

You didn't have time to think about how unhappy you were. It was afterwards, when you couldn't go to sleep . . . here you were without sleep for thirty-six hours, lying in your bed expecting sleep to overwhelm you, but you couldn't fall asleep because you were so tensed and stressed from what you saw. I knew I had a problem the day I was with a nurse I was training who was going to replace someone else. I remember I had completed this amputation and I had the soldier's leg under my arm. I was holding the leg because I had to

dress it up and give it to graves registration. They'd handle all the severed limbs in a respectful manner. They wouldn't just throw them in
the garbage pile and burn them. They were specially labeled and handled the good old government way.

I remember this nurse came in and she was scheduled to take the
place of another nurse. When she saw me, I went to greet her and I
had this leg under my arm. She collapsed on the ground in a dead
faint. I thought, "What could possibly be wrong with her?" There I
was trying to figure out what's wrong with her, not realizing that here
I had this leg with a combat boot still on and half this man's combat fatigue still on, blood dripping over the exposed end. And I had no idea
this might bother her.

We had a lot of big parties, too. The Army had all these rules
about fraternization, how officers couldn't fraternize with enlisted. In
Quang Tri, we were just one big family. You didn't worry about who
had an E-2 stripe or who had the colonel's insignia. I'm not saying we
didn't have problems with officers and enlisted people or things like
insubordination. But everybody partied together.

I never had a sexual relationship over there. You have to remember how Catholic I was. Dating, well, you'd walk around bunkers and
talk about home. Every hooch had a bunker, so you'd bring a bottle of
wine and he'd bring glasses and—this sounds gross, I guess—you'd
sit and watch the B-52s bomb across the DMZ. It produced this northern lights effect. The sky would light up in different colors and you'd
sit and watch the fireworks. I know it sounds strange, watching somebody's village get blown up. We didn't want to think about the lives
being lost.

The grunts always knew where the female nurses were. They all
knew that at the hospital there was a good chance of seeing a "round-
eye." Once, during monsoon season, we received a dust off call saying
there'd been a truck convoy ambush involving forty or fifty guys.
They were in bad shape but not far from the hospital, maybe seven or
eight miles. We could stand on the tops of our bunkers and see flashes
of light from where they were fighting the VC. One of these deuce-
and-a-half trucks with a load of wounded came barreling up right into
our triage area. Like I said, they all knew where the hospital was. The
truck's canvas and wood back part were all on fire. Evidently they had
just thrown the wounded in back and driven straight for us.

We were concerned about the truck, about getting it out of the 25
way, but we were also trying to get to the wounded. There were two
guys in the back, standing up. There was a third guy we couldn't see,
and the first two were carrying him and shrieking at the top of their
lungs. One was holding the upper part of his torso, under the arms,
and the other held the legs. Their eyes were wild and they were
screaming. I couldn't see what was wrong with the guy they were

carrying. Everyone else on the truck was jumping off. We were shouting to these guys to get off too, that the truck was about to explode.
We were screaming, "You're OK, you're at the hospital."

Two of the corpsmen got up in the truck, grabbing them to let go
and get moving. The corpsmen literally had to pick them up and
throw them off the truck. Once they were off, they sat down in a heap,
still shrieking. It wasn't until then that I got a look at the wounded
one. He didn't have a head. He must have been a buddy of theirs. The
buddy system was very strong, and these two evidently weren't going
to leave without their friend. We brought them to the docs and had
them sedated. We didn't have any psychiatric facilities, so we got
them evac'd to Da Nang. We never heard what happened to them.

After awhile in Vietnam, I guess I wasn't so young anymore. I was
seeing things, doing things that I never imagined could happen to
anyone. I had to do a lot of things on my own, making snap decisions
that could end up saving someone or costing him his life. Like once,
when I'd been there about seven months, they brought in this guy
who'd been shot square in the face. It was the middle of the night and
I was on duty with a medical corpsman, no doctors around at all. They
were sleeping, saving their strength. We got the call from dust off that
this guy was coming in. Apparently he'd been shot by a sniper. Amaz-
ingly enough, he was conscious when they brought him in. As a matter of fact, he was sitting up on the stretcher. It was incredible.

His face was a huge hole, covered with blood. You couldn't see his
eyes, his nose, or his mouth. There was no support for his jaw and his
tongue was just hanging. You could hear the sound of blood gurgling
as he took a breath, which meant he was taking blood into his lungs.
We were afraid he'd aspirate. The corpsman was this older guy, over
40 anyway, an experienced sergeant. I took a look at this guy and
knew we'd have to do a trach on him pretty fast. He couldn't hear us
and we couldn't get him to lie down.

I told the sergeant, "We gotta call the doc in." He told me we
didn't have time for that. We had to stabilize him with a trach and
ship him out to Da Nang. I told the corpsman that the only time I'd
ever done a trach was on a goat back in basic training at Fort Sam
Houston. The corpsman said, "If you don't do it, he'll die." So he put
my gloves on for me, and handed me the scalpel. I was shaking so
badly I thought I'd cut his throat. I remember making the incision, and
hearing him cough. The blood came out of the hole, he was coughing
out everything he was breathing in. The drops flew into my eyes, spot-
ting my contact lenses. After the blood finished spurting out, we slid
the tube in. He laid back and I worried, "What's going on?"

But he was breathing. He didn't have to fight or struggle for 30
breath anymore. I could see the air was escaping from the trach, just
like it was supposed to. It was a beautiful feeling, believe me. We

packed his face with four-by-fours and roller gauze to stop the bleeding. We told him what we were doing and he nodded his head. When they finally loaded him up for the trip to Da Nang, I was shaking pretty badly. The whole thing had taken less than forty-five minutes, from the time dust off landed to the time we packed him off. We never did get his name.

But three months later, I was sitting in the mess hall in Da Nang, waiting to take a C-130 to Hong Kong for R&R. I'd been in country ten months by then, and I was in the mess hall alone, drinking coffee and eating lunch, still in my fatigues. Somebody tapped me on the shoulder. I remember turning around. You have to remember, I was used to guys being friendly. I saw this guy standing there in hospital pajamas, the green-gray kind with the medical corps insignia on it. He had blond hair on the sides, bald on top. His face was a mass of scars, and you could see the outline of a jaw and chin. He had lips and a mouth, but no teeth. He looked like he had been badly burned, with a lot of scar tissue. You couldn't really tell where his lips began and the scar tissue ended.

The rest of his body was fine, and he could talk. "Do you remember me?" I was used to that, too, people coming up to me and saying, "Hey, I drove that tank by you the other day. . . ." Then he pointed to his trach scar and I said, "You can't be the same guy." He said something like, "I'll never forget you." I asked him how he knew who I was, because, I mean, there had been nothing left of his face. Apparently, the shot had flipped this skin flap up over his eyes so he could still see through the corners. I couldn't believe it. They called my flight right then, so I started saying a hasty goodbye. He mumbled something about how they had taken his ribs from his ribcage and artificially made a jawbone, and reconstructed portions of his face, taking skin from the lower legs, the buttocks.

Well, they began calling my name over the loud speaker. I remember giving him a big hug, saying I wished I had more time to talk to him. I wanted to learn his name, but I don't think he ever said it. I wanted to go back to the hospital and tell the others, "Hey, you remember what's-his-name? He's from Arkansas and he's doing fine." We always wanted to put names to faces, but we rarely got a chance to do it. You kept believing that everyone who left the hospital actually lived. When you found out someone actually had survived, it helped staff morale.

I came back home on a Friday, on a Pan American flight that landed in Seattle. I remember how we were told not to wear our uniforms, not to go out into the streets with our uniforms on. That made us feel worthless. There was no welcome home, not even from the Army people who processed your papers to terminate your time in the service. That was something. I felt like I had just lost my best friend. I decided to fly home to upstate New York in my uniform anyway. Nobody said anything. There were no dirty looks or comments. I was kind of excited. I wanted to say to people, "I just got back from Vietnam." Nobody cared. When I got home, my parents had a big banner strung up across the garage, "Welcome Home, Jacque." But that was about it. My parents were proud of me, of course. But other civilians? "Oh, you were in Vietnam? That's right, I remember reading something in the newspaper about you going there. That's nice." And then they'd go on talking about something else.

You were hungry to talk about it. You wanted so badly to say, 35 "Gee, don't you want to hear about what's going on there, and what we did, and how proud you should be of your soldiers and your nurses and your doctors?" I expected them to be waiting there, waving the flag. I remember all those films of World War II, with the tape that flew from the buildings in New York City, the motorcades. Of course, I had my mother. My mom was always willing to listen, but of course she couldn't understand it when I started talking about "frag wounds" or "claymore mines." There was no way she could.

The first six months at home, I just wanted to go back to Vietnam. I wanted to go back to where I was needed, where I felt important. The first job I took was in San Francisco. It was awful. Nobody cared who I was. I remember the trouble I got into because I was doing more than a nurse was supposed to do. I got in trouble because I was a "mini-doctor." They kept saying, "You're acting like you're a doctor! You're doing all these things a doctor is supposed to do. What's the big idea? You're a nurse, not a doctor." And I thought, how can I forget all the stuff I learned—putting in chest tubes, doing trachs. True, doctors only do that, but how do you prevent yourself from doing things that came automatically to you for eighteen months? How do you stop the wheels, and become the kind of nurse you were before you left?

I was completely different. Even my parents didn't recognize me as the immature little girl who left Albion, New York, just out of nursing school. San Francisco was a bomb, and there wasn't an Army post for miles around Albion. So that's why I came back to San Antonio. All my friends were back in and around Fort Sam Houston, so I just naturally gravitated back toward my network. I came to San Antonio in 1974 to get my B.S. in nursing from Incarnate Word College. The best thing I did was to get into the reserve unit there. That's where I met my husband. It gave me a chance to share my feelings with other Vietnam veterans. It kept me in touch with Army life, the good things and the bad. It was like a family.

On weekends at North Fort Hood, we really do sit around the campfire and talk about 'Nam, about what we as reservists can do to be better prepared than we were back there. If there is another Vietnam-type war, God forbid, I just know I'd want to be part of it. I couldn't sit on the sidelines. We usually just talk about these things among ourselves. I think the reason a lot of people are hesitant to talk about it is that they don't know anyone who wants to listen. A lot of people don't want to hear those kinds of stories. A lot of people just want to forget that time altogether. I don't know why. I guess I'm just not like that.

I'm not saying you don't pay a price for your memories. Last year, I had an intense flashback while flying on a Huey (helicopter) around North Fort Hood. It was the last day of this reserve unit exercise and I was invited on this tour of the area. We were flying a dust off, a medevac helicopter, just like the ones we had back then. It was my first time up in a helicopter since. I thought, "Gee, this is going to be great." One of the other nurses said to me, "Are you sure you want to do this? You're pretty tired." I brushed her aside, "No problem." We sat in back in seats strapped in next to where they held the litters. I was sitting in the seat, the helicopter was revving up . . . I don't know how to describe it. It was like a slide show, one of the old-fashioned kind where you go through this quick sequence . . . flick, flick, flick . . . now I know where they got the term flashback.

At first, it was as though I was daydreaming. What scared me to 40 death was that I couldn't turn it off. I couldn't control my mind. The cow grazing in the field became a water buffalo. Fields marked off and cross-sectioned became cemeteries. We flew over this tent, it was the 114th (reserve hospital unit) and suddenly it became the 18th surg. I was scared. All I could do was grasp the hand of this friend of mine. We couldn't talk above the helicopter roar. I just started to cry, I couldn't control myself. I saw blood coming down onto the windshield and the wiper blades swishing over it. There was blood on the floor, all over the passenger area where we were sitting. The stretchers clicked into place had bodies on top of them. I was crying. The nurse next to me kept shouting about whether I was all right. My contacts were swimming around, I wanted the ride to end. I could see why GIs felt scared . . . I couldn't just turn around and open up to the nurse sitting next to me. How could you explain something like that?

I had had a flashback or two before, but the difference was I could control them. Even when the nurse started shaking me, I couldn't turn it off. I just looked past her toward the racks in the helicopter, with bodies on stretchers, body bags on the floor, blood everywhere. When we landed, everyone saw I was visibly upset. The pilot came over to see if I was OK. The only thing I could say was, "It brought back a lot of memories." How could I explain my feelings to these people at North Fort Hood. A lot of them were too young to remember Vietnam as anything more than some dim kind of image on the nightly news. I was scared to death, because all these feelings were brought back that I never knew I had.

I still try to think of the good memories from Vietnam, the people we were able to save. A flashback has certain negative connotations.

It's a flashback when they can't think of another way of explaining it. I guess I'm lucky it took fourteen years for it to hit me like that. The one positive thing I can say about it is that it felt awfully good to come back and hover down to that red cross on the top of the tent. It felt good to come home.

For Journals

Do you know anyone who served in Vietnam? Do you know anyone who is a nurse or a nursing student? In what ways does this person talk about his or her work?

For Discussion

1. What is your personal response to the story that Rhoads tells and the ways in which she relates it? In what ways does her story either confirm or dispute what you have heard about the Vietnam War?

2. Rhoads is a woman telling about an experience more often associated with men. In what ways do you think her perspective differs from or is similar to that of the men who served in Vietnam, leaving aside, for the moment, considerations of age and rank?

3. Thinks about the participation of women in the Iraq War, considering both the types of work that they do and the attention that their service has attracted. You might consider, for example, the Jessica Lynch story and the experience of women implicated in the Iraq prison abuse scandal.

4. Doctors and nurses who serve in the military have in some ways a fundamentally different mission from that of the soldiers whose job, in the words of an army colonel, is to "kill people and break things." What kinds of personal conflicts do you imagine existed for the military health-care workers in Vietnam? In what ways do you think they might have resolved this conflict?

5. The personal narrative can bring geopolitical conflict to a human scale. Examine the ways in which Rhoads clarifies your understanding of both the human cost of war and the painful homecoming of returning Vietnam veterans.

6. In what ways does Rhoads seem transformed by her experience? Do you sense a shift in her perspective, in her approach or attitudes, as she tells the story of her tour of duty?

For Writing

1. Interview someone who served in Vietnam or in some other war, using the oral history technique. Write up the oral history, and then compose a brief analysis that responds to the following questions: In what ways is the individual's story similar to, or different from, Rhoads's story? In what ways does your interviewee's language compare with Rhoads's style?

2. Research newspaper and magazine articles from the late 1960s and early 1970s, selecting articles and opinion pieces that covered the Vietnam War. Examine the language in which stories about Vietnam are conveyed, and write an essay analyzing the attitudes about the war and about the Vietnam service personnel that you find in the press coverage. Alternatively, explore the ways in which the wars in Afghanistan and Iraq have been represented in the media, and consider comparing the language and content of news accounts from both Vietnam and the more recent conflicts.

❊❊❊ *Type-Casting* (1989)

PAUL FUSSELL

A native of Pasadena, California, Paul Fussell (1924–) earned his Ph.D. in education from Harvard University in 1952. In 1976, he won the National Book Award and National Book Critics Circle Award for The Great War and Modern Memory. *In addition to being a Fulbright lecturer and Guggenheim fellow, Fussell was a member of the U.S. Army during World War II and was the recipient of two Purple Hearts. More recently, he edited* The Norton Book of Modern War *(1991). His work reflects profoundly on the effect that war has on the individual and society. The selection that follows is from* Wartime *(1989).*

"The Chinese are fine fighting men," declares one of Horatio Stubbs's fellow soldiers. "Your Chink is brought up to fight on a handful of rice a day. A Chink'll go for days on just a handful of rice."[1] That's an example, if a rather low one, of the kind of cliché classifications indispensable in wartime. If war is a political, social, and psychological disaster, it is also a perceptual and rhetorical scandal from which total recovery is unlikely. Looking out upon the wartime world, soldiers and civilians alike reduce it to a simplified sketch featuring a limited series of classifications into which people, in the process dehumanized and deprived of individuality or eccentricity, are fitted. In the Second World War many more things than conscripts underwent classifications from 1-A to 4-F. The British working girl Louie, in Elizabeth Bowen's *The Heat of the Day* (1948), receives the classifications determining her vision in 1942 from the newspapers she follows devotedly:

> Was she not a worker, a soldier's lonely wife, a war orphan, a pedestrian, a Londoner, a home and animal-lover, a thinking democrat, a

movie-goer, a woman of Britain, a letter-writer, a fuel-saver and a housewife?[2]

Within the soldier's world, the classifications are clearly indicated by insignia of rank and branch of service. The result is that with people, you always know what to expect. A captain of artillery will be a certain type, and so will a major in the Judge Advocate General's department, a first lieutenant of Ordinance, and an infantry staff-sergeant. You can count on it. And gazing outward toward the civilian scene, the soldierly imagination rudely consigns people to four categories:

1. The female, consisting of mother, grandmother, and sister, on the one hand, and, on the other, agents of sexual solace.
2. Elderly men, who are running the draft boards, as well as the rationing, transportation, and propaganda apparatus.
3. The infantine, who will be in the war if it lasts long enough.
4. And the most despised of categories, the 4-F or physically unfit and thus defective, the more despicable the more invisible the defect, like a heart murmur, punctured ear-drum, or flat feet.

One might think the most vigorous soldierly contempt might be directed at conscientious objectors, but no: since most of them were set to hard labor in camps, they were regarded as virtually members, if a bit disgraced, of the armed services, and their circumstances were conceived to be little more degrading than those of the troops in, say, the non-combatant quartermaster corps. That the COs endured lots of chickenshit made them like brothers. Civilians were different, more like "foreigners," indeed rather like the enemy.

For the war to be prosecuted at all, the enemy of course had to be severely dehumanized and demeaned, and in different ways, depending on different presumed national characteristics. One way of classifying the Axis enemy was to arrange it by nationalities along a scale running from courage down to cowardice. The Japanese were at the brave end, the Italians at the pusillanimous, and the Germans were in the middle. This symmetrical arrangement also implied a scale of animalism, with the Japanese accorded the most feral qualities and the Italians the most human, including a love of music, ice-cream, and ostentatious dress.

Americans detested the Japanese the most, for only they had had the effrontery to attack the United States directly, sinking ships, killing sailors, and embarrassing American pretenses to alertness and combat adequacy. They must be animals to behave thus, and cruel ones at that. "Bestial apes"—that is what Admiral William F. Halsey termed them and added the good news that "we are drowning and burning

[them] all over the Pacific, and it is just as much pleasure to burn them as to drown them."[3] A marine on Guadalcanal could perceive the Japanese only as beasts of various species. He told John Hersey, "They hide up in the trees like wildcats. Sometimes when they attack, they scream like a bunch of terrified cattle in a slaughter house." Another said, "I wish we were fighting against Germans. They are human beings, like us. . . . But the Japs are like animals. . . . They take to the jungle as if they had been bred there, and like some beasts you never see them until they are dead."[4] What harm, then, in cleaning, polishing, and sending home their animal skulls as souvenirs, so that a standard snapshot depicts a soldier or marine proudly exhibiting a cleansed Japanese skull, while a poem of the period, by Winfield Townley Scott, meditates without moral comment on "The U.S. Sailor with the Japanese Skull":

> our
> Bluejacket, I mean, aged 20, in August strolled
> Among the little bodies on the sand and hunted
> Souvenirs: teeth, tags, diaries, boots; but bolder still
> Hacked off this head and under a Ginkgo tree skinned it.[5]

Then dragged it behind his ship for many days and finally scrubbed it thoroughly with lye and had a perfect souvenir. Dealing that way with the skull of a German or Italian, that is, "a white man," would be clearly inappropriate, perhaps sacrilegious. This treatment of Japanese corpses as if they were animal became so flagrant as early as September, 1942, that the Commander in Chief of the Pacific Fleet ordered that "No part of the enemy's body may be used as a souvenir. Unit Commanders will take stern disciplinary action. . . ."[6]

The civil, unbloodthirsty American sailor James J. Fahey, a Roman 5
Catholic from Waltham, Massachusetts, and a respecter of all the decencies, after a *kamikaze* attack on his ship wrote home that "one of the men on our [gun] mount got a Jap rib and cleaned it up" because "his sister wants part of a Jap body."[7] No censorious reaction whatever from Fahey, for that rib is like one you can buy in a meat market. "Oh, the inhuman brutes!" exclaimed Mrs. John Milburn, as news of Japanese behavior reached the United Kingdom.[8] Among the Allies the Japanese were also known as "jackals" or "monkey-men" or "subhumans," the term of course used by the Germans for Russians, Poles, and assorted Slavs, amply justifying their vivisection. Personnel of the United States Marine Corps sought to popularize the term *Japes* (Japs + apes), but the word never caught on, and the Japanese remained *Japs*, or, slightly less contemptuously, *Nips*. Like the *Huns* of the Great War, *Japs*—"the yellow Huns of the East," Australian General Gordon Bennett called them[9]—was a brisk monosyllable handy for slogans like "Rap the Jap" or "Let's Blast the Jap Clean Off the Map," the last a virtual prophecy of Hiroshima. It is a truism of military propaganda that

monosyllabic enemies are easier to despise than others. A *kraut* or *wop* is instantly disposable in a way a German or Italian isn't quite, just as in the Great War a *boche* or a *hun* betrayed by their very names their vileness and worthlessness. Like the later *gook*. In July, 1943, a large sign on the damaged bow of the U.S. Cruiser *Honolulu* quoted Admiral Halsey urging everyone to

> Kill Japs.   Kill Japs.
> Kill More Japs.[10]

Because they were animals, Japanese troops had certain advantages over Americans. They could see in the dark, it was believed, and survive on a diet of roots and grubs. The very tiny-ness of the Japanese was another reason for contempt. They were little the way insects and rodents are little—little but nasty. In 1942, in the pamphlet *Individual Battle Doctrine,* the United States Marine Corps assured its members of Japanese combat inferiority by pointing out that "the Jap is much too short to enter the Marine Corps." One result of this puniness is that "he is really a poor bayonet fighter." Americans held in Japanese prison camps noticed the way their captors liked to get up onto something, a box, podium, platform, or stand, when haranguing the prisoners. "They loved to elevate themselves," one prisoner said.[11] Americans of standard height could understand the Japanese problem immediately as the "Runt's Complex," familiar from high school, the need of the short to "get back at" people of normal height and their customary use of guile or fraud to do so. The "sneak attack" on Pearl Harbor thus explains itself.

A rumor popular during the war told of a mother receiving a letter from her soldier son in a Japanese POW camp. He tells her that he is well and surviving OK and not to worry, and he adds that she might like to soak off the stamp on the envelope to give a friend who's a collector. When she does so, she finds written under the stamp, "THEY HAVE CUT OUT MY TONGUE." Given the notorious cruelty of the Japanese, in wartime that story could be received as entirely credible, making everyone forget that letters from captured soldiers bear no postage stamps. Typecasting assured that the Pacific War would be particularly cruel, and the cruelty was on both sides. The Japanese, as former marine E. B. Sledge says, "killed solely for the sake of killing, without hope and without higher purpose," and so did the Americans. The Japanese fired programmatically on stretcher-bearers and tortured to death Americans who fell into their hands. Sledge once encountered a group of dead marines whose bodies had been defiled, one man's penis having been sliced off and inserted in his mouth, another man's head and hands having been chopped off.[12] Similarly, the marines loved to use the few Japs who came forward to surrender as amusing rifle targets, just as they felt intense satisfaction watching them twist and writhe when set afire by the napalm of the flame-thrower. Japanese skulls were not the only desirable trophies: treasured also were Japanese gold teeth, knocked out, sometimes from the mouths of the still-living, by a USMC Ka-bar knife-hilt. During wartime it was impossible to complicate "the Japanese character" in any way, to recognize that the same auspices were behind the Bataan Death March and the Noh drama. It was not to be widely publicized that the same "types" who had bayoneted hospital patients in Hong Kong also flew out over the sea where they had sunk HMS *Repulse* and *Prince of Wales* and dropped a memorial wreath on the water. Once the war was over and the Americans were installed on the home islands as occupiers, the Japanese capacity for subtlety and delicacy could again be recognized. Then, Admiral Nimitz, doubtless with Halsey and such in mind, reminded his subordinates that "the use of insulting epithets in connection with the Japanese as a race or individuals does not now become the officers of the United States Navy."[13]

If the Japanese were type-cast as animals of an especially dwarfish but vicious species, the Germans were recognized to be human beings, but of a perverse type, cold, diagrammatic, pedantic, unimaginative, and thoroughly sinister. We had submarines, but they had U-boats. Their instinct for discipline made them especially dangerous, and their admitted distinction in technology made their cruelty uniquely effective. That it was the same people who were shooting hostages and hanging Poles and gassing Jews, on the one hand, and enjoying Beethoven and Schubert, on the other, was a complication too difficult to be faced during wartime. In March, 1942, John Steinbeck found that he had seriously misjudged the popular necessity of type-casting German troops as simply wicked. In his novella (later a play) *The Moon Is Down*, he depicted the Germans occupying a Norwegian town as human, subject like other people to emotions of love, pride, envy, and jealousy. None was characterized as an anti-Semitic monster. To his astonishment, a cascade of intellectual and moral abuse fell upon him. Artistically he may have deserved it: *The Moon Is Down* is a sort of narrative *Our Town* relocated to a wartime Continent. The story overflows with folksiness and jocosity, and the small-town scene is peopled with sentimental would-be lovable characters. But the badness of the book lies rather in its aesthetic clumsiness than in any ideological defect. As a writer dependent on popular suffrage, Steinbeck had simply not noticed that the days of light duty were past and henceforth Germans, all Germans—Wehrmacht, SS, sailors, housewives, hikers, the lot—had to be cast as confirmed enemies of human decency.

In normal times, the characteristic most often imputed to the Germans, thoroughness, would have constituted a compliment. But in wartime it was a moral defect, implying an inhuman mechanism,

monotony, and rigidity. Heartless classification and analysis were considered a German specialty, and German soldiers were said to have a
passion for straight lines and rigid postures. In one British theater
showing a newsreel scene of German soldiers standing at exaggerated
attention, someone was heard to shout, "Take t'coat hanger out
then."[14] RAF bomber crews were not often deceived by decoy burning
cities located five to ten miles from the actual ones because the fake
fires were disposed in lines that were too straight. One photograph in
Len Deighton's *Fighter* (1977) carries this legend:

> *Junkers JU 88 Bomber Crews Go to Work.* Most of the photographs . . . of
> the airmen, German and British . . . are strikingly alike—as the fliers
> pat their dogs, play chess, or relax near their aircraft—but it would be
> difficult to imagine RAF crews marching to their aircraft in the long
> rays of the early-morning sun singing as these men do.[15]

The German aircrewmen depicted there are marching in three precise
files, an officer at their head, past a line-up of planes. And of course
the group singing of such troops was more objectionably disciplined
than that of the British or Americans could ever be. British General Sir
John Hackett heard a lot of German army singing during his months
as a prisoner of war, and he found himself offended by the communal
abrupt "shortening of the final note of any line, as though according to
a drill."[16] As a German characteristic, "thoroughness" was recognized
even by the Germans. Visiting a Luftwaffe establishment in France in
1940, Josef Goebbels notes with satisfaction that it's operated with
"German thoroughness," although it is "a very complex organizational machine."[17] Popular historiography especially preserves the
German reputation for being foolishly "methodical." Thus Seymour
Reit's *Masquerade: The Amazing Camouflage Deceptions of World War II*
(1978) speaks critically of "the very methodical and systematic way"
the Germans went about their visual deceptions. "Teutonic thoroughness" is the term for their technique,[18] and there is clearly something
reprehensible about it.

   While the Japanese were calumniated for being animals, the Ger-   10
mans were simply "sick," the very embodiment of disease. Hearing
that the Germans have been manacling British prisoners of war (actually in retaliation for the British order to handcuff prisoners taken at
Dieppe), Mrs. Milburn explodes: "One can't think of anything bad
enough for these diseased Germans. Their minds are all wrong."[19]
Indeed, "They are like a loathsome disease spreading and spreading
over Europe."[20] And a disease is what they were held to resemble in a
whimsical "receipt" by which General Troy Middleton took over the
town of Bastogne from the 101st Airborne Division in January, 1945.
The condition of the town was said to be "Used but Serviceable," and
it was held to be "Kraut Disinfected."[21] Sick or not, the Germans were

different in every way. Even their planes sounded different. Flying over England, their motors seemed to throb, sounding like "grunt-a-grunt-a-grunt-a-grunt-a." Some heard in the throbbing sound the message, "It's for you, It's for you, It's for you." One report printed in a newspaper ("ROUGED GERMAN AIRMEN") could never have been fastened on the bestial Japanese, namely, that some captured German fliers were found to have rouged cheeks, together with waved hair, lipstick, and painted finger- and toenails.[22]

Social envy and social snobbery, respectively, seem to lie behind Hitler's view of Churchill as "a superannuated drunkard supported by Jewish gold" and Churchill's view of Hitler as a "bloodthirsty guttersnipe."[23] Down below, where the troops were, the Germans had some respect for British soldiers but none for Americans. The Americans were spoiled, lazy, ignorant, unpolitical loud-mouths, and, as Goebbels put it, they seemed afflicted with "a spiritual emptiness that really makes you shake your head."[24] Few in Germany had any idea why the Americans had invaded Europe. One German officer could conclude only, as he told his interrogator, that they had attacked the Reich "in order to save Churchill and the Yews."[25] It was only their superiority in numbers, ordnance, and equipment that brought any victories to the Americans—and the British as well. High British officers privately admitted as much. Max Hastings observes of the state of Allied sensibility just before the invasion of Normandy:

> Four years of war against the Wehrmacht had convinced Britain's commanders that Allied troops should engage and could defeat their principal enemy only on the most absolutely favorable terms. Throughout the Second World War, whenever British or American troops met the Germans in anything like equal strength, the Germans prevailed.[26]

It was only wealth that tipped the scales in favor of the Allies.

A sensitive German woman, Christabel Bielenberg, accidentally came upon an American flier hidden in a room in her small town. She instantly perceived that the war was lost when she observed "the general air of health and well being, of affluence, about him." What struck her was

> the quality of the stuff his overalls were made of, his boots and the silk scarf which he had tied into his belt, and a soft leather wallet he held in one hand. Suddenly I felt shabby, old, dilapidated, and defeated. Everything he had on was so real: real wool, real leather, real silk—so real and he looked so young.[27]

German troops could often tell when the "Amis" were nearby. Their positions seemed to give off a sweet smell, probably because they smoked Virginia, rather than "Turkish" and ersatz, tobacco.

Those fighting on the same side type-cast each other just as enemies did. One reason the Italians were in such contempt by the Germans is that they seemed to resemble the Americans, with their
unmilitary concern with comfort and their lack of the sacrificial impulse. But the Italians were patronized even by the Americans. One
American officer in the North African desert was outraged to hear a
German prisoner, asked what he thought of the American troops he'd
encountered, assert: "The Americans are to us what the Italians are to
you."[28] If the Germans were sadists and bullies, the Italians were
dandies motivated by both vainglory and cowardice. Popular culture
had them surrendering not just en masse but pomaded and scented,
accompanied by framed pictures, birdcages, and similar domestic
amenities, their elegant spare uniforms neatly folded in extra suitcases
and trunks. One British prisoner of the Italians who was often moved
from camp to camp was astonished at the Italian understanding of the
comforts appropriate to commissioned rank, even when held by an
enemy. He was allowed two suitcases, a pack, a blanket roll, and a
case of books. "It never seemed to worry the Italians how much kit we
took," he says, "since they regarded it as quite normal for officers.
Their own took thirty large trunks, mostly full of different uniforms,
wherever they moved, even on active service."[29]

Since it was not until late in the war that the Allies entered France,
and since by that time there was little food there, Italy, even afflicted
as it was by widespread starvation, became a place where the troops'
food fantasies could sometimes be realized. In Taranto in June, 1944,
one British soldier had an experience he set down in his diary this
way: "Wonderful meal in T. Steak—eggs—cherries—white wine—
macaroni—and Marsala." He added: "We should never have fought
these people."[30] The Italian reputation as the surviving custodians of
the cuisine depended in part on their fame in London as waiters and
chefs and restaurant owners. Many were interned in the United Kingdom to be shipped to Canada out of harm's way. When a ship carrying them, the *Arandora Star*, was torpedoed and sunk, "a number of
London's most famous *restaurateurs*," says Vera Brittain, "perished in
the Atlantic."[31] Because the Italians were also associated with ice
cream—making it, selling it, and eating it—British soldiers seldom let
the idea of "Italians" pass through their understandings without some
half-melancholy, half-contemptuous allusion to ice cream, a commod-
ity rare in the British army. In one battalion magazine for February,
1941, a comic story, "Wops in Action," introduces its characters thus;
"Alphonse and Toni were two soldiers in a crack Wop infantry regiment. On their right arms they wore three enamel ice cream cones,
awarded by their C.O. for the smartest pair of heels."[32]

If the Germans were held to sing with conspicuous group disci- 15
pline, "shortening . . . the final note of any line, as though according to

a drill," the Italians were likely to burst into song out of the sheer "Latin" joy of being alive, a feeling intensified beyond measure by the hazards of wartime. When Farley Mowat's unit invaded the Italian mainland near Messina, there were no Germans about, and "since the Italian troops manning the coast defenses already knew that Mussolini had fallen, they were in no mood to die heroically in a lost cause." Thus,

> As the Allied column labored upward like an attenuated khaki-colored snake, another descended parallel to it, this one bluish-green in hue. The Italian soldiers came down from the hills, not like members of a defeated army but in a mood of fiesta, marching raggedly along with their personal possessions slung about them, filling the air with laughter and song.[33]

"A lot of opera singers" was Roosevelt's characterization of resident Italian aliens as he decided not to intern them in 1942.[34] And speaking of the association between wartime and cliché, *"O Sole Mio"* was the song actually being sung when Edward Blishen saw a group of Italian prisoners in England for the first time,[35] while some of the British in North Africa maintained that it was "to the strains of *Aida"* that the Italians planned to march triumphantly into Egypt. Says Tanker H. L. Sykes, "We actually found the music, the instruments, and the ceremonial dress they intended to use."[36]

When in the earlier war Frederic Henry, in Hemingway's *A Farewell to Arms* (1929), feels some guilt about deserting, Catherine Barkley comforts him by reminding him that "It's only the Italian army."[37] This myth of Italian military haplessness served a useful psychological function in the Second World War, helping secretly to define what Allied soldiers wanted the "enemy" universally to be—pacifists, dandies, sensitive and civilized non-ideologues, even clowns. The antithesis of committed, fanatic National Socialists. At the same time the Italians could serve as the definition of incompetence, fraudulence, and cowardice: no one really wanted to be like them to be sure, but how everyone wished it were possible! The world was laughing at Italy, and yet the Italians were sensibly declining to be murdered. The Allied soldier couldn't help wondering that if contempt and ridicule are the price of staying alive, perhaps the price is worth paying. While constituting one of the war's most simple-minded clichés, the Italians thus posed a challenge to cliché, shaking up and complicating the standard uncomplex attitude toward "the enemy." It was their presence in the war that kept a degree of ambiguity and paradox alive in a wartime world of stark and easily dealt-with oppositions. Were the Italians properly sized up by ridicule, as in the popular London dance-step The Tuscana ("based on the Italians' way of fighting, . . . one step forward, two steps back")?[38] Was A. P. Herbert right to refer to Mussolini on the BBC as "the Top Wop"? Or were they a serious enemy,

more correctly treated respectfully? One who fought them, Peter
Cochrane, in his book *Charlie Company* (1977), praises their courage,
flair, and discipline, and goes out of his way to celebrate Italian skill in
road engineering and artillery ranging and to note Italian compassion
toward wounded prisoners. Is that the correct view? Or did General
Montgomery have the right attitude when he told the troops preparing to invade Sicily,

> "Someone said to me a few days ago that the Italians are really de-
> cent people and that if we treat them properly they will come over to
> us. I disagree with him. Our job is to kill them. That is what we have
> to do. Once we have killed them we can see if they are good fellows
> or not. But they must be killed first."[39]

Whatever the Italians actually were, the myth that they were the
sweetest people in the war survives. The cover illustration of the
American magazine *Men Today* for July, 1963, depicts a scene from one
of the sadoerotic narratives within. Two girls are busy torturing an
American soldier of the Second World War. He is tied to a chair. One
girl, dressed in tight blouse and short shorts, is playing a blowtorch
over his chest. The other looks on, coiled whip at the ready. The first
girl is shouting, "Scream for my kisses, Amerikaner Soldat!" She wears
a swastika armband. The other girl wears a German officer's jacket
and cap.[40] The Italian wartime image becomes doubly clear if one tries
to imagine the insignia and trappings of Italian fascism used with sig-
nifications like these. They would produce not a frisson or even an
erection but a laugh.

The force and to a degree the validity of wartime type-casting can
be appreciated by trying to imagine German troops crawling on their
stomachs through the malarial jungles of the South Pacific. Just as
hard to conceive as Japanese soldiers defending the Apennines from
behind mountain barricades built up from stones of determined Italian
youths resisting to the death the American assault on the Rhine or the
Russian assault on Berlin. Each enemy has taken on the characteristics
of primary geography, both literal and otherwise, and it is impossible
to imagine them any other way. Similarly it is impossible to believe
about one enemy what it is easy to believe about another. For example:
according to Captain M. J. Brown, British troops once came up highly
desirable billet abandoned by the Germans whose front was invitingly
half-open. Entering cautiously through a window to avoid the likely
booby-trap, they approached the front door from inside and found attached to it the expected explosive charge set to go off when the door
was moved. They left the house carefully and tied a string to the outside knob of the front door, taking cover in a slit-trench across the
road. When they were all in the slit-trench, they pulled the string and
the slit-trench exploded, killing them all. "The layer of the trap had an-

ticipated their process of reasoning," notes Captain Brown, "step by step."[41] The Japanese would probably not think such a caper funny enough to be worthwhile. The Italians would, but would be too "unmethodical" to set it up efficiently. The Americans and British would like the idea but would be too lazy to waste time on it. But assigned to the Germans, the story, apocryphal as it may be, rings true.

And although a whole book could be devoted to the sort of stereotyping necessary for Americans (and British) to see themselves as attractive, moral, and exemplary, some of the conventions can be noted briefly. A good way to get a feel for the subject would be to go through any number of *Life* magazine, or *Look,* or *Collier's,* or *The Saturday Evening Post* issued from 1942 to 1945. Attending to the display advertisements, mostly in color, one would immediately understand the wartime thrill Americans achieved by imagining themselves good-looking Aryans blond and tall, beloved by slim blonde women and surrounded by much-desired consumer goods. If the illustrations are to be believed, all young men are in the Air Corps, where they are officers almost by definition (or, in 1942, cadets destined soon to be officers). If by some misfortune they are in any other part of the army, they are almost never privates or NCOs but young officers beaming on their fiancée's assiduity in accumulating flatware of International Sterling. Notable is the absence of any features which might be interpreted as Jewish, or Central European, or in any remote way "Colored." The people on whose behalf the war is being fought are Anglo-Saxons, "nice people"—that is, upper-middle class. Readers of these advertisements could not help inferring that the war was designed primarily to defend and advance the interests of such tall, clean blondes, as well as the suppliers of the cars, tires, and refrigerators the blonds will own and exhibit once the war is won. If the Jews, like those in New York, liked to think the war was in some way about them, it's clear that most people didn't want to be like them in any way or even reminded of them. You could spend your life studying the magazine ads of wartime without once coming upon a yarmulkah or prayer shawl, or even features suggestive of Jewishness. Philip Roth's Alexander Portnoy, too young for the war but not too young to associate himself with the thrill of being on the winning and the righteous side, conceives of it as entirely an upper-middle-class Anglophile-American victory, less about the right to wear phylacteries than argyle socks and loafers.

The advertising artists sometimes had to face facts and recognize that many of those fighting the Axis were, regrettably, quite unromantic enlisted men, but such are generally depicted without women and usually alone, unwrapping a gift watch sent by the folks, celebrating the possession of a candy bar ("Boy! I'm strong for Milky Ways"), enjoying being included at a strange family's dinner table at Thanksgiving, waiting to board a train which, it is to be hoped, is not already full of idle civilians, or delighting in the Chelsea cigarettes included in a K-ration. The man shown in bed enjoying the luxury of Pacific Sheets is a Pfc., not an officer, because he is alone. Yawning and stretching in an ad in *Life* in February, 1945, he thinks, "'Hallelujah, what a day is coming! A day when a fellow can drop his gear in his tracks, climb into a real bed as soft as a marshmallow, and s-t-r-e-t-c-h every last muscle! A day when he can feel again the caress of sleek, soft, white Pacific Sheets against his tired body.'" But when women enter, the male models get promoted instantly to officer rank, and their looks improve, too. Thus the woman enjoying a Honeymoon in Mexico on behalf of DuBarry Beauty Preparations is attended by her young naval-officer husband in whites. A young woman fortunate enough to have found a lover who appreciates the benefits of an extremely smooth Barbasol Shave is doubly blessed, for he is also an officer (branch of service not revealed). One young woman appearing on behalf of a brand of woolen goods is being met at her front door at a snowy Christmastime by a young man in a sleigh bearing a Christmas tree. At first glance he seems to be wearing an enlisted soldier's rough overcoat, but the ad-man has saved the day by remembering to affix a gold bar to his shoulder. Another young woman, lonely, has been left behind as a result of Rough Hands, but in the background wiser women who have learned to use Campana Balm swarm past in crowds, each with her date: only two are servicemen, but one is a naval ensign, the other a commissioned Air Corps pilot. If an enlisted man must be depicted in close proximity to a desirable woman, as in one ad for Chesterfield cigarettes, the situation can be salvaged by displaying on his shoulder the insignia ("patch") not, surely, of the 3rd Armored Division but of the United States Army Air Corps. In fiction or film, the GI might be Jewish or Italian, Polish or Hispanic or "Colored," but never in advertising, a medium where only ideal imagery can be allowed to enter. In advertising, the Allied war is fought by white Anglo-Saxons, officers or aviators, with neat, short hair, clear eyes, gleaming teeth, and well-defined jawlines. That is the wartime "we," fighting against the beast-like yellow-skinned Japanese, the "sick" Germans, and the preposterous Italians. Naturally we won. As Admiral Halsey said in his victory message to his fleet when the Japanese surrendered, "The forces of righteousness and decency have triumphed."[42]

Endnotes

1. *A Soldier Erect, or Further Adventures of the Hand-Reared Boy* (London, 1971).
2. (New York, 1948 [1979]), 134.
3. Dwight Macdonald, *Memoirs of a Revolutionist: Essays in Political Criticism* (New York, 1957), 93.
4. *Into the Valley* (New York, 1943), 20, 56.

5. *Collected Poems: 1937–1962* (New York, 1962), 121.

6. Samuel Cosman Papers, U.S. Marine Corps Historical Center, Washington, D.C.

7. James Fahey, *Pacific War Diary* (New York, 1963), 231.

8. Peter Donnelly, ed., *Mrs. Milburn's Diaries: An Englishwoman's Day-to-Day Reflections, 1939–1945* (London, 1979 [1980]), 248.

9. *Why Singapore Fell* (Bombay, 1945), 58.

10. John W. Dower, *War Without Mercy: Race and Power in the Pacific War* (New York, 1986), 36.

11. Donald Knox, *Death March* (New York, 1981), 364.

12. *With the Old Breed* (Novato, Calif., 1981), 142, 148.

13. John Costello, *The Pacific War* (New York, 1981), 616.

14. Norman Longmate, *How We Lived Then* (London, 1971), 404.

15. No. 51, between pp. 248–49.

16. *I was a Stranger* (London, 1977 [1979]), 74–75.

17. Fred Taylor, ed., *The Goebbels Diaries, 1939–1941* (New York, 1983), 148.

18. (1980), 5, 148.

19. Donnelly, *Mrs. Milburn's Diaries*, 216.

20. *Ibid.*, 185.

21. Napier Crookenden, *The Battle of the Bulge* (New York, 1980), 124.

22. Arthur Marshall, "Odd Man In," *New Statesman*, Nov. 21, 1980, p. 15.

23. John Strawson, *Hitler's Battles for Europe* (New York, 1971), 113.

24. Louis Lochner, ed., *The Goebbels Diaries, 1942–1943* (Garden City, N.Y., 1948), 317.

25. Franklyn Johnson, *One More Hill* (New York, 1949), 157.

26. Hastings, *Overlord* (New York, 1984), 24.

27. *The Past Is Myself* (London, 1970), 148.

28. M. J. Brown, Diary, IWM.

29. Anthony Deane-Drummond, *Return Ticket* (London, 1953 [1967]), 82.

30. Oliver Carpenter, Diary, IWM.

31. *Testament of Experience*, 258.

32. C. C. Rand, *The Ordinary Fellow* (Magazine of the 1st Bn., London Irish Rifles), I, #5, 54–55.

33. *And No Birds Sang* (Boston, 1979), 143.

34. James MacGregor Burns, *Roosevelt: The Soldier of Freedom* (New York, 1970), 214.

35. Edward Blishen, *A Cackhanded War* (London, 1972), 119.

36. Memoir, IWM.

37. (New York, 1929), 260.

38. Longmate, *How We Lived Then*, 422.

39. Neil McCallum, *Journey with a Pistol* (London, 1959), 145.

40. Gillian Freeman, *The Undergrowth of Literature* (London, 1967), facing p. 86.

41. Diary, IWM.

42. E. B. Potter, *Bull Halsey* (Annapolis, Md., 1985), 348.

For Journals

Write about some common stereotypes that you are aware of and the ways in which they are depicted in film, paintings, advertisements, posters, or other media.

For Discussion

1. In view of Fussell's essay, discuss some kinds of typecasting or stereotyping that are familiar to you. Consider recent world events and conflicts, such as in the Middle East, in your discussion.

2. In what ways is constructing an "other," especially an enemy, similar to or different from the process of establishing a national identity? Review the readings in Chapter 5 as needed.

3. Fussell's preface to the book *Wartime,* from which this excerpt is taken, notes that the book is about "the rationalizations and euphemisms people needed to deal with an unacceptable actuality from 1939 to 1945." Does Fussell achieve his purpose of exposing such rationalizations and euphemisms? Are you aware of such rationalizations in recent news reports and political discourse around the conflicts since 9/11?

4. In what ways, according to Fussell, are people "dehumanized and deprived of individuality" in wartime? Examine this claim, citing specific examples that you find especially convincing, again drawing from recent events as appropriate, including images from war in Iraq.

5. Identify and analyze some of the metaphors used to stereotype different nationalities during World War II. From your own observation and experience, are any of these stereotypes still in popular use? Have other stereotypes emerged?

6. Contrast other nation's impressions of American soldiers in World War II with impressions you may have already gained from American popular culture—films, photographs, books and the like, or from family narratives.

For Writing

1. Follow Fussell's suggestion, and research American popular magazines published during World War II—*Life* or *Time,* for example. You will find collections in your college library or in a public library, and you may need to work with microfilm or microfiche. A local historian may have information to share. Browse through a number of magazines, taking notes on what you see, particularly in the advertisements, but also reading editorials and letters to the editor as they seem relevant. Develop an essay based on your findings, focusing on some theme or aspect of your findings and supporting your core assertion with examples from your research.

2. Interview people who lived during World War II about their perceptions of the enemy during the war. Alternatively, conduct research among your college population or neighborhood, using a tape recorder or taking notes and then reviewing your interviews to see whether common themes or metaphors emerge. Write up and document your findings, using specific examples and quotations as appropriate.

❀❀❀ Propaganda in Roosevelt's "Pearl Harbor Address" (2000)

NEIL A. VAN OS

Neil A. Van Os (1981–) is a college student attending a California university. He wrote this essay for an assignment in his writing class where he was asked to select one or more background texts and apply their principles to a primary text. He chose Roosevelt's Pearl Harbor Address, which his class had examined both in text and in an audio recording.

On December 7, 1941, Japanese forces launched a surprise offensive against the United States of America at Pearl Harbor, Hawaii. The attack was recognized as a premeditated act of aggression against the United States, and thus a declaration of war against Japan became virtually inevitable. The attention of the American people was promptly directed toward President Roosevelt, but it is not the role of the president to declare war; the Constitution reserves this power for Congress. However, the president can address an emergency session of Congress and ask that such a declaration be made. In making this speech, Roosevelt knew that he would be addressing not only one room of Congressmen, but also millions of citizens listening to the radio as he spoke and reading newspapers the next day. In his address to Congress on December 8, 1941, President Roosevelt utilizes strategies of propaganda to portray the Japanese as inhuman aggressors while moving the American people to unite against them.

The notion that a president would intentionally manipulate the thoughts and emotions of U.S. citizens is disconcerting at first. Through propaganda, however, a government can add conviction to a cause and strength to a unified people. Propaganda exists to spread and promote a certain idea, cause, or policy through the populace. Effective propaganda is the greatest social weapon conceivable, for it is the force that reforms the minds of a people from individuals into elements of a unified whole, giving citizens beliefs and convictions that the government wants them to have, according to Jacques Ellul, author of *Propaganda: The Formation of Men's Attitudes*. To lead American forces to victory in the pending war, propaganda was the right tool at the right time.

President Roosevelt would deliver this speech to an enormous audience with anxious, attentive ears. The effectiveness of propaganda grows as the size and attention of the audience grows and, historically, propaganda is most useful in a state of war, a time when the unification of a nation is critical. Despite the undesirable circumstances, Roosevelt had an ideal opportunity to unite the Americans against their new foe, the Japanese.

Roosevelt begins by portraying the Japanese Empire as a heartless, faceless aggressor, a technique emphasized in the film, *Faces of the Enemy*. After setting a historical context with the words, "Yesterday, December 7, 1941,—a date which will live in infamy," he states that the "Empire of Japan" had "deliberately attacked" the United States of America. The president uses *empire* instead of *nation* or *people* because *empire* has a less appealing, imperialistic connotation. He does not want Americans to see the Japanese as individual people. A human being feels compassion and sympathizes with other human beings, and such feelings toward the Japanese, according to *Faces of the Enemy*, would only hinder this new American agenda to defeat them. Roosevelt's insinuation of an inhuman nature in the Japanese serves a further purpose. It suggests that the Japanese do not feel sympathy and compassion as Americans do. Therefore, the Japanese Empire seems even more evil and appears to pose a more aggressive threat to the United States. Stating that the empire had "deliberately attacked" American forces reminds the audience that this was not a random, accidental incident. The Japanese made a specific effort to strike against the United States.

Roosevelt now shifts his focus to accentuate the premeditated be- 5 trayal of trust committed by the Japanese. He explains that "the United States was at peace with that nation and, at the solicitation of Japan, was still in conversation with its government and its emperor looking toward the maintenance of peace in the Pacific." He focuses on this point for a relatively long time, approximately one-third of his speech. The idea that the Japanese were hiding behind a mask of peaceful intention while actually planning aggressive action against the United States makes them more despicable in the eyes of an American citizen. Roosevelt reinforces his claims against Japan through appeals to logos when he says:

> It will be recorded that the distance of Hawaii from Japan makes it obvious that the attack was deliberately planned many days or even weeks ago. During the intervening time the Japanese government had deliberately sought to deceive the United States by false statements and expressions of hope for continued peace.

Roosevelt simultaneously makes appeals to pathos, provoking emotional response with charged words such as *deliberately* and *deceived* contrasting sharply with *hope* and *peace*. The Japanese Empire is again depicted as an aggressive and deceitful opponent with no sense of truce or negotiation. This causes citizens of the United States to feel even further removed from their new Japanese foes, an aspect of propaganda that *Faces of the Enemy* claims is essential.

President Roosevelt's next tactic is to remind his audience that the Japanese are not only attacking, but they are also killing as well. He says that the surprise attack "caused severe damage to American naval and military forces." More importantly, however, he makes the situation more real in saying, "I regret to tell you that very many American lives have been lost." Roosevelt's disclosure that "American lives have been lost" informs the people that this is not simply a fight between warships and airplanes, but a real attack with real consequences. To say that "very many American lives have been lost" adds still more to the seriousness of the situation. He wants America to know that the Japanese, like savages, have killed the sons, friends, and neighbors of many of the people listening to the address. This approach combines intellectual and emotional messages to the audience, an idea stressed by Ellul's *Propaganda.*

Roosevelt proceeds to broaden the scope of the Japanese aggression beyond one attack in Hawaii. He explains that the threat of the Japanese is not limited to one distant naval base. The President asserts that the Japanese threat is spreading like a plague of violence, and brings the threat closer to the common American by reporting that "American ships have been reported torpedoed on the high seas between San Francisco and Honolulu." The reference to San Francisco includes the continental United States as an area under threat by the Japanese, even though there had been no real fighting near San Francisco. Using anaphora to make a stronger impact, Roosevelt lists other recent victims of Japanese attack: "Last night Japanese forces attacked Hong Kong. Last night Japanese forces attacked. . . ." These devices add a sense of urgency to the situation. With the attitude Roosevelt encourages, an attitude explained in *Faces of the Enemy,* Americans would feel compelled to stop the Japanese "monster" before it grew too large.

Now that he has created this image of a demonic, bloodthirsty Empire of Japan and ignited a fire of fear, anger, and hatred among millions of Americans, Roosevelt's final task is to give direction to the people and unite them under the cause of war. He leaves no room for argument regarding interpretation of the Japanese action: "The facts of yesterday speak for themselves." He tells the American people that they "have already formed their opinions and well understand the implications to the very life and safety of our nation." Not every American has actually formed an opinion, but Roosevelt conveys the mentality that no real citizen would have any convictions other than those which he is expressing. He says "our nation" to tie the people to the cause on a more personal level. Ellul addresses this aspect of social manipulation on page 11 of *Propaganda:*

Not only does propaganda seek to invade the whole man, to lead him to adopt a mystical attitude and reach him through all possible psychological channels, but, more, it speaks to all men. Propaganda cannot be satisfied with partial successes, for it does not tolerate discussion; by its very nature, it excludes contradiction and discussion.

Roosevelt makes an appeal to ethos in the next sentence, reminding the audience that he is "commander in chief of the army and navy" and therefore the utmost authority in matters of national defense. He then takes another jab at the Japanese while again reinforcing the historical significance of recent events. "Always will we remember the character of the onslaught against us," he says. Roosevelt addresses the American people as a part of a whole, as propaganda is ineffective when applied toward an individual without direct association with the nation. The intended mentality is that the individual is only valuable as a part of the cause or idea presented; one man alone is not even worth mentioning. Roosevelt concludes by promoting the "righteous might" of the American people, implying that God is with the Americans, and emphasizes that they will win this fight not just to the point of victory, but to the point of "absolute victory." Both *Faces of the Enemy* and *Propaganda: The Formation of Men's Attitudes* acknowledge the significance of this image: the nation as a whole, not individuals, fighting on the side of righteousness.

No small event has the power to reform the mind-set of a nation 10 from relative peace to ambitions of "absolute victory" over an adversary in two days' time. The December 7 bombing of Pearl Harbor was among the most unsettling events in modern American history, and the shock of the attack evoked a range of emotions, from fear and confusion to anger and hatred, among millions of U.S. citizens. Public reaction could have amounted to chaos unless these emotions were channeled and the people united by common attitudes and goals. President Roosevelt recognized that America would prove triumphant in the war not as a random collection of individual ideals and intentions, but only as one collective whole: a nation. Roosevelt's use of propaganda brought the nation together to give Americans an advantage of unity and resolve that they would need in the years to follow.

Works Cited

Ellul, Jacques. *Propaganda: The Formation of Men's Attitudes.* Translated from the French by Konrad Kellen and Jean Lerner. With an introd. by Konrad Kellen. New York: Vintage Books, 1973, c1975.

Jersey, Bill. *Faces of the Enemy* [videorecording]. A Quest production for the Catticaus Corporation; produced and directed by Bill Jersey; edited and codirected by Jeffrey Friedman. Narrated by Sam Keen. 1987.

For Journals

Do you ever think of your country's political leaders as engaging in propaganda?

For Discussion

1. How would you define strategies of propaganda? Do you accept the author's use of the term? What is your reaction to Van Os's thesis that an American president has engaged in techniques of propaganda? Do you agree? Why, or why not?

2. Van Os appeals to authority by citing his secondary sources. To what degree do these strengthen his argument?

For Writing

1. Write a response to Van Os, critiquing his essay. Consider thesis or overall point, his assumptions, the integration of evidence, and essay structure, including introduction, body of essay, and conclusion.

2. Select a speech following 9/11, the invasion of Afghanistan, or the war in Iraq, and, using secondary sources as appropriate, critique the persuasive strategies of the speech.

✱✱✱ *Address to Joint Session of Congress, September* 20, 2001

GEORGE W. BUSH

George Walker Bush (1946–) became the forty-third president of the United States of America in 2001 in one of the closest elections in American history. The Republican candidate, despite losing the popular vote, defeated Democratic Vice President Albert Gore by five electoral votes. The election results were contested for several weeks until December 12, 2000, when the U.S. Supreme Court ruled in favor of Bush in the case Bush v. Gore. *Bush took office on January 20, 2001. George W. Bush was born in Connecticut and grew up in Midland and Houston, Texas. His father, George H. W. Bush, was the forty-first president of the United States. His brother Jeb Bush has served as governor of Florida, the site of the contested election results. Bush received a B.A. in 1968 from Yale University and an M.B.A. from Harvard Business School. He enrolled in the Texas Air National Guard during the Vietnam War and served as an F-102 pilot for a period until he was grounded after failing to appear for a mandatory physical exam and drug test. He worked in the oil industry, and with a partnership he purchased the Texas Rangers baseball team. In 1994 he was elected governor of Texas over incumbent Ann Richards. He identifies himself as a born-again Christian. Following the September 11 attacks, President Bush held the highest approval ratings in history; high approval ratings are historically common for wartime presidents when both leaders and everyday citizens tend to rally around the president. The following speech is Bush's address to a joint session of Congress and the American people on September 20, 2001.*

Mr. Speaker, Mr. President Pro Tempore, members of Congress, and fellow Americans:

In the normal course of events, Presidents come to this chamber to report on the state of the Union. Tonight, no such report is needed. It has already been delivered by the American people.

We have seen it in the courage of passengers, who rushed terrorists to save others on the ground—passengers like an exceptional man named Todd Beamer. And would you please help me to welcome his wife, Lisa Beamer, here tonight. (Applause.)

We have seen the state of our Union in the endurance of rescuers, working past exhaustion. We have seen the unfurling of flags, the lighting of candles, the giving of blood, the saying of prayers—in English, Hebrew, and Arabic. We have seen the decency of a loving and giving people who have made the grief of strangers their own.

My fellow citizens, for the last nine days, the entire world has seen ⁵ for itself the state of our Union—and it is strong. (Applause.)

Tonight we are a country awakened to danger and called to defend freedom. Our grief has turned to anger, and anger to resolution. Whether we bring our enemies to justice, or bring justice to our enemies, justice will be done. (Applause.)

I thank the Congress for its leadership at such an important time. All of America was touched on the evening of the tragedy to see Republicans and Democrats joined together on the steps of this Capitol, singing "God Bless America." And you did more than sing; you acted, by delivering $40 billion to rebuild our communities and meet the needs of our military.

Speaker Hastert, Minority Leader Gephardt, Majority Leader Daschle and Senator Lott, I thank you for your friendship, for your leadership and for your service to our country. (Applause.)

And on behalf of the American people, I thank the world for its outpouring of support. America will never forget the sounds of our National Anthem playing at Buckingham Palace, on the streets of Paris, and at Berlin's Brandenburg Gate.

We will not forget South Korean children gathering to pray outside our embassy in Seoul, or the prayers of sympathy offered at a mosque in Cairo. We will not forget moments of silence and days of mourning in Australia and Africa and Latin America.

Nor will we forget the citizens of 80 other nations who died with our own: dozens of Pakistanis; more than 130 Israelis; more than 250 citizens of India; men and women from El Salvador, Iran, Mexico and Japan; and hundreds of British citizens. America has no truer friend than Great Britain. (Applause.) Once again, we are joined together in a great cause—so honored the British Prime Minister has crossed an ocean to show his unity of purpose with America. Thank you for coming, friend. (Applause.)

On September the 11th, enemies of freedom committed an act of war against our country. Americans have known wars—but for the past 136 years, they have been wars on foreign soil, except for one Sunday in 1941. Americans have known the casualties of war—but not at the center of a great city on a peaceful morning. Americans have known surprise attacks—but never before on thousands of civilians. All of this was brought upon us in a single day—and night fell on a different world, a world where freedom itself is under attack.

Americans have many questions tonight. Americans are asking: Who attacked our country? The evidence we have gathered all points to a collection of loosely affiliated terrorist organizations known as al Qaeda. They are the same murderers indicted for bombing American embassies in Tanzania and Kenya, and responsible for bombing the *USS Cole.*

Al Qaeda is to terror what the mafia is to crime. But its goal is not making money; its goal is remaking the world—and imposing its radical beliefs on people everywhere.

The terrorists practice a fringe form of Islamic extremism that has   15 been rejected by Muslim scholars and the vast majority of Muslim clerics—a fringe movement that perverts the peaceful teachings of Islam. The terrorists' directive commands them to kill Christians and Jews, to kill all Americans, and make no distinction among military and civilians, including women and children.

This group and its leader—a person named Osama bin Laden—are linked to many other organizations in different countries, including the Egyptian Islamic Jihad and the Islamic Movement of Uzbekistan. There are thousands of these terrorists in more than 60 countries. They are recruited from their own nations and neighborhoods and brought to camps in places like Afghanistan, where they are trained in the tactics of terror. They are sent back to their homes or sent to hide in countries around the world to plot evil and destruction.

The leadership of al Qaeda has great influence in Afghanistan and supports the Taliban regime in controlling most of that country. In Afghanistan, we see al Qaeda's vision for the world.

Afghanistan's people have been brutalized—many are starving and many have fled. Women are not allowed to attend school. You can be jailed for owning a television. Religion can be practiced only as their leaders dictate. A man can be jailed in Afghanistan if his beard is not long enough.

The United States respects the people of Afghanistan—after all, we are currently its largest source of humanitarian aid—but we condemn the Taliban regime. (Applause.) It is not only repressing its own people, it is threatening people everywhere by sponsoring and sheltering and supplying terrorists. By aiding and abetting murder, the Taliban regime is committing murder.

And tonight, the United States of America makes the following 20 demands on the Taliban: Deliver to United States authorities all the leaders of al Qaeda who hide in your land. (Applause.) Release all foreign nationals, including American citizens, you have unjustly imprisoned. Protect foreign journalists, diplomats and aid workers in your country. Close immediately and permanently every terrorist training camp in Afghanistan, and hand over every terrorist, and every person in their support structure, to appropriate authorities. (Applause.) Give the United States full access to terrorist training camps, so we can make sure they are no longer operating.

These demands are not open to negotiation or discussion. (Applause.) The Taliban must act, and act immediately. They will hand over the terrorists, or they will share in their fate.

I also want to speak tonight directly to Muslims throughout the world. We respect your faith. It's practiced freely by many millions of Americans, and by millions more in countries that America counts as friends. Its teachings are good and peaceful, and those who commit evil in the name of Allah blaspheme the name of Allah. (Applause.) The terrorists are traitors to their own faith, trying, in effect, to hijack Islam itself. The enemy of America is not our many Muslim friends; it is not our many Arab friends. Our enemy is a radical network of terrorists, and every government that supports them. (Applause.)

Our war on terror begins with al Qaeda, but it does not end there. It will not end until every terrorist group of global reach has been found, stopped and defeated. (Applause.)

Americans are asking, why do they hate us? They hate what we see right here in this chamber—a democratically elected government. Their leaders are self-appointed. They hate our freedoms—our freedom of religion, our freedom of speech, our freedom to vote and assemble and disagree with each other.

They want to overthrow existing governments in many Muslim 25 countries, such as Egypt, Saudi Arabia, and Jordan. They want to drive Israel out of the Middle East. They want to drive Christians and Jews out of vast regions of Asia and Africa.

These terrorists kill not merely to end lives, but to disrupt and end a way of life. With every atrocity, they hope that America grows fearful, retreating from the world and forsaking our friends. They stand against us, because we stand in their way.

We are not deceived by their pretenses to piety. We have seen their kind before. They are the heirs of all the murderous ideologies of the 20th century. By sacrificing human life to serve their radical visions—by abandoning every value except the will to power—they follow in the path of fascism, and Nazism, and totalitarianism. And they will follow that path all the way, to where it ends: in history's unmarked grave of discarded lies. (Applause.)

Americans are asking: How will we fight and win this war? We will direct every resource at our command—every means of diplomacy, every tool of intelligence, every instrument of law enforcement, every financial influence, and every necessary weapon of war—to the disruption and to the defeat of the global terror network.

This war will not be like the war against Iraq a decade ago, with a decisive liberation of territory and a swift conclusion. It will not look like the air war above Kosovo two years ago, where no ground troops were used and not a single American was lost in combat.

Our response involves far more than instant retaliation and iso- 30 lated strikes. Americans should not expect one battle, but a lengthy campaign, unlike any other we have ever seen. It may include dramatic strikes, visible on TV, and covert operations, secret even in success. We will starve terrorists of funding, turn them one against another, drive them from place to place, until there is no refuge or no rest. And we will pursue nations that provide aid or safe haven to terrorism. Every nation, in every region, now has a decision to make. Either you are with us, or you are with the terrorists. (Applause.) From this day forward, any nation that continues to harbor or support terrorism will be regarded by the United States as a hostile regime.

Our nation has been put on notice: We are not immune from attack. We will take defensive measures against terrorism to protect Americans. Today, dozens of federal departments and agencies, as well as state and local governments, have responsibilities affecting homeland security. These efforts must be coordinated at the highest level. So tonight I announce the creation of a Cabinet-level position reporting directly to me—the Office of Homeland Security.

And tonight I also announce a distinguished American to lead this effort, to strengthen American security: a military veteran, an effective governor, a true patriot, a trusted friend—Pennsylvania's Tom Ridge. (Applause.) He will lead, oversee and coordinate a comprehensive national strategy to safeguard our country against terrorism, and respond to any attacks that may come.

These measures are essential. But the only way to defeat terrorism as a threat to our way of life is to stop it, eliminate it, and destroy it where it grows. (Applause.)

Many will be involved in this effort, from FBI agents to intelligence operatives to the reservists we have called to active duty. All deserve our thanks, and all have our prayers. And tonight, a few miles from the damaged Pentagon, I have a message for our military: Be ready. I've called the Armed Forces to alert, and there is a reason. The hour is coming when America will act, and you will make us proud. (Applause.)

This is not, however, just America's fight. And what is at stake is 35 not just America's freedom. This is the world's fight. This is civilization's fight. This is the fight of all who believe in progress and pluralism, tolerance and freedom.

We ask every nation to join us. We will ask, and we will need, the help of police forces, intelligence services, and banking systems around the world. The United States is grateful that many nations and many international organizations have already responded—with sympathy and with support. Nations from Latin America, to Asia, to Africa, to Europe, to the Islamic world. Perhaps the NATO Charter reflects best the attitude of the world: An attack on one is an attack on all.

The civilized world is rallying to America's side. They understand that if this terror goes unpunished, their own cities, their own citizens may be next. Terror, unanswered, can not only bring down buildings, it can threaten the stability of legitimate governments. And you know what—we're not going to allow it. (Applause.)

Americans are asking: What is expected of us? I ask you to live your lives, and hug your children. I know many citizens have fears tonight, and I ask you to be calm and resolute, even in the face of a continuing threat.

I ask you to uphold the values of America, and remember why so many have come here. We are in a fight for our principles, and our first responsibility is to live by them. No one should be singled out for unfair treatment or unkind words because of their ethnic background or religious faith. (Applause.)

I ask you to continue to support the victims of this tragedy with 40 your contributions. Those who want to give can go to a central source of information, *libertyunites.org*, to find the names of groups providing direct help in New York, Pennsylvania, and Virginia.

The thousands of FBI agents who are now at work in this investigation may need your cooperation, and I ask you to give it.

I ask for your patience, with the delays and inconveniences that may accompany tighter security; and for your patience in what will be a long struggle.

I ask your continued participation and confidence in the American economy. Terrorists attacked a symbol of American prosperity. They did not touch its source. America is successful because of the hard work, and creativity, and enterprise of our people. These were the true strengths of our economy before September 11th, and they are our strengths today. (Applause.)

And, finally, please continue praying for the victims of terror and their families, for those in uniform, and for our great country. Prayer has comforted us in sorrow, and will help strengthen us for the journey ahead.

Tonight I thank my fellow Americans for what you have already done and for what you will do. And ladies and gentlemen of the Congress, I thank you, their representatives, for what you have already done and for what we will do together.

Tonight, we face new and sudden national challenges. We will come together to improve air safety, to dramatically expand the number of air marshals on domestic flights, and take new measures to prevent hijacking. We will come together to promote stability and keep our airlines flying, with direct assistance during this emergency. (Applause.)

We will come together to give law enforcement the additional tools it needs to track down terror here at home. (Applause.) We will come together to strengthen our intelligence capabilities to know the plans of terrorists before they act, and find them before they strike. (Applause.)

We will come together to take active steps that strengthen America's economy, and put our people back to work.

Tonight we welcome two leaders who embody the extraordinary spirit of all New Yorkers: Governor George Pataki, and Mayor Rudolph Giuliani. (Applause.) As a symbol of America's resolve, my administration will work with Congress, and these two leaders, to show the world that we will rebuild New York City. (Applause.)

After all that has just passed—all the lives taken, and all the possibilities and hopes that died with them—it is natural to wonder if America's future is one of fear. Some speak of an age of terror. I know there are struggles ahead, and dangers to face. But this country will define our times, not be defined by them. As long as the United States of America is determined and strong, this will not be an age of terror; this will be an age of liberty, here and across the world. (Applause.)

Great harm has been done to us. We have suffered great loss. And in our grief and anger we have found our mission and our moment. Freedom and fear are at war. The advance of human freedom—the great achievement of our time, and the great hope of every time—now depends on us. Our nation—this generation—will lift a dark threat of violence from our people and our future. We will rally the world to this cause by our efforts, by our courage. We will not tire, we will not falter, and we will not fail. (Applause.)

It is my hope that in the months and years ahead, life will return almost to normal. We'll go back to our lives and routines, and that is good. Even grief recedes with time and grace. But our resolve must not pass. Each of us will remember what happened that day, and to whom it happened. We'll remember the moment the news came— where we were and what we were doing. Some will remember an image of a fire, or a story of rescue. Some will carry memories of a face and a voice gone forever.

And I will carry this: It is the police shield of a man named George Howard, who died at the World Trade Center trying to save others. It was given to me by his mom, Arlene, as a proud memorial to her son. This is my reminder of lives that ended, and a task that does not end. (Applause.)

I will not forget this wound to our country or those who inflicted it. I will not yield; I will not rest; I will not relent in waging this struggle for freedom and security for the American people.

The course of this conflict is not known, yet its outcome is certain. 55 Freedom and fear, justice and cruelty, have always been at war, and we know that God is not neutral between them. (Applause.)

Fellow citizens, we'll meet violence with patient justice—assured of the rightness of our cause, and confident of the victories to come. In all that lies before us, may God grant us wisdom, and may He watch over the United States of America.

Thank you. (Applause.)

For Journals

Did you hear this speech as it was delivered shortly after the terrorist attacks? If so, do you recall how you responded to it?

For Discussion

1.   To whom was this speech directed in addition to the immediate audience in the Capitol? Consider multiple extended audiences. What elements of the speech seem targeted to the difference audiences? How does Bush meet the potentially divergent interests of his audiences?

2.   What strategies and appeals does Bush use to unite both Americans and their allies? How does he characterize the enemy? How does he differentiate between friends and enemies of the Muslim faith? Why was it important to do so? After reading or listening to this whole speech, go over the text again, and analyze the ways in which appeals to authority and common values, emotions, and logic contribute to the speech's effectiveness.

3.   Evaluate how the structures in the speech contribute to its persuasiveness. Consider overall structure—introduction, body, conclusion— and sentence-level strategies, such as repetition, parallel construction, and short sentences.

For Writing

1. Drawing on your responses to the discussion questions, write an essay in which you analyze the persuasive appeals in this speech. Consider focusing on stylistic issues, such as anaphora (sentence-opener repetition), parallelism, and diction; or on logic, such as structure of argument and logical fallacies.

2. Compare and contrast the appeals in this speech with those in the speech of Franklin Delano Roosevelt, earlier in this chapter, or John F. Kennedy's Inaugural Address, Chapter 5.

禁禁 *The Real War* (2001)

THOMAS FRIEDMAN

Thomas L. Friedman (1953–) is a journalist with the New York Times *and a three-time winner of the Pulitzer Prize. He earned a B.A. in Mediterranean studies from Brandeis University in 1975 and a Master of Philosophy degree in Modern Middle East studies from Oxford University in 1978. From 1979 to 1984, Friedman reported from war-torn Beirut, Lebanon, leaving after a mortar attack on his neighbor hood. Friedman went on to Jerusalem, where until 1988 he served as* The New York Times' *Israel Bureau Chief. Although of Jewish-American heritage, Friedman is considered an unbiased and critical investigator of the Middle East conflict. Friedman's books include* From Beirut to Jerusalem *(1983), which chronicles his ten years in the Middle East and his transformation from admirer of Israeli policy to its public detractor. He also wrote* The Lexus and the Olive Tree *(2000), which has been translated into twenty languages. The following essay was published in the* New York Times *on November 27, 2001.*

If 9/11 was indeed the onset of World War III, we have to understand what this war is about. We're not fighting to eradicate "terrorism." Terrorism is just a tool. We're fighting to defeat an ideology: religious totalitarianism. World War II and the cold war were fought to defeat secular totalitarianism, Nazism and Communism, and World War III is a battle against religious totalitarianism, a view of the world that my faith must reign supreme and can be affirmed and held passionately only if all others are negated. That's bin Ladenism. But unlike Nazism, religious totalitarianism can't be fought by armies alone. It has to be fought in schools, mosques, churches and synagogues, and can be defeated only with the help of imams, rabbis and priests.

The generals we need to fight this war are people like Rabbi David Hartman, from the Shalom Hartman Institute in Jerusalem. What first attracted me to Rabbi Hartman when I reported from Jerusalem was his contention that unless Jews reinterpreted their faith in a way that embraced modernity, without weakening religious passion, and in a way that affirmed that God speaks multiple languages and is not exhausted by just one faith, they would have no future in the land of Israel. And what also impressed me was that he knew where the battlefield was. He set up his own schools in Israel to compete with fundamentalist Jews, Muslims and Christians, who used their schools to preach exclusivist religious visions.

After recently visiting the Islamic madrasa in Pakistan where many Taliban leaders were educated, and seeing the fundamentalist religious education the young boys there were being given, I telephoned Rabbi Hartman and asked: How do we battle religious totalitarianism?

He answered: "All faiths that come out of the biblical tradition—Judaism, Christianity and Islam—have the tendency to believe that they have the exclusive truth. When the Taliban wiped out the Buddhist statues, that's what they were saying. But others have said it too. The opposite of religious totalitarianism is an ideology of pluralism, an ideology that embraces religious diversity and the idea that my faith can be nurtured without claiming exclusive truth. America is the Mecca of that ideology, and that is what bin Laden hates and that is why America had to be destroyed."

The future of the world may well be decided by how we fight this 5 war. Can Islam, Christianity and Judaism know that God speaks Arabic on Fridays, Hebrew on Saturdays and Latin on Sundays, and that he welcomes different human beings approaching him through their own history, out of their language and cultural heritage? "Is single-minded fanaticism a necessity for passion and religious survival, or can we have a multilingual view of God, a notion that God is not exhausted by just one religious path?" asked Rabbi Hartman.

Many Jews and Christians have already argued that the answer to that question is yes, and some have gone back to their sacred texts to reinterpret their traditions to embrace modernity and pluralism, and to create space for secularism and alternative faiths. Other Christian and Jewish fundamentalists have rejected this notion, and that is what the battle is about within their faiths.

What is different about Islam is that while there have been a few attempts at such a reformation, none have flowered or found the support of a Muslim state. We patronize Islam, and mislead ourselves, by repeating the mantra that Islam is a faith with no serious problems accepting the secular West, modernity and pluralism, and the only problem is a few bin Ladens. Although there is a deep moral impulse in Islam for justice, charity and compassion, Islam has not developed a dominant religious philosophy that allows equal recognition of alternative faith communities. Bin Laden reflects the most extreme version of that exclusivity, and he hit us in the face with it on 9/11.

Christianity and Judaism struggled with this issue for centuries, but a similar internal struggle within Islam to re-examine its texts and articulate a path for how one can accept pluralism and modernity and still be a passionate, devout Muslim has not surfaced in any serious way. One hopes that now that the world spotlight has been put on this issue, mainstream Muslims too will realize that their future in this integrated, globalized world depends on their ability to reinterpret their past.

For Journals

Write about your understanding of conflict in the Middle East region. Of which conflicts are you aware? What do you believe are the main issues in these conflicts? What do you think are the underlying issues regarding 9/11?

For Discussion

1. What is the real war that Friedman describes? Why does he call it a war? How does it relate to other conflicts with which you are familiar?

2. According to Friedman, how can reinterpreting religious texts allow for "plurality and diversity"?

3. Would you agree with Rabbi Hartman that one's "faith can be nurtured without claiming exclusive truth"? Does Friedman offer ways to implement this view?

4. Do you think that Friedman's position is persuasive? If not, on what other bases might he argue that Islam should accept plurality and diversity?

For Writing

1. Friedman uses the metaphor of war in this essay. In class or in small groups, develop a list of alternative metaphors, and select one to use in rewriting his argument. To get some ideas, consider rereading some of the essays in this book that are highly metaphorical, such as the Martin Luther King, Jr., reading in Chapter 9.

2. This essay originally appeared as commentary in the *New York Times*. Write a response to Friedman as an op-ed column, agreeing or disagreeing with him or pointing out alternative views.

❋❋ Listening to the Bad Guys (2002)

KATHLEEN LACAMERA

Kathleen LaCamera is a minister and television producer, as well as a United Methodist News Service correspondent based in England. In the article that follows, she reports on the efforts at critical reflection and the attempts to build bridges between the two communities hurt by thirty years of violence in the Northern Ireland conflict known as "The Troubles."

Belfast, Northern Ireland—"Why are Americans giving money to terrorists to kill our children?" As an American journalist working in Britain, I've been asked this question over and over again during the nine years I've been coming to Northern Ireland. Today the question comes out of the mouths of Loyalist paramilitary members, people who themselves have been labelled "terrorists." I'm sitting around a table with a dozen top Loyalist paramilitary leaders—part of a newly formed "Loyalist Commission" as they discuss how they feel the official peace process has betrayed them. At least that's what I thought was the plan. But the conversation quickly begins to focus on me, the American in their midst. Suddenly I'm the one being grilled.

Their question is about the perception that across the U.S., especially in cities like New York, Boston and Chicago with strong Irish immigrant roots, Americans are stuffing cash into boxes that fund the IRA's fight for a united Ireland. My gut reaction is to wonder what gives these guys the right to ask such a question when guns and bombs also have been part and parcel of their Loyalist paramilitary trade for some many years. Then I take a deep breath and remember I'm sitting with people who—no less than their Republican counterparts—are also fathers, brothers, sons, uncles, nephews, and friends to those murdered and injured in the thirty years of Northern Ireland's Troubles.

The answer I give them reflects much of what compels me to write about this and other troubled spots around the world year after year after year. It responds to the kernel of truth that is real and the mountain of misunderstanding and vacuum of information that distorts it. It relates to the need inside so many of us to label some of the worst atrocities in Ireland, the Balkans, the Middle East, in Rwanda and even at Ground Zero as "pure evil" or "senseless destruction." For someone out there, those actions made sense. Understanding how that is possible does not condone it, but gives us a power to prevent it from repeating itself.

With regard to Americans raising money for the IRA? It's true. American money has helped fuel the conflict in Northern Ireland for years. We've bought into the image of the Brad Pitt–beautiful freedom fighter, who is, sure, misguided, but in his heart of hearts, a decent, caring soul who wouldn't hurt a fly if he weren't forced into it. Listening to Loyalist paramilitaries talk about the loss and pain their community has suffered at the hands of the IRA is worth doing. It helps to understand why what seems like such a senseless conflict, continues. It *does not* in any way justify the Loyalists' equally destructive activities perpetrated on Catholics and Protestants, including children, over the years.

Despite that fact that we Americans are notoriously uninterested 5 in much beyond our borders, Loyalists talk as if all 280 million Americans actively see them as the bad guys. This perception only contributes to the feeling amongst Loyalists that they have been backed into a tight, lonely corner. The truth is that most Americans don't know or don't care much about Northern Ireland (whether that's good or bad is another story). But here is the tragic irony: Loyalists' misperception of the extent of U.S. support for "the other side" actually contributes to the real, increasing alienation and desperation of the Loyalist Protestant community. That in turn affects the peace process. That's amazing! That's awful!

So where does that leave us in a world full of conflict and terror? I think it leaves us with a mandate to listen, particularly when we don't want to. Especially when the actions of those asking for our ear (and sometimes they do that with violence) repel or baffle or terrify us. We have to talk to those we think of as "the bad guys" as well as those who are their "victims." We need to know more about who they are and what they are thinking. Dare I resort to the old cliché; we need to walk a mile (or two) in their shoes. And we need to do it as directly and as personally as it is possible.

It also means turning to more than just our local newspapers and regular television news and radio reports for information. Through the internet, the world's media is at our fingertips. Why not log on and see what *both* Irish and South African newspapers are saying about peace talks in Northern Ireland? While you're at it, have a look at what newspapers in England are saying about the US war in Afghanistan. Then check out the Hong Kong papers for stories about the Palestinian/Israeli conflict. Don't forget you can log on to radio worldwide through the Internet as well. I've lived for ten years in Europe and, believe me, there is a whole world of stories and opinions reported that Americans rarely see or hear. No doubt the reverse is true as well. There are many stories reported within the US that the rest of the world never get a look at. Information gaps—they are dangerous.

Daniel Holloway works with a group in Northern Ireland called Community Dialogue. It specializes in bringing together people on all sides of Northern Ireland's conflict to hear each other's story. With a laugh, Holloway told me that through dialogue at the very least "people come to know better why they want to kill each other." But more often, he reported, telling their stories means that people who were once just "the other side" begin to have a human face and the common ground that links one to the other becomes more obvious.

"There's nothing mysterious going on here in Northern Ireland," said Holloway. While specifics change, the basics of conflict and reconciliation are remarkably similar whether you're in the Northern Ireland or the Middle East, Kosovo or Afghanistan, South Africa or New York City. The way to peace almost always involves sitting down, talking and then listening to those we see as the bad guys.

Conflicts like those in Northern Ireland can seem far too complex, 10 deep rooted and down right confusing for us to engage. They are not. We don't have to wait for Colin Powell, or Yasser Arafat or Gerry Adams to enter into the process of making peace. We can begin today, listening deeply to people on all sides, even the ones we suspect are the bad guys.

For Journals

What do you know about the conflict in Northern Ireland? Do you see one side or the other as the good side or bad side?

For Discussion

1. How do the first-person point of view and the reported personal experience affect the article's authority and persuasiveness?

2. Does the author appear to take sides on the Protestant/Catholic conflict, or rather to maintain a relatively neutral stance? What in the text supports your view?

3. Do you agree with the author's premise that understanding why atrocities occur, rather than just labeling them, may lead to preventing future violence? Why, or why not?

4. According to La Camera, what is the role of the media in finding ways to listen to others and to their points of view? How can media help people see the "other side"?

For Writing

1. Research the history of the conflict in Northern Ireland, focusing on some particular aspect, such as the Good Friday Accords, the role of paramilitary groups, or the role of American financial support in fueling the conflict. Alternatively, research the Community Dialogue project that the author describes or the Forgiveness Project and its work with survivors of violence in Northern Ireland.

2.   Write an opinion piece, such as an op-ed essay or a letter to the editor, focusing on listening to some other "bad guys" in the current political landscape.

❀❀❀ *Film: We Were Soldiers* (2002)

Paramount Pictures and Icon Productions, an Icon/Wheelhouse Entertainment production, a Randall Wallace film. Producers, Bruce Davey, Stephen McEveety, Randall Wallace; written for the screen and directed by Randall Wallace. Hollywood, Calif. (138 min.). With Mel Gibson, Madeleine Stowe, Greg Kinnear, Sam Elliott, Chris Klein, Keri Russell, Barry Pepper, Don Duong, Ryan Hurst. This film is based on the book We Were Soldiers Once . . . and Young, *by Lt. Gen. Harold G. Moore (ret.) and Joseph L. Galloway. In the film, which is mainly set in 1965, Lt. Col. Hal Moore, commander of the First Battalion, Seventh Cavalry, is assigned to action in the Ia Drang Valley, an area known to be overrun by North Vietnamese troops and nicknamed "The Valley of Death."*

For Journals

Write a personal reflection of your response to this film, to one or more of the characters or situations involved, or to the ways in which the film represented the events in the story.

For Discussion

1.   Compare the portrayals of each side's foot soldiers in this film. Is each a capable and worthy adversary of the other? How do you assess the characterization of each side? How does the film develop these characterizations?

2.   How does the film portray the "domestic" side of military life? Do you suspect that it is a fair and complete portrait?

3.   Do you believe that the film takes a stance on the Vietnam War, or on war in general? Do you think that this film is pro-war or antiwar? Neither? Does it take a pro-America or an anti-America stance?

4.   Without seeing *The Green Berets* (1968, with John Wayne), do you suspect that the North Vietnamese received a different portrayal in that earlier film? How do you think that Ron Kovic, the author of *Born on the Fourth of July*, might respond to this film?

For Writing

1.   Write a review of this film for your campus or local newspaper. A review generally introduces your topic, briefly summarizes the story (without giving away any surprises), and then critiques the film by

commenting on noteworthy aspects of it such as plot, characterization, acting, cinematography, and the like. Review the section on films in Chapter 2 for useful elements of film analysis and for appropriate terminology.

2. Research the Vietnam War, focusing on some aspect such as this location and battle, military strategy, Vietnam veterans, Vietnam today, or another topic of concern to you, such as the war on terror, the Afghanistan campaign, or the Iraq War. Consider using available documents from both sides of the conflict, including Moore's original story on which this film is based, government documents, and the like.

Chapter Writing Assignments

1. There are any number of films that you, your classmates, or your instructor may recommend for viewing. Whichever film you select, try to analyze the film in view of some principles discussed in this chapter, such as in the Fussell selection. Some possibilities are *The Guns of Navaronne, Bridge on the River Kwai, Casablanca, Apocalypse Now, Platoon,* and *Full Metal Jacket.*

2. Drawing from secondary sources that you research, write a documented essay analyzing several propaganda posters or one of the text selections in this chapter, integrating the secondary source as evidence to support your assessment of the propaganda. You may find it helpful to review the Fussell reading or to find and review Jacques Ellul's book *Propaganda: The Formation of Men's Attitudes* or to view Sam Keen's film or to read his book entitled *Faces of the Enemy.*

3. Select a political event or an issue of current interest, such as the 2000 presidential election and the vote-counting fracas that followed. Then select several magazines with divergent political viewpoints— *National Review, US News and World Report, Newsweek, New Republic,* or *The Nation.* Compare the coverage of events in the different sources. Do a close textual analysis of the sources, and write an essay presenting your findings.

4. Researching articles, Web pages, and news accounts, try to determine the ways in which the conflict in Northern Ireland is represented in the U.S. media. Consider not only the volume of articles and information about the conflict but also the tone, stance, and language in which the conflict and the major players are represented.

5. Drawing from the Internet or library sources, review a number of propaganda posters, either from one country or region, or from across different cultures and time frames. In the former, assess whether certain strategies or themes about the enemy persist throughout different posters and campaigns; in the latter, try to identify the common denominators in creating images of friends and enemies. Support the inferences you draw with examples from the images themselves, taking care to document sources and, if possible, including the images in the text or in an appendix.

Web Sites for Further Exploration

U.S. National Archives and Record Administration
http://www.archives.gov/index.html

U.S. Civil War Center
http://www.cwc.lsu.edu/

World War I
http://www.ku.edu/%7Ekansite/ww_one/photos/greatwar.htm

United States Institute of Peace
http://www.usip.org/

U.S. Army War College
http://carlisle-www.army.mil/library/

Smithsonian National Museum of American History
http://americanhistory.si.edu/

U.S. Holocaust Memorial Museum
http://www.ushmm.org/

September 11 Digital Archive
http://www.911digitalarchive.org/

11
※※※

Frontiers

At the beginning of the nineteenth century, New York State was on the frontier, and most people thought that it would take a hundred years to get to the Pacific, if in fact they ever thought in those terms at all. They certainly would have been surprised to learn that by 1849, Americans had moved across the entire continent, all the way to California, thanks to the political and economic charms of expansion and the incentive of the Gold Rush. What they would have found even more unlikely is that a hundred years after the frontier had ceased to exist as a geographic marker, Americans would still be so attached to it, or to what it represents, that the search for new frontiers—even technological ones—continues to occupy the American vocabulary and the American psyche.

The American idea of frontier is of an invisible border between settled and unsettled, civilized and uncivilized areas. It is recognized more by what it is not than by what it is: it's not civilization as you know it, it's not domesticated, it's not safe. Of course, the idea of the frontier was a reality only to the European settlers who saw themselves as the bearers of culture and developers of empty country, not to Native Americans who had their own indigenous cultures and knew that the country wasn't empty, because they were already there.

Whether everyone accepted the idea of a frontier—receding before the development of towns and farms but always out there somewhere, leading to newer undiscovered places—it became so embedded in our culture that it is what Americans think they know best about their own country, and it is the way we are identified by the rest of the world. In Germany, for example, there are vacation places complete with wigwams so that tourists can play cowboys and Indians. Blue jeans, invented by young merchant Levi Strauss during the Gold Rush so that prospectors could put ore in their pockets without tearing them, are an American national uniform and a status symbol in eastern Europe and Russia. American theme parks have frontier towns;

movie studios have mock shoot-outs between good guys and bad
guys; and Americans have been watching Western movies as long as
there have been movies to watch.

How much all of this recreation has to do with what the frontier
was actually like seems to matter much less than what most people
prefer to think it was like. Wherever Americans live, they infuse some
sense of the centrality of the frontier into their image of the United
States. Whatever changes are wrought in that image are the cause of
pitched emotional and intellectual battles between groups with an interest in preserving the idea of the frontier. In the last forty or fifty
years, many scholars have explored the difference between the actual
American frontier and the frontier of the American imagination, and
many Native Americans have campaigned successfully for reevalua-
tions of the image of Indians in American history.

Frontiers through History

Most Americans never saw the frontier, wherever it happened to
be at the time. In the eighteenth and most of the nineteenth centuries,
whether they lived in towns, on farms and in rural areas, or in the bigger eastern cities, they got their information about the frontier from
newspaper reports, narratives—accurate or exaggerated—paintings
by artists who had accompanied expeditions, and eventually from
photographs.

The people who knew the frontier from firsthand experience were
not only the settlers, trappers, hunters, and seekers for gold, and the
frontier was not just the Far West. It existed as a permeable border between the white settlers and the Native Americans or the Mexicans, or
the English and the French, or wherever issues of control, power, and
settlement arose, and it moved irregularly from the East Coast to the
West Coast over a period of almost three hundred years. In the early
nineteenth century, the first great white exploration of the frontier was
the Lewis and Clark expedition, which was sent by President Jefferson
to do a scientific and military study of the Louisiana Purchase. In fact,
it went all the way to the West Coast, and, as William Kittredge has
observed, it opened the West to settlement by white pioneers. A mere
forty-two years after the expedition was completed, gold was discovered in California, and the frontier everyone had expected to take a
hundred years to cover receded with astonishing speed as far as it
could go—to the Pacific Ocean.

For a lucky few, the idea of the frontier was an adventure of absolutely glorious proportions, and no one left a record of a better time
than the young Samuel Clemens, otherwise known as Mark Twain. In
1861, accompanying his brother, who had been appointed secretary to

the governor of the Nevada Territory, Clemens saw the continent as few other people except the Native Americans had ever been privileged to see it—stagecoaches, the Pony Express, the Southwest, clear lakes full of fish, early San Francisco, silver mining in Nevada, even Hawaii. His early book, *Roughing It,* is ironic from title to finish, but Twain's irrepressible humor communicates the reality of the frontier at the same time that it embroiders and sustains the mythology.

Twain could find amusement in almost anything, but the trip was extremely difficult, and relations between settlers and Indians deteriorated in proportion to the number of settlers who arrived and the realization that they were not going to stop coming. Some settlers both feared and pitied the Indians, but for Americans back East, the picture was less complicated. People who went through their entire lives without ever seeing an Indian believed in the popular image of crazed savages bent on destroying civilization. There were real instances of brutality as competition for diminishing natural resources raised the stakes on both sides. But the tabloid newspapers such as the *Police Gazette* knew their audience and catered to its prejudices. In a typical example, the *Gazette* gives its version of a clash between U.S. Cavalry and Indians in South Dakota, complete with headline ("Indian Treachery and Bloodshed") and violent illustration.

A different and sadder image of a changing West is the subject of Albert Bierstadt's spectacular painting, *The Last of the Buffalo.* Painted about the same time that the *Police Gazette* was appealing to the lowest common denominator, this picture gives us a sense of the symbiotic relationship between the Indians, buffalo, and a disappearing way of life.

By 1893, the frontier was essentially closed. Oklahoma would not become a state until 1912, but the Indians were no longer a factor; the railroad had long since become transcontinental; industrialization had transformed American cities and multiplied their populations; and people who wanted to see Indians could buy a ticket to Buffalo Bill's show—the great Indian chief Sitting Bull was one of his acts.

Chicago, the youngest of America's great cities, celebrated its status by holding a World's Fair in 1893. A brilliant young professor, Frederick Jackson Turner, took the opportunity to speak about the impact that the closing of the frontier had on the American consciousness. The result, his essay "The Significance of the Frontier in American History," is the first and still the most famous analysis of the frontier. Turner's address had profound effects on the development of economics as a discipline, as well as on the study of American history, and the argument he started about the significance of the frontier to the development of American character and democracy has continued ever since. Richard Hofstadter's response that follows is the most famous, but it is only one of many.

Among the significant social changes that followed the closing of the frontier was the imaginative transformation of the West from a place of danger into one where a spectacular landscape and an exotic past—colonial Spanish and Mexican ranch life, cowboys and Indians, Gold Rush prospecting—became a subject for nostalgia and a tourist attraction. There are many examples of this kind of cultural reduction—posters inviting tourists to California to see a real Mexican fiesta, staged for their benefit; or paintings of Mexican grandees, aristocratic and gracious, on their enormous estates, even though those estates had been taken by Americans almost a half century ago in the wake of the Gold Rush.

The greatest degree of nostalgia, of course, was reserved for Native Americans. Because they had been perceived by whites as the greatest threat, they became, once they were powerless, the people who were the most thoroughly romanticized and fondly remembered. This change is not as strange as it sounds; it was, in a way, the strongest evidence of how completely they had been dismantled. The stereotypical image of the bloodthirsty savage was replaced by the equally stereotypical image of the noble savage. Indians maidens were now always pictured as beautiful and demure, and Indian men as handsome and courageous.

One of the most interesting and aesthetically pleasing sources of romanticized Indian images was the ephemeral creations of the 1920s and 1930s known as crate labels. These packing labels, put on the sides of fruit and vegetable crates to make them recognizable and saleable at food auctions, are now collectors' items. The example in this chapter, called "Indian Belle," is a beautifully colored advertisement for navel oranges grown in central California for the consumption of easterners. It is not clear whether the farmers and the largely anonymous artists they hired realized that they were selling not only the fruit inside the cartons but also the fantasy that decorated them.

Once the actual frontier was gone, and with it the real conflict between whites and Indians, the need to preserve some portion of a pristine landscape grew, with the West and Far West as the primary beneficiaries. A conservationist movement led by the naturalist and writer John Muir successfully campaigned for Yosemite and the Sequoias in California, which were declared national parks in 1890. The size of the parks system has gradually increased over the years, but not without debate about the need for development versus the need for open space. One Western writer who dedicated much of his work to the significance of the wilderness in an industrialized America was the novelist and conservationist Wallace Stegner. In his famous "Coda: Wilderness Letter," Stegner argues not just for the wilderness but for the *idea* of the wilderness, even for Americans who have never seen it and don't really want to, except in the movies.

Then in the late 1970s, the naturalist and writer Edward Abbey, who is closer to Twain in his combination of irony and immense appreciation than he is to anyone else, celebrated the deserts of the West in an idiosyncratic, beautiful, and highly enjoyable article, "The Great American Desert."

For real Native Americans, movies provided one of their few chances to see themselves reflected in popular culture, but that reflection was, for many years, as much of a distortion as the overly idealized images on fruit crates. (In that sense, their portrayals had much in common with that of African Americans, who were limited to movie roles as maids and servants, happy poor people, and entertainers.) Actors playing the parts of Indians were invariably dressed in the clothing of Plains Indians no matter where the movie was set; and in the 1940s and 1950s, their chief function seemed to be that they got shot off their horses in battle scenes by members of the U.S. cavalry in general, and John Wayne in particular. In her poem "Dear John Wayne," writer Louise Erdrich captures the ironic experience of American Indian teenagers who go to a drive-in movie in the Southwest to watch Hollywood versions of what happened to their ancestors.

Thanks to the Gold Rush, the creation of the movie industry, and its enormous economic and social influence, California is the place most Americans think of as the end of the frontier, the place, writer Joan Didion says, where "we have to get it right because this is where we run out of room." And, in fact, writing about California, like everything else about California, is more abundant than writing about the rest of the West Coast. But it isn't and never will be the whole Western frontier. In fact, as Edward Abbey points out in one of his lovely and playful articles about nature in the West, "The Great American Desert" covers parts of Mexico and twelve states, and contains enough natural wonders for all of them. At the same time, Oregon and Washington State—much more sparsely populated than California and less a part of the general imagination than desert—have taken on the role of refugees from California's success, its crowds, its development, and what they perceive as its lost promise.

Irritated natives have bumper stickers on their cars asking that their states not be "Californiacated." Loggers fight with environmentalists about jobs versus old growth timber, livelihoods versus open space. Perhaps only someone who is not a Westerner—like English writer Jonathan Raban—could explain these conflicts, as he does in his article about Washington State, Wyoming, and Montana, "The Next Last Frontier." Observant, curious, and a good listener, he is enough of an outsider to have the ear of both sides; coming from England, which would fit easily into one corner of Montana and which hasn't had a wilderness for a thousand years, he is visibly struck by the size and variety of the country, and his descriptions have the freshness of genuine surprise.

Ultimately, what may be most remarkable about the idea of the frontier is its incredible staying power. It has remained in our consciousness and our sense of ourselves, not only in the elegantly ironic poetry of Louise Erdrich, but also in every level of American culture, from high to low. Historian Patricia Nelson Limerick, in one of a series of essays on the frontier in American culture, writes in "Frontier Headlines" about the varied and sometimes ridiculous ways that Americans contrive to identify every activity or product from the significant to the trivial with the frontier spirit.

Like any other powerful idea, though, the concept of the frontier must constantly be reexamined and reinterpreted in order to be meaningful. The Frontierland area at Disneyland or the fake shoot-outs staged for tourists in Western ghost towns may be entertaining, but they are no more useful in that regard than the fake Mexican fiestas staged for tourists a century ago. Now the relationship of whites and Indians has taken a turn in a direction no one could have anticipated. Indian tribes who have established claims to their ancestral lands or other Indian lands through the Bureau of Indian Affairs have been able to construct casinos on reservations, and the casinos, like casinos in the rest of the country, are making a great deal of money for their investors. But as a recent *Time* magazine cover story asks, is this finally a case in which a lot of Indians are finally entering the financial mainstream, or are only a few profiting while most Indians don't get anything? A more intriguing approach comes from Clint Eastwood's revisionist Western movie about the frontier, *Unforgiven.* Eastwood became a movie star in a delightfully cynical series of Italian "spaghetti" Westerns in which he played the ultimate silent gunfighter, inscrutable and alone, and a killer, but essentially heroic. In this film, he makes use of many of the elements of the traditional Western, including the gunslinger, women in distress, good guys and bad guys, and the big gunfight at the end. But he turns many of those same elements on their heads: the good guy is a retired killer who is useless as a farmer, can barely get on a horse, and would rather stay home with his two children; the ladies in distress are prostitutes who hire him to kill a man who mutilated one of them; the most brutal character in the movie is the sheriff; and the epilogue to the film, which describes the gunslinger's change of career after all this is over, is a comic reversal of frontier clichés. The result is a movie that simultaneously revises, criticizes, and yet validates the frontier of myth. It may or may not be any more accurate than all the other versions of the frontier that have been with us for more than three hundred years, but it is another proof of our need for its continued presence, and for what we believe it tells us about who we are, or who we could be.

✹✹✹ FROM *The Journals of Lewis and Clark* (1805)

MERIWETHER LEWIS AND WILLIAM CLARK

After President Thomas Jefferson negotiated the Louisiana Purchase with France in 1803 and thus effectively doubled the size of the United States, he commissioned an exploratory expedition led by William Clark and Meriwether Lewis. Lewis was Jefferson's personal secretary and a scientist, and Lewis had experience as a map maker and navigator, as well as a negotiator with the Indians.

Tuesday, May 28th

The weather was dark and cloudy; the air smoky, and there fell a few drops of rain. At ten o'clock we had again a slight sprinkling of rain, attended with distant thunder, which is the first we have heard since leaving the Mandans. We employed the line generally, with the addition of the pole at the ripples and rocky points, which we find more numerous and troublesome than those we passed yesterday. The water is very rapid round these points, and we are sometimes obliged to steer the canoes through the points of sharp rocks rising a few inches above the surface of the water, and so near to each other that if our ropes give way the force of the current drives the sides of the canoe against them, and must inevitably upset them or dash them to pieces. These cords are very slender, being almost all made of elkskin, and much worn and rotted by exposure to the weather: several times they gave way, but fortunately always in places where there was room for the canoe to turn without striking the rock; yet with all our precautions it was with infinite risk and labour that we passed these points. An Indian pole for building floated down the river, and was worn at one end as if dragged along the ground in travelling; several other articles were also brought down by the current, which indicate that the Indians are probably at no great distance above us, and judging from a football which resembles those used by the Minnetarees near the Mandans, we conjecture that they must be a band of the Minnetarees of fort de Prairie.

The appearance of the river and the surrounding country continued as usual, till towards evening, at about fifteen miles, we reached a large creek on the north thirty-five yards wide, discharging some water, and named after one of our men Thompson's creek. Here the country assumed a totally different aspect; the hills retired on both sides from the river which now spreads to more than three times its former size, and is filled with a number of small handsome islands covered with cottonwood. The low grounds on the river are again wide, fertile, and enriched with trees; those on the north are particularly wide, the hills being comparatively low and opening into three large vallies, which extend themselves for a considerable distance towards the north: these appearances of vegetation are delightful after the dreary hills over which we have passed, and we have now to congratulate ourselves at having escaped from the last ridges of the Black mountains. On leaving Thompson's creek we passed two small islands, and at twenty-three miles distance encamped among some timber on the north, opposite to a small creek, which we named Bull creek. The bighorn is in great quantities, and must bring forth their young at a very early season, as they are now half grown. One of the party saw a large bear also, but being at a distance from the river, and having no timber to conceal him, he would not venture to fire.

Wednesday, May 29th

Last night we were alarmed by a new sort of enemy. A buffalo swam over from the opposite side and to the spot where lay one of our canoes, over which he clambered to the shore; then taking fright he ran full speed up the bank towards our fires, and passed within eighteen inches of the heads of some of the men, before the sentinel could make him change his course: still more alarmed he ran down between four fires and within a few inches of the heads of a second row of the men, and would have broken into our lodge if the barking of the dog had not stopped him. He suddenly turned to the right and was out of sight in a moment, leaving us all in confusion, every one seizing his rifle and inquiring the cause of the alarm. On learning what had happened, we had to rejoice at suffering no more injury than the damage to some guns which were in the canoe which the buffalo crossed.

In the morning early we left our camp, and proceeded as usual by the cord. We passed an island and two sandbars, and at the distance of two and a half miles we came to a handsome river which discharges itself on the south, and which we ascended to the distance of a mile and a half: we called it Judith's river: it rises in the Rock mountains in about the same place with the Muscleshell and near the Yellowstone river. Its entrance is one hundred yards wide from one bank to the other, the water occupying about seventy-five yards, and in greater quantity than that of the Muscleshell river, and though more rapid equally navigable, there being no stones or rocks in the bed, which is composed entirely of gravel and mud with some sand: the water too is clearer than any which we have yet seen; and the low grounds, as far as we could discern, wider and more woody than those of the Missouri: along its banks we observed some box-alder intermixed with the cottonwood and the willow; the undergrowth consisting of rose-bushes, honeysuckles, and a little red willow. There was a great abundance of the argalea or big-horned animals in the high country through which it passes, and a great number of the beaver in its waters.

Just above the entrance of it we saw the fires of one hundred and twenty-six lodges, which appeared to have been deserted about twelve or fifteen days, and on the other side of the Missouri a large encampment, apparently made by the same nation. On examining some moccasins which we found there, our Indian woman said that they do not belong to her own nation the Snake Indians, but she thought that they indicated a tribe on this side of the Rocky mountains, and to the north of the Missouri; indeed it is probable that these are the Minnetarees of fort de Prairie.

At the distance of six and a half miles the hills again approached the brink of the river, and the stones and rocks washed down from them form a very bad rapid, with rocks and ripples more numerous and difficult than those we passed on the *27th* and *28th:* here the same scene was renewed, and we had again to struggle and labour to preserve our small craft from being lost. Near this spot are a few trees of the ash, the first we have seen for a great distance, and from which we named the place Ash Rapids. On these hills there is but little timber, but the salts, coal, and other mineral appearances continue.

On the north we passed a precipice about one hundred and twenty feet high, under which lay scattered the fragments of at least one hundred carcases of buffaloes, although the water which had washed away the lower part of the hill must have carried off many of the dead. These buffaloes had been chased down the precipice in a way very common on the Missouri, and by which vast herds are destroyed in a moment. The mode of hunting is to select one of the most active and fleet young men, who is disguised by a buffalo skin round his body; the skin of the head with the ears and horns fastened on his own head in such a way as to deceive the buffalo: thus dressed, he fixes himself at a convenient distance between a herd of buffalo and any of the river precipices, which sometimes extend for some miles. His companions in the meantime get in the rear and side of the herd, and at a given signal show themselves, and advance towards the buffalo: they instantly take the alarm, and finding the hunters beside them, they run towards the disguised Indian or decoy, who leads them on at full speed towards the river, when suddenly securing himself in some crevice of the cliff which he had previously fixed on, the herd is left on the brink of the precipice: it is then in vain for the foremost to retreat or even to stop; they are pressed on by the hindmost rank, who, seeing no danger but from the hunters, goad on those before them till the whole are precipitated and the shore is strewed with their dead bodies. Sometimes in this perilous seduction the Indian is himself either trodden underfoot by the rapid movements of the buffalo, or missing his footing in the cliff is urged down the precipice by the falling herd. The Indians then select as much meat as they wish, and the rest is abandoned to the wolves, and creates a most dreadful stench. The wolves who had been feasting on these carcases were very fat, and so gentle that one of them was killed with a spontoon.

Above this place we came to for dinner at the distance of seventeen miles, opposite to a bold running river of twenty yards wide, and falling in on the south. From the objects we had just passed we called this stream Slaughter river. Its low grounds are narrow, and contain scarcely any timber. Soon after landing it began to blow and rain, and as there was no prospect of getting wood for fuel farther on, we fixed our camp on the north, three quarters of a mile above Slaughter river. After the labours of the day we gave to each man a dram, and such was the effect of long abstinence from spirituous liquors, that from the small quantity of half a gill of rum, several of the men were considerably affected by it, and all very much exhilarated. Our game to-day consisted of an elk and two beaver.

For Journals

What part of the journey would you like to have experienced yourself? Why?

For Discussion

1. One purpose of the trip was to observe and record what the expedition saw. How good do you think this selection is at creating a scientific and visual record? Look for and read aloud a couple of paragraphs that seem to you particularly strong, and identify what it is about the language that you find appealing or convincing.

2. Look for all the references you can find in this selection to the Indians, their culture, and their way of life. What images of them do you see represented here? Which one made the strongest impression on you?

3. The expedition really had very little idea of what it was going to find. What do you think seems most impressive to them, or most educational, or most dramatic?

4. Do you think that Clark is a colorful writer? Look ahead to the next reading, from Mark Twain's own trip across the country about half a century later, and find one of his descriptive paragraphs. What differences do you see in word choice, rhythm, vernacular, and tone?

For Writing

1. Check one of the Lewis and Clark Web sites, like *www .lewisandclark200.gov* developed to coordinate all the celebrations, re-creations, and events commemorating the two-hundredth anniversary of the start of the expedition. The Web sites come with maps and routes marked. With one or two other people in your class, write a mini-brochure with illustrations to explain the significance of one section of the trip and the reason that people should be interested in traveling on it. To do this well, you will also need to look at the Journals to see what Lewis and Clark wrote about the section of the trip that you are advertising.

2. Write an essay based on discussion question number 2.

3. Write a rhetorical analysis of one section from this selection, and consider the following questions: What is the most significant information being communicated? How is the section ordered, that is, what are the turning points in the section; what is the drama, if any; and what is the attitude of the writer toward what he is observing or experiencing? Is this narrative or objective reporting? Pick a section that you either liked a lot or didn't like much; either way will help you focus your analysis.

❋❋❋ FROM *Roughing It* (1872)

MARK TWAIN

Mark Twain (pseudonym of Samuel Clemens, 1835–1910), humorist, novelist, satirist, and lecturer, is one of the foremost writers in American literature, and probably the most beloved. He grew up in Missouri before the Civil War and worked as a printer and a Mississippi riverboat pilot before accompanying his brother Orion to Nevada in 1862. Roughing It, *with its adventures, tall tales, and absolutely American voice, came out in 1872.*

By eight o'clock everything was ready, and we were on the other side of the river. We jumped into the stage, the driver cracked his whip, and we bowled away and left "the States" behind us. It was a superb summer morning, and all the landscape was brilliant with sunshine. There was a freshness and breeziness, too, and an exhilarating sense of emancipation from all sorts of cares and responsibilities, that almost made us feel that the years we had spent in the close, hot city, toiling and slaving, had been wasted and thrown away. We were spinning along through Kansas, and in the course of an hour and a half we were fairly abroad on the great Plains. Just here the land was rolling—a grand sweep of regular elevations and depressions as far as the eye could reach—like the stately heave and swell of the ocean's bosom after a storm. And everywhere were cornfields, accenting with squares of deeper green, this limitless expanse of grassy land. But presently this sea upon dry ground was to lose its "rolling" character and stretch away for seven hundred miles as level as a floor!

Our coach was a great swinging and swaying stage, of the most sumptuous description—an imposing cradle on wheels. It was drawn by six handsome horses, and by the side of the driver sat the "conductor," the legitimate captain of the craft; for it was his business to take charge and care of the mails, baggage, express matter, and passengers. We three were the only passengers, this trip. We sat on the back seat, inside. About all the rest of the coach was full of mail-bags—for we had three days' delayed mails with us. Almost touching our knees, a perpendicular wall of mail matter rose up to the roof. There was a great pile of it strapped on top of the stage, and both the fore and hind boots were full. We had twenty-seven hundred pounds of it aboard, the driver said—"a little for Brigham, and Carson, and 'Frisco, but the heft of it for the Injuns, which is powerful troublesome 'thout they get plenty of truck to read." But as he just then got up a fearful convulsion of his countenance which was suggestive of a wink being swallowed by an earthquake, we guessed that his remark was intended to be facetious, and to mean that we would unload the most of our mail matter somewhere on the Plains and leave it to the Indians, or whosoever wanted it.

We changed horses every ten miles, all day long, and fairly flew over the hard, level road. We jumped out and stretched our legs every time the coach stopped, and so the night found us still vivacious and unfatigued.

It was now just dawn; and as we stretched our cramped legs full length on the mail-sacks, and gazed out through the windows across the wide wastes of greensward clad in cool, powdery mist, to where there was an expectant look in the eastern horizon, our perfect enjoyment took the form of a tranquil and contended ecstasy. The stage whirled along at a spanking gait, the breeze flapping curtains and suspended coats in a most exhilarating way; the cradle swayed and swung luxuriously, the pattering of the horses' hoofs, the cracking of the driver's whip, and his "Hi-yi! g'lang!" were music; the spinning ground and the waltzing trees appeared to give us a mute hurrah as we went by, and then slack up and look after us with interest, or envy, or something; and as we lay and smoked the pipe of peace and compared all this luxury with the years of tiresome city life that had gone before it, we felt that there was only one complete and satisfying happiness in the world, and we had found it. . . .

Really and truly, two thirds of the talk of drivers and conductors 5 had been about this man Slade, ever since the day before we reached Julesburg. In order that the Eastern reader may have a clear conception of what a Rocky Mountain desperado is, in his highest state of development, I will reduce all this mass of Overland gossip to one straight-forward narrative, and present it in the following shape:

Slade was born in Illinois, of good parentage. At about twenty-six years of age he killed a man in a quarrel and fled the country. At St. Joseph, Missouri, he joined one of the early California-bound emigrant trains, and was given the post of trainmaster. One day on the Plains he had an angry dispute with one of his wagon-drivers, and both drew their revolvers. But the driver was the quicker artist, and had his weapon cocked first. So Slade said it was a pity to waste life on so small a matter, and proposed that the pistols be thrown on the ground and the quarrel settled by a fist-fight. The unsuspecting driver agreed, and threw down his pistol—whereupon Slade laughed at his simplicity, and shot him dead!

He made his escape, and lived a wild life for a while, dividing his time between fighting Indians and avoiding an Illinois sheriff, who had been sent to arrest him for his first murder. It is said that in one Indian battle he killed three savages with his own hand, and afterward cut their ears off and sent them, with his compliments, to the chief of the tribe.

Slade soon gained a name for fearless resolution, and this was sufficient merit to procure for him the important post of Overland division-agent at Julesburg, in place of Mr. Jules, removed. For some time previously, the company's horses had been frequently stolen, and the coaches delayed, by gangs of outlaws, who were wont to laugh at the idea of any man's having the temerity to resent such outrages. Slade resented them promptly. The outlaws soon found that the new agent was a man who did not fear anything that breathed the breath of life. He made short work of all offenders. The result was that delays ceased, the company's property was let alone, and no matter what happened or who suffered, Slade's coaches went through, every time! True, in order to bring about this wholesome change, Slade had to kill several men—some say three, others say four, and others six—but the world was the richer for their loss. The first prominent difficulty he had was with the ex-agent Jules, who bore the reputation of being a reckless and desperate man himself. Jules hated Slade for supplanting him, and a good fair occasion for a fight was all he was waiting for. By and by Slade dared to employ a man whom Jules had once discharged. Next, Slade seized a team of stage-horses which he accused Jules of having driven off and hidden somewhere for his own use. War was declared, and for a day or two the two men walked warily about the streets, seeking each other, Jules armed with a double-barreled shotgun, and Slade with his history-creating revolver. Finally, as Slade stepped into a store, Jules poured the contents of his gun into him from behind the door. Slade was pluck, and Jules got several bad pistol wounds in return. Then both men fell, and were carried to their respective lodgings, both swearing that better aim should do deadlier work next time. Both were bedridden a long time, but Jules got on his feet first, and gathering his possessions together, packed them on a couple of mules, and fled to the Rocky Mountains to gather strength in safety against the day of reckoning. For many months he was not seen or heard of, and was gradually dropped out of the remembrance of all save Slade himself. But Slade was not the man to forget him. On the contrary, common report said that Slade kept a reward standing for his capture, dead or alive!

After a while, seeing that Slade's energetic administration had restored peace and order to one of the worst divisions of the road, the Overland Stage Company transferred him to the Rocky Ridge division in the Rocky Mountains, to see if he could perform a like miracle there. It was the very paradise of outlaws and desperadoes. There was absolutely no semblance of law there. Violence was the rule. Force was the only recognized authority. The commonest misunderstandings were settled on the spot with the revolver or the knife. Murders were done in open day, and with sparkling frequency, and nobody thought of inquiring into them. It was considered that the parties who did the killing had their private reasons for it; for other people to meddle would have been looked upon as indelicate. After a murder, all that Rocky Mountain etiquette required of a spectator was, that he should help the gentleman bury his game—otherwise his churlishness would surely be remembered against him the first time he killed a man himself and needed a neighborly turn in interring him.

Slade took up his residence sweetly and peacefully in the midst of 10 this hive of horse-thieves and assassins, and the very first time one of them aired his insolent swaggerings in his presence he shot him dead! He began a raid on the outlaws, and in a singularly short space of time he had completely stopped their depredations on the stage stock, recovered a large number of stolen horses, killed several of the worst desperadoes of the district, and gained such a dread ascendancy over the rest that they respected him, admired him, feared him, obeyed him! He wrought the same marvelous change in the ways of the community that had marked his administration at Overland City. He captured two men who had stolen Overland stock, and with his own hands he hanged them. He was supreme judge in his district, and he was jury and executioner likewise—and not only in the case of offences against his employers, but against passing emigrants as well. On one occasion some emigrants had their stock lost or stolen, and told Slade, who chanced to visit their camp. With a single companion he rode to a ranch, the owners of which he suspected, and opening the door, commenced firing, killing three, and wounding the fourth.

From a bloodthirstily interesting little Montana book* I take this paragraph:

> While on the road, Slade held absolute sway. He would ride down to a station, get into a quarrel, turn the house out of windows, and mal-treat the occupants most cruelly. The unfortunates had no means of redress, and were compelled to recuperate as best they could. On one of these occasions, it is said, he killed the father of the fine little half-breed boy, Jemmy, whom he adopted, and who lived with his widow after his execution. Stories of Slade's hanging men, and of innumer-able assaults, shootings, stabbings and beatings, in which he was a principal actor, form part of the legends of the stage line. As for minor quarrels and shootings, it is absolutely certain that a minute history of Slade's life would be one long record of such practices.

Slade was a matchless marksman with a navy revolver. The leg-ends say that one morning at Rocky Ridge, when he was feeling com-fortable, he saw a man approaching who had offended him some days before—observe the fine memory he had for matters like that—and, "Gentlemen," said Slade, drawing, "it is a good twenty-yard shot—I'll clip the third button on his coat!" Which he did. The bystanders all ad-mired it. And they all attended the funeral, too.

On one occasion a man who kept a little whiskey shelf at the sta-tion did something which angered Slade—and went and made his will. A day or two afterward Slade came in and called for some brandy. The man reached under the counter (ostensibly to get a bot-tle—possibly to get something else), but Slade smiled upon him that peculiarly bland and satisfied smile of his which the neighbors had long ago learned to recognize as a death-warrant in disguise, and told him to "none of that!—pass out the high-priced article." So the poor bar-keeper had to turn his back and get the high-priced brandy from the shelf; and when he faced around again he was looking into the muzzle of Slade's pistol. "And the next instant," added my informant, impressively, "he was one of the deadest men that ever lived."

The stage-drivers and conductors told us that sometimes Slade would leave a hated enemy wholly unmolested, unnoticed and un-mentioned, for weeks together—had done it once or twice at any rate. And some said they believed he did it in order to lull the victims into unwatchfulness, so that he could get the advantage of them, and oth-ers said they believed he saved up an enemy that way, just as a school-boy saves up a cake, and made the pleasure go as far as it would by gloating over the anticipation. One of these cases was that of a French-man who had offended Slade. To the surprise of everybody Slade did not kill him on the spot, but let him alone for a considerable time.

The Vigilantes of Montana, by Prof. Thos. J. Dimsdale. [Author's note]

Finally, however, he went to the Frenchman's house very late one night, knocked, and when his enemy opened the door, shot him dead—pushed the corpse inside the door with his foot, set the house on fire and burned up the dead man, his widow and three children! I heard this story from several different people, and they evidently believed what they were saying. It may be true, and it may not. "Give a dog a bad name," etc.

Slade was captured, once, by a party of men who intended to lynch   15
him. They disarmed him, and shut him up in a strong log-house, and placed a guard over him. He prevailed on his captors to send for his wife, so that he might have a last interview with her. She was a brave, loving, spirited woman. She jumped on a horse and rode for life and death. When she arrived they let her in without searching her, and before the door could be closed she whipped out a couple of revolvers, and she and her lord marched forth defying the party. And then, under a brisk fire, they mounted double and galloped away unharmed!

In the fulness of time Slade's myrmidons captured his ancient enemy Jules, whom they found in a well-chosen hiding-place in the remote fastnesses of the mountains, gaining a precarious livelihood with his rifle. They brought him to Rocky Ridge, bound hand and foot, and deposited him in the middle of the cattle-yard with his back against a post. It is said that the pleasure that lit Slade's face when he heard of it was something fearful to contemplate. He examined his enemy to see that he was securely tied, and then went to bed, content to wait till morning before enjoying the luxury of killing him. Jules spent the night in the cattle-yard, and it is a region where warm nights are never known. In the morning Slade practised on him with his revolver, nipping the flesh here and there, and occasionally clipping off a finger, while Jules begged him to kill him outright and put him out of his misery. Finally Slade reloaded, and walking up close to his victim, made some characteristic remarks and then dispatched him. The body lay there half a day, nobody venturing to touch it without orders, and then Slade detailed a party and assisted at the burial himself. But he first cut off the dead man's ears and put them in his vest pocket, where he carried them for some time with great satisfaction. That is the story as I have frequently heard it told and seen it in print in California newspapers. It is doubtless correct in all essential particulars.

In due time we rattled up to a stage station, and sat down to breakfast with a half-savage, half-civilized company of armed and bearded mountaineers, ranchmen and station employ[ees]. The most gentlemanly-appearing, quiet and affable officer we had yet found along the road in the Overland Company's service was the person who sat at the head of the table, at my elbow. Never youth stared and shivered as I did when I heard them call him SLADE!

Here was romance, and I sitting face to face with it!—looking upon it—touching it—hobnobbing with it, as it were! Here, right by my side, was the actual ogre who, in fights and brawls and various ways, *had taken the lives of twenty-six human beings,* or all men lied about him! I suppose I was the proudest stripling that ever traveled to see strange lands and wonderful people.

He was so friendly and so gentle-spoken that I warmed to him in spite of his awful history. It was hardly possible to realize that this pleasant person was the pitiless scourge of the outlaws, the raw-head-and-bloody-bones the nursing mothers of the mountains terrified their children with. And to this day I can remember nothing remarkable about Slade except that his face was rather broad across the cheek bones, and that the cheek bones were low and the lips peculiarly thin and straight. But that was enough to leave something of an effect upon me, for since then I seldom see a face possessing those characteristics without fancying that the owner of it is a dangerous man.

The coffee ran out. At least it was reduced to one tin-cupful, and 20 Slade was about to take it when he saw that my cup was empty. He politely offered to fill it, but although I wanted it, I politely declined. I was afraid he had not killed anybody that morning, and might be needing diversion. But still with firm politeness he insisted on filling my cup, and said I had traveled all night and better deserved it than he—and while he talked he placidly poured the fluid, to the last drop. I thanked him and drank it, but it gave me no comfort, for I could not feel sure that he would not be sorry, presently, that he had given it away, and proceed to kill me to distract his thoughts from the loss. But nothing of the kind occurred. We left him with only twenty-six dead people to account for, and I felt a tranquil satisfaction in the thought that in so judiciously taking care of No. 1 at that breakfast-table I had pleasantly escaped being No. 27. Slade came out to the coach and saw us off, first ordering certain rearrangements of the mail-bags for our comfort, and then we took leave of him.

For Journals

What had you previously read of Twain's works? What did you know about him or his work?

For Discussion

1. Tall tales are very characteristic of Twain and of Western humor. Why do you think that the frontier lent itself to such wildly exaggerated stories about people and places?

2. How do you respond to the idea that giving a biography to Slade or any other western character gives a history to a frontier that doesn't have any history of its own?

3. How does Twain's encounter with the real Slade make us revise our expectations of what he would be like?

4. What image of the frontier do you think Twain's eastern readers had? Does Twain's way of writing reinforce or revise that image?

5. How does Twain's humor contribute to his portrait of himself as a man who knows absolutely nothing about the frontier? Why do you think he chose that way of presenting himself?

For Writing

1. Read a couple of other chapters from *Roughing It*—for example, on Mono Lake, on an earthquake in San Francisco, on Hawaii, on the desert, on striking it rich for ten days in a silver mine—and write a paper on how these episodes support or contradict your own expectations of what the frontier was like, what frontier heroes were like, and what American values these heroes lived by.

2. Write an essay about a trip you took when you were younger to a place—a national park or a city, for example—that made a big impression on you at the time. Write a paragraph about it as you experienced it in childhood and a paragraph on the same experience as you recall it now. Analyze both paragraphs, and write an essay examining the ways you revised your understanding of your own experience.

The Last of the Buffalo (1889)

ALBERT BIERSTADT

Albert Bierstadt (1830–1902), was born in Germany but became famous in America as a painter of Western scenery. After traveling and sketching the mountains of Europe, he went on a trail-making expedition to the West in 1859. He painted huge grand canvases, whose subjects included a Shoshone village, redwood trees of the buffalo, the Rocky Mountains, and Yosemite. When he painted this picture, his style and subject matter were out of fashion, but The Last of the Buffalo *is now one of his most famous works. (See Color Plate V for a color image of this painting.)*

For Journals

Who do you think was the original audience for this painting? What was your own first reaction to it?

Albert Bierstadt (1830–1902), "The Last of the Buffalo," 1889. Oil on canvas, six feet by ten feet. Courtesy of the Corcoran Gallery, Washington D.C.

547

For Discussion

1. You're seeing this painting in a book, but it is actually six feet tall and ten feet wide. How do you think seeing it in person would affect your impression of it?

2. How would the dramatic impact of the picture be changed if the hunters in it were white rather than Native American? Why do you think Bierstadt made the choice he did?

3. What words would you use to describe the mood or emotion conveyed by this painting? How do its features—the angle from which you view it, the placement of the skeletons near the buffalo, the way the buffalo about to be killed and the one to our left are positioned—contribute to that mood?

4. Faced with the spectacular western scenery of paintings like Bierstadt's, viewers often couldn't believe their eyes until they saw photographs of the same places. What would be the advantages and disadvantages of viewing a photograph of a scene like this versus a painting?

For Writing

1. Bierstadt wrote about this painting: "I have endeavored to show the buffalo in all his aspects and depict the cruel slaughter of a noble animal now almost extinct." Write a reflective essay in which you explain why you think he did or didn't succeed in his aim. To do this, you will need to examine the painting closely. Given its scope, you could divide it in thirds across the width of the painting, and examine each part more closely in relation to the others. Or you could analyze individual elements, like the landscape, all the buffalo, the hunters, and the central dramatic episode of the buffalo being killed. Finally, you could read this painting as a narrative—a story about a specific moment in time that won't come again. Whatever you choose, refer to details, and explain what they contribute to the whole.

2. Write an essay comparing the Lewis and Clark episode on buffalo hunting earlier in this chapter with this image. Consider, for example, what mood is conveyed by the Lewis and Clark journal: Are the explorers scared? impressed? curious? exhilarated? And what words would you use to describe the mood in the painting? You will need quotes from the journal to back up your assertions, and you will need details from the painting (the background, the activity of the hunter and the behavior of the buffalo, the choice of title, etc.) to prove your points about it.

3. In 1840 there were approximately 20 million buffalo. This painting prompted the government to take a census of the buffalo population in

1889, and there were a total of 551 survivors. Today there are more buffalo than at any time since that count was taken. Research the resurgence of the buffalo, and write a paper about the factors involved, like the reconversion of former farm land to prairie land, the interest of tourism, and the experiments in raising buffalo as a newly fashionable food source.

✸✸✸ *Indian Treachery and Bloodshed* (1891)

POLICE GAZETTE

The Police Gazette *was a popular and lurid newspaper that was begun in 1846 but was at its height—or depth—in the 1880s and 1890s. It specialized in stories about crime, prostitution, and sports; was copiously illustrated; never had a story without a melodramatic title; and freely expressed the biases of its publisher, James Fox, who entertained lifelong prejudices against Chinese, African Americans, Jews, Native Americans, ministers, and college students, among others.*

The Indian war in South Dakota, so long anticipated, has at last become a reality, and with it has come the death of a number of brave troops of the United States Cavalry. The leader of the warriors was Big Foot and he and his braves tricked the troops into ambush. Then a wholesale slaughter began, the Indians being nearly annihilated, those who were not killed seeking refuge in the Bad Lands, where they will be frozen or starved out. As soon as the troops had cornered the Indians they fell upon them with Hotchkiss guns. The Indians fell in heaps but, determined to the last, they fought to the death even after being sorely wounded.

The saddest scene of the carnage was the killing of Captain George D. Wallace of the Seventh Cavalry, who was brutally tomahawked. Captain Wallace was appointed to the Military Academy from South Carolina in 1868 and upon being graduated in 1872 was commissioned a second lieutenant in the Seventh. He received his promotion to first lieutenant in 1876 and was commissioned captain in September 1885.

It is said that General Sheridan first remarked that "a dead Indian is the best Indian" and the action of the soldiers appears to coincide with Little Phil's views. The action teaches the lesson that if the Sioux are of any use at all they should be fairly dealt with, and if not, that they should at once be given free passes to the happy hunting grounds. As they speak highly of the happy hunting grounds, it might be as well to start them on the journey in any case, and then, if the decision be found unjust, to write them an apology.

For Journals

How does the news style of the *Police Gazette* compare with that of contemporary tabloid newspapers and magazines? Which tabloids now do you consider the most sensational?

For Discussion

1.   How would you describe the author's attitude toward the Indians? What values do you think that the writer places on the lives of both Indians and soldiers?

2.   How closely do you think that the contents of the article and the illustration are related? What would you describe as the theme of the article? Of the illustration?

3.   Look at the headline of the article and then at the first paragraph. How does the article support or revise the sentiments in the headline? Given the headline, what would you have expected?

4.   Look at the illustration, starting at the top and working down to the bottom. How successfully does each grouping convey violent action? If there were no headline for the picture and text, what headline would you supply?

5.   Who do you think read the *Police Gazette?* What would its audience have to do with the kinds of articles it published?

6.   Suppose that Indians were writing the article and drawing the illustrations. In what specific ways do you think they would have revised the results?

For Writing

1.   At the library, look at a book with copies of George Catlin's paintings of Native Americans—*North American Indians* or *Catlin's Indians,* for example—and write a paper in which you discuss and compare any two of the portraits. Among the points for you to consider are these: What is your impression of the character and personality of the Native Americans in the pictures? How different do they look from the Plains Indians in this illustration? How does the color of the paintings affect your impression of the Indian in the Catlin portrait? Your college library would be a good source of material on the history of the various tribes and on Catlin's artistry. The Smithsonian Museum is another source, and its Web site can lead to information about the tribes Catlin painted and to images of the paintings.

2.   Research the development of the idea of the reservation: how it was developed, what treaties surrounded the setting up of reservations, or what conditions prevail on reservations today. If you write about reservations today, focus on one area of the country or one or two reservations. You will get different viewpoints on this issue, depending on where you look; for example, the Bureau of Indian Affairs saw its mission one way, but the tribal leaders saw the question of what to do about the "Indian Problem" very differently.

3.   Write a paper based on discussion question number 6.

❋❋❋ The Significance of the Frontier in American History (1893)

FREDERICK JACKSON TURNER

Frederick Jackson Turner (1862–1932) was born in Wisconsin and taught at the University of Wisconsin and Harvard. He presented this paper during the Chicago World's Fair of 1893 before the American Historical Association. Although Jackson did not publish a great deal, this essay alone made him one of the most famous historians in American studies.

In a recent bulletin of the Superintendent of the Census for 1890 appear these significant words: "Up to and including 1880 the country had a frontier of settlement, but at present the unsettled area has been so broken into by isolated bodies of settlement that there can hardly be said to be a frontier line. In the discussion of its extent, its westward movement, etc., it can not therefore, any longer have a place in the census reports." This brief official statement marks the closing of a great historic movement. Up to our own day American history has been in a large degree the history of the colonization of the Great West. The existence of an area of free land, its continuous recession, and the advance of American settlement westward, explain American development.

Behind institutions, behind constitutional forms and modifications, lie the vital forces that call these organs into life and shape them to meet changing conditions. The peculiarity of American institutions is, the fact that they have been compelled to adapt themselves to the changes of an expanding people—to the changes involved in crossing a continent, in winning a wilderness, and in developing at each area of this progress out of the primitive economic and political conditions of the frontier into the complexity of city life. Said Calhoun in 1817, "We are great, and rapidly—I was about to say fearfully—growing!" So saying, he touched the distinguishing feature of American life. All peoples show development; the germ theory of politics has been sufficiently emphasized. In the case of most nations, however, the development has occurred in a limited area; and if the nation has expanded, it has met other growing peoples whom it has conquered. But in the case of the United States we have a different phenomenon. Limiting our attention to the Atlantic coast, we have the familiar phenomenon of the evolution of institutions in a limited area, such as the rise of representative government; the differentiation of simple colonial governments into complex organs; the progress from primitive industrial society, without division of labor, up to manufacturing civilization. But we have in addition to this a recurrence of the process of evolution in each western area reached in the process of expansion. Thus American development has exhibited not merely advance along a single line, but a return to primitive conditions on a continually advancing frontier line, and a new development for that area. American social development has been continually beginning over again on the frontier. This perennial rebirth, this fluidity of American life, this expansion westward with its new opportunities, its continuous touch with the simplicity of primitive society, furnish the forces dominating American character. The true point of view in the history of this nation is not the Atlantic coast, it is the great West. Even the slavery struggle, which is made so exclusive an object of attention by writers like Professor von Holst, occupies its important place in American history because of its relation to westward expansion.

In this advance, the frontier is the outer edge of the wave—the meeting point between savagery and civilization. Much has been written about the frontier from the point of view of border warfare and the chase, but as a field for the serious study of the economist and the historian it has been neglected.

The American frontier is sharply distinguished from the European frontier—a fortified boundary line running through dense populations. The most significant thing about the American frontier is, that it lies at the hither edge of free land. In the census reports it is treated as the margin of that settlement which has a density of two or more to the square mile. The term is an elastic one, and for our purposes does not need sharp definition. We shall consider the whole frontier belt, including the Indian country and the outer margin of the "settled area" of the census reports. This paper will make no attempt to treat the subject exhaustively; its aim is simply to call attention to the frontier as a fertile field for investigation, and to suggest some of the problems which arise in connection with it.

In the settlement of America we have to observe how European 5 life entered the continent, and how America modified and developed that life and reacted on Europe. Our early history is the study of European germs developing in an American environment. Too exclusive attention has been paid by institutional students to the Germanic origins, too little to the American factors. The frontier is the line of most rapid and effective Americanization. The wilderness masters the colonist. It finds him a European in dress, industries, tools, modes of travel, and thought. It takes him from the railroad car and puts him in the birch canoe. It strips off the garments of civilization and arrays him in the hunting shirt and the moccasin. It puts him in the log cabin of the Cherokee and Iroquois and runs an Indian palisade around him. Before long he has gone to planting Indian corn and plowing with a sharp stick; he shouts the war cry and takes the scalp in orthodox Indian fashion. In short, at the frontier the environment is at first too strong for the man. He must accept the conditions which it furnishes, or perish, and so he fits himself into the Indian clearings and follows the Indian trails. Little by little he transforms the wilderness, but the outcome is not the old Europe, not simply the development of Germanic germs, any more than the first phenomenon was a case of reversion to the Germanic mark. The fact is, that here is a new product that is American. At first, the frontier was the Atlantic coast. It was the frontier of Europe in a very real sense. Moving westward, the frontier became more and more American. As successive terminal moraines result from successive glaciations, so each frontier leaves its traces behind it, and when it becomes a settled area the region still partakes of the frontier characteristics. Thus the advance of the frontier has meant a steady movement away from the influence of Europe, a steady growth of independence on American lines. And to study this advance, the men who grew up under these conditions, and the political, economic, and social results of it, is to study the really American part of our history. . . .

The Frontier Furnishes a Field for Comparative Study of Social Development

At the Atlantic frontier one can study the germs of processes repeated at each successive frontier. We have the complex European life sharply precipitated by the wilderness into the simplicity of primitive conditions. The first frontier had to meet its Indian question, its question of the disposition of the public domain, of the means of intercourse with older settlements, of the extension of political organization, of religious and educational activity. And the settlement of these and similar questions for one frontier served as a guide for the next. The American student needs not to go to the "prim little townships of Sleswick" for illustrations of the law of continuity and development. For example, he may study the origin of our land policies in the colonial land policy; he may see how the system grew by adapting the statutes to the customs of the successive frontiers. He may see how the mining experience in the lead regions of Wisconsin, Illinois, and Iowa was applied to the mining laws of the Rockies, and how our Indian policy has been a series of experimentations on successive frontiers. Each tier of new States has found in the older ones material for its constitutions. Each frontier has made similar contributions to American character, as will be discussed farther on.

But with all these similarities there are essential differences, due to the place element and the time element. It is evident that the farming frontier of the Mississippi Valley presents different conditions from the mining frontier of the Rocky Mountains. The frontier reached by the Pacific Railroad, surveyed into rectangles, guarded by the United

States Army, and recruited by the daily immigrant ship, moves forward at a swifter pace and in a different way than the frontier reached by the birch canoe or the pack horse. The geologist traces patiently the shores of ancient seas, maps their areas, and compares the older and the newer. It would be a work worth the historian's labors to mark these various frontiers and in detail compare one with another. Not only would there result a more adequate conception of American development and characteristics, but invaluable additions would be made to the history of society.

Loria, the Italian economist, has urged the study of colonial life as an aid in understanding the stages of European development, affirming that colonial settlement is for economic science what the mountain is for geology, bringing to light primitive stratifications. "America," he says, "has the key to the historical enigma which Europe has sought for centuries in vain, and the land which has no history reveals luminously the course of universal history." There is much truth in this. The United States lies like a huge page in the history of society. Line by line as we read this continental page from west to east we find the record of social evolution. It begins with the Indian and the hunter; it goes on to tell of the disintegration of savagery by the entrance of the trader, the pathfinder of civilization; we read the annals of the pastoral stage in ranch life; the exploitation of the soil by the raising of unrotated crops of corn and wheat in sparsely settled farming communities; the intensive culture of the denser farm settlement; and finally the manufacturing organization with city and factory system. This page is familiar to the student of census statistics, but how little of it has been used by our historians. Particularly in eastern States this page is a palimpsest. What is now a manufacturing State was in an earlier decade an area of intensive farming. Earlier yet it had been a wheat area, and still earlier the "range" had attracted the cattle herder. Thus Wisconsin, now developing manufacture, is a State with varied agricultural interests. But earlier it was given over to almost exclusive grain-raising, like North Dakota at the present time.

Each of these areas has had an influence in our economic and political history; the evolution of each into a higher stage has worked political transformations. But what constitutional historian has made any adequate attempt to interpret political facts by the light of these social areas and changes?

The Atlantic frontier was compounded of fisherman, fur-trader, 10 miner, cattle-raiser, and farmer. Excepting the fisherman, each type of industry was on the march toward the West, impelled by an irresistible attraction. Each passed in successive waves across the continent. Stand at Cumberland Gap and watch the procession of civilization, marching single file—the buffalo following the trail to the salt springs, the Indian, the fur-trader and hunter, the cattle-raiser, the pioneer farmer—and the frontier has passed by. Stand at South Pass in the Rockies a century later and see the same procession with wider intervals between. The unequal rate of advance compels us to distinguish the frontier into the trader's frontier, the rancher's frontier, or the miner's frontier, and the farmer's frontier. When the mines and the cow pens were still near the fall line the traders' pack trains were tinkling across the Alleghenies, and the French on the Great Lakes were fortifying their posts, alarmed by the British trader's birch canoe. When the trappers scaled the Rockies, the farmer was still near the mouth of the Missouri. . . .

Land

The exploitation of the beasts took hunter and trader to the west, the exploitation of the grasses took the rancher west, and the exploitation of the virgin soil of the river valleys and prairies attracted the farmer. Good soils have been the most continuous attraction to the farmer's frontier. The land hunger of the Virginians drew them down the rivers into Carolina, in early colonial days; the search for soils took the Massachusetts men to Pennsylvania and to New York. As the eastern lands were taken up migration flowed across them to the west. Daniel Boone, the great backwoodsman, who combined the occupations of hunter, trader, cattle-raiser, farmer, and surveyor—learning, probably from the traders, of the fertility of the lands on the upper Yadkin, where the traders were wont to rest as they took their way to the Indians, left his Pennsylvania home with his father, and passed down the Great Valley road to that stream. Learning from a trader whose posts were on the Red River in Kentucky of its game and rich pastures, he pioneered the way for the farmers to that region. Thence he passed to the frontier of Missouri, where his settlement was long a landmark on the frontier. Here again he helped to open the way for civilization, finding salt licks, and trails, and land. His son was among the earliest trappers in the passes of the Rocky Mountains, and his party are said to have been the first to camp on the present site of Denver. His grandson, Col. A. J. Boone, of Colorado, was a power among the Indians of the Rocky Mountains, and was appointed an agent by the Government. Kit Carson's mother was a Boone. Thus this family epitomizes the backwoodsman's advance across the continent. . . .

Composite Nationality

First, we note that the frontier promoted the formation of a composite nationality for the American people. The coast was preponderantly English, but the later tides of continental immigration flowed across to the free lands. This was the case from the early colonial days.

The Scotch-Irish and the Palatine Germans, or "Pennsylvania Dutch," furnished the dominant element in the stock of the colonial frontier. With these peoples were also the freed indentured servants, or redemptioners, who at the expiration of their time of service passed to the frontier. Governor Spottswood of Virginia writes in 1717, "The inhabitants of our frontiers are composed generally of such as have been transported hither as servants, and, being out of their time, settle themselves where land is to be taken up and that will produce the necessarys of life with little labour." Very generally these redemptioners were of non-English stock. In the crucible of the frontier the immigrants were Americanized, liberated, and fused into a mixed race, English in neither nationality nor characteristics. The process has gone on from the early days to our own. Burke and other writers in the middle of the eighteenth century believed that Pennsylvania was "threatened with the danger of being wholly foreign in language, manners, and perhaps even inclinations." The German and Scotch-Irish elements in the frontier of the South were only less great. In the middle of the present century the German element in Wisconsin was already so considerable that leading publicists looked to the creation of a German state out of the commonwealth by concentrating their colonization. Such examples teach us to beware of misinterpreting the fact that there is a common English speech in America into a belief that the stock is also English.

Industrial Independence

In another way the advance of the frontier decreased our dependence on England. The coast, particularly of the South, lacked diversified industries, and was dependent on England for the bulk of its supplies. In the South there was even a dependence on the Northern colonies for articles of food. Governor Glenn, of South Carolina, writes in the middle of the eighteenth century: "Our trade with New York and Philadelphia was of this sort, draining us of all the little money and bills we could gather from other places for their bread, flour, beer, hams, bacon, and other things of their produce, all which, except beer, our new townships begin to supply us with, which are settled with very industrious and thriving Germans. This no doubt diminishes the number of shipping and the appearance of our trade, but it is far from being a detriment to us." Before long the frontier created a demand for merchants. As it retreated from the coast it became less and less possible for England to bring her supplies directly to the consumer's wharfs, and carry away staple crops, and staple crops began to give way to diversified agriculture for a time. The effect of this phase of the frontier action upon the northern section is perceived when we realize how the advance of the frontier aroused seaboard cities like Boston,

New York, and Baltimore, to engage in rivalry for what Washington called "the extensive and valuable trade of a rising empire." . . .

Growth of Democracy

But the most important effect of the frontier has been in the promotion of democracy here and in Europe. As has been indicated, the frontier is productive of individualism. Complex society is precipitated by the wilderness into a kind of primitive organization based on the family. The tendency is anti-social. It produces antipathy to control, and particularly to any direct control. The tax gatherer is viewed as a representative of oppression. Professor Osgood, in an able article, has pointed out that the frontier conditions prevalent in the colonies are important factors in the explanation of the American Revolution, where individual liberty was sometimes confused with absence of all effective government. The same conditions aid in explaining the difficulty of instituting a strong government in the period of the confederacy. The frontier individualism has from the beginning promoted democracy.

The frontier States that came into the Union in the first quarter of 15 a century of its existence came in with democratic suffrage provisions, and had reactive effects of the highest importance upon the older States whose peoples were being attracted there. An extension of the franchise became essential. It was *western* New York that forced an extension of suffrage in the constitutional convention of that State in 1821; and it was *western* Virginia that compelled the tide-water region to put a more liberal suffrage provision in the constitution framed in 1830, and to give to the frontier region a more nearly proportionate representation with the tide-water aristocracy. The rise of democracy as an effective force in the nation came in with western preponderance under Jackson and William Henry Harrison, and it meant the triumph of the frontier—with all of its good and with all of its evil elements. . . .

So long as free land exists, the opportunity for a competency exists, and economic power secures political power. But the democracy born of free land, strong in selfishness and individualism, intolerant of administrative experience and education, and pressing individual liberty beyond its proper bounds, has its dangers as well as its benefits. Individualism in America has allowed a laxity in regard to governmental affairs which has rendered possible the spoils system and all the manifest evils that follow from the lack of a highly developed civic spirit. In this connection may be noted also the influence of frontier conditions in permitting lax business honor, inflated paper currency and wild-cat banking. The colonial and revolutionary frontier was the region whence emanated many of the worst forms of an evil currency.

The West in the War of 1812 repeated the phenomenon on the frontier of that day, while the speculation and the wild-cat banking of the period of the crisis of 1837 occurred on the new frontier belt of the next tier of States. Thus each one of the periods of lax financial integrity coincides with periods when a new set of frontier communities had arisen, and coincides in area with these successive frontiers, for the most part. The recent Populist agitation is a case in point. Many a State that now declines any connection with the tenets of the Populists, itself adhered to such ideas in an earlier stage of the development of the State. A primitive society can hardly be expected to show the intelligent appreciation of the complexity of business interests in a developed society. The continual recurrence of these areas of paper-money agitation is another evidence that the frontier can be isolated and studied as a factor in American history of the highest importance. . . .

Intellectual Traits

From the conditions of frontier life came intellectual traits of profound importance. The works of travelers along each frontier from colonial days onward describe certain common traits, and these traits have, while softening down, still persisted as survivals in the place of their origin, even when a higher social organization succeeded. The result is that to the frontier the American intellect owes its striking characteristics. That coarseness and strength combined with acuteness and inquisitiveness; that practical, inventive turn of mind, quick to find expedients; that masterful grasp of material things, lacking in the artistic but powerful to effect great ends; that restless, nervous energy; that dominant individualism, working for good and for evil, and withal that buoyancy and exuberance which comes with freedom—these are traits of the frontier. Since the days when the fleet of Columbus sailed into the waters of the New World, America has been another name for opportunity, and the people of the United States have taken their tone from the incessant expansion which has not only been open but has even been forced upon them. He would be a rash prophet who should assert that the expansive character of American life has now entirely ceased. Movement has been its dominant fact, and, unless this training has no effect upon a people, the American energy will continually demand a wider field for its exercise. But never again will such gifts of free land offer themselves. For a moment, at the frontier, the bonds of custom are broken and unrestraint is triumphant. There is not *tabula rasa*. The stubborn American environment is there with its imperious summons to accept its conditions; the inherited ways of doing things are also there; and yet, in spite of environment, and in spite of custom, each frontier did indeed furnish a new field of opportunity, a gate of escape from the bondage of the past; and freshness, and confidence, and scorn of older society, impatience of its restraints and its ideas, and indifference to its lessons, have accompanied the frontier. What the Mediterranean Sea was to the Greeks, breaking the bond of custom, offering new experiences, calling out new institutions and activities, that, and more, the ever retreating frontier has been to the United States directly, and to the nations of Europe more remotely. And now, four centuries from the discovery of America, at the end of a hundred years of life under the Constitution, the frontier has gone, and with its going has closed the first period of American history.

For Journals

What is your own idea of what the American frontier represents? Cowboys and Indians? The Gold Rush? The space program? Western movies?

For Discussion

1. Turner saw the existence of a frontier as crucial to the formation of the American character and American democracy. What are his premises in this argument? What evidence does he provide to support them?

2. How do you respond to Turner's assertion that the frontier was the meeting point between civilization and savagery "the outer edge of the wave—" (paragraph 3)? How positively do you regard the idea of settlers moving through the frontier in order to create a different and distinctly American civilization?

3. Why does Turner see the life of Daniel Boone as a prototype of the frontiersman? What combination of elements makes Boone, in Turner's thesis, so suitable an example of the positive side of westward expansion?

4. How do you think Turner defines the idea of progress in American civilization? Progress from what to what? What do you think of as an example of progress in America?

5. One writer has said that Turner's essay is not *an* explanation of American history but rather *the* explanation of American history. Why would an analysis of the frontier be an analysis of American history altogether?

6. Turner said that the frontier had made the American character expansive, and that once the free land disappeared, Americans would have to find other ways of stretching their horizons. Where do you think Americans have turned to find psychological substitutions for the western frontier?

For Writing

1. Watch a video of one of the following movies: *High Noon; Shane; A Fistful of Dollars; Little Big Man; She Wore a Yellow Ribbon; Unforgiven.* Then write an essay in which you address the following issues: What picture does the movie give of life in the West? How closely does that picture coincide with your own idea of that life? What are the primary ethical and social values expressed in the movie, and who in the film embodies them?

2. Since it was written, there have been many revisions of Turner's thesis. Look at David Potter's *People of Plenty* or Richard Slotkin's *Gunfighter Nation*, and pick one chapter to read that relates to the author's ideas on Turner's thesis. Next, write your own evaluation of whether the author refutes all of Turner's claims effectively. Then write your own response to Turner's ideas.

✳✳✳ The Thesis Disputed (1949)

RICHARD HOFSTADTER

> *Richard Hofstadter (1916–1970) was a highly original American historian who spent his career at Columbia University. His amazingly diverse body of work paid particular attention to the importance of ideas in American history and to the development of political institutions. He won the Pulitzer Prize twice. When he wrote this essay, which is the most famous analysis of Frederick Jackson Turner's thesis on the role of the frontier in American history, the thesis had just undergone a period of attack by other historians. Hofstadter was able to appreciate the significance as well as the faults of Turner's theory.*

American historical writing in the past century has produced two major theories or models of understanding, the economic interpretation of politics associated with Charles A. Beard, and the frontier interpretation of American development identified with Frederick Jackson Turner. Both views have had a pervasive influence upon American thinking, but Beard himself felt that Turner's original essay on the frontier had "a more profound influence on thought about American history than any other essay or volume ever written on the subject." It is the frontier thesis that has embodied the predominant American view of the American past. . . .

American evolution, Turner believed, had been a repeated return to primitive conditions on a continually receding frontier line, a constant repetition of development from simple conditions to a complex society. From this perennial rebirth and fluidity of American life, and from its continual re-exposure to the simplicity of primitive society, had come the forces dominant in the American character. And as the frontier advanced, society moved steadily away from European influences, grew steadily on distinctive American lines. To study this advance and the men who had been fashioned by it was "to study the really American part of our history."

Of all the effects of the frontier, the most important was that it promoted democracy and individualism. So long as free land existed, there was always opportunity for a man to acquire a competency, and economic power secured political power. Each succeeding frontier furnished "a new field of opportunity, a gate of escape from the bondage of the past." The lack of binding tradition and organized restraints promoted a distinctively American passion for individual freedom, antipathy to direct control from outside, aggressive self-interest, and intolerance of education and administrative experience. But by the year 1890, this process had come to an end; the frontier, the hither edge of unsettled land, no longer existed, and with its passing the first epoch of American history had closed. . . .

The initial plausibility of the Turner thesis lies in the patent fact that no nation could spend more than a century developing an immense continental empire without being deeply affected by it. Few critics question the great importance of the inland empire, or that Turner originally performed a service for historical writing by directing attention to it. Many accept Turner's emphasis on the frontier as one of several valid but limited perspectives on American history. But it has been forcefully denied that the frontier deserves any special preeminence among several major factors in "explaining" American development. The question has also been raised (and frequently answered in the negative) whether Turner analyzed the frontier process itself clearly or correctly.

It became plain, as new thought and research was brought to bear 5 upon the problem, that the frontier theory, as an analytic device, was a blunt instrument. The terms with which the Turnerians dealt—the frontier, the West, individualism, the American character—were vague at the outset, and as the Turnerian exposition developed, they did not receive increasingly sharp definition. Precisely because Turner defined the frontier so loosely ("the term," he said, "is an elastic one"), he could claim so much for it. At times he referred to the frontier literally as the edge of the settled territory having a population density of two to the square mile. But frequently he identified "the frontier" and "the West," so that areas actually long settled could be referred to as frontier. At times he spoke of both the "frontier" and the "West" not as places or areas, but as a social process: "The West, at bottom, is a form of society rather than an area." When this definition is followed to its logical conclusion, the development of American society is "explained" by "a form of society"—certainly a barren tautology. Again, at times Turner assimilated such natural resources as coal, oil, timber, to the idea of "the West"; in this way the truism that natural wealth has an important bearing upon a nation's development and characteristics was subtly absorbed into the mystique of the frontier and took on the guise of a major insight.

However, the central weakness of Turner's thesis was in its intellectual isolationism. Having committed himself to an initial overemphasis on the uniqueness of the historical development of the United States, Turner compounded the error by overemphasizing the frontier as a factor in this development. The obsession with uniqueness, the subtly demagogic stress on "the truly American part of our history," diverted the attention of historical scholarship from the possibilities of comparative social history; it offered no opportunity to explain why so many features of American development—for example, the rise of democracy in the nineteenth century—were parallel to changes in countries that did not have a contiguous frontier. Historians were encouraged to omit a host of basic influences common to both American and Western European development—the influence of Protestantism and the Protestant ethic, the inheritance from English republicanism, the growth of industrialism and urbanism. More than this, factors outside the frontier process that contributed to the singularity of American history were skipped over: the peculiar American federal structure, the slave system and the Southern caste complex, immigration and ethnic heterogeneity, the unusually capitalistic and speculative character of American agriculture, the American inheritance of *laissez faire*. The interpretation seems particularly weak for the corporate-industrial phase of American history that followed the Civil War. Indeed, if the historian's range of vision had to be limited to one explanatory idea, as it fortunately does not, one could easily argue that the business corporation was the dominant dynamic factor in American development during this period.

As a form of geographical determinism, the frontier interpretation is vulnerable on still another ground. If the frontier alone was a self-sufficient source of democracy and individualism, whatever the institutions and ideas the frontiersmen brought with them, frontiers elsewhere ought to have had a similar effect. The early frontier of seignorial French Canada, the South American frontier, and the Siberian frontier should have fostered democracy and individualism. The frontier should have forged the same kind of democracy when planters came to Mississippi as when yeomen farmers came to Illinois. Turner's dictum, "American democracy came out of the American forest," proved to be a questionable improvement upon the notion of his predecessors that it came out of the German forest. Plainly the whole complex of institutions, habits and ideas that men brought to the frontier was left out of his formula, and it was these things, not bare geography, that had been decisive. Turner's analysis, as George Warren Pierson aptly put it, hung too much on real estate, not enough on a state of mind. . . .

One of the most criticized aspects of Turner's conception of American history, the so-called safety-valve thesis, maintains that the availability of free land as a refuge for the oppressed and discontented has alleviated American social conflicts, minimized industrial strife, and contributed to the backwardness of the American labor movement. As Turner expressed it, the American worker was never compelled to accept inferior wages because he could "with a slight effort" reach free country and set up in farming. "Whenever social conditions tended to crystallize in the East, whenever capital tended to impede the freedom of the mass, there was this gate of escape to the free conditions of the frontier," where "free lands promoted individualism, economic equality, freedom to rise, democracy."

The expression "free land" is itself misleading. Land was relatively cheap in the United States during the nineteenth century, but the difference between free land and cheap land was crucial. Up to 1820 the basic price of land was $2.00 an acre, and for years afterward it was $1.25. Slight as it may seem, this represented a large sum to the Eastern worker, whose wage was generally about $1.00 a day. Economic historians have estimated that during the 1850s, $1,000 represented a fairly typical cost for setting up a farm on virgin prairie land, or buying an established one; and the cost of transporting a worker's family from, say, Massachusetts or New York to Illinois or Iowa was a serious additional burden. Farming, moreover, is no enterprise for an amateur, nor one at which he has a good chance of success. The value of "free land" in alleviating distress has been challenged by several writers who have pointed out that periods of depression were the very periods when it was most difficult for the Eastern worker to move. Scattered instances of working-class migration to the West can be pointed to, but detailed studies of the origins of migrants have failed to substantiate the Turner thesis. . . .

Finally, Turner acknowledged but failed to see the full importance 10 for his thesis of the fact that the United States not only had a frontier but was a frontier—a major outlet for the countries of Western Europe during the nineteenth century. From 1820 to 1929, the total European emigration to the United States was more than 37,500,000—a number only a million short of the entire population of the United States in 1870. In one decade alone, 1901–1910, 8,795,000 people came from Europe. If Europe shared to such a major extent in this safety-valve economy, its uniqueness for American development must be considerably modified. The mingling of peoples that took place in the United States must be placed alongside the presence of "free land" in explaining

American development; the closure of the American gates after the First World War becomes an historical event of broader significance than the disappearance of the frontier line in 1890. And the facts of immigration probably provide a better key to the character of the American labor movement than any speculation about the effects of "free land" upon workers who could not reach it.

It should be added, in justice to Turner, that his historical writing was better than his frontier thesis, and not least because he regularly made use in practice of historical factors which were not accounted for in his theory. Although he often stated his ideas with the vigor of a propagandist, his was not a doctrinaire mind, and he was willing, as time went on, to add new concepts to his analysis. In 1925 he went so far as to admit the need of "an urban reinterpretation of our history." "I hope," he frequently said, "to propagate inquiry, not to produce disciples." In fact he did both, but he propagated less inquiry among his disciples than among his critics.

For Journals

Hofstadter says that he is revising Turner, but in effect he comes up with a thesis of his own. How would you state Hofstadter's central idea?

For Discussion

1. What do you think Hofstadter means when he states that, as an analytic device, Turner's frontier theory is "a blunt instrument" (paragraph 5)? What kinds of problems in Turner's approach does that phrase suggest?

2. Hofstadter accuses Turner of intellectual isolationism. In revising Turner's thesis, what kinds of evidence does he include that he says Turner failed to consider in developing his ideas?

3. Hofstadter revises Turner but does not reject him. Where do you find points of agreement or overlap in their theories?

4. Hofstadter thought that Turner overstated the significance of rural life in American history at the expense of the city. Which do you think—rural life or urban life—was more significant as a source of values? Of power?

5. On the basis of your other readings in this book, what do you think of Hofstadter's assertion that emigration to America of millions of people from Europe is a better key to the American character than the idea of available free land in the West?

6. Look back over Turner's thesis and Hofstadter's revision. Which one is more satisfying to you? Intellectually, are they equally interesting? Which one coincides more with your own ideas about why America developed as it did?

For Writing

1. Write a persuasive essay in which you compare two of the central points in Turner's argument with two points of Hofstadter's that disagree. Make clear what each man's assertions are, and decide who you think has the more convincing evidence and why.

2. In your college library, look for primary and secondary materials, including books, periodicals, or photographs, as material for a research paper on one of the following topics: African American cowboys and the West; the great Mexican ranches of California; the Indian cultures of the Southwest; or any other group that is not a part of Turner's thesis. You could focus on an aspect of this group's life in frontier days (for example, influential individuals, significant events, or contributions to American culture). How does being aware of the group cause you to revise your image of the frontier?

3. Turner and Hofstadter are both interested in the idea of American progress. Write an essay about a change in American life that has come about in your own lifetime that you think represents real progress. Is it a result of technology, or of social and political change? Why do you think that this change is important? For contrast, you might ask someone in your parents' generation what he or she thinks of as a major contribution to progress in America.

✿✿✿ *"Indian Belle" crate label* (ca. 1920)

Decorative labels for wooden fruit and vegetable crates were designed to attract attention to a grower's produce at food auctions and to distinguish the grower's produce from that of other farmers. The labels remained very popular before World War II, when wood was needed for the war effort and wooden crates were replaced by metal ones. The labels had as their subjects anything from ethnic stereotypes to famous presidents to animals, flowers, and scenery. Porterville, California, the source of the oranges being advertised, is in the Central Valley, which became the richest agricultural land in the United States in the twentieth century. (See Color Plate VI for a color image of this crate label.)

For Journals

What do you think that an honest and/or attractive image of your state would be? Why?

For Discussion

1. Look up the term "belle" in the dictionary. How was it traditionally applied, and why is it being used here?

2. Look at the young Indian couple. How would you describe their clothing, their posture, and their expressions? How would they be dressed if they were a white courting couple?

3. Crate labels are now much prized by collectors. Why do you think that people want to have them?

For Writing

1. Research and write a paper on crate labels from your state or your part of the country, or from another state such as Florida, New York, California, Pennsylvania, Georgia, and others. There are several books with color illustrations of crate label art from different parts of the country, including *Fruit Crate Art,* by Joe Davidson. You can also write to the American Antiques Graphic Society, P.O. Box 924, Medina, Ohio 44256, for further information on crate labels or other ephemera (perishable older items such as games, dolls, plastics, etc.). Points to consider include exactly what the label or other ephemera looks like; what its intended use was; who was expected to either buy or use it; whether it is a beautiful or an enjoyable creation; and what became of the category to which it belongs. For example, if you did a paper on yoyos, you'd want to see what the newest ones look like, and whether there was any improvement over the originals.

2. Write an essay based on discussion question number 2.

❊❊❊ Coda: *Wilderness Letter* (1960)

WALLACE STEGNER

Wallace Stegner (1909–1993) grew up in Canada and Utah, and much of his writing, including his novels and essays, reflects his love for the wilderness. Stegner was active in the conservationist movement, often working with photographer Ansel Adams to promote national parks and a balance between development and the preservation of open space. The recipient of both the National Book Award and the Pulitzer Prize, Stegner founded the Creative Writing Program at Stanford University.

Los Altos, Calif.
December 3, 1960

David E. Pesonen
Wildland Research Center
Agricultural Experiment Station
243 Mulford Hall
University of California
Berkeley 4, Calif.

Dear Mr. Pesonen:

I believe that you are working on the wilderness portion of the Outdoor Recreation Resources Review Commission's report. If I may, I should like to urge some arguments for wilderness preservation that involve recreation, as it is ordinarily conceived, hardly at all. Hunting, fishing, hiking, mountain-climbing, camping, photography, and the enjoyment of natural scenery will all, surely, figure in your report. So will the wilderness as a genetic reserve, a scientific yardstick by which we may measure the world in its natural balance against the world in its manmade imbalance. What I want to speak for is not so much the wilderness uses, valuable as those are, but the wilderness *idea*, which is a resource in itself. Being an intangible and spiritual resource, it will seem mystical to the practical-minded—but then anything that cannot be moved by a bulldozer is likely to seem mystical to them.

I want to speak for the wilderness idea as something that has helped form our character and that has certainly shaped our history as a people. It has no more to do with recreation than churches have to do with recreation, or than the strenuousness and optimism and expansiveness of what historians call the "American Dream" have to do with recreation. Nevertheless, since it is only in this recreation survey that the values of wilderness are being compiled, I hope you will permit me to insert this idea between the leaves, as it were, of the recreation report.

Something will have gone out of us as a people if we ever let the remaining wilderness be destroyed; if we permit the last virgin forests to be turned into comic books and plastic cigarette cases; if we drive the few remaining members of the wild species into zoos or to extinction; if we pollute the last clear air and dirty the last clean streams and push our paved roads through the last of the silence, so that never again will Americans be free in their own country from the noise, the exhausts, the stinks of human and automotive waste. And so that never again can we have the chance to see ourselves single, separate, vertical and individual in the world, part of the environment of trees and rocks and soil, brother to the other animals, part of the natural world and competent to belong in it. . . . We need wilderness preserved—as much of it as is still left, and as many kinds—because it was the challenge against which our character as a people was formed. The reminder and the reassurance that it is still there is good for our spiritual health even if we never once in ten years set foot in it. It is good for us when we are young, because of the incomparable sanity it can bring briefly, as vacation and rest, into our insane lives. It is important to us when we are old simply because it is there—important, that is, simply as idea.

. . . Not many people are likely, any more, to look upon what we call "progress" as an unmixed blessing. Just as surely as it has brought us increased comfort and more material goods, it has brought us spiritual losses, and it threatens now to become the Frankenstein that will destroy us. One means of sanity is to retain a hold on the natural world, to remain, insofar as we can, good animals. Americans still have that chance, more than many peoples; for while we were demonstrating ourselves the most efficient and ruthless environment-busters in history, and slashing and burning and cutting our way through a wilderness continent, the wilderness was working on us. It remains in us as surely as Indian names remain on the land. If the abstract dream of human liberty and human dignity became, in America, something more than an abstract dream, mark it down at least partially to the fact that we were in subtle ways subdued by what we conquered. . . .

. . . For an American, insofar as he is new and different at all, is a ⁵ civilized man who has renewed himself in the wild. The American experience has been the confrontation by old peoples and cultures of a world as new as if it had just risen from the sea. That gave us our hope and our excitement, and the hope and excitement can be passed on to newer Americans, Americans who never saw any phase of the frontier. But only so long as we keep the remainder of our wild as a reserve and a promise—a sort of wilderness bank. . . . We need to demonstrate our acceptance of the natural world, including ourselves; we need the spiritual refreshment that being natural can produce. And one of the best places for us to get that is in the wilderness where the fun houses, the bulldozers, and the pavements of our civilization are shut out. . . .

. . . For myself, I grew up on the empty plains of Saskatchewan and Montana and in the mountains of Utah, and I put a very high valuation on what those places gave me. And if I had not been able periodically to renew myself in the mountains and deserts of western America I would be very nearly bughouse. Even when I can't get to the back country, the thought of the colored deserts of southern Utah, or the reassurance that there are still stretches of prairie where the world can be instantaneously perceived as disk and bowl, and where the little but intensely important human being is exposed to the five directions and the thirty-six winds, is a positive consolation. The idea alone can sustain me. But as the wilderness areas are progressively exploited or "improved," as the jeeps and bulldozers of uranium prospectors scar up the deserts and the roads are cut into the alpine timberlands, and as the remnants of the unspoiled and natural world are progressively eroded, every such loss is a little death in me. In us.

I am not moved by the argument that those wilderness areas which have already been exposed to grazing or mining are already deflowered, and so might as well be "harvested." For mining I cannot say much good except that its operations are generally short-lived. The extractable wealth is taken and the shafts, the tailings, and the ruins left, and in a dry country such as the American West the wounds men make in the earth do not quickly heal. Still, they are only wounds; they aren't absolutely mortal. Better a wounded wilderness than none at all. And as for grazing, if it is strictly controlled so that it does not destroy the ground cover, damage the ecology, or compete with the wildlife it is in itself nothing that need conflict with the wilderness feeling or the validity of the wilderness experience. I have known enough range cattle to recognize them as wild animals; and the people who herd them have, in the wilderness context, the dignity of rareness; they belong on the frontier, moreover, and have a look of rightness. The invasion they make on the virgin country is a sort of invasion that is as old as Neolithic man, and they can, in moderation, even emphasize a man's feeling of belonging to the natural world. Under surveillance, they can belong; under control, they need not deface or mar. I do not believe that in wilderness areas where grazing has never been permitted, it should be permitted; but I do not believe either that an otherwise untouched wilderness should be eliminated from the preservation plan because of limited existing uses such as grazing which are in consonance with the frontier condition and image.

Let me say something on the subject of the kinds of wilderness worth preserving. Most of those areas contemplated are in the national forests and in high mountain country. For all the usual recreational purposes, the alpine and forest wildernesses are obviously the most important, both as genetic banks and as beauty spots. But for the spiritual renewal, the recognition of identity, the birth of awe, other kinds will serve every bit as well. Perhaps, because they are less friendly to life, more abstractly nonhuman, they will serve even better. On our Saskatchewan prairie, the nearest neighbor was four miles away, and at night we saw only two lights on all the dark rounding earth. The earth was full of animals—field mice, ground squirrels, weasels, ferrets, badgers, coyotes, burrowing owls, snakes. . . .

So are great reaches of our western deserts, scarred somewhat by prospectors but otherwise open, beautiful, waiting, close to whatever God you want to see in them. Just as a sample, let me suggest the Robbers' Roost country in Wayne County, Utah, near the Capitol Reef National Monument. In that desert climate the dozer and jeep tracks will not soon melt back into the earth, but the country has a way of making the scars insignificant. It is a lovely and terrible wilderness, such a wilderness as Christ and the prophets went out into; harshly and beautifully colored, broken and worn until its bones are exposed, its great sky without a smudge or taint from Technocracy, and in hidden corners and pockets under its cliffs the sudden poetry of springs. Save a piece of country like that intact, and it does not matter in the slightest that only a few people every year will go into it. That is precisely its value. Roads would be a desecration, crowds would ruin it. But those who haven't the strength or youth to go into it and live can simply sit and look. They can look two hundred miles, clear into Colorado; and looking down over the cliffs and canyons of the San Rafael Swell and the Robbers' Roost they can also look as deeply into themselves as anywhere I know. And if they can't even get to the places on the Aquarius Plateau where the present roads will carry them, they can simply contemplate the *idea,* take pleasure in the fact that such a timeless and uncontrolled part of earth is still there.

These are some of the things wilderness can do for us. That is the 10 reason we need to put into effect, for its preservation, some other principle than the principles of exploitation or "usefulness" or even recreation. We simply need that wild country available to us, even if we never do more than drive to its edge and look in. For it can be a means of reassuring ourselves of our sanity as creatures, a part of the geography of hope.

Very sincerely yours,
WALLACE STEGNER

For Journals

Do you go hiking or camping in national parks or other wilderness areas? If not, do you nevertheless support the idea of saving wilderness?

For Discussion

1. Stegner says that he wants to argue not for the wilderness but for the idea of the wilderness (paragraph 1). What do you think he means by the idea as opposed to the reality of the wilderness? Why should the idea be protected?

2. How did you respond to Stegner's assertion that Americans—even Americans who have never set foot in the wilderness—will lose the wilderness if it is destroyed?

3. How does Stegner think the development of technology and urban life have affected Americans? What advantage does he feel that Americans who were exposed to the frontier gained?

4. Why does Stegner think that the relatively undramatic prairies and the deserts are as worthy of preservation as the more spectacular forest and alpine areas? How does emphasizing them help or harm his thesis?

5. Stegner was always interested in conflicting attitudes toward nature and development. Where do his sympathies lie? Yours?

6. Stegner says that ". . . an American, insofar as he is new and different at all, is a civilized man who has renewed himself in the wild." According to that definition, where does that leave the Indians and the city dwellers? What kinds of Americans are they?

For Writing

1. Write an essay about an urban place you know—an open space, a part of an old neighborhood, a small city park, a favorite store, a place that a parent used to take you to or that you shared with a childhood friend—and you want to see preserved. Explain what its emotional and spiritual value are to you and why you would like it to stay the way it is. Your research may include firsthand observation, interviews with other people familiar with the place, and library research. For example, if you are interested in an old movie theater, look for source materials on historic preservation and old movie palaces.

2. Write a paper in which you compare Stegner's and Turner's ideas of the how the wilderness has shaped American character. In which instances does Stegner sound like Turner? How does each of them define what makes an American different? (Just use one section of Turner for purposes of this comparison, like the ones on national character or democracy).

3. Write a reflective essay comparing what Stegner loves about the wilderness with what Edward Abbey loves about the desert. Choose two, or at the most three, examples from each as evidence, and explain which author's attitude is more moving or convincing to you.

✼✼ *The Great American Desert* (1977)

EDWARD ABBEY

Edward Abbey (1927–1989) was born in Pennsylvania but fell in love with the West as a teenager after he had hitchhiked around it. As an environmentalist he loved the wilderness, but he writes with joy at what he sees, as well as with the exactness of a great observer. This essay is from his book The Journey Home: Essays in Defense of the American West *(1977).*

In my case it was love at first sight. This desert, all deserts, any desert. No matter where my head and feet may go, my heart and my entrails stay behind, here on the clean, true, comfortable rock, under the black sun of God's forsaken country. When I take on my next incarnation, my bones will remain bleaching nicely in a stone gulch under the rim of some faraway plateau, way out there in the back of beyond. An unrequited and excessive love, inhuman no doubt but painful anyhow, especially when I see my desert under attack. "The one death I cannot bear," said the Sonoran-Arizonan poet Richard Shelton. The kind of love that makes a man selfish, possessive, irritable. If you're thinking of a visit, my natural reaction is like a rattlesnake's—to warn you off. What I want to say goes something like this.

Survival Hint #1: Stay out of there. Don't go. Stay home and read a good book, this one for example. The Great American Desert is an awful place. People get hurt, get sick, get lost out there. Even if you survive, which is not certain, you will have a miserable time. The desert is for movies and God-intoxicated mystics, not for family recreation.

Let me enumerate the hazards. First the Walapai tiger, also known as conenose kissing bug. *Triatoma protracta* is a true bug, black as sin, and it flies through the night quiet as an assassin. It does not attack directly like a mosquito or deerfly, but alights at a discreet distance, undetected, and creeps upon you, its hairy little feet making not the slightest noise. The kissing bug is fond of warmth and like Dracula requires mammalian blood for sustenance. When it reaches you the bug crawls onto your skin so gently, so softly that unless your senses are hyperacute you feel nothing. Selecting a tender point, the bug slips its conical proboscis into your flesh, injecting a poisonous anesthetic. If you are asleep you will feel nothing. If you happen to be awake you may notice the faintest of pinpricks, hardly more than a brief ticklish sensation, which you will probably disregard. But the bug is already at work. Having numbed the nerves near the point of entry the bug proceeds (with a sigh of satisfaction, no doubt) to withdraw blood. When its belly is filled, it pulls out, backs off, and waddles away, so drunk and gorged it cannot fly.

At about this time the victim awakes, scratching at a furious itch. If you recognize the symptoms at once, you can sometimes find the bug in your vicinity and destroy it. But revenge will be your only satisfaction. Your night is ruined. If you are of average sensitivity to a kissing bug's poison, your entire body breaks out in hives, skin aflame from head to toe. Some people become seriously ill, in many cases requiring hospitalization. Others recover fully after five or six hours except for a hard and itchy swelling, which may endure for a week.

After the kissing bug, you should beware of rattlesnakes; we have 5 half a dozen species, all offensive and dangerous, plus centipedes, millipedes, tarantulas, black widows, brown recluses, Gila monsters, the deadly poisonous coral snakes, and giant hairy desert scorpions. Plus an immense variety and near-infinite number of ants, midges, gnats, bloodsucking flies, and blood-guzzling mosquitoes. (You might think the desert would be spared at least mosquitoes? Not so. Peer in any water hole by day: swarming with mosquito larvae. Venture out on a summer's eve: The air vibrates with their mournful keening.) Finally, where the desert meets the sea, as on the coasts of Sonora and Baja California, we have the usual assortment of obnoxious marine life: sandflies, ghost crabs, stingrays, electric jellyfish, spiny sea urchins, man-eating sharks, and other creatures so distasteful one prefers not even to name them.

It has been said, and truly, that everything in the desert either stings, stabs, stinks, or sticks. You will find the flora here as venomous, hooked barbed, thorny, prickly, needled, saw-toothed, hairy, stickered, mean, bitter, sharp, wiry, and fierce as the animals. Something about the desert inclines all living things to harshness and acerbity. The soft evolve out. Except for sleek and oily growths like the poison ivy—oh yes, indeed—that flourish in sinister profusion on the dank walls above the quicksand down in those corridors of gloom and labyrinthine monotony that men call canyons.

We come now to the third major hazard, which is sunshine. Too much of a good thing can be fatal. Sunstroke, heatstroke, and dehydration are common misfortunes in the bright American Southwest. If you can avoid the insects, reptiles, and arachnids, the cactus and the ivy, the smog of the southwestern cities, and the lung fungus of the desert valleys (carried by dust in the air), you cannot escape the desert sun. Too much exposure to it eventually causes, quite literally, not merely sunburn but skin cancer.

Much sun, little rain also means an arid climate. Compared with the high humidity of more hospitable regions, the dry heat of the desert seems at first not terribly uncomfortable—sometimes even pleasant. But that sensation of comfort is false, a deception, and therefore all the more dangerous, for it induces overexertion and an insufficient consumption of water, even when water is available. This leads to various internal complications, some immediate—sunstroke, for example—and some not apparent until much later. Mild but prolonged dehydration, continued over a span of months or years, leads to the crystallization of mineral solutions in the urinary tract, that is, to what urologists call urinary calculi or kidney stones. A disability common in all the world's arid regions. Kidney stones, in case you haven't met one, come in many shapes and sizes, from pellets smooth as BB shot to highly irregular calcifications resembling asteroids, Vietcong shrapnel, and crown-of-thorns starfish. Some of these objects may be "passed" naturally; others can be removed only by means of the Davis stone basket or by surgery. Me—I was lucky; I passed mine with only a groan, my forehead pressed against the wall of a pissoir in the rear of a Tucson bar that I cannot recommend.

You may be getting the impression by now that the desert is not the most suitable of environments for human habitation. Correct. Of all the Earth's climatic zones, excepting only the Antarctic, the deserts are the least inhabited, the least "developed," for reasons that should now be clear.

You may wish to ask, Yes, okay, but among North American 10
deserts which is the *worst*? A good question—and I am happy to attempt to answer.

Geographers generally divide the North American desert—what was once termed "the Great American Desert"—into four distinct regions or subdeserts. These are the Sonoran Desert, which comprises southern Arizona, Baja California, and the state of Sonora in Mexico; the Chihuahuan Desert, which includes west Texas, southern New Mexico, and the states of Chihuahua and Coahuila in Mexico; the Mojave Desert, which includes southeastern California and small portions of Nevada, Utah, and Arizona; and the Great Basin Desert, which includes most of Utah and Nevada, northern Arizona, northwestern New Mexico, and much of Idaho and eastern Oregon.

Privately, I prefer my own categories. Up north in Utah somewhere is the canyon country—places like Zeke's Hole, Death Hollow, Pucker Pass, Buckskin Gulch, Nausea Crick, Wolf Hole,

Mollie's Nipple, Dirty Devil River, Horse Canyon, Horseshoe Canyon, Lost Horse Canyon, Horsethief Canyon, and Horseshit Canyon, to name only the more classic places. Down in Arizona and Sonora there's the cactus country; if you have nothing better to do, you might take a look at High Tanks, Salome Creek, Tortilla Flat, Esperero ("Hoper") Canyon, Holy Joe Peak, Depression Canyon, Painted Cave, Hell Hole Canyon, Hell's Half Acre, Iceberg Canyon, Tiburon (Shark) Island, Pinacate Peak, Infernal Valley, Sykes Crater, Montezuma's Head, Gu Oidak, Kuakatch, Pisinimo, and Baboquivari Mountain, for example.

Then there's The Canyon. *The* Canyon. The Grand. That's one world. And North Rim—that's another. And Death Valley, still another, where I lived one winter near Furnace Creek and climbed the Funeral Mountains, tasted Badwater, looked into the Devil's Hole, hollered up Echo Canyon, searched for and never did find Seldom Seen Slim. Looked for *satori* near Vana, Nevada, and found a ghost town named Bonnie Claire. Never made it to Winnemucca. Drove through the Smoke Creek Desert and down through Big Pine and Lone Pine and home across the Panamints to Death Valley again— home sweet home that winter.

And which of these deserts is the worst? I find it hard to judge. They're all bad—not half bad but all bad. In the Sonoran Desert, Phoenix will get you if the sun, snakes, bugs, and arthropods don't. In the Mojave Desert, it's Las Vegas, more sickening by far than the Glauber's salt in the Death Valley sinkholes. Go to Chihuahua and you're liable to get busted in El Paso and sandbagged in Ciudad Juárez—where all old whores go to die. Up north in the Great Basin Desert, on the Plateau Province, in the canyon country, your heart will break, seeing the strip mines open up and the power plants rise where only cowboys and Indians and J. Wesley Powell ever roamed before.

Nevertheless, all is not lost; much remains, and I welcome the 15 prospect of an army of lug-soled hiker's boots on the desert trails. To save what wilderness is left in the American Southwest—and in the American Southwest only the wilderness is worth saving—we are going to need all the recruits we can get. All the hands, heads, bodies, time, money, effort we can find. Presumably—and the Sierra Club, the Wilderness Society, the Friends of the Earth, the Audubon Society, the Defenders of Wildlife operate on this theory—those who learn to love what is spare, rough, wild, undeveloped, and unbroken will be willing to fight for it, will help resist the strip miners, highway builders, land developers, weapons testers, power producers, tree chainers, clear cutters, oil drillers, dam beavers, subdividers—the list goes on and on— before that zinc-hearted, termite-brained, squint-eyed, nearsighted, greedy crew succeeds in completely californicating what still survives of the Great American Desert.

So much for the Good Cause. Now what about desert hiking itself, you may ask. I'm glad you asked that question. I firmly believe that one should never—I repeated *never*—go out into that formidable wasteland of cactus, heat, serpents, rock, scrub, and thorn without careful planning, thorough and cautious preparation, and complete—never mind the expense!—*complete* equipment. My motto is: Be Prepared.

That is my belief and that is my motto. My practice, however, is a little different. I tend to go off in a more or less random direction myself, half-baked, half-assed, half-cocked, and half-ripped. Why? Well, because I have an indolent and melancholy nature and don't care to be bothered getting all those *things* together—all that bloody *gear*—maps, compass, binoculars, poncho, pup tent, shoes, first-aid kit, rope, flashlight, inspirational poetry, water, food—and because anyhow I approach nature with a certain surly ill-will, daring Her to make trouble. Later when I'm deep into Natural Bridges Natural Moneymint or Zion National Parkinglot or say General Shithead National Forest Land of Many Abuses why then, of course, when it's a bit late, then I may wish I had packed that something extra: matches perhaps, to mention one useful item, or maybe a spoon to eat my gruel with.

If I hike with another person it's usually the same; most of my friends have indolent and melancholy natures too. A cursed lot, all of them. I think of my comrade John De Puy, for example, sloping along for mile after mile like a goddamned camel—indefatigable—with those J. C. Penney hightops on his feet and that plastic pack on his back he got with five books of Green Stamps and nothing inside it but a sketchbook, some homemade jerky and a few cans of green chiles. Or Douglas Peacock, ex-Green Beret, just the opposite. Built like a buffalo, he loads a ninety-pound canvas pannier on his back at trailhead, loaded with guns, ammunition, bayonet, pitons and carabiners, cameras, field books, a 150-foot rope, geologist's sledge, rock samples, assay kit, field glasses, two gallons of water in steel canteens, jungle boots, a case of C-rations, rope hammock, pharmaceuticals in a pig-iron box, raincoat, overcoat, two-man mountain tent, Dutch oven, hibachi, shovel, ax, inflatable boat, and near the top of the load and distributed through side and back pockets, easily accessible, a case of beer. Not because he enjoys or needs all that weight—he may never get to the bottom of that cargo on a ten-day outing—but simply because Douglas uses his packbag for general storage both at home and on the trail and prefers not to have to rearrange everything from time to time merely for the purposes of a hike. Thus my friends De Puy and Peacock; you may wish to avoid such extremes.

A few tips on desert etiquette:

1. Carry a cooking stove, if you must cook. Do not burn desert wood, which is rare and beautiful and required ages for its creation (an ironwood tree lives for over 1,000 years and juniper almost as long).

2. If you must, out of need, build a fire, then for God's sake allow it to burn itself out before you leave—do not bury it, as Boy Scouts and Campfire Girls do, under a heap of mud or sand. Scatter the ashes; replace any rocks you may have used in constructing a fireplace; do all you can to obliterate the evidence that you camped here. (The Search & Rescue Team may be looking for you.)

3. Do not bury garbage—the wildlife will only dig it up again. Burn what will burn and pack out the rest. The same goes for toilet paper: Don't bury it, *burn it.*

4. Do not bathe in desert pools, natural tanks, *tinajas,* potholes. Drink what water you need, take what you need, and leave the rest for the next hiker and more important for the bees, birds, and animals—bighorn sheep, coyotes, lions, foxes, badgers, deer, wild pigs, wild horses—whose *lives* depend on that water.

5. Always remove and destroy survey stakes, flagging, advertising signboards, mining claim markers, animal traps, poisoned bait, seismic exploration geophones, and other such artifacts of industrialism. The men who put those things there are up to no good and it is our duty to confound them. Keep America Beautiful. Grow a Beard. Take a Bath. Burn a Billboard.

Anyway—why go into the desert? Really, why do it? That sun, [20] roaring at you all day long. The fetid, tepid, vapid little water holes slowly evaporating under a scum of grease, full of cannibal beetles, spotted toads, horsehair worms, liver flukes, and down at the bottom, inevitably, the pale cadaver of a ten-inch centipede. Those pink rattlesnakes down in The Canyon, those diamondback monsters thick as a truck driver's wrist that lurk in shady places along the trail, those unpleasant solpugids and unnecessary Jerusalem crickets that scurry on dirty claws across your face at night. Why? The rain that comes down like lead shot and wrecks the trail, those sudden rockfalls of obscure origin that crash like thunder ten feet behind you in the heart of a dead-still afternoon. The ubiquitous buzzard, so patient—but only so patient. The sullen and hostile Indians, all on welfare. The ragweed, the tumbleweed, the Jimson weed, the snakeweed. The scorpion in your shoe at dawn. The dreary wind that blows all spring, the psychedelic Joshua trees waving their arms at you on moonlight nights. Sand in the soup du jour. Halazone tablets in your canteen. The barren hills that always go up, which is bad, or down, which is worse. Those canyons like catacombs with quicksand lapping at your crotch. Hollow, mummified horses with forelegs casually crossed, dead for ten years, leaning against the corner of a barbed-wire fence. Packhorses at night, iron-shod, clattering over the slickrock through your camp. The last tin of tuna, two flat tires, not enough water and a forty-mile trek to Tule Well. An osprey on a cardón cactus, snatching the head off a living fish—always the best part first. The hawk sailing by at 200 feet, a squirming snake in its talons. Salt in the drinking water. Salt, selenium, arsenic, radon and radium in the water, in the gravel, in your bones. Water so hard it bends light, drills holes in rock and chokes up your radiator. Why go there? Those places with the hardcase names: Starvation Creek, Poverty Knoll, Hungry Valley, Bitter Springs, Last Chance Canyon, Dungeon Canyon, Whipsaw Flat, Dead Horse Point, Scorpion Flat, Dead Man Draw, Stinking Spring, Camino del Diablo, Jornado del Muerto . . . Death Valley.

Well then, why indeed go walking into the desert, that grim ground, that bleak and lonesome land where, as Genghis Khan said of India, "the heat is bad and the water makes men sick"?

Why the desert, when you could be strolling along the golden beaches of California? Camping by a stream of pure Rocky Mountain spring water in colorful Colorado? Loafing through a laurel slick in the misty hills of North Carolina? Or getting your head mashed in the greasy alley behind the Élysium Bar and Grill in Hoboken, New Jersey? Why the desert, given a world of such splendor and variety?

A friend and I took a walk around the base of a mountain up beyond Coconino County, Arizona. This was a mountain we'd been planning to circumambulate for years. Finally we put on our walking shoes and did it. About halfway around this mountain, on the third or fourth day, we paused for a while—two days—by the side of a stream, which the Navajos call Nasja because of the amber color of the water. (Caused perhaps by juniper roots—the water seems safe enough to drink.) On our second day there I walked down the stream, alone, to look at the canyon beyond. I entered the canyon and followed it for half the afternoon, for three or four miles, maybe, until it became a gorge so deep, narrow and dark, full of water and the inevitable quagmires of quicksand, that I turned around and looked for a way out. A route other than the way I'd come, which was crooked and uncomfortable and buried—I wanted to see what was up on top of this world. I found a sort of chimney flue on the east wall, which looked plausible, and sweated and cursed my way up through that until I reached a point where I could walk upright, like a human being. Another 300 feet of scrambling brought me to the rim of the canyon. No one, I felt certain, had ever before departed Nasja Canyon by that route.

But someone had. Near the summit I found an arrow sign, three feet long, formed of stones and pointing off into the north toward those same old purple vistas, so grand, immense, and mysterious, of more canyons, more mesas and plateaus, more mountains, more cloud-dappled sun-spangled leagues of desert sand and desert rock, under the same old wide and aching sky.

The arrow pointed into the north. But what was it pointing *at?* I 25 looked at the sign closely and saw that those dark, desert-varnished stones had been in place for a long, long, time; they rested in compacted dust. They must have been there for a century at least. I followed the direction indicated and came promptly to the rim of another canyon and a drop-off straight down of a good 500 feet. Not that way, surely. Across this canyon was nothing of any unusual interest that I could see—only the familiar sun-blasted sandstone, a few scrubby clumps of blackbrush and prickly pear, a few acres of nothing where only a lizard could graze, surrounded by a few square miles of more nothingness interesting chiefly to horned toads. I returned to the arrow and checked again, this time with field glasses, looking away for as far as my aided eyes could see toward the north, for ten, twenty, forty miles into the distance. I studied the scene with care, looking for an ancient Indian ruin, a significant cairn, perhaps an abandoned mine, a hidden treasure of some inconceivable wealth, the mother of all mother lodes. . . .

But there was nothing out there. Nothing at all. Nothing but the desert. Nothing but the silent world.

That's why.

For Journals

At the very end of the essay, Abbey says, "That's why." What question is he answering?

For Discussion

1.   What are the three major "hazards" that Abbey describes as reasons to stay away from the desert?

2.   Abbey explains how people usually define the Great American Desert; why do you think he likes to categorize it differently? What does the way he categorizes tell you about his relationship with the place?

3.   Why does Abbey tell us all the things that are wrong with the desert? Is he serious about discouraging us from coming? What do you think he would like our response to be?

4.   What's Abbey's explanation for not following his own good advice about how to go camping in the desert?

For Writing

1.   Take one section of Abbey's essay and analyze it, for the appeals it makes, for its use of humor or irony, for its diction, and for whatever else about it strikes you as noteworthy. Some possible sections are these: the kissing bug; desert etiquette; and how not to go camping

2.   Critics have noticed that, like Twain, Abbey can write about nature beautifully but also humorously. Find a passage in which Abbey accomplishes this and read it aloud. Then write an essay in which you analyze the rhetorical strategies he uses—persuasiveness, irony, choice of detail, language, and so on—to write a close description of a natural phenomenon with humor.

3.   Abbey, Twain, Lewis and Clark, Stegner—all place a high value on the wilderness. Take Abbey and one of the other writers, and explain what you think that the psychological, spiritual, or social values of the wilderness are to them. They may have different reasons, and the times or circumstances in which they live certainly affect how they respond, but concentrate on what you think are the most important aspects of the wilderness to their wholeness as human beings. Use short quotations as appropriate to act as evidence for your claims.

✵✵ *Dear John Wayne* (1984)

LOUISE ERDRICH

Louise Erdrich (1954–) is a Native American novelist, poet, and essayist who teaches at Dartmouth College. She was born in Minnesota and grew up near a reservation in North Dakota, where her Native American mother and German father worked for the Bureau of Indian Affairs. She is the author of the novels Love Medicine *(1984),* The Beet Queen *(1986),* The Bingo Palace *(1994),* The Blue Jay's Dance *(1995), and* The Antelope Wife *(1998), as well as short stories and poems. She and her deceased husband, Michael Dorris, coauthored a novel,* The Crown of Columbus *(1991). "Dear John Wayne" is a wonderful example of Erdrich's ability to explore how differently white Americans and American Indians experience the mythology of the frontier.*

August and the drive-in picture is packed.
We lounge on the hood of the Pontiac
surrounded by the slow-burning spirals they sell

at the window, to vanquish the hordes of mosquitoes.
Nothing works. They break through the smoke-screen   5
   for blood.

Always the look-out spots the Indians first,
spread north to south, barring progress.
The Sioux, or Cheyenne, or some bunch
in spectacular columns, arranged like SAC missiles,
their feathers bristling in the meaningful sunset.   10

The drum breaks. There will be no parlance.
Only the arrows whining, a death-cloud of nerves
swarming down on the settlers
who die beautifully, tumbling like dust weeds
into the history that brought us all here   15
together: this wide screen beneath the sign of the bear.

The sky fills, acres of blue squint and eye
that the crowd cheers. His face moves over us,
a thick cloud of vengeance, pitted
like the land that was once flesh. Each rut,   20
each scar makes a promise: *It is*
not over, this fight, not as long as you resist.

Everything we see belongs to us.
A few laughing Indians fall over the hood
slipping in the hot spilled butter.   25
The eye sees a lot, John, but the heart is so blind.
How will you know what you own?
He smiles, a horizon of teeth
the credits reel over, and then the white fields
again blowing in the true-to-life dark.   30
The dark films over everything.
We get into the car
scratching our mosquito bites, speechless and small
as people are when the movie is done.
We are back in ourselves.   35

How can we help but keep hearing his voice,
the flip side of the sound-track, still playing:
Come on, boys, we've got them
where we want them, drunk, running.
They will give us what we want, what we need: 40
The heart is a strange wood inside of everything
we see, burning, doubling, splitting out of its skin.

For Journals

Where do your own ideas of the West come from? Movies? If so, which ones? What other sources? Where else could you find information about the West?

For Discussion

1. Read the poem out loud, all the way through. Then go back to the beginning, and in each stanza find three or four words that are either unexpected or particularly effective. What do they contribute to the theme of each stanza? How?

2. Compare this poem with the article and illustration from the *Police Gazette*. How does the view of Indians in the *Gazette* compare with the portrayal of them in the John Wayne movie? With the Indians watching the movie at the drive-in?

3. What values does the image of John Wayne usually represent? How does Erdrich's attitude toward him revise that image?

4. How do you think that Erdrich would see the settling of the West compared with the way Turner sees it? Whose evidence do you find more persuasive? Why?

5. If the Indians had written the film script, how do you think they would write the battle scene? What kind of movie do you think they could make about whites and Indians on the frontier?

6. How does Erdrich use ironic details like the drive-in movie and the fact that the American Indians have a car named for an Indian chief to suggest Indians' ambivalence toward American culture and their place in it? What other examples of this irony can you find in the poem?

For Writing

1. Investigate books and scholarly articles for material on the Battle of Little Big Horn. Write a documented paper in which you compare an earlier version of the story—from newspaper stories at the time of the battle, or older books about it—with recent versions, such as Evan Connell's *Son of the Morning Star*. How have evaluations of Custer, his strategy, and the battle been revised?

2. Watch a John Wayne Western, like *She Wore a Yellow Ribbon*, and then write an essay in which you examine his character's relationship with the Indians, the battle scene, and the dialogue that is spoken by the Indians, if any. Does it support Erdrich's revisionist view of Wayne as the archetypal Western movie star? Are the Indians the enemy, or is the situation more complicated than that?

❀❀ *The Next Last Frontier* (1993)

JONATHAN RABAN

Jonathan Raban (1942–) was born in Great Britain but lives in Seattle. He is the author of novels, literary criticism, and works of social commentary, travel, and exploration. This selection is from an article he wrote for Harper's magazine, after he had traveled through the Northwest from Washington State to Idaho to Montana.

In the spring of 1990 I packed up as much of my life in London as would fit into four tea chests and flew to Seattle to set up house. It was a selfish and irregular move. I had "met someone" and liked what I'd seen of the Pacific Northwest during a two-month stay there in the autumn of 1989: the aquarium lighting, the sawtooth alps forested with black firs, the compact cities encrusted in Romanesque stucco. Most of all, I liked the place's wateriness. At forty-seven I felt cracked and dry. My new home territory was as rainy as Ireland, puddled with lakes and veined with big rivers. Seattle was built out on pilings over the sea, and at high tide the whole city seemed to come afloat like a ship lifting free from a mud berth and swaying in its chains.

We took a house on the wrong side of Queen Anne, the innermost of Seattle's hilltop suburbs. The tall wooden house, built like a boat from massive scantlings of Douglas fir, carvel-planked with cedar, had been put up in 1906, in the wake of the Yukon gold rush, when the hill was logged. It had warped and settled through a string of minor earthquakes: the floors sloped, doors hung askew in their frames. In the silence of the night, the house groaned and whiffled like a sleeping dog.

Barely a mile from the new banking and insurance skyscrapers of downtown, the house felt hidden away in the woods. Shaggy conifers, survivors of the original forest, darkened the views from every window. The study looked down over the Ship Canal, where trawlers stalked through an avenue of poplars on their way to the Alaskan fishing grounds, eight hundred miles to the north. From the deck on the top floor, one could see out over the pale suburbs, like shell middens, to the serrated line of the Cascade mountains, still snowcapped in May.

For someone fresh off the plane from London, it was a big prospect to take in, and a hard one in which to make oneself at home. It had been fine to be a tourist in this landscape, when I had been enjoyably awed by its far-western heights and distances; but now that I'd signed up as a permanent resident, the view from the window seemed only to reflect my own displacement here.

Even the very near-at-hand was strange. I kept Peterson's *Western* 5 *Birds* and the Audubon Society's *Western Forests* by the typewriter. I made lists, and pinned them to the wall. *Redwood, cedar, cypress, dog-*

wood, laurel, madrona, maple, I wrote, trying to distinguish individual personalities in the jumble of damp and muddy greens framed by the window. I took the tree book down to the garden and matched the real-life barks with their pictures; the peeling, fish-scale skin of the lodge-pole pine, the frayed hemp rope of the coast redwood. It took a month, at least, to be able to see the black-crested Steller's jay in the madrona with something like the comfortable indifference with which I'd used to notice a song thrush in the sycamore in Battersea. It took a good deal longer to adjust to the way the rufous hummingbird, like a tiny thrashing autogiro, redisposed itself in space, zapping from point to point too fast for the eye to follow. Glancing up from the typewriter, stuck for a phrase, I'd sight a bald eagle, circling on a thermal over the Ship Canal on huge stiff ragged wings, and lose the logic of the sentence to another bout of ornithology.

The German word for "uncanny," as in Freud's famous essay on the Uncanny, is *unheimlich*—unhomely. The tourist thrives on the uncanny, moving happily through a phenomenal world of effects without causes. This world, in which he has no experience and no memory, is presented to him as a supernatural domain: the language of travel advertising hawks the uncanny as part of the deal. Experience the *magic* of Bali! the *wonders* of Hawaii! the *enchantment* of Bavaria!

But for the newly arrived immigrant, this magic stuff is like a curse. He's faced at every turn with the unhomelikeness of things, in an uncanny realm where the familiar house sparrows have all fled, to be replaced by hummingbirds and eagles. The immigrant needs to grow a memory, and grow it fast. Somehow or other, he must learn to convert the uncanny into the homely, in order to find a stable footing in his new land. . . .

November 1992 and the snow level, said Harry Wappler, our TV weatherman, was down to 3,500 feet and dropping fast. In a week the mountain passes would be tricky and the back roads closed for the winter. I dug out of storage my never-used box of tire chains and set off on a wide swing around the neighborhood.

It was high time to make the trip: though I had been living in Seattle for more than two years, I was still confused as to its whereabouts. I knew the city better than its cabdrivers (a very modest boast), but I'd barely begun to work out how Seattle fitted into the larger story. A long drive, on empty western roads where it's still possible to think with one's foot down, would, with luck, thread the oddly assorted bits of the Pacific Northwest onto one string and set them in narrative order.

The afternoon rush hour had started by the time I got away, and 10 on Interstate 90 heading east, the cars were locked bumper-to-bumper on the floating bridge over Lake Washington. The sky was lightless, and the windshield wipers scraped on the glass in the fall moisture, typical of these parts, that was something more than mist and less than rain. The traffic jam was typical of these parts, too: a ceremonious procession, like a funeral, of VWs with ski racks on their tops and I'D RATHER BE SAILING stickers on their rear ends. A lot of higher education was stuck on the bridge that afternoon. The names of the universities from which the drivers had graduated were posted in their back windows—faraway schools, mostly, like Syracuse, M.I.T., Columbia, Missouri, Michigan.

My own car, a low-slung, thirsty, black Dodge Daytona with a working ashtray, marked me out as a Yahoo among the Houyhnhnms— too old, dirty, and wasteful to pass as a member of Seattle's uniquely refined middle class. Stuffed into the book bag beside the work of the northwestern writers whom I had brought along for the ride (Richard Hugo, Ursula K. Le Guin, Raymond Carver, Katherine Dunn, William Stafford, Norman Maclean, James Welch, James Crumley) was a bottle of Teacher's, two-thirds full, which would have been okay by the northwestern writers but thought a very low touch by these northwestern drivers. In Seattle, a double shot of non-decaffeinated espresso was thought to be pushing the boat out farther than was wise.

In shifts and starts, we lurched into Eastside Seattle, Houyhnhnm country, where the VWs began to peel off to the Bellevue exits. Bellevue and its satellites were not suburbs so much as—in the rising term—an "edge city," with its own economy, sociology, and architecture. Things made on the Eastside were odorless, labor-intensive, and credit-card thin, like computer software and aerospace-related electronics gear. They were assembled in low, tree-shaded factories, whose grounds were known as "campuses"—for in Bellevue all work was graduate work, and the jargon of college leaked naturally into the workplace. Seen from an elevated-freeway distance, Bellevue looked like one of its own products: a giant circuit board of color-coded diodes and resistors, connected by a mazy grid of filaments.

During the presidential campaign, Bill Clinton had jetted around the country, calling for the advent of the "high-growth, high-wage, smart-work society"—a fair description of Bellevue, with its lightly rooted, highly trained workforce, its safe streets, its scented malls sprayed with composerless light orchestral music, its air of bland good conscience. Bellevue was the new and hopeful face of American capitalism, and it had a strongly Japanese cast to its features. The one-and two-story campuses with their radial walkways reflected a style of business management that was closer to the industrial collectives of Tokyo than to the moribund hierarchies of Detroit and the American Rust Belt.

The place looked like somebody's utopia, more a model city than an actual one, and it was inhabited by the kinds of people whom architects like to place as strolling figures in the foregrounds of watercolor sketches of their projects. Wherever the eye wandered in Bellevue, it lit on another 31C\v-year-old, with a master's if not a doctorate, dressed for work in hiking shoes and chunky sweater. Thousands of these diagrammatic people were housed along I-90 in white-painted, shingled faux–New England condo blocks called "villages." Lakefront Village . . . Redwood Village . . . Olde Towne Village . . . communities in which the villagers met in the evenings at neighboring Exercycles in the village health club or at a pre-breakfast tee-off on the village driving range.

Eastside Seattle was a new kind of American city, though it had a 15 lot in common with the long-established retirement paradises of Florida and southern California. People in their twenties and thirties were now moving (as their parents had done only toward the ends of their lives) for the sake of the climate and the natural amenities of a place rather than just for the jobs offered there. They were coming to Seattle in much the same way as people had gone to Venice, California, and to Miami Beach; the difference was that they were coming at the beginnings of their careers. So they arrived, as kayakers, hikers, balloonists, bird-watchers, skiers, and mountain bikers who also happened to have degrees in math and marketing and computer science. Their Pacific Northwest was really a civic park, roughly the same size as France, equipped with golf courses, hiking trails, rock-climbing routes, boat-launch ramps, ski lifts, campgrounds, and scenic overlooks. This great migration of open-air hobbyists (which dated from about 1980—the early Reagan years) had won Seattle a curious niche in urban history, as the first big city to which people had fled in order to be closer to nature.

Sixteen miles out of Seattle the eastward march of the city was stopped in its tracks by the foothills of the Cascades. Beyond Issaquah the black cliffs of the forest began, and the social character of the road abruptly changed, as the last of the VWs melted into the last of the white condo blocks. Up till now I'd been in the fast lane; no longer. Mud-slathered pickups with jumbo tires charged past the Dodge wearing angry slogans on their tailgates: JOBS BEFORE OWLS. SUPPORT THE TIMBER INDUSTRY. SAVE A LOGGER—SHOOT AN OWL. Behind the glass of a cab window, a Zippo lighter flashed in the gloaming.

Small charcoal-colored clouds were snagged in the firs. We were climbing steadily now, the road wet, the light failing fast. Each bend in the road opened on another wall of Douglas fir, the trees as dense and regularly spaced as the bristles on a broom.

This wasn't true forest; it was a "tree farm"—a second- or third-growth plantation, now ready for "harvesting." The terms were those of the industry, and after two years of seeing them in use, I still found myself putting quotation marks around them in my head. To me, farm and harvest meant a two-acre wheat field in Essex, with rabbits scarpering from between the cornstalks, and the words refused to stick when I tried to attach them to a mountain range with 150-foot trees, where bears and cougars ran out in place of rabbits and twin-rotor helicopters served as baling machines. . . .

That night I put up at a motel in Forks, twelve miles inland, on the slope of the invisible Olympics. It was a timber town, and a minor classic in its genre. I had been driving through timber towns all day and seen them at every stage of their evolution. Forks was the most highly evolved version so far.

The lowest form of timber-industry social life was a camp of trail- 20 ers parked in line along the roadside. It became a town with a name when the trailers were joined by three or four prefabricated ranch-style bungalows and a 7-Eleven convenience store with a gas pump out front. The next stage up the ladder required the addition of a gas station with a "deli" (which in these parts meant not a delicatessen but a basic horseshoe-counter diner, serving steak-and-egg breakfasts and sandwiches). Serious civic ambitions set in with the arrival of the video store and the motel. After that came the sculpture.

The sculpture was as formalized in its way as the statue of the bronze infantryman atop the war memorial in small English market towns. I'd seen a dozen variants of it in Oregon, Washington, and British Columbia. It was carved from a section of old-growth Douglas fir of massive diameter, and it represented, in heavy relief, sometimes painted and sometimes in bare varnished wood, a logger with an ax cutting down an old-growth Douglas fir.

The example outside the motel was a beauty, for Forks was the metropolis of the logging camps—a mile-long strip of neon business signs, with three stoplights and a string of tenebrous beer joints. But the carved and painted logger, a figure of heroic pastoral, was way out of tune with his real-life counterparts, who gloomed disconsolately over their drinks in the bars. None were Paul Bunyan types. The loggers were journeyman employees of billion-dollar outfits like the Weyerhaeuser Corporation, and they gave off the sour smell of years of negative profits, evaporating cash flows, and hard bottom lines.

They were now the endangered species. They put up homemade signs on their lawns that said THIS FAMILY LIVES ON TIMBER DOLLARS— and I'd find myself peering in at the windows of these houses as if, indeed, I might catch a glimpse of some rare owlish birds pecking at a tray of timber dollars while *Wheel of Fortune* played in the background.

The sculptures (and all the ones I saw were recently carved) were part of the counter-preservationist movement. They owed a lot to the carved totemic ravens and thunderbirds with which the local Indian tribes announced their special status. They made the assertion that timber-industry workers, like the Indians, had, in one of the hardest-worked American phrases of the late twentieth century, a unique and historic *culture*. Deny me my job, and you deny me my culture, my past, my ethnic identity. So the logging communities were busy manu-facturing craft objects that gave them a tribal history and the right to be regarded as yet another beleaguered minority threatened with extinction.

It took some imaginative effort to identify the Weyerhaeuser fork-   25 lift operators and helicopter crews with the carved figures of lone brawny woodsmen swinging axes. The sculptures seemed to me to be self-defeating: they came across as sentimental tributes to a past so long gone that it was far beyond the reach of preservation.

I picked at a meal in an overlit, almost empty restaurant. The view through the window was of pickups and logging trucks plowing through the wet and dark. The chicken and French fries tasted of saw-dust and wood pulp. The only other customer removed his teeth and pocketed them after he'd finished dining. Forks in the rain was an unlovely place.

An elderly blue VW Beetle was stopped at the light. Its back end was pasted over with slogans that looked misplaced in Forks: anti-nuke, Clinton/Gore, and the brightest piece of folk wisdom that I'd yet seen on the tribulations of the timber industry, SAVE A LOGGER & A WHALE—SINK A JAPANESE SHIP.

For Journals

What is your reaction to the idea of limiting logging as a livelihood in order to preserve a natural setting? To save a species?

For Discussion

1.   The author is an Englishman who moved to Seattle from London. How does his status as an outsider help him assess the beliefs and ex-periences of loggers and conservationists? Is he in any way at a disad-vantage in trying to understand them?

2.   Explain the title of the essay; does it undercut or support the no-tion of the American frontier? How many frontiers do you think there have been or will be in the future?

3.   Compare the arguments of Wallace Stegner versus those of the loggers in Raban's article; what are the most persuasive points each makes? Try to consider both arguments in their own terms—that is, on the basis of the different assumptions about environment and liveli-hood that each side starts out with.

4. Protest sculptures of loggers felling Douglas firs remind Raban of Indian totems; in what way is this an ironic comparison, and how do you think that the loggers would respond to it?

For Writing

1. Going back to discussion question number 2, write an essay in which you compare and contrast Wallace Stegner's passionate letter for preservation of the wilderness with the loggers' equally passionate stance against conservationists. Try to present each side's assertions in the best possible light before you evaluate them.

2. Raban mentions that Paul Bunyan, a logger, used to be a folklore hero. Write an essay in which you address the following issues: Why did the logger go from being a larger-than-life hero to a larger-than-life villain? What ideas and myths about the frontier did Bunyan's character represent to most Americans in the past? What does his image seem to represent now?

❋❋ *The Headline Frontier* (1994)

PATRICIA NELSON LIMERICK

Patricia Nelson Limerick (1951–) is one of the United States's foremost historians of the American frontier. She is the author or editor of nine books, including The Legacy of Conquest: The Unbroken Past of the American West *(1985);* Trails: Toward a New Western History *(1991); and* The Frontier in American Culture *(1994) from which the following essay is excerpted.*

The headlines in 1986 looked as if they had been co-authored by Frederick Jackson Turner and the director of the 1890 census:

Frontier's Fate Still Uncertain

Frontier Still Has a Chance for Survival

Frontier Verges on Collapse

Time Runs Out for Frontier

Frontier Shuts Down

Too Late for Frontier

Frontier Throws in the Towel

Frontier Files for Bankruptcy

Politics Killed Frontier

Frontier Legacy Lives

The entity in question was Frontier Airlines, struggling for financial survival. For readers in Colorado in 1986, the fate of the airline was a subject of some anxiety; the ironic historical resonance of these headlines offered little in the way of consolation or diversion.

Seldom recognized for its ironic implications, the word "frontier" appears frequently in headlines. To serve their function, headlines have to convey some trustworthy clue to the contents of the story they introduce. But headlines are very short; they are virtually a freeze-dried form of communication. Thus, their writers tap out their message in a kind of code. In the necessary economy of the headline, the writers go in search of words that will convey big meanings. They have, under those circumstances, little interest in treacherous words, words that stand a chance of betraying their users.

Headline writers are, predictably, heavy users of the words "frontier" and "pioneer." They trust those words, and the words repay that trust. They are words that carry the master key to the reader's mind; with that key, they can slip into the mind and deposit their meanings before anyone quite knows they are there.

To assemble a set of artifacts demonstrating the persistent and widespread power of these words, I looked at roughly four thousand headlines, from 1988 through the first half of 1993, that made use of "frontier" and "pioneer." The first time through, I made a strategic error, and simply looked to see how silly these references were. This was an easy exercise, because many of the usages are indeed goofy. But at the end of the exercise, I had to realize that simply chuckling over these phrases was not accomplishing much for the cause of understanding.

The next time, then, I tried to find the patterns in the usage of 5 these words. What seems to be going on in people's minds in the late twentieth century when they call someone a pioneer or refer to an activity or an enterprise as a frontier? Answering this question can illuminate even the sillier usages, showing just how far from historical reality this historical reference has strayed. This exercise works best if the reader picks a nineteenth-century pioneer and then imagines how that pioneer might respond to his or her twentieth-century descendants. Or one might think only of Frederick Jackson Turner and imagine his response to what the twentieth century has done to his favorite term and his favorite people.

Let us begin on the comparatively neutral frontier of food. "Eating to Heal: The New Frontiers," the *New York Times* announced in 1990. Apparently fighting on the wrong side of this frontier was the "Cookie Pioneer," "creator of the fortune cookie folding machine and a line of risqué fortune cookies." The Cookie Pioneer may have held only a superficial kinship to the Cinnamon Roll Pioneers, but all of these pioneers could have joined forces with the Fast Food Pioneer and the

Pioneer of the Snack Food Industry to defend their turf against the insinuations of the Natural Foods Pioneer, the Vegetarian Pioneer, and the Pioneer of the Edible Landscape. Occupying less contested territory were the Pasta Pioneers, the Potato Pioneer, and the Microwave Popcorn Pioneer, and surely the most memorable of the food pioneers—the Pioneer of the South Philadelphia Hoagie.

As striking as the food pioneers are the "lifestyle pioneers": the Passionate Pioneer of Fitness Franchising (the woman who founded Jazzercise Inc.); the Surfing Pioneer ("he pioneered a whole way of surfing for thousands"); the Psychedelic Pioneer; the New Age Pioneer; the Sex-Change Pioneer; the Porn Pioneer; the Pioneer in the Crack Business; and the Peekaboo Pioneer, the founder of Frederick's of Hollywood. Frederick's pioneering work did not exhaust the possibilities of the underwear frontier: "Underwear Pioneers Targeting Men," one headline reads, and the story opens with this promising line: "The two designing women who revolutionized the bra industry in the 1970s with the invention of the first jogging bra have turned their talents to men's underwear." On the subject of fabrics and new materials, there is the memorable Polyester Pioneer, as well as a Pioneer of Plastics and a Stainless Steel Cookware Pioneer.

Forced into the discomfort and disorientation of time travel, Frederick Jackson Turner, or any of his contemporaries, would have to experience astonishment at the applications of the word "pioneer" in the late twentieth century, at this implied kinship between overland travelers and marketers of underwear, stainless steel, and hoagies. Of all these contestants, the award for the most unsettling pioneer would have to go to Dr. Louis Irwin Grossman, Pioneer in Root Canal Dentistry. And if there were an award for the twentieth-century pioneer of the product that nineteenth-century pioneers would have had the most occasions to appreciate, then that prize would go to Bernard Castro, described as the Pioneer of the Sleeper-Sofa.

Beneath and beyond the silliness of these references lies a clear set of patterns. The pioneers and frontiers cluster in particular areas and enterprises. Art, music, sports, fashion, commerce, law, and labor activism get their full share of the analogy. Technology holds the biggest cluster: technology of transportation (bicycles, automobiles, helicopters, airplanes, rockets, and spacecraft); technology of communications and information (radio, television, talk shows, CD players, laser discs, computers, software, programming); technology of medicine (heart transplants, plastic surgery, headache treatment, weight reduction, gene therapy); technology of weaponry (rocketry, atomic bombs). Indeed, it is impossible to read all these references to the frontiers of technology without recognizing that the American public has genuinely and completely accepted, ratified, and bought the notion that the American frontiering spirit, sometime in the last century, picked itself up and made a definitive relocation—from territorial expansion to technological and commercial expansion.

In November 1944, as the end of World War II neared, President Franklin Roosevelt asked Vannevar Bush, director of the Office of Scientific Research and Development, to report on the prospects for American science after the war. "New frontiers of the mind," Roosevelt said, "are before us, and if they are pioneered with the same vision, boldness, and drive with which we have waged this war we can create a fuller and more fruitful employment and a fuller and more fruitful life." Called *Science—The Endless Frontier,* Bush's response to Roosevelt's request set the agenda for federally funded science. "It is in keeping with basic United States policy," Bush wrote, "that the Government should foster the opening of new frontiers," and federal investment in science "is the modern way to do it." Casting science as the nation's new frontier, a frontier maintained by hearty federal funding, Vannevar Bush captured and promoted the popular understanding of the frontier's relocation after Turner.

Certainly the space program has provided the best example of this pattern. The promoters of space exploration and development may well qualify as the nation's most committed and persistent users of the frontier analogy. *Pioneering the Space Frontier,* the 1986 Paine commission report on the future of the space program, shows the analogy at its most fervent. The story of the American nation, as imagined by the Paine commissioners, was a triumphant and glorious story of success, with the complex stories of Indian conquest and African American slavery simply ignored and eliminated. "The promise of virgin lands and the opportunity to live in freedom," the commissioners declared, "brought our ancestor to the shores of North America." The frontiers have not closed, and Manifest Destiny has just taken a turn skyward: "Now space technology has freed humankind to move outward from Earth as a species destined to expand to other worlds." The best that the Paine commissioners could offer in recognizing that frontiers might not always be vacant was this memorable line: "As we move outward into the Solar System, we must remain true to our values as Americans: To go forward peacefully and to respect the integrity of planetary bodies and alien life forms, with equality of opportunity for all." If one thinks of the devastation of Indians by disease, alcohol, war, loss of territory, and coercive assimilation, and then places that reality next to the Paine commissioners' pious intentions, one feels some obligation to take up the mission of warning the "alien life forms," to suggest that they keep their many eyes on their wallets when they hear these intentions invoked, especially the line about "equality of opportunity for all."

However this frontier experience plays out for alien life forms, the mental act of equating the frontier of westward expansion with the development of space proved to be an enterprise that ran itself. In the selling of space as "the final frontier," the aerospace industry, the National Aeronautics and Space Administration, presidents, the news media, and the entertainment business collaborated with perfect harmony, with no need for centralized direction or planning, with a seamless match in their methods and goals. The split infinitive was regrettable, but the writers of *Star Trek* came up with the phrase to capture the essential idea brought to mind at the mention of the words "frontier" and "pioneer": "to boldly go where no man has gone before."

For Journals

Of all the examples Limerick gives of how the frontier idea gets used, which did you think was the most amusing? The most understandable?

For Discussion

1.   What point do you think Limerick was trying to make in choosing the example she did to begin this essay?

2.   Why do you think that the concept of the frontier is still important to Americans? What meanings does it seem to have for us that no other word possesses?

3.   Limerick gives many examples of how the word "frontier" is attached to all kinds of activities and businesses. What definition or definitions of "frontier" can you come up with that make sense to you?

For Writing

1.   Look through some newspapers and magazines for the word "frontier"; write an essay in which you explain how it is used in one or two articles you find, and why you think that the way it is used does or doesn't make sense. You may find yourself agreeing or disagreeing with Limerick. In any case, state what Limerick's assertions are about how the frontier concept is being manipulated in contemporary America, and then use your article(s) to either support or refute her argument. If you want, you can follow the same form in your essay that Limerick does, and start by quoting the best newspaper headlines you find.

2.   Write an essay based on discussion question number 3, but once you've written about what you think frontier means, pick one or two other words or terms that are similarly important to Americans, for example, pursuit of happiness, all men are created equal, and freedom of speech. Choose whatever term or word you want, but in order to keep this essay from becoming too abstract, give specific examples of what

it means to you, your friends, or members of your family. You can interview people you know at school or elsewhere and ask them significant questions.

3. Assume that you are in charge of an advertising campaign for one of your favorite products—a food, a kind of clothing, a song or CD you really like, a movie, and so on—and that the frontier, in whatever way you choose to use it, is going to be at the heart of your campaign. Write a memorandum to your boss explaining why the frontier would be a good analogy for your ad campaign, who your audience is, and how you intend to incorporate the frontier into the slogan for your ad. Illustrate your memorandum by doing a version of the ad, including the slogan. You can look to Limerick's examples to give you ideas.

�֍֍ *Wheel of Misfortune* (2002)

DONALD L. BARTLETT

This article was the cover story in Time *magazine on December 16, 2002.*

Imagine, if you will, Congress passing a bill to make Indian tribes more self-sufficient that gives billions of dollars to the white backers of Indian businesses—and nothing to hundreds of thousands of Native Americans living in poverty. Or a bill that gives hundreds of millions of dollars to one Indian tribe with a few dozen members—and not a penny to a tribe with hundreds of thousands of members. Or a bill that allows select Indian tribes to create businesses that reap millions of dollars in profits and pay no federal income tax—at the same time that the tribes collect millions in aid from American taxpayers. Can't imagine Congress passing such a bill? It did. Here's how it happened—and what it means.

Maryann Martin presides over America's smallest tribe. Raised in Los Angeles in an African-American family, she knew little of her Indian ancestry until 1986, when at age 22 she learned that her mother had been the last surviving member of the Augustine Band of Cahuilla Mission Indians. In 1991, the Bureau of Indian Affairs (BIA) certified Martin and her two younger brothers as members of the tribe. Federal recognition of tribal status opened the door for Martin and her siblings to qualify for certain types of government aid. And with it, a far more lucrative lure beckoned: the right to operate casinos on an Indian reservation.

As Indian casinos popped up like new housing developments across Southern California, Martin moved a trailer onto the long-abandoned Augustine reservation in Coachella, a 500-acre desert tract then littered with garbage, discarded household appliances and junk cars, about 25 miles southeast of Palm Springs. There she lived with her three children and African-American husband William Ray Vance. In 1994, membership in the tiny tribe dwindled from three adults to one when Martin's two brothers were killed during separate street shootings in Banning, Calif. Police said both men were involved in drug deals and were members of a violent Los Angeles street gang.

Subsequently, Martin negotiated a deal with Paragon Gaming, a Las Vegas company, to develop and manage a casino. Paragon is headed by Diana Bennett, a gaming executive and daughter of Vegas veteran and co-founder of the Circus Circus Casino William Bennett. Martin's Augustine Casino opened last July. With 349 slot machines and 10 gaming tables, it's the fifth and by far the most modest casino in the Palm Springs area. But it stands to make a lot of non-Indian investors—and one Indian adult—rich.

And get this: Martin still qualifies for federal aid, in amounts far   5 greater than what many needy Native Americans could even dream of getting. In 1999 and 2000 alone, government audit reports show, she pulled in more than $1 million from Washington—$476,000 for housing, $400,000 for tribal government and $146,000 for environmental programs.

It wasn't supposed to be this way. At the end of the 1980s, in a frenzy of cost cutting and privatization, Washington perceived gaming on reservations as a cheap way to wean tribes from government handouts, encourage economic development and promote tribal self-sufficiency. After policy initiatives by the Reagan Administration and two U.S. Supreme Court rulings that approved gambling on Indian reservations, Congress enacted the Indian Gaming Regulatory Act in 1988. It was so riddled with loopholes, so poorly written, so discriminatory and subject to such conflicting interpretations that 14 years later, armies of high-priced lawyers are still debating the definition of a slot machine.

Instead of regulating Indian gambling, the act has created chaos and a system tailor-made for abuse. It set up a powerless and underfunded watchdog and dispersed oversight responsibilities among a hopelessly conflicting hierarchy of local, state and federal agencies. It created a system so skewed—only a few small tribes and their backers are getting rich—that it has changed the face of Indian country. Some long-dispersed tribes, aided by new, non-Indian financial godfathers, are regrouping to benefit from the gaming windfall. Others are seeking new reservations—some in areas where they never lived, occasionally even in other states—solely to build a casino. And leaders of small, newly wealthy tribes now have so much unregulated cash and political clout that they can ride roughshod over neighboring communities, poorer tribes and even their own members.

The amount of money involved is staggering. Last year 290 Indian casinos in 28 states pulled in at least $12.7 billion in revenue. Of that sum, *Time* estimates, the casinos kept more than $5 billion as profit. That would place overall Indian gaming among *Fortune* magazine's 20 most profitable U.S. corporations, with earnings exceeding those of J. P. Morgan Chase & Co., Merrill Lynch, American Express and Lehman Bros. Holdings combined.

But who, exactly, is benefiting? Certainly Indians in a few tribes have prospered. In California, Christmas came early this year for the 100 members of the Table Mountain Rancheria, who over Thanksgiving picked up bonus checks of $200,000 each as their share of the Table Mountain Casino's profits. That was in addition to the monthly stipend of $15,000 each member receives. But even those amounts pale beside the fortunes made by the behind-the-scenes investors who bankroll the gaming palaces. They walk away with up to hundreds of millions of dollars.

Meanwhile, the overwhelming majority of Indians get nothing. Only half of all tribes—which have a total of 1.8 million members— have casinos. Some large tribes like the Navajo oppose gambling for religious reasons. Dozens of casinos do little better than break even because they are too small or located too far from population centers. The upshot is that a small number of gaming operations are making most of the money. Last year just 39 casinos generated $8.4 billion. In short, 13% of the casinos accounted for 66% of the take. All of which helps explain why Indian gaming has failed to raise most Native Americans out of poverty. What has happened instead is this: 10

A Losing Hand. Revenue from gaming is so lopsided that Indian casinos in five states with almost half the Native American population—Montana, Nevada, North Dakota, Oklahoma and South Dakota—account for less than 3% of all casino proceeds. On average, they produce the equivalent of about $400 in revenue per Indian. Meanwhile, casinos in California, Connecticut and Florida—states with only 3% of the Indian population—haul in 44% of all revenue, an average of $100,000 per Indian. In California, the casino run by the San Manuel Band of Mission Indians pulls in well over $100 million a year. That's about $900,000 per member.

The Rich Get Richer. While federal recognition entitles tribes to a broad range of government benefits, there is no means testing. In 2001, aid to Indians amounted to $9.4 billion, but in many cases more money went to wealthy members of tribes with lucrative casinos than to destitute Indians. From 1995 to 2001, the Indian Health Service, the agency responsible for looking after the medical needs of Native Americans, spent an average of $2,100 a year on each of the 2,800 members of the

Seminole tribe in Florida. The Seminoles' multiple casinos generated $216 million in profits last year, and each tribe member collected $35,000 in casino dividends. During the same six years, the health service spent an annual average of just $470 on each of the 52,000 members of the Muscogee (Creek) Nation in Oklahoma, whose tiny casinos do little more than break even.

Buying Politicians. Wealthy Indian gaming tribes suddenly are pouring millions of dollars into political campaigns at both state and federal levels. They are also influencing gaming and other policies affecting Native Americans by handing out large sums to influential lobbying firms. In 2000 alone, tribes spent $9.5 million on Washington lobbying. Altogether they spend more to influence legislation than such longtime heavyweights as General Motors, Boeing, AT&T—or even Enron in its heyday.

Gaming Tribes as Exclusive Clubs. Tribal leaders are free to set their own whimsical rules for admission, without regard to Indian heritage. They may exclude rivals, potential whistle-blowers and other legitimate claimants. The fewer tribe members, the larger the cut for the rest. Some tribes are booting out members, while others are limiting membership. Among them: the Pechanga Band of Mission Indians in Riverside County, Calif., whose new Las Vegas–style gaming palace, the Pechanga Resort & Casino, is expected to produce well over $100 million in revenue.

Gold Rush. Since only a federally recognized tribe can open a casino, scores of groups—including long-defunct tribes and extended families—have flocked to the BIA or Congress seeking certification. Since 1979, as gambling has boomed, the number of recognized tribes on the U.S. mainland has spiked 23%, to a total of 337. About 200 additional groups have petitioned the bureau for recognition. Perhaps the most notorious example of tribal resurrection: the Mashantucket Pequots of Connecticut, proud owners of the world's largest casino, Foxwoods. The now billion-dollar tribe had ceased to exist until Congress re-created it in 1983. The current tribe members had never lived together on a reservation. Many of them would not even qualify for government assistance as Indians.

The Impotent Enforcer. Congress created the National Indian Gaming Commission (NIGC) to be the Federal Government's principal oversight-and-enforcement agency for Indian gaming—and then guaranteed that it could do neither. With a budget capped at $8 million, the agency has 63 employees to monitor the $12.7 billion all-cash business in more than 300 casinos and small gaming establishments nationwide. The New Jersey Casino Control Commission, by contrast, has a $59 million budget and a staff of 720 to monitor 12 casinos in Atlantic City that produce one-third the revenue. The NIGC has yet to discover a single major case of corruption—despite numerous complaints from tribe members.

The White Man Wins Again. While most Indians continue to live in poverty, many non-Indian investors are extracting hundreds of millions of dollars—sometimes in violation of legal limits—from casinos they helped establish, either by taking advantage of regulatory loopholes or cutting backroom deals. More than 90% of the contracts between tribes and outside gaming-management companies operate with no oversight. That means investors' identities are often secret, as are their financial arrangements and their share of the revenue. Whatever else Congress had in mind when it passed the regulatory act, presumably the idea was not to line the pockets of a Malaysian gambling magnate, a South African millionaire or a Minnesota leather-apparel king.

Fraud, Corruption, Intimidation. The tribes' secrecy about financial affairs—and the complicity of government oversight agencies—has guaranteed that abuses in Indian country growing out of the surge in gaming riches go undetected, unreported and unprosecuted. Tribal leaders sometimes rule with an iron fist. Dissent is crushed. Cronyism flourishes. Those who question how much the casinos really make, where the money goes or even tribal operations in general may be banished. Indians who challenge the system are often intimidated, harassed and threatened with reprisals or physical harm. They risk the loss of their jobs, homes and income. Margarite Faras, a member of the San Carlos Apache tribe, which owns the Apache Gold Casino in San Carlos, Ariz., was ousted from the tribal council after exposing corruption that led to the imprisonment of a former tribal leader. For three years, Faras says, those in control mounted nighttime demonstrations at her home, complete with loudspeakers. They initiated a boycott of her taco business, telling everyone she used cat meat. They telephoned her with death threats. Says Faras: "I don't know what else to say, other than it's been a nightmare."

For Journals

Have you or anyone in your circle ever gambled at Las Vegas, Atlantic City, a church bingo game, an Indian casino, or a riverboat casino? Have you ever bought a lottery ticket?

For Discussion

1. Do you disapprove of gambling or see it as entertainment? Why?

2. The author chose to open the article with a series of situations that he asks us to imagine. What do those situations have in common? By choosing them, what kind of appeal—to logic, ethics, or emotion—do the authors make?

3.   The first part of the article revolves around Maryann Martin and what it means when the BIA (Bureau of Indian Affairs) certifies someone as a member of an Indian tribe. What ethical problems are raised in this episode, and what details does the author select that are particularly pointed against Martin?

4.   A lot of the article is given over to what is wrong with the Gaming Regulatory Act of 1988, which made it possible for Indians to put casinos on reservations. Either on your own or working in small groups in class, make up two lists: the first made up of what the Act was supposed to do, and the second of what went wrong with it, according to the author.

5.   Look at the headings in the list that begins with "A Losing Hand." Why do you think that each of them was chosen? What does each one suggest to you?

For Writing

1.   Look back earlier in this chapter for other juxtapositions of relationships between Indians and whites, including the selection by Frederick Jackson Turner, the *Police Gazette* article "Indian Treachery and Bloodshed," and Louise Erdrich's "Dear John Wayne" poem. Pick one, and compare two or three points that it makes about the Indian experience directly with two or three points made in this article about the same subject. You should identify your points of comparison clearly, by number if necessary, and also be clear about whether you think that the issues here are similar to or different from the ones you found in the other reading you choose.

2.   Write an argumentative essay in which you take a side in the casino issue on whether it is or isn't a good idea in terms of financial return, equity, and who gets what. For sources, you can use Google; or if you have access to any databases, you can use Academic Premier or Expanded Academic, for example, which would lead to articles from newspapers and magazines about the nature of the disagreement and provide you with background material. *Time, Newsweek*, the *New York Times* (which is on the Web in its entirety), and the *Los Angeles Times* have articles that could be useful to you.

✻✻ *Film: Unforgiven* (1993)

Two retired, down-on-their luck outlaws pick up their guns one last time to collect a bounty offered by the vengeful prostitutes of the remote Wyoming town of Big Whiskey. (131 minutes)

For Journals

Why do you think that this movie is called *Unforgiven?* How many people are unforgiven, and for what?

For Discussion

1. In older Westerns, the good guys wore white hats, and the bad guys wore black hats, so that the audience would always know who was who. In this movie, the hero is a killer; what does Eastwood, both as director and as actor, do with the character to make him heroic?

2. Two young people have significant parts in this movie: a near-sighted gunslinger who pretends he is an experienced killer, and a nearsighted writer who is enchanted with the idea of meeting a real killer. In a way, both become accomplices to what happens. Look closely at the scenes in which they appear: Who is the more innocent? Who is more corrupted by the West? What kind of harm does each of them do?

3. There are considerable comic touches in the film: Will Monny can't ride a horse well, and the Scofield Kid can't see what he's shoot-ing at. How do these touches play against the usual stereotypes of Western gunslingers? What parts of the movie reinforce those images?

4. The movie begins and ends with a peaceful scene of Will's farm, accompanied by words on the screen. Look at what the words say in the beginning and in the end; who do you think is supposed to be the author of those words? Why does it sound like part of a novel? What point do you think that Eastwood is making about the fictionalization of the frontier?

For Writing

1. View one of Eastwood's earlier spaghetti Westerns or one of his early American Westerns, such as *A Fistful of Dollars* (1964), *For a Few Dollars More* (1966), *Hang 'Em High* (1968), and *The Good, the Bad, and the Ugly* (1967). Take two or three scenes from one of those films and two or three scenes from *Unforgiven,* and write an essay in which you compare them for the presence or absence of the following themes: guilt, conscience, memory, or a frontier ethic. How has Eastwood's ar-chetype of the Western hero evolved since the earlier films?

2. The Western is one of the primary American film traditions; that role has made it a target for humor and satire. Look at Mel Brook's *Blazing Saddles* (1974), the single most parodic version of a Western ever made. Write an essay in which you identify as many stereotypes as you can and the way that Brooks treats them: for example, cowboys and Indians, whites and blacks, the gunslinger, the crooked politician.

Chapter Writing Assignments

1. Write an essay on an issue you feel strongly about, but take a stand absolutely against your usual position. Analyze a poem, take a side of a debate, or examine an advertisement from the perspective of someone with a background or gender different from yours. Your paper can be research-oriented, expository, or narrative. Then write a reflective essay on how the change in perspective affected your writing process and your conclusions, and whether or how it caused you to revise your previous certainties on the topic.

2. Go through copies of old magazines—*Century* or *McClure's* from the early twentieth century, or *Colliers, Harper's, and Saturday Evening Post* through the 1950s and 1960s—and look for images of Native Americans in advertisements. Write a paper in which you include your reflections on the following questions: What are the Native Americans being used to sell? If there are any whites in the ads, what is the relationship between them and the Native Americans? What stereotypes or clichés do you find in these ads? If you were writing any of these advertisements, how would you revise the pictures or the text, or both?

3. Try to locate any of the following: the old television series on Daniel Boone and Davy Crockett (starring, incidentally, the same actor, Fess Parker, as though these historical figures were interchangeable) or the musical based on the life of Annie Oakley, *Annie Get Your Gun*. How does the image of these figures that are put forth by articles and books revise or coincide with the image of them in television and theater? What do you think is lost or gained when the revised versions of their lives become more important than the reality?

4. Write an essay in which you discuss the negative stereotyping of any group to which you belong: your gender, your racial heritage, the region of the country you come from, your religious affiliation, or your love of computers. Consider the following questions: How do you think that your group is perceived by others? What stereotyping, negative and positive, do you have to contend with? How would you revise the stereotype to make it a more accurate reflection of reality?

5. Research any American hero or heroine in sports, movies, politics, or some other area who has become the subject of a mythology. Some of the most obvious are Elvis Presley, Marilyn Monroe, F. Scott Fitzgerald, and John F. Kennedy, but anyone who can persistently fascinate the American public and is the subject of endless restructuring and remaking would be a good subject. Concentrate on separating some of the reality from the subsequent revision or on the way your subject's standing is revised positively or negatively in people's estimation. What, would you argue, is the cultural significance of your subject to America?

Web Sites for Further Exploration

Lewis and Clark

www.pbs.org/lewisandclark/
www.lewis-clark.org/

Mark Twain

etext.lib.virginia.edu/railton/index2.html
www.marktwainhouse.org/

Albert Bierstadt

www.artchive.com/artchive/B/bierstadt.html

Frederick Jackson Turner

www.pbs.org/weta/thewest/people/s_z/turner.htm

Wallace Stegner

gill.stanford.edu/depts/hasrg/ablit/amerlit/stegner.html

Edward Abbey

www.canyoncountryzephyr.com/archives/abbey-interview.html

Louise Erdrich

www.salon.com/weekly/interview960506.html

Acknowledgments

✿✿

Text

Edward Abbey, "The Great American Desert," from *The Journey Home* by Edward Abbey, copyright © 1977 by Edward Abbey. Used by permission of Dutton, a division of Penguin Group (USA) Inc.

Donald L. Bartlett, "Wheel of Misfortune," from *Time*, December 16, 2002. © 2002 Time Magazine, Inc. Reprinted by permission.

John Rowe, Marisa Rowe, and Sabin Streeter, "The High School Basketball Coach," from *Gig* by John Bowe, Marisa Bowe, and Sabin Streeter, copyright © 2000, 2001 by John Bowe, Marisa Bowe, and Sabin Streeter. Used permission of Crown Publishers, a division of Random House, Inc.

Clayborne Carson, "March on Washington: A Look Back After 40 Years," *San Francisco Chronicle*, 24 August 2003. Reprinted courtesy of Dr. Clayborne Carson.

Gail Collins, "African American Women: Life in Bondage," from *America's Women: Four Hundred Years of Dolls, Drudges, Helpmates, and Heroines* by Gail Collins. Copyright © 2003 by Gail Collins. Reprinted by permission of HarperCollins Publishers Inc.

Dinesh D'Souza, "In Praise of American Empire," *Christian Science Monitor* (April 26, 2002). Reprinted by permission of the author.

Alan M. Dershowitz, "What is hate speech?" from *The San Francisco Chronicle* (July 22, 1993). Reprinted with the permission of the author.

Marian Wright Edelman, "A Family Legacy," from *The Measure of Our Success* by Marian Wright Edelman. Copyright © 1992 by Marian Wright Edelman. Reprinted by permission of Beacon Press, Boston.

Barbara Ehrenreich, "Serving in Florida," from *Nickel and Dimed: On (Not) Getting By in America* by Barbara Ehrenreich, © 2001 by Barbara Ehrenreich. Reprinted by permission of Henry Holt and Company, LLC.

Louise Erdrich, "Dear John Wayne" from *Jacklight* (New York: Henry Holt and Company, 1984). Copyright © 1984 by Louise Erdrich, reprinted with the permission of The Wylie Agency, Inc.

Chronicle. Reprinted by permission of The San Francisco Chronicle via The Copyright Clearance Center.

Kevin Phillips, "Hegemony, Hubris, and Overreach" from *The Iraq War Reader.* Reprinted by permission of the author.

Mary Pipher, "Saplings in the Storm" from *Reviving Ophelia* by Mary Pipher, Ph.D., copyright © 1994 by Mary Pipher, Ph.D. Used by permission of G.P. Putnam's Sons, a division of Penguin Group (USA) Inc.

Robert D. Putnam, excerpt from *Bowling Alone* (New York: Simon & Schuster, 2000), pp. 402-406. Reprinted with the permission of Simon & Schuster Adult Publishing Group from *Bowling Alone: The Collapse and Revival of American Community* by Robert D. Putnam. Copyright © 2000 by Robert D. Putnam.

Jonathan Raban, "The Next Last Frontier" from *Harper's.* Copyright © 1993 by *Harper's Magazine.* All rights reserved. Reproduced by special permission.

Jacqueline Navarra Rhoads, "Nurses in Vietnam," from Dan Freedman and Jacqueline Rhoads, *Nurses in Vietnam: The Forgotten Veterans* (Houston: Gulf Publishing, 1987). Copyright © 1987 by Dan Freedman and Jaccqueline Rhoads. Reprinted with the permission of Dan Freedman and Jacqueline Rhoads.

Richard Rodriguez, "Disunited We Stand—America's Diversity Is Its Strength," Pacific News Service. Copyright © 2001 by Richard Rodriguez. Reprinted by permission of Georges Borchardt, Inc., for the author.

Witold Rybczynski, "Tomorrowland" from *The New Yorker,* July 22, 1996. Copyright © 1996 by Witold Rybczynski. Reprinted with the permission of the author.

Arthur M. Schlesinger, Jr., "The Cult of Ethnicity," from *Time* (7/8/1991). © 1991 Time Inc. Reprinted by permission.

Luther Standing Bear, "What the Indian Means to America," from *Land of the Spotted Eagle* by Luther Standing Bear by permission of the University of Nebraska Press. Copyright 1933 by Luther Standing Bear. Renewal copyright, 1960, by May Jones.

Wallace Stegner, "Coda: The Wilderness Letter" from *The Sound of Mountain Water* by Wallace Stegner, copyright © 1969 by Wallace Stegner. Used by permission of Doubleday, a division of Random House, Inc.

Thomas Stoddard, "Marriage Is a Fundamental Right" from *The New York Times* (1989). Copyright © 1989 by The New York Times. Reprinted with permission.

Studs Terkel, "The Stonemason" from *Working: People Talk About What They Do All Day and How They Feel About What They Do* (New York: Pantheon Books, 1974). Copyright © 1972, 1974 by Studs Terkel. Reprinted with the permission of Donadio & Ashworth.

Jacob Weisberg, "United Shareholders of America" from *The New York Times* (1/25/1998). Copyright © 1998 by The New York Times. Reprinted with permission.

Cornel West, "Affirmative Action in Context" from George E. Curry, ed., *The Affirmative Action Debate* (Reading, Mass.: Addison-Wesley, 1996). Reprinted by permission of the author.

Art

No Dumping, Drains to Bay. Courtesy of Ann Watters.

Slow for Kids. Courtesy of Ann Watters.

IKEA—Help keep prices low. Courtesy of Ann Watters.

CAUTION, Dangerous Cliff. Courtesy of Ann Watters.

"I Want You for U.S. Army." Courtesy of the Library of Congress.

"I Want Out." Courtesy of the Library of Congress.

Hasten the Homecoming by Norman Rockwell. Reprinted by permission of the Norman Rockwell Family Trust. Copyright © 1943 the Norman Rockwell Family Trust. Photo: FDR Library.

Join, or Die. Courtesy of the Library of Congress.

Americans All! Victory Liberty Loan poster by Howard Chandler Christy. Reprinted by permission of Culver Pictures, Inc.

America: Open for Business. © 2001 Craig Frazier. www.craigfrazier. com.

There's No Way Like the American Way by Margaret Bourke-White. Getty Images/Time Life Pictures.

Edward Hopper (1882-1967), "Office in a Small City," 1953. Oil on canvas, H. 28 in. W. 40 in. Signed (lower left) Edward Hopper. The Metropolitan Museum of Art, George A. Hearn Fund, 1953. (53.183)

"Keep Within Compass," England, 1785-1805. Graphic on laid paper, H. 9.310 cm. Courtesy, Winterthur Museum. 1954.0093.001A

Enlist—On Which Side of the Window Are YOU? Courtesy of the Poster Collection, Hoover Institution Archives.

More Help for Busy Mothers. The Fuller Brush Company.

Young Women Picking Tobacco Leaves. Courtesy of the Library of Congress.

Three Women at a Parachute Plant in San Diego, California. Courtesy of the Library of Congress.

Advertisement of Wife and Her New Gibson Ultra 600 Electric Range. Courtesy of Gibson.

Dolls by Eudora Welty. Reprinted by permission of the Eudora Welty Collection, Mississippi Department of Archives and History.

Destroy This Mad Brute. Enlist. by H. R. Hopps. Courtesy of the Poster Collection, Hoover Institution Archives.

"Deliver Us from Evil. Buy War Bonds." Courtesy of the Poster Collection, Hoover Institution Archives.

Saigon Execution by Edward T. Adams. Reprinted by permission of AP/Wide World Photos.

The Terror of War by Huynh Cong "Nick" Ut. Reprinted by permission of AP/Wide World Photos.

Albert Bierstadt (1830-1902), "The Last of the Buffalo," 1889. Oil on canvas, six feet by ten feet. Courtesy of the Corcoran Gallery of Art, Washington, D.C. Gift of Mary (Mrs. Albert) Bierstadt.

Indian Treachery and Bloodshed. The National Police Gazette, edited by Gene Smith and Jayne Barry Smith. Courtesy of the Library of Congress.

Indian Belle crate label. Courtesy of American Antique Graphics Society.

Index of Authors
and Titles

❊❊❊

Index of Rhetorical Terms
❋❋❋